MODERN PLAYWRIGHTS AT WORK

MODERN PLAYWRIGHTS
AT WORK

Volume I

by

J. WILLIAM MILLER
Ph.D.

S A M U E L   F R E N C H ,   I N C .

25 West 45th Street   New York 10036
7623 Sunset Boulevard   Hollywood 90046

LONDON   TORONTO

Acknowledgements

Just as a lens may focus enough light into heat to kindle a fire, so in a sense this study has attempted to focus enough flashes of the lives of playwrights into the warmth or even fire of their living presence. Without the wide, thoughtful, and often generous granting of a great many permissions from those who control these "flashes of life," this study could never have come about. In this view, the permissions comprise the most important, single part of this entire book. Acknowledgements are most gratefully made immediately after each section in which the direct quotes appear. But one great acknowledgement made the bulk of these others, in a way, possible, and that is the help of the New York City Public Library at 42nd Street and Fifth Avenue and its branches whose resources are second only to the Library of Congress and whose patience, courtesy, and consideration are second to none. I acknowledge, too, the discipline of scholarship I acquired under the inspired but very demanding late Prof. Alexander Magnus Drummond and the late Prof. Henry Alonzo Myers of Cornell University. I acknowledge also the regard of the late Prof. John Gassner, who read the manuscript, suggested revisions, and encouraged publication. Finally, I acknowledge the indulgence and patience of M. M. whose facilities went a long way toward making this study possible.

Preface

WHY another book on playwriting?

This study started, continued, and reached fulfillment from the author's long felt need for a work which is as necessary to a serious student of playwriting as a record of the most successful mountain climbers might be to anyone considering an ascent ranging from High Tor to Mount Everest. "I wrote my first play in ten days of spring vacation," recalled Arthur Miller of his undergraduate days at the University of Michigan. "I had seen but one play in my life and had read the tragedies of Shakespeare. The play won several prizes," continued Miller, "and made me confident that I could go ahead from there. It left me with the belief that the ability to write plays is born into one, and that it is a kind of sport of the mind, as though one had to be knocked on the head in a certain way before one can practice the craft." [1] About eight years after writing his first play, Miller was thinking of giving up playwriting, for he had been knocked on the head in another way, what with the failure of his first Broadway production, *The Man Who Had All the Luck*. About two years later, Miller had his first Broadway success, *All My Sons*. Miller's pattern of experience is rather common even among the most gifted.

This study attempts to compile into a single book a kaleidoscope of the most authoritative information on modern playwriting and to give it a meaningful continuity in a flowing, related, comprehensive picture. If a talented person wanted to study an art, he would at best want to study with a master. But no master has for the record taken on any apprentice. Still the implication is plain, since playwrights in general have had so much to say of the growth of their creative spirit and how they have gone about playwriting, that the information was given out with some hope of helping those in need of help about such matters. The plays, themselves, provide the finished models. In addition to these chief sources—the playwright and his work—this study also relies upon the reaction of representative critics and the testimony of the playwright's associates, for example, husband or wife, children, friends, relatives, employees, and reporters.

This study in no way attempts to downgrade other studies; it is simply a new approach to solving the common problems of playwriting. William Archer's *Playwriting, a Manual of Craftsmanship,* George Pierce Baker's *Dramatic Technique* and John Howard Lawson's *Theory and Technique of Playwriting* provide another kind of window and view of creation in playwriting. The illustrative material of these studies, however, cannot help but often be dated. "If one counted the dramatists which can still move the public," remarked Eugene Ionesco in the *Tulane Drama Review,* "one would find through the centuries about twenty or thirty at the most." [2] Few plays live beyond one or two generations, for plays tend to a full life rather than a long one. The anthology, *Playwrights on Playwriting,* consists of short articles by playwrights with no attempt at correlation or continuity and differs from my study in the way a series of snapshots or short-short movies might differ from a documentary. All the studies mentioned take care to offer no specific exercises guaranteed to evolve a playwright as one might, for instance, evolve a chemist. Indeed, any presumption of a "text" on playwriting suggests the dubious business of trading in gold-bricks. Playwrights can no more be made by texts than can composers, painters, sculptors, or any artists.

The *Saturday Review* printed the answers to a questionnaire Henry Hewes sent out to twenty leading American playwrights asking, among other things, what advice they would give aspiring playwrights. The most common piece of advice in composite was, "Read the best plays. Develop a critical sense. Mature. Get 'know-how' backstage. Write plays and get them produced whenever you can." "Read plays, see plays, think plays, talk plays," for instance advised John Van Druten; "read all good dramatic criticism." [3] "Work backstage—as actor, stage manager, stagehand," urged Thornton Wilder. "An hour working there is worth a hundred as a member of the audience." "Write as much as you can as well as you can," counselled William Inge, "and get produced whenever you can." "Mature," was implied advice, for all the playwrights were well over twenty-one. "Write plays," is obviously the playwright's chief function.

Modern Playwrights at Work attempts to guide the aspiring playwright in directions suggested by successful playwrights themselves. The approach is one of self-help. To assist the aspirant in his need to read and analyze the best of plays, the appendix of this book offers a selected list of notable plays and dramatic criticism. The appendix also includes a pattern of play analysis based on the full study, substantiated by the great majority of plays, and is in itself a guide to form in playwriting. "Know-how" must be acquired by aspirants on their own from working backstage in the theatre, and from seeing their plays produced whenever possible; the chance turns up usually in school, college, or community theatre. Maturity is a gift of time.

When it comes to settling down and writing plays, the study should prove most helpful. It provides authoritative answers to very bothersome and searching questions about the growth of the playwrights' creative spirit in life, their considerations dealing with plays as merchandise and plays as art, and finally their ways of approaching the challenge of playwriting itself. The appendix has a special section containing a breakdown of all these matters in terms of key questions in playwriting with their answers indicated directly after each question by page numbers in the text. For any particular question uppermost in a playwright's mind at some moment, the key to a composite answer of modern playwrights and their associates is at the reader's finger-tips. "All arts are mysteries," said Granville Barker in his book of lectures, *On Dramatic Method,* "the way into their service is by initiation, not learning, and the adept hugs his secrets." [4] This study suggests the pattern of "initiation" and the "secrets."

This book is not to be read necessarily in the sequence in which it is written, but to satisfy a need. Some might argue that it devotes too much space to matters which do not immediately concern the playwright, such as the growth of the playwright's creative spirit in life or the background of his career. "If the writing is honest," said Tennessee Williams, "it cannot be separated from the man who wrote it. It isn't so much his mirror as it is the distillation, the essence of what is strongest and purest in his nature . . ." [5] "A tremendous amount of living goes into it," Robert Woodruff Anderson commented of writing a play when interviewed by Gilbert Millstein for *The New York Times;* "and a play has to emerge from what you are." [6] All this is an echo of Ibsen's own contention late in middle-age—"And as regards the thing which has been lived through, that is just the secret of the literature of modern times." [7] Once bitten by the bug to write plays, people often are prone to a recurrence of the creative fever or rapture —it can be both—for the rest of their lives. This book and a good deal more that it suggests are sooner or later bound to satisfy a real need for every seriously aspiring playwright. It suggests means of self-discovery and even survival.

Modern Playwrights at Work centers on eight distinguished mod-

ern playwrights and rounds out with a more cursory approach to
many others of perhaps less significance. Each of the select eight is
given a separate chapter and their order is based upon their chrono-
logical success in modern playwriting: Henrik Ibsen, August Strindberg, Anton Chekhov, Bernard Shaw, John Galsworthy, Luigi Pirandello, Eugene O'Neill and Tennessee Williams. "After Ibsen," wrote
Walter Kerr, the drama critic, "Chekhov is the most widely imitated
of playwrights in the contemporary theatre. . . ." [8] Kerr, incidentally,
was not happy about this state of affairs. "To go from the work of
Strindberg, Chekhov and Shaw to that of Luigi Pirandello," observed
Allan Lewis in *The Contemporary Theatre,* "is to explore the full
range of possibility in form and meaning in the contemporary theatre." [9] Shaw, Galsworthy, Pirandello and O'Neill have each won the
Nobel Prize in Literature. Tennessee Williams is probably too close to
us to allow for an uncontroversial judgment as to his lasting merits;
of all living, modern dramatists, nevertheless, he is generally acknowledged to have come nearest to distinction in our time what with winning four Drama Critics' Circle Awards to date. Arthur Miller,
though distinguished, has been far less productive than Williams and
is given special attention in the multiple study. All of the playwrights
selected for intensive study rank as pioneers in technique and as authors of plays repeatedly revived or at least widely read. If Galsworthy's plays seem somewhat dated, it is, of course, because the conditions they helped correct, like the struggle between capital and labor,
as in *Strife,* seem at the moment corrected; yet Galsworthy's naturalistic method is as valid as ever for dramatizing urgent, current problems, and to deny it an honored place in a serious study of playwriting is artificially to exclude from the drama the treatment of subject
matter relating to the very life and death of society in these days of
potential atomic war. What folly to think of drama as best only when
dealing with "lasting" subjects, when for failure to deal with the most
explosive subjects of the moment our civilization, itself, might not
last!

The many playwrights given a cursory inspection were chosen because they were notably successful either financially or artistically or
both. The majority are from the United States or England, and a
common language and often common cultural values allow for a relatively easy visa to each other's stages. In the multiple survey, other
than English-speaking playwrights have had to overcome the special
barriers of translation from a foreign language and a foreign culture

markedly different from America's mother country, England. Although the same pattern of analysis for the whole study is difficult and in part impossible to follow, a rather consistent pattern recurs. The chief trouble in giving each playwright a proper due has been in rounding up enough first hand source material, and also in not needlessly laboring illustration by drawing on playwrights like Pinero, for example, whose work has proven to be apparently so ephemeral.

All of the material in this study will share the inaccuracy and incompleteness of fragmentary personal reports on the creative process. It will be very long, if ever, before the secrets of creative artists can be revealed in controlled laboratory experiments. A second volume along the lines of *Modern Playwrights at Work* is planned to include such names for detailed study as: Brecht, O'Casey, Camus, Giraudoux, Wilder, Sartre, Ionesco, Beckett, Anouilh, Genet, Betti, Osborne, Duerrenmatt, Pinter, Weiss and Albee.

When should a writer start writing plays if he hasn't already started? Moss Hart said, "Plunge. There are no rules." Perhaps in first attempting a monologue, then a skit, then a scene hinging upon some revelation of character, then a short play, then a long play, can an aspiring playwright, through degrees as it were, come to face on a larger and larger scale the full array of problems posed by increasingly difficult forms of dramatic writing. And yet, as the study will show, a good many playwrights were writing "tragedies" and "sex farces" at the ages of seven to twelve. When the problem becomes his own by experience, then the aspiring playwright finds the strongest motivation and possibly learning from reading of others' initiation and secrets. An artist does not need a huge canvas to acquire technique and exercise a passion for expression. A small canvas can be the severest challenge to make the most of every stroke. A large canvas may only suggest a pretentious beginner. Early works should be considered exercises in self-discovery and not "for the ages." Leading dramatists as a rule have either destroyed, "lost," or refused to allow the publication of their earliest plays.

Some tyro playwright is always bound to say, "I can only work from inspiration. I can't work from technique." Inspiration is always the best thing to work from. A primitive person waiting for lightning to start a fire might have to wait pretty long. The person who discovered how to twirl a stick in a hollow of wood with dry shavings to start a fire at will, was better off. And the person who invented matches was a modern Prometheus. There is some truth in this analogy to the technique of playwriting. The professional knows the best means of controlling inspiration and acquires a passion for its discipline and due respect.

Playwriting has often been called "one of the loneliest professions," but many playwrights feel like Ibsen, O'Neill, or Albee. Ibsen said on his seventieth birthday that he had really never taken a vacation from "the exciting and exhausting writing of dramas." [10] "Writing is my vacation from living," said O'Neill, "—so I don't need vacations." [11] And Albee confessed, "Writing in itself is exhilarating, absorbing, involving. I can't think of anything else that I'd rather do." [12] The reason many playwrights have come to be happiest at their work is implied in Edith Hamilton's translation of an old Greek definition of happiness— "The exercise of vital powers along lines of excellence in a life affording them scope." [13]

1. Stanley J. Kunitz and Vineta Colby, *Twentieth Century Authors, First Supplement* (New York 1955), p. 669

2. Eugene Ionesco translated by Leonard Pronko, "Discovering the Theatre," *Tulane Drama Review* (September 1959), 9

3. Henry Hewes, "American Playwrights Self-Appraised," *Saturday Review* (September 3, 1955), 18

4. Harley Granville-Barker, *On Dramatic Method* (New York 1956), 17

5. William Inge, *The Dark at the Top of the Stairs* with an introduction by Tennessee Williams (New York 1958), vii

6. Gilbert Millstein, "Ten Playwrights Tell How It Starts," *New York Times Magazine* (December 6, 1959), 63

7. Arne Kildal, *Speeches and New Letters of Henrik Ibsen* (Boston 1919), 49

8. Walter Kerr, *How Not to Write a Play* (New York 1955), 32

9. Allan Lewis, *The Contemporary Theatre* (New York 1962), 127

10. Kildal, 58

11. Arthur and Barbara Gelb, *O'Neill* (New York 1962), 235

12. R. S. Stewart, "John Gielgud and Edward Albee Talk about the Theatre," *Atlantic* (April 1965), 63

13. Edith Hamilton, *The Greek Way to Western Civilization* (New York 1930), p. 21

If the word and example of the foremost playwrights can't help you in playwriting, whose word and example can?

Contents

Illustrations

Following page 14

*Illustrations printed through the
courtesy of the New York Public
Library Picture Collection.*

Chapter I

Henrik Ibsen

IF EVER there was proof of the value of subsidizing promising talent in playwriting, that proof was Henrik Ibsen, "The Father of Modern Drama." At the age of thirty-eight in his petition for a poet's pension of 400 specie dollars a year, Ibsen on April 15, 1866, wrote Charles XV, King of Sweden and Norway, "It is not for a care-free existence I am fighting, but for the possibility of devoting myself to the task which I believe and know has been laid upon me by God—the work which seems to me more important and needful in Norway than any other, that of arousing the nation and leading it to think great thoughts." [1] Ibsen turned to the King as "my one last hope" without whose help he would "suffer the bitterest disappointment which can befall a human soul—the disappointment of having to give up my life-work." [2] Ibsen got the poet's pension for life. Not until he was fifty-one did he write a play which earned international fame—*A Doll's House*. By the age of seventy, Ibsen has so fulfilled himself that on March 23, 1898, at a state dinner in Christiania, now called Oslo, he could speak to the gathering of "that rare fairytale fate which I have had: to gain fame and name in many lands. And I have gained warm, understanding hearts out there, too. *That* first and foremost." [3] When he died eight years later, Ibsen was as famous as the near mythical Tolstoy or even Victor Hugo. As "The Father of Modern Drama," Ibsen has been fused heart and soul into that drama's life-stream as surely as this can be done by heredity in literature.

I

THE GROWTH OF IBSEN'S CREATIVE SPIRIT IN LIFE

Not before the winter of 1848–49, when he was twenty years old, did Ibsen write his first play. In the seaport of snowbound Grimstad, Norway, as a lonely apprentice to an apothecary, Ibsen in his little

1

back-room concocted quite a literary pharmaceutical—a full-length tragedy in turgid blank verse, *Catiline*. He showed *Catiline* to a friend, Ole Schulerud who, as a law student at Christiania University and a native of Grimstad, believed *Catiline* was worthy of production by the Christiania Theatre. The Theatre ruled out the play as inept. *Catiline,* however, had let out Ibsen's genii, and it would never again quite go back into his apothecary's bottles.

Henrik Ibsen was born on March 20, 1828, to Knud and Marichen Ibsen in the Norwegian town of Skien at the head of a long narrow fjord opening to the sea in the South of Norway. Generations of Ibsens had kept shop or in the Viking heritage sailed the seas. On his mother's side, Ibsen was of German blood, and on his father's side, a medley of German, Scotch and Danish blood. The Ibsen home at Henrik's birth was a center of social life, and among the town's 3,200 or so people, the Ibsens were elite. "My father was a merchant with a large business and wide connections," recalled Ibsen, "and he enjoyed dispensing reckless hospitality." [4] Ibsen thought of himself as very well born. "My parents both belonged to the most respected families of the Skien of their day. Chief Magistrate Paus, who for many years represented the town in the Storthing, and his brother, Judge Paus, were my father's half-brothers and my mother's cousins," wrote Ibsen on September 21, 1882, from Gossensass to his friend, Georg Brandes. "And my parents were just as nearly related to the Plesner, von der Lippe, Cappelen, and Blom families—that is to say, to almost all the patrician families who were at that time the most influential in the town and neighborhood." [5] In her book, *The Three Ibsens,* Bergliot Ibsen, who was a daughter of the writer, Björnsterne Björnson, and who married Ibsen's only child, Sigurd, reminisced of Ibsen's gifts, "Like his mother, he could draw and paint, and he had his father's liking to tell stories; but with him it became poetry." [6]

Henrik was the Ibsens' eldest living child. His father, Knud, was short, clever, outgoing and liked showing the world a big front; his mother, Marichen, was a quiet, gentle family-woman who saw in everything the moving hand of a Lutheran Providence. In 1826 the couple had a first child that died within a month after Henrik was born. Then after Henrik's birth in 1828 came contestants in the game of sibling rivalry: John Andreas in 1830; Hedvig in 1832; Nicolai Alexander in 1834; and Ole Paulus in 1836. As the eldest child, Henrik tried to find security in being domineering, arrogant, and difficult. "To all of us," wrote his sister Hedvig of Henrik's fondness for shutting himself in his room with his books, "he was a most unsympathetic boy, and we used to do everything in our power to disturb him, throwing stones and snowballs at the walls and door of his room in the hope of forcing him to join us in our games." And Hedvig recollected, "When he could bear the onslaughts no longer, he would rush out into the courtyard after us. But as he was not at all agile, and violence was entirely foreign to his nature, his attack did not go beyond this." [7]

As a child, Ibsen exercised his imagination and fantasy especially by playing magician, toying with paste-board figures mounted on wooden blocks, painting water colors, scrutinizing old prints, and reading books. These were the only signs of any marked visual or dramatic sense. Likely Henrik's childhood curiosity about human motives was very often sharply prodded, for he spent his formative years living in a house facing the market place which also served as the town square. "Stockman's Court, it was then called," Ibsen reminisced in January of 1881. "The court faced the church, with its high steps and its noteworthy tower. At the right of the church stood the town pillory, and at the left, the town hall, with the lock-up and the madhouse. The fourth side of the marketplace was occupied by the common and the Latin schools. The church stood in a clear place in the middle." [8] Through his early years, Ibsen could not but see and hear of just about everything exciting that went on in his hometown. Even though the Ibsens moved to a still bigger and finer house when he was about four, Ibsen recalled, "The market-place, where the two biggest schools were situated, was the natural meeting place and field of battle for the village youth." [9] Skien's typically Norwegian geography of North Sea, mountains, fjords and waterfalls came to mean home to Ibsen's spirit. All day long he could hear the muffled roar of the Langefos and the Klosterfos and lesser waterfalls with the intermittent shrill shrieking of literally hundreds of saw-mills located within ear-shot.

When Ibsen was eight, he was in for a traumatic experience. Through questionable business practices, his father went bankrupt. The family managed somehow to keep a small, run-down farm at Venstob on the outskirts of Skien. Snubbed and humiliated with the stigma that usually goes with bankruptcy, tantamount in a small town to a kind of legalized thievery, the once socially elite Ibsens were now driven to eke out a bare livelihood on marginal land. The Ibsens' rich relatives simply dropped them. They repeatedly turned a deaf ear to Knud's pleas for a new start. Ibsen's father grew bitter; his mother, melancholic; and Ibsen, abandoned and mocked by his friends among the children, was hurt profoundly for a lifetime. At the age of eight, Ibsen felt as he later put it in a poem, "an outcast . . . rejected as a guest at the sumptuous banquet of life." [10]

"From my fourteenth year, I was thrown upon my own resources," wrote Ibsen on November 18, 1877, to his uncle, Christian Paus; "it has been a long, hard struggle that I have won my way to where I stand now." [11] Ibsen was a self-made man. His lifelong appetite for fame and his great delight in all kinds of honors might have been a compensation for his terrible suffering as a child from society's sudden rejection of him. All his life, Ibsen had to prove through his talents that he both could and would win society's love and respect, but on his own terms and, in fact, by rebelling against the very values of the society that had rejected him in childhood.

On October 1, 1843, the Ibsens moved back to Skien. Magistrate Paus, the half-brother of Ibsen's father, opened his heart and purse enough to buy the Ibsens a humble home. Henrik dreamed of becoming a painter, but instead, his now practical family bundled him off as an apprentice to an apothecary in the neighboring town of Grimstad. Ibsen arrived there on January 3, 1844. He saw a port town on the North Sea with roughly one fourth of Skien's population, only 800 people, who for the most part earned a modest living from salt, flax, and herring. Ibsen soon found that just about everyone in Grimstad had been born there, expected to die there, and knew everyone else's business. Gossips gathered at the apothecary's shop. How deeply one native bowed to another, showed who had what bank balance; workmen bowed deeply to shipowners who nodded indulgently in return.

Gossip over his father's bankruptcy didn't help Ibsen; one lady described Ibsen as going around town "like an enigma, secured with seven seals." For about five years Ibsen lived out his adolescence on the verge of poverty in the provincial philistinism of tiny Grimstad. He "tried to do without underclothing and finally even without stockings . . . and in winter he went without an overcoat." [12] Days Ibsen worked for the apothecary, "a kind and good-natured man." Nights Ibsen studied his *Materia Medica*. He also prepared for university entrance examinations by studying Cicero and Seneca in Latin on his own, for Ibsen had notions of becoming a doctor. For recreation, he drew cartoons, read the *Bible,* Voltaire, the plays of Holberg and Oehlenschläger, and tried writing poetry himself. "His working power and physical endurance were phenomenal," noted C. L. Due, then

Ibsen's close friend, as reported in *The Critic* of July, 1906. "With the exception of only the earliest morning hours, he was at work by day and night." [13]

In his loneliness, Ibsen took special comfort in the company of the apothecary's hired girl, Else Borkedal, ten years his senior. Recent research has turned up this entry in the records of the Church of East Moland near Grimstad, dated October 9, 1846: "Baptized. Hans Jacob, the son of Else Borkedal and Henrik Ibsen." [14] Ibsen was eighteen. He stayed in Grimstad until the end of 1849. The whole matter was apparently hushed up, but by law, Ibsen still had to support the child until it was fourteen. Ibsen never in his lifetime acknowledged this child. Perhaps this helps explain why he confessed that throughout his career he lived "in constant apprehension of anything that might terminate his work as a writer, such as illness or accident" [15] and especially, "scandal."

In the winter of 1848–49, "*Catiline* was written in a little provincial town," said Ibsen to Peter Hansen in a letter of October 28, 1870, "where it was impossible for me to give expression to all that fermented in me except by mad, riotous pranks, which brought down upon me the ill will of all the respectable citizens, who could not enter into that world which I was wrestling with alone." [16]

By March of 1850, Ibsen was in Christiania and rooming with his friend, Ole Schulerud; Ibsen attended Heltberg's "student factory," a cram school to qualify candidates for college entrance examinations. Even though the Christiania Theatre turned down *Catiline,* Schulerud, in a gesture of wild confidence, paid out of his own near empty pocket for an edition of 250 copies; *Catiline* came off the press April 12, 1850, and sold in all 45 copies. The hungry Ibsen and Schulerud kept 50 copies but marketed the rest to an enterprising huckster for wrapping paper. Ibsen said, "In the days immediately following we lacked none of the first necessities of life." [17] *Catiline* sounded the defiantly probing key-note of much of Ibsen's work to come. Ibsen identified his own hatred of society's hypocrisy and cant with Catiline's, and to Ibsen, Cicero became the villain as the living symbol of a questionable *status quo.*

Although Ibsen failed his entrance examinations in Greek and mathematics, he passed everything else. In the summer of 1850, Ibsen had recovered enough from *Catiline's* death by neglect to write a short play, *The Viking's Barrow,* for the current Christiania Theatre's playwriting contest. Ibsen won a prize, and he saw the Christiania

Theatre produce his play on September 26, 1850, for a run of three performances. The biographer, Henrik Jaeger, who knew Ibsen personally, wrote, "All thought of taking up his studies at the University was abandoned once and for all." [18] When he wasn't writing plays, Ibsen was one of three contributing editors to a satirical newspaper, *The Man* (*Andhrimmer*), which had a short life. Now Ibsen really had "bread-worries."

Ibsen's rejection of medicine for playwriting marked the beginning of just about a lifelong alienation from his family in Skien. If they had forgiven the prodigal for having at the age of eighteen fathered a child out of wedlock, they did not forgive him for abandoning the respectability of medicine for the notoriety of the theatre of the mid-nineteenth century. To the end of his life, Ibsen's family looked upon him as "a lost soul." [19] For all their respectability, his parents in their late years separated, and his mother went to live with her daughter Hedvig, who had married a well-to-do merchant in Skien. Ibsen's father remained alone, embittered as ever, improvident, drunken, and lecherous. Ibsen's family had given him an object lesson in the nature of middle-class respectability that he was never to forget, though in later years he somewhat forgave.

The famous Norwegian violin virtuoso of the day, Ole Bull, was at this time a zealot for playing his magic fiddle to help promote Norwegian culture. He was especially transported by the notion of a national drama fusing Norway's folk arts. He saw in the twenty-three year old Ibsen enough signs of talent to engage him as "theatre poet" at the National Theatre in Bergen for five years at a salary of 300 specie dollars a year. Ibsen officially assumed his duties on November 6, 1851. During the theatrical season in this town of 25,000, performances took place only two or three times a week, obviously on week-ends. The National Theatre had been founded on January 2, 1850, and it was Ibsen's chief duty to commemorate "Foundation Day," each January 2nd, with an original national drama. Ole Bull in a small way was to Ibsen what Lorenzo de Medici was to young Michelangelo; Ibsen was literally subsidized in the European tradition of a poor artist having a rich patron. Ole Bull was soon impressed enough with Ibsen's work to grant him a traveling fellowship of 45 pounds so that from April to September, of 1852, Ibsen might study the full flow of theatrical production at Copenhagen and Dresden.

When Ibsen returned to Bergen, he was not only "theatre poet" but also "skene instruktor," the equivalent of scene designer and technical director. "Those years at Bergen were indeed my apprenticeship," [20] said Ibsen to the English drama critic and Ibsen's authorized English translator, William Archer. During his five years at the National Theatre, Ibsen had a hand in every aspect of the production of 29 plays each year. "Of these more than half were French," recorded Archer, "21 being by Scribe, himself, while at least half of the remainder were by adepts of his school." [21] The other playwrights produced were Shakespeare, Holberg, Oehlenschläger, Heiberg, Björnson, and, of course, Henrik Ibsen.

Ibsen studied dramatic literature by using the stage, itself, for his library and laboratory. For each January 2nd of his contract, Ibsen wrote, helped stage, and in the end, directed:

St. John's Night (1853)	*The Feast at Solhaug* (1856)
The Warrior's Barrow (1854,	*Olaf Liljekrans* (1857)
revised *Viking's Barrow*)	*Lady Inger of Östraat* (1855)

Ibsen's one hit was *The Feast at Solhaug,* which ran for six performances and which was the first play of Ibsen to reach the wider public of Christiania, Copenhagen and Stockholm. Ibsen survived at Bergen only by going into debt.

In 1857 Christiania's Norwegian Theatre was in financial hot water and, hoping to make matters more temperate, offered Ibsen double his salary to come to the capitol city as the new stage manager. Though already engaged to Suzannah Thoresen of Bergen, he accepted what must have appeared a fine opportunity. He assumed full duties on September 3, 1857, and married Suzannah on June 18, 1858. On December 23, 1859, they had their first and only child, Sigurd.

Magdalene Thoresen was the author of three plays Ibsen's theatre had produced in Bergen, and Ibsen met Suzannah at a party her stepmother, Magdalene, gave on January 7, 1856. It was love at first sight for Ibsen. On the second date with Suzannah at a ball in Bergen, he told her, as Bergliot Ibsen heard the story, "that if she would join him, he would become something really great in the world." [22] What Suzannah somewhat lacked in looks, she more than made up for in personality. "Hers is exactly the character desired by a man of mind," said Ibsen of Suzannah, then already long his wife, in writing of her to Peter Hansen, on October 28, 1870, "—she is illogical, but has a strong poetic instinct, a broad and liberal mind, and an almost violent antipathy to all petty considerations." [23] Ibsen had two pet names for his Suzannah: "Cat," suggesting her animal domesticity; and "Eagle," suggesting a rather dominating nobility. Bergliot Ibsen thought Suzannah had "a great sense of humor."

Theodore Jorgenson cites the period of 1859–60 as when things almost blacked out for Ibsen. Everything seemed to go wrong. His new play, *The Vikings of Helgeland,* launched at the Norwegian Theatre on November 24, 1858, financially foundered. The theme was the surrender of a man's real love for material considerations. What's more, so many plays that Ibsen produced foundered that the Norwegian Theatre was soon deeper in its old trouble. The Board of Directors charged Ibsen with bad judgment, idleness, and incompetence, and threatened his dismissal. To freshen his whole outlook, he in vain petitioned the Norwegian government on August 6, 1860, for a traveling stipend to study theatrical production throughout Europe. Climaxing these frustrations, Ibsen had found that, as a playwright, for three years he was creatively impotent. Finally in acute depression Ibsen told his wife he was going to kill himself and ran out of the house into the street. Suzannah's legs and good sense somehow headed Ibsen off.[24]

The Norwegian Theatre finally got out of hot water in the summer of 1862 by going bankrupt. Ibsen found the solution quite chilling, for his salary was far in arrears. Ibsen and his family somehow managed to live from a number of petty incomes: a grant in 1862 from the University of Christiania for Ibsen to compile Norwegian folk songs and folk stories by field work; the publication in December, 1862, of Ibsen's new play, *Love's Comedy,* a work in rhymed verse on the theme that when marriage makes love official, the glorious union becomes a casualty of babies, bills, and routine living; another grant from Christiania University on May 23, 1863, again to gather Norwegian folk songs and folk stories in the field; and finally in October, 1863, the publication of Ibsen's play, *The Pretenders,* portraying the power struggle between the aggressive King Haakon and the Hamlet-like Earl Skule—two sides of Ibsen's nature at war at the time.

After repeated petitions from Ibsen, the Norwegian Parliament, the Storthing, on September 12, 1863, finally granted him a traveling stipend, but still withheld the funds until the following April. On April 5, 1864, Ibsen set out alone for Rome, leaving behind his family and debts of over 500 specie dollars. His creditor was a lawyer named J. Nandrup of Christiania; Nandrup probably knew of the bankruptcy of Ibsen's father and now must have feared that Ibsen's wife and child might skip town with him. Nandrup foreclosed on the Ibsens; he had all their household effects sold at public auction. Suzannah and her child, Sigurd, were practically put out on the street, and quite dependent upon the kindness of friends and relatives.

In Rome, Ibsen had meanwhile begun his long poetic drama, *Brand,* of which he said, "This poem is not intended for the stage . . ." *Brand* had as its theme a man of unyielding principle who lives like an unloveable superman by the creed of all or nothing. Ibsen had so far written ten full length plays and literally had nothing. "I did not bewail the loss of the furniture, and things of that kind," wrote Ibsen to Björnson from Rome in October, 1866, upon hearing of the auction of all his household effects, "but to think that my private letters, and literary and other papers were in goodness knows whose hands, annoyed me excessively, as did also the loss of many things the value of which to me was not their money-value." [25] According to Bergliot Ibsen, Ibsen at this period could not even afford a postage stamp; but somehow his wife and child through his traveling stipend managed to join Ibsen.

He sent his completed *Brand* to his friend, Björnson, who liked it enough to submit it to his own publisher, Frederik Hegel of Gyldenals Publishing House in Copenhagen. After repeated, nerve-racking postponements for Ibsen, Hegel finally published *Brand* on March 15, 1866, to score a sensational run-away success of three editions in the first year. Then with what must have seemed to Ibsen the slowness of a Norwegian glacier, the Storthing, upon due recommendation of the King and his cabinet, on May 12, 1866, finally granted Ibsen a poet's pension of 400 specie dollars a year for life. "My future is now assured," said the thirty-eight year old Ibsen, "and I can pursue my vocation undisturbed." [26]

Ibsen followed *Brand* with *Peer Gynt;* the unloveable superman gave way to a reverse Norwegian character, a grown up Peter Pan always on the run from his responsibilities, never realizing himself, and in the end winding up as human bone-scrap for the Button-Moulder to recast in his ladle. *Peer Gynt* was published on November 14, 1867, and Norway's most influential critic, Clemens Petersen, called it "not poetry" and, "Full of riddles which are insoluble because there is nothing in them at all." [27] "I shall try my luck as a photographer," wrote the quite embittered Ibsen to Björnson from Rome on December 9, 1867, in Janko Lavrin's translation. "My contemporaries in the North I shall take in hand one after the other. I will not spare the child in the mother's womb, nor the thought or feeling that lies under the word of any living soul that deserves the honour of my notice." [28]

Ibsen's first play as "a photographer" came out on September 30, 1869, *The League of Youth,* a satire on small town politics and snobbery of the Grimstad variety, done with a fumbling focus. It would take Ibsen years to become an expert "photographer."

"The work which I am now bringing out will be my chief work," said Ibsen of *Emperor and Galilean* in writing to Ludvig Dae from Dresden on February 23, 1873; Ibsen brought out the play on October 16, 1873. A historical tragedy in the modern idiom, *Emperor and Galilean* had taken Ibsen ten years of working on and off at actually two plays, *Caesar's Apostasy* and *Emperor Julian.* Ibsen believed the play to be a "world drama" because of its universal theme of paganism at war with Christianity. *Emperor and Galilean* was never produced.

"*Peer Gynt* is not intended for the stage at all," [29] said Ibsen in a letter of August 17, 1881 to the publisher, Ludwig Passarge. In 1874, however, Ibsen corresponded with Edvard Grieg suggesting he compose music for *Peer Gynt* and even specifying what kind and just where to insert it. *Peer Gynt* with Grieg's music opened on February 24, 1876, at the Christiania Theatre and ran for an almost unheard of 37 performances. Clemens Petersen must have felt quite ill. Thereafter, as if there was a kind of time span in his creative *accouchements,* with few exceptions, Ibsen continued to give birth mentally to a new brain-child in the modern idiom every two years or so:

The Pillars of Society (1877)	*The Lady from the Sea* (1888)
A Doll's House (1879)	*Hedda Gabler* (1890)
Ghosts (1881)	*The Master Builder* (1892)
An Enemy of the People (1882)	*Little Eyolf* (1894)
The Wild Duck (1884)	*John Gabriel Borkman* (1896)
Rosmersholm (1886)	*When We Dead Awaken* (1899)

For roughly twenty-seven years beginning in April of 1864 Ibsen, except for two short visits, chose to live away from Norway while receiving a poet's pension and writing almost only of Norwegians. With his family by him, he found he did his best work abroad. "The world can thank my mother that it has one less indifferent painter," said Sigurd Ibsen, "and one more great poet." [30] In self-exile, the three Ibsens made up a rather charmed family circle; Bergliot Ibsen declared, "they loathed publicity." Though they lived chiefly in Munich and Dresden, they also lived at some time in Capri, Sorrento, Rome and Gossensass. Ibsen, himself, travelled much to be present at premieres of his plays. In 1880, Sigurd planned to study law at Christiania University; Ibsen then thought of repatriating but gave up the idea in disgust because of trouble in transferring his son's credits from a transient and foreign educational background.

"I have always loved stormy weather," wrote Ibsen to his sister, Hedvig Stousland, from Munich on March 13, 1891, "to this, a part of my literary production bears witness."[31] *The Pillars of Society* first set Scandinavia in a Wotan mood toward Ibsen: the wealthy shipbuilder, Consul Bernick, a pillar of society, is portrayed as nobly impressive on the outside but hollowly selfish within, while Lona Hessel, returning from America as an emancipated woman, sees the fraud in Bernick and calls society's real pillars "truth and freedom." *A Doll's House,* with Lona Hessel possibly suggesting Nora, set off a whole international hot and cold front of tempests: Nora as a woman believed she had just as much right to self-realization and self respect as did her husband, even if it meant walking out on her family. "After Nora, Mrs. Alving had to come," Ibsen wrote Sophie Adlersparre from Rome on June 24, 1882, in Sprinchorn's translation.[32] Nora left home, but Mrs. Alving stayed to conform to society's ideals of respectability, and so Mrs. Alving brings on her only child, Oswald, a hereditary fate from a syphillitic father. The first edition of *Ghosts* was published in December, 1881, and wasn't sold out until 1894; on December 22, 1881, Ibsen wrote Ludwig Passarge from Rome, "My new play has now appeared and has occasioned a terrible uproar in the Scandinavian press." What an uproar may be gathered from Ibsen's remark in a letter to Olaf Skavlan from Rome on January 24, 1882— "The only man in Norway who has stood up frankly, boldly, and courageously for me is Björnson."[33] Shaw could recall when Ibsen was denounced "as an obscene and malignant lunatic."[34] Oswald in *Ghosts,* made necessary Dr. Stockman in Ibsen's next play, *An Enemy of the People,* in which the public hue and cry reaches a crescendo against the doctor who discovers diseased waters at a health resort and refuses to hush it up. As Ibsen said, "I have always loved stormy weather."[35] He also said, according to Bergliot Ibsen, "I have become famous by constant abuse."[36]

At the zenith of his career in his mid-fifties, Ibsen appeared undersized, a broad shouldered and slightly stooped gentleman with a dome-like brow, bushy gray whiskers, and a formidable reserve and dignity behind his gold-rimmed spectacles and piercing, small, light-

blue eyes. They called him "The Sphinx." "Nearly all these amiable
fabulists revamp the stock stories about his drinking alternate drafts
of brandy and beer," reported *The Critic* of July, 1906, "or about his
having a plate glass mirror inside his hat and contemplating his coun-
tenance with approval every few minutes." [37] Tone-deaf to music,
according to Gosse, and reading little but the daily newspaper and his
Bible, Ibsen until the last five years was hardly sick a day in his life. He
took good care of himself. "A man's gifts are not a property," Ibsen
wrote Björnson from Rome on December 28, 1867; "they are a duty." [38]

"Friends are an expensive luxury," said Ibsen in a letter to Georg
Brandes from Dresden on March 6, 1870; "and when a man's whole
capital is invested in a calling and a mission in life, he cannot afford
to keep them." [39] Ibsen found friends kept him from being himself
out of regard for them. Over the years he had very few close friends:
Ole Bull, his first patron; Björnsterne Björnson, the Norwegian writer
and critic; Georg Brandes, the Danish Shakespearean scholar and
Ibsen champion; and Frederik Hegel, Ibsen's publisher.

Ibsen was charged with a thirst for decorations and a vanity for
displaying them across his chest on public occasions. Bergliot Ibsen
believed these honors were Ibsen's way of proving to the world that
he had rubbed out the blotch on his family's honor from his father's
bankruptcy at Skien. They were also proof of Ibsen's dearly earned
merit and of literature worthy of the highest recognition in a society
too prone to ignore it. "I do not see in this homage which is paid me
here a mere personal homage," said Ibsen in a speech at a banquet in
his honor on April 13, 1898, at Stockholm, attended by Oscar II, King
of Norway and Sweden. "I see in it an approval of literature as a cultural power expressed by the Swedish people." [40] Ibsen's chief honors
were: Knight of the Order of St. Olaf, the Vasa Order, the Ernestine
Order, an honorary doctoral degree in letters from the University of
Uppsala, the Grand Cross of the Dannebrog Order, and the Order of
the Northern Star. "It is true that Ibsen himself sews on his vagrant
buttons," John Paulsen recalls Fru Ibsen saying; "but the fact that
they hold so well is *my* doing, for without his knowledge, I always
'finish them off,' which he forgets to do. But don't disturb the conviction: it makes him so happy." [41] Ibsen believed his greatness related to
such trivia as sewing on his own buttons. "One should never let
others do what one can do oneself," he told Paulsen. "If you begin
with blacking your boots, you will get on to putting your room in
order, laying the fire, etc. In this way, you will at last find yourself an
emancipated man, independent of Tom, Dick, or Harry." [42]

"My life has been like a long, long Holy Week," said Ibsen at seventy, "and now in the real Passion Week, my life is transformed into a fairy play." [43] Though Ibsen became world-famous, his personal life was neither easy nor necessarily happy. He had lived hand to mouth for years. There was the illegitimate child by Else Borkedal. Ibsen had cut himself off from his own family to fulfill his "mission" in life, a devil's disciple to many in those days. His mother had died on June 3, 1869, and not until September 26, 1869, did he write his sister Hedvig from Stockholm, "So our dear old Mother is dead. I thank you for having so lovingly fulfilled the duties which were incumbent on us all. You are certainly the best!" [44] Upon his father's death, Ibsen wrote his uncle Christian Paus from Munich on November 18, 1887, "My chief reason for writing home so very seldom during all these years of struggle was that I could offer no assistance of any kind to my parents . . . It has been a great consolation to me to know that my parents were surrounded by attached relatives . . . a great support to me during my toils and endeavours, and has furthered the accomplishment of my work in this world." [45] Ibsen knew that at least he had given his parents a kind of distinction; Aase in *Peer Gynt,* for instance, he said was modelled after his mother, and *John Gabriel Borkman* suggests his father's troubles.

Ibsen's son, Sigurd, was denied a professorship at Christiania University and was long distrusted in Norwegian politics for his foreign rearing and education. "I will save every penny," Ibsen often told his daughter-in-law, Bergliot, "so that Sigurd can be independent of that rabble." [46] Ibsen's wife, Suzannah, became increasingly a gout-ridden invalid. The Ibsens stopped having "at homes" when guests gossiped about the simple refreshments; Ibsen had skimped for so long to survive that once he could afford better, he still made a virtue of Spartan living and kept careful account of every penny spent.

In his sixties, Ibsen had an affair of sorts with Emilie Bardach, an eighteen year old Austrian refugee at Gossensass, with talk of his divorce in the air. At his death, Ibsen left an estate of about 50,000 specie dollars. The "Father of Modern Drama" had human frailties along with a distinguished talent.

In March of 1900, for the first time Ibsen's health failed him when erysipelas struck, and then in 1901 a stroke really felled him. Ibsen recovered, but another stroke hit even harder in 1903 leaving him mentally at loss and too paralyzed to walk. On May 23, 1906, Henrik Ibsen died at the age of seventy-eight. Norway gave him a state funeral in Christiania, and the mourners included just about every Nor-

wegian dignitary from King Haakon and Queen Maud on down.
Foreign nations also sent representatives.

II

COMMERCIAL CONSIDERATIONS AFFECTING IBSEN'S PLAYWRITING

Ibsen was always his own literary agent, for in his day there were
no literary agents to relieve an author of business head-aches for a 10%
fee of the gross from his properties. Ibsen was long poor in spite of
his success for one reason: legal, literary piracy. The nature of Ibsen's
circumstance is vital information for any dramatist today who has any
illusions about how many would run up the "Jolly Roger" once they
spotted on attractive property on the literary high seas outside of international copyright agreements. Russia's flag is red, but to any dramatist whose work the Russians admire and who is no Russian, that
flag, for all the royalty he gets, might as well be the "Jolly Roger."
Here is a revealing excerpt from Ibsen's plea to the Storthing for an
increase in his poet's pension and written March 27, 1881, as translated
by John Laurvik and Mary Morison:

> From the Christiania Theatre we, as a rule, received a small payment,
> once for all, for our plays. For *The Vikings* they offered me 30 specie
> dollars, informing me at the same time that if I was not satisfied with
> this, they would, being legally entitled to do so, pay the piece without
> giving me any compensation whatever. The other theatres in Norway,
> and the traveling theatrical companies, naturally paid nothing; and the
> same state of matters prevailed throughout Sweden and Denmark, as far
> as the smaller theatres were concerned.[47]

True, Ibsen received his "poet's pension" of 400 specie dollars a year
from Norway effective 1866 for life. Ibsen still felt that he was entitled
to a higher poet's pension as a form of indemnity his country's parliament owed by failing to protect the fruits of his labor. The Berne
Convention, establishing international copyright laws for all subscrib-
ing nations and thereby an enforcement of royalty payments, was not
signed by Denmark, lawfully the country of Ibsen's publisher, Hegel,
until after Ibsen's lifework was done.

Ibsen received nothing for hundreds of performances of his plays in
the United States during his life-time; and afterwards, his heirs received nothing. A translator, nevertheless, might make money and

HENRIK IBSEN
1870

AUGUST STRINDBERG
1907

ANTON CHEKHOV
(*undated*)
1860-1904

BERNARD SHAW
c. 1912

Luigi Pirandello
(*undated*)
1867-1936

John Galsworthy
c. 1913

EUGENE O'NEILL
c. 1915

TENNESSEE WILLIAMS
(*undated*)
1911-

even acquire rights to Ibsen's work by foreign law. So, for instance, William Archer acquired full rights to royalties from Ibsen's plays performed in England. According to Bergliot Ibsen, from eighteen Russian editions of Ibsen's collected works neither Ibsen nor his heirs received a kopeck in royalties. The biggest money Ibsen ever earned came from the Gyldenals Publishing House, paying him or his heirs in equal installments over twenty years the sum of 200,000 kroner, roughly 50,000 specie dollars, for full rights to publication of Ibsen's collected works. If the dramatist is somewhat protected now by international copyright agreements, part of his fight was fought by "The Father of Modern Drama," Ibsen. "In theatre work," said Ibsen in Koht's translation, "one learns to be practical, one grows accustomed to admit the power of circumstances and temporarily to renounce higher considerations when it cannot be otherwise." [48] Note the word, "temporarily."

In his five years at Bergen, Ibsen wrote Norwegian national dramas to please his patron, Ole Bull, but Ibsen's biographer, Halvdan Koht, said, "Ibsen regarded it clearly as his mission to write national drama." [49] "I will not be an antiquary or a geographer," [50] insisted Ibsen of dealing with Norwegian history and folk-tales; he was certain he could overcome the limitations of his subject matter by changing it, as he put it, "into higher symbolic truth which should retain its vitality in the future." [51] "The national writer," Ibsen told Georg Brandes of his overall intent, "is he who can impart to his work the underlying tone which comes to us from sea and mountain, shore and valley and, above all, from our soul." [52] Ibsen was plainly trying to find the deepest, widest, truest identification of his plays with his prospective public.

At times, Ibsen's prospective public deeply disturbed him. While weathering the gales of abuse his play, *Ghosts,* stirred up, he wrote Georg Brandes from Rome on January 3, 1882:

> When I think how slow and heavy and dull the general intelligence is at home, when I notice the low standard by which everything is judged, a deep despondency comes over me, and it often seems to me that I might just as well end my literary activity at once. They really do not need poetry at home . . .[53]

This despairing note, in fact, sounded much earlier in a letter to Clemens Peterson from Christiania on August 10, 1863: "it would be difficult to convince you who do not know," wrote Ibsen, "of how terrible a degree I feel intellectually alone up here." [54] As a dramatist, Ibsen definitely felt that he was what is today called "avant-garde." "I maintain that a fighter in the intellectual vanguard can never collect a majority around him," wrote Ibsen to Georg Brandes from Rome on June 12, 1883. "At the point where I stood when I wrote each of my books, there now stands a tolerably compact crowd; but I myself am no longer there; I am elsewhere; farther ahead, I hope." [55]

But if Ibsen put himself in the vanguard, he was still ready to be "practical" and to "temporarily renounce higher considerations when it cannot be otherwise." In his lifetime, Ibsen's biggest commercial success, though it gave rise to violent dispute, was *A Doll's House*. On their own, many theatrical managers and stars chose to rewrite the ending so Nora returned to her family. "This much is certain," Ibsen said in correspondence with Heinrich Lauber from Munich on February 18, 1880; "that the play with its present ending has had an almost unprecedented success in Stockholm, Christiania, and Copenhagen." Ibsen then admitted, "The alternative ending I have prepared, not because I thought it was required, but simply at the request of a North German manager and of an actress who is going on tour in North Germany as 'Nora.' I herewith send you a copy of the altered scene, on reading which you will, I hope, acknowledge that the effect of the piece can only be weakened by employing it. I trust that you will decide to produce the play in its original form." [56] But when *Ghosts* went unproduced for two years in Scandinavia and for almost six years in Germany, Ibsen didn't change a word. "The future belongs to my book," he wrote Frederik Hegel from Rome on March 16, 1882. "Those fellows who have bellowed so about it, have no real connection with the life of their own day." [57] Venereal disease was rampant in Europe; Nietzsche with his doctrine of the superman was to die of it. The public wouldn't tolerate bringing it onstage.

Ibsen implied he never tried to get a play produced by deliberately tailoring a role to smartly fit a star even when the star was a manager, too. At a banquet the star, Constance Brun, told the then famous Ibsen that she and her friends liked best to act "parts" in his plays, and he replied, possibly chilling the gathering, "May I be allowed to remark that in all my life I have never written 'parts' but that I merely try to draw human beings? I have never written a play with an actor or actress in mind." [58] "I have quite definite conceptions of my own characters," Ibsen told Archer, "and the actors come between me and these conceptions, in some cases permanently distorting or obscuring them." Ibsen had drawn life, and he saw his characters "acted;" O'Neill decades later complained despondently of the same thing. And yet at Bergen's National Theatre, Ibsen had to submit to the discipline of writing for a repertory theatre with the same eight men and five women when he tried to fulfill his contract of writing one new play a year. Why specify balsa with only Norwegian oak or birch or spruce available? Ibsen also had to stay within the staging limits of a fixed budget. Certainly once Ibsen began writing his highly controversial plays in the modern idiom, he seldom used more than seven characters and often only one or at most two settings to lure managers to produce his plays at a minimum risk.

Critics were always a potential commercial as well as aesthetic problem to Ibsen, to put it mildly. At Christiania in the years 1858 to 1862, Ibsen heard critics call his work, as the biographer Jaeger recorded, "Norwegian weeds," "Norwegian trash," and pass such judgment as, "Herr Ibsen as a dramatic author is a complete nonentity about whom the nation can hardly be expected to plant a protecting hedge."[59] "Your review will be a decisive factor in my countrymen's reception of the poem," Ibsen wrote Copenhagen's chief critic, Clemens Petersen, on December 4, 1865, regarding *Brand* in a letter that few if any playwrights today would dare write a critic.[60] In a letter to his mother-in-law, Magdalene Thoresen, from Dresden on May 29, 1870, to encourage her writing regardless of what critics said, Ibsen commented:

> Most critical fault-finding, when reduced to its essentials, simply amounts to reproach of the author because he is himself—thinks, feels, sees, and creates, as himself, instead of seeing and creating in the way the critic would have done—if he had been able.[61]

In Ibsen's case, critics came to have a fantastically paradoxical effect. "My enemies have helped me greatly," Ibsen told Bergliot Ibsen. "They attacked me so viciously that in the end people wanted to know who this man was they kept shouting at."[62]

Ibsen was so often attacked by critics that to survive he acquired a technique for dealing with them like crashing a paper barrier. From Dresden, he wrote Georg Brandes on April 4, 1872:

> As regards the agitation against you, the lies, calumnies, etc., I will give you a piece of advice which I know from personal experience to be the best possible. Be dignified. Dignity is the only weapon against such

assaults. Look straight ahead; never reply in the newspapers . . . in
short, behave as though you had no idea that you had any antagonists
. . . In the old days, when I read an attack on myself in the morning, I
thought: I am ruined; my reputation will never survive this. But it did
survive it; and now no one remembers what was written—even I myself
have long ago forgotten it. Therefore, do not demean yourself by bandy-
ing words with this, that, or the other person . . . Do you believe that
what is worm-eaten has any real power of resistance! [63]

No record exists to show that Ibsen ever invested his own money in
the production of his plays. The bankruptcy of the Norwegian Theatre in 1862 in Christiania and his own personal bankruptcy there in
1864 as a kind of chain-reaction, reminded Ibsen what a risky business
theatrical production could be. Ibsen perhaps felt thereafter that he
had risked all he could afford to by devoting roughly two years to
writing each of his plays; the gambler in talent refused to gamble
with the little money he had to sustain it.

III

AESTHETIC CONSIDERATIONS AFFECTING
IBSEN'S PLAYWRITING

In his first four months of working at *Brand* in Rome, Ibsen in leisure moments got to see much ancient and renaissance art, and on
September 16, 1864, he wrote Björnson, "I can often see only conventions where others profess to find laws." [64] Four more years in Rome
spent largely in studies involving *Emperor and Galilean* only confirmed this opinion for Ibsen. When the influential Clemens Petersen
condemned *Peer Gynt* as "not poetry," Ibsen wrote to Björnson on
December 9, 1867, "The conception of poetry in our country, in Norway, shall be made to conform to the book. There is no stability in
the world of ideas. The Scandinavians of this century are not
Greeks." [65] "In my opinion no one has sinned more against the established conventions of beauty than he," Ibsen said of Michelangelo in
later writing to Brandes from Dresden on July 15, 1869; "nevertheless
everything which he has created is beautiful, because it is full of character. Raphael's art has never really warmed me," confessed Ibsen;
"his personages belong to a period before the fall of man." [66] Ibsen
said, "to us, conventional ugliness may be beautiful by virtue of its inherent truth." Ibsen became much taken with the notion of a kind of

evolutionary change in aesthetics. "For art forms become extinct," he wrote the actress Lucie Wolf from Rome on May 25, 1883, "just as the preposterous animal forms of prehistoric times became extinct when their day was over." [67] Late in life, Ibsen refused to formulate any universally binding precepts about anything because he didn't believe such precepts existed. "Aesthetics," he wrote Björnson, "are as great a curse to poetry as theology to religion." [68]

Although aesthetics might change with the artist and his times, Ibsen believed that the artist, himself, had certain fixed traits. "So to conduct one's life as to realize one's self," wrote Ibsen to Björnson from Gossensass on August 8, 1882, "—this seems to me the highest attainment possible to a human being. It is the task of one and all of us, but most of us bungle it." [69] "What makes a work of art the spiritual property of its creator," said Ibsen, "is the fact that he has imprinted on it the stamp of his own personality." [70]

When Laura Petersen asked Ibsen for advice about pursuing a career as author, he replied from Dresden on June 11, 1870, "It is always a risky thing to give advice . . . The great thing is to become honest and truthful in dealing with one's self." And then Ibsen elucidated,— "not to determine to do this or determine to do that, but to do what one *must* do because one is one's self. All the rest simply leads to falsehood." [71] Ibsen also cautioned Laura Petersen on the need to be mature. "One must have something to create from, some life-experience," warned Ibsen. "The author who has not that, does not create; he only writes books." [72]

On September 10, 1874, Ibsen on the spur of the moment was asked to speak to a gathering of Norwegian students honoring him at Christiania with a torchlight procession after viewing a performance of his play, *The League of Youth.* "And what is it then that constitutes a poet?" asked Ibsen. "As for me, it was a long time before I realized that to be a poet, that is chiefly to see, but mark well, to see in such a manner that the thing seen is perceived by his audience just as the poet saw it." And then Ibsen made quite a revelation: "And as regards the thing which has been lived through, that is just the secret of the literature of modern times. . . . But no poet lives through anything isolated," Ibsen went on. "What he lives through, all of his countrymen live through together with him." [73] Here, to Ibsen, was the bridge of understanding between poet and public. Though many saw in Ibsen's work the propaganda they looked for, Ibsen said quite emphatically in a speech to the Women's Rights League in Christiania on May 26, 1898, "My task has been the *description of humanity.*"[74] His last public sentiment about the author as an artist, Ibsen stated in a speech to the Author's League in Stockholm, April 11, 1898, at the age of seventy: "authors must go their own wild ways—," said this Norwegian maverick, "ay, as wild as they can ever wish, if they are to fulfill the mission of their lives."[75]

Ibsen's view of life slanted his perspective and somehow colored the light of all his plays. "From special reforms, I expect nothing," wrote Ibsen to Brandes from Dresden on September 24, 1871. "The whole race is on the wrong track. Or is there really anything tenable in the present situation—with its unattainable ideals, etc.?"[76] In an earlier letter to Brandes on December 20, 1870, Ibsen said, "Yes—I must confess that the only thing I love about liberty is the struggle for it; I care nothing for the possession of it." On January 3, 1882, in the state of mind that was to show in *An Enemy of the People,* Ibsen wrote to Georg Brandes:

> I, at any rate, shall never be able to join a party which has the majority on its side. Björnson says, "The majority is always right," and as a practical politician he is bound, I suppose, to say so. I, on the contrary, of necessity say, "The minority is always right." Naturally I am not thinking of that minority of stagnationists who are left behind by the great middle party, which with us is called Liberal; I mean that minority which leads the van, and pushes on to points which the majority has not yet reached. I hold that man is in the right who is more clearly in league with the future.[77]

A society to Ibsen could be no greater than the individuals making it up. "An element of nobility must enter into our political life, our administration, our representation, and our press," Ibsen told a gathering of workingmen at Trondhjem, June 14, 1885, and he specified, "I think of the nobility of character, of the nobility of will and mind. That alone it is which can make us free. . . . It will come to us from our women and from our workingmen."[78] "It has been said of me on different occasions that I am a pessimist," Ibsen remarked in a speech at a banquet in Stockholm on September 24, 1887. "And so I am in so far as I do not believe in the everlastingness of human ideals. But I am also an optimist," he carefully qualified himself, "in so far as I firmly believe in the capacity for procreation and development of ideals."[79]

IV

IBSEN'S WORKING METHODS IN PLAYWRITING

Genesis

When the writer, Peter Hansen, asked the then forty-two year old Ibsen the nature of his working methods, Ibsen replied on October 28, 1870, in one of his most searching letters on the subject. He wrote Hansen of keeping bottled up on his desk a live scorpion, perhaps not so unusual a pet for one periodically so envenomed as Ibsen was psychologically for years. When the scorpion regularly fell ill, Ibsen would relieve the insect by dropping near it a bit of tender fruit into which the scorpion would violently empty its poison and then return to health. "Does not something of the same kind happen with us poets?" asked Ibsen. "The laws of nature regulate the spiritual world also." [80]

In his speech to the Norwegian students after their torchlight procession honoring him on September 10, 1874, Ibsen, enlarging upon the experience of genesis of his plays said:

> Partly I have written on that which only by glimpses and at my best moments I have felt stirring vividly within me as something great and beautiful. I have written on that which, so to speak, has stood higher than my daily self, and I have written on this in order to fasten it over against and within myself.
>
> But I have also written on the opposite, on that which to introspective contemplation appears as the dregs and sediments of one's nature. The work of writing has in this case been to me like a bath which I have felt to leave cleaner, healthier, and freer.[81]

On June 16, 1880, Ibsen penned a letter to Ludwig Passarge from Munich and reaffirmed his earlier testimony about genesis: "in every new poem or play I have aimed at my own spiritual emancipation and purification—for a man shares the responsibility and guilt of the society to which he belongs,"—a position, of course, almost identically to be that of Arthur Miller.[82]

The nature of the creative drive had minor variations. "I am revolving in my mind just now, the plan for a new dramatic work in four acts," Ibsen wrote Georg Brandes from Rome on June 12, 1883. "From time to time a variety of whimsies gathers in one's mind, and one wants to find an outlet for them." [83] His "whimsies" he elsewhere referred to as "some tomfoolery" and also "deviltry." The call to new battles might catch his ear. After finishing what was to be his last play, *When We Dead Awaken,* Ibsen in a letter to Count Prozor in March 1900, said, "I do not imagine that I shall be able to keep permanently away from old battlefields. However, if I were to make my appearance again, it would be with new weapons and in new armor." [84] Ibsen, incidentally, was practising his realism beginning with *The League of Youth* in 1869; not until 1881 did Zola write his famous essay, "Naturalism on the Stage" emphasizing the need of modern drama to rely upon modern science to approach the truth. "Zola descends into the sewer to take a bath," said Ibsen; "I do in order to scour it." [85]

For Ibsen, a special set of personal attitudes were at work not only in genesis but throughout the whole of his creating a play. He declared on his seventieth birthday, that he had never really taken a vacation "from the exciting and exhausting writing of dramas." [86] Ibsen always had his work on his mind. Self-exile from Norway he found good for him. "Life there . . . has something unspeakably wearing about it," he said of his country, ". . . it is the curse of narrow circumstances that they make the soul narrow." [87] "I could not write freely and unreservedly and fully up there," Ibsen noted to Björnson in a letter of September 29, 1884, "which is the same as saying that I could not write at all." [88] "We see most clearly at a distance," Ibsen penned Laura Petersen from Dresden on June 11, 1870; "the details confuse; we must be away from what we desire to judge." [89] Although self-exiled for almost twenty-seven years, Ibsen in his intense concern with Norwegian life became more Norwegian than ever. "He never became what in German is called 'eingeburget'," said Koht, "spiritually at home in any one of the foreign countries—Germany or Italy—in which he lived." [90] "I understand clearly," said Ibsen, "that it is really only in the solitude of my own thoughts that I am myself." [91]

To these attitudes, Ibsen needed also the love, peace of mind, and encouragement of his wife and son. "Quite seriously I believe that if Mother had not compelled him to sit down at his desk every morning," recollected Sigurd of his father, "half of his work might never have been written." And Sigurd went on, "She knew what fate had entrusted to her care, and she regarded it as her task in life." [92]

Ibsen relied upon a routine work day with habits trial and error had proved to him most conducive to good work. He appeared to live with the regularity of a self-winding clock. Usually, as Ibsen wrote his son from Gossensass on July 20, 1884, "I get up every day at 6 a. m. at the latest . . . sometimes earlier." According to Jaeger, Ibsen found dressing so helpful in resolving creative problems that had troubled him the night before, that he spent an hour or so getting into his clothes.[93] Sometimes, as in creating *Brand* and *Peer Gynt,* Ibsen might take long walks along the seashore in the solitude of dawn breaking. "When he sets about the execution of one of his plans, he takes only what food is absolutely necessary," reported Jaeger of Ibsen. "A small piece of bread and half a cup of black coffee is all that he takes before sitting down to his desk in the morning. He thinks he would be impeded in his work if he were to eat more." [94]

By 9 a. m. at latest, Ibsen would be settled down in his study. Creative stimulation for him came not only from an almost empty stomach but, according to Archer, "He couldn't work without smoking—not cigars, but a short pipe." [95] Some thought Ibsen also drank to work; Archer thought Ibsen's health suffered from drinking, and Shaw, the teetotaller, thought Ibsen drank too much. "Environment has a great influence upon the forms in which the imagination creates," wrote Ibsen to Peter Hansen on October 28, 1870. "Can not I, in the style of Christoff in *Jacob V. Tyboe,* point at *Brand* and *Peer Gynt,* and say, 'See, wine did this?' And is there not something in *The League of Youth* which reminds one of sausage and beer?" [96] Friends recall Ibsen on occasion at cafes drinking thin Italian wine, or beer, or cognac. Ibsen's carefully kept accounts show no extraordinary outlay for alcohol. Not to drink on the continent where the drinking water was often contaminated, might even be unwise.

"He has to pace back and forth through three or four rooms while writing his plays," related Jaeger. "So he spends four hours every forenoon, pacing and writing, writing and pacing, now and then taking a pull at a pipe. Otherwise, he never smokes tobacco." [97] Rumor had it that on his desk Ibsen kept a variety of carved wooden figures including a cat, a bear, a rabbit, a dog, and even Satan, and that Ibsen kindled his imagination by warmly identifying the characters of his current play with these figures and manipulating them in combinations to strike a creative fire. Henderson thought the rumors true and that Ibsen found in these figures the equivalent of the pasteboard ones of his childhood days. "I never saw anything of the kind," observed Archer, "either in Rome, Munich, or Christiania; and photographs of his study in Christiania confirm my skepticism." [98] And yet, oddly enough, in his very last play, *When We Dead Awaken,* Ibsen has his counterpart, Professor Rubek say of making to order portrait busts of ladies and gentlemen—and this is Archer's translation—"To order, yes. With animals' faces behind the masks. Those I threw in gratis —into the bargain, you understand." [99] Ibsen's study was quite bare except for a desk, a chair, his writing materials, and a large brass-bound, family-type *Bible* with gilt edged pages.

At 1 p. m., Ibsen would take a walk. "When he has selected his material, he turns it over in his mind for a long while before setting pen to paper," said Jaeger after interviewing Ibsen. "A great deal of this thinking is done while taking long and solitary walks." [100] Ibsen would then lunch, and spend his afternoons reading and walking with a special fascination for the movement of the sea if it happened to be near. He could sit alone and watch the sea for hours; Koht thought Ibsen saw in the sea the symbolic ancestral home of man, an association picked up from Darwin. Ibsen said, "The sea I love." Ibsen would then sup, drink sparingly at his usual cafe; the Scandinavian Club or the Cafe Nationale, for instance in Dresden, or the Cafe Maximillian in Munich, and always only between 6:30 and 8:30 p. m. Ibsen then would go home and retire early, mulling over the latest problems of his new play. He usually spent winters in dreaming up his plays and summers in writing and rewriting them. Day in, day out, for decades, this approximated Ibsen's routine working day.

"Everything which I have created as a poet," Ibsen wrote Peter Hansen in that memorable letter of October 28, 1870, "has had its origin in a frame of mind and a situation in life. I never wrote because I had, as they say, 'found a good subject.' " [101] Here are some illustrative excerpts from the letter as translated by Laurvik and Morison:

> *Lady Inger of Östraat* is the result of a love affair hastily entered into and violently broken off . . . *The Vikings at Helgeland* I wrote whilst I was engaged to be married. For Hjordis I had the same model as I took afterwards for Svanhild in *Love's Comedy* . . . Not until I was married did more serious interests take possession of my life . . . The desire for emancipation . . . did not, however, receive its full expression until I wrote *Love's Comedy,* a book which gave rise to much talk in Norway . . . The fact that all were against me—that there was no longer anyone outside my own family circle of whom I could say: 'He believes in me'—must, as you can easily see, have aroused a mood which found its outlet in *The Pretenders.* But enough of this subject . . .[102]

Ibsen used different starting points to get different plays under way. In his early romantic works, ranging from *The Viking's Barrow* through *Emperor and Galilean,* Ibsen found a theme with which he could deeply identify; much of his story, many of his characters, and the setting and atmosphere being from history and legend. N. M. Petersen's *Historical Tales of the Icelanders at Home and Abroad* and Landstad's *Norwegian Popular Songs* proved especially worthwhile. In his search for material, Ibsen still had to submit to all the hard work of exploring promising ore, and whether he struck it rich or not, he had to use his own judgment as to when to stop digging and when to go on. He wrote, for instance, in Archer's translation:

> In 1854, I had written *Lady Inger of Östraat.* This was a task which had obliged me to devote much attention to the literature and history of Norway during the Middle Ages, especially the latter part of that period. I did my utmost to familiarize myself with the manners and the customs, with the emotions, thoughts, and language, of the men of those days.
>
> The period, however, is not one over which the student is tempted to linger, nor does it present much material suitable for dramatic treatment.
>
> Consequently I soon deserted it for the Saga period. But the Sagas of the Kings, and in general the more strictly historical traditions of that far-off age, did not attract me greatly; at that time I was unable to put the quarrels between kings and chieftains, parties and clans, to any dramatic purpose. This was to happen later.
>
> In the Icelandic 'family' Sagas, on the other hand, I found in abundance what I required in the shape of human garb for the moods, conceptions, and thoughts which at that time occupied me, or were, at least, more or less distinctly present in my mind. . . . But now N. M. Petersen's excellent translation—excellent, at least, as far as the style is concerned—fell into my hands. In the pages of these family chronicles with their variety of scenes and relations between man and man, between woman and woman, in short between human being and human being, there met me a personal, eventful, really living life . . .[103]

When Ibsen wrote *Olaf Liljekrans,* he also wrote an essay on aesthetics, "Upon the Battle Song and Its Poetic Significance"; Ibsen here suggests his approach to prospecting a vein of nationalism (Payne's translation):

> The time will come when the national poetry will turn to the folksong as to an inexhaustible gold mine and when the latter, refined, restored to its pristine purity, and exalted by art, will again take hold of the people . . . The saga is wholly epic while the battle-song has the lyric elements—has it although not as the drama has it—and the dramatic poet who takes his material from the song, does not need to

remodel his material as much as does the poet who takes it from the saga. This circumstance is advantageous to the poet, for it enables him to reproduce in his work a more exact and more intimate picture of the age and the events with which he deals; by this means (if he be otherwise competent) he can present his hero to the public as the public already knows him from folk-song . . . National poetry in Norway began with the saga; the turn of the battle-song has now come.[104]

Some of Ibsen's historical plays came with astonishing spontaneity, as *The Pretenders* did. Jaeger confirmed with Ibsen, himself, for example, that "so easily did the material take shape that six weeks sufficed for its completion." A play, like the gargantuan *Emperor and Galilean,* by contrast was a labor of Hercules and never reached production. "During my four years' stay in Rome," Ibsen wrote Julius Hoffory from Munich on February 26, 1888, "I had occupied myself with all kinds of historical studies in view of writing *Emperor and Galilean* and made notes for it; but I had evolved no distinct plan or plot, much less written any part of the drama." [105] Ibsen could not be sure he even "had a play," as the expression goes; genesis was a gigantic labor on a hunch.

Ibsen had to find intense self-identification and also a journalistic timeliness in his material as this excerpt implies in his letter to Edmund Gosse from Dresden, referring to *Emperor and Galilean* and dated October 14, 1872: "It is a part of my own spiritual life which I am putting into this book; what I depict I have, under different conditions, gone through myself." And Ibsen noted, "the historical subject chosen has a much more intimate connection with the movements of our own time than one might at first imagine. The establishment of such a connection I regard as imperative in any modern poetical treatment of such a remote subject, if it is to arouse interest at all." [106]

"Whatever he may have been in youth," said Archer, "Henrik Ibsen in maturity and age, was the most reticent of artists." [107] In genesis and throughout creation, Ibsen usually was a sphinx of ferocious secretiveness; perhaps he feared aborting his brain-child by inviting its premature criticism. John Paulsen tells the anecdote of Ibsen traveling in a railroad carriage compartment with his wife and son and of Ibsen accidentally dropping a scrap of paper as he left the compartment for a few moments. Ibsen's wife picked up the paper and found these few words, "The doctor says . . ." When Ibsen returned to the compartment, Suzannah asked, "What doctor is it that figures in your new piece? I am sure he must have many interesting things to say." [108]

Ibsen almost threw a fit, what with raging over being spied upon by his own wife. Suzannah simply showed Ibsen the scrap of paper he had dropped, and he became meekly penitent. Ironically, Ibsen was to reveal a great deal not only in his letters but especially in his "foreworks," his personal papers which he had long accumulated in the unrealized hope of someday linking "my life and my writings together into an explanatory whole." "These are very important things," said Ibsen of his foreworks, which he bequeathed to his son, Sigurd, "perhaps the most important of all." [109]

The foreworks offer a probing insight into the genesis of Ibsen's plays of contemporary life which have made him a modern classic. A sampling of his notes on genesis for these plays suggests practises not deeply unlike from play to play. And yet the "sphinx" persists in Ibsen's foreworks for they omit the actual "soul-experience" which Ibsen said he found absolutely necessary for creation. Perhaps Ibsen kept quiet to avoid law suits and even scandal. Details persist as to the actual person, incident, or newspaper story that somehow directly or indirectly amounted to Ibsen's own soul-experience.

A Doll's House was long rumored to be drawn from the life of Laura Kieler Petersen who at eighteen so admired *Brand* that she wrote *The Daughters of Brand,* dedicated it to Ibsen, and sent him a copy. Ibsen corresponded with Laura as excerpts already cited from letters testify. He met her, too, and after she married School Superintendent Kieler, Ibsen was a guest at their home. When a reporter for the Copenhagen *Berglinske Tidende* asked Laura if Ibsen wrote *A Doll's House* about "a real event in your life," Laura answered:

> Yes. Ibsen wrote his *Doll's House* about a tragic event in my life. My experience was similar to that of Nora. My husband was ill, and to save him, I contracted, without his knowledge, certain debts. When this was discovered, various enemies I had made among the then all-powerful Brandes Party, by writing Nationalistic articles, utilized the opportunity to spread the rumor that I had written falsehoods, which I had not done. These rumors reached Ibsen, and he wrote *A Doll's House* . . . Those were hard years for me. The Larkbird had a difficult time.[110]

When asked if her husband had taken the attitude of Helmer in the play, Laura replied:

> Yes, for a while. He was Ibsen's model for the character of Helmer. It was hard to bear, and still harder when *A Doll's House* became a success and all of Denmark and Norway knew that I was the model for Nora.

When Ibsen, himself, was then asked to comment on Laura's story, he said cagily:

> If untruthful rumors have been circulated in Copenhagen to the effect that in an earlier period of her life something happened that had some similarity to the check story in *A Doll's House,* then she herself, or her husband, or best of all, both together, are the only ones who by an open and firm denial can down these false rumors.[111]

"A newspaper clipping revealed that the lady, like Nora, had obtained money by forgery," said Georg Brandes, Ibsen's close friend, ". . . not in order to save her husband's life, but in order to beautify her home. Her husband is said to have been furious when he found out."[112]

If Laura inspired Ibsen's Nora, Ibsen certainly made major changes in his model. Laura Kieler did not leave home like Nora but simply worked to help pay off her rather feather-brained debts. Ibsen put a strain of the unyielding Brand in his Nora. Ten years before even writing *A Doll's House,* Ibsen has Selma in *The League of Youth*— without the assistance of Laura Kieler—tell Selma's husband and father-in-law, "You have dressed me up like a doll; you have played with me as you would play with a child. Oh, what a joy it would have been to me to take my share in your burdens."[113]

Now perhaps the earliest memoranda for *A Doll's House* from the foreworks have more meaning. They suggest the play's key-note, theme, leading characters, main action, outcome—a vaguely stirring, complete, living embryo of a famous brain-child:

NOTES FOR THE TRAGEDY OF TODAY

There are two kinds of spiritual laws, two kinds of conscience, one in men and a quite different one in women. They do not understand each other; but the woman is judged in practical life according to the man's law, as if she were not a woman but a man.

The wife in the play finds herself at last entirely at sea as to what is right and what wrong; natural feeling on the one side, and belief in authority on the other, leave her in utter bewilderment.

A woman cannot be herself in the society of to-day, which is exclusively a masculine society, with laws written by men, and with accusers and judges who judge feminine conduct from the masculine standpoint.

She has committed forgery, and it is her pride; for she did it for love of her husband, and to save his life. But this husband, full of everyday rectitude, stands on the basis of the law and regards the matter with a masculine eye.

Soul-struggles. Oppressed and bewildered by belief in authority, she loves her faith in her own moral right and ability to bring up her children. Bitterness. A mother in the society of today, like certain insects (ought to) go away and die when she has done her duty towards the continuance of the species. Love of life, of home, of husband and children and kin. Now and then a womanlike shaking off of cares. Then a sudden apprehension and dread. She must bear it all alone. The catastrophe approaches inexorably, inevitably. Despair, struggle, and disaster.[114]

The earliest memoranda of *Ghosts* show an astonishing similarity of form to those of the play immediately preceding, *A Doll's House*. Ibsen was a highly disciplined craftsmen who knew what he was doing. He himself wrote Sophie Adlersparre on June 24, 1882, "After Nora, Mrs. Alving had to come." [115] If much of Europe was outraged that Nora left her family, in the succeeding play Ibsen showed the effects of a woman who stays with her family for a lifetime of sham respectability. It appears he created his plays in a chain-reaction.

As for the soul-experience involved, Ibsen himself, when a young man, had with a servant girl begotten an illegitimate child in a seaport town. Captain Alving's sickness was then common to sailors, and Ibsen came of a partly nautical family. The male forebears of his father, Knud, for 100 years were all skippers. Ibsen's own mother had stayed with her husband till for her he became impossible.

The complete *Ghosts* should be read with these earliest memoranda before the aspiring playwright's eyes, even as likely Ibsen had them in his mind's eye as he wrote the play. Archer, incidentally, noted the unpredictability of Ibsen's insights in that some of these notes were jotted down on the back of an envelope addressed to "Madam Ibsen, 75 via Capo le Case, Citta (Rome)":

> The piece will be like an image of life. Faith undermined. But it does not do to say so. "The Asylum"—for the sake of others. They shall be happy—but this also is only an appearance—it is all ghosts.
> One main point. She has been believing and romantic—this is not wholly obliterated by the stand-point afterward attained—"It is all ghosts."
> It brings a Nemesis on the offspring to marry for external reasons, even if they be religious or moral.
> She the illegitimate child, may be saved by being married to—the son—but then—?
> He was in his youth dissipated and worn out; then she, the religiously awakened, appeared; she saved him; she was rich. He had wanted to marry a girl who was thought unworthy. He had a son in his marriage; then he returned to the girl; a daughter—

These women of to-day, ill-treated as daughters, as sisters, as wives, not educated according to their gifts, withheld from their vocation, deprived of their heritage, embittered in mind—these it is who furnish the mothers of a new generation. What will be the consequence?

The fundamental note shall be the richly flourishing spiritual life among us in literature, arts, etc.; and then, as a contrast, all humanity astray on wrong paths.

The complete human being is no longer a natural product, but a product of art, as corn is, and fruit-trees, and the creole race, and the higher breeds of horses and dogs, the vine, etc.

The fault lies in the fact that all humanity has miscarried. When a man demands to live and develop humanly, it is megalomania. All humanity, and most of all the Christians, suffer from megalomania.

Among us we place monuments over the dead, for we recognize duties towards them; we allow people only fit for the hospital (literally lepers) to marry: but their offspring—? The unborn—? [116]

These few notes are, when seen alongside the play, almost the literal bone-structure of the chief characters and their struggle to live out their lives—nearly a microcosm of the play.

Ibsen's concern with "soul-experience" led increasingly to his obsession with psychology, as in *Hedda Gabler*. Certain people and incidents were from the first associated with the genesis of the play. They suggest the deep calling to the deep, and more than the shallows answering in Ibsen's own soul-experience. Ibsen knew the story of a "well-known" Norwegian composer who had made his wife so furiously jealous by staying so much away from home that, in revenge, she took the manuscript of a symphony he had just completed and burned it. She quite likely suspected that the music was the inspiration of another woman upon her husband's creative talent. The soul-revelation of destroying a brain-child out of envy was all Ibsen kept of this for *Hedda Gabler;* Ibsen quite altered the circumstances under which Hedda burns Lövborg's manuscript.[117]

According to Brandes, another story excited Ibsen, and had in it a climax of soul-revelation. Ibsen had heard how a very intelligent and beautiful woman, married to an alcoholic celebrity, helped him conquer his thirst, and then to flout her mastery over him as well as to test his self-mastery, rolled into his study on his birthday a small keg of brandy. The wife then left. When she returned, she found her husband lying on the floor of the study, stone-drunk. Ibsen, of course, was no teetotaller. The story of this lady suggested a strong trait in Hedda and also her own deliberate exposure of Eilert Lövborg to the temptation of liquor after Thea supposedly had helped him "cure" his terrible thirst; it also suggested Lövborg's ruin.

Brandes believed Ibsen drew added traits of Eilert Lövborg from a friend in Munich, a young Danish writer, Dr. Holm, who one day posted Ibsen a packet of correspondence including a photograph. Intrigued as to motive, Ibsen asked the hotel-clerk at Holm's quarters what the clerk knew of Holm's habits. "When Dr. Holm wakes up, he orders a bottle of port," said the clerk, "at lunch, a bottle of wine; at dinner a bottle of red wine; and in the evening, another bottle or two of port." [118] Gifted, erudite, imaginative, Dr. Holm after a heavy drinking bout with friends one night actually lost a manuscript he had been working on. Holm also mailed Ibsen his will, naming Ibsen as executor and many frauleins as legatees; the frauleins, Brandes thought, suggested Lövborg's Madame Diana and her *soirée* in *Hedda Gabler*. Now perhaps Ibsen's first memoranda in his fore-works to *Hedda Gabler* make more sense; like the foreworks of earlier plays cited, they also suggest leading characters, chief action, soul-revelations in the climaxes, and the very end, too (A. G. Chater's translation):

The pale, apparently cold beauty. Expects great things of life and the joy of life.
The man who has finally won her, homely in appearance, but honorable, and a gifted, liberal-minded man of science.

HEDDA: I have no gift for anything but being bored. That life should have nothing in the world to offer one. Supposing he were to go in for politics.
BRACK: That is not in his line.
HEDDA: But perhaps I could get him into it. Do you think he would ever get into the ministry?
BRACK: For that he would have to be a very rich man.
HEDDA: Yes and then—I doubt if it would bring me any satisfaction in the long run.

LÖVBORG: I have led a rather wild life, they say. Now I have to make amends. But I cannot renounce.

Brack had always thought that Hedda's short engagement to Tesman would come to nothing.
Hedda speaks of how she felt herself set aside, step by step, when her father was no longer in favour, when he retired and died without leaving anything. —It then came upon her, in her bitterness, that it was

for his sake she had been made much of. —And then she was already between 25 and 26, in danger of becoming an old maid.

She thinks that in reality Tesman only feels a vain pride in having won her. His solicitude for her is the same as is shown for a thoroughbred horse or a valuable sporting dog. —This, however, does not offend her. She merely regards it as a fact.

Hedda says to Brack that she does not think Tesman can be called ridiculous. But in reality she finds him so. Later on she finds him pitiable as well. . . .

In the 3rd act one thing after another comes to light about Lövborg's adventures in the course of the night. At last he comes himself, in quiet despair. "Where is the manuscript?" "Did I not leave it behind me here?" He does not know that he has done so.

But after all, of what use is the manuscript to him now! He is writing of the "moral doctrine of the future!" When he has just been let out of the police cells!

Hedda's despair is that there are doubtless so many chances of happiness in the world, but that she cannot discover them. It is the want of an object in life that torments her.

When Hedda beguiles T. into leading E. L. into ruin, it is done to test T.'s character.

It is in Hedda's presence that the irresistible craving for excess always comes over E. L.

Tesman cannot understand that E. L. could wish to base his future on injury to another.[119]

A most revealing entry is found about one-third of the way through a little black notebook which Ibsen later bequeathed to Sigurd and which Ibsen supposedly carried with him during the creation of *Hedda Gabler.* The entry proves that relatively early Ibsen was aware of the very end of his play, as shown in this translation by Evert Sprinchorn of notes included in *Playwrights on Playwriting:*

In the last act as Tesman, Mrs. Elvsted, and Miss Rysing are consulting, Hedda plays in the small room at the back. She stops. The conversation continues. She appears in the doorway—Good night—I'm going now. Do you need me for anything? Tesman: no, nothing at all. Good night, my dear! . . . The shot is fired—

Conclusion: All rush into the back room. Brack sinks as if paralyzed into a chair near the stove: But God have mercy—people don't *do* such things! [120]

With the end of his play well in mind, Ibsen continued developing earlier action deviously as his muse prompted and as illustrated in these entries immediately following the above entry:

When Hedda hints at her ideas to Brack, he says: Yes, yes. That's extraordinarily amusing—Ha, ha, ha! He does not understand that she is quite serious.

Hedda is right in this: There is no love on Tesman's part. Nor on the Aunt's part. However full of love she may be.

Eilert Lövborg has a double nature. It is a fiction that one loves only *one* person. He loves two—or many—alternately (to put it frivolously).

All of the first memoranda of plays already dealt with, *A Doll's House, Ghosts,* and *Hedda Gabler,* are highly significant. They show the form in which Ibsen's creative spirit worked in genesis at the height of his powers.

Incubation and Characterization

"Different plans and ideas, he admits, often flow together," Archer said from talking with Ibsen, "and the play he ultimately produces is sometimes very unlike the intention with which he set out." [121] Some notes end up unused: *Rosmersholm,* for instance, drops the "elder daughter" and the "younger daughter" mentioned in the foreworks; new characters emerge, for example, Tesman's memorable Aunt Julia in *Hedda Gabler.*

For all his self-discipline as an artist, Ibsen was still somewhat at the mercy of his "fancies." He wrote Emilie Bardach, who was to be his model for Hilda Wangel in *The Master Builder,* to illustrate this in a letter of October 15, 1889:

> Here I sit as usual at my writing-table. Now I would fain work, but am unable to. My fancy, indeed, is very active. But it always wanders away. It wanders where it has no business to wander during working hours. I cannot suppress my summer memories—nor do I wish to. I live through my experiences again and again and yet again. To transmute it all into a poem, I find, in the meantime, impossible.[122]

In his next letter to Emilie, dated October 29, 1889, Ibsen wrote:

> Do not be troubled because I cannot, in the meantime, create (*dichten*). In reality I am forever creating, or, at any rate, dreaming of something which, when in the fulness of time it ripens, will reveal itself as a creation (*Dichtung*).

To dream away Ibsen knew was the only road to revelation. He wrote Emilie on November 19, 1889, "I am very busily occupied with preparations for my new poem. I sit almost the whole day at my writing table. Go out only in the evening for a little while." [123] On September 18, 1890, Ibsen wrote Emilie of what was to be *The Master Builder,* "The new play on which I am at present engaged will probably not be ready until November, though I sit at my writing-table daily, and almost the whole day long." In the quotes just cited, Ibsen at sixty-one implies he had learned to dispense with walking in his study and adjoining rooms to stimulate incubation; simply sitting at his desk now released his fancies.[124]

The time from incubation to scenario varied from play to play. After four years of gathering material for *Emperor and Galilean,* Ibsen still lacked "any clear plan for its working out." In this impasse, came *Brand:* "I suddenly saw in strong clear outlines what I had to say." [125] Ibsen still thought it much harder to develop a unified, organic, historical play like the heavily documented *Emperor and Galilean* than an episodic play like *Brand.*[126] The research for *Brand,* as for *Peer Gynt,* Ibsen had largely done in his own living and especially in his travels through Norway in search of folk-material.

For Ibsen, the leading characters really made the play. As a disciplined artist, he knew what he must do for each character (A. E. Zucker's translation in *Ibsen: The Master-Builder*):

> Before I write down one word, I have to have the character in mind through and through. I must penetrate into the last wrinkle of his soul. I always proceed from the individual; the stage setting, the dramatic ensemble, all of that comes naturally and does not cause me any worry, as soon as I am certain of the individual in every aspect of his humanity. But I have to have his exterior in mind also, down to the last button, how he stands and walks, how he conducts himself, what his voice sounds like. Then I do not let him go until his fate is fulfilled.[127]

It is no exaggeration to say Ibsen knew his characters down to their last button; in his years of producing plays at Bergen and Oslo, he drew many costume-plates which are now extant. Shaw observed, "Ibsen . . . devotes two years to the production of a three act play, the extraordinary quality of which . . . can only be achieved by working out a good deal of the family and personal history of the individuals represented." [128] Ibsen's acute interest in detail is suggested in Bergliot Ibsen's observation: "The strange thing about Ibsen was that he seemed slow at grasping things," she recalled. "One had to tell them twice to him. The first time he just listened, the second time he asked for further and more minute details." Ibsen flourished on details. "He took note of all the details; one could almost see him swallow them." [129]

"People in Norway will perhaps say I have depicted real persons and circumstances. This is not the case," insisted Ibsen. "I have, however, used models, which are as indispensable to the writer of comedy as to the painter or sculptor." [130] Ibsen's characters grew from hybrids or composites of models drawn from life, literature, history, and above all, from himself. He bred his characters, it seems, for dominant blood strains through association even as they selectively might biologically be bred in other animal-life; in fact, the likeness of people to other animals fascinated Ibsen. "Nobody can poetically present that to which he has not a certain degree and at least at times the model within himself," said Ibsen. [131]

The locale of *Brand* was Ibsen's by upbringing. Danish critics thought Ibsen drew Brand from their philosopher, Soren Kierkegaard; Ibsen wrote Hansen, "Brand is myself in my best moments." The syllogism implied in *Brand* is: a man of principle stands firm at any price; Brand is a man of principle; Brand stands firm at any price. "I could have applied the syllogism just as well to a sculptor, or a politician, as to a priest," Ibsen told Georg Brandes, and Ibsen believed Galileo would certainly do, "—assuming, of course, that he should stand firm and not concede the fixity of the earth." [132] "Do you know that I have cut myself off for good from my parents and from my whole kindred," Ibsen wrote Björnson on December 9, 1867, like Brand talking, "because I could not be at rest in a relation of half-understanding?" [133]

Norwegians believed Brand was in part drawn from their heretic Pastor Lammers who delivered jeremiads against the State Church for throttling the individual's conscience and finally founded his own church. But Lammers deserted his flock, and was fond of music and theatre—a far call from the unyielding pietist, Brand. As a representative of the highly controversial man of unyielding principle, like a Samson in the temple, Brand still lives on today, for all the play's shambles of structure.

Peer Gynt followed *Brand* in a chain-reaction of character-creation. The fantastic success of the unyielding Brand put Ibsen in the carefree mood of Peer Gynt, who compromises about every principle and ends up a human cipher. Ibsen wrote Hegel from Rome in January 1867:

I must tell you that my new work is well under way, and will, if nothing untoward happens, be finished early in the summer. It is to be a long dramatic poem, having as its chief figure one of the Norwegian peasantry's half-mythical, fantastic heroes of *recent* times. It will bear no resemblance to *Brand,* contains no direct polemics and so forth. I have long had the subject in my thoughts; now the entire plan is worked out and written down, and the first act begun. The thing grows as I work at it, and I am certain that you will be satisfied with it.[134]

In 1882, Ibsen confided in Brandes, "In writing *Peer Gynt,* I had the circumstances and memories of my own childhood before me when I described the life in the house of 'the rich Jon Gynt'." [135] Like Peer, Ibsen in his youth lived on a farm of stony acreage, was wild in the eyes of his mother and the world, fathered an illegitimate child, and made himself a hero in his fantasies of Norwegian folklore. Brandes thought Ibsen found another model for Peer in a handsome, young Danish acquaintance full of such devices as telling his girl-friends that his father was a bosom friend of the King of Denmark, though actually his father was a humble school-master.

In creating Peer Gynt, as in creating Brand and all of his best characters to come, Ibsen worked for a spirit of "higher symbolic truth which should retain its vitality in the future." Norwegians, in fact, recognized some of themselves in Peer's life—loveable rascality with no more heart than an onion. "But if the Norwegians of the present time recognize themselves," wrote Ibsen on February 24, 1868, in a letter to Hegel, "as it would appear they do, in the character of Peer Gynt, that is the good people's own affair." [136]

The character of Hilda Wangel in *The Master Builder* is especially intriguing because Ibsen's soul-experience that made it possible is well substantiated. "Do you know, my next play is already hovering before me—of course in vague outline," Dr. Julius Elias reported Ibsen as telling him, while the two waited for a train following the Berlin opening of *Hedda Gabler.* "But of one thing I have got firm hold," said Ibsen, "an experience: a woman's figure. Very interesting, very interesting, indeed. Again a spice of deviltry in it." [137]

As Elias recalled the incident, Ibsen told him of meeting in the Austrian Tyrol at the resort town of Gossensass, a young lady who immediately unburdened her whole heart to him. She didn't plan at all on marrying; what she most enjoyed was luring husbands away from their wives, a kind of Lorelei who had Ibsen next on her list. "She did not get hold of me," Ibsen told Elias, "but I got hold of her

—for my play. Then I fancy (here he chuckled again) she consoled herself with someone else." "Thus Ibsen spoke," recollected Elias, "calmly and cooly, gazing as it were into the far distance, like an artist taking an objective view of some experience—like Rubek speaking of his soul-thefts. He had stolen a soul and put it to a double employment. Thea Elvsted and Hilda Wangel are intimately related—are, indeed, only different expressions of the same nature." [138]

The young lady was eighteen years old, well-born, quite innocent looking and in the sympathetic plight of an Austrian war refugee. "Never in his life," wrote this young lady, Emilie Bardach, of Ibsen in her diary, "he says, had he felt so much joy in knowing anyone. . . . He means to possess me. This is his absolute will." [139] The sixty-one year old Ibsen was old enough to be Emilie's grandfather. When they parted in the Tyrol on September 27, 1889, he gave Emilie his picture and on the back wrote, *"Au die Maisonne eines Septemberlebens*—(To the May-sun of a September romance)." In Emilie's album, he also wrote, *"Hohes, Schmerzliches Gluck—um das Unerreichbare zu ringen!* (High, painful happiness—to struggle for the unattainable!)" [140]

Ibsen wrote Emilie twelve letters, then stopped. Her identification with Hilda Wangel is quite clear. In the 5th letter, for instance, Emilie is "an enigmatic Princess." [141] In the sixth, "my dear Princess." In the 9th, dated February 6, 1890, his conscience, like Halvard Solness' conscience, leads him to write, "I feel it a matter of conscience to end, or at any rate, to restrict, our correspondence." In his 11th letter, dated December 30, 1890, he pleaded, "Please, for the present, do not write me again . . . I will soon send you my new play (*Hedda Gabler*). Receive it in friendship, but in silence!" [142] When *The Master Builder* appeared, Emilie sent Ibsen her photograph with her inscription, "Princess of Orangia"—Hilda Wangel's title in daydreams.

In *The Master Builder,* Hilda's hypnotic powers drive Solness to dare climb to the top of the tower of his latest building in a public ceremony, and he falls to his death; Ibsen doubtless feared an approximation of this if he stayed around Emilie Bardach too long. In fact, Solness is modelled on Ibsen, himself, the master-builder. The sequence of buildings in Solness' life parallels Ibsen's plays; in youth, the churches or his romantic early plays; later, "the homes for human beings," his dramas about society; and finally, the houses with high towers rising to castles in the air, his dramas of the human spirit. Ibsen said, "The conscience is very conservative." [143] His affair with

Emilie matched his "very conservative" conscience against her amoral conscience. The whole struggle to Solness' mind is ambiguously angelic-daemonic, like Emilie Bardach's mixed intentions. "Oh, there are devils innumerable abroad in the world, Hilda, that one never sees! . . . If only you could always tell whether it is the light or dark ones that have got hold of you!"[144]

"And as regards the thing which has been lived through—that is just the secret of the literature of modern times," said Ibsen in September, 1874; in his letter of May 29, 1870, to Magdalene Thoresen, he had cautioned, "be extremely careful in discriminating between what one has observed and what one has experienced; because only this last can be the theme for creative work."[145] Ibsen was deeply involved with Emilie Bardach. In fact, his own wife's attitude might easily have been that of Halvard Solness' wife. "Ibsen (I have often said to him)," Fru Ibsen confessed to Dr. Elias, "Ibsen, keep these swarms of over-strained womenfolk at arm's length. 'Oh, no (he would reply), let them alone. I want to observe them more closely.'" And then Dr. Elias said, perhaps with a bit of uneasiness, "His observations would take a longer or shorter time as the case might be, and would always contribute to some work of art."[146] In the case of Emilie Bardach, it also contributed to talk of divorce for the Ibsens.

Sources of Ibsen's Freshness

To Shaw, "The giants of the theatre of our time are Ibsen and Strindberg."[147] The distinguished novelist, Henry James, who failed repeatedly as a dramatist, thought that in Ibsen's plays "the lamps of the spirit burn as in tasteless parlors with the flame practically exposed."[148]

However they burn to James' Boston Brahmin taste, they refuse to go out. Ibsen's works are done in college and university playhouses, in repertory, and on radio and television. In rank, he has challenged the best dramatists of any age, and to this has also attracted such giants as Shaw and lesser figures like Miller and Hellman, who have chosen to inherit a powerful Ibsen strain. Hardly a single playwright of any distinction is free of some spiritual debt to Ibsen for showing how to bring poetry out of modern life without verse and with a consummate naturalism. Pirandello said, "After Shakespeare, I unhesitatingly place Ibsen first."[149] "A Doll's House," Shaw conceded, "will be flat as ditch-water when A Midsummer Night's Dream will still be fresh as paint, but it will have done more work in the world; and that is enough for genius." [150] Ibsen is timeless and timely. He offers techniques for being both.

The modern plays in which Ibsen's world-wide fame still lives on have the modern spirit of Socrates' credo—"Follow wheresoever the questioning may lead," and, "All things are to be examined and called into question. There are no limits set to thought." [151] Ibsen at best, did this to probe the values of society and the individual. In *A Doll's House*, for instance, he found that marriage and a family can be deeply dissatisfying for a wife. In *Ghosts*, respectability at any price can destroy the soul. In *An Enemy of the People*, government by the majority can be evil in its self-interest. In *The Wild Duck*, complete truthfulness in human relations can be murderous folly. In *Hedda Gabler*, an "emancipated" woman can make nothing of all her opportunities but fatal boredom. "What Ibsen insists," wrote Shaw in *The Quintessence of Ibsenism*, "is that there is no golden rule; that conduct must justify itself by its effect upon life and not by its conformity to any rule of ideal." [152] What Ibsen says at best is no more stale than the Socratic spirit.

Before Ibsen, the middle-class public who supported the 19th century commercial theatre were content with the expert sleight-of-hand dramaturgy of the acknowledged masters of the well-made play, Sardou and Scribe. Television and grade B movies today offer an equivalent slick entertainment with assembly-line expertness. Such theatre is usually no more true than catsup is blood. Speed and polish try to hide a lack of reality.

Archer believed that Ibsen made his great technical advance by combining the technique of the well-made play with superb insight into the revelation of character. "I owe absolutely nothing to Dumas in respect to dramatic form," Ibsen told Archer of this master of the well-made play—and he might have included Sardou and Scribe, too—"except that I learnt from him to avoid certain glaring errors and clumsiness of which he is not infrequently guilty." [153] Ibsen learned by falling into the trap so badly in his early plays, that he never quite forgot the teeth. *Catiline, Lady Inger of Östraat*, and *The Vikings of Helgeland*, for instance, all rely heavily upon such theatrical defects of the "well-made" play as poorly motivated character, extravagant action, complicated plots and counter-plots, the long arm of coincidence, and a busy, well-oiled *deus ex machina*.

A Doll's House, however, and practically all of Ibsen's best plays to follow, still use conventional techniques found not only in the "well-made" play but in Sophocles and Shakespeare, too. For instance: an opening exposition of servants, telling all the facts by being at odds over their master, strong leads, a confidant, a recognition scene, and a major climax with a direct confrontation of the leading characters—a device the critic Sarcey called "the obligatory scene."

What was so fresh in Ibsen's technique? In his best modern plays, Ibsen characteristically begins the plot by showing the story in its last climactic hours in an approximation of the classical unities of time, place and action as found in Greek tragedy. And yet Ibsen's exposition, was an innovation modelled most likely after life's catastrophes as Ibsen had experienced them. He did not give the whole exposition at the beginning of his best plays but, as in *Hedda Gabler,* exposed the past bit by bit through the current action. Both past and present action are like streams running side by side, one periodically overflowing into the other. Clayton Hamilton wrote in *Problems of the Playwright:*

> Ibsen caught his story very late in its career, and revealed the antecedent incidents in little gleams of backward-looking dialogue. . . . instead of compacting his exposition into the first act—according to the formula of Scribe—he revealed it, little by little, throughout the progress of the play.

Usually Ibsen's leads reveal one major aspect of character in each scene. The revelation, for instance, of Hedda's horror of scandal is ordered, for most effectiveness of plot, to near the very end of the play, and this revelation, of course, suits her whole previously established character as a near bankrupt aristocrat with little left but her honor; in this sense, plot was, it appears, the most important of all elements of a play to Ibsen.

Ibsen's freshness also shows in that instead of dramatizing only folklore or history as does, for example, Sophocles in *Oedipus the King,* he realistically dramatized contemporary Norwegian life which in its basic truth was that of human beings with the values of western civilization. There were and are certainly millions of near-kin to Nora outside of Norway; in Nora, Ibsen put the millions onstage.

Brandes believed that Ibsen's leading characters moved in a lifelike perspective outstripping the reality of any other dramatist of the day. To Henderson, "It is this which makes the dramas of Ibsen so supremely great: the characters are not creatures of the situation as in Scribe and Sardou, but the situation, the plot is the inevitable consequence of the characters." [154] "Many a play is like a painted back-drop," said Minnie Maddern Fiske, who in her day won fame and fortune acting female leads in Ibsen's plays; "An Ibsen play is like a black forest. . . . And once inside, you find such wonderful glades and such beautiful sunlit places." [155] Ibsen said his task was "the description of humanity." His freshness lies in the extraordinary life of such characters with mass identification as Peer Gynt, Nora, Mrs. Oswald, Hedda. When these characters die, Ibsen dies.

In his best plays, Ibsen worked for the "common touch" in characterization to make archetypes live in the flesh by excellent illustrative detail. "As for symbolism," Archer recollected of Ibsen, "he says that life is full of it, though critics insist on discovering all sorts of esoteric meanings in his work of which he is entirely innocent." [156] Archer was much upset when, to his mind, Ibsen in *When We Dead Awaken* became obscurely symbolic. "This is an abandonment of the fundamental principle which Ibsen over and over again emphatically expressed," said Archer, "—namely, that any symbolism his work might be found to contain was entirely incidental, and subordinate to the truth and consistency of his picture of life." [157]

Each of Ibsen's modern plays uses a central symbol giving a natural, visual statement of the theme at the major climax. In *A Doll's House,* Nora walks out on her "doll's house." Her hope of being treated as a human being with self-respect equal to her husband's, rather than as a criminal who might corrupt her children, leads her —once her potential black-mailer, Krogstad, drops his plans—to try to find a place for herself in the world outside. In *Hedda Gabler,* the brace of pistols that General Gabler bequeathed to his daughter comes by association to epitomize her whole view of life. One pistol apparently symbolizes Hedda's bungling, destructive wish to control at least one somewhat fine human destiny, Lövborg's, in envy of his dependence on Thea and as a vicarious suicide for Hedda drifting into a dreary, bourgeois marriage; this pistol is found and brings only scandal, for Lövborg dies ignobly shot in the stomach, climaxing a sordid brawl at a high class prostitute's quarters. The second pistol apparently symbolizes Hedda's grandstand play at hari kari, a bullet through the temple, suggesting she had to prove her honor as an aristocrat, and yet in a sense blame the society that found no place for her.

The play's very title, *Hedda Gabler,* was naturally symbolic, for on December 4, 1890, Ibsen wrote his French translator, Count Snoilsky, "The title of the play is *Hedda Gabler*. My intention in giving it this name was to indicate that Hedda, as a personality, is to be regarded rather as her father's daughter than as her husband's wife." In *The Master Builder,* to cite one more illustration of Ibsen's fondness for a natural, central symbol, Solness is almost hypnotically enticed by Hilda to climb to the top of the very high tower he himself has built; and so Solness climbs, only to reach the top and, from vertigo, tumble to his death into the quarry below. In this major climax, Solness symbolized his lifelong wish to do the impossible and his coupled fear of personal failure.

Writing and Rewriting

When a young playwright called upon Ibsen and asked him to read his play, Ibsen supposedly replied, "Show me the scenario (disposition) of your comedy." [158] The young man answered that he wrote only from inspiration. Ibsen promptly showed him the door. Ibsen informed his German publisher, Hegel, from Dresden on October 31, 1868 regarding *The League of Youth,* "The whole outline is finished and written down." The scenario of only *A Doll's House* is extant, the very barest bones of a skeleton, if even that. It is assumed that Ibsen must have destroyed a great many scenarios, once the plays were written and they had served their purpose.

"It is said to have been his habit," remarked Archer of Ibsen, "before setting to work on a play, to 'crystallize in a poem the mood which then possessed him'," [159] and Archer literally translated the only such extant poem, that for *The Master-Builder:*

They Sat There, the Two—

They sat there, the two, in so cosy a house, through autumn and winter days. Then the house burned down. Everything lies in ruins. The two must grope among the ashes.

For among them is hidden a jewel—a jewel that can never burn. And if they search faithfully, it may easily happen that he or she may find it.

But even should they find it, the burnt-out two—find this precious unburnable jewel—never will she find her burnt faith; he, never his burnt happiness. [160]

Archer, incidentally, also translated a very early poem of Ibsen as possibly germinal to about every play he was to write; for those interested in such speculation, here is the poem:

Building-Plans

I remember as clearly as if it had been today the evening when, in the paper, I saw my first poem in print. There I sat in my den, and, with long-drawn puffs, I smoked and I dreamed in blissful self-complacency. I will build a cloud-castle. It shall shine all over the North. It shall have two wings: one little and one great. The great wing shall shelter a deathless poet; the little wing shall serve as a young girl's bower.

The plan seemed to me nobly harmonious; but as time went on it fell into confusion. When the master grew reasonable, the castle turned utterly crazy; the great wing became too little, the little wing fell to ruin . . .[161]

In the actual writing of his plays, Ibsen gave his stage directions the care he gave to characterization. In 1899 Ibsen told Gosse that it was futile to try to perform Holberg's comedies properly because, "There were no stage directions and the tradition was lost." [162]

Before *Peer Gynt*, Ibsen in writing dialogue had used verse in all of his historical and romantic plays. "The characteristic quality of the poet's achievement," noted Archer of *Peer Gynt's* diction, "lay precisely in his having, by the aid of rhythm and rhyme transfigured the most easy and natural dialogue without the least sacrifice of its naturalness." [163] *Peer Gynt,* its later success with Grieg's music notwithstanding, originally failed with the Norwegian critics and public, and led Ibsen to a fateful change for modern drama. "I shall try my luck as a photographer," he said and aimed to give the effect of real things happening to real people, free of all the artifice of rhythm and verse, yet retaining the colloquial quality of *Peer Gynt*.

The English speaking world knows Ibsen only in translation. "It is my opinion," said Ibsen advising his translator, Fredrik Gjertsen in a letter of March 21, 1872, "that a poem should be translated in the style in which the author would have written it himself had he belonged to the nation to read him in the translation." [164] Ibsen's diction sometimes seems a bit stiff in translation. "Ibsen is at once extremely easy, and extremely difficult to translate," said Archer in the preface to the *Works*. "It is extremely easy in his prose plays, to realize his meaning; it is often extremely difficult to convey it in natural colloquial, and yet not too colloquial, English." [165]

What was Ibsen's intent? In replying to the English critic, Edmund Gosse's charge that *Emperor and Galilean* should have been written in verse, Ibsen wrote from Dresden on January 15, 1874, "The illusion which I wanted to produce was that of reality . . . If I had employed verse, I should have counteracted my intention." [166] "Speaking generally," continued Ibsen, "the style must conform to the degree of ideality which pervades the representation . . . What I desired to depict were human beings, and therefore, I would not let them talk the 'language of the Gods'." "I myself have for the last seven or eight years hardly written a single verse," said Ibsen in corresponding with the actress Lucie Wolf on May 25, 1883; "I have exclusively cultivated the very much more difficult art of writing the genuine, plain language spoken in real life." [167] To give up verse entirely in his plays did not mean for Ibsen giving up poetry. He always called himself "a poet" and found in the *Bible* exemplary prose poetry. By 1884, he withdrew his condemnation of verse as diction in the drama: "I have long since ceased to formulate universally binding precepts because I no longer believe that one can with any inner right formulate them." [168]

In the actual writing and rewriting, Ibsen tended to three drafts. The first, for getting "acquainted with the characters, to know their dispositions, and to feel sure of the manner in which they will express themselves." The added two, as Ibsen noted in a letter to Theodor Caspara, from Rome on June 27, 1884, were for "the more energetic individualization of the characters and their mode of expression." [169] Writing was an experience in the revelation of character. Less than three drafts meant cutting short the revelation. Ibsen specified (Zucker's translation):

> As a rule, I make three drafts of my dramas which differ very much from each other in characterization, not in action. When I proceed to the first sketch of the material I feel as though I had the degree of acquaintance with my characters that one acquires on a railway journey; one has met and chatted about this or that. With the next draft I see everything more clearly, I know the characters just about as one would know them after a few weeks' stay in a spa; I have learned the fundamental traits in their characters as well as their little peculiarities; yet it is not impossible that I might make an error in some essential matter. In the last draft, finally, I stand at the limit of knowledge; I know my people from close and long association—they are my intimate friends, who will not disappoint me in any way; in the manner in which I see them now, I shall always see them.[170]

How objective Ibsen liked to think he was toward his characters in writing and rewriting may be gathered from his remark to Schandorph, a Danish novelist, in a letter dated January 6, 1882, concerning the Scandinavian reviewers' reaction to *Ghosts:*

> They endeavour to make me responsible for the opinions which certain of the personages of my drama express. And yet there is not in the whole book a single opinion, a single utterance, which can be laid to the account of the author. The very method, the technique which imposes its form upon the play, forbids the author to appear in the speeches of his characters. My object was to make the reader feel that he was going through a piece of real experience.[171]

"My new play is finished," wrote Ibsen of *Hedda Gabler* to Count Prozor from Munich on November 20, 1890. And then suggesting how Ibsen literally had to live in the imagined world of his characters and how deeply this affected him, he confessed, "It gives me a curious feeling of emptiness to find myself suddenly separated from a work that has occupied my time and thoughts for several months to the exclusion of everything else. But on the other hand, it is good to have done with it," admitted Ibsen. "Living every moment of my life with these fictitious characters was beginning to make me more than a little nervous . . ."[172] The fine line between the imagined and the real was growing less and less distinct to Ibsen at times, much to his dismay.

Ibsen's foreworks show his progress in writing and rewriting. Space allows only for special study of his first great international success and likely his best known play, *A Doll's House,* and, often rated his finest play, *Hedda Gabler.* To evaluate differences from draft to draft, we must keep Ibsen's stated intention in mind: "to draw human beings." What helped, Ibsen kept. What didn't help, Ibsen cut or changed to his intent.

A comparison of the final draft to the one available earlier draft of *A Doll's House* shows that, while the big scenes are basically the same, only in the final draft did Ibsen get around to individualizing his characters with these memorable bits of illustrative action: Nora eats macaroons on the sly to keep her husband from scolding her for risking tooth decay; [173] Nora decorates the Christmas tree while her husband tells her how such forgers as Krogstad are poisonous to a home.[174] Well into Act II, Helmer hears Nora's plea that he keep Krogstad on the job at the bank as a subordinate, and then objects:

> . . . he was a college chum of mine—there was one of those rash friendships between us that one so often repents of later. . . . He de-

lights in putting on airs of familiarity—Torvald here, Torvald there! I
assure you it's most painful to me. He would make my position at the
Bank perfectly unendurable.[175]

Most notably about mid Act III in the earlier draft, when Helmer receives Nora's forged IOU from Krogstad, Helmer says, "You are
saved, Nora, you are saved." In the final draft, Helmer points up his
whole character,—"I am saved, Nora, I am saved!" [176]

Other refinements appear from the earlier to the final draft. Ibsen
greatly compressed some speeches for proper emphasis. In the earlier
draft, for example, about mid Act I Dr. Rank inveighs against Nora's
sympathy for Krogstad:

> DR. RANK: There we have it! This damned humanity! Excuse me if
> I express myself rather strongly. But it makes me wild when I
> hear—. Who are the people who will suffer? Incapable or disorderly
> individuals, drunkards many of them, persons who take advantage
> of the weakness of their superiors to obtain advances or loans that
> they can never repay.
> STENBORG: Yes, you're not far from the truth.
> DR. RANK: And then, who is it that will suffer next? Why the share-
> holders, myself and a lot of other honest men. We are the people
> who are robbed by incapacity and irregularity and apathy, so that
> we never see a penny of our deposits. But nobody pities us. No, of
> course not; we are not failures; we are not drunkards, forgers, dis-
> charged convicts; and these are the sort of fellows who have a mon-
> opoly of pity in our humane age.

In the final draft, this whole stew is reduced to a meaty morsel:

> MRS. LINDE: Well, I suppose—the delicate characters require the most
> care.
> DR. RANK: (*shrugs his shoulders*) There we have it! It's that notion
> that makes society a hospital.[177]

Ibsen reduced the time span of *A Doll's House* to heighten tension.
In the earlier draft, Act II began a week after Act I, and in the interval, the anxious Nora took desperately to party-going in the Christmas season as a form of whistling in the dark. In the final draft, Act
II begins directly after Act I, and Nora's anxiety is at its highest pitch
without the distractions of a week of party-going.

A comparison of the earlier and the final draft also shows that
Ibsen sustained the tone of *A Doll's House* by cutting melodramatic
passages or by making them more realistic. For instance, in the final

draft he cut this passage from the earlier draft very near the start of Act II, portraying Nora as despondent over Krogstad's threats of blackmail:

> NURSE: What is it, ma'am? You're white as a sheet.
> NORA: Oh, it was fearful.
> NURSE: What? What was it?
> NORA: I was thinking of the terrible story you told me when I was little.
> NURSE: I?
> NORA: Don't you remember the girl who lived near us, who had helped to murder her father and was executed? When they came to fetch her, she screamed: "No, not now in the spring-time! Not now in the sunshine!"—Yes, it is terrible to die in the springtime and in the sunshine.[178]

In the final draft, moreover, Ibsen revised the following passage from late in Act II of the earlier draft, with Krogstad picturing for Nora her suicide should she fail to meet his blackmail:

> KROGSTAD: . . . Poison? Not so easy to get. Shoot yourself? That wants some practice, Mrs. Helmer. Hanging? Fie, there's something ugly about it—you get cut down; you would never bring yourself to do that.
> NORA: Do you hear it roaring?
> KROGSTAD: The river? Yes, of course, that is what you've been thinking of. But haven't you thought just casually—think now, of putting it into execution—out of the house at night—into the foaming black water—to be carried along, dragged under the ice—to struggle, to be suffocated, and to be fished up—some day, from far below—and in what a state—.

In the final draft, Ibsen turned all this gloating villainy into a macabre bit of realism:

> KROGSTAD: Under the ice, perhaps? Down into the cold, black water? And next Spring to come up again, ugly, hairless, unrecognizable . . .
> NORA: You can't terrify me.[179]

From the earlier to the final draft, Ibsen also cut needless scenes and added scenes to strengthen probability. In the final draft, for instance, he cut the scene from the earlier draft opening Act II in which Helmer urges Nora to return to the ball. He added, however, two short scenes to strengthen probability: in one, Mrs. Linde suggests that Nora solve her troubles by borrowing money from Dr. Rank; in the other, Dr. Rank confesses to Nora that he secretly loved her and so makes it impossible for her to accept his loan.

A comparison of successive drafts of *Hedda Gabler* shows similar progress. Ibsen created many of his best touches of characterization only in the final draft. For instance, Tesman's trivial ways and failure to understand Hedda, his Aunt Julia's sentimentality, and Hedda's unhappiness with Tesman as well as her disgust with the banality at hand, are illustrated for the first time in this memorable bit appearing well into Act I:

> TESMAN: My old morning-shoes! My slippers.
> HEDDA: Indeed. I remember you often spoke of them while we were abroad.
> TESMAN: Yes, I missed them terribly. (*goes up to her*) Now you shall see them, Hedda.
> HEDDA: (*going toward the stove*) Thanks, I really don't care about it.
> TESMAN: (*following her*) Only think—ill as she was, Aunt Rina embroidered these for me. Oh, you can't think how many associations cling to them.
> HEDDA: (*at the table*) Scarcely for me.[180]

Hedda's destructive envy even as a school girl comes through only in the final draft about the middle of Act I with this bit:

> MRS. ELVSTED: . . . for when we met on the stairs, you used always to pull my hair.
> HEDDA: Did I really?
> MRS. ELVSTED: Yes, and once you said you would burn it off my head.
> HEDDA: Oh, that was all nonsense of course.[181]

Hedda's avoidance of unpleasantness is also emphasized with this speech found only in the final draft in the middle of Act III when Hedda refuses to see Tesman's dying Aunt Rina:

> HEDDA: (*rises and says wearily, repelling the idea*) No, no, don't ask me. I will not look upon sickness and death. I loathe all sorts of ugliness.[182]

Ibsen also enriched the final draft of Hedda Gabler with lively detail. In the earlier draft, Berta and Miss Rising not far into Act I discuss Hedda as George's wife:

BERTA: Most like she'll be terrible grand in her ways.
MISS RISING: Well, you can't wonder at that. Think of the sort of
life she was accustomed to in her father's time.

In the final draft, Miss Rising, renamed "Miss Tesman" says:

MISS TESSMAN: Well, you can't wonder at that—General Gabler's
daughter! Think of the sort of life she was accustomed to in her
father's time. Don't you remember how we used to see her riding
down the road along with the General? In that long black habit—
and with feathers in her hat? [183]

Similarly, in an earlier draft, Thea near the close of Act II says of
Lövborg attending Brack's stag party:

THEA: Hedda—Hedda—what will come of all this?
HEDDA: We shall see about ten o'clock.

In the final draft, Hedda adds the now famous bacchanalian detail:

HEDDA: At ten o'clock—he will be here. I can see him already—with
vine leaves in his hair—flushed and fearless.[184]

Ibsen developed some scenes in *Hedda Gabler* to give proper emphasis. In the earlier draft, Judge Brack in Act III tells of what took
place after Eilert Lövborg left the Judge's apartment with some old
acquaintances:

BRACK: They paid a visit to some singing girl, I think.
HEDDA: Or something of the sort, yes. And afterwards?
BRACK: An orgie, presumably. Followed by the customary free fight
with the resultant ejection. Then a street row outside. Windows
smashed. Police called. And so on to the lock-up.

This incident brings Hedda's life to its major crisis; therefore, in the
final draft, Ibsen develops the scene with specific sordid detail that
makes us feel more powerfully its impact upon Hedda:

BRACK: To make a long story short—he landed at last in Mademoiselle
Diana's rooms.
HEDDA: Mademoiselle Diana's?
BRACK: It was Mademoiselle Diana that was giving the *soirée* to a
select circle of her admirers and her lady friends.
HEDDA: Is she a red-haired woman?

BRACK: Precisely.

HEDDA: A sort of—singer?

BRACK: Oh, yes,—in her leisure moments. And moreover a mighty huntress of men—Mrs. Hedda. You have no doubt heard of her. Eilert Lövborg was one of her most enthusiastic protectors—in the days of his glory.

HEDDA: And how did all this end?

BRACK: Far from amicably, it appears. After a most tender meeting they seem to have come to blows—

HEDDA: Lövborg and she?

BRACK: Yes. He accused her or her friends of having robbed him. He declared that his pocketbook had disappeared—and other things as well. In short, he seems to have caused a furious disturbance.

HEDDA: And what came of it all?

BRACK: It came to general scrimmage, in which the ladies as well as the gentlemen took part. Fortunately, the police at last appeared on the scene.[185]

In the final draft, to sustain the play's tone, Ibsen cut all caricature and absurdity from the earlier draft. In the earlier draft, Brack at the opening of Act II calls upon Hedda when she is at pistol practice and asks for her husband, George:

HEDDA: He rushed out of the house as soon as I took up the pistol case.

In the final draft, the facetious hint has been removed:

HEDDA: He rushed off to his Aunt's directly after lunch; he didn't expect you so early.[186]

Near the close of Act III, Ibsen also cut from the earlier draft the ludicrous portion of Judge Brack's proposal to Hedda that she, he and Tesman form a "triangular relationship:"

HEDDA: Oh, come, I am sure you have plenty of other comfortable homes about town.

BRACK: No, unfortunately. Not now; in the last six months I have lost no fewer than three. And those among the best.

HEDDA: Oh, did intruding cocks come into those baskets, too?

BRACK: No, but other intruders arrived—

HEDDA: Of what kind?

BRACK: Children.

HEDDA: Indeed? But what have those children to do with you?

BRACK: (laughingly) They have nothing to do with me. That's why I call them intruders.[187]

Ibsen took care, too, to make changes clarifying motivation. In the final draft, for instance, he blue-pencilled the earlier draft's insinuations that Tesman helped Hedda burn Lövborg's manuscript and that Tesman knew of Lövborg's passion for Hedda.

No record is at present revealed as to just how much Ibsen revised his plays during rehearsal of their premiere. He was much too much the master craftsman to allow pride to paralyze his better judgment. In his own day, stars and managers were far too powerful anyway for Ibsen to quite control when they chose to do a play of his. His printed plays at least contain his ultimate effort.

My grateful acknowledgement is extended to the following sources of quotations:
THE BOOKMAN, June 1910, "How Ibsen Made His Plays" by Archibald
Henderson. Reprinted by permission.
CENTURY magazine:
"Henrik Ibsen, Personal Reminiscences and Remarks on His Plays" by George
Brandes, February 1917
"Mrs. Fiske on Ibsen the Popular," a conversation recorded by Alexander Wooll-
cott, February 1917
"Ibsen and Emilie Bardach, Part II" by Basil King, October 1923
Extracts from Volumes I, III, IV, V, VI, VII, VIII, X, XI and XII of THE
COLLECTED WORKS OF HENRIK IBSEN, revised and edited by William
Archer, are used by permission of Charles Scribner's Sons and William Heine-
mann, Ltd.
THE CRITIC, July 1906, "Ibsen's Early Youth—An Old Friend's Recollection of
Grimstad Days" by C. L. Due
FORTNIGHTLY REVIEW:
"Ibsen's Apprenticeship" by William Archer, January 1904
"Ibsen in His Letters" by William Archer, March 1905
"Ibsen's Craftsmanship" by William Archer, July 1906
"From Ibsen's Workshop" by William Archer, December 1909
Reprinted by permission of Contemporary Review Company, Ltd.
HENRIK IBSEN by Edmund Gosse, Charles Scribner's Sons, 1907
HENRIK IBSEN, 1828–1888, A Critical Biography, by Henrik Jaeger translated
from the Norwegian by William Morton Payne, McClurg & Co., 1890
HENRIK IBSEN, A Study in Art and Personality, by Theodore Jorgenson, St.
Olaf Press, 1945
IBSEN AND STRINDBERG by F. L. Lucas. (c) 1962. Reprinted by permis-
sion of Cassell & Co., Ltd.
IBSEN AND HIS CREATIONS by Janko Lavrin, S. W. Collins Sons & Co.
IBSEN LETTERS AND SPEECHES edited and translated by Evert Sprinchorn,
a Dramabook. Copyright 1964. Reprinted by permission of Hill and Wang.
INTERPRETERS OF LIFE AND THE MODERN SPIRIT by Archibald
Henderson, Kennerly, 1911

IBSEN: THE MASTER-BUILDER by A. E. Zucker. Copyright 1929. Reprinted by permission of Holt, Rinehart and Winston, Inc.

Extracts from LETTERS OF HENRIK IBSEN translated and edited by John Nilsen Laurvik and Mary Morison, Fox, Duffield & Co., 1905. Some letters repeated in THE CORRESPONDENCE OF HENRIK IBSEN translated and edited by Mary Morison. Copyright 1905. Reprinted by permission of Hodder & Stoughton, Ltd.

THE LIFE OF HENRIK IBSEN, I, II, by Halvdan Koht. Copyright 1931. Reprinted by permission of W. W. Norton & Co., Inc.

THE LIFE-WORK OF HENDRIK IBSEN from the Russian of D. S. Merejkowski by G. A. Mounsey. The De La Mare Press.

LIVING AGE:

"Ibsen in Transformation" by Erik Lee, May 21, 1921, reprinted from BERLINE TAGEBLATTER of April 3, 1921

"Sidelights on Ibsen, I" by Georg Brandes, November 3, 1923, reprinted from NEUE FREIE PRESSE of August 5, 11, 1923

"The Real Doll's House" by Xiane, March 1, 1924, reprinted from BERLINGSKE TIDENDE of January 6, 1924

"Ibsen Discusses A DOLL'S HOUSE," March 8, 1924

THE MONTHLY REVIEW, June 1906, "Ibsen as I Knew Him" by William Archer

PLAYWRIGHTS ON PLAYWRITING edited by Toby Cole. Copyright 1961, a Dramabook, Hill and Wang. Reprinted by permission of Evert Sprinchorn.

PROBLEMS OF THE PLAYWRIGHT by Clayton Hamilton, Henry Holt & Co., 1917

SPEECHES AND NEW LETTERS OF HENRIK IBSEN translated by Arne Kildal, Richard G. Badger, Publisher, 1909

THE THREE IBSENS by Bergliot Ibsen, translated from the Norwegian by Gerik Schjelderup. Copyright 1952. Reprinted by permission of Hutchinson & Co., Ltd.

1. Mary Morison, *The Correspondence of Henrik Ibsen* (Hodder & Stoughton, London 1905), 102
2. Ibid.
3. Kildal, 60
4. John Laurvik and Mary Morison, *The Letters of Henrik Ibsen* (New York 1905), 361
5. Ibid.
6. Bergliot Ibsen, *The Three Ibsens* (London 1952), 10
7. Merejkowski, *The Life of Hendrik Ibsen* (London), 4
8. Henrik Jaeger, *Henrik Ibsen* (Chicago 1890), 18
9. Ibid. 21
10. Ibid., 18
11. Laurvik and Morison, 313
12. C. L. Due, "Ibsen's Early Youth," *The Critic* (July 1906), 37
13. Ibid., 35
14. Theodore Jorgenson, *Henrik Ibsen, a Study in Art and Personality* (Northfield 1945), 56
15. Halvdan Koht, *The Life of Henrik Ibsen* (New York 1931), II, 2
16. Laurvik and Morison, 198
17. William Archer, *The Collected Works of Henrik Ibsen* (New York 1912), I, 7.
18. Jaeger, 71
19. Koht, I, 25
20. Ibid., 83
21. William Archer, "Ibsen's Apprenticeship," *Fortnightly Review* (January 1904), 31
22. Bergliot Ibsen, 15
23. Laurvik and Morison, 199
24. Jorgenson, 125; Koht, I, 181
25. Laurvik and Morison, 129
26. Archer, "Ibsen in His Letters," *Fortnightly Review* (March 1905), 430
27. *The Collected Works of Henrik Ibsen*, IV, 9
28. Janko Lavrin, *Ibsen and His Creations* (Glasgow), 38

29. Laurvik and Morison, 344; Morison, 271
30. Bergliot Ibsen, 34
31. Laurvik and Morison, 439
32. Evert Sprinchorn, *Ibsen Letters and Speeches* (New York 1964), 208
33. Laurvik and Morison, 354
34. E. J. West, *Shaw on Theatre* (New York 1958), 238
35. Laurvik and Morison, 438
36. Bergliot Ibsen, 5
37. *The Critic* (July 1906), 249
38. Laurvik and Morison, 150
39. Ibid., 183
40. Kildal, 64
41. *The Collected Works of Henrik Ibsen,* VIII, 228, 229
42. Ibid., 229
43. Sprinchorn, 336
44. Laurvik and Morison, 178
45. Ibid., 313
46. Bergliot Ibsen, 20
47. Laurvik and Morison, 338
48. Koht, I, 146
49. Ibid., 88
50. Ibid., II, 49
51. Ibid.
52. Ibid., I, 88
53. Laurvik and Morison, 350
54. Kildal, 69
55. Laurvik and Morison, 370
56. Ibid., 327
57. Ibid., 358
58. William Archer, "Ibsen as I Knew Him," *Monthly Review* (June 1906), 18; Arthur and Barbara Gelb, *O'Neill* (New York 1962), 325-6
59. Jaeger, 153
60. Kildal, 71
61. Laurvik and Morison, 190
62. Bergliot Ibsen, 35
63. Laurvik and Morison, 234
64. *Fortnightly Review* (March 1905), 434
65. Laurvik and Morison, 145
66. Ibid., 176
67. Ibid., 367
68. *The Collected Works of Henrik Ibsen,* III, 8
69. Laurvik and Morison, 359
70. *The Collected Works of Henrik Ibsen,* I, 200
71. Laurvik and Morison, 194

72. Ibid., 193
73. Kildal, 49
74. Ibid., 65
75. Ibid., 62
76. Laurvik and Morison, 218
77. *The Collected Works of Henrik Ibsen,* VIII, 5
78. Kildal, 53, 54
79. Ibid., 57
80. Laurvik and Morison, 200
81. Kildal, 50
82. Laurvik and Morison, 334
83. *The Collected Works of Henrik Ibsen,* VIII, 221
84. Ibid., XI, 356
85. Brian Downs, *Ibsen, the Intellectual Background* (London 1948), 155
86. Kildal, 58
87. Koht, II, 2
88. Ibid., 3
89. Laurvik and Morison, 193
90. Koht, II, 3
91. Ibid.
92. Bergliot Ibsen, 136
93. Jaeger, 272
94. Ibid., 272, 274
95. *The Monthly Review* (June 1906), 4
96. Laurvik and Morison, 200
97. Jaeger, 274
98. *The Monthly Review* (June 1906), 7
99. *The Collected Works of Henrik Ibsen,* XI, 428
100. Jaeger, 273
101. Laurvik and Morison, 198
102. Ibid.
103. *The Collected Works of Henrik Ibsen,* I, 201, 202
104. Jaeger, 108
105. Laurvik and Morison, 413
106. Ibid., 248
107. *The Collected Works of Henrik Ibsen,* XII, 5
108. Ibid., VIII, 3, 4
109. Archibald Henderson, "How Ibsen Made His Plays," *The Bookman* (June 1910), p. 493
110. Xiane, "The Real Doll's House," *Living Age* (March 1, 1924), 415
111. "Ibsen Discusses A Doll's House," *Living Age* (March 8, 1924), 477
112. Georg Brandes, "Henrik Ibsen, Personal Reminiscences and Remarks on His Plays," *Century* (February 1917), 542
113. *The Collected Works of Henrik Ibsen,* VI, 153

114. Ibid., VII, 4, 5
115. Sprinchorn, 208
116. *The Collected Works of Henrik Ibsen,* VII, 195–6
117. Brandes, 544
118. Ibid.
119. *The Collected Works of Henrik Ibsen,* XII, 381–3
120. Toby Cole, *Playwrights on Playwriting* (New York 1961), 162
121. *The Monthly Review* (June 1906), 13
122. *The Collected Works of Henrik Ibsen,* X, 5
123. Ibid.
124. Ibid.
125. *Fortnightly Review* (March 1905), 431
126. *The Monthly Review* (June 1906), 18
127. A. E. Zucker, *Ibsen: The Master Builder* (New York 1929), 194
128. Bernard Shaw, *Plays Pleasant and Unpleasant* (New York 1898), II, xxiii
129. Bergliot Ibsen, 107
130. *Fortnightly Review* (January 1904), 434
131. Kildal, 50
132. *The Collected Works of Henrik Ibsen,* III, 10
133. *The Monthly Review* (June 1906), 8
134. *The Collected Works of Henrik Ibsen,* IV, 4
135. Ibid., 6
136. Ibid., 16
137. Ibid., X, 232, 233
138. Ibid., 23
139. Basil King, "Ibsen and Emilie Bardach," *Century* (October 1923), 810
140. *The Collected Works of Henrik Ibsen,* X, 231
141. Ibid.
142. Ibid., 232
143. Ibid., 238
144. Ibid., X, 367
145. Laurvik and Morison, 190; Kildal, 49
146. *The Collected Works of Henrik Ibsen,* X, 230
147. Lewis, p. 59; quote from Shaw's speech of acceptance of Nobel Prize in Literature, 1925
148. Eric Bentley, *The Playwright as Thinker* (New York 1946), 336
149. F. L. Lucas, *Ibsen and Strindberg* (London 1962), 1
150. Lewis, 59
151. Hamilton, 23
152. Bernard Shaw, *The Quintessence of Ibsenism* (New York 1957), 156–7
153. *Fortnightly Review* (July 1906), 101, 102
154. *The Bookman* (June 1910), 497
155. "Mrs. Fiske on Ibsen the Popular," *Century* (February 1917), 535
156. *The Monthly Review* (June 1906), 13

157. *The Collected Works of Henrik Ibsen*, XI, 357
158. *The Bookman* (June 1910), 495
159. *The Collected Works of Henrik Ibsen*, X, 228
160. Ibid., 229
161. Ibid.
162. Edmund Gosse, *Henrik Ibsen* (New York 1907), 241
163. *The Collected Works of Henrik Ibsen*, IV, 29
164. Laurvik and Morison, 228
165. *The Collected Works of Henrik Ibsen*, I, xi
166. Laurvik and Morison, 269
167. Ibid., 367–8
168. Koht, II, 196; cf. *Fortnightly Review* (March 1905), 432
169. *Fortnightly Review* (March 1905), 433
170. Zucker, 208
171. Albert Sturtevant, "Henrik Ibsen: Some Aspects of His Life and Works," *Scandinavian Studies* (August 1928), 76
172. Sprinchorn, 295
173. Cf. *The Collected Works of Henrik Ibsen*, VII, 27, 33 with XII, 97
174. Cf. ibid., VII, 81 with XII, 124
175. Cf. ibid., VII, 104 with XII, 130
176. Cf. ibid., XII, 162 with VII, 173
177. Cf. ibid., XII, 112 with VII, 59
178. Cf. ibid., XII, 126–7 with VII, 89, 90
179. Cf. ibid., XII, 142 with VII, 128
180. Ibid., X, 41
181. Ibid., 60
182. Ibid., 162
183. Cf. ibid., XII, 384 with X, 24
184. Cf. ibid., XII, 424 with X, 144
185. Cf. ibid., XII, 432 with X, 167–9
186. Cf. ibid., XII, 400 with X, 88
187. Ibid., XII, 435

Chapter II

August Strindberg

IN A love-letter dated March 12, 1876, August Strindberg, then twenty-seven years old, wrote the married Baroness Wrangel, "I will, I will be mad! . . . I love you!!!" [1] . . . my fire is the greatest in Sweden," and, in Elizabeth Sprigge's translation, offered the Baroness a role as his muse, "—you who can give this country its greatest author—." [2] From his first play, *A Name-Day Gift,* written at the age of twenty, to his first successful long play, *Master Olof,* written at the age of twenty-three but not produced until nine years later, how Strindberg thought he had learned playwriting is suggested in his book, *The Confession of a Fool.* "I had provided her with the masterpieces of all literature," he said of his futile efforts to teach the Baroness to write, "had taught her the first principles of literary composition by furnishing endless summaries, commentaries and analyses, to which I added advice and practical illustrations." [3] To Eugene O'Neill, "Strindberg was the precursor of all modernity in our present theatre . . . ," [4] and to Shaw, by an evaluation made at the age of seventy, "the only genuine Shakespearean modern dramatist." [5] To F. L. Lucas in a recent appraisal, "Strindberg often, I think, over-rated as a writer, remains as a personality far more extraordinary than any of his works." [6] Ironically, no other modern dramatist, not even O'Neill, has so openly identified his life with his work as Strindberg.

I

THE GROWTH OF STRINDBERG'S CREATIVE SPIRIT IN LIFE

Strindberg's ultimate conviction about the circuitous nature of human destiny is illustrated in how he came to write his first play: the aftermath of an attempt at suicide. Impoverished and checkmated first in his medical career and then as an aspiring actor, Strindberg relates in Claud Field's translation of *The Growth of a Soul* that, "He wept for rage, went home and took an opium pill which he had long kept by him, but without effect; then a friend took him out and he got intoxicated." [7] The next morning, ashamed and near collapse, Strindberg read Topelius' *The Stories of a Barber-Surgeon,* about the reconciliation of a step-mother and a step-son—one of Strindberg's problems—and in a few hours he dreamed up a two-act comedy that took him four days to write. After reading the play, *A Name-Day Gift,* to his friends, Strindberg fell on his knees and thanked God— "At last he had found his calling." [8]

Plato said there were two inscriptions on the shrine of the oracle at Delphi: "Know thyself," and, "Nothing in excess." [9] Strindberg was obsessed with the first and largely ignored the second. The biographies of Martin Lamm in Swedish and of Elizabeth Sprigge in English are reputed the best in revealing the true Strindberg, and both draw heavily upon his work. "Strindberg," concluded Sprigge in *The Strange Life of August Strindberg,* "chose the form of the novel for his autobiographies." [10] Strindberg's changing self-portrait is somewhat a figure of incantation seen by his mind's eye in the cave of his imagination by the flickering light of his own highly inflammable emotions.

Christened Johan August Strindberg, the dramatist was born in "the Venice of the North," Stockholm, in mid-winter on January 22, 1849, a seven-month baby. Strindberg was the fourth child of Carl Oscar Strindberg, an aristocratic shipping agent, and his plebeian mistress, the waitress and bar-maid, Ulrika Eleonora Norling. The parents married only shortly before Strindberg was born. Europe at the time was going into a chronic climate of thunder, lightning, and violent storms of social change with Karl Marx's *Communist Manifesto,* published in 1849, adding to the turbulence. Strindberg was born when his father was in bankruptcy. "Do you know there is a legend in my family," says the Stranger, obviously Strindberg, in his play, *To Damascus I,* "that I am a changeling? . . . a child that has been exchanged by the elves for the child that was born?" [11] In *The Growth of a Soul,* Strindberg says of himself, "His face had no resemblance to that of his father or mother. Since he had not seen his grandparents, he could not judge whether there was resemblance to them." [12] In *The Confession of a Fool* he wrote, "I was developed far in advance of my years . . . perhaps even attempt had been made to suppress life before it could properly be said to have come into existence. Such things happen only too frequently in large families." [13] And very late in his life, in *Zones of the Spirit,* a compilation of notes from his *Bluebooks,* Strindberg possibly made a Freudian slip and implied his long muted cry in the whole matter. "If for fifty years I have cherished the memory of my parents," he said, "and my family, property, and honour is based on my relationship to them, and then someone comes and tells me I am not my father's son, he has killed me; the whole edifice of my emotional life collapses." [14] Strindberg did not apparently in his opinion ever really look like a Strindberg. This shocking uncertainty provides a neglected master-key to help unlock the very complex and baffling character of the dramatist. From earliest memories, he was to feel unwanted, hated, and even persecuted. "Most of my misfortunes have been imaginary," Strindberg wrote at fifty in Klaf's translation, "but they have had the same effect as real ones because I came to the consciousness of my own wrong-doing." [15] Strindberg euphemistically born "a changeling" was practically "a misogynist" by self-discovery.

Perhaps Strindberg's lifelong tendency to enjoy suffering came from his first few months of life following his premature birth when he literally fought for survival, and like an Indian fakir had to learn to enjoy his bed of nails or die. "The child's first impressions," Strindberg said in *The Son of a Servant,* "were, as he remembered afterwards, fear and hunger." [16] The bells of the clock-tower of the nearby Clara Church relentlessly bonged out the hours, quarter-hours, church occasions, and local alarms of fire and drownings, like some divine, shattering mouth-piece. "He seemed to have been born frightened," Strindberg said of himself, "and lived in continual fear of life and of men." [17]

His mother's favorite was his eldest brother, and his father's favorite, his second brother. The father's side of the family refused to mix with his wife, "a fallen woman;" Strindberg's mother was to die of consumption when he was thirteen and only then did his father's family show their forgiveness by allowing her burial in their uncle's family plot. The Strindbergs prospered; the once bankrupt relatives dispersed; the Strindbergs had in all twelve children of whom five died in infancy. Strindberg's father, a weary, taciturn gentleman, appeared only at meal-time, usually ate in deathly silence, and punished the children as his easily excited and quickly quieted wife thought right. The home atmosphere was one of Lutheran Pietism. "Strict obedience prevailed in the house," recalled Strindberg; "falsehood and disobedience were severely punished." [18] Strindberg's rebellion against all authority, even for a while against God the Father, might go back to being caned through childhood. He called his brain "a revolutionary's from birth." [19] In *The Growth of a Soul* he considered that two traits especially set his life's course: "Doubt" and "Sensitiveness to pressure." [20] Both could surely be nurtured by not looking like a Strindberg.

Oscar Strindberg's shame over his bankruptcy and his touchiness over his marriage led him to invite almost no one to his home for years. He deliberately moved his family to get away from people. First, the Strindbergs moved to the suburb of Nortullsgata till Strindberg was about ten, and then they moved to an even more isolated suburb, Stora Grabergsgata, in the thick of tobacco farms. When Strindberg's mother died, his father remarried within six months, and the family moved back to Nortullsgata.

At what time Strindberg exactly discovered his family's wayward past, is not clear, but at twelve he realized that he was sent for the summer to a school at Mariefred run by a parish clerk for only illegitimate children. Worse yet, with his aristocratic-servile blood, he felt he belonged neither to the aristocracy of his father nor to the menial class of his mother, and he said, "That becomes one of the struggles of his life." [21] At his mother's death, he thought of her as "a good and conscientious woman;" [22] she warned him against onanism and brothels, and also, "He was to beware of intellectual pride and always to remain simple." [23] Again and again while growing up Strindberg found in his parents not the sense of security most children find, but a continual insecurity plunging his soul into torment and later distinguishing his plays, a state of ambivalence and inner conflict. "Family," Strindberg wrote in *The Son of a Servant,* "thou art the home of all social evil, a charitable institution for indolent women, an anchorage for fathers, and a hell for children." [24] But in *The Confession of a Fool* he wrote, "What inexpressible happiness it is to be married! . . . It is as if one had regained the home of one's childhood, with its sheltering love . . ." [25]

Strindberg's attitude toward his mother was critical for determining his attitude toward all women. "Her image seems glorified and draws him with unbreakable cords of longing," he wrote of his mother in *The Son of a Servant.* "This feeling of loneliness and longing after his mother followed him all through his life." And then Strindberg said of himself, "He remained, as it were, a mistletoe, which could not grow except upon a tree; he was a climbing plant, which must seek support. He was naturally weak and timid." [26] Strindberg often wrote of his mother as the "madonna," suggesting the model of womanhood among many Christians, the Virgin Mary; but in his adolescent experience from picking up bar-maids and waitresses and in his "changeling" fears, his mother probably had an ambivalent image. Each woman Strindberg was to marry, he was attracted to as "the madonna," come in heaven's plan to redeem him; then he suspected each of coquetry; and in time, he told off each in effect, "You whore!"

Though Strindberg as a child loved his toy theatre and play-acted with an older brother in the attic, and though a paternal grandfather had once written plays for amateur actors, and a distant relative had become an unsuccessful actor, Strindberg found only one powerful sign in himself of a dramatist. "It was a peculiar trait of John's character," noted Strindberg, "that he identified himself with others, suffered for them, and felt ashamed on their behalf." [27]

Strindberg's "changeling" status might have given him a fierce lifelong drive to clear up all mysteries, even that of the universe itself. "He had a mania for explaining and knowing everything," Strindberg said of himself.[28] And this "mania" was to isolate him even more. A precocious child, Strindberg was admitted to the Clara School at seven, passed the year's work and then, lest he be the youngest in the next class, was forced to repeat the completed year's work. He quickly hated formal schooling as an affliction of wearisome rote learning, vicious punishment by the rod, and senseless delay. "Solitude," he wrote, "had to take for him the place of desert-wandering . . ." [29] He excelled in geography, languages, and natural science, and by his tenth year, his relatives nicknamed him "the professor;" when his family moved to a more secluded and poorer neighborhood with larger quarters, Strindberg attended the Jacob School whose humble student body caused more fortunate outsiders to dub it "the louts' school."

Strindberg's brilliance only further set him at home and in school alone on a spiritual island. His favorite books suggest his disposition then: *Robinson Crusoe, Discovery of America* and *The Scalp Hunter*. He also collected insects, minerals and herbs, as well as practised piano and the guitar—all potentially solo occupations. His father soon transferred Strindberg to a private school for mostly aristocrats, from which Strindberg at fifteen graduated. But now he had to wait until eighteen to qualify to take the admission examinations of Uppsala University.

Even when Strindberg was twelve his father had opened his bookcase to him. He read books on physics and chemistry, built Leyden jars and detonated gases. By fifteen, Strindberg had "swallowed Shakespeare whole" and found it largely indigestible. His fare of mental nourishment, all from his father's book-case, came to include such banqueting as Cervantes, Byron, Scott, Dumas, Dickens, Sue and books on botany, anatomy, geography, aesthetics, painting, and music. When Strindberg's father married his housekeeper so soon after his first wife's death, Strindberg turned even more to his books; he refused to kiss his stepmother at the wedding or to call her "mother," and he believed his father had him wearing his elder brothers' cast-off clothes and sweeping the stable as a punishment.

Strindberg, like all boys, suffered growing pains sexually. When thirteen, he borrowed from his older brother a book that was to haunt him for many years with fears of insanity: *Warning of a Friend of Youth against the Most Dangerous Enemy of Youth*. The enemy was onanism, and the warning was death or lunacy by twenty-five—"His spinal marrow and his brain would disappear . . . the cure was—Christ." [30] At fifteen, Strindberg became infatuated with the thirty-year-old daughter of his landlord. Their affair consisted of studying French and Pietism together. That year, a young engineer switched Strindberg from Pietism to free-thinking by way of the Unitarian sermons of Theodore Parker and Rousseau's *Confessions*. Another friend, the materialistic Fritz with pince-nez, took Strindberg from his new terminal to "balls" and "punch evenings" and to getting on with the girls. "All northerners are born of generations of drinkers from early heathen times," wrote Strindberg; ". . . with John, it was an imperious need." [31]

In the summer of his eighteenth year and before entering Uppsala University, Strindberg got his first job, tutoring a Baron's son. Typical of just about everything that was to happen to Strindberg for the rest of his life, the experience ended in disillusionment. The aristocrats treated Strindberg like a servant and dismissed him when he refused to stand by and let an innocent steward take the blame for a missing pair of driver's gloves that the son of the Baron had stolen.

When Strindberg entered Uppsala that fall with only 80 kronas for a whole term's expenses, he learned he couldn't afford to buy books, and he had to half-starve to live. After one semester he left Uppsala, appalled by its great-toed-sloth's pace of instruction and the faculty-student courtly system of back-scratching. In the spring of 1868 while reading on his own for a doctorate degree—an approximation of today's American doctorate—Strindberg taught elementary classes at his old Clara School in Stockholm; he soon realized that to survive as a teacher he had to adopt the repressive practices he, himself, as a student had hated. Strindberg also became convinced that improvement in society had to come from above, not from below, for the poor are too ignorant, diseased, and handicapped to lift themselves by bootstraps without boots.

In the summer of 1868, Dr. Axel Lamm, a prosperous Jewish physician, offered to prepare Strindberg for medical studies in exchange for Strindberg's tutoring Lamm's children. Strindberg thrived in the cosmopolitan spirit of the Lamms' cultured home. He shared equality as a guest at gatherings of artists and professional men, attended the theatre twice a week, read freely from Mrs. Lamm's library, and became more interested in art than in medicine. Strindberg's disillusionment with medicine was complete when he failed his qualifying examination in chemistry because he couldn't tell the examining professor at Uppsala how to begin to construct a salt-petre factory. Shades of Freud! "Why read so much unnecessary stuff," thought Strindberg, ". . . and slave in order to enter this dirty profession where one had to analyse urine, pick about in vomit, poke about in all the recesses of the body! Faugh!" [32] He would, of course, be doing exactly this figuratively in playwriting.

On impulse upon seeing a happy troupe of Levasseur's French actors pass by on the street, Strindberg decided now to become an actor. Without formal training, he took bit parts at the Royal Theatre and after an utterly humiliating try-out for a lead, was told to study acting for a year at the Academy. As earlier related, Strindberg then in a tearful rage tried to end his life and woke up, with a terrible hang-over, to write his first play, *A Name-Day Gift*. The director of the Royal Theatre in Stockholm turned down the play but advised Strindberg to return to Uppsala to study dramaturgy. In this, too, Strindberg was to be disillusioned. On his own, he wrote: two comedies; a tragedy, *Hermione;* a tragedy about Demosthenes and Philip of Macedonia; and a play about Jesus which he destroyed as lacking scholarship.

At twenty-one Strindberg, now come of age, inherited a few hundred krona from his deceased mother, and in the fall of 1870 enrolled at Uppsala again. Extant known plays he wrote there are:

In Rome (1870)	*The Outlaw* (1871)
The Free Thinker	*Master Olof* (1872)

The Royal Theatre first produced his one-act in verse, *In Rome,* in 1870, and the one-act, *The Outlaw,* in 1871. King Carl XV himself summoned the astounded Strindberg to award him a stipend. Then Strindberg's fortunes took a reverse turn. His proposed doctorate dissertation on Oehlenschläger's play, *"Haakon Jarl,* Idealism or Realism," written as an exchange of letters, was rejected as mere journalism. The Royal Theatre turned down *Master Olof.* Strindberg's stipend stopped. In debt and quite distraught, he wrote a physician as to his sanity and was reassured that he suffered only from a sensitive nature. "The University is a combination of cloister, tavern and brothel," he wrote in *The Gothic Rooms* in 1904; "the University is a school—a school of pride, oppression, frivolity, envy, and toadyism."[33]

Strindberg had no choice but to withdraw from Uppsala University to read philology on his own. He turned to journalism to earn his bread and never took a degree. He came to write highly controversial criticism even for the radical *Riksdag* and then for the *Dagens Nyheter.* In 1874 he was appointed Assistant in the Royal Library at Stockholm, a post he was to keep until 1882 and which now provided him with the biggest bookcase of his life, a King's, and an *entrée* to correspond with writers all over the world. He taught himself Chinese and classified the chaotic Chinese collection. He did a monograph, *Sweden's Relation to China and the Tartar Lands,* which led the Imperial Russian Geographical Society to award him a medal. He read on his own not only the best of dramatic literature but writings whose viewpoint was to profoundly affect his own perspective by suiting his earliest disposition as "a changeling." He found new spiritual vision in Buckle, Darwin, Rousseau, Buddha, Kierkegaard, Nietzsche, Poe, and Charcot.

While an Assistant at the Royal Library, Strindberg until 1878 tried unsuccessfully to revise *Master Olof.* He lived hand to mouth. "I had the greatest difficulty to make ends meet," he confessed. He regarded himself as a free-thinker, a bohemian, and a member of a secret society to further free-love. This last dubious distinction it seems led Strindberg to receive in 1875 a letter from an anonymous lady who eventually introduced him to the young and very beautiful, Finnish-born Baroness Wrangel. Siri von Essen, the Baroness, presumably was familiar with Strindberg's plays and wanted to talk to him as a potential patron to help produce his *Master Olof.* The Baroness was to be the greatest disillusionment of Strindberg's whole life.

In the eerie pattern of linked destinies, parallel incident, and recurrence—the circuitous fate which Strindberg eventually decided controlled human life—he found the Wrangels living at his family's old address at 12 Nortullsgata. With the philandering Baron's obvious encouragement, Strindberg fell in love with the Baroness. The Wrangels were suddenly nearly bankrupt from a fraudulent stock in which the Baron had invested his wife's dowry. The Baroness divorced her husband in 1876. Just as his own father had done with Strindberg's mother, Strindberg now got Siri pregnant out of wedlock; likely with his "changeling" fears, he believed that the Baron was actually the father of Siri's foetus. To avoid scandal, Strindberg married Siri on December 31, 1877; her child died prematurely. To Strindberg, this was a divine punishment. The marriage ended in divorce in 1891 like something of a dream tour involving heaven and hell. Siri bore Strindberg three children: Karin, Greta, and Hans. Strindberg later claimed they were not his.

By 1879 Strindberg had even acquired a name as "the Swedish Zola." He had written a sensationally successful novel, *The Red Room,* viewing the way of the world in Stockholm as seen through the eyes of a struggling young writer, Arvid Falk, with bohemian friends and a style anticipating *The New Yorker* magazine. Strindberg created plays to give Siri a firmament to twinkle in: *The Secret of the Guild* (1880); *Herr Bengt's Wife* (1882); and *Lucky Per's Journey* (1882). *Master Olof,* meanwhile, opening in the prose version of 1872, scored such a success in 1881 that Strindberg seemed to have crashed the literary Valhalla while alive. Then his miscellany, *The New Kingdom,* in 1882 brought his expulsion.

The Strindbergs fled to Switzerland and a six year exile in twenty or so "homes." The chief tremor that brought down Strindberg's world came in 1884 when his volume of stories, *Married,* satirized among other things the earthly commerce involved in the wafers and wine used in Holy Communion. Strindberg was arrested on a charge of blasphemy, and to save his Swedish publisher, Bonnier, stood trial in Stockholm as his own attorney October 2–17, 1884. Strindberg was acquitted, but no Swedish publisher dared offer him to the public until he had proved his repentance in *Inferno* in 1897, and especially in *To Damascus I,* in 1898.

By 1886 Nietzsche, who was suffering from tertiary syphilis, went quite mad; Siri, aware of Strindberg's correspondence with Nietzsche, consulted a Swiss doctor about Strindberg's sanity. By 1887, in an atmosphere of rising marital tension and with poverty and hate closing in on them like the walls in a Poe horror story, the Strindbergs moved to a dilapidated castle in Holte near Copenhagen where living costs were very modest. In record time Strindberg dashed off some of his best plays, and all somehow involved the fierce love-hate ambivalence of his marriage; an asterisk indicates a long play:

The Father (1887) *	*The People of Hemsö*
Comrades (1888) *	*The Keys of Heaven* (1892)
Miss Julie	*The First Warning*
Creditors *	*Debit and Credit*
The Stronger (1889)	*In the Face of Death*
Pariah	*A Mother's Love*
Simoon	*Playing with Fire*
	The Bond

Strindberg was not to write another play for six years. A whole drawer-full waited, ignored or unprofitable.

Divorced, notorious, with a flat purse and alimony in arrears, Strindberg managed to get to Berlin to try to promote production of his plays. His charm and literary charisma were so potent that he fascinated and then, by 1893, married Frida Uhl, a twenty-one year old Austrian journalist. Very pretty and vivacious, Frida came from a home broken by divorce. Her father was a State Counselor to the Emperor Franz Josef, and her mother had parents with a huge estate on the Danube River. Seven weeks after their marriage, Strindberg and his Frida had gone to London to try to promote the English production of his plays, and wound up in a summer heat wave, stranded and broke. Frida, disobeying Strindberg, read an advance copy of his book, *The Confession of a Fool,* detailing the story of his marriage to Siri and charging her with being a Lesbian between adulteries; Frida saw herself as this literary Blue-beard's next victim.

To be quit of Strindberg and to try to help him, she quickly for five pounds pawned just about all of her belongings including her wedding ring, and sent him alone to friends on the Continent. She remained in London to try to promote the sale of Strindberg's literary wares. The Strindbergs soon wound up at her grandparents' estate on the Danube, beggars at their table. The story is all brought out in *To Damascus I.* Frida became pregnant, and Strindberg became obsessed with experiments to transmute sulphur into gold and to anaesthetize plants with morphine. Their little guest-cottage, what with Strindberg's experiments involving burning sulphur, could not but smell often of sulphur dioxide—"stink-bombs." The publication of *Anti-barbarus,* a summation of his experiments on transmuting elements, prophetically forecast some great modern discoveries but was slighted by professional chemists as the work of a dilletante.

"I have no more illusions as to my finances," Strindberg wrote Frida. "Everything has gone to pieces in Germany, in Scandinavia, in Italy, in England." He had even tried selling his paintings, done often with the abandon of modern "abstracts." Frida finally separated from Strindberg in 1894 when her grandmother, fearing the squandering of her ancestral fortune, said, "Either you give up your husband or you leave tomorrow morning, along with the child." [34]

Nearly destitute, Strindberg lived in "flea-bag" hotels on the Left Bank in Paris. He continued his chemical experiments supported somewhat by a Swedish benefactor, the theosophist, Torsten Hedlund. Paris was then Europe's show-case of culture and, for Strindberg, the scene of his famous if unprofitable triumph at Antoine's Théâtre Libre with *Miss Julie,* which opened January 16, 1893, and at Lugné-Poe's Théâtre de l'Oeuvre with *The Father,* which opened December 13, 1894.

One thing Strindberg got from Frida's grandparents—again confirming his notion of circuitous destiny at work—their enthusiasm for Swedenborg's mystical Christianity as expounded in books Strindberg read in their library, like *Arcana Celestia.* Strindberg devoutly came to believe that all of his Parisian "inferno" was to expiate his terrible sins. In his mind, he had through deed or wish broken about every one of the Ten Commandments. How completely damned Strindberg felt may be gathered from Act III, Scene 2, of *To Damascus I.* In the refectory of the cloister, the Stranger hears the Confessor read a curse Strindberg heard read through childhood in church at Lent, the most terrible curse in all of *Deuteronomy,* and laid on those who break the Commandments.

In January 1895, Strindberg wound up at the Hôpital Saint Louis in Paris, a charity case of the Swedish colony. He was suffering from malnutrition, blood-poisoning of the hands induced by his experiments with sulphur, and delusions of persecution. After several months he was well enough to take further treatment from the alienist, Dr. Anders Eliasson, at the seaside town of Ystad, Norway.

In 1896 Strindberg moved to Lund, a University town in Sweden. From May through June of 1897, he wrote his "Poem in Prose: called *Inferno;*" actually, he assembled notes he had taken of his sufferings in Paris. "I was excluded from society by my pitiable and scandalous poverty," wrote Strindberg.[35] The effect of such poverty Strindberg anticipated in a letter he wrote to a friend on April 10, 1875: "Poverty makes people very evil, or if not evil, mean and petty. One doesn't see much of the world from a dung heap." [36] Poverty now meant to Strindberg isolation, desperate loneliness, and obsession by guilt. With Swedenborg his seer, Strindberg saw everywhere signs but not the actual "Unknown Powers." To illustrate, he saw the devil in the whorled shape of his pillow chastening his pride, foiling his transmutation of sulphur into gold, visiting him with electrical current emanating from the walls, and giving him powers of tele-evil—killing his enemies by wishing them dead from a long distance. For Strindberg, the *Bible* opened at random now became "always my oracle." [37]

Frida received her final decree of divorce in 1897 and by 1898 Strindberg's creative spirit seemed to have taken a new lease on life. In 1899, the Vasa Theatre successfully revived his early drama of nationalism, *Master Olof;* that year in a recurrence of his nationalism, Strindberg finished a new historical drama of Shakespearean dimensions but in prose, *Gustav Vasa,* and the Swedish Theatre produced the play immediately. Between 1898 and 1904 Strindberg was to pour from his pen:

To Damascus I, II (1898)	*Charles XII*
Crime and Crime	*The Bridal Crown*
Advent (1899)	*Swanwhite*
Gustav Vasa	*A Dream Play*
The Saga of the Folkungs	*Queen Christina* (1903)
Eric XIV	*Gustavus III*
Midsummer (1900)	*Exodus*
Gustavus Adolphus	*Hellas*
Easter	*The Lamb and the Beast*
Casper's Shrove Tuesday	*The Nightingale of Wittenberg*
The Dance of Death (1901)	*To Damascus III* (1904)
Engelbrecht	

In 1900 while in Stockholm searching for an actress to play the Lady in a production of *To Damascus I,* Strindberg picked a twenty year old Norwegian, Harriet Bosse, whom he saw performing Puck in *A Midsummer Night's Dream.* About three months later Strindberg said, "Would you like to have a little child with me, Miss Bosse?" [38] On May 1, 1901, they were married. Harriet Bosse was to inspire a number of starring roles in the plays just mentioned. Even as

Strindberg had tried to give Siri a theatrical firmament to twinkle in, he set to do the same for Harriet. Within a few months of their marriage, however, the pair separated; Harriet was pregnant and again Strindberg wasn't sure who was the father. A child, Anne Marie, was born on March 25, 1902. Divorce was final in 1904. Harriet grew tired of being cooped up while Strindberg did his writing and regulated their lives from spotting Swedenborgian portents everywhere, for instance in the grain of a wooden cabinet or in the formations of fleeting clouds. Harriet became unable to cope with Strindberg's jealousy after she had been out of his sight awhile. And when in his sight, she found his mania for cleanliness too much. Separated, they remained amicable for years.

In 1907 August Falck, a young actor and stage director, after a successful tour of Sweden with *Miss Julie* in 1906, founded The Intimate Theatre in Stockholm. He rented a store and remodelled it into a theatre. Strindberg gave Falck's venture his blessing and cooperation. Till 1910 when Falck abandoned the effort, he had produced exclusively twenty-four plays of Strindberg drawn from his entire output of previous work and his new output of final work. The new plays were:

The Storm (1907)	*The Last Night*
The Burned Lot	*The Earl of Bjalbo*
The Ghost Sonata	*The Regent*
The Pelican	*The Black Glove* (1909)
Abu Ben Casem's Slipper (1908)	*The Great Highway*

In 1910 Strindberg moved to a second floor apartment at the home of Fanny Falkner, an eighteen year old actress from the Intimate Theatre. Fanny's mother kept house for Strindberg in his "Blue Tower." Strindberg called Fanny his "little protegee." Soon talk had Strindberg cradle-snatching, but he told Fanny, "I am not fit company for a young girl," and did not marry her. To make up for his neglect of workingmen's causes, Strindberg turned again to the socialism of his youth, and for three years he wrote a newspaper column in the old vein. In his last two years of life, torchlight processions and wide public performance of his plays marked his birthday in Stockholm.

Complex, ambivalent, volatile, Strindberg was most at home only in his imagination. His complete works, put out by Bonnier in Sweden from 1912–20 in John Landquist's edition, total 55 volumes. In middle-age, Strindberg appeared somewhat the actor—blond, wavy hair in poetic disarray, piercingly blue and manic eyes, a forehead as expansive as Beethoven's, a voluptuary's full lips, and a comically spare moustache rather like Peter Rabbit's. In a lifetime of changing fortunes, he intensely identified himself with such an array of personalities as Hamlet, Sir Francis Bacon, Lord Byron, Emanuel Swedenborg, Edgar Allan Poe, Dr. Faustus, Prometheus, the Wandering Jew, the Flying Dutchman, Satan, Job, Jacob, Ishmael, and the suffering Christ. Strindberg could sing pleasantly and accompany himself well on the guitar and the piano.

From childhood, Strindberg had eczema on the mound of the thumb of his right hand and on the second joint of the fingers. He also suffered from agrophobia, a kind of hysterical paralysis in crowds, and from aphasia during examinations at school. Strindberg's best friends were apparently the two critics, the Brandes brothers, Georg and Edward; the writers, Björnstern Björnson, Jonas Lie, and Knut Hamsun; and the actor-manager, August Falck. Between marriages Strindberg loved the drinking and conviviality of the bohemian gathering places like the Red Room at Bern's Restaurant in Stockholm, the Schwarze Ferkele (Black Pig) in Berlin, and the sidewalk cafes of the Left Bank in Paris. "When I am alone in a great city," he told Frida, "the tavern alone saves me from suicide." [39] Strindberg met about every talent of any account in the world of art and letters of his day. "I am swift in attack," Strindberg wrote Edward Brandes on July 29, 1880, "but then comes my humanity and I suffer from having scourged my fellow beings even when they deserved it. Therefore I cannot be a trustworthy friend nor an enduring enemy . . ." [40] "You tell me he has a grudge against you. But I scarcely know anyone against whom he hasn't a grudge," wrote Hamsun to Adolph Paul in asking for help for Strindberg during his 'inferno' days. "He doesn't like me either. . . . In spite of everything he is August Strindberg." [41]

Strindberg died in Stockholm on the morning of May 14, 1912; he was heavily dosed with morphine to endure cancer of the stomach. *The Artonbladet* reported him in his last moments as holding his *Bible* to him and saying, "I have done with life and closed the account. This is the only truth." [42] On the morning of May 19, 1912, a procession of an estimated 30,000 mourners—mostly students, workers, artists, musicians, writers, and dignitaries from near and far—followed the hearse from the "Blue Tower" to the New Church Cemetery where, as Strindberg had asked, he was buried among the poor.

On his grave was placed only a cross of dark oak, with these words carved out: "Ave Crux Spes Unica" ("Hail Cross, Our Only Hope"). Strindberg was not buried with his family. Perhaps he felt he had returned to the one Father he was quite sure of and that to his own family he was still, as in his plays, *To Damascus, I, II, III,* for eternity "a changeling" and the Stranger.

II

COMMERCIAL CONSIDERATIONS AFFECTING STRINDBERG'S PLAYWRITING

Like Ibsen, Strindberg was his own literary agent, for there were no literary agents in Strindberg's day. The national and international copyright laws that for most of his literary life left Ibsen rich only in fame, made a similar victim of Strindberg. "The bread of the literary man was certainly hard earned," wrote Strindberg, ". . . the profession was also despised."[43] How little Strindberg earned from his plays abroad may be gathered from Frida Strindberg's book, *Marriage with Genius.* Frida, for instance, was puzzled by Strindberg's royalty from the Parisian production opening December 13, 1894, at the Théâtre Nouveau seating 1,800: *"The Father* only realized 300 francs in spite of ten performances—I don't know why."[44]

In 1899 when Hjalmar Brantin planned to ask the Swedish Riksdag to grant Strindberg a pension, Strindberg stopped him. "The liberty to grow that I reserved for others," said Strindberg, "I reserved for myself. I must decline."[45] "He is unfit to deal with managers and publishers, his nerves cannot stand it," wrote Frida's mother of Strindberg with the eye of a spy. "As a result, he earns almost nothing. He has piles of manuscripts, stories, plays; he is the hardest worker in the world, but he is no business man."[46] Evidently Strindberg wouldn't be "bought" and couldn't "sell." The best Strindberg could do was complain, "According to Swedish and natural law, the man who has been robbed is no more guilty than the man born poor. I am therefore not ashamed of my poverty."[47]

Strindberg thought he knew just what the public and the managers wanted. "People are constantly clamoring pretentiously for the *joy of life,*" Strindberg wrote in the preface to *Miss Julie* in Paulson's translation, "and play producers keep demanding farces." "For my part," wrote Strindberg, "I find the joy of life in the hard and cruel battles of life; and to be able to add to my store of knowledge, to learn something, is enjoyment to me." [48] Did Strindberg consider himself a kind of freak on this account? "It was a sceptical and materialistic period," he said of himself in *The Growth of a Soul;* ". . . he had unconsciously developed into a man of his time." [49] The hardest and cruelest battles of life Strindberg found to be those of the sexes and those of the social classes. Combining these conflicts, escalated the drama into the most intense kind of personal warfare.

"Modernity," Strindberg wrote for the newspaper, *Figaro,* in Paris, "at any period implies in art the idea of expression best fitted to stir contemporaries." [50] "I seem to have observed," he wrote in the preface to *Miss Julie,* "that the psychological course of events is what interests the people of our time most. I have also noticed that our souls, so hungry for knowledge, find no satisfaction in merely seeing something done." He went on, "we want to know *how* and *why* it is done!" [51] In giving the public what he construed to be the hardest and cruelest battles of contemporary life, Strindberg felt he offered great public identification bound to command public attention on his own terms.

What went wrong? "But a drama written for the average man who has ready made views on all subjects," Strindberg remarked in *The Growth of a Soul,* "must at least take sides with one of its characters in order to win the excitable and partisan public." And then Strindberg sized up his special strength and weakness throughout his writing career. "John could not do this, because he believed in no absolute right or wrong, for the simple reason that all these ideas are relative. One may be right as regards to the future, and wrong as regards the present." [52] Strindberg, whose birth virtually made him a doubter, then says, "Why do men hate and despise the doubter? Because doubt is the seed of development and progress, and the average man hates development because it disturbs his quiet." [53] In Shakespeare's greatest play, Hamlet is a doubter, yet the sympathy of the audience is still with him to avenge his murdered father. In practically all of Strindberg's finest plays, however, he drew his leading characters so ambivalently, for instance, in *The Father, Miss Julie, The Dance of Death, To Damascus I, Creditors, Crime and Crime, The Ghost Sonata,* that Strindberg made not only anti-heroes and anti-heroines but usually anti-villains, too. The public, as a rule, likes to take sides in the hardest and cruelest battles of life.

Why did Strindberg keep writing, if intermittently, for a public that he knew was not ready for him? " 'If you will not be with us,' society says, 'then go into the woods,'" said Strindberg in *The Growth of a Soul*, ". . . and from its own point of view society is right and always will be right. But the society of the future," specified Strindberg, "will celebrate the revolter, the individual who has brought about social improvement, and the revolter is justified long after his death." [54] The public did send Strindberg into the woods, and according to Paulson, "Actually, it was only during the last five years of his life that he received the public acclaim that his genius deserved." [55]

Roughly half of Strindberg's literary output was plays; the rest was in the more easily marketable merchandise of short stories, novels, poems, essays, history, and scientific studies. Some of his plays had marathon runs for their day. *Master Olof,* for instance, in 1881–2, ran for 47 performances in the Dramatic Theatre in Stockholm. *Creditors* in January, 1893, opened at the Berlin Residenz Theatre for a run of 100 performances. "After Paris," Strindberg wrote Frida in December, 1894, *"Father* is going on tour to Brussels, London, all over France, and further." [56] Strindberg's zenith of popularity came in Germany of World War I during the years of 1913–1915 when twenty-four of his plays ran for a total of 1,035 performances in sixty-two cities and towns. [57]

In Sweden, Strindberg is the nearest they have to a Shakespeare; outside of Sweden today, Strindberg is very close to those disenchanted with our times and ready to look at human nature in plain daylight to see what it really is on occasion. Consider what his best known plays show in the candid spirit we now call "existential." In *The Father*, the female proves more deadly than the male in a love-hate war of matrimony. In *Miss Julie*, a decadent aristocratic girl dies by her dated code of honor while her servant seducer survives by natural selection. In *To Damascus I*, a tormented soul is saved by a creedless faith. In *The Dance of Death*, an aging married couple torture each other with recriminations suggesting that life is hell on earth, and death may be the only hope. In *A Dream Play*, the inherent troubles of the world mean mankind is to be pitied. In *The Ghost Sonata*, every value in life, even love, proves to be an illusion calling for prayers of mercy.

When Strindberg in 1907 had twenty-six or so unproduced plays on his hands, he was willing to allow experimental production in August Falck's Intimate Theatre, a converted store seating roughly 160 people. Possibly Falck was the only one who wanted to produce him, and

Strindberg wanted his plays done. Falck's productions must also have pleased Strindberg. But what could a literary giant gain by appearing in a kind of theatrical rabbit-hutch? Strindberg must have known from the example of Antoine's Théâtre Libre in Paris that a chain reaction of many similar productions of his plays could follow in capitol cities. Antoine, in fact, by example fathered the whole Little Theatre movement though this exclusiveness has been challenged.

How did Strindberg's "name" or "image" affect his commercial success as a dramatist? Strindberg did not get a long play produced until he first had a "name" as the writer of a best-seller, the novel, *The Red Room*. On the title page of this book, he entered the remark of Voltaire: *"Rien n'êst pas si désagréable que d'être pendu obscurement*. (Nothing is so disagreeable as to be hanged obscurely.)" [58] Whenever in his literary career Strindberg felt that his enemies were out to hang him obscurely or otherwise, he candidly told the terrible truth about himself in another new book, so that though his feet seemed to dance in mid-air, he was actually on his toes. "For retaliation is a natural instinct with me," he wrote Frida. "It is an irresistible one and plays the part of justice." [59]

Sooner or later, Strindberg got around to hanging just about every enemy in print, and seldom obscurely. At the height of his new and dizzying success in 1882, to illustrate, Strindberg chose to write *The New Kingdom* and left so many of his fancied and powerful enemies figuratively hanging in mid-air that he and his family as a result had to flee to Switzerland in virtual exile. In 1907 Strindberg, resettled in Stockholm, could not resist writing *Black Banners,* a satirical novel that left Gustaf af Geijerstam, a major literary factotum in Stockholm, virtually publicly hanged. Strindberg blamed this man for having forced him to write *The Confession of a Fool* by threatening to use the material himself for a novel.[60]

The only public image Strindberg ever had was his private one; in his work, he always more or less held up another mirror to his tormented soul for the public view. From his blasphemy trial, he was left with the public image of "a blasphemer." From *The Father*, "the mad misogynist." From *Inferno*, "the mad penitent." Strindberg was always his own press agent for better or worse, and the "image" he now has, whatever it is, he must himself take chief responsibility for as both model and artist. During his lifetime his "name" alone kept people away from his plays; he redeemed himself publicly by showing that like Saint Paul he, too, had been to Damascus.

Did Strindberg never show any commercial sense? Only on his own terms. *In Rome,* for instance, his first play to win a professional production, was a one-act in verse about the Scandinavian equivalent to Michelangelo, the Danish sculptor Thorwaldsen, whose centenary was that very year, 1870. The play centered typically for Strindberg on a strong lead in a psychological crisis—the destruction of the Jason statue in a new resolve to create a still finer work. Strindberg's whole scattered series of plays about Swedish national heroes, such as *Master Olof, Gustav Vasa,* and *Queen Christina,* offered strong leading roles with broad public identification in the tradition of Shakespeare's chronicle plays. Unlike Shakespeare, Strindberg used not verse but idiomatic prose diction, though like Shakespeare he searched for human motives in history. Strindberg's historical plays, however, are today of limited interest outside Sweden.

Strindberg wrote some of his best roles to show the radiance of his current wife as a star; he wrote Miss Julie in *Miss Julie* for Siri and Indra's Daughter in *A Dream Play* for Harriet. Strindberg's "chamber plays," like *The Ghost Sonata,* were created to suggest in their quality the equivalent of chamber music for a few performers, a tiny stage, a small audience, and the limitations of the talents of a repertory company with the shoe-string budget of The Intimate Theatre. Ironically, the biggest hits of The Intimate Theatre proved to be plays Strindberg had written earlier with large houses in mind: *Miss Julie, Easter, The Dance of Death* and *The Father.*

"Were you to control yourself, write an Ibsen play for example," said Edward Brandes to Strindberg (McGill's translation in *August Strindberg, The Bedeviled Viking*), "you might become the greatest figure of our time. You have it in your power to become a dictator, yet you choose to follow your whims." [61] Strindberg's "whims" were as much a part of Strindberg as his heart, itself.

III

AESTHETIC CONSIDERATIONS AFFECTING STRINDBERG'S PLAYWRITING

Late in life, Strindberg became convinced that as an artist he was God's instrument. "Of this Someone," Strindberg wrote Harriet Bosse on September 16, 1905, in Paulson's translation, "I know only that He rules my fate, and ever leads me to the goal, although circuitously." [62] More than once the goal appeared to be a dead-end; in *Swedish Des-*

tinies, Strindberg in 1890 regarded art as a primitive throw-back become a toy for the rich, and in *Inferno,* he cried out, "Seek God and find the Devil." [63] On quite another note, Strindberg wrote in *The Red Room* at the age of thirty in his counterpart, Olle, a struggling artist, "I can analyse the much talked of artistic instinct because I was endowed with it myself. It rests on a broad base of longing for freedom, freedom from profitable labour. . . . Furthermore the instinct rests on pride; man wants to play God in art, not that he wants to create anything new—he can't do that—but because he wants to improve, to arrange, to re-create . . . Everything is full of faults and he longs to correct them." [64]

The complexity of Strindberg's ambivalent feelings toward art is further suggested in *The Growth of a Soul,* "But he was a truthseeker, and did not shrink from looking into the abyss of contradictions." [65] If the abyss gave him occasional vertigo, he could speak to Siri as an artist of his "freedom of body and soul," and he could write her on March 12, 1876, "—don't they tell you, all those works of art, how much one must suffer and dare if one wants to be more than the crowd?" [66] In his preface to *Miss Julie,* Strindberg again modified his view of the artist: "the playwright has the semblance of being a lay preacher," he wrote, "presenting the views and sentiments of his time in popular form—and in a form sufficiently popular so that the middle classes, from which theatre audiences are chiefly drawn, can understand what it is all about without racking their brains." [67]

In 1899, when declining an appeal in his behalf for a pension, Strindberg wrote, " 'No programme' was my old motto and still is." If Strindberg had a new motto, it was, "Freedom!" [68] "Now a poet is something different from a recluse," Strindberg jotted down in his very late *Zones of the Spirit,* "and in order to be able to describe life in all its aspects and dangers, he must first have lived it." [69] "He who does not approach men in a spirit of sympathy," insisted the ambivalent Strindberg, "finds no point of contact with them." [70] "A real poet must sacrifice his person for his work," he told Schering in a letter in 1900; must have "made his pilgrimage through all the stages of human development in order to be able to *depict people.*" [71] Life, to Strindberg, existed for his art. "Artistic creation is a delicate and sensitive undertaking," Strindberg entered in his "Notes for an Intimate Theatre," as translated by Evert Sprinchorn and Seabury Quinn, Jr. in *The Chamber Plays,* "and nearly all artists seek solitude and seclusion" —Strindberg's was enough to produce 55 volumes.[72]

He called his power "the author-mesmerizer's suggestive influence." [73] "He [the poet] should only live in his works, if they possess
vital power," observed Strindberg in *Zones of the Spirit;* "Men should
accustom themselves to look upon him as something different from
an ordinary man; they ought not to judge him but regard him as
something which they cannot understand." [74] Once famous as well as
infamous, Strindberg found people a real problem. "Persons of our
prominence are never surrounded by friends," he wrote Harriet, "only
by secret police who worm out the significance of the smallest word.
Loneliness is the lot of the famous. Hate is their reward, and treachery their bread . . . Flies pick out mirrors and gilt surfaces to speck
because they are glossy and shine brightly." [75]

Strindberg's ambivalent attitude toward just about everything, even
God, extended as already implied to the theatre itself. "The novel intrigues me most. I detest the theatre. Pose—superficiality—contrivance!" he wrote Harriet, April 15, 1906. "Most people go around like
stupid cattle that you can beguile into believing anything." [76] Yet in
1897 when interviewed by George Brocker and asked his favorite occupation, Strindberg said, "Writing plays." When asked what position
he would most like to have held, Strindberg answered, "That of a
constantly performed dramatist." [77]

Obviously Strindberg was incurably stage-struck. "In common with
art generally," he wrote, "the theatre has long seemed to me to be a
bilblia pauperum, i. e. a bible in pictures for those who cannot read
the written or printed word." [78] In the same breath, he noted, "when
the rudimentary, immature way of thinking (which is a process of
imagination) appears to be developing into reflection, inquiry and
analysis—the theatre, like religion, is in the throes of being abandoned
as a moribund form of art for which we lack the conditions requisite
to enjoyment." [79]

New content dictated new form; conceivably a jet engine would be
misplaced in a horse's hide. The chief outward distinction of the new
form, Strindberg noted in his letter to Adolf Paul, of January 6, 1907,
was this: *"Miss Julie* (without intermission) has gone through its
ordeal by fire and shown itself to be the kind of drama demanded by
the impatient man of today: thorough but brief." [80] This phrase,
"thorough but brief," describes just about Strindberg's whole effort in
experimenting in playwriting from almost his earliest plays to his last,
the chamber plays. "Already in 1872, in one of my earlier playwriting
experiments, *The Outlaw,"* he wrote, "I tried using this concentrated

form, although without much success." He then tells of burning the play originally written in five acts and of rewriting it into a one-act. "While the form of *Miss Julie* is not absolutely original," Strindberg admitted, "it nevertheless seems to be my own innovation; and as public taste appears to be changing, there may be prospects for its being accepted in our time." [81]

Strindberg's experiments in form, continuing in his "pilgrimage plays" and on through his "chamber plays," were to keep up with the changing times. "It falls to my share to strike out a path between naturalism and supernaturalism," he wrote in *Legends* in 1898, "by expounding the latter as a development of the former." [82] The earth-bound naturalist became a kind of Swedenborgian sky-pilot. Strindberg, the one-time "free-thinking" student, could write, "All 'free-thinking' is foolishness, for thought is not free, but bound by the laws of thought, by logic, just as nature is bound by the laws of nature." [83] If Strindberg had any credo of the theatre, he seems closest to stating it fully in his "Notes for an Intimate Theatre:"

> It is impossible to lay down any valid rules for the art of the theatre. But in order to move us, it must be in tune with the times. For instance: if the age is skeptical, insensitive, and democratic, as our age is, the fancy stuff is not going to work . . . Tragedy itself adopts the tone of light conversation . . . Verse gives way to prose; genres are mixed; kings don't dare set themselves above the mob; everybody talks the same language and nobody is finicky about the words he uses . . . The wise thing to do is to wait for the moment when the noises of the present begin to be drowned out by the voices of the future. The growing artist who is constantly renewing himself knows he must keep up with the times.[84]

The artist who doesn't keep up with the times can only be out of date, even a museum-piece.

Too often, Strindberg's whole view of life reflected in his plays is thought to be contained in the content of this passage from his *Zones of the Spirit:*

> This agrees with what every thinking man observes, that lying and deceit are universal. The whole of life—politics, society, marriage, the family—is counterfeit. Views which universally prevail are based upon false history; scientific theories are found in error; the truth today is discovered to be a lie tomorrow; the hero turns out to be a coward; the martyr a hypocrite.[85]

Yet Strindberg, himself, believed his pessimism had a happy ending as he noted in his "Summa summarum" in *Zones of the Spirit* and as he implied from his pilgrimage plays through his chamber plays:

> Pray, *but* work; suffer *but* hope; keeping both the earth and the stars in view. Do not try and settle permanently, for it is a place of pilgrimage; not a home, but a halting-place. Seek truth, for it is to be found but only in one place, with Him who Himself is the Way, the Truth and the Life.[86]

In fact in two of his plays, when he was living buoyantly in the ozone atmosphere of love, Strindberg was markedly optimistic. In *Lucky Per's Journey*, portraying an innocent fifteen year old boy's search for happiness with a magic wishing ring in a workaday world, Per discovers happiness only in love. And in *Swanwhite*, the Princess finds that love conquers all, even bringing the dead back to life.

Strindberg's extensive study of aesthetics through philology convinced him of what a quagmire of words aesthetics could become for the unwary traveler: "Ljunggren, in two closely printed volumes, containing the view of all philosophers on the Beautiful," Strindberg noted with astonishment, still found "no satisfactory definition of it . . ."[87] Strindberg pondered, for example, over how a pothouse scene could be ugly in reality, and yet when painted realistically in the Dutch genre could suddenly become to critics "Beautiful!" "But a strong suspicion had been aroused in John," Strindberg decided of himself, "that the 'Beautiful' was not always beautiful." He wrote Edward Brandes, "You Danes are still suffering from these wretched 'Aesthetics.' You worship form, Beauty, but that is only the exterior . . ."[88]

"When as a playwright I saw one of my own works performed and was satisfied with the presentation," Strindberg remarked, "I could not understand how the critics could possibly be dissatisfied. But when I saw how the same production could be praised by one critic and denounced by another, I understood the difference of opinion was due entirely to subjective considerations."[89] These Strindberg noted as taste, malice toward content and outright prejudice. Almost thirty years later, Strindberg was sounding the same complaint against the critics of his last works, the chamber plays. "A blind man does not readily judge colour," Strindberg wrote in "Open Letters to the Intimate Theater," "but if he should agree to be a critic of an art exhibition he must be prepared to put up with a reminder that he is blind, even if at other times it's unkind to draw attention to physical defects." In reply to those critics who had denounced his chamber plays as "decadent," he continued, "If a tipsy or deaf person comes to the theatre and sets about writing (and having printed) a review of the play after a single performance, then I as the accused have the right to challenge the evidence or the judgment. 'He's drunk. He's deaf. Throw him out'," [90] Strindberg kept a long friendship with only two critics, Georg and Edward Brandes who believed in him. "You are the man who will awaken Swedish literature and become the leader of the future," Edward had written Strindberg after the publication of *The Red Room,* ". . . Your strength, your will, is not less than that of Björnson's or Ibsen's, your cultivation much greater." [91]

WORKING METHODS OF STRINDBERG IN PLAYWRITING

Genesis and Incubation

If Strindberg found life so full of suffering, how could he bear to keep writing of it? In *The Growth of a Soul* he said, "authorship, in spite of all its pains, was a wonderful enjoyment." [92] "This is a terrible book," he said of *The Confession of a Fool;* "I had to wash my corpse before it was laid in its coffin." [93] In a letter to Harriet written April 1, 1906, Strindberg in referring to *A Dream Play* spoke of "the surging joy during the conception of it." [94] In his *Legends,* Strindberg let out, "it is enough that my sin be publicly acknowledged in writing." [95] For Strindberg, literary creation meant a great pleasure and a spiritual catharsis making life's suffering bearable.

"A work of art begins to exist," Strindberg told Frida, "the moment it kindles—and no sooner." [96] "The final act is the most important one in a drama," Strindberg declared in *Zones of the Spirit* when he was fifty-nine, "and a dramatist generally begins his work at the end." [97] In *Legends,* he spoke further: "In the great crises of life, when existence itself is threatened, the soul attains transcendent power." [98] No wonder Strindberg wrote in the preface to *Miss Julie,* "For my part, I find the joy of life in the hard and cruel battles of life; and to be able to add to my stores of knowledge, to learn something, is enjoyment to me." [99] The "end" at which a play begins could only be the major climax of the last act, for here is the peak of life's battles at their hardest and cruelest, and here Strindberg learned something new, a psychological revelation of a human soul at a transcendent moment. Strindberg told each of his wives before marriage, in effect, "You will redeem me," and each time, though the marriage failed, the woman did redeem him, for he used the terrible stresses and strains of his marriages to find what the human soul was made of. Strindberg wrote Schering, his German translator, on March 27, 1907, "My whole life often strikes me as if it were put on stage for me, both to make me suffer and to make me write it down." [100]

Strindberg knew a regimen favored his creative work. He confided in Frida's mother, "All I want is quiet and peace enough to work, enough money so as not to starve, and a wife who will let me love her and will not hate me in return. As a rule woman hates man because he is her superior." [101] "I am a man of very regular habits," he confessed in *Inferno,* "and like to live by the clock." [102]

His study throughout his writing career was severely simple, orderly, and immaculate, a Spartan vestibule to his real home—his imagination. In his apprentice years, Strindberg lived in a series of attic rooms sometimes rat-infested, with a bed made of planks, and light after dark from a candle stuck in a bottle. "He is living like a monk, and is supposed to have lived that way since his divorce and previous to it," Frida's mother observed of him.[103] Pictures of Strindberg's study in Stockholm show few amenities more than a table, a chair, a desk, and a couch. He had as fetishes a stuffed owl, a figure of Buddha, and a death-mask of Beethoven. To him the imaginative life became so real that a real person was often very jarring. "I believe it is my fate to be solitary, and that it is best for me," he wrote as translated by Klaf from *Alone,* "spinning oneself into the silken web of one's soul, spinning a cocoon and waiting for the transformation." [104]

Harriet reported Strindberg's routine (Paulson's translation):

> The daily morning walks between seven and nine were practically the only outdoor exercise that Strindberg took. He would rise at half past six, brew his own coffee in a Russian coffee urn, and then set off promptly on the road toward Djurgården. It was during these walks he planned and sketched his work for the day. He could take these walks in peace and quiet, as Djurgården was almost entirely asleep at this hour of the day.[105]

The monotonous, rhythmical exercise of walking seemed hypnotically to limber up Strindberg's unconscious for work. He wrote in *Inferno:*

> Ever since my youth my morning walk has been dedicated to medita-
> tion as a preparation for the day's work. I have never allowed anyone to
> accompany me, not even my wife . . . It is for me the hour of inward
> concentration, the hour of prayer, of worship.[106]

Strindberg apparently had nothing for breakfast but coffee, likely a
continuation of his student habits imposed by poverty and found
good for creating. Frida noted the great importance that Strindberg
put upon the ritual of his diet—"as every disturbance of his physical
well-being puts a brake on his intellectual activities," she wrote, "he
regards unsuitable diet as an attack on his genius." [107] Harriet continues:

> On arriving home from his walk, he would immediately seat himself
> at his writing table, charged with intensity and ready to work. From then
> on he would write furiously, feverishly, smoking his Finnish cigarettes.
> Generally he would have the outline and dialogue clear in his mind
> before he commenced to write; this accounts for the very few changes in
> his manuscripts. While he was at work, no one was permitted to disturb
> him—i.e., no one but myself. At noon, he took a brief pause, after which
> he set to work again.

Apparently Strindberg ate no lunch except perhaps coffee from his
Russian coffee urn. Strindberg not only smoked cigarettes but occasionally cigars and a pipe and was to die of cancer of the stomach; he
told Falck, "the Hindus cure all complaints with tobacco." Did
Strindberg drink while working? In *To Damascus I,* the Lady asks
the Stranger if it's true that he does a good deal of drinking, and he
replies, "A good deal, yes! The wine frees my soul from my body—I
fly into the ether—I see what no one ever divined—hear what no one
ever heard . . ." [108] Strindberg from his *Red Room* days drank ab-
sinthe until, in his *Inferno* period, the resultant visions so frightened
him that he quit for fear of going mad. "Lying flat on his back,"
recollected Frida, "he could always think best." [109] Strindberg usually
had a couch or bed in his study though sometimes he just lay on the
floor for his "trance;" "I possess the remarkable gift," he said, "of becoming blind and deaf when it suits me." [110] Except for the hypnotic
evocation of walking, he found that physical inactivity stimulated the
brain "into systems, into thought-combinations, into hallucinations
which haunt painters, sculptors, and poets." [111]

"The afternoons he would spend reading, preparing for the next
day's task," Harriet relates. "He never wrote in the afternoon

(Strindberg's habit at this particular period of his life)." Strindberg's evening meal was, it seems, his only sizeable one when working. Asked what his favorite drink and food was, he answered, "Ale and fish dishes." [112] Frida's mother reported that he "lives on almost nothing: vegetables, fish, claret." [113] Fish, more easily digested than meat, seemed to least upset his creative thinking, and the wine satisfied his "imperative need" as a "Northerner."

Of evenings, Harriet said:

> When evening came, he would walk back and forth in the apartment, although mostly round the dining-room table, and up and down in that room. In order to walk softly and with ease, he would wear white rubber soled shoes indoors.[114]

Strindberg relaxed with flowers, fruits, and wine on the table and liked especially to listen to music or play the piano, favoring Grieg, Schumann, Schubert and, most of all, Beethoven.

With his Pegasus harnessed by his regimen, Strindberg could take off and land best. Very few accounts of actual genesis remain, but these in the larger picture imply much. To the preliminaries earlier mentioned, here is Strindberg's record of writing his first play, *A Name-Day Gift*:

> While thus lying on the sofa he felt an unusual degree of fever during which his brain seemed to work at arranging memories of the past, cutting out some scenes, and adding others. New minor characters entered; he saw them mixing in the action, and heard them speaking, just as he had done on the stage. After one or two hours had passed, he had a comedy in two acts ready in his head. This was both a painful and pleasurable form of work if it could be called a work; for it went forward of itself, without his will or co-operation.[115]

In a letter written late in his career and as translated by Sprinchorn and Quinn, Strindberg again described the creative experience of playwriting:

> Something begins to ferment within me, a not unpleasant kind of fever, which is transformed into an ecstasy or intoxication. Sometimes it's like a seed that suddenly sprouts, sends down roots, draws to it all my experiences—but all the while selecting and rejecting. Sometimes I think of myself as a medium: everything comes so easily, half unconsciously with just a little bit of planning and calculation. But at best this lasts for only three hours (nine to twelve in the morning usually). And

when it's over, things are a little dull and boring until the next time it happens. But it doesn't come when ordered, and it doesn't come when it pleases *me*. It comes when *it* wants to come. But most frequently and with greatest impact after the major catastrophes in my life.[116]

Though roughly thirty years apart, the two accounts of the creative experience are about the same. But was the experience really so automatic or capricious? Through his formal and self-education in philology, Strindberg was quite likely familiar with the best in world drama and aesthetics, had watched many plays with the Lamms, had attempted acting, and could not but have acquired a genuine sense of dramatic form. A key passage only of the second account but implied in the actual experience of the first account is, "It comes when *it* wants to come. But most frequently and with greatest impact after the major catastrophes in my life."

How does all this help us understand Strindberg's genesis of his plays? If "a dramatist generally begins his work at the end," then *The Father,* for example, began with the Captain's paralytic stroke after being fitted into the camisole with the old Nurse helping the wife to trap him through gentle subterfuge. This fear, of course, approximated Strindberg's that his wife would have him committed at this very time. She actually wrote a Swiss doctor in 1886 about Strindberg's sanity, and he suspected her of opening his mail to and from Nietzsche who went mad that year. How much did Nietzsche influence the conception of *The Father*? Strindberg wrote Brandes, "my spirit life has received in its uterus a tremendous outpouring of seed from Friedrich Nietzsche, so that I feel as full as a pregnant bitch."[117] In *Thus Spake Zarathustra,* Nietzsche wrote, "and thou goest to women? Remember thy whip!" The Captain in *The Father* forgot his whip and certainly his pistol; he was no match for Laura's schemes. Strindberg's daughter, Karin, recollected that in the winter of 1887-8 Strindberg came home drunk one night and tried to get Siri to go upstairs with him. Siri, however, managed to lock her children and herself in her room, and then turned out the lamp because Strindberg had threatened to throw it at her.[118] "Placed between two alternatives, either to kill a woman or be killed by her," Strindberg wrote, "I took a third one—I left her, and my first marriage was dissolved."[119] The Captain stayed. "I don't know if *The Father* is an invention or if my life has been so," Strindberg wrote Axel Lundegarde on December 12, 1887, "but I feel at a given moment, not far off, this will be revealed to me, and then I shall crash either into insanity from agony of conscience or into suicide."[120]

In the prospective genesis of *The Father* are suggested two basic sources of inspiration for Strindberg: life and literature. "The brain produces of itself very little, perhaps nothing," Strindberg wrote in *The Growth of a Soul:* "in order to make combinations it must be supplied with material from without." [121] "But no doubt for the development of the soul into a rich and free life, much social intercourse is necessary." And Strindberg continued of himself, "after he had spent some time in the rush, he withdrew into solitude for a day or two to digest his impressions." [122] In his novel, *The Red Room,* Strindberg has his self-portrait, Arvid Falk, suggest what he learned from journalism:

> He has seen humanity under many aspects, aspects which are only revealed to the eye of the poor man's doctor or the journalist, with the only difference that the journalist generally sees men as they are. He had every opportunity to study man as a social animal in all possible guises. He had been present at Parliamentary meetings, church councils, general meetings of workingmen . . .[123]

Though Strindberg knew he must rely upon life for raw material to excite creation and feed it, he showed his usual ambivalence toward this practice in *The Confession of a Fool:*

> Can you still be surprised that I am done with les belles lettres? This literature disgusts me! Think of the horrors of that profession! To skin one's nearest and dearest and then offer the skin for sale . . . To spy out people's secrets, to find the moles on a woman's body, to vivisect humans like rabbits, to kill, to violate, to burn down—ugh! [124]

The other source of creative excitement for Strindberg was literature, itself, the end product of the creative process of someone else's experience in life. He read especially for the latest ideas to reveal the truth. Among dramatists, Strindberg notably read Ibsen, whom he called "the Great Norwegian blue-stocking" in contempt for Ibsen's apparent advocacy of women's emancipation in the vastly popular *A Doll's House*.[125] Strindberg's Laura in *The Father* might well have been part of Strindberg's violent reaction to Ibsen's Nora; "Give women emancipation," Strindberg might as well have said, "and see what they'll do to you!" Strindberg himself admitted or implied some measure of literary semination from Ibsen: *Master Olof* from Ibsen's *Brand; Lucky Per's Journey* from Ibsen's *Peer Gynt; To Damascus I* from Ibsen's realistic mysticism as in *The Master-Builder*. In fact, Strindberg sent a copy of *To Damascus I* to Ibsen with the inscription, "To the Master from whom I have learnt so much." [126] "See how my seed has fallen in Ibsen's brain-pan—and germinated," Strindberg wrote the Swedish author, Birger Mörner, referring to Ibsen's *Hedda* as kin to Laura in *The Father* and Tekla in *Creditors*.[127]

A curious spiritual cross-semination, indeed, involved Ibsen and Strindberg who were long outright enemies. "I cannot write a line," said Ibsen to a friend late in the 1890's, as Ibsen indicated Krog's portrait of Strindberg in his study, "except when this bold man with his mad eyes looks down on me." [128] What was the affinity of Ibsen and Strindberg? A simple but revealing clue is suggested in a letter Ibsen wrote Passarge from Munich, June 16, 1880, which included this passage that Strindberg himself might have penned:

> Everything that I have written has the closest possible connection with what I have lived through, even if it has not been my own personal experience; in every new poem or play, I have aimed at my own spiritual emancipation and purification . . . Hence I once wrote the following dedicatory lines in a copy of one of my books:
>
>> To *live*—is to war with fiends
>> That infest the brain and the heart;
>> To *write*—is to summon one's self,
>> And play the judge's part.[129]

Strindberg's wide reading from the age of twelve, and especially since his days as Assistant at the Royal Library in Stockholm, opened him at various times to certain powerful minds that swayed his thinking in spells like so many master spirits. " 'No system' is Buckle's motto," wrote Strindberg of Buckle's *History of Civilization in England*. "Doubt is the beginning of all wisdom." [130] Buckle's determinism advanced the idea that as an individual's circumstances and social position changed, the truth, too, changed for him. Darwin's *Origin of the Species* opened Strindberg's eyes to see life as a continuous struggle of natural selection. Rousseau's work presented man as born naturally good but corrupted by civilization with escape possible only by a return to nature. The Danish theologian Kierkegaard's *Either-Or* displayed life as opposing alternatives demanding commitments. Buddhism contemplated life as a mystic illusion with only the after-life as real. Poe's stories of the occult, Nietzsche's *Thus Spake Zarathustra* with its superman and anti-Christ, and Charcot, Bernheim and the Nancy School of psychologists on hypnotism, all at some period obsessed Strindberg's thoughts. Swedenborg's mystic

Christianity and Maeterlinck's sense of unseen powers at work also haunted Strindberg. And always the voices and images of the *Bible,* especially the Pietism of Strindberg's childhood, tantalized his conscience. If Strindberg read Freud, he never said so, yet Freud's pioneer work, *The Interpretation of Dreams,* came out in 1899; German was a second language for Strindberg, and ideas about truth, a staple of his diet. Strindberg by his own close observation had anticipated many of Freud's insights. "For many years I have taken notes of all my dreams," Strindberg said in *Legends* (1898), "and I have arrived at the conviction that man leads a double life, that imaginations, fancies and dreams possess a kind of reality." [131]

The only filing system Strindberg seemed to have kept for prospective genesis of his material, other than in his mind, was in his Green Bag. Strindberg associated the color green with wizards, and so, of course, with himself. The bag was about a yard long with a black button fastener and made of dark green glazed linen; Frida wrote, "it embodies the spell on which August Strindberg's life depends." What was in the bag? She wrote, "hundreds of little notes, rapid sketches and thoughts, caught and pinned down and stored away on his way through life." [132] It also held the manuscripts of his latest work. For fear the bag might be lost or stolen, Strindberg in traveling never checked it but kept it by his side. He used random note paper because parchment was bulky and expensive. The Green Bag suggests that Strindberg's writing was far from automatic. He used it to store exciting experience for mass incubation of the imaginative lives that he as an "author-mesmerizer" tried to conjure for the public. Frida thought Strindberg had as many as twenty projects going at once. With one play finished, he could rather readily go right on to another with many imaginative characters cross-breeding and maturing for his purposes.

Space allows only for concentrating now upon Strindberg's creation of two of his most distinguished plays, showing him at his best in his chief modern distinction: as a naturalist, in *Miss Julie;* and as an expressionist, in *The Ghost Sonata.*

"When I chose this theme from real life—as I heard it related a number of years ago, at which time I was greatly moved by the story," wrote Strindberg in his preface to *Miss Julie* which appeared with the play's publication in 1888, "—I saw in it the ingredients of a tragic drama." [133] Here Strindberg plainly implies that he had the play growing in his mind or in notes in his Green Bag "a number of years," and as he earlier said of genesis, "Sometimes it's like a seed that suddenly sprouts, sends down roots, draws to it all my experiences—but all the while selecting and rejecting."

What was the "story" Strindberg had heard? In the spring of 1888 the Strindbergs and their three children, like refugees from a hostile Sweden, to live most frugally took quarters at Skovlyst near Holte a few miles from Copenhagen in a dilapidated castle. The landlady was Fröken Frankenau, the only surviving child of a so-called Count and Countess Frankenau. Word had it, and Strindberg evidently heard the story several years *before* moving to the castle, that in her desperate, genteel poverty and loneliness, Fröken Frankenau had given herself to the bailiff who now ran her estate. When Strindberg first met the principals of the story, Fröken Frankenau was forty years old, half-crazed, and showering her affection on such pets as a senile rooster she called "my angel-boy." Fröken Frankenau's "lover," the bailiff, was then twenty-nine; their "affair" had been going four years.[134]

The important thing is that upon hearing the story Strindberg, always alert for dramatic material, saw in it a great modern theme: a declining and decadent aristocracy, trying to be at home in a world of vital if vulgar and aggressive democracy; a theme, incidentally, that some of the greatest modern plays had been or would be about—*Hedda Gabler, The Cherry Orchard,* and *A Streetcar Named Desire.* "To see an individual on whom fortune has heaped an abundance of gifts go to her ruin and destruction, leaves us with a tragic feeling," wrote Strindberg; "to see a whole line die out is still more tragic."[135] If we take Strindberg at his word, that "the final act is the most important one in a drama and a dramatist generally begins his work at the end," then most likely Strindberg started the growth of *Miss Julie* with Jean, her father's valet, handing her his razor to do away with herself in the barn. For Strindberg, the play's whole development then was to make this major climax plausible and even inevitable. He had the theme, the leading characters and the basic story in mind almost from the very start. He was also "greatly moved."

Certainly what also helped excite Strindberg was his intense identification of the principal characters with himself and his own wife. "The son of the people," he wrote in *The Confession of a Fool,* referring to his marriage to the Baroness, "had carried off the whiteskin, the plebeian had won the aristocrat, the swineherd had mated with the princess! But he had paid a heavy price."[136] The suggesion of the valet to Miss Julie, that she clean matters up by cutting her own throat, was even possibly Strindberg's death-wish for Siri at the time when his marriage had, as he said, come to the stage of "kill or be killed."

But why Strindberg's central concern with love in this play, as in about all his best known plays? "Love," Strindberg told the Baroness he ultimately married, "is a passion stronger than all others, a force of nature, absolutely irresistible." [137] "Friendship can exist only between persons with similar interests and points of view," said Strindberg in *The Son of a Servant.* "Man and woman by the conventions of society are born with different interests and different points of view." [138] For Strindberg, only as a home-maker could a wife quite identify with her husband's interest and viewpoint; otherwise a wife became a competitor. "Struggle between opposites produces energy," says the Daughter of Indra in *A Dream Play,* "—just as fire and water generate steam." [139] In Jean and Miss Julie, Strindberg created opposite leads, with social class and love providing the hardest and cruelest of life's battles; how hard and cruel, Strindberg knew too well.

In developing *Miss Julie,* Strindberg seemed to have uppermost in his mind a desire to please Zola, the acknowledged master of naturalism who, though he admired *The Father,* wrote Strindberg critically, "You know that I am not much for abstraction. I like my characters to have a complete social setting that we may elbow them and feel that they are soaked in our air . . ." [140] In *Miss Julie,* more than in any other of his plays, Strindberg provides for his characters "a complete social setting." He found many motivations for Miss Julie's implied suicide, but the one with a most lifelike validity and providing him with a lasting creative drive was "that innate or acquired sense of honor which the upper classes have as their inheritance." [141] Miss Julie's code was not "Death before dishonor," but like the Japanese aristocracy, "Death after dishonor."

Since the play's whole action builds to a major psychological crisis of the antagonists, Strindberg worked for modern insight into their behavior—"my motivation is not a simple one," he noted, and added this now famous comment:

A happening in life—and this is a fairly recent discovery!—is generally brought about by a whole series of more or less deep-lying motives; but as a rule the spectator selects the one which in his opinion seems the easiest to understand or that is most flattering to his own best judgment. A suicide takes place. "Bad business!" says the burgher. "Unrequited love!" say the women. "Physical illness!" says the invalid. "Crushed

hopes!" says the human derelict. But now it is possible the motive may
be all or none of these things, and that the deceased may have concealed
the actual motive by letting another be known that would cast a more
favorable light over his memory! [142]

Strindberg then details how as "author-mesmerizer," through accumulated suggestion, he makes Miss Julie and the audience accept her
end:

> The sad fate of Miss Julie I have motivated by a host of circumstances:
> the mother's fundamental instincts, the father's wrong upbringing of the
> girl, her own strange nature, and the suggestive influence of her fiancé
> upon an insipid, vapid degenerated mind. In addition, and more di-
> rectly, the festal mood of Midsummer Eve, the absence of her father, her
> monthly period, her preoccupancy with animals, the excitement of the
> dance, the long twilight of the night, the strongly aphrodisiac influence
> of the flowers, and lastly the chance bringing together of the two alone
> in a secluded room—not to mention the aroused passion of a bold and
> aggressive man. Consequently my mode of procedure has been neither
> one-sidedly physiological nor psychological . . .[143]

The character of Jean, the Count's valet, is a perfect foil for Miss
Julie. Only physical attraction, recollected daydreams of childhood,
and chance bring them together; reality drives them apart. She is a
Count's daughter; he, a farmer's son. She is romantic, self-indulgent,
decorative, and refuses to bear children; he is a ruthless realist, ambitious in a petty bourgeois way to be an inn-keeper, and will breed like
a cock of the roost. She dreams of new values for her dying feudal
ones; he dreams of bourgeois success to mimic his betters, even to
buying a Roumanian title someday. The concentration on these two
leads gives the play time for an astonishing degree of fullness of character drawing and revelation. Karin, the cook, who pilfers from the
Count's kitchen and who often sleeps with Jean, is the only other
character, really, in the play, and she largely emphasizes the other
two—Miss Julie's degradation and the valet's venality. Karin, with her
smug, lower class morality, believes in forgiveness for her own sins,
but not for those of the nobility who she thinks are supposed to be
really noble.

"In this attempt of mine," Strindberg confessed of a literary seminal
influence upon *Miss Julie,* "I have had in mind the brothers de Gon-
court's monographic novels which, among all literature of modern
times, have appealed to me most." [144] The play also has spiritual
chromosomes suggesting Darwin, Buckle, and Nietzsche, all strong in

Strindberg's mind at the time; Miss Julie's fall might as well be that of just a rotting tree in the national forest, for another or other forms of life will take up the sunshine her place left.

"In the great crises of life, when existence itself is threatened," wrote Strindberg, "the soul attains transcendent power." Where is the "transcendent power" of *Miss Julie?* It can only be in its burst of inner light upon the human conscience as the secret place where modern man must pay for his acts at the bar of society's judgment if not God's. "The Naturalist has done away with the idea of guilt, as well as God," Strindberg wrote; "but the consequences of the act: punishment, imprisonment (or fear of it)—*that* he cannot do away with for the simple reason that they are bound to remain." [145] Strindberg himself learned of the power of society's judgment from the repercussions of his trial for blasphemy and the public revulsion especially from *The Confession of a Fool.* Strindberg's odyssey of suffering from guilt in search of atonement, the need to be socially punished, is as psychiatrists have found often a sickness of the modern soul. In *Miss Julie,* Strindberg transcendentally offered himself and Siri up for social punishment in the sublimation of art.

A letter from Strindberg to Adolf Paul, dated January 6, 1907, suggests how clear a total conception Strindberg recollected he had of *Miss Julie* before actually doing the writing:

> intimate in form; a simple theme treated with thoroughness; few characters; vast perspectives; freely imaginative, but built on observations, experiences, carefully studied; simple, but not too simple; no huge apparatus; no superfluous minor parts; none of those 'old machines' or five-acters built according to the rules; none of those drawn-out plays lasting all night. *Miss Julie* (without intermission) has gone through its ordeal by fire and shown itself to be the kind of drama demanded by the impatient man of today: thorough but brief.[146]

Miss Julie, as part of being "thorough but brief," to Strindberg took the form of the unities in time, place and action.

This account of the creation of *Miss Julie* has one highly ironic postscript. The "story" Strindberg originally heard that left him "greatly moved" and so led to the creation of *Miss Julie,* was, according to Jacobsen's *Digteren of fantasen,* published in Copenhagen in 1945, not the true story of Fröken Frankenau and her "lover" at all. The true story was that Frau Frankenau's "lover" was actually only her half-brother whom her father had illegitimately begotten with a girl whom he married off somehow to another man. Fröken Frankenau knew all this but chose to conceal it from the villagers very likely to spare her half-brother, herself, and the memory of her father's name.[147] She persuaded her half-brother eventually to come live with her and to help manage her estate in her lonely and genteel poverty; the villagers invented the whole "affair." The truth would have made a Pirandello play.

"The higher phantasy," wrote the aging Strindberg in Sprigge's translation, "has a greater reality than this actuality. These banal accidents are not essential life. My whole life is a dream."[148] The dream-plays, *The Ghost Sonata* included, were to him "a greater reality" and so, of course, an advance over the naturalism of *Miss Julie* and an extension of his notion of "the kind of drama demanded by the impatient man of today: thorough but brief." Strindberg's proclamation of what has since come to be called "expressionism" is best stated in his own preface to *A Dream Play* (Paulson's translation):

> As in his previous dream play, *To Damascus,* the author has in *A Dream Play* attempted to reproduce the detached and disunited—although apparently logical—form of dreams. Anything is apt to happen, anything seems possible and probable. Time and space do not exist. On a flimsy foundation of actual happenings, imagination spins and weaves in new patterns: an intermingling of remembrances, experiences, whims, fancies, ideas, fantastic absurdities and improvisations, and original inventions of the mind.
>
> The personalities split, take on duality, multiply, vanish, intensify, diffuse and disperse, and are brought into a focus. There is, however, one single-minded consciousness that exercises a dominance over the characters: the dreamer's. There are for the dreamer no secrets, no consequences, no scruples, no laws. He neither pronounces judgment nor exonerates; he merely narrates.
>
> Since dreams most frequently are filled with pain, and less often with joy, a note of melancholy and a compassion for all living things runs through the limping story. Sleep, the liberator, often appears as a tormentor, a torturer, but when the agony is most oppressive the awakening rescues the sufferer and reconciles him to reality. No matter how agonizing reality may be, it will at this moment be welcomed cheerfully as a release from the painful dream.[149]

"Strindberg fathered out of necessity," commented Allan Lewis, "what is now called expressionism, to reveal the illogic of dreams and the disconnectedness of the subconscious."[150]

Strindberg wrote his chamber plays as a counterpart in drama to the chamber music of Beethoven's "last" sonatas. He explicitly said (Sprinchorn and Quinn's translation):

If you were to ask me what the aim of an intimate theatre is and what is meant by a chamber play, I would say that in this kind of drama we single out the significant and over-riding theme but treat it with moderation. In handling it we avoid all ostentation—all the calculated effects, the bravura roles, the solo numbers for the stars, and the cues for applause. The author rejects all predetermined forms because the theme determines the form. Hence he has complete freedom in handling the theme as long as unity and style of the original idea are not violated.[151]

Probably the most common charge brought against expressionism and Strindberg's no less is: "You, the author, may know what you mean by your dream play, but who else knows?" The only defense can be, "People are far more alike than different and so actually think, dream, and act largely in archetypical ways." Confusion from personal associations can still never be quite removed, especially from a different period and culture; a milk-maid, for instance, who figures in *The Ghost Sonata,* is an anachronism in many countries today and even unheard of among backward nations.

If for Strindberg theme determines form in the chamber plays, as he thought theme did in music, what for Strindberg germinated the theme? The chamber plays are all concerned, like Beethoven's "last" sonatas, with death. The themes of these plays are all variations of Strindberg's dominant thoughts on the meaning of death, and so of life, itself. *The Ghost Sonata* plays variations upon chiefly two themes: before we leave this world, all scores are evened; and even for the innocent, life on earth is hell, a pilgrimage offering hope for a better world only through prayer not unlike, "Kyrie, eléison. Christe, eléison. (Lord, have mercy on us. Christ, have mercy on us.)" Upon dying, Strindberg is reported to have said, "I have done with life and closed the account," and holding the *Bible* to him, added, "This is the only truth." The themes of *The Ghost Sonata,* indeed, haunted Strindberg's mind through: *To Damascus I, II, III, A Dream Play, The Dance of Death,* and the lesser chamber plays like *The Storm, The Burned Site* and *The Pelican.*

If Strindberg began at the "end"—"We sit out a long evening at the theatre in order to see the last act or 'how it will go'"—then Strindberg first thought of the death of the Young Lady at the end of Act III in *The Ghost Sonata.* The Young Lady lives in a modern, romantic, narcissistic and illusory world of her own, and when forced to hear the truth about herself—in a sense the very climax of *Miss Julie*—the Young Lady dies of the shock. The minor climax preceding this comes at the end of Act II. In this climax, which Strindberg possibly thought of early as a kind of preliminary "end," old Hummel exposes almost everybody at the ghost supper, only to have the Mummy expose old Hummel as a soul-merchant. To escape his public guilt, old Hummel hangs himself in the Mummy's closet. These climaxes are both predicated on a basic situation substantiating Strindberg's conviction that in life all scores are evened before death: rich old Hummel tries to do penance for his lifetime of crimes by marrying the Student to old Hummel's illegitimate offspring, the Young Lady whom old Hummel once begot with the one-time beauty, now the Mummy.

The play's development proceeds in the line of a circuitous destiny controlling everybody, especially through the eerie phenomena Strindberg saw operate in his own life—linked destinies, parallel incident, and recurrence. In *Alone,* Strindberg had written, as translated by Klaf, "In dreams my innermost feelings are reflected, and therefore I can use them as I do my mirror while shaving." [152]

The Ghost Sonata moves along these basic lines with characters guided by "Unknown Powers," invoking the dream-quality we have come to call "surrealistic." Strindberg, "the author-mesmerizer," uses illustrative action in a hypnotically elusive way, and yet, as Olle in *The Red Room* says of the aim of art, in such a manner as "to imprison the idea in a sensuous form so as to make it visible." [153] Insinuations of the fleeting unreal reality of what is happening pervade the play as various characters say in effect, "Am I dreaming?", "Are you crazy?" "You see it, but I don't." The ancestry of such dreamlike technique surely goes back to Aeschylus' depicting the Furies tormenting Orestes in the trilogy, *The Oresteia,* and continues as in Shakespeare's portrayal of Macbeth reacting to hallucinations of Banquo's ghost. Oriental and ritual drama have used visible symbols for ages. Strindberg, however, was the first to create a whole modern play with an original story in the spirit of visual-aural short-hand likened to music.

Visible symbols are active everywhere in the flow of *The Ghost Sonata.* The Consul, who is dead and wrapped in a shroud, comes out of the house to see if the flag is at half-mast for his funeral and perhaps symbolizes his lifelong vanity. The Colonel's wife, the Mummy, is swathed like a Mummy, lives in a closet concealed in the wall, talks often like her parrot, says her name is "Amalia" (Soul) and has been carrying on so for forty years. She seems to symbolize the living-dead who withdraw from life for such reasons as fear, shame, and guilt. "I am spending most of my life now in the closet there," says the Mummy, "—not only not to see, but to avoid being seen." [154] During the ghost supper, a clock is heard ticking away in the wall suggesting the consuming power of time, and old Hummel says, "Do you hear what it says? Time—time! Time—time! In a few moments—when it strikes—your time will be up—and then you may go—but not before...." [155] Those who attend the ghost supper, to which old Hummel brings the Student, have been coming for twenty years, saying and doing the same things, suggesting how automated people might become through long and very close association. The Student likely symbolizes the truth-seeker, risking his life to save others from the collapse of their houses, wanting no reward, innocent and poor. Strindberg, himself, noted how conclusively inconclusive he meant the play to be in a letter he wrote Schering, April 7, 1907 (Sprinchorn and Quinn's translation):

> As far as *The Ghost Sonata* is concerned, don't ask me what it is about. *Discrétion, s'il vous plaît!* One enters a world of intimations where one expresses oneself in halftones and with a soft pedal since one is ashamed to be a human being. [156]

Character

To what has already been said, little can be added that is really new as to Strindberg's method of characterization. "A man's character is his destiny," was a favorite proverb in Strindberg's day, and in the preface to *Miss Julie* Strindberg rejected this because "character and automation seem often synonymous." He found men's motives much too complex and, later, "Unseen Powers" too powerful to ignore in his own destiny. He wrote:

> In the course of time the word *character* has been given many meanings. Originally it no doubt denoted the dominant trait in the soul-complex and was confused with temperament. With time it became the middle-class term for an automaton, an individual who had become so fixed in his nature—or who had adapted himself to a particular role in life and who, in a word, had ceased to grow—that people called him *a character*. On the other hand, a man who continued to develop, an able navigator on the river of life, who sailed not with sheets set fast but who veered down the wind to steer closer to the wind again—this man was called lacking in character. . . .
>
> This bourgeois notion of the fixed state of the soul was transmitted to the stage, where the middle-class element has always been in dominance. [157]

Yet it cannot be denied that in his expressionist plays like *The Ghost Sonata,* in typical ambivalent fashion, Strindberg returned somewhat to character as destiny, for instance in the romantic, narcisistic Young Lady who dies of hearing the truth about herself. Strindberg also regards human beings as automated, for instance, in the guests at the ghost supper, repeating themselves for twenty years. "John had discovered that men in general were automata," Strindberg had written of himself about twenty years earlier in *The Growth of a Soul.* "All thought the same; all judged in the same fashion; and the more learned they were, the less independence of mind they displayed." [158]

Strindberg was in enough trouble most of his life without frankly identifying every model he used to create his characters. Strindberg did, nevertheless, admit that the model for Eleonora, the female lead in *Easter,* was his demented sister, Elizabeth, whose wits went awry after a series of family disasters. "She suffers with all living things," Strindberg wrote Harriet Bosse, "in other words, she manifests Christ in man." [159] Elizabeth, whom Strindberg called his *"Easter* girl," died in a mental asylum in 1904. Strindberg let out how many models he might use in creating even a single character in this comment, as translated by Edwin Björkman, concerning the source material for the sophisticated fairy-tale play, *Swanwhite*.

> Pushed ahead by the *impression* made on me by Maeterlinck, and borrowing his divining-rod for my purposes, I turned to such sources [i.e. of Swedish folk-lore] as the works of Geijer, Afeelius and Dybeck. There I found a superabundance of princes and princesses . . . I poured it all into my separator . . . and in a short while the cream began to flow—and for that reason the story is my own. . . . I have lived through the tale in my fancy—a spring in time of winter! [160]

The fifty-one year old Strindberg was then, in fact, experiencing "a spring in time of winter." He was in love with the twenty-one year old Harriet Bosse. He is obviously in part the Prince in the play, and Harriet is in part Swanwhite who restores him from death through her love. The Stranger in *To Damascus I, II,* and *III,* is as plain as day Strindberg himself, stripping his soul naked, showing his damnation and redemption in essentially the action of his very own life. The Lady in *To Damascus I* is almost as plain as a photograph, a composite of the Baroness Wrangel and Frida.

Strindberg drew characters by selecting and rearranging memories, especially those relating to "major crises" in his life. How intensely

Strindberg believed he identified himself with his characters is clear from this passage in *Alone* in Sprigge's translation:

> I live the manifold lives of all the people I described, happy with those who are happy, evil with the evil ones, good with the good; I creep out of my own personality and speak with the mouths of children, of women, of old men: I am king and beggar, I have worldly power, I am the tyrant and the down-trodden hater of the tyrant; I hold all opinions and profess all religions; I live in all times and have myself ceased to be. This is a state which brings indescribable happiness.[161]

Strindberg showed a phenomenal resourcefulness in making the most of a few people who brought about the major crises in his life and so his soul-revelations: Strindberg, himself; his mother and his father; Siri von Essen; the Baron Wrangel; Frida Uhl; Frida's grandparents; and Harriet Bosse. Strindberg, of course, noted "a dramatist generally begins his work at the end." What he did, it appears, was to conceive of a wide variety of endings for the people he knew best, put into different basic situations. Many of his plays are variations on the central theme of the ambivalent battle of the sexes, with the hand that loved, coming to bear a weapon, most often a psychological one but potentially lethal if at times funny in the way it is brandished. It is as if Strindberg said, "Now suppose I took the characters in *The Father,* changed them somewhat from added memories, and showed them fifteen years later in a life that ended in a stale-mate of torment. *How* and *why* could this have come about?" The answer would be found in *The Dance of Death.*

Other plays provide other answers. In *Comrades,* the painter Axel Alberg, obviously Strindberg, and his bride, his competitor in painting, clash ambivalently to the end that a man wants in a wife a comrade not a competitor, or else he prefers a mistress to a wife. In *The Stronger,* Mrs. X, a married actress, addresses Miss Y, an unmarried actress, extolling the joys of marriage that Miss Y missed in passing up Mrs. X's husband as a mate; but Mrs. X winds up by revealing that to keep that husband's love, she now must act like his former mistress, Miss Y. In *The Bond,* the Baron and Baroness agree to keep their private lives out of the court divorce proceedings to protect their one child from scandal, but once in court, the pair fall into a duel of recriminations that brings out the worst in each, with long litigation ahead over the custody of their child. In *Creditors,* Gustav, the athletic ex-husband of Tekla, a female writer, comes to visit her new husband, Adolph, a man of slight build. The men agree that to find the truth from Tekla as to what she thinks of each, Gustav and Adolph will take turns hiding in the adjoining room to overhear what the other draws out about his rival. The outcome is very funny in some ways, yet the truth finally might kill Adolph by giving him a heart attack. Strindberg got a great deal of mileage from the people and situations he knew best. His work shows the potential for variations upon a single theme, especially that of the ambivalent and sometimes spent but ever-renewed battle of the sexes.

Sources of Freshness

John Gassner said of Strindberg, "it is plainly his comprehension of ambivalence and inner conflict that made him the prime creator of modern psychological drama. His mastery of his *métier* has not yet found its match in the work of his twentieth-century successors in the theatre despite the exertions of Wedekind, O'Neill, Williams, and others, and despite the vogue of Freudian depth-psychology." [162] And Gassner continued, "Strindberg is doubly celebrated as the first modern master of both psychological realism and expressionism." [163] Strindberg will always be at least a playwright's playwright. When will he be more of a popular playwright?

"I feel it is my calling to persuade humanity that the world we live in is not the best, and that another world, a better one is awaiting us," Strindberg wrote Harriet, June 4–6, 1904. "It is a gospel of hope, and that is my doctrine. In gratitude they strike me in the face, the fools." Strindberg went on, "And this has been my teaching throughout my writings, not least in my latest work." [164] Has the public stopped striking Strindberg in the face and taken more to patting him on the back? He never pretended to be saying anything really new. The ambivalent battle of the sexes that is the sign of his fame to many, he saw in Hercules and Omphale, Agamemnon and Clytemnestra, Samson and Delilah, Antony and Cleopatra.

Strindberg's disillusionment with life is in the very spirit of *Ecclesiastes*—, "Vanity of vanities . . . all is vanity!" In *Inferno,* Strindberg, like a modern soul searching desperately for the truth yet sooner or later only lost again, concludes with something very close to the present day Theatre of the Absurd; he says of "the Powers:"

> In my youth I was a true believer and you made of me a free-thinker. Of the free-thinker you made an atheist, of the atheist a monk. Inspired by the humanitarians, I extolled socialism. Five years later you showed me the absurdity of socialism. You have cut the ground from under all

my enthusiasms, and suppose that I now dedicate myself to religion: I know for a certainty that before ten years have passed you will prove to me that religion is false.

Are not the Gods jesting with us mortals, and is that why we too, sharing the jest, are able to laugh in the most tormented moments of our lives? [165]

Since the discovery of how to control atomic energy and to make bigger and better bombs, the prospect of modern science making earth either a heaven or hell is nearer than ever to Strindberg's ambivalent spirit of hopeful pessimism. Does Strindberg have something to say to the common man in these days of a world-wide revolution of expectations? "Everything's a racket!" and "The world is full of phonies!" and "What a mess the world's in today!" are not uncommon on men's lips. Strindberg thinks all men must wind up this way. Are totalitarian countries ready for Strindberg's spirit? His power is more likely to crack than preserve a monolithic state.

"Apart from this intensity," said F. L. Lucas, "the other main secret of Strindberg's success may be, as I have said, his style." [166] "No Swedish author," wrote Alrik Gustafson in his *A History of Swedish Literature,* "has the stylistic variety and range, the spontaneity, directness and economy of phrasing that Strindberg commands." [167] Another Swedish critic summed up Strindberg's style, "no one has a shorter way from the blood to the ink." Strindberg is the nearest Sweden has to Shakespeare and is bound to suffer as much from translation. Something of Strindberg's own awareness of the power of his style is suggested in this excerpt from a love letter to Siri, written March 12, 1876, and here translated by Sprigge. "Oh, don't you know that I have a magic wand that strikes water from the rock?" wrote Strindberg, "—that I can get poetry out of filth if I must? Oh, I shall grind a coffee mill so that it sounds like music—." [168] Strindberg owes his intensity of effect not only to words, but to his obsession with the soul as revealed by life's hardest and cruellest battles. "Ibsen, Strindberg and Tolstoy," observed Shaw in the London *Mercury* of 1921, "wrote tragi-comedies, supplying a much grimmer entertainment than tragedy." [169]

Writing and Rewriting

Strindberg let his plays grow sometimes for years, sometimes far less, before he felt in his mind that his brain-child was ready to be delivered. "The work of the author has often been compared to child-birth," he wrote in *The Growth of a Soul*, "and the comparison has something to justify it." Strindberg added, upon finishing his first play, "He felt a kind of peace like that which follows parturition." [170]

"He writes without a pause," reported Frida, "almost without stopping, does not even read over what he has written, to say nothing of correcting it. It is like harvest-time when the fruit has ripened." [171] But Strindberg himself implied great reservations about such ease in having his brain-children. "The Creator, that great artist who Himself develops as He creates," wrote Strindberg in *Inferno* in Mary Sandbach's translation, "who makes rough drafts only to cast them aside, who takes up abortive ideas afresh, . . . perfects and multiplies His primitive conceptions." [172] In likening God to an artist, Strindberg implied his own problems with his brainchildren. True, he could on occasion write a first and final draft at a breathless speed. In 1907, for instance, as he wrote his chamber plays, including *The Ghost Sonata*, he would let each page of freshly written manuscript flutter to the floor as he went on to a new page; August Falck, his actor-manager, who was sitting outside the study, then would quietly enter, pick up each newly written page with the ink still wet, and quietly exit to read it. But Strindberg's semi-automatic writing in which he likened himself sometimes to a "medium" came from a stern discipline he acquired as an "author mesmerizer."

"Toiling with a lexicon and investigating roots of words," he said of his university studies, "had become painful to him, but he enjoyed this pain and disciplined his imagination by hard work, looking upon it as his professional duty." [173] Of writing even his first play, *A Name-Day Gift*, in four days he said, "Had he not formed his style through reading, translating, and writing for the papers?" [174] "Thought is an act of the mind, and words are congealed thoughts," he said of his word-mastery in *Zones of the Spirit*, and always likening himself to a wizard of words he wrote, "The uttered word can have an effect like a charm or an adjuration . . . A word may kill." [175] He spoke, in Klaf's translation, of "bombs out of my ink bottle," [176] and said, "When I take my pen in hand, I become the devil." He wrote with a quill pen sometimes made from a feather of his wife's hat, as Harriet was to learn. [177]

Strindberg put as much care into detailing his setting, stage directions, and stage business as into his dialogue. He knew that every visual detail essential to a play could speak sometimes far more effectively than dialogue. In *Miss Julie*, for instance, the Count's kitchen is grand yet menial, and so suggests the level into which Miss Julie falls in her own eyes by going there for company. The time is Midsummer Night's Eve; anything can happen in the wild festivities of that holiday from the mingling of the social classes. The first thing Miss Julie does upon entering is the key-note to her nature: she flips her fine handkerchief in the face of Jean, the Count's valet, and he immediately notes its aphrodisiac quality. "Ah—," he says, "what lovely fragrance—the smell of violets—." [178] When Miss Julie wants to take her little bird, Sérine, with her in its cage and run off with Jean, Jean quickly settles the nuisance of the bird: "(*He lets the hatchet fall on the bird's neck.*)." [179] Much of Jean's character and his whole social status is revealed in a simple stage direction near the end: "(*Two abrupt rings interrupt him. Julie jumps to her feet; Jean quickly changes his coat.*)." [180] The Count is impatiently summoning Jean who quite loses his bravado and becomes servile. At the very end, to make matters right his way, Jean sends Miss Julie out to the barn with his razor to cut her own throat: "(*Miss Julie, with the razor in her hand, walks firmly out through the door.*)." [181]

In the dream-plays, the detail is at least as great, for each bit must be an essence free of the excessive detail of reality. A white marble statue of a young lady, for instance, is seen in *The Ghost Sonata* in the perfectly round room, and the Mummy points out the statue as being of her in virginal youth. The colonel has a toupée, false teeth, and wears iron stays to look smart. Though the milk-maid gives the Student a drink of water from her dipper, old Hummel can't see her; but at the ghost supper she appears as a ghost only to old Hummel, a ghost of a girl he in his youth drowned in a canal to cover other crimes. Strindberg had learned the power of visual effects in the theatre to hit the mind with a quintessential reality having the speed of light.

If Strindberg had an ideal for his dialogue, it seems suggested in this excerpt from a love-letter he wrote to Harriet on April 10, 1908. "I find in these letters the very finest in us," he said, "our souls in holiday dress, as life in the flesh seldom is. It is no poetic imagery; it is true to life. There is no posing (in them), no illusions—and if by illusion is meant something unreal, then this is the very highest reality." "Words and tongue are so impure," said Strindberg implying dissatisfaction with his diction, "that they are unable to express the most sublime." [182] In *A Dream Play*, Strindberg has this self-revealing bit:

> DAUGHTER OF INDRA: . . . Could your words, even once, for a
> fleeting moment, impart the full and true meaning of your
> thoughts?
> POET: No . . . I have always seemed to myself a mere deaf-
> mute! [183]

What stymied Strindberg about his diction, for all his practice and
calculation? He said, "the creative process is just as much a mystery
to me now as it was forty years ago, whether it takes place with clear
deliberation and complete consciousness or not." [184] Even so, he did
his best to match his dialogue to his over-all intent. So, for instance, in
the naturalism of *Miss Julie* we might as well have our ear to the
door, as illustrated in this excerpt:

> MISS JULIE: (*Paces back and forth*) Could there be anyone in this
> world more miserable than I am?
> JEAN. Why be miserable—after a conquest like yours? Think of
> Kristin in there—don't you think that she, too, has feelings . . .
> MISS JULIE. I used to think so, but I no longer do! No—once a ser-
> vant, always a servant!
> JEAN. And once a whore—always a whore!
> MISS JULIE. (*on her knees, her hands clasped*) Oh, God in heaven
> —put an end to my miserable life! Take me away from this filth
> —I am sinking down in it! Help me! Save me!
> JEAN. I can't help feeling sorry for you. . . . When I lay in the
> onion bed and watched you in the rose garden, I—yes, I can tell
> you now—I had the same nasty thoughts that all boys have.
> MISS JULIE. And you—you wanted to die for me!
> JEAN. You mean in the oats-bin? I just made that up!
> MISS JULIE. Just a lie, then! [185]

Important things come through in this translation by Paulson—not
merely the obvious tricks of conversation—broken phrases, exclamations, interjections, outbursts of feeling. The dialogue moves in a psychological give and take, a kind of hypnotic drift of implied meaning
to reach stark revelations of character.

As for long speeches, Strindberg has one in *Miss Julie* running to
about three minutes. "The monologue has now been condemned by
our realists as not being true to life," Strindberg noticed, "but if its motivation is sound, it can be made believable, and consequently it can
be used to good advantage." [186] Strindberg's all time *tour de force* in
what amounts to a monologue is his one-act play, *The Stronger,* in
which Mrs. X, the married actress, does all the talking, and Miss Y
responds simply by sipping her chocolate, laughing, or gazing fixedly

and curiously at Mrs. X. The speech of Mrs. X, about eighteen minutes long, undoubtedly influenced such efforts as O'Neill's *After Breakfast*, Rice's *The Adding Machine*, and Williams' *Suddenly Last Summer*.

In the dream plays, exemplified by *The Ghost Sonata*, a kind of living surrealism is suggested in this excerpt:

> MUMMY. (*from the closet*) Pretty Polly!
> HUMMEL. (*Shrinks back*) What was that? Is there a parrot in the room? I don't see it!
> MUMMY. Is Jacob there?
> HUMMEL. Spooks!
> MUMMY. Jacob!
> HUMMEL. This is frightening! . . . So—it is secrets of this kind they guard in this house! (*He goes over to look at a painting and stands with his back turned to the closet.*) There he is! . . . He!
> MUMMY. (*Comes out of the closet and steals up behind Hummel, pulling at his wig*) Currrr! Is it you—Currrr?
> HUMMEL. (*Leaps, frightened out of his senses*) Lord in heaven!— What is it?
> MUMMY. (*in a normal, human voice*) Is it Jacob?
> HUMMEL. Yes—that's my name—actually, yes. . . .
> MUMMY. (*with deep emotion*) And my name is Amalia!
> HUMMEL. No, no, no . . . Oh God, oh God!
> MUMMY. This is the way I look now! Yes!—And that is how I used to look! (*She points to the marble figure*) Life teaches us many things, doesn't it? I am spending most of my life now in the closet there—not only not to see, but to avoid being seen. . . .[187]

Every device of naturalistic dialogue is used here to help give the sense of reality to the unreality. Strindberg likened *The Ghost Sonata* to Beethoven's Sonata 17, Opus 31, "The Tempest." Certainly the visual is highly exploited in the quoted excerpt, as it should be in good theatre, the word, "theatre," itself meaning "a place to see." The analogy to music is necessarily more figurative than real, and yet music, Plato noted in *The Republic,* can most intimately involve the movements of the soul; so a startling likeness of soul-struggles in drama to music is perhaps quite possible.

"Strindberg's stylistic skill," wrote Alrik Gustafson, "is the despair of the translator."[188] Edwin Björkman, the first authorized translator of Strindberg's plays into English, believed the chief trouble in translation came from Swedish and English having a quite different natural, basic rhythm:

But the rhythm dearest and most natural to the genius of the Swedish language seems to be the falling pulse-beat manifested in the true trochée. The swing and motion of English, on the other hand, is almost exclusively, commandingly iambic. And it was not until I made the iambic rising movement prevail in my translation that I felt myself approaching the impression made on me by the original.[189]

To best savor the full flavor of Strindberg one should, of course, know Swedish as a native or second tongue.

During his university days, Strindberg tested such new plays as *In Rome, The Outlaw* and *Master Olof* by reading them aloud to a small circle of friends for a reaction. Then he tried to revise. Afterward, Strindberg is said to have done no revision because he had thought out each play so thoroughly before putting his pen to paper that to revise might offend the "Unseen Powers" he believed guided his pen. Ordinarily Strindberg attended rehearsals and tried to take a hand in casting, especially in the days of The Intimate Theatre. Strindberg seemed to know a good deal about what he didn't want in the way of acting and directing, but he was not skilled enough to always get what he wanted. He was no Max Reinhardt in production. If Strindberg did rewrite, he would do so only when his script proved lacking when properly cast. "You can pick out the *first-rate* actor as soon as he makes his entrance," Strindberg said. "When he comes on, he lifts up the whole show." [190] The fact that Strindberg was happy to work with The Intimate Theatre, to see a great many of his unproduced plays produced for the first time, suggests that he did not quite feel his brain-children were really delivered until he saw them on the stage, for better or worse.

My grateful acknowledgement is here extended to the following sources for the use of quotations:

AUGUST STRINDBERG, The Bedeviled Viking by V. J. McGill. Russell & Russell, New York, 1965

THE CHAMBER PLAYS OF STRINDBERG translated by Evert Sprinchorn and Seabury Quinn, Jr. Copyright (c) 1962 by Evert Sprinchorn and Seabury Quinn, Jr. Dutton Paperback Series. Reprinted by permission of E. P. Dutton & Co., Inc.

9 brief excerpts from THE CONFESSION OF A FOOL by August Strindberg, translated by Ellie Schleussner. Copyright 1925 by The Viking Press, Inc. All rights reserved. Reprinted by permission of The Viking Press, Inc.

THE GROWTH OF A SOUL by August Strindberg, translated by Claud Field, London, William Rider & Sons, Ltd., 1913

A HISTORY OF SWEDISH LITERATURE by Alrik Gustafson. Copyright 1964. Reprinted by permission of the American Scandinavian Foundation and the University of Minnesota Press

IBSEN AND STRINDBERG by F. L. Lucas, London, Cassell & Co., Ltd., 1962. Reprinted by permission of Cassell & Co., Ltd.

INFERNO by August Strindberg, translated by Mary Sandbach. Copyright 1962. Reprinted by permission of Hutchinson & Co., Ltd.

LEGENDS by August Strindberg, autobiographical sketches, London, Andrew Melrose Ltd., 1912

Reprinted from LETTERS OF STRINDBERG TO HARRIET BOSSE, Edited and translated by Arvid Paulson, (c) 1959 by Arvid Paulson. Universal Library Edition published by Grosset & Dunlap, Inc.

MARRIAGE WITH GENIUS by Frida Strindberg. Copyright 1937. Reprinted by permission of Jonathan Cape Ltd. and Curtis Brown Ltd.

PLAYS BY AUGUST STRINDBERG translated from the Swedish with an introduction by Edwin Björkman, authorized edition. Copyright 1913. Reprinted by permission of Charles Scribner's Sons

THE RED ROOM by August Strindberg, authorized translation by Ellie Schleussner, New York, G. P. Putnam's Sons, 1913

Reprinted from SEVEN PLAYS BY AUGUST STRINDBERG, translated by

1. Elizabeth Sprigge, *The Strange Life of August Strindberg* (London 1949), 70
2. Ibid., 73
3. August Strindberg translated by Ellie Schleussner, *The Confession of a Fool* (New York 1925), 40
4. Lewis, 59
5. Ibid.
6. F. L. Lucas, *Ibsen and Strindberg* (London 1962), 305
7. August Strindberg translated by Claud Field, *The Growth of a Soul* (London 1913), 119
8. Ibid., 124
9. Hamilton, 25
10. Sprigge, vii
11. August Strindberg translated by Arvid Paulson, *Strindberg: Eight Expressionist Plays* (New York 1965), 142
12. *The Growth of a Soul,* 261
13. *The Confession of a Fool,* 72
14. August Strindberg translated by Claud Field, *Zones of the Spirit* (New York 1913), 119
15. Franklin S. Klaf, M. D., *Strindberg, the Origin of Psychology in Modern Drama* (New York 1963), 151
16. August Strindberg translated by Claud Field, *The Son of a Servant* (New York 1913), 1
17. Ibid., 53
18. Ibid., 11
19. Ibid., 156
20. *The Growth of a Soul,* 261
21. *The Son of a Servant,* 35
22. *The Son of a Servant,* 113
23. Ibid., 101
24. Ibid., 14
25. *The Confession of a Fool,* 179
26. *The Son of a Servant,* 51

27. Ibid., 255
28. Ibid., 114
29. Ibid., 65
30. Ibid., 131
31. *The Growth of a Soul*, 39
32. Ibid., 87
33. V. J. McGill, *August Strindberg: The Bedeviled Viking* (New York 1965), 54
34. Frida Strindberg, *Marriage with Genius* (London 1937), 388
35. August Strindberg translated by Mary Sandbach, *Inferno* (London 1962), 32
36. Sprigge, 57
37. *Inferno*, 150
38. August Strindberg translated by Arvid Paulson, *Letters of Strindberg to Harriet Bosse* (New York 1959), 26
39. Frida Strindberg, 379
40. Sprigge, 87
41. Ibid., 159
42. Klaf, 152
43. *The Growth of a Soul*, 209
44. Frida Strindberg, 410
45. Sprigge, 182-3
46. Frida Strindberg, 138
47. Ibid., 411
48. August Strindberg translated by Arvid Paulson, *Seven Plays by August Strindberg* (New York 1960), 64
49. *The Growth of a Soul*, 226
50. Sprigge, 356
51. *Seven Plays by August Strindberg*, 70
52. *The Growth of a Soul*, 189
53. Ibid.
54. Ibid., 52, 53
55. *Seven Plays by August Strindberg*, i
56. Frida Strindberg, 396
57. Lucas, 473
58. Alrik Gustafson, *A History of Swedish Literature* (Minneapolis 1964), 258
59. Frida Strindberg, 382
60. *The Confession of a Fool*, 317
61. McGill, 11
62. *Letters of Strindberg to Harriet Bosse*, 125
63. *Inferno*, 167
64. August Strindberg translated by Ellie Schleussner, *The Red Room* (New York 1913), 369, 370
65. *The Growth of a Soul*, 216

66. Sprigge, 72
67. *Seven Plays by August Strindberg*, 62
68. Sprigge, 182–3
69. *Zones of the Spirit*, 83
70. Ibid., 99
71. Ibid., 84
72. August Strindberg translated by Evert Sprinchorn and Seabury Quinn, Jr., *The Chamber Plays of Strindberg* (New York 1962), 216
73. *Seven Plays by August Strindberg*, 71
74. *Zones of the Spirit*, 127
75. *Letters of Strindberg to Harriet Bosse*, 155
76. Ibid., 153
77. Sprigge, unnumbered supplement at close
78. *Seven Plays by August Strindberg*, 62
79. Ibid.
80. *The Chamber Plays of Strindberg*, vii
81. *Seven Plays by August Strindberg*, 71
82. August Strindberg, *Legends* (London 1912), **6**
83. *Zones of the Spirit*, 75
84. *The Chamber Plays of Strindberg*, 217–8
85. *Zones of the Spirit*, 42
86. Ibid., 293
87. *The Growth of a Soul*, 156
88. Sprigge, 87
89. *The Chamber Plays of Strindberg*, 215
90. Sprigge, 213
91. McGill, 156
92. *The Growth of a Soul*, 168
93. *The Confession of a Fool*, 317
94. *Letters of Strindberg to Harriet Bosse*, **151**
95. *Legends*, 144
96. Frida Strindberg, 339
97. *Zones of the Spirit*, 247
98. *Legends*, 89
99. *Seven Plays by August Strindberg*, 64
100. *The Chamber Plays of Strindberg*, xvi
101. Frida Strindberg, 150
102. *Inferno*, 130
103. Frida Strindberg, 138
104. Klaf, 145
105. *Letters of Strindberg to Harriet Bosse*, 90
106. *Inferno*, 130, 131
107. Frida Strindberg, 183
108. *Strindberg: Eight Expressionist Plays*, 148

109. Frida Strindberg, 270
110. *The Confession of a Fool,* 76
111. *The Growth of a Soul,* 48
112. Sprigge, unnumbered supplement at close
113. Frida Strindberg, 139
114. *Letters of Strindberg to Harriet Bosse,* 91
115. *The Growth of a Soul,* 120
116. *The Chamber Plays of Strindberg,* xiii
117. Sprigge, 130
118. Lucas, 349
119. Klaf, 92
120. Sprigge, 116
121. *The Growth of a Soul,* 13
122. Ibid., 58
123. *The Red Room,* 218
124. *The Confession of a Fool,* 75
125. McGill, 11
126. Lucas, 465
127. Sprigge, 130
128. McGill, 11
129. Laurvik and Morison, 334
130. *The Growth of a Soul,* 214
131. *Legends,* 96
132. Frida Strindberg, 117
133. *Seven Plays by August Strindberg,* 63
134. Lucas, 364–5
135. *Seven Plays by August Strindberg,* 63
136. *The Confession of a Fool,* 127
137. McGill, 135
138. *The Son of a Servant,* 166
139. *Strindberg: Eight Expressionist Plays,* 401
140. Eric Bentley, *The Playwright as Thinker* (New York 1946), 317; Lucas, 359
141. *Seven Plays by August Strindberg,* 67
142. Ibid., 64
143. Ibid., 65
144. Ibid., 70
145. Ibid., 67
146. *The Chamber Plays of Strindberg,* vii
147. Lucas, 365, 366
148. Sprigge, 187
149. *Strindberg: Eight Expressionist Plays,* 343
150. Lewis, 56
151. *The Chamber Plays of Strindberg,* 207

152. Klaf, 131
153. *The Red Room*, 371
154. *Strindberg: Eight Expressionist Plays*, 478
155. Ibid., 484
156. *The Chamber Plays of Strindberg*, xix
157. *Seven Plays by August Strindberg*, 65
158. *The Growth of a Soul*, 238
159. *Letters of Strindberg to Harriet Bosse*, 19
160. August Strindberg translated by Edwin Björkman, *Plays by August Strindberg* (New York 1913), 4
161. Sprigge, 206
162. *Seven Plays by August Strindberg*, xiii
163. Ibid., vii
164. *Letters of Strindberg to Harriet Bosse*, 103
165. *Inferno*, 165
166. Lucas, 458
167. Gustafson, 255
168. Sprigge, 73
169. *Seven Plays by August Strindberg*, xvii
170. *The Growth of a Soul*, 122
171. Frida Strindberg, 168
172. *Inferno*, 88
173. *The Growth of a Soul*, 185
174. Ibid., 122
175. *Zones of the Spirit*, 119
176. Klaf, 93
177. *Letters of Strindberg to Harriet Bosse*, 17
178. *Seven Plays by August Strindberg*, 80
179. Ibid., 108
180. Ibid., 114
181. Ibid., 116
182. *Letters of Strindberg to Harriet Bosse*, 171
183. *Strindberg: Eight Expressionist Plays*, 401
184. *The Chamber Plays of Strindberg*, xiv
185. *Seven Plays by August Strindberg*, 96
186. Ibid., 71
187. *Strindberg: Eight Expressionist Plays*, 478
188. Gustafson, 255
189. *Plays by August Strindberg*, 5
190. *The Chamber Plays of Strindberg*, 214

Chapter III

Anton Chekhov

"To write a good play for the theatre," said Anton Chekhov, "one must have a special talent . . ." [1] He thought that the dramatist, like other artists, works by instinct. Any attempt of science to find out the organic laws of art, Chekhov surmised, could only wind up in a wild goose chase among nerve cells and nerve centers. The sensible alternative, as he expressed in an article in November 1888, was to discover the common element in the best works of art: "That common element will be the law." [2] Chekhov implies that in the drama "the law" would be found among the masterpieces. Even at thirty-eight with *The Sea Gull* and *Uncle Vanya* to his credit, Chekhov doubted his talent in playwriting. "My attitude toward my plays," he said, "is in general cold." [3] And in Koteliansky's translation, Chekhov noted, "All that I have written will be forgotten in five or ten years, but the paths paved by me, will remain safe and sound—therein is my only merit." [4]

Today, Chekhov's later long plays are considered modern classics; some critics don't think so, yet still concede his genius. Tolstoy, for instance, called Chekhov "an incomparable artist" in his stories and novels, but upon seeing *Uncle Vanya* performed January 27, 1900, he told Chekhov, "I cannot bear Shakespeare, you know, but your plays are even worse." [5] Shaw, however, remarked of Chekhov, "He makes me feel like a beginner." [6] "It has even been suggested," said F. L. Lucas of Chekhov in 1963, "that today his popularity surpasses that of Dostoievsky, Tolstoy, and other giants of Russian literature." [7]

I

THE GROWTH OF CHEKHOV'S CREATIVE SPIRIT IN LIFE

Chekhov first tried his hand at playwriting when he was eighteen years old. In a futile attempt to help his near destitute family, he wrote three plays—all now lost—whose titles suggest his own hard lot

114

at the time: *Without Fathers, Diamond Cuts Diamond,* and *Laugh It off If You Can.* Chekhov's earliest bent for drama showed in his funny improvisations and imitations of townspeople for an audience of his family and friends. He would, for example, play a dentist and perform prolonged dental surgery on his brother Alexander by putting a coal tong into his mouth and finally, after a struggle, extract a very troublesome tooth—a bottle cork.

Born in the port town of Taganrog on the Sea of Azov, January 17, 1860, Anton Pavlovich Chekhov was the son of a petty grocer, Pavel Yegorovich Chekhov, whose father was an emancipated serf. Anton grew up in the highly status-conscious and autocratic Russia of Czar Alexander II. Chekhov's lifelong dedication to good works and his struggle for fame against great handicaps suggest he was driven by a fierce inner compulsion; as he put it, "this young man squeezed the slave out of himself drop by drop." [8]

"Our talents we got from our father," said Chekhov in Constance Garnett's compilation and translation, *Letters of Anton Chekhov to His Family and Friends,* "but our soul from our mother." [9] Anton's mother, Eugeniya Yakovlevna Morozova, the daughter of a local dry-goods merchant, was a very gentle woman and a lover of nature. His father, although only a grocer, was also an amateur painter, a violinist, and a choirmaster who never hesitated about giving a flogging. "I myself was taught like that," he told his sons, "and you see I have turned out a man. One beaten man is worth two unbeaten ones." [10] Anton was the third of six children born over a ten year span to his overworked mother. In order of birth, the children were: Alexander, Nikolai, Anton, Ivan, Mariya and Mikhail. The Chekhov children were forbidden to play games or fool away their time. Morning and evening they attended church services and read psalms. When they weren't at school, they were expected to help at the grocery store. From the age of eight, Chekhov helped clerk at the grocery which was open from five in the morning until usually eleven at night. Chekhov wrote his brother Alexander, "Despotism and lies so disfigured our childhood that it makes me sick and horrified to think of it." [11] Another time, Chekhov reminisced, "In my childhood, I had no childhood." [12] No wonder that as a man he felt intensely, "People must never be humiliated. That is the main thing." [13]

Perhaps Chekhov's literary drive was in part from his lifelong attempt to make up through fantasy for his unhappy childhood. "He was the liveliest and most original of the children," commented Ernest Simmons, Chekhov's excellent and definitive biographer, "always ready for a joke or a humorous enterprise—a characteristic that remained with him throughout his life." [14]

Chekhov was sixteen years old when his father went bankrupt from a 500 ruble debt he contracted to build a new house for his family. To escape debtor's prison, Chekhov's father sneaked out of town on a train to Moscow. Soon afterward, all of the Chekhov family but Anton joined the father. Anton stayed behind in Taganrog to finish his preparatory schooling. For the next three years, Anton especially learned self-reliance by tutoring for his room and board. He grew up poor, shy, sensitive, fond of people, and fun-loving. He completed his studies with a record of B—. In punctuality, diligence and curiosity, he was rated excellent. His tutoring likely kept him from giving full time to his studies. He made friends by his knack for telling funny stories and by mimicking local characters like his teachers and the town mayor. His love of the theatre showed up in his disguising himself in a long coat and dark glasses and joining other students, also disguised, to attend the local playhouse in violation of the school rules. From the front row of the gallery, Chekhov saw such theatrical magic as Offenbach's *Fair Helen,* Gogol's *The Inspector General,* and Shakespeare's *Richard III.* "He liked nothing better," wrote Simmons, "than to imitate at home the characters he saw on the stage." [15]

From Moscow, meanwhile, Anton's family sent him a steady stream of letters detailing their poverty, sickness, and despair. Anton's chief diversion became the books in the town's free library. He read such Russian classics as Turgenev, Dostoievsky, and Tolstoy, as well as literary criticism. How much Chekhov felt he owed the Taganrog library as his "open sesame" to culture is best shown in the money he repeatedly gave to help it once he became famous and well-to-do.

In spite of poverty and misfortune, Chekhov's parents seem somehow always to have inspired their children to try to better themselves. Alexander eventually became a journalist and an author; Nikolai, a gifted artist; Anton, a doctor and a great writer; Ivan, a teacher; Mariya, a teacher; and Mikhail, a well known lawyer. The success of the Chekhov children and especially of Chekhov, himself, for all its undertones of deep suffering, has the cheerful quality of an American success story and suggests that talent, even in times of despotism, somehow had laurels within reach.

Chekhov's interest in a medical career seems to date from the sum-

mer of 1875 when his school physician, Dr. Schrempf, helped save his
life from an attack of peritonitis. His mother told him, "And as you
respect me, mind that you enter the Medical School; it is the best career." [16] How deeply Chekhov respected and loved his mother is suggested in his comment to his cousin Mikhail in a letter in 1877: "In
this unhappy world there is no one dearer to us than our mother
. . ." [17] Probably with the approval of its school physician, the town of
Taganrog actually paid Chekhov's tuition at medical college by granting him a special scholarship of 25 rubles a month. Chekhov never
forgot this kindness that made all the difference in his life, and once
he became a successful doctor and a famous author as well, he could
never quite abandon medicine and took care to contribute generously
toward better local schools. He also helped pay for the education of
his brothers and his sister. No wonder that in his plays Chekhov repeatedly has his characters lay their finest hopes for a better world in
work and especially in education. This was Chekhov's down-to-earth
formula for Utopia.

In the fall of 1879 at the age of nineteen, Chekhov entered the University of Moscow to study medicine. The Chekhovs lived almost
elbow to elbow in a small basement apartment located in a licensed
"red light district" of Moscow. For a while, they were so poor that
they slept on the floor with no blankets but their overcoats. They were
literally a doorstep from destitution. Chekhov took no part in social
or political activities at the University; the assassination of Czar Alexander II, in 1881, brought stern repression upon all suspects from his
successor, Czar Alexander III. During his four years as a medical student, Chekhov was the chief bread-winner of his family. At every free
moment from his studies, he scribbled humorous sketches like so
many free-hand drawings to make a fast ruble; he portrayed such
local sources of amusement as drunks, prostitutes, tradesmen and
housewives. Even as a freshman, Chekhov with the pseudonym,
Chekonte, was a regular contributor to Moscow's humor magazines,
such as *Alarm Clock, Dragonfly,* and *Fragments.*

In 1881, Chekhov in high spirits dashed off his first full length play,
Platonov, and rushed it to the Moscow Imperial Maly Theatre. The
return post brought him the manuscript rejected. In a seizure of despair, the twenty-one year old medical student tore up *Platonov.* "It
was a very unwieldy play," recalled his brother Mikhail, "with a railway train, horse thieves, and the lynching of a gypsy." [18] A still extant

rough draft of *Platonov* is about three full plays in length. "I have only one secret illness which torments me like an aching tooth," said Chekhov of writing potboilers, "—lack of money."

From 1880 to 1884, Chekhov sold nearly 300 sketches and short stories to humor magazines.[19] He confessed, "I do not recall a *single* tale of mine over which I worked more than a day." [20] He did not try his hand at another play until 1884 when he wrote the one-act drama, *On the Highway*, based upon his successful story, *In the Autumn*. The theatre censor banned *On the Highway* as setting a bad example in depicting a ruffian trying to kill a noblewoman who had driven her husband to alcoholism and a ruinous crack-up. As a medical student, Chekhov must have found that plays were not a very dependable way to bring home the groceries. All through his university days and practically to the very end of his life, he lived under the same roof with most of his family or at least with his parents and his sister Mariya. He called his family "my benignant tumor." [21]

On June 23, 1884, at the age of 24, Chekhov became Dr. Anton Chekhov, and he interned at Voskresensk (New Jerusalem), a town near Moscow. To supplement his meager medical fees, Chekhov in his spare time again took to writing stories. Then on March 25, 1886, the celebrated author, Grigorovitch, wrote Dr. Anton Chekhov a fan letter twenty pages long, inspired by the publication of his writings over the years. "You possess, dear sir, a very exceptional talent," was Grigorovitch's theme to Chekhov, "which I am convinced has no need to recoil from the most difficult tasks." [22] The effect upon Chekhov, a man of science, was somewhat apocalyptic. "I felt that I had a gift," replied Chekhov to Grigorovitch on March 28, 1886, in a daze of euphoria, "but I had got into the habit of thinking it was insignificant." [23] A celebrity had recognized in Chekhov a kinship of talent!

Chekhov never quite gave up the practice of medicine, yet in all he came to write over 4,000 letters to hundreds of people, more than 900 stories, and all of his plays.[24] As a doctor whose townspeople had helped pay for his medical education, Chekhov while his health permitted could never with a clear conscience quite turn from his suffering countrymen. "Even without the plague, only about four hundred out of every thousand children survive to the age of five in our district," said Chekhov in Magarshack's translation, "and in the villages and the factories and backstreets of our towns, you will not find one healthy woman." [25] At the age of twenty-nine, Chekhov showed definite symptoms of tuberculosis,—bloody sputum and a continual, hack-ing cough. Chances are that he had become a casualty as a doctor on the field of battle against disease. He must have known his own prognosis. Of the old Russian proverb, "You cannot chase two hares at one time," Chekhov said in Garnett's translation, "the proverb about trying to catch two hares has given to no one more sleepless nights than to me." [26] Chekhov's medicine might save his countrymen's lives; his writing might give him some measure of immortality.

On October 7, 1888, the Division of Russian Language and Letters of the Academy of Sciences awarded Chekhov the distinguished Pushkin Prize for his story *In the Twilight*. All the doors of Russia's literary powers now were more or less open to him. He made close friends with one of the leading editors and publishers in Moscow, A. S. Suvorin. Chekhov was widely acknowledged as possibly a major, new, literary talent yet he never suffered from a swelled head, nor lost his distinct sense of balance.

Chekhov's favorite authors were Maupassant, Flaubert, Korolenko and Tolstoy. In honest realism, he belongs to the tradition of Pushkin, Gogol, Turgenev, and Dostoievsky. In form, however, even Tolstoy regarded Chekhov as a unique impressionist. In the hectic activity of his double career, Chekhov wrote these extant plays—the long plays marked with a single asterisk:

Platonov or	*The Proposal* (1889)
A Country Scandal (1881)*	*Tatyana Repina*
On the Highway (1885)	*The Wood Demon**
On the Harmfulness of Tobacco	*The Wedding* (1890)
(1886–1903)	*The Anniversary* (1892)
Swan Song (1887)	*The Night Before the Trial* (1895)
*Ivanov**	*The Sea Gull* (1896)*
The Bear (1888)	*Uncle Vanya* (1898)*
The Tragedian in Spite of Him-	*The Three Sisters* (1900)*
self	*The Cherry Orchard* (1904)*

A major turning point in Chekhov's life came in 1889 when his taste of literary fame gave him a guilty conscience as a doctor. From his reading, Chekhov realized that millions of Russians were freighted off to penal servitude in Siberian exile. He arranged to cross Siberia to study Russia's cruellest penal colony, Sahalin Island. "I want to write some 100 or 200 pages," he said in Garnett's translation of a letter to Suvorin, dated March 9, 1889, "and so do something, however little, for medical science, which as you are aware, I have neglected shockingly . . ." [27] That year, his brother, Nikolai, died of tuberculosis. Perhaps Chekhov was also thinking of what had happened to quite a few students at the University of Moscow as an aftermath of the assassination of Czar Alexander II. For all his precarious health, Chekhov seemed to find in his robust purpose a palladium against the hazards of a 10,000 mile journey to Sahalin Island through drought, flood and blizzard over plains, mountains, and rivers, traveling by carriage, horseback, sleigh, boat, and on foot. He started about April 15, 1890, and arrived on July 11. He stayed at Sahalin Island for three months.

"I made the rounds of every settlement, entered every cabin and spoke with every individual; I used a card system and have already accounted for approximately ten thousand convicts and penal settlers," Chekhov wrote Suvorin on September 11, 1890.[28] He observed convict life at its most commonplace: flogging, obscenity, poverty, forced labor, child prostitution, ignorance and apish brutality. Sahalin gave Chekhov a spiritual rebirth whose aura was to show in his plays. He rebelled against Tolstoy's doctrine of non-resistance as the best way to overcome evil; at Sahalin Island, he had seen non-resistance steadily degrade human beings to beasts. Chekhov became a humanist, declaring, "The highest and most sacred task of civilized man is to serve his neighbor and we are endeavoring to serve as best we can."[29]

Chekhov set out for home by way of boat, making port in Asia, sailing through the Suez Canal, and winding up in Italy which he toured. He took a train home to Moscow, arriving on December 8, 1890. His report, *The Island of Sahalin,* appeared in 1893, and the shocking, sensational realities forced some reform. In the cholera years of 1892 to 1893, Chekhov from his country home at Melikhovo gave free medical treatment to hundreds of peasants, helped check the epidemic in a territory of twenty-five villages, and followed through by assisting in organizing famine relief. "Work is what is wanted," he wrote A. S. Suvorin December 9, 1890, "and the rest can go to the devil."[30] On March 27th, 1894, Chekhov reaffirmed his transformation in a letter to Suvorin, "—in electricity and heat and love of man there is something greater than chastity and abstinence from meat."[31]

Chekhov went on writing to greater and greater public acclaim and financial success, the kind given to literary demi-gods. Fyodor Marx, one of Russia's leading publishers, on January 26, 1899, contracted with Chekhov to pay him 75,000 rubles for the right to publish his collected works, and all works to come. Chekhov must have had his prognosis in mind.

During his days at medical school, frantic with almost instant journalism in his stories, Chekhov and his family kept a kind of perpetual open house. They didn't have much, but everyone was welcome. The congeniality continued in more affluent days at Melikhovo and Yalta. "I positively cannot live without guests. When I am alone, for some reason," said Chekhov in Simmons' translation, "I become terrified just as though I were alone in a frail little boat on a great ocean." [32] Chekhov had hundreds of friends as his correspondence shows, but his closest friends were: the publishing tycoon, Suvorin; the literary titan, Tolstoy; the landscape painter, Levitan; and the married lady and would-be writer, Lydia Avilova.

Of his own disposition, Chekhov wrote Suvorin in Garnett's translation, "In women I love beauty above all things; and in the history of mankind, culture, expressed in carpets, carriages with springs, and keenness of wit." [33] Once when asked why he was so fond of churchbells, Chekhov replied after a pause, "That is all that is left to me of religion."

By 1897, Chekhov's tuberculosis took a critical turn for the worse, and under strict doctor's orders, he went to the sunny, gentle, and healthful climate of Yalta in the Crimea. Hemorrhoids and heart palpitations made his ill health worse.

In September of 1898, at rehearsals of *The Sea Gull*, he met the leading lady of the Moscow Art Theatre, Olga Knipper. The two fell deeply in love and were married in a Moscow church on May 25, 1901. Olga did not need Chekhov's support, for she continued to earn 25,000 to 40,000 rubles each winter season as the star of the Moscow Art Theatre. Chekhov remained largely isolated at Yalta to keep his tuberculosis in check. [34]

On July 2, 1904, Chekhov died of tuberculosis at Baden Weiler in the Black Forest, muttering, "Ich sterbe," and sipping a glass of champagne—a kind of gallant final gesture suggesting that, after all, perhaps he had squeezed the last drop of serf's blood out of him. Chekhov's body was brought to Moscow in a railway freight car marked "Fresh Oysters" likely with ice packing. In a further grim, farcical twist as incredible as life, the coffin of a General Keller, a casualty of the Manchurian War, was mistaken for Chekhov's, and part of the crowd of 200 or so, assembled at the railroad station in Moscow to mourn Chekhov, went marching off after the General. [35] Chekhov was buried beside his father at the Nvodevichii Convent in Moscow.

Chekhov used irony very much in his plays, perhaps because he saw so much irony in his own life. He won great literary distinction with the Pushkin Prize at twenty-eight, but tuberculosis was soon to become his inseparable, grim companion and eventually kill him. He was a successful physician who had the greatest success as a writer, but many writers so envied him that Chekhov said, "If I were to shoot myself I would give nine-tenths of my friends and admirers the greatest satisfaction." [36] He was desperately racing against time, but he found time to constructively criticize the work of many aspiring writers. His sister, Mariya, or "Masha" as he endearingly called her, gave him the best years of her life taking care of all his trivia so he would be free to work his talent. When Chekhov married Olga Knipper, "Masha" was left a bitter spinster. He came to earn huge sums of money but could not live within his income. He had perhaps one of his dearest friends in Suvorin, but he broke with Suvorin over Suvorin's press policy of anti-Semitism during the Dreyfus affair. Chekhov was made an honorary literary member of the St. Petersburg Academy of Science, but when the Czar annulled Gorky's membership on political grounds, Chekhov in protest resigned. Chekhov became great by writing, but he said, "It's hard to combine a desire to live and a desire to write." [37] He had married Olga Knipper hoping that she would bear him a son before he died, but Olga suffered a miscarriage and was left barren. So often in a play of Chekhov's, a character has only to want something very much, and we may be reasonably sure that he will not get it. After all, Chekhov himself didn't.

II

COMMERCIAL CONSIDERATIONS AFFECTING CHEKHOV'S PLAYWRITING

Chekhov's fame, and so his commercial value, in a sense has grown steadily since his death. In Russia he is in a state of communist canonization. Ilya Ehrenburg estimated that the total soviet publication of Chekhov's works has reached about 50,000,000 copies. If the total is less in any other one country, the sum total of other countries is undoubtedly greater than in Russia alone. There is hardly a reputable repertory theatre in the world that does not include some play by Chekhov.

Usually the most saleable of all literary wares even today is humor. As a medical student, Chekhov found in his natural bent for making others laugh a quick remedy for his own and his family's chronic financial troubles, which he likened to an aching tooth. He catered to a ready and steady market for laughs with humorous sketches specifically drawn up for such magazines as *Alarm Clock*, *Dragon Fly*, and *Fragments*. From the rejection of his two early efforts in playwriting —*Platonov*, by the Moscow Imperial Maly Theatre, and *On the High Road*, by the censor—he learned to shy away from playwriting for the more saleable humorous journalism which he later called "all sorts of rubbish." [38]

When Chekhov returned to playwriting on February 17, 1886, with the monologue, *On the Harmfulness of Tobacco*, published in *The St. Petersburg Gazette*, he had a career in medicine and wrote as a lucrative hobby. His new bid in drama was in the humblest form of all, the stage monologue, doubling, in fact, as journalism. In early January of 1887, Chekhov turned out another monologue, *Swansong*, based upon his story, *Kalhas*, written in 1886. *Swansong* depicted the conditions of the Russian stage as seen through the diagnostic eye of an aging alcoholic actor on his last legs.

Chekhov returned to more ambitious playwriting only when the then important Moscow theatre manager, F. A. Korsh, twice in two years asked him to write a play. "I wrote the play quite unexpectedly," Chekhov informed his brother, Alexander, in a letter dated October 10-12, 1887, "after a conversation with Korsh." [39] The first draft took only ten days; the work, *Ivanov*, was to yield Chekhov 8% of the box-office gross. Korsh produced the play in Moscow on November 19, 1887, to a widely mixed reception. Chekhov revised the play to meet criticism, especially of the ending in which Ivanov patly dropped dead of a heart attack just before his wedding. He learned the commercial value of revision in playwriting when the new version scored a smash-hit in its opening night at St. Petersburg on January 31, 1889; most reviews agreed with that of *The Petersburg Gazette*: "the triumph of a truly powerful talent . . . Its success was colossal . . ." [40] The revival on Broadway in May, 1966, starring John Gielgud and Vivien Leigh, demonstrates that for today the ending is still "wrong;" Ivanov's suicide offstage just before his wedding shows that, for all its excellent sums along the way, the whole play still doesn't add up right.

What kept Chekhov writing plays? The virtual certainty of Korsh producing them; furthermore by October 7, 1888, Chekhov was in demand as winner of the Pushkin Prize. "The Novel is a lawful wife,"

Chekhov wrote Pleshchev on January 15, 1889, showing he had a dubious attitude toward the stage, "but the stage is a noisy, flashy, insolent mistress." [41]

Beginning with *The Bear,* written on February 22, 1888, Chekhov in the course of the next four years turned out a series of one-act plays or, as he called them, "vaudevilles," with a sharp eye for the market. *The Bear,* itself, was built of proven guts and fur. Chekhov had seen N. N. Solovtsov, a huge actor with a voice like a double-bass, portraying an unruly sea-dog being tamed by a society woman in a Russian version of Pierre Berton's farce, *Les Jirons de Cadillac;* Chekhov's *The Bear,* or *The Boor* as it is often called, was deliberately drawn as the Russian equivalent of the French model of the beast.

The Bear became Chekhov's most successful one-act play and still is. Like it, his later one-acts were meant for variety shows or for curtain-raisers to long plays, and featured Chekhov's most saleable commodity—his warm humor. They offered Russian characters with broad public identification in romance, Russian style. They had the vitality of heady leading roles. They were usually based upon his successful stories. In late 1888, to illustrate, Chekhov wrote *The Proposal,* a kind of repeat of *The Bear,* a battle of the sexes, ending in capitulation with a marriage proposal. On May 3, 1889, he wrote *The Tragedian in Spite of Himself* based upon his short story, *One of Many,* written in 1887 and telling of a Russian suburban commuter who must remember his wife's and her friend's errands for him to do in town. In October, 1889, he wrote *The Wedding,* based upon two short stories written five years earlier, *A Marriage of Convenience* and *A Wedding with a General. The Wedding* lampoons the lower middle-class custom of hiring some retired, high ranking military figure to attend a shop-keeper's marriage to give it a high-class tone. Chekhov wrote his last one-act play, *The Anniversary,* in December, 1891, basing it on his short story, *A Helpless Creature,* published four years earlier. *The Anniversary* cordially pokes fun at a Russian private banker in his family life and in his dealings with his customers and hired help. *The Bear* had shown Chekhov there was fun and quick money in vaudevilles, and he wrote Suvorin on December 23, 1888, "Subjects for one-act plays sprout out of me like oil from the soil of Baku." [42]

A commercial failure very nearly crippled Chekhov's creative sensibilities for more playwriting. A few weeks before Christmas of 1889, the actor-manager Solovtsov read Chekhov's play, *The Wood Demon,* based on an abandoned collaboration with Suvorin. Solovtsov found enough of Chekhov's spell-binding in the play to pay him 1,000 rubles to revise the work in time for a Christmas opening. Chekhov completed the revision in four days. Put into a slap-dash production, *The Wood Demon* opened on December 27, 1889, and fell apart. "My *Wood Demon*," said Chekhov in despair, "is flopped and bust." [43] The great shock of the failure kept Chekhov from ever allowing the play to be published in his lifetime. It also tempered his judgment so he did not release another full length play for about six years. In fact, it took some of Chekhov's powerful friends in the Moscow theatre, —Suvorin, Nemirovich-Danchenko, and Sumatov-Yuzhin—to rally his spirits for another try.

Chekhov's *The Sea Gull* opened in St. Petersburg on October 17, 1896, at the Alexandrinsky Theatre, and this second failure of a full length play left Chekhov, already in failing health, all but shattered psychologically. "After the performance that night and next day," Chekhov wrote A. F. Koni on November 11, 1896, "I was assured I had hatched out nothing but idiots, that my play was clumsy from the stage point of view, that it was not clever, that it was even senseless, and so on and so on." [44] Chekhov also wrote Nemirovich-Danchenko, "Never will I write these plays, or try to produce them, not if I live to be 700 years old." [45] Possibly Chekhov might have kept his word if the Moscow Art Theatre hadn't come along.

What won Chekhov over to another venture with the once downed *The Sea Gull* was the persistent and enthusiastic pleading of Nemirovich-Danchenko, Stanislavsky's co-producer at the Moscow Art Theatre. *The Sea Gull* as performed by the Moscow Art Theatre opened on December 17, 1898, and this time the bird took off on the kind of flight reserved for classics. The power of *The Sea Gull*'s success literally lifted the Moscow Art Theatre from the verge of bankruptcy, for their previous five plays in repertory had been abysmal failures. What made all the difference was the new Stanislavsky-Danchenko approach to directing the play, an approach that was to revolutionize modern acting and directing. Stanislavsky and Danchenko now took over the function that Korsh originally had in luring Chekhov to write plays.

Chekhov's liaison with the Moscow Art Theatre almost ended after *The Sea Gull* because Chekhov thought Stanislavsky had misinterpreted the role of Trigorin. Chekhov actually offered his next play, *Uncle Vanya,* to the Moscow Imperial Maly Theatre; his play was accepted on condition that he alter it to satisfy the objection that in Czarist Russia no cultivated person would try to shoot an ex-professor, for a professor emeritus had the august equivalent rank of a general. Chekhov turned his back on the Maly Theatre and returned to the Moscow Art Theatre for *Uncle Vanya*'s production. Chekhov thereafter wrote all his plays with the Moscow Art Theatre in mind as his producer. Stanislavsky confided in his star, Olga Knipper, who was later to marry Chekhov, "However you regard it, our theatre is Chekhov's, and without him it will go badly for us." [46]

In writing his plays, Chekhov was practical enough to deliberately create roles with an eye to suitable and available acting talent. In creating *The Bear,* for instance, he fashioned the central role of Madam Popov to suit Korsh's leading lady, Rhychinskaya, and the complementary role of Smirnov, to suit Korsh's leading man, a giant with a basso profundo voice, Solovstov. Chekhov wrote Stanislavsky, "When I was writing Lopahin, I thought of it as a part for you." [47] And of the leading lady in *The Cherry Orchard,* he wrote Olga Knipper in Garnett's translation, *Letters of Anton P. Tchekhov to Olga L. Knipper,* "Lyubov Andreyevna will be played by you. . ."

Chekhov thought he really knew what the public wanted. "The bourgeoisie is very fond of so-called practical types and novels with happy endings," he wrote Suvorin on April 26, 1893, "since they soothe it with the idea that one can both accumulate capital and preserve innocence, be a beast and at the same time be happy." [48] Chekhov, however, wrote Nemirovich-Danchenko on November 2, 1903, "the whole idea of a 'people's' theatre and 'people's' literature is foolishness and lollipops for the people. We musn't bring Gogol down to the people but raise the people up to Gogol." [49] "The public has always been a flock which neeeded good shepherds and dogs," he wrote in a letter to Suvorin November 7, 1888, "and it has always gone in the direction in which the shepherds and dogs drove it." [50]

Critics surely had a powerful effect at the box-office for Chekhov, but after writing for twenty-five years he told Gorky, "Critics are like horse flies which prevent the horse from ploughing." [51] "I don't remember a single remark of any value," recollected Chekhov of critics, "or one word of valuable advice." [52] The critics Chekhov came across did not meet his standards, for he believed that just as whole civilizations had vanished from the face of the earth for lack of historians, "In the same way," Chekhov wrote to Suvorin on December 23, 1888, "a number of lives and works of art disappear before our very eyes owing to the complete absence of criticism." [53] Chekhov admitted he needed criticism: "And then I would take trouble over my work, and I should know what I was working for . . ." Censorship, itself, Chekhov thought, would be unnecessary if critics as well as authors were on the job: "no thinking will discover a better police for literature than the critics and the author's own conscience." [54]

III

AESTHETIC CONSIDERATIONS AFFECTING CHEKHOV'S PLAYWRITING

Aesthetics struck Chekhov as mainly a kind of highflown double-talk. Terms like "tendency," "realism," "artistic," and "dramatic" he found to be wearisome half-truths. "I divide all works into two classes: those I like and those I don't," he wrote Shtecheglov on March 22, 1890; "I have no other criterion, and if you ask me why I like Shakespeare and don't like Zlatovratsky, I don't venture to answer . . ." [55]

Chekhov distrusted aesthetics, but he still had a definite credo as an artist:

> My holy of holies is the human body, health, intelligence, talent, inspiration, love, and the most absolute freedom—freedom from violence and lying, whatever forms they may take. This is the program I would follow if I were a great artist.[56]

He amplified this program largely piece-meal in his letters. "An artist must always work, always think," he told Ladzhensky, "for he can't live otherwise." [57]

Like the classicists, Chekhov believed that the artist sees life clearly and sees it whole; "muck heaps play a very respectable part in the landscape," he wrote Madam Keselyov on January 14, 1887, ". . . the evil passions are as inherent in life as the good ones." [58] Chekhov, moreover, wrote Suvorin on May 30, 1888, "The artist must not be the judge of his characters and of their conversations, but merely an impartial witness . . ." [59]

Chekhov believed that the tell-tale sign of the artist is plasticity of perception in his work; "you feel superbly," he wrote Gorky from Yalta on December 3, 1898, "you are plastic; that is, when you describe a thing, you see it and touch it with your hands. That is real art." [60] Chekhov believed that the great artist has an objective which the public senses with all its being. "One who wants nothing, hopes for nothing, and fears nothing," Chekhov confided in Suvorin by letter in November 1892, "cannot be an artist." [61] "It is bad for an artist to tackle what he does not understand," Chekhov wrote Suvorin from Moscow on October 27, 1888, in Lederer's translation, *Selected Letters of Anton Chekhov*, ". . . his circle is as limited as that of any other specialist—this I repeat and on this I always insist." [62] This might explain why Chekhov never wrote a costume drama.

As for politics and the writer, Chekhov penned Suvorin from Nice on February 6, 1898, "But great writers and artists should engage in politics only to the extent necessary to defend themselves against politics." [63] As a struggling medical student, Chekhov had kept quite clear of politics, but once famous and rather secure, though he never wrote to propagandize, he dared house Gorky when the Czarist regime had him under police surveillance. Did Chekhov believe the artist did nothing to influence his society in vital matters? He wrote Tikhonov in 1902:

> You tell me that people cry at my plays. But that was not why I wrote them. It is Alexeyev [Stanislavsky] who made my characters into crybabies. Also I wanted to say honestly to people—"Take a look at yourselves, see how bad and dreary are your lives." The important thing is for people to realize *that;* for, when they do, they will most certainly create another, better life for themselves. I shall not live to see it, but I know that it will be quite different, quite unlike our present life.[64]

Of the nature of drama, Chekhov told Mme V. S. Boutov, "Drama takes place inside a man and not in external manifestations." And Chekhov in a letter to Gorky, dated April 25, 1899, from Moscow, recalled a very astute comment by Tolstoy about Gorky's work: "He said, 'You can invent anything you please, but not psychology, and Gorky is full of psychological inventions. He has described what he hasn't felt.'" [65]

Art, itself, Chekhov thought unpredictable. "Art, especially the stage," he pictured to Olga Knipper in October, 1899, in Nabokoff's translation, "is a region where it is impossible to walk without stumbling . . . Should you think that *Uncle Vanya* did not have the success you expected, please go to bed and sleep soundly." [66] And Chekhov became convinced from his early failures, "Talent and freshness can spoil many a good work . . . Maturity is needed——secondly . . . the sense of personal freedom." [67] The dramatist also needed a pioneering spirit. "The drama must either degenerate completely, or assume a completely new form," said Chekhov in Kotliansky's translation. "We cannot even imagine what the theatre will be like in a hundred years." [68]

IV

CHEKHOV'S WORKING METHODS IN PLAYWRITING

Genesis

Chekhov more or less stimulated his creative spirit by relying upon a fixed, daily working schedule. "One has to work very hard," he told Bunin. "Every day. One must work without fail." [69] He generally rose at seven in the morning, and he ate very sparingly. "Coffee in the morning and chicken broth at mid-day," he told Bunin. "If I don't, my work suffers." [70] By eight or nine in the morning Chekhov was at his work table. "To work and to look as though I were working, from nine in the morning till dinner," said Chekhov in Garnett's translation, "and from evening tea till bedtime, has become a habit with me, and in that respect I am just like a government clerk." [71] Though his working hours were fixed, his mind never was quite at rest. "An artist must always work, always think, for he can't live otherwise," Chekhov told Ladzhensky.

This heavy working schedule was typical of Chekhov only while writing was his career and when ill health made medicine more of an avocation. When writing was his avocation and medicine his career, Chekhov wrote at leisure two or three hours a day and a little at night, time enough only for minor efforts. For relaxation and to invigorate his subconscious mind to solve his writing problems, Chekhov was given to walking, watching the sea, gardening, reading, or possibly visiting. He preferred to write in summer, for then he felt the fine weather gave him a greater objectivity and freedom. He smoked, and occasionally he drank liquor. Once tuberculosis struck him hard, he had to quit smoking. He was so delicately adjusted to work only in the familiar surroundings of his study that in strange surroundings he could work only with great difficulty, if at all.

"An artist observes, selects, guesses, and combines," Chekhov wrote describing his creative activity to Suvorin in correspondence, October 27, 1888, "—and this in itself presupposes a problem." [72] Then Chekhov elaborated, "To deny that artistic creation involves problems and purposes would be to admit that an artist creates without reflection, without design, under a spell . . ." "The important thing," said Chekhov, "is to have a play in which one can feel the author's shaping idea." [73] Concerning the origin of the "problem" or "the author's shaping idea," Chekhov said, "I can only write from reminiscences, and I have never written directly from nature." [74] Where did Chekhov get his reminiscences? "I am convinced," recollected Alexander Kuprin of his friendship with Chekhov, "that Chekhov talked to a scholar and a peddler, a beggar and a litterateur, with a prominent Zemstvo worker and a suspicious monk or shop assistant or a small postman with the same attention and curiosity." [75]

A few of Chekhov's notebooks remain to illustrate the kind of observation he jotted down and no doubt chose to reminisce about. He noted prospective titles like "The title of a play: The Bat." [76] He noted expressive names like "Rosalie Ossipovna Aromat." [77] He noted little impressions of character like: "A play: to avoid having visitors, Z pretends to be a regular tippler, although he drinks nothing." [78] He noted fragmentary action like:

> N. rings at the door of an actress. He is nervous. His heart beats; at the critical moment he gets into a panic and runs away. The maid opens the door and sees nobody. He returns, rings again, but has not the courage to go in. In the end, the porter comes out and gives him a thrashing.[79]

He noted observations suggesting basic truths or prospective themes or insights like: "Love, friendship, respect, do not unite people as much as common hatred for something." [80]

Incubation and Characterization

Having posed the "problem" or "the author's shaping idea" through reminiscence, Chekhov hinted he found the answer or development the same way. "To write a play in the contemporary style or taste," Chekhov said in Friedland's translation, "there is one secret that you must know . . . one must write the play with closed eyes." [81] Kuprin noticed that every moment Chekhov seemed preoccupied with weighing, defining, remembering. V. Tkonov also noticed that Chekhov always seemed to be thinking. "The big things will remain," Chekhov said to Kuprin of reminiscence, "and the details you can always invent or find." [82]

Broadly speaking, Chekhov adapted to the drama his technique of creating a short story or a novel. He wrote to his brother Alexander on May 10, 1886, to help Alexander's writing (Simmons' translation):

> In my opinion, a true description of nature must be very brief and possess the character of relevance . . . commonplaces must be excluded . . . one ought to seize upon the little particulars, grouping them in such a way that when you close your eyes after reading, you see a picture . . . Details are also the thing in the sphere of psychology. God preserve us from generalizations. Best of all, avoid depicting the hero's state of mind; you ought to make it clear from the hero's actions. It is not necessary to portray many active figures. The center of gravity should be two persons—he and she.[83]

Chekhov elaborated his method of planning a story in a letter to Suvorin of October 27, 1888 (Garnett's translation):

> And so in planning a story one is bound to think first about its framework: from a crowd of leading or subordinate characters one selects one person only—wife or husband; one puts him on the canvas and paints him alone, making him prominent, while the others one scatters over the canvas like small coin, and the result is something like the vault of heaven; one big moon and a number of very small stars around it. But the moon . . . can only be understood if the stars, too, are intelligible . . .[84]

Throughout the creation of a play Chekhov kept in mind, "The stage reflects in itself the quintessence of life so one must not include on it anything that is superfluous." [85] To try to achieve this aim, Chekhov became convinced that "the drama must either degenerate completely or assume a completely new form;" a suggestion of that "new form" for Chekhov is found in a letter of February 18, 1889, which he wrote to Leonyev and which is translated by Magarshack in his book, *Chekhov, the Dramatist*:

> It is necessary that on the stage everything should be as complex and as simple as in life. People are having dinner, and while they're having it, their future happiness may be decided or their lives may be about to be shattered.[86]

Chekhov's conception of the very nature of drama is implied in this continued observation so typical of his own method of developing a play:

> The demand is made that the hero and heroine (of a play) should be dramatically effective. But in life, people do not shoot themselves or

hang themselves, or fall in love, or deliver themselves of clever sayings every minute. They spend most of their time eating, drinking, running after women or men, talking nonsense. It is therefore necessary that this should be shown on stage. A play ought to be written in which the people come and go, dine, talk of the weather or play cards not because the author wants it but because that is what happens in real life. Life on the stage should be as it really is and the people, too, should be as they are and not stilted.[87]

Chekhov found that his medical studies had a "great influence" upon his writing. In a letter to G. I. Rossolimo from Yalta on October 11, 1899, he said, "It is probably due to my close association with medicine that I have succeeded in avoiding many mistakes."[88] Medicine forced him to see things as they really were if he were to help human beings in crisis; he must have developed a physician's detachment yet zeal for noticing symptoms and seeing troubled human beings at all levels of life in terms of a case history.

Chekhov told Kuprin, "For God's sake don't read your work to anyone till it is published."[89] Perhaps Chekhov was tight-lipped for fear of diverting his creative drive or inviting premature criticism. During incubation, Chekhov worked on and off at a number of creations, thereby readying a new work for the time when the work already in hand was finished. "Subjects for five stories and two novels are languishing in my head," said Chekhov, ". . . and some of the characters have grown old without managing to be written. In my head there is a whole army of people asking to be let out."[90]

How much Ibsen affected Chekhov's thinking during incubation is conjectural. Chekhov on November 7, 1903, did write a letter to Vishnevski, an actor with the Moscow Art Theatre, and say, "Since I am coming to Moscow soon, please set aside one seat for me for *Pillars of Society*. I want to have a look at this amazing Norwegian play and will even pay for the privilege. Ibsen is my favorite author, you know."[91] But according to Nemirovich-Danchenko, Chekhov said of Ibsen's *Wild Duck* during a rehearsal, "Look here, Ibsen does not know life. In life it does not happen like that."[92]

Knowledge of the incubation of specific plays of Chekhov is fragmentary. Certainly reminiscence to create a "shaping idea" preceded the actual writing. In his early efforts, Chekhov suggests he created as he wrote—"I wrote as a bird sings."[93] He could even work somehow in his family's crowded, noisy apartment with continual distractions. In his later and great plays, however, the incubation was long, tortuous, and often tantalizing. So, for example, Chekhov told his brother

Alexander that he wrote the long, early play, *Ivanov,* quite by surprise after talking with the theatrical manager, Korsh—"went to bed, thought of a theme, and wrote it." [94] The first draft was almost simultaneous with genesis and incubation and took him only ten days with a break of three or four days in which he did nothing or worked at something else. But after the failure of *The Wood Demon,* Chekhov in a much chastened mood wrote Suvorin in December of 1889, "There is not a single line that has a serious literary significance in my eyes . . . I have to write conscientiously, completely, and with feeling, write not five sheets in one month but one sheet in five months." [95]

Chekhov now required much time and the solitude of his study to write plays to his satisfaction. *The Sea Gull,* for instance, the very first of his long plays to be regarded a modern classic, took about three years for genesis and incubation, in recollecting incidents and people widely separated in time and place, quite apart from the actual writing. Perhaps the first experience exciting the creation of *The Sea Gull* was Chekhov's recollection of the deep poignancy of an innocent creature's death and Chekhov's own part in it. On April 1, 1892, Chekhov went hunting with his artist friend, Isaak Levitan, at Chekhov's country estate, Melikhovo. Levitan shot but did not quite kill a beautifully plumed wood-cock. When Chekhov picked up the bleeding bird, it fixed its black eyes pathetically upon him. The guilt-stricken Levitan then begged Chekhov to kill the bird and end its suffering. Chekhov killed it. "One lovely, amorous creature less in the world," Chekhov wrote Suvorin on April 18, 1892, "and two fools returned home and sat down to supper." [96]

By June 3, 1892, Chekhov again wrote Suvorin: "I have an interesting subject for a comedy, but I haven't thought of its ending so far . . . I can't get those endings right! The hero has either to get married or shoot himself. There is no other solution." [97] The hero, Konstantin, in *The Sea Gull* was to shoot himself at the very end; the quote suggests how early in a play's conception Chekhov was concerned with the end for its influence upon the total effect. A quick review of the endings of some of Chekhov's other long plays shows he tended to favor the hero to shoot himself—or the equivalent. *Ivanov* is about to end in Ivanov's remarriage, but the guilt-stricken Ivanov shoots himself. In *Uncle Vanya,* we have a variation: the disillusioned Uncle Vanya tries to shoot the pretentious Professor Serebyrakov twice but, in bungling ineffectuality, misses. The attempt at murder nevertheless reinforces the Professor and his wife Elena's decision to leave their country estate, for Uncle Vanya might not miss the next time. In *The Three Sisters,* the Baron Tusenbach really takes his own life by deliberately dueling with a man he knows is a far better duelist. In *The Cherry Orchard,* no one dies at the end except that a whole social order is on its death-bed, and another is well out of the delivery-room and growing fast. What made all the difference in the endings of each play was Chekhov's belief that, through the implications of marriage or self-destruction, men made a choice most revealing of their soul-struggles.

To return to the incubation of *The Sea Gull,* Chekhov in the three years following the death of the wood-cock added new characters and incidents drawn from life. So, for example, the character of the village schoolteacher, Medvendenko, is suggested in a letter Chekhov wrote Suvorin on November 27, 1894, directly after Chekhov had visited a village school. The teacher was grey at thirty, tried to support a wife, four children, and himself, on a salary of 23 rubles a month and, no matter what turn the conversation took, changed it to mention his miserable salary. Besides, Chekhov's brother, Ivan, was a teacher and so was his sister, Mariya. In the summer of 1895, several things happened suggesting the final action of *The Sea Gull.* For one thing, the artist Levitan was visiting at the estate of a rich woman, A. N. Turchaninova, who with her daughter so competed for Levitan's affection that in a quixotic gesture of despair he shot himself in the head and suffered a superficial scalp wound. As Levitan's close friend, Chekhov was quickly summoned and stayed for five days to doctor him and listen to his troubles. For another thing, two friends of Chekhov—a playwright, Ignatius Potapenko, and his mistress, Lydia Mizinov, a jolly stout blond—had an unhappy love affair paralleling that of the novelist, Trigorin, and the struggling actress, Nina, in *The Sea Gull.* The shooting of the wood-cock (some accounts make it a sea gull), the competition of A. N. Turchaninova and her daughter for Levitan's love, Levitan's attempted "suicide," the setting of that very country estate in the lake district of Novgorod province, and the unhappy romance of Potapenko and Lydia, all contributed to the structure of *The Sea Gull* over a three year period of coalescing through reminiscence. Furthermore, as Magarshack suggests, Nina has a counterpart in Chekhov's story written six years earlier, *A Boring Story,* in the character of Katya, a stage-struck young lady who is made pregnant, is jilted, loses her child, and then in despair decides she is through with the stage, for she had no talent really. Nina, by contrast, in Chekhov's emphasis upon redemption through work, chooses to carry on.

In writing his next play, *The Three Sisters,* Chekhov worked from reminiscence about fifteen years old. In this perspective of time, Chekhov recollected his experiences at Voskresnesk near Moscow where he had his first medical practice and, quite likely through a medical visit, had come to meet the commander of the local battery, Colonel Mayevsky, who had three young daughters and a lively circle of military friends; Chekhov might have known them well socially, for he was "good company." Chekhov had written a short story, *Children,* about these sisters. In *The Three Sisters* they emerged full grown as if Chekhov had revisited them. The affair of Masha parallels that of one of the officers, Lt. E. P. Yegorov. The cry of the daughters, "To Moscow, to Moscow!" is presumed a yearning of Chekhov's own exile which his illness imposed upon him at Yalta. "To Moscow, to Moscow!" Chekhov wrote Olga Knipper in November, 1903, in Simmons' translation. "That is not said by *Three Sisters* but by *One Husband.*" [98]

The genesis of *The Cherry Orchard,* and its incubation as well, seem to have been perfectly in the spirit of Chekhov's state of mind at the time. Throughout his life, as Chekhov himself said, he "squeezed the slave out of himself drop by drop," and now, in what he knew was his terminal tuberculosis, Chekhov through *The Cherry Orchard* gave his *apologia pro sua vita.* The play tells of the decline of the Russian aristocracy and the rise of the former serf class, and is written by a consummate artist of serf descent. The setting, the mood, and the theme of *The Cherry Orchard* took life from Chekhov's reminiscence of the summer of 1889 and from his abortive full length play of 1881, *Platonov.* In 1889, a noble family in Luke, Kharkov province, was so hard up that it rented its run-down estate to Chekhov and his family for the summer. The people of the community must have provided echoes of the noble family's days of glory and its attempt to adjust to a new world of business values. About twelve years later during a rehearsal of *The Three Sisters* (January 1901), Chekhov gave members of the Moscow Art Theatre a few hints about his new play as Stanislavsky recollected:

An open window, a branch of white cherries in blossom creeping into the room from the garden. Artiom (one of the actors of the Moscow

Art Theatre) as butler or steward. His master or mistress is ever in need of money, and in critical moments she turns for help to her butler or steward, who has managed to save up quite a considerable sum.[99]

It was only when the play was finally given a reading by the company that the full implication of this and other remarks could be appreciated, for Stanislavsky admitted that though Chekhov gave the company a few fleeting glimpses of the play he "gave us no notion at all of what it was to be about." According to Princess Nina Toumanova, Chekhov had spent many summers of his youth in Kharkov province where his favorite brother, the artist Nikolai, had died of tuberculosis. The drowning of little Grischa was probably something Chekhov remembered as a doctor called in on an emergency fairly common in the country. The auctioning off of the Ranevsky estate has a parallel in the life of the spendthrift, Sergei, in *Platonov,* which Chekhov had written as his first long play at twenty-one.

On October 1, 1902, Chekhov wrote Stanislavsky of *The Cherry Orchard,* "I have already a theme . . ."[100] In the next month or so, Chekhov's general health was so upset by the ravages of tuberculosis that he could hardly eat, yet he continued to dream up *The Cherry Orchard.* By January of 1903, Chekhov wrote the actress Komissarshevskaya, "It is quite true that I have already planned out my play and that I even have a title for it (*The Cherry Orchard*—this is still a secret), but I shall probably begin to write it not later than the end of February provided, of course, my health is good."[101] *The Cherry Orchard* was a good three years in growing from genesis through incubation before coming to fruition as a play.

Characterization

As earlier suggested in Chekhov's comment on story development, he tried usually to concentrate upon full portraiture of two leading characters, "he and she," with lesser characters sketched in for a meaningful background in depth. Chekhov modelled his characters after persons he had known and recollected—peasants, students, landowners, professors, doctors, literary men, military men, nobility, artists, and lovers. He shunned stereotypes. "Retired captains in the reserve, with huge red noses, newspaper reporters who drink, starving authors, consumptive women-toilers, honest young people without a flaw in their make-up, ideal maidens, good natured nurses," he cautioned, "all these have been described again and again and should be avoided as a pitfall."[102] "It is easier to write about Socrates," commented

Chekhov in 1894, "than about a lady or a cook." [103] Chekhov thought pretentious authors always try to create the great because they cannot create the little; he also implies that the public could immediately detect the falseness to life of a lady or a cook but not of a remote figure like Socrates.

Extant information about the development of Ivanov, in *Ivanov,* suggests Chekhov's approach to drawing a major character. "I have been cherishing the bold dream of summing up all that has hitherto been written about whining, miserable people," Chekhov wrote Suvorin in a letter on January 7, 1889, "and with my Ivanov saying the last word." [104] In a letter he had sent Suvorin a week earlier, Chekhov noted, "Ivanov and Lvov appear to my imagination to be living people . . . They are the result of observing and studying life." [105] The very significance of Ivanov's character gave the play a vital comment on the futility of the intelligentsia and of uselessness, a kind of conspicuous waste expected of a gentleman at the time. Ivanov marries a beautiful Jewess of rich family, expecting a large dowry, but finds instead that his wife is disinherited. The play shows his lost love, and his indifference and cruelty toward a wife dying from tuberculosis, as he carries on a love affair with another young heiress. Only the imminent marriage ceremony at the end, after Ivanov has buried his first wife, shows Ivanov his selfish, cruel, and crass nature. Then, no longer able to face his own soul, he kills himself. Chekhov called the suicide a "stage lie" and the play "my abortion." [106] The drawing of the character of Ivanov taught Chekhov the absolute need for adequate and truthful motivation in a major character's action.

In creating the characters for his next full length play, *The Wood Demon,* as indeed he did also with *Ivanov,* Chekhov left thumbnail sketches of each character. The importance he put upon these preliminary sketches may be gathered in his comment to Suvorin at the end of the sketches for *The Wood Demon:* "That is the whole scenario." Here, for instance, is Blagosvyetlov as noted by Chekhov on October 18, 1888, in Friedland's translation:

Alexander Platonich Blagosveyetlov, a member of the Imperial Council, has the White Eagle, receives a pension of 7,200 rubles. Deriving from the clergy, he has received his education at the seminary. The position he occupies has been attained through personal effort. In the past, not one blot on his scutcheon. Suffers from gout, rheumatism, insomnia, ringing in the ears. Acquired his real estate as a marriage portion. Has positive intellect. Can't stand mystics, fantastics, the possessed, lyrical people, bigots; does not believe in God, is accustomed to looking at the whole universe from the standpoint of business. Business, business, business, business—everything else is nonsense or charlatanism.[107]

This man, incidentally, seems in some traits a forerunner of Lopahin in *The Cherry Orchard,* with his emphasis upon "business."

The character sketches show that Chekhov repeatedly used contrast so that the characters were foils, crossed to conflict and so promote drama. The match for the businesslike Blagosvyetlov is his foolish, spendthrift son, Boris. Blagosvyetlov's well educated, lazy and bored daughter, Nastya, contrasts with the peasant-bred, hardworking, energetic Luba. The merry old Anuchin, who after a narrow escape from death believes that sincerity solves everything, is the opposite of the eighty-year-old pilgrim, Fedosia, an ex-soldier who gave his fortune to a monastery, and thinks the world is full of lying scoundrels. Finally there is Korovin, a young and poetic landowner who feels, like Chekhov, that culture is measured by the conservation of woodlands and who is almost the contrary of his competitor for Nastya's hand—Galakhov, a very rich State Councillor, official to the core, eager to enjoy life but unaware of quite how to go about it. The brief impressions of each character include such strokes as: age, status, income, occupation, health, family, desires, integrity, sincerity, frustrations, eating habits, behavior in public, sensibilities, and temperament. "I want Blagosvyetlov to feel he is surrounded by a lot of cranks," said Chekhov suggesting the point of view of his whole play. "We must show how Wood Demons affect women." [108]

With representative yet individually contrasted characters assembled to answer the problem posed in reminiscence, Chekhov expected the play to grow spontaneously. *The Wood Demon* did grow and fantastically fast. "After dinner, marching to and fro," said Chekhov, "I managed to slap together the first three acts, and I have just made a preliminary sketch of the fourth." [109] But the play proved to be faulty when tested on the public and taught Chekhov to distrust such speed in growth; the revision of the characterizations into *Uncle Vanya* suggested the value of time and maturation.

Throughout characterization Chekhov must have kept in mind, "The important thing is to have a play in which one can feel the author's shaping idea." [110] In his scenario, whether in his mind or in characterizations on paper, Chekhov's "shaping idea" worked out with the irony that he saw so deeply characteristic of his own life and of the life about him. "I am always in a good mood while I work," he said. "It has been pointed out that sombre, melancholy people always write gaily, while the works of cheerful souls are always depressing. And I am a joyous person." [111] Much of Chekhov's later life, of course, was one long whistle by a graveyard. Chekhovian irony is as typical of Chekhov's great plays as chiaroscuro is of Rembrandt's masterpieces. This irony therefore deserves very marked consideration for showing his way of thinking in developing the action from characterization, before beginning the dialogue. The method is plainly implied in the completed plays.

In *The Sea Gull*, for example, at first Nina and Konstantin are two young people so blissfully in love that he says of her, "I cannot live without her . . . ," [112] and she says to him, "My heart is full of you." [113] But once Nina has come to know the famous writer, Trigorin, she ironically gives up Konstantin for Trigorin, whom she now is sure fulfills her innocent dream of love. Trigorin, however, only has a backstreet affair with Nina for want of anything better to do, and possibly for "copy." Later he discards her.

Konstantin, as the son of the famous stage star, Arkadina, is so belittled by his mother about his playwriting, and so in despair over his love for Nina, that after one unsuccessful attempt he finally kills himself with a pistol. His mother says to Dr. Dorn, "I feel uneasy. Tell me, what's wrong with my son?" [114] But she knows she is stingy and unloving toward him, especially because his presence reminds both her and the public of her age. He calls her, "You miser!" [115] and she calls him, "You ragged beggar!" [116] and then they weep and comfort each other and ask forgiveness.

Nina admires Trigorin for his fame, glory, and happiness, which he tells her are to him "like a sweetmeat which I never taste." [117] He says of his work, "as soon as it is published I can't endure it, and I see that it is all wrong . . ." [118] Nina, like so many of Chekhov's leads, finds redemption not in love but in work—in her own instance through her acting, which deep suffering in love has vastly improved.

Even the image of the sea gull comes to have ironically different meanings to those most vitally concerned. Early in the action, Konstantin brings the dead sea gull to Nina's feet and says, "I was so mean as to kill this bird today . . . Soon I shall kill myself in the same way." [119] Trigorin, however, after talking with Nina about the dead sea gull says, "Oh, I am only making a note. A subject struck me (*putting away the note-book*). A subject for a short story: a young girl, such as you, has lived all her life beside a lake; she loves the lake like a sea gull, and is as free and happy as a sea gull. But a man comes by chance, sees her, and having nothing better to do, destroys her like that sea gull here." [120] After Nina's affair with Trigorin has resulted in a dead illegitimate child and Trigorin has left her, Konstantin says of Nina, "in her letters she kept repeating that she was a sea gull." [121] When Shamreyeff two years later shows Trigorin the stuffed sea gull, Trigorin ironically says of the whole incident, "I don't remember." [122] Finally, of course, Konstantin does kill himself, echoing his comment early in the play, "Soon I shall kill myself in the same way."

In *Uncle Vanya* the ironies of time never let up, like a hand that inevitably withers even as it grows more practiced. The aging Uncle Vanya finally realizes he has sacrificed the best years of his life managing the estate of his sister, Professor Serebryakov's deceased first wife, just to support the Professor to write now quite passé books on aesthetics: "The man has been lecturing and writing about art for twenty-five years, though he knows absolutely nothing about art." [123] Uncle Vanya, hopelessly in love with the retired professor's second wife, the twenty-seven year old, very beautiful Yelena, sees in this charming woman the happiness he missed in life. Yelena does not return Uncle Vanya's love. Sonya, however, the Professor's daughter by his first wife, loves Dr. Astrov who is the family physician and unhappily in love with Yelena. Yelena, in turn, loves Dr. Astrov but remains faithful to her gout-ridden, rheumatic, despotic old husband from a strict sense of decency. "I was attracted by him as a learned, celebrated man," Yelena tells Sonya in her big scene of reconciliation with Sonya. "It was not real love, it was all made up; but I fancied at the time it was real." [124] Yelena now ironically confesses, "I am very, very unhappy!" [125] The plain-looking Sonya says, "Oh, how awful it is that I am not beautiful!" [126] She could be loved by Dr. Astrov if only she were beautiful, for he himself told her, "What still affects me is beauty. That does stir me." [127]

Once Yelena discovers Uncle Vanya's and Dr. Astrov's unrequited love for her, she is determined to leave her country home to escape further temptation. The Professor is in the dark about all this. To please his wife, he decides to sell the estate and go to Kharkov if his in-laws allow it; and ironically, Uncle Vanya bitterly reminds the Professor, "The estate is free from debt and in good condition only owing to my personal efforts. And now that I am old I am to be kicked out of it!" [128] Uncle Vanya, enraged, gets his pistol to shoot the Professor for his ingratitude and, in his ineffectual way, misses twice. The only salvation for Uncle Vanya and Sonya, they each decide, is in work. "Those who will live a hundred or two hundred years after us," says Dr. Astrov, ". . . they will, perhaps, find a means of being happy." [129] As in *The Sea Gull*, happiness is not in the uncertainty of love, but in work.

In *The Three Sisters*, Chekhov again finds time dealing with human destinies quite ironically. Only the presence of the battery of soldiers in town makes the dreary provincial life at all somewhat lively and bearable for the three sisters, Olga, Masha, and Irina Prozorov, children of the former Brigadier General in command in the town and himself deceased a year. The three sisters carry on in the hope of returning to Moscow, whence they had come eleven years earlier; or as Olga says, "And only one yearning grows stronger and stronger . . . ," and Irina interrupts, "To go back to Moscow. To sell the house, to make an end of everything here, and off to Moscow . . ." [130] By the play's end, none of the sisters gets to go to Moscow or is likely to.

Lt. Colonel Vershinin, the new battery commander, is married to a suicidal, jealous wife, and carries on a hopeless love affair with Masha. The future to Vershinin will be indescribably beautiful in a few hundred years. Masha's husband, Kuligin, is naïve and boring to her. The brother, Andrey, blissfully marries the outwardly shy and insecure Natasha. But once she has a child, Natasha becomes loud-mouthed, brassy, shrewish, unfaithful and downright mean. Irina, whose faith is in redemption through work, and who labors diligently at the telegraph station, hopes to marry the reformed idler, aristocrat, and soldier, Baron Tusenbach, not out of love but out of loneliness; while the Baron ultimately becomes involved in a love-duel with staff Captain Solyony over Irina, and is shot to death. Olga, as headmistress in a girls' high school, finds herself a frustrated spinster—like Chekhov's sister, Masha. Love is not the answer for lasting happiness in this or in any play by Chekhov; love brings disillusionment to Masha, misery to Colonel Vershinin, regret to Andrey, bereavement to Irina, and unfulfilled longing to Olga. To Vershinin, "We must work and work, and happiness is the portion of our remote descendants."

When the town is half ravaged by fire, the disaster brings out the best and worst in people. The soldiers, ironically, save many civilians. Natasha, the civilian, however, uses the emergency to throw out poor old Anfisa, the three sisters' nurse and house-maid for thirty years, telling her, "Don't dare to sit down in my presence! Get up! Get out of the room!" [131] Andrey, who had hoped for a Moscow Professor-ship, has settled for a secretaryship on the local District School Board; he tries to drown his sorrows in drink and find luck in gambling ruinous to him. When Andrey had proposed to Natasha, he said, "I love you . . . as I have never loved anyone . . ." [132] but by the fourth act, he says of Natasha, now his wife, "A wife is a wife. She is a straightforward, upright woman, good natured perhaps, but for all that there is something in her which makes her no better than some petty, blind, hairy animal. Anyway, she is not a human being!" [133] When Tchebutykin brings word that the Baron was killed in a duel with Solyony, Irina weeps quietly and says, "I knew, I knew . . . ," [134] as if sure that the Baron wanted to be killed, knowing that Irina didn't really love him at all.

As the battery departs and the music fades away, the town goes into doldrums. Irina and Olga now see only work as redemption. "Life for us three sisters," Irina said earlier, "has not been beautiful yet; we have been stifled by it as plants are choked by weeds." [135]

In *The Cherry Orchard,* Chekhov's irony perhaps reaches its finest fulfillment in visual and psychological terms. Though warned re-peatedly by Lopahin of the outcome if she fails to be businesslike, Madame Ranevsky, who cannot come to terms with reality, finally finds that her ancestral home with its blossoming cherry orchard has been sold at auction. The purchaser is Lopahin, whose an-cestors were once serfs of the Ranevskys and who plans to do just what he advised Madame Ranevsky to do—to cut down the blossom-ing cherry trees and change the acreage into plots for week-end villas. Lopahin long expected to marry Madame Ranevsky's adopted daugh-ter, Varya, but sensing Varya's superior airs and antagonism toward him, he never proposed. Upon hearing at the farewell party that Lopahin had bought the Ranevsky estate, Varya cast down her house-keeper's keys in the middle of the ball-room floor, a public gesture of contempt not lost on the peasant-born Lopahin, who eventually picks up the keys and says with a smile, "She threw away the keys; she means to show she's not the housewife now (*jingles the keys*). Well, no matter." [136]

Telegraph lines stretch across the landscape as a sign of progress, but in the play they are used only to receive Madame Ranevsky's daily telegram from her worthless lover in France, a man she calls "my millstone" and to whom she eventually returns. Trofimov sees society's only hope in truth and hard work, but he himself is a "perpetual student," poor, mangy, somewhat confused, who has made his means in effect his end. In the third act, the farewell party of the Ranevskys goes on ironically in sham high spirits even as the estate is being auctioned off; ironically, too, as the old retainer, Firs, notes, "In old days we used to have generals, barons and admirals dancing at our balls, and now we send for the post-office clerk and the station master, and even they're not over-anxious to come." [137]

As in all his other plays, love promises happiness, but what happiness it might bring doesn't last: Madame Ranevsky has thrown away her life and her fortune on a gigolo; Lopahin would have possibly married Varya had she been more kind and less a snob; Trofimov and Anya are infatuated, but he cannot support her and his love is platonic. The impoverished country Squire, Semyonov-Pishtchik, who always believes something good will turn up, actually has a stroke of great fortune when English option-holders find aluminum on his land. Firs, who has viewed the emancipation of the Russian serf as "the great misfortune," is forgotten by the bankrupt aristocrats, the Ranevskys, who think he's off to the hospital and lock him up unwittingly in the liquidated mansion. The very symbolism of the title, *The Cherry Orchard,* has a great irony implied. The sentimental, charming, improvident aristocrat, Madame Ranevsky, says, "I love this house. I can't conceive of life without the cherry orchard, and if it really must be sold, then sell me with the orchard." [138] The seeker of truth, the student Trofimov, says, "Think only, Anya, your grandfather and great grandfather, and all your ancestors were slave-owners—the owners of living souls—and from every cherry in the orchard, from every leaf, from every trunk there are human creatures looking at you. Cannot you hear their voices? Oh, it's awful." [139]

Ironies of every size are implicit in the characters and their actions, as if life were basically "an unweeded garden"—a phrase Chekhov used and found in *Hamlet,* too—with the cross-pollination left to the winds of chance, and blooming at the mercy of the weather, insects, and animals. Love is always portrayed as unpredictably disappointing, and happiness lies only in work, especially in education, a kind of paraphrase of "good works." The unweeded garden needs much cultivation.

Is irony a cliché in Chekhov? No more a cliché than in life. The Hegelian dialectic, incidentally, was to see life entirely in terms of irony: thesis, antithesis, synthesis,—with the cycle repeating itself forever. Karl Marx's dialectical materialism implied the process stops in the communists' favor: a biased notion, like believing that time stands still. Aristotle, of course, observed that in the drama of his day the most powerful means of accelerating the action was through discovery and reversal, especially when combined in a climax; each of these devices, as in *Oedipus the King,* can be entirely ironical.

Chekhov's Sources of Freshness

Chekhov's distinctive impressionism has a protean quality depending somewhat upon the observer's eye. For Gorky, "No one understood as clearly and finely as Anton Chekhov the tragedy of life's trivialities, no one before him showed men with such merciless truth the terrible and shameful picture of their life in the dim chaos of bourgeois, everyday existence." [140] For Vladimir Nemirovich-Danchenko, Chekhov's excellence lay in "seeing life not only through its rising peaks and sinking abysses but also through surrounding ordinary everyday life" and in revealing "hidden, inward psychological movement." For Stanislavsky, who became the most famous and successful if somewhat controversial interpreter of Chekhov's plays, they were unique:

> Their charm does not lie in the dialogue; it lies in the meaning behind the dialogue, in the pauses, in the looks of the actors, in the way they display emotions. Everything comes to life in these plays; the properties, the sounds, the scenery, the images created by the players, the play itself. Here is a case of creative intuition in artistic feeling.[141]

Chekhov said of his own life, "No vile deeds and no glorious exploits—I am just like the majority." And his plays mirror this kind of life. Toumanova noted, "The unity of mood that replaced the unity of action was generally acclaimed." Tolstoy in a minority view told Chekhov after seeing *The Sea Gull:*

> I cannot bear Shakespeare, you know, but your plays are even worse. Shakespeare, for all that, takes the reader by the neck and leads him to a certain goal, and does not let him turn aside. And where does one go with your heroes? From the sofa where they are lying to the closet and back.[142]

A certain ambiguity of effect is inherent in Chekhov's distinctive quality. No more phenomenal instance of this can be found than in

Stanislavsky's original production of *The Cherry Orchard*. To Chekhov, this play was "a comedy . . . in places even a farce." [143] To Stanislavsky it was a tragedy, the quintessence of the passing of the Russian nobility. As Magarshack points out, Stanislavsky by blood was an
aristocrat while Chekhov was a peasant; therefore to Stanislavsky the
passing of the aristocracy was basically tragic, while to Chekhov it
was basically comic or even farcical. Chekhov's plays have something
of the ambiguity of life itself. He made them that way. In a letter that
provides a kind of summer lightning of revelation in this matter,
Chekhov wrote Suvorin on May 30, 1888, in Garnett's translation, "it
is time that writers, especially those who are artists, recognized that
there is no making out anything in this world, as once Socrates recognized it, and Voltaire, too." [144] In that same letter he also wrote, "The
artist must not be the judge of his characters and of their conversations, but merely an impartial witness . . ."

Writing and Rewriting

"To write a play in the contemporary style or taste," Chekhov advised, "there is one secret you must know . . . one must write the
play with closed eyes." [145] In his writing and rewriting, his mind's
eye was on reminiscence. "I must write without a break," Chekhov
confided in his beloved Olga in Magarshack's translation, "or nothing I
do comes off." [146] He wrote the monologue, *Swansong,* in one hour
and five minutes; the first draft of *Ivanov,* in ten days; *The Bear,* in
one afternoon. "In my opinion," said Chekhov, "writing at a terrific
speed is not . . . a blemish but a special gift." [147] Chekhov learned, of
course, that genesis and incubation at a "terrific speed" and "writing
at a terrific speed" were two different things; they might be simultaneous and good for a short work, but a long work required long
maturation of character and action before "writing at a terrific speed"
came off, and even then, very extensive rewriting was necessary.

He noted in a letter to Suvorin in December, 1889, after the failure
of *The Wood Demon,* "I must write with all my conscience, with
feeling, with gusto, not eighty pages a month, but sixteen pages in
five months." The first draft of *Ivanov* took only ten days, but there
are now from Chekhov's hand seven revised editions of *Ivanov* extant.
In 1889, Chekhov advised his brother, Alexander, who was attempting
playwriting, "The large number of revisions need not trouble you."
And then noted a most profound observation for anyone trying to
learn playwriting: "the more of a mosaic the work is, the better. The

characters stand to gain by this." [148] Characterization is the art of afterthoughts and rearrangement. Chekhov had seen what revision did for his *Ivanov;* the mixed success in Moscow became a "colossal success" in St. Petersburg. "I have made a new Sasha, changed Act IV so that it can't be recognized," said Chekhov, "and polished off Ivanov, himself." [149]

Chekhov's finished plays are the sum total of his writing and rewriting. "Avoid 'choice' diction," said Chekhov. "The language should be simple and forceful." [150] Stanislavsky found that Chekhov spoke in the same style as he wrote. During a run of *The Sea Gull,* for instance, Stanislavsky, who played Trigorin, asked Chekhov for criticism of his interpretation of the role, and Chekhov replied, "Wonderful! Listen, it was wonderful! Only you need torn shoes and checked trousers." [151] After much thought, Stanislavsky decided that this clothing typified the adolescent bohemianism with which Trigorin intrigued romantic girls. To Leonid Andreyev, Chekhov's dialogue was pan-psychic, "Everything is alive, has a soul and a voice." [152] Stark Young called the technique "realistic psychological," because real things had an associated inner meaning.[153] Bruford calls it "psychological naturalism." [154] When actors asked Chekhov to clarify the substance of a speech, he often would only answer, "Look here, I have written there all I know." [155] Chekhov himself had advised a fellow dramatist, "The more compact and the tighter a play is, the brighter and more expressive it is." [156]

Chekhov, of course, had developed his impressionistic technique through years of application. When a worried young writer told Chekhov of writing that didn't come off, Chekhov replied, "Later it will come off. The chief thing is do not waste your youth and elasticity ... You must acquire words and turns of speech and for this you must write every day." [157] "It is of more use to young people to write critical articles," said Chekhov in 1888, "than poetry." [158]

The Cherry Orchard is probably Chekhov's best known long play and, according to Stanislavsky, his finest and most beautiful work. The very opening of the script in Constance Garnett's translation is excellent for illustrating Chekhov's technique in using setting, stage directions, dialogue—the whole of his script—to dramatize for the stage "the quintessence of life."

> (*A room, which has always been called the nursery. One of the doors leads into Anya's room. Dawn, sun rises during the scene. May, the cherry trees in flower, but it is cold in the garden with the frost of early morning. Windows closed.*) [159]

The nursery of the Ranevsky estate, unused for years, is full of child-hood memories. Through the windows, a new day is seen dawning, just as in a sense a new day is dawning for Russia with ominous im-plications, for there is frost in the air and the cherry orchard of the Ranevsky estate is in full bloom. Not a word has been said, but the play's theme is already visually implied, and the dialogue will shortly intimate this more clearly as well as sound the key-note.

"(*Enter Dunyasha with a candle and Lopahin with a book in his hand.*)" The candle suggests the period of the late 1880's. Lopahin appearing with a book at his first entrance suggests his businesslike punctuality, his peasant manners, his abandoned pretense at culture, but above all, his concern—even a kind of love for the Ranevskys:

> LOPAHIN: The train's in, thank God. What time is it?
> DUNYASHA: Nearly two o'clock. (*Puts out candle*) It's daylight already.
> LOPAHIN: The train's late! Two hours, at least. (*Yawns and stretches*) I'm a pretty one; what a fool I've been. Came here on purpose to meet them at the station and dropped asleep . . . Dozed off as I sat in the chair. It's annoying . . . You might have waked me.
> DUNYASHA: I thought you had gone. (*Listens*) There, I do be-lieve they're coming! [160]

Dunyasha in putting out the candle already suggests her kopeck pinching economy, possibly an attempt to do her bit with the Ranev-skys so hard up. Why didn't Lopahin meet the Ranevskys? Has he worked too hard at business that day or might he inwardly resent the obeisance suggested by meeting the bankrupt aristocrats at the train station, or is it both reasons? Here is a suggestion of Chekhov's am-biguity and elusiveness so like life. Lopahin's next speech builds up the entrance of the leading character, Madame Lyubov Andreyevna Ranevsky, and further depicts the other leading character in the play, Lopahin; the speech also demonstrates Chekhov's comment, "the more of a mosaic the work is, the better. The characters stand to gain by this."

> LOPAHIN: (*Listens*) No, what with the luggage and one thing and another. (*A pause*) Lyubov Andreyevna has been abroad five years; I don't know what she is like now . . . She's a splendid woman. A good-natured, kind-hearted woman. I remember when I was a lad of fifteen, my poor father—he used to keep a little shop here in the village in those days—gave me a punch in the face with his fist and made my nose bleed. We were in the yard here, I forget what we'd come about—he had had a drop. Lyubov Andreyevna—I

can see her now—she was a slim young girl then—took me to wash my face, and then brought me into this very room, into the nursery. "Don't cry, little peasant," says she, "It will be well in time for your wedding." . . . (*A pause*) Little peasant . . . My father was a peasant, it's true, but here am I in a white waistcoat and brown shoes, like a pig in a bun shop. Yes, I'm a rich man, but for all my money, come to think, a peasant I was, and a peasant I am. (*Turns over the pages of the book*) I've been reading this book, and I can't make head or tail of it. I fell asleep over it. (*Pause*) [161]

Epihodov, the clerk, soon comes in with a nosegay from the gardener for Dunyasha to put in the dining-room. The theme and very spirit of the play are then struck in the frost on the flowering cherry orchard:

EPIHODOV: It's chilly this morning, three degrees of frost, though the cherries are all in flower. I can't say much for our climate. (*Sighs*) I can't. Our climate is not often propitious to the occasion. Yermolay Alexevitch, permit me to call your attention to the fact that I purchased myself a pair of boots the day before yesterday, and they creak, I venture to assure you, so that there's no tolerating them. What ought I to grease them with?

LOPAHIN: Oh, shut up! Don't bother me.[162]

This brief passage from the opening of *The Cherry Orchard,* can barely suggest Chekhov's method. To fully appreciate the method would require the intensive study that a director would have to give the play, and yet no director, not even Stanislavsky, could possibly find in the script what Chekhov had not put there. Virginia Woolf has said of Chekhov's technique in her book, *The Common Reader:*

The method which at first seemed so casual, inconclusive, occupied with trifles, now appears the result of an exquisitely original and fascinating taste, choosing boldly, arranging infallibly and controlled by an honesty for which we can find no match save among the Russians themselves.[163]

Chekhov's writing and rewriting of his long plays suggests how fluid his scenario was. In 1896, he wrote Suvorin that his new play, *Uncle Vanya,* was about ready to go to press; calling the revision of *The Wood Demon* "a new play" was doubtless to remove from it the stigma of failure in Moscow on December 27, 1889. Chekhov likened trying to turn a bad play into a good one to trying to turn a soldier's pair of old pants into a frock coat; the dramatist had to "take a new focus, cross out, add, insert monologues, revive the dead and bury the living . . ."[164] Instead of showing "how Wood Demons affect women," Chekhov's new focus was to show how a good, kind hero-worshipper, Uncle Vanya, ironically finds that the intellectual hero he has sacrificed so many years of his life for, Prof. Serebryakov, is really only a pedantic old fraud on the subject of his presumed specialty —art. The subject was timely in a Russia trying to be culture conscious; Tolstoy, Chekhov's friend, had for twenty-five years been reading about and pondering over art, and in 1897 came out with his still highly provocative reaction, a book, *What Is Art?*

A comparison of *The Wood Demon* with *Uncle Vanya* shows Chekhov's chief changes. He salvaged Acts II and IV almost intact. To focus on his new theme, he had to "revive the dead and bury the living." He dropped such characters from *The Wood Demon* as Fyodor Orlovsky, and Leonid Zheltoukhin, and his sister, Julia. Kruschov, the original "wood demon," was like Chekhov a doctor obsessed with the importance of forest conservation as a measure of a nation's culture. Kruschov, the central figure, becomes the minor figure, Dr. Astrov, an idealistic country doctor who treats the ailing professor. Chekhov revitalized with new growth the roles of Prof. Serebryakov, Elena and Uncle Vanya. Elena, for instance, originally gave in to the seducer, Ilya Dyadin, an omitted figure in the revision; the revised Elena's virtuous avoidance of seduction becomes one of the chief concerns of the whole play, for this young and beautiful wife of the old professor tempts a number of men but gives in to none. George Voinitsky, the original Uncle Vanya, committed suicide in the third act over love for Elena; Chekhov revived this dead man and left him a frustrated lover who saw happiness pass him by and has to turn to work. Today *The Wood Demon* is almost never performed. *Uncle Vanya* is often revived. "My *Uncle Vanya* is played all over the provinces and is everywhere a success," Chekhov wrote his brother, Alexander. "One never knows where one finds and where one loses. I never counted on that play."[165]

Chekhov began the actual writing of *The Sea Gull* in October of 1895, and by the following November 21st he had already sent Suvorin a first draft, commenting in Garnett's translation, "a plan which will be altered a million times before next season." By early April of 1896, Chekhov had revised the play enough to submit it to his friend Potapenko for clearance; rumor had it that Potapenko was part model for Trigorin, and Chekhov took care to avoid any libelous likeness. Potapenko approved. Produced on October 17, 1896, at the Alexandrinksky Theatre in Petersburg, *The Sea Gull* failed. Produced by the Moscow Art Theatre on December 17, 1898, it was a great success. Chekhov did not rewrite the version of the earlier faliure at all; the play was only interpreted freshly. This proves that when Chekhov felt that as an artist he was right, he would not revise; if he felt that as an artist he was wrong, as with *The Wood Demon,* he might revise at great length and over many years.

The writing and rewriting of *The Three Sisters* shows that even when Chekhov thought he had a play "crystallized" in his head and "ready" to be written, the characters in the course of the actual writing might run wild. "It is not a play, but a sort of tangle," Chekhov noted of his progress. "There are a great many characters—perhaps I shall get in a muddle and give it up." [166] On September 9, 1900, he wrote "Masha," "I find it very difficult to write *The Three Sisters,* much more difficult than any other of my plays . . . I feel as though I had no object in writing; what I wrote yesterday, I don't like today . . ." [167] Chekhov even considered postponing the whole revision—"If the play won't come right, I shall put it away till next year." [168]

When *The Three Sisters* went into rehearsal early in December of 1900, Olga kept Chekhov posted on its progress; Chekhov did not quite trust Stanislavsky. Chekhov also corresponded with individual actors in answer to their questions about interpreting their roles. At Chekhov's personal request, his friend Colonel Victor Petrov attended rehearsals to check the authenticity of the play's artillerymen. Chekhov did not see the play's premiere on January 31, 1901, a middling success.

In writing and rewriting *The Cherry Orchard,* Chekhov showed an almost superhuman stamina. With terminal tuberculosis, he worked as if the fates might never let him complete his project. The first draft must have come very slowly, for in February, 1903, with the scenario quite in mind, Chekhov began the actual writing and by March 21, 1903, he wrote Olga, *"The Cherry Orchard* will come off; I'm trying to have as few characters as possible; this will make it more intimate." [169] Some days Chekhov's health was so poor that he could write only four lines and, as he put it, "with almost unendurable torment." [170] By September 15th, 1903, he wrote Stanislavsky's wife, "Not a drama but a comedy has emerged from me, in places even a farce." [171] By September 26th, he wrote Olga that he didn't like some passages at all and was rewriting them. By October 8th, he wrote her that his second act was as tiring and wearisome as "a spider's web" and that the third act was "the least boring." But the very next day he wrote her, "The play is growing better and better and the characters are clear now." [172] By October 10th, he accounted for his delay in finishing the play by explaining that he was rewriting it a second time. On October 12th, he wrote Olga, "The worst thing about the play is that I have not written it at one sitting, but over a long, long period, so that it is bound to seem spun out. Oh, how hard it was for me to write this play." [173] The first draft had taken from February to September. Revision came faster.

Chekhov said, "I never consider a play ready for publication until it has been revised during rehearsal." [174] The rehearsal of *The Cherry Orchard* was especially a trial for the very ill Chekhov. "Nemirovich-Danchenko and Stanislavsky see in my play something absolutely different from what I have written," complained Chekhov of the play's interpretation as a tragedy rather than as a comedy, "and I'm willing to stake my word on it that neither of them has once read my play through attentively." [175]

Chekhov allowed only minor changes in the script during rehearsal, except for the second act in which Stanislavsky insisted on cutting the whole final scene. In the published version of *The Cherry Orchard,* Chekhov used part of this emended scene to open Act II with Charlotte's now well-known soliloquy. "The blossoms had only just begun to appear," recorded Stanislavsky of his run-in with Chekhov at rehearsal, "when the author arrived and messed up everything for us. The blossoms vanished and only now are new buds starting to show themselves." [176] Four days before the play's opening on January 17, 1904, Chekhov wrote to his old friend, the principal of the Yalta school, "I expect no particular success, the thing is going poorly." [177] Chekhov did not rewrite further. He felt secure that "the paths paved by me will remain safe and sound."

It is a Chekhovian irony that Chekhov and Stanislavsky, who owed each other so much, should have at times fallen out so bitterly as to not be on speaking terms. The trouble seems to have started when, in Chekhov's opinion, Stanislavsky as director began to usurp the boundaries of Chekhov as author. In the staging of *The Sea Gull,* for instance, Stanislavsky planned realistic evocative touches like frogs croaking, grasshoppers chirring, and dogs barking. "But the stage is art," said Chekhov obviously quite peeved. "Kramskoy has a picture on which the faces are painted beautifully. What would happen if one cut out the nose of one of the faces and substituted a real one for it? The nose would be realistic, but the picture would be ruined." [178] The falling out grew worse when Chekhov read that Stanislavsky was portraying Trigorin in *The Sea Gull* as a sort of weakling author. "Trigorin appeals to women; he is captivating and charming; in short, only a third-rate and unthinking actor could act him as a flabby weakling." [179] It is a curious tribute to Chekhov and Stanislavsky that in spite of their differences they recognized each other's value and did not part. In his book, *My Life in Art,* Stanislavsky implies their mutual great debt:

> It was Chekhov who suggested to me the line of intuition and feeling. To reveal the inner contents of his plays, it is necessary to delve into the depths of his soul . . . there are no other ways in his case . . . All the theatres in Russia and a great many in Europe tried to interpret Chekhov with other methods of acting. . . . They failed . . . The Art Theatre is the only one to have succeeded. . . . The reason is that we have discovered a new approach to Chekhov, an altogether different approach, and that is our main contribution to dramatic art.[180]

What was the "new approach"? It is now called "the Stanislavsky System," and it has revolutionized modern acting. The basic tenets of the system were literally dictated by the individuality of Chekhov's plays in the writing and rewriting: absolute sincerity; the accumulation of trifles to sum up the quintessence of character; lifelike ambiguity of motivation; continuity suggested mosaic fashion; an absolute rejection of clichés and stereotypes; a reliance upon reminiscence, "memory of emotion" to Stanislavsky; and a complete responsiveness of the body to externalize the thoughts and feelings of the actor in a fresh way. If Chekhov had not pursued his course in writing and rewriting, it is doubtful that Stanislavsky would ever have discovered his famous system. And without Stanislavsky, it is doubtful if Chekhov would have continued writing for the theatre.

CHAPTER III: ACKNOWLEDGEMENTS

My grateful acknowledgement is extended to the following sources for the use of quotations:

ANTONY TCHEKHOV, LITERARY AND THEATRICAL REMINIS-CENCES translated and edited by S. S. Koteliansky, G. H. Doran and Co., 1927. Reprinted by Blom Inc., New York, 1964. Reprinted by permission of Routledge and Kegan Paul Ltd.

ANTON CHEKHOV, THE VOICE OF TWILIGHT RUSSIA by Princess Nina Toumanova. Copyright 1937. Reprinted by permission of Columbia University Press

CHEKHOV, A Biography by Ernest J. Simmons, Copyright (c) 1962 by Ernest J. Simmons, Reprinted by permission of Atlantic-Little, Brown, publishers, and by permission of Jonathan Cape Ltd.

CHEKHOV, A LIFE by David Magarshak. Copyright 1952. Reprinted by per-mission of Faber and Faber Ltd.

CHEKHOV, THE DRAMATIST by David Magarshack. Copyright 1960. Re-printed by permission of Hill and Wang and John Lehman Ltd.

THE COMMON READER, "The Russian Point of View" by Virginia Woolf. Copyright 1925. Reprinted by permission of Harcourt, Brace & World and the Hogarth Press

CONTEMPORARY REVIEW, February 1924, "Chekhov and His Plays" by C. Nabokoff

THE DRAMA OF CHEKHOV, SYNGE, YEATS AND PIRANDELLO by F. L. Lucas, copyright 1963. Reprinted by permission of Cassell & Co., Ltd.

THE LAST ESSAYS by Thomas Mann translated from the German by Richard and Clara Winsten and Tannie and James Stern. Copyright 1959. Reprinted by permission of Alfred A. Knopf, Inc.

LETTERS OF ANTON CHEKHOV TO HIS FAMILY AND FRIENDS trans-lated by Constance Garnett. Copyright 1920. Reprinted by permission of Chatto and Windus Ltd. and A. P. Watt & Son, Literary Agents to Mr. David Garnett, C. B. E.

LETTERS OF ANTON P. TCHEKHOV TO OLGA L. KNIPPER translated by Constance Garnett. Copyright 1925. Reprinted by permission of Doubleday & Co. and Chatto and Windus Ltd. and A. P. Watt & Son, Literary Agents for the Garnett Estate

153

LETTERS ON THE SHORT STORY, THE DRAMA AND OTHER LITERARY TOPICS by Anton Chekhov, selected and edited by Louis S. Friedland, Minton Balch & Co., 1924. Reprinted by permission of Geoffrey Bles Ltd.

MY LIFE IN ART by Constantin Stanislavski, translated from the Russian by G. Ivanov-Murmiev, Moscow, Foreign Language Publishing House, 1921

MY LIFE IN THE RUSSIAN THEATRE by Vladimir Nemirovich-Danchenko, translated by John Cournos. Copyright 1936. Reprinted by permission of Marjorie Barkinton, Representative for the Estate of Vladimir Nemirovich-Danchenko

THE NOTE-BOOKS OF ANTON TCHEKHOV translated by S. S. Koteliansky and Leonard Woolf. Copyright 1921. Reprinted by permission of Hogarth Press

Extracts from THE PLAYS OF ANTON TCHEKHOV translated by Constance Garnett, a Modern Library Book, copyright 1930. Reprinted by permission of Chatto and Windus Ltd. and A. P. Watt & Son, literary agents for David Garnett, C. B. E.

10 brief excerpts from REMINISCENCES OF CHEKHOV from REMINISCENCES OF TOLSTOY, CHEKHOV AND ANDREYEV by Maxim Gorky, translated by S. S. Koteliansky and Leonard Woolf. Copyright 1921 by B. W. Huebsch, Inc., 1949 by S. S. Koteliansky and Leonard Woolf. Reprinted by permission of The Viking Press, Inc.

Reprinted from THE SELECTED LETTERS OF ANTON CHEKHOV, Edited by Lillian Hellman and Translated by Sidonie Lederer, by permission of Farrar, Straus & Giroux, Inc. Copyright 1955 by Lillian Hellman

STUDIES IN MODERN EUROPEAN LITERATURE edited by Erich Heller, "Anton Chekhov" by W. H. Buford, Yale University Press, 1957

THEATRE ARTS MONTHLY, February 1924, "Tchehoff Letters" by L. S. Friedland

1. Louis S. Friedland, editor and translator, *Letters on the Short Story, the Drama and Other Literary Topics by Anton Chekhov* (London 1924), 192
2. Constance Garnett, editor and translator, *Letters of Anton Chekhov to His Family and Friends* (London 1920), 105
3. Friedland, 118, 153
4. S. S. Koteliansky, editor and translator, *Literary and Theatrical Reminiscences* (New York 1927), 4
5. Princess Nina Toumanova, *Anton Chekhov, the Voice of Twilight Russia* (New York 1937), 4, 173
6. Hesketh Pearson, *George Bernard Shaw, His Life and Personality* (New York 1963), 330
7. F. L. Lucas, *The Drama of Chekhov, Synge, Yeats and Pirandello* (London 1963), 145
8. Lillian Hellman editor and Sidonie Lederer translator, *The Selected Letters of Anton Chekhov* (New York 1955), xviii
9. Garnett, 4
10. Koteliansky, xxiv
11. David Magarshack, *Chekhov, a Life* (London 1952), 15
12. Koteliansky, xxiii
13. Magarshack, 18
14. Ernest Simmons, *Chekhov, a Biography* (Boston 1962), 18
15. Ibid., 20
16. Ibid., 32
17. Ibid., 31
18. David Magarshack, *Chekhov, the Dramatist* (London 1960), p. 67
19. Simmons, 72
20. Ibid., 98
21. *Chekhov, a Life,* 139
22. Thomas Mann, *Last Essays* (New York 1959), 185
23. Ibid.
24. *New York Times Book Review* (October 12, 1962), 60
25. *Chekhov, a Life,* 299
26. Garnett, 44
27. Ibid.

28. Hellman and Lederer, 130

29. Simmons, 361

30. Garnett, 269

31. Ibid.

32. Simmons, 114

33. Garnett, 269

34. Simmons, 590

35. Maxim Gorky translated by S. S. Koteliansky and Leonard Woolf, *Reminiscences of Chekhov* from *Reminiscences of Tolstoy, Chekhov and Andreyev* (New York 1921, 1949), 119

36. Simmons, 236

37. Garnett, 327

38. Koteliansky, 4

39. *Chekhov, the Dramatist,* 91

40. Simmons, 176

41. Marian Fell, editor and translator, *Five Famous Plays* (London 1939), 11

42. Simmons, 171

43. *Chekhov, the Dramatist,* 128

44. Friedland, 149

45. Vladimir Nemirovich-Danchenko, *My Life in the Russian Theatre* (Boston 1936), 66

46. Simmons, 603

47. Garnett, 407

48. Garnett, 336

49. Ibid., 408

50. Ibid., 106

51. Gorky, 17

52. Ibid.

53. Garnett, 110

54. Ibid., 58

55. Friedland, 283

56. Garnett, 127

57. Gorky, 8

58. Garnett, 57

59. Koteliansky, 14

60. Garnett, 360

61. Ibid., 310

62. Hellman and Lederer, 56

63. Ibid., 219

64. Lucas, 135

65. Hellman and Lederer, 241

66. C. Nabokoff, "Chekhov and His Plays," *Contemporary Review* (February 1924), 345

67. Gorky, 12
68. Ibid., 78; Koteliansky, 4
69. Ibid., 8
70. Ibid., 92
71. Garnett, 122
72. Ibid., 100
73. Friedland, 201
74. Garnett, 352
75. Gorky, 66, 67
76. S. S. Koteliansky and Leonard Woolf, translators, *The Note-Books of Anton Tchekhov* (London 1921), 65
77. Ibid., 14
78. Ibid., 45
79. Ibid., 25
80. Ibid., 13
81. Friedland, 202
82. Koteliansky, 87
83. Simmons, 129
84. Garnett, 101
85. Simmons, 430–431
86. *Chekhov, the Dramatist,* 118
87. Ibid., 84
88. Friedland, 36
89. Gorky, 70
90. Garnett, 103
91. Hellman and Lederer, 64
92. Koteliansky, 161
93. Ibid., 6
94. Friedland, 129
95. *Chekhov, a Life,* 187
96. Simmons, 279
97. *Chekhov, the Dramatist,* 174
98. Simmons, 611
99. Koteliansky, 161
100. Toumanova, 198
101. *Chekhov, the Dramatist,* 265
102. Friedland, 171
103. Ibid., 94
104. Garnett, 119
105. Ibid., 111
106. *Chekhov, the Dramatist,* 90, 98
107. L. S. Friedland, "A Tchehoff Scenario," *Theatre Arts Monthly* (April 1924), 234
108. Friedland, 123

109. Ibid., 124
110. Ibid., 201
111. Hellman and Lederer, 212
112. Anton Tchekhov translated by Constance Garnett, *The Plays of Anton Tchekhov* (New York 1930), 7. All of the dialogue cited in illustrating Chekhov's irony is drawn from Constance Garnett's famous translation in *The Plays of Anton Chekhov*. These translations proved their first-rate stage worthiness, for instance, in Eva Le Gallienne's excellent productions of Chekhov by The Civic Repertory Theatre Company of New York; productions of these translations established Chekhov's fame as a playwright in English-speaking countries. Laurence Olivier's all-star production of *Uncle Vanya,* shown incidentally on National Educational Television, used Constance Garnett's translation.
113. Ibid., 8
114. Ibid., 20, 21
115. Ibid., 37
116. Ibid.
117. Ibid., 27
118. Ibid., 28
119. Ibid., 25
120. Ibid., 30
121. Ibid., 48
122. Ibid., 58
123. Ibid., 193
124. Ibid., 212
125. Ibid., 213
126. Ibid., 211
127. Ibid.
128. Ibid., 225
129. Ibid., 232
130. Ibid., 120
131. Ibid., 158
132. Ibid., 137
133. Ibid., 176
134. Ibid., 184
135. Ibid., 134
136. Ibid., 103
137. Ibid., 99
138. Ibid., 96–7
139. Ibid., 90
140. Gorky, 22
141. Constantin Stanislavsky translated by G. Ivanov-Murmieve, *My Life in Art* (Moscow 1921), 260
142. Toumanova, 173; Friedland, 283
143. Simmons, 604

144. Garnett, 89
145. Friedland, 42
146. *Chekhov, the Dramatist,* 174
147. Constance Garnett, translator and editor, *The Letters of Anton P. Tchekhov to Olga L. Knipper* (London 1925), 46
148. Friedland, 171
149. Koteliansky, 9
150. Friedland, 171
151. Stanislavsky, 270
152. Koteliansky, 174
153. Anton Tchekhov translated by Stark Young, *The Sea Gull* (New York 1939), 1
154. W. H. Bruford, "Anton Chekhov," *Studies in Modern European Literature* (New Haven 1957), 43
155. Koteliansky, 158
156. *Chekhov, the Dramatist,* 45
157. Gorky, 74–5
158. *Letters of Anton Chekhov to His Family and Friends,* 105
159. *The Plays of Anton Tchekhov,* 61
160. Ibid.
161. Ibid., 61–2
162. Ibid.
163. Virginia Woolf, *The Common Reader* (New York 1925), 249
164. Friedland, 192
165. *Contemporary Review* (February 1924), 342
166. *Letters of Anton P. Tchekhov to Olga L. Knipper,* 40
167. *Letters of Anton Tchekhov to His Family and Friends,* 399
168. Ibid., 44
169. *Chekhov, the Dramatist,* 266
170. Nemirovich-Danchenko, 214
171. Simmons, 604
172. *Chekhov, the Dramatist,* 268
173. Ibid., 267
174. Ibid., 21; Friedland, 127
175. Simmons, 617
176. Ibid., 612
177. Ibid., 613
178. *Chekhov, a Life,* 322
179. Ibid., 337
180. Stanislavski, 260

Chapter IV

Bernard Shaw

"Unless nature has done ninety-nine percent of the work," said Bernard Shaw of playwriting, ". . . the one percent which can be taught or learned is not worth studying."[1] That one percent to Shaw was a bagful of stage tricks gathered from taking part in many productions. Yet if nature had done ninety-nine percent of the work to make Shaw a playwright, this effort was long concealed from Shaw himself. From the age of twenty to twenty-nine, Shaw wrote four novels which publishers rejected; his output of over a million words earned him in all six pounds or so. At twenty-nine, he tried his first play, a collaboration with the drama critic, William Archer—the plot to be Archer's, the dialogue Shaw's. When Archer heard Shaw read aloud the first two acts, Archer simply fell asleep, and the collaboration died of Shaw's deep shame. Shaw's dismay kept him from trying another play until seven years later when he was thirty-six. And he did not score his first success until he was thirty-eight, when Richard Mansfield, as Bluntschli, triumphantly toured America with *Arms and the Man*. Does this seem as if nature did ninety-nine percent of the work? England did not really wake up to Shaw until he was forty-eight. In 1925, at the age of seventy, Shaw won the Nobel Prize for Literature.

"After Shaw," remarked Chesterton in his biography, *George Bernard Shaw,* "one may say, there is nothing that cannot be introduced into a play if one can make it decent, amusing, and relevant."[2] Shaw ultimately felt so sure of his greatness in modern drama that with unabashed modesty he said, "The apostolic succession from Eschylus to myself is as serious and as continuously inspired as that younger institution, the apostolic succession of the Christian Church."[3]

I

THE GROWTH OF SHAW'S CREATIVE SPIRIT IN LIFE

Every 4 to 6 weeks from his 20th until his 70th year, Shaw suffered such severe headaches that he had to lie prostrate in a darkened room for a full day or so.[4] Doctors might find the headaches psychosomatic. The headaches stopped when Shaw was seventy, the very year he won the Nobel Prize. Shaw tried to attribute their disappearance to eating less protein and more uncooked fruits and vegetables; the completion of his tract, *The Intelligent Woman's Guide to Socialism and Capitalism,* he also thought helped end his headaches—"I transferred them to my readers." [5]

George Bernard Shaw was born on July 26, 1856, to Elizabeth Gurly Shaw and George Carr Shaw at 3 Upper Synge Street, Dublin, the couple's third child in four years. Lucinda Francis and Elinor Agnes preceded George Bernard.

The Shaw family lived in genteel poverty and disillusionment. On both sides of the family, the Shaws came of solid, respectable, middle-class, Irish Protestant stock. The paternal grandfather, a high sheriff of Kilkenny, unfortunately had a business partner whom he failed to watch closely, for this partner embezzled over 50,000 pounds of the firm's and the clients' money. This paternal grandfather still mustered courage enough to father fourteen children, of whom George Carr Shaw was the eighth. Gifted with an anti-climactic sense of humor as strong as his brogue, the ineffectual George Carr Shaw clerked in the Dublin law courts and summed up most of life with his pet phrase, "It's all a pack of lies." [6] George Carr Shaw finally became a dealer in the Dublin Wholesale Corn Exchange and, at thirty-eight, courted and married the twenty-two year old, very wilful, cool-headed Lucinda Elizabeth Gurly, the daughter of a debt-ridden country squire. Lucinda was strictly brought up by her rich Aunt Ellen, and from what Shaw learned in time, he judged that at her betrothal his mother knew "nothing about marriage, nor housekeeping, nor anything unladylike." She married George Carr Shaw against her father's advice, and he, on the basis of rumors that George Carr was a drunkard, tried to undo a bequest under her Grandfather Whitcroft's will; according to definitive records revealed in B. C. Rosset's book, *Shaw of Dublin: The Formative Years,* Lucinda was endowed with "1,500 pounds." [7] Lucinda thought she would surely be also her Aunt Ellen's

heiress, but as Shaw came to note, "My mother was embittered because she expected money to be left to her, and it didn't happen, and
we all suffered for it." [8] Economics was vitally to affect the lives of all
of Shaw's characters in his plays.

Shaw's father seems to have solved his problems by turning more
and more to an alcoholic's world of values. Shaw recalls that when he
was a little boy his father took him for a walk, and in a moment of
alcoholic fun on the bridge of a canal, threatened to toss George Bernard into the water. Upon reaching home, the little boy reported,
"Mama, I think Papa's drunk;" to which Mama replied, "When is he
ever anything else?" [9] Shaw in late years said that this early disillusionment with his father's perfection and omniscience left him at a
loss to believe in anything at all. "Once, in a rare mood of bitterness,"
recalled St. John Ervine in his biography, *Bernard Shaw*, "G. B. S. asserted that he had been begotten after a brawl when his father was
fuddled with drink." [10] Shaw was the last child his mother had; he
chose to be a lifelong teetotaller.

"The adult who has been poor as a child," Shaw told his friend of
forty years, Ervine, "will never get the chill of poverty out of his
bones." [11] Shaw never did, and it is most likely this chill that turned
Shaw eventually to what he believed the far healthier climate of socialism. His mother had been so despotically overtrained in correct-
ness by her Aunt Ellen that she deliberately left the Shaw children to
learn on their own, abandoning them in effect to Irish servants, in
Shaw's words, "whose wage was 8 pounds a year and could neither
write nor read." [12] Shaw's lifelong hatred of poverty also came from
"the slums into which my nursemaid took me on her visits to her
friends when she was supposed to be exercising me in the parks." [13]
For the mature Shaw, the mother of all crimes was poverty, and to be
content with poverty was, in itself, a crime.

Attempts of well-to-do-relatives to entertain the hard-up Shaws
went awry. "At one of the family parties at Bushy Park," Shaw related of his father, "he got so drunk that he was written off as socially
impossible." [14] Shaw remembered his father snobbishly, if somewhat
incongruously insisting that no Shaw children could play with the
children of Roman Catholics or shop-keepers. "From my mother, I
derive my brains and character which do her credit," said Shaw; [15]
yet he wrote Ellen Terry of his childhood, "Oh, a devil of a childhood, Ellen, rich only in dreams, frightful and loveless in realities." [16]

By the time Shaw was ten, his parents had given up even a pretense of church-going, and Shaw recalled, "Our family atmosphere was one of derisive free thinking." [17] The fun in the house was in conversation and especially in good music. George Vandaleur Lee at the time was a prominent Catholic, orchestral conductor in Dublin; a man of volcanic spirit and energy, Lee found in Shaw's mother a mezzo soprano voice of unusual purity of tone. Lee set to training this voice by unorthodox but effective methods. "Your mother will sing one day in London before the Queen," Lee told the Shaw children.[18] From the age of six, Shaw had recollections of Lee. As an adult, Shaw believed that in his way Lee was a "true genius." Through Lee and Shaw's mother, music became Shaw's daily spiritual food, or as Chesterton put it, "the imaginative safety-valve of the rationalistic Irishman." [19] Shaw's father objected to his children playing with Catholics but plainly had no control over his wife's dealings with Lee, a Catholic.

Lee started a music school in the new Shaw residence at 1 Hatch Street; Lee also moved in. Shaw is certain that romantically Lee could have done no better with his mother than with the wooden virgin of Nuremberg. Delivering her from her hell of matrimony, Lee became Mrs. Shaw's salvation professionally and financially. She made money as she copied his orchestral parts, scored his songs, led his choruses, starred in his operas and oratorios, and helped out in his teaching. With rehearsals often going on right in the Shaw home, Shaw from childhood sang along and committed whole musical scores to his photographic memory.

Lee was so grateful and indebted to Mrs. Shaw for her indispensable help in his growing success that he invited the Shaw family to share his Torca Cottage about nine miles from Dublin, commanding a magnificent view of Killiney Bay and the Whitlow Mountains. "I had one moment of ecstatic happiness in my childhood," Shaw recollected, "when my mother told me we were going to live in Dalkey. I had only to open my eyes there to see such pictures as no painter could make for me." [20] Rosset thinks maturity opened Shaw's eyes to the gross impropriety of Lee and the Shaws sharing homes.

Shaw's formal education left him with a lifelong violent distaste for schools as prisons, and for teachers as little more than keepers. In his lifetime, he was to refuse all honorary degrees and declared, "no book of mine shall ever with my consent be that damnable thing, the schoolbook." [21] To Shaw, "without living experience no person is educated," and the way to fine minds was by breeding. "Fancy trying to produce a greyhound or a racehorse by education!" said Shaw.[22]

Shaw's formal education began in Dublin's Wesleyan Connexional School where through boredom and defiance he remained "generally near or at the bottom of his classes." His parents sent him at thirteen to the Central Model Boys School, a *de facto* segregated Catholic school for children of petty shopkeepers and tradesmen. After six months Shaw was so miserable, his parents transferred him to the *de facto* Protestant school, the Dublin English Scientific and Commercial Day School, where he remained till he was fifteen years old—the last year of his formal education.[23]

Then Shaw's uncle, Frederick Shaw, got the fifteen year old nephew his first position, a junior clerkship in the exclusive estate office of C. Uniacke Townshend & Company. Shaw remained there for five years, daily associating with young men graduated from Trinity College, Dublin. "I have discovered all my powers from the outside, with incredulous astonishment," observed Shaw, "or rather I have discovered that everybody else hasn't got them."

When Shaw was sixteen years old his family broke up. In 1872, Vandaleur Lee, who had been footing much of the Shaws' rent through his musical activities at their home, decided to advance himself further musically by moving to London. Mrs. Shaw immediately followed as Lee's assistant and took along her two daughters. After twenty years of marriage, Shaw's parents separated but never were divorced. Shaw remained behind in Dublin in very modest quarters at a lodging-house on 61 Harcourt Street; he lived for the next four years with his improvident, alcoholic father who periodically took and kept the "pledge" of abstinence. On March 27, 1876, Shaw's sister Elinor Agnes died of tuberculosis at Balmoral House on the Isle of Wight. By March 31, 1876, Shaw officially resigned from Townshend's to join his mother and sister Lucy in London.

Lucy warned Shaw, "You won't be able to pretend in London as you did in Dublin that you are a genius." [24] He had not really pretended. After one year at Townshend's as junior clerk, he temporarily filled the position of head cashier, and so impressed Townshend that eventually he offered Shaw not only a partnership, but also his daughter's hand. Shaw wanted neither. What he wanted was to find exactly in what he was a genius. "I was chronically ashamed and even miserable," confessed Shaw, "simply because I couldn't do anything." [25] He hoped to sing opera, play the oboe, or paint pictures; but he lacked an operatic voice, could not afford an oboe, and was short of talent in drawing. Shaw did have some accomplishments in music, art, speech and drama, and these were to reveal themselves as roadmarks to his future success. From listening and singing along to his mother's music, Shaw had even at fifteen memorized at least one major work each of Handel, Verdi, Gounod, Mendelssohn, Meyerbeer, Mozart, and Beethoven. His operatic dreams had led him to study voice production and phonetics with a Dublin neighbor, Chichester Bell, a cousin of Alexander Graham Bell and a doctor of medicine and physicist-chemist in his own right.

Shaw had also spent so many leisure hours attending the admission-free National Gallery of Ireland that he had in his poverty become an authority of sorts on Flemish and Italian painting. As for literary attainments, Shaw at twenty claimed he knew the people in Shakespeare "from Hamlet to Abhorson much more intimately than I knew my living contemporaries." [26] Shaw's only writing to date had been in keeping a diary and in corresponding at great length with an old schoolmate, Mathew Edward McNulty. In London, Shaw finally decided that because he didn't have money to do anything else and because it came easiest to his hand, he would become a writer.

Shaw's literary apprenticeship lasted roughly from 1876 to 1885. "I have a notion hazy," said Shaw, "that mother thinks me crazy and Lucy thinks me lazy." [27] Shaw's mother regarded Lucy as a prospective star of musical comedy and the family's brightest hope; Lucy dimmed out. Shaw, however, diligently applied himself to write at least five pages of roughly 2,000 words every single day. "My mother and I lived together," Shaw told Ervine, "but there was hardly a word between us. She was a disillusioned woman." [28] By Rosset's definitive calculations, "Mrs. Shaw's annual income during the early London years . . . probably did not amount to more than 100 pounds." [29] The Shaws lived in "respectable" poverty. Mrs. Shaw broke with Lee when he betrayed his "method" and became a charlatan promising singers results in sixteen weeks that she knew must take at least four years; and Lucy found Lee's attentions unwelcome.

In nine years, Shaw's writing earned him six pounds from two pamphlets he was commissioned to write: one condemning slaughter houses; another condemning patent medicines. His mother supported him. He briefly tried clerking in a music shop and for about six months sold subscriptions to Bell's telephone. From 1879 to 1883, Shaw wrote four novels which publishers rejected; Shaw later admitted that even the rats couldn't finish his first novel, *Immaturity*.

For dress clothes, Shaw trimmed his fraying cuffs and wore an all purpose black coat finally "green with decay." His only relatives in London were a hard-drinking, Rabelaisian uncle, Dr. Gurly, and a cousin, Cashel Hoey, who as a minor novelist knew many literary figures, but introduced her struggling nephew to none. In his late eighties, Shaw said, "My timid want to push kept me a penniless burden on my harassed parents until I was nearly thirty." [30]

"When he first went to London," Chesterton said of Shaw, "he mixed with every kind of revolutionary society, and met every kind of person except the ordinary person." Shaw had very little money, but in London all kinds of intellectual pleasures were free. He mined for source material at the British Museum. He attended exciting meetings of the Browning Society, the Shakespeare Society, the Shelley Society, and most notably, starting in 1879, the no-holds-barred Zetetical ("truth-seeking") Society, which freely debated politics, religion and sex. Shaw was testing his convictions and his friends. England in 1879 was in the grip of a great depression equalled only in 1931. Henry George's lectures sold Shaw on the Single Tax. A reading of a French translation of *Das Kapital* in the British Museum left Shaw a lifelong Marxist; a suggestion of how he reconciled this with later being a millionaire is in his comment, "Money is worth nothing to the man who has more than enough; and the wisdom with which it is spent is the sole justification for leaving him in possession of it." [31]

At the Zetetical Society Shaw met Sidney Webb, whom he later called "the ablest man in England," and Shaw believed, "Without him, I might have been a mere literary wisecracker, like Carlyle and Ruskin." [32] In 1884, Webb, Shaw and other socialists from the Zetetical Society founded the Fabian Society which through writing, speaking and organization rallied to attack the *status quo,* and in time became the most powerful single force in England promoting socialism as a cure for society's ills. Their doctrine was, "For the right moment you must wait, as Fabius did most patiently when warring against Hannibal, though many censured his delays; but when the time comes, you must strike hard, as Fabius did, or your waiting will be in vain and fruitless . . ." [33] The Fabian Society became Shaw's University. "My colleagues knocked much nonsense, ignorance, and vulgar provinciality out of me," confessed Shaw; "for we were on quite ruthless critical terms with one another." [34] Shaw with intellectual passion wrote socialist tracts and regularly addressed at least two or three audiences every fortnight for almost ten years on problems of the day;

his audiences ranged from washerwomen to University dons, and he never asked for or accepted a fee.

In 1885, as earlier related, William Archer by accident left ajar the door to a whole imaginative world in playwriting that was to lead Shaw to greatness. Seven years after Archer slept, Shaw was to make his first solo try as a playwright to wake the whole world. Jack Grein, an Anglo-Dutch Ibsen enthusiast, in 1892 founded the Independent Theatre in London modelled after Le Théâtre Libre in Paris; Grein had publicly said that backward managers had rejected hundreds of fine modern plays in England. In his journalistic columns, Shaw trumpeted in witty clarion notes for England's neglected modern playwrights to come to Grein. None came. Said Shaw, "I had rashly taken up the case; and rather than let it collapse, I manufactured the evidence." [35] Shaw opened his trunk, took out the two-act collaboration with Archer, wrote a third act, retitled the work *Widowers' Houses,* drawing heavily on his experiences as a rent collector in Dublin, and Grein produced the play on December 9, 1892 for a run of two performances; "unless I could produce at least half a dozen plays before I was forty," resolved Shaw with mixed emotions toward his brain-children on the stage, "I had better let playwriting alone." [36]

In his four year period of grace, Shaw wrote:

The Philanderer (1893)	*Candida*
Mrs Warren's Profession	*The Man of Destiny* (1895)
Arms and the Man (1894)	*You Never Can Tell* (1896)

Of these, immediate success came only to *Arms and the Man* in Richard Mansfield's tour of the United States in 1894 as Bluntschli. Until 1904, England's theatre managers treated Shaw's steady outpouring of plays as if they had been written in a recondite dialect of Sanskrit.

Shaw meanwhile supported himself chiefly as a critic in journalism, exploiting his youthfully acquired qualifications in art, books, music and drama. In 1885, Shaw ghost-wrote an art criticism for his friend, William Archer, in *The World*. Very soon after, Shaw shed this literary ectoplasm. He became art critic for *The World,* book reviewer for *The Pall Mall Gazette* and, by 1888, music critic with a pseudonym, "Corno di Bassetto" (Italian for "basset horn"), for *The Star*. The success of these assignments led Shaw in 1895 to his virtuoso engagement as it were, drama critic with an international stage and audience offered by *The Saturday Review of Literature* through special courtesy of its editor and Shaw's friend, Frank Harris.

By April, 1898, Shaw's hectic activities—reviewing, playwriting, tract-writing, speechifying, socializing—and an infected left foot snarled him into a nervous breakdown. Necrosis of the bone set in so the foot required two operations; for eighteen months Shaw was on crutches and in danger of having to have the left foot amputated. The Irish millionairess, Charlotte Frances Payne-Townshend, whom Shaw had met through the Fabian Society, now rushed to nurse her highly distressed "genius."

Charlotte, the heiress and spinster of 41, nursing Shaw, the comparatively poor bachelor of 42, could only end in one of two ways as Shaw saw it—scandal or marriage. Charlotte chose marriage, and on June 1, 1898, at the Strand Registry Office in London, Shaw stood up on crutches and said, "I do." [37] "She had none of the feminine traits that I had expected," Shaw said fondly of Charlotte, "and all the human qualities I had only hoped for."

Charlotte insisted that her "genius" give up all other activities but his playwriting. "As man and wife," said Shaw in his *Sixteen Self-Sketches,* "we found a new relation in which sex had no part." [38] Charlotte's family for a while suspected Shaw of being a fortune-hunter. Shaw seemed rather happy with his platonic marriage lasting over forty years; he had intense intellectual pleasure from his writing.

He also had a gallery of recollections of physical pleasures. He frankly admitted he was "a virgin" until he was twenty-nine, because he didn't have the money to entertain attractive young ladies and his taste was too fastidious for those otherwise available. Then a "sexually insatiable" widow named Jenny Patterson, now presumed to have been about forty-four years old, led Shaw into her pleasures. [39] At thirty-two, Shaw placidly counted six love affairs in varying blaze at once, so that Sidney Webb told him, "My! You do warm both hands at the fire of life!" [40] But it seems Shaw never got burned. He claimed women always pursued him, and he proved exceptional in flight if he chose.

In *The Loves of George Bernard Shaw,* C. B. L. DuCann suggests that Shaw drew about all the women in his love-life from three chief preserves: his mother's singing students, like his first love, Alice Lockett, and then Jenny Patterson; his zealous associates in economics and politics, like Annie Besant, Geraldine Spooner, May Morris, Eleonor

Marx, and Edith Nesbit; and finally, his bevy of young actresses who were promising leading ladies for his plays, like Florence Farr, Janet Achurch, Ellen Terry, and Mrs. Patrick Campbell. Mrs. Sidney Webb, after putting her cold, statistical eye upon Shaw with the ladies, decided he was only "a sprite" on the hunt for literary game, not cuckoldry. Shaw admitted a great weakness for married women, and apparently entranced quite a few with the feast of his wit and intellect, tossed off for them in such a manner that their husbands' performances were a sorry spectacle of cold beef and mashed potatoes. Shaw in some measure so treated Florence Farr, May Morris, Edith Nesbit, and Janet Achurch.

Charlotte's letter to T. E. Lawrence, the Lawrence of Arabia, written when she was seventy and given to the British Museum after her death on September 12, 1943, clears up some of the mystery of Charlotte's unconsummated marriage to Shaw and suggests his physical frustration. "I had a perfectly hellish childhood and youth," Charlotte wrote. "My mother was a terribly strong character—managing and domineering. She could not bear opposition; if it was offered, she either became quite violent, or she cried. She constantly cried," recalled Charlotte. "She felt (genuinely felt) that she had sacrificed her life for us . . ." [41] Charlotte thought her mother literally killed her father by wearing him down and then in guilt undid herself through illness. "But anyway, my own home life made me firmly resolve," Charlotte confided in Lawrence, "never to be the mother of a child who might suffer as I had suffered." [42]

Charlotte, incidentally, failed to invite Shaw's mother or sister Lucy to her home; Lucy called Charlotte "the drop of gall in our cup." Charlotte's diary disappeared after her death. According to DuCann, Charlotte had many times threatened to walk out on Shaw, especially over his infatuation with Mrs. Patrick Campbell and his continued correspondence with her over a period of forty years. "Of all the women I have known (and I have known many)," said Shaw after Charlotte's death, "I knew Charlotte least of all." [43]

On November 29, 1904, the experimental management of John Vedrenne and Harley Granville-Barker at the Court Theatre began their own and Shaw's rocket to celebrity in England with a special matinee performance of *Candida*. In its span of life, the Vedrenne-Barker management produced thirty modern works with eleven from their most profitable playwright, "Bernard Shaw." Shaw chose to drop "George" as part of his pen-name; now no one could call him

"Sonny," his childhood nick-name, or "Junior," for he was forty-eight years old.

Shaw's complete output of plays shows a man of Puritan industry and protean accomplishment; titles with one asterisk after them are short plays or one-acts:

Widowers' Houses (1892)
The Philanderer (1893)
Mrs. Warren's Profession
Arms and the Man (1894)
Candida
The Man of Destiny (1895)*
You Never Can Tell (1896)
The Devil's Disciple (1897)
Caesar and Cleopatra (1898)
Captain Brassbound's Conversion
The Admirable Bashville (1901)*
Man and Superman (1901-1903)
John Bull's Other Island (1904)
How He Lied to Her Husband
Major Barbara (1905)
Passion, Poison, and Petrifaction
The Doctor's Dilemma (1906)
Interlude at the Playhouse (1907)*
Getting Married (1908)
The Shewing up of Blanco Posnet
Press Cuttings
The Fascinating Foundling
A Glimpse of Reality
The Dark Lady of the Sonnets (1910) *
Misalliance
Fanny's First Play (1911)
Androcles and the Lion (1912)*

Pygmalion
Over-Ruled
Great Catherine (1913)*
Heartbreak House (1913-1918)
The Music Cure (1914)*
O'Flaherty, V.C. (1915)*
The Inca of Perusalem
Augustus Does His Bit (1916)*
The Bolshevik Empress (1917)*
Back to Methuselah (1917-1921)
A Glimpse of the Domesticity of Franklin Barnabas (1921)*
Saint Joan (1923)
Jitta's Atonement (1926) (translation)
The Applecart (1930)
Too True to Be Good (1931)
Beauty's Duty
Village Wooing (1933)*
On the Rocks
The Six of Calais
The Simpleton of the Unexpected Isles (1935)
The Millionairess (1936)
Geneva (1938)
In Good King Charles' Golden Days (1939)
Buoyant Billions (1948)

From an early age, Shaw was as leery of death as a treasure laden person might be of a bandit. He openly admitted being "a coward" as a boy, "lest I throw away my genius in some pugnacious adventure." [44] The death of his sister, Elinor Agnes, at the age of twenty from tuberculosis was no assurance that a like end wasn't to be his. Whatever the cause, headaches disabled Shaw for a day or so every month to six weeks, from the age of about twenty till he was seventy; for awhile, he must have dreaded tumor on the brain. Shaw especially feared the early forties because he was aware that at this age men of genius, like Mozart and Schiller, were often prey to a critical illness. He almost drowned on August 12, 1907, when at the age of fifty-one he went swimming and was swept far out to sea on a strong tide, and left exhausted on a sandbar. Shaw dreamed often of death at sixty-three, and at eighty-eight prepared for Golders Green Crematorium. His wife, Charlotte, died at eighty-six of a bone-crippling disease, osteitis deformans. Shaw survived her for seven years.

Throughout his adult life, Shaw let fly violently a critical barrage against alcohol, tobacco, vivisection, inoculation, vaccination, meat-eating, Darwinism, chauvinism, capitalism, and fascism among other fierce antipathies. Oddly enough Shaw had some words of praise for anarchy, monarchy, Mussolini, Hitler and Stalin. Shaw did change his mind. "Once when we had a bonfire going," noted his gardener, for instance, "he said he'd like to put Hitler on top of it with all the other weeds and things."[45] Shaw gave perhaps his own best explanation for his often mystifying and infuriating stands: "It annoys me to see people comfortable," he said, "when they ought to be uncomfortable; and I insist on making them think in order to bring them to conviction of sin."[46] "An excellent man," Oscar Wilde said of Shaw, "he has no enemies. And none of his friends like him."

Actually Shaw never lacked for enemies, nor for friends either, although his authorized biographer, Archibald Henderson, wrote of him, "Fastidiousness and corporeal aloofness stamp his temperament."[47] Shaw's friendships were of the intellectually "hot" kind. His best friends were: the socialist Webbs; the artist, William Morris; the actor, Sir Barry Jackson; the witty parliamentarian, Lady Astor; the high churchman, Dean Inge; and the disillusioned man in rebellion against England's broken promises, Lawrence of Arabia. Shaw also knew more or less intimately such names of doers in the roster of politics and the arts as: Annie Besant, St. John Ervine, A. B. Walkley, Ellen Terry, Frank Harris, H. W. Massingham, Lila McCarthy, Gilbert Murray, Sybil Thorndike, G. K. Chesterton, Harley Granville-Barker, Lady Gregory, Sir Edward Elgar, Mrs. Patrick Campbell, Arthur Balfour, Arthur Wing Pinero, James Barrie, Henry Arthur Jones, and John Galsworthy. Shaw's anti-imperialist writings in World War I, cooled many of his friends never to warm again, for instance, Jones, Kipling, and Wells.

Shaw's flaming red beard, originally grown in 1881 to hide an attack of small-pox, became with his sharp, grey-blue eyes, his shaggy eyebrows, and his iconoclastic wit a kind of Mephistophelean public image; when the silky beard and hair whitened, he looked more the

sage. He held no grudges and could laugh at himself; villagers at
Ayot called him "Old Hair and Teeth." [48]

By 1908, Shaw found the world beat a path to his door, along with
such a stream of mail that he claims he could have written twenty
more plays in the time it took him to answer his correspondence with
usually only a post-card. Proof of the affection he and his wife could
inspire is in the devoted years of service of his household staff; for instance, Henry Higgs, his head-gardener, 42 years; Fred Day, his
chauffeur, 31 years; Blanche Patch, his secretary, 30 years. His hobbies
were photography, motoring, bee-keeping, and raising fan-tail pi-
geons. He travelled to please his wife, Charlotte, and in 1933 made a
world tour. "She was always discontented, with everything in the
world to make her happy," said Shaw after her death. "But she had
the idea that happiness was always in the place she wished to be or
had just left." [49]

Once married, Shaw settled down to a puritanical simplicity of living at two addresses: 31 Adelphi Terrace, his London home; and
Shaw's Corner at Ayot, St. Lawrence, Hertfordshire. He had read a
headstone in Ayot's graveyard: "Mary South . . . Born March 5, 1825 -
Died March 13, 1895 . . . Her Time Was Short." Shaw said, "I thought
. . . then this was just exactly the climate for me." [50]

Shaw found a rich literary inheritance in the work of figures his
childhood had disposed him to. In Shelley, a vegetarianism against
the needless inflicting of pain on life, a rebellion against convention,
and a universal sympathy. In Samuel Butler, lifelike models of ironic
paradox satirizing bourgeois life. In Dickens, a whole world of
warmly alive if somewhat caricatured people. And in Ibsen and
Strindberg, the techniques to dramatize the modern mind. Early
Shaw, in fact, was called "The Laughing Ibsen."

"As long as I live, I must write," Shaw said in his nineties. "If I
stopped writing, I should die for want of something to do." [51] Shaw's
sense of his literary immortality led him to pose for many works of
art, but the one he most admired was Rodin's bust of him. Shaw had
no reservations about this work, saying, perhaps for once in his life,
"Just as I am, without one plea." [52] Ironically for the man who wrote
Back to Methuselah, the ailing and enfeebled Shaw wearied of life at
94 and, refusing to eat, died on November 2, 1950. As he had willed,
Shaw was cremated and then buried, not as some wished in Westminster
Abbey, but in his own garden at Ayot, at the foot of the statue of
Joan of Arc. There in a symbol of perfect sentiment, for one so often

charged with lacking any sentiment, Shaw's ashes were mixed with his wife's.

II

COMMERCIAL CONSIDERATIONS AFFECTING SHAW'S PLAYWRITING

Shaw was always his own literary agent, and a very shrewd one, too, although in his late years he harried himself with fears of poverty from high taxes. While other playwrights received roughly 10% of a play's gross, Shaw usually contracted for roughly 15%, and he never sold motion picture rights to his plays but granted only limited licenses.[53] His estate at his death was 367,233 pounds or about $1,222,-000 before taxes. Shaw had, indeed, carefully analyzed the wants of those crucial to his success: the theatrical managers, the public, himself, the actors, the critics and the censor.

"No one can foresee the fate of a play," said Shaw, and he rated English theatrical management "one of the most desperate commercial forms of gambling."[54] To satisfy the public, in Shaw's opinion, most managers wanted what amounted to a nice play about sex: "nice" so as not to offend the people who could afford to pay admission and who enjoyed seeing their genteel lives onstage; "about sex" because nothing else could excite and interest the highly mixed audience of playgoers. "Can any dilemma be more complete?" asked Shaw. "Love is assumed to be the only theme that touches all your audience infallibly, young and old, rich and poor. And yet love is the one subject that the drawing-room drama dare not present."[55] Shaw thought that managers tried to solve their dilemma by the legerdemain of the romantic play, "the play in which love is carefully kept off the stage whilst it is alleged as the motive of all the actions presented to the audience."[56] The more the romance, the better the box-office, the more tractable the manager, thought Shaw. "If the twin flats and twin beds produce a guinea more than Shakespear," commented Shaw, "out goes Shakespear, and in come the twin flats and the twin beds."[57] The greediest and most cynical of managers, Shaw believed, tried for the biggest box-office at the least risk by building musicals around a lurid love story. The most public-spirited of managers, in contrast, drew from the best of dramatic literature and current culture at a much higher risk of failure. Most managers, as Shaw viewed them, were between these extremes.

The commercial theatre as a matter of fact depended upon a public whose taste, Shaw believed, was plain in its reading. "What they like to read," he observed, "is the police intelligence, especially the murder cases and divorce cases." [58] Shaw, moreover, thought that Shakespeare for just this reason built his plays from the tales of envy and murder current in his day. "Without such allurements," remarked Shaw, "Shakespear could not have lived by his plays. And if he had been rich enough to disregard this consideration, he would still have had to provide sensation enough to induce people to listen to what he was inspired to say." [59] Shaw claimed, "Nobody goes to the theatre except the people who also go to Madame Tussaud's." [60] He elaborated this: "most people go to the theatre to escape reality." What is more, the escape must be complete or it is no good. "The theatre is a place which people can only endure when they forget themselves," said Shaw; "that is when their attention is entirely captured . . ." [61] Some of the public, Shaw noted, wanted "food" for their "starving souls." [62]

Shaw was to come to terms with the theatre managers and the public—his own terms. He wanted to write modern drama with the pioneering spirit of Ibsen and Chekhov. Though Shaw first let Jack Grein produce *Widowers' Houses* and then *The Philanderer* on a shoestring and for very short runs, when he observed Mansfield's success in the American tour of *Arms and the Man,* in 1894, he took a new view toward allowing the production of his plays. He wrote Ellen Terry, "in art what poverty can do only unhandsomely and stingily, it should not do at all." [63] Until England's qualified theatre managers were ready for him, Shaw chose to settle for intelligent English readers. The publisher, William Heinemann, however, warned Shaw that even Pinero's plays failed to sell as books. In 1898 a daring novice at publishing, Grant Richards, put out Shaw's first volume of plays, *Plays Pleasant and Unpleasant,* and in time it succeeded. In later years, Shaw became his own publisher in England and commissioned Constable and Company to handle the printing and distribution. "I had to give my plays a complete artistic existence as printed books," Shaw told Frank Harris, "because I could not get my plays performed in England at all, and in America and Germany where they first gained their hold on the stage, I could not superintend their production personally." [64] Shaw wrote imaginative and appealing stage directions, and for each play a witty and informative preface. According to Shaw's secretary, Blanche Patch, Shaw usually included three plays in a single volume to give the public the feeling that it was getting its money's worth.

For seekers of pure amusement, Shaw said, "I can no more write what they want than Joachim can put aside his fiddle and oblige a happy company of beanfeasters with a marching tune on the German concertina. They must keep away from my plays; that is all." [65] "To laugh without sympathy," Shaw specified, "is a ruinous abuse of a noble function; and the degradation of any race may be measured by the degree of their addiction to it." Shaw, for instance, did not like *The Importance of Being Earnest* because "unless comedy touches me as well as amuses me, it leaves me with a sense of having wasted my evening." [66]

As Shaw struggled for his integrity and a public, a twenty-five year old German so admired him that he pleaded for permission to translate his works. "He had begun by pooh poohing the whole proposal," said Patch of Shaw's reaction to Siegfried Trebitsch, "and it was only Trebitsch's faith and drive that carried it through and won the world for Shaw." [67] Thanks to Trebitsch, Germany read and produced Shaw long before England did.

The experimental Vedrenne-Barker management at the Court Theatre in 1904 gave Shaw his first commercial production in London, a matinee try-out of *Candida*. This play set off the Shaw craze in England, and by 1908 he had established his literary reputation. Shaw, himself, did more than just write the plays. He took active part in supervising casting and rehearsals, too. "Get your cast wrong," he wrote Granville-Barker, "and you wreck your play just to the extent to which the cast is wrong." [68] Shaw would let no one "wreck" his plays, if he could help it. He believed that his plays needed unusually energetic and lively acting and that, though stars might guarantee bankruptcy, they could not always guarantee success. The Court Theatre introduced eleven of Shaw's plays with as a rule young and highly talented casts, avoiding if possible high-priced stars. Asked why the commercial managers hadn't produced him before, Shaw replied of his plays, "There were no murders, no adulteries, no sexual intrigues in them," and he noted further, "The heroines were not like heroines; they were like women." [69] In 1908 Shaw was quite shocked when the Vedrenne-Barker management went bankrupt after hiring three West End Theatres that season and scoring three successive failures, none of them Shaw's. "Vedrenne got out with nothing but a reputation," Shaw said with some concern; "Barker had to pawn his clothes; and I disgorged most of my royalties. But the creditors were paid in full." [70]

Shaw deplored commercial managers who wouldn't produce his plays, but he wanted none of their fearful headaches; he had his own. "I made a vow early in life never to put a farthing in any form of public entertainment, especially theatrical entertainment," Shaw confessed late in life; "Hence my present solvency." [71] Shaw's investment of time in his plays was the most he would invest in the theatre.

For all his implied independence of managers' wants, Shaw in his best plays obviously was meeting the wants of these very managers but on his own terms: *Pygmalion, Man and Superman, Heartbreak House* and *Saint Joan.* The first three are really "nice" plays "about sex;" and *Saint Joan* is drawn directly from international "police intelligence." But in each instance Shaw made his own interpretation of life an organic part of the entertainment. As Frank Harris intimated, Shaw knew that "Shakespeare and Molière's plays—ninety percent of them were potboilers." Shaw was much too proud to live off his millionairess wife; "the pot must be boiled," he told Hesketh Pearson, "and even my pot au feu has some chunks of fresh meat in it." [72]

To win to him indifferent theatrical managers and the public, Shaw again and again tried the magic of hitching his wagon to a "star." He believed the true pioneers in advancing the drama were daring actors and actresses, who said, "I do so long to play Nora, or Hedda Gabler; and I must try whether the public will support me in it." [73] If a playwright wrote a play that fascinated a star into saying, "I must play that role," Shaw believed that play would get produced. The device was especially potent in Shaw's prime when so many stars were also theatrical managers, such as Beerbohm Tree, Henry Irving, Lewis Waller and Granville-Barker. Yet the hitching to a "star" sometimes uncoupled for altogether unforeseen reasons; Sir Henry Irving would have none of Napoleon in Shaw's *Man of Destiny* after Shaw, in a review of Irving's *Richard III,* implied that Irving in the title role was drunk with more than power. To cite a few instances of Shaw deliberately hitching his wagon to a "star," Shaw wrote Dick Dudgeon in *The Devil's Disciple* for William Terris; Candida in *Candida* for Janet Achurch; Caesar in *Caesar and Cleopatra* for Forbes Robertson; Cicely Wayneflette in *Captain Brassbound's Conversation* for Ellen Terry; Catherine the Great in *Great Catherine* for Gertrude Kingston; and Joan in *Saint Joan* for Sybil Thorndike. He told Ellen Terry, "I am a good ladies' tailor," and he could have added, "—gentlemen's, too." [74]

"The more exactly I reproduce objective life for him on the stage," Shaw wrote of the run-of-the-mill drama critic, "the more certain he is to call my play an extravaganza." [75] Shaw believed this came from drama critics seeing so much of life onstage, and so little of it offstage, that they judged a true stage portrayal of human beings by spurious standards and wound up talking gibberish. The remedy for this, Shaw thought as a one-time drama critic himself, was to have standards to qualify a man to be a drama critic. For Shaw, a drama critic should have high ethics, a comprehensive knowledge and experience in the theatre, and a true understanding of life. As a dramatist-drama critic, Shaw lived by his ethics in refusing to accept from a theatre manager anything but royalties or percentages from actual performances of his own plays; "advances," Shaw felt, might be construed as a trick to bribe him to give a good notice to other productions of the manager that Shaw, as critic, might have to review. Shaw believed a qualified drama critic is someone who has written, adapted, translated, and produced plays himself. Such a critic would take a serious rather than a flippant view of his task. In Shaw's opinion, the first moral and technical qualification of the critic was: "The determination to have every play as well done as possible and the knowledge of what is standing in the way of that consummation." [76] The drama critic also must make "good or bad" art a "personal" matter. "Criticism cannot give an absolutely true and just account of any artist," Shaw asserted; "it can at best explain its point of view and then describe the artist from that point of view." [77] Such criticism would be "medicinally salutary" for art and also have the excitement of gladiatorial combat. No genuine drama critic, Shaw was convinced, is soft:

> Those who think the things I say severe or even malicious should see the things I do not say. I do my best to be partial, to hit out at remediable abuses rather than at accidental shortcomings, and at strong and responsible people rather than weak and helpless ones.[78]

English censorship of plays, in Shaw's view, was a kind of star chamber proceeding with no recourse in law. The theatre was literally at the censor's mercy because unless the Lord Chamberlain licensed a play's performance at his own discretion or that of his aids, the public could not see that play performed. Shaw thought that like books, plays should be censored only by the writer, the publisher, and the reading public, and that plaintiffs should have similar recourse in law. Shaw himself experienced the vagaries of censorship. *Mrs. Warren's*

Profession and *The Shewing Up of Blanco Posnet,* to illustrate, were censored at first and then licensed decades later. Shaw called this "A detestable censorship, a public nuisance of which it seems impossible to rid ourselves under existing parliamentary conditions." [79]

III

AESTHETIC CONSIDERATIONS AFFECTING SHAW'S PLAYWRITING

In *Man and Superman* a speech of the artist, Tanner, runs so true to Shaw's life in many respects that Shaw likely meant it to be taken as faithfully depicting the artist's nature:

> The true artist will let his wife starve, his children go barefoot, his mother drudge for his living at seventy sooner than work at anything but his art. To women he is half vivisector, half vampire. He gets into intimate relations with them to study them, to strip the mask of convention from them, to surprise their inmost secret, knowing they have the power to rouse his deepest creative energies . . . Perish the race and wither a thousand women if only the sacrifice of one of them enables him to act Hamlet better, to paint a finer picture, to write a deeper poem, a greater play, a profounder philosophy! For mark you, Tavy, the artist's work is to shew us ourselves as we really are.

In *The Doctor's Dilemma* the dying Dubedat states his credo as an artist:

> I believe in Michael Angelo, Velasquez, and Rembrandt; in the might of design, the mystery of color, the redemption of all things by Beauty everlasting, and the message of Art that has made these hands blessed. Amen.[80]

Shaw himself notes in *The Sanity of Art* that the artist does not neglect to feed men's moral as well as physical senses, whether the feasts range from dress to drama. The truly great artist, in Shaw's opinion, creates work of extraordinary interest, beauty and individuality, and so literally extends the public's sensibilities. The public sees, for instance, what it was blind to before.

For Shaw, a play is an interpretation of life presented within the physical limitations of the theatre and requiring conflict, a significant ordering of events, a display of acting, and above all, truth. "Life as we see it," said Shaw, "is so haphazard that it is only by pickout of its key situations and arranging them in significant order (which is never how they actually occur) that it can be made intelligible." [81] Shaw believed, "the great dramatist has something better to do than to amuse himself or his audience. He has to interpret life." And he poses the problem in this famous quotation:

> Life as it appears to us in our daily experience is an unintelligible chaos of happenings . . . To attempt to understand life from merely looking on at it as it happens in the streets is as hopeless as trying to understand public questions by studying snap-shots of public demonstrations.[82]

Shuffling "key situations" reveals the playwright's point of view. A farce-writer, thinks Shaw, will see life as nonsense; a concocter of melodrama, as thrills; a pornographer, as lewdness; and a tragic poet, as sublimity. The view is not static; Shaw says, "no conflict, no drama." "As I write my plays," Shaw admits, too, "it is continually in my mind, and very much to my taste . . . to provide an exhibition of the art of acting." [83] This consideration, Shaw recalls, was uppermost in playwrights' minds from Shakespeare's time to the mid-nineteenth century, and in Shaw's opinion accounts for the survival of bad plays with good parts like *Richelieu* and *The School for Scandal*. Finally, through implication, Shaw asks for a play to be truthful above all. "That's what they all want," Shaw wrote Ellen Terry of theatre managers, "—a play in which pretty lies will make as much effect as awful truths. But it's impossible." [84]

Shaw regarded his own plays as "sui generis." [85] For him, dramatic form was convention which those who can, may make or break. His basic view of comedy and tragedy suggests his very free interpretation of traditional dramatic form:

> To me the tragedy and comedy of life lie in the consequences, sometimes terrible, sometimes ludicrous of our persistent attempts to found our institutions on the ideals suggested to our imaginations by our half-satisfied passions, instead of on a genuinely scientific natural history.[86]

Shaw justified his right to fresh form in the drama by insisting there was no future in parroting the past. "What is the use of writing plays," said Shaw, almost out of patience, "or painting frescoes if you have nothing more to say or shew than was said and shewn by Shakespear, Michael Angelo, and Raphael?" [87] Each generation, Shaw thought, had new things that needed to be said, and the artist had to keep in contact with the life of his time or find no public. The first great artist on the scene reaped the whole harvest of new thought and feeling and left only stripped fields for those following him. Shaw thought that modern man's one new message was his loss of faith, and that without faith a playwright was denied the quality of the sublime. He sincerely believed he was a prophet because he had invented or discovered a faith for moderns, "Creative Evolution," a rational passion for the science of natural history.

IV

SHAW'S WORKING METHODS IN PLAYWRITING

Genesis

For Shaw, in Blanche Patch's words, "An author's children were his books, and his wife had quite enough trouble nursing him through his confinements without having any of her own." [88] Shaw's wife, Charlotte, nursed him through "confinements" with such tender, loving care as shutting out unwelcome visitors, regulating the whole household staff of two maids, a house-keeper and a gardener, putting her time and money at Shaw's disposal, jotting down Shaw's memorable remarks, listing friends to cultivate and friends to brush off at Shaw's will, and suggesting subjects for plays or writing of another kind. [89] Charlotte must have also been a consummate companion for her to suit Shaw for about forty-five years, and for him to suit her. She made a platonic married life most congenial for his "brain-children" and a continuous creative *accouchement*.

Hinting why he wrote for the theatre, Shaw said, "Nobody writes for it, unless he is hopelessly stage struck and cannot help himself." [90] This "hopelessly stage-struck" condition seems all Shaw ever needed. Stimulants were not for him. As a man of the world of communication, however, he said, "Most of the activity of the Press, the Pulpit, and the Platform, and the Theatre is only a symptom of the activity of the drug trade, the tea trade, and the tobacco trade, and the liquor trade . . . Nowadays you get drunk to enable you to begin work." This reliance upon stimulants, Shaw also noticed, led to blurring the artist in his self-criticism and to bigger and bigger doses for less and less work, and finally to complete physical deterioration.

Though Shaw deplored the price many artists paid for creativeness, he frankly told how they went about it. "There are two ways of setting in motion the mystical agency that changes a mere human animal into a writer, a composer, an actor, a painter, a poet or what not," wrote Shaw in his introduction to Harris' *Oscar Wilde*. "There is the natural and sacred one, the application of one's own inner force by one's own inner light. The other is the way of sorcery: the resort to stimulants and drugs." [91] Wilde, of course, depended completely upon liquor, and without drink, he could neither talk nor write. Shaw depended completely upon his own "inner light."

"I never eat supper; I never smoke; I drink water . . ." [92] Shaw was a frugal vegetarian writing on practically an empty stomach. "His meals being so light," noted Blanche Patch, "and eating so frugally, he never weighed much more than nine stone (126 pounds)." [93] Shaw was six foot, one inch tall. Upon first seeing him, Alfred Hitchcock, the rotund motion picture producer-director, said, "One look at you, and I know there's famine in the land;" to which Shaw replied, "One look at you, Mr. Hitchcock, and I know who caused it." [94] "He lived on soups, eggs, milk, honey, cheese, fruit, cream, and lemon juice," reported his housekeeper, Mrs. Alice Laden, in Allan Chappelow's *Shaw, the Villager and Human Being*. "He had difficulty in eating nuts in his later years." [95]

Shaw led such a very busy life involving so much transportation to keep engagements that he said, "I had either to write under all circumstances or not to write at all . . ." [96] In fact, Shaw revealed, "A very considerable part of my plays has been written in railway carriages between King's Cross and Hatfield, and it is no worse than what I have written in the Suez and Panama Canals."

Shaw's study at 31 Adelphi Terrace, London, was a fourth floor "cubby-hole" overlooking the Thames River. His study at Ayot from 1906 until his death in 1950 was in a separate little summer house, a hut actually, that could be turned to face the sun: "He liked to 'go out to work' every day—away from home (even if only a short way)," wrote Chappelow. [97] Both studies were simple, small, furnished just with basic needs like a flat-topped desk for Shaw, another desk for his secretary, and plenty of books haphazardly stowed away on shelves. Blanche Patch found Ayot "deadly dull;" Shaw found the remote town with its rather fixed population of 100 "ideal."

Whatever the path of his imagination, Shaw's working day followed a routine. In London he would wake early, go for a swim at the Royal Automobile Club, take a stroll down Pall Mall, and be breakfasting and reading his newspaper, *The Daily News,* or in later years, *The Daily Herald,* by nine in the morning. By ten o'clock, Shaw was at his desk writing and kept at it till twelve or sometimes even until one p.m. Then Shaw lunched meagerly, napped, relaxed, and took care of his mail. At six p.m. he might put in another hour's work writing before a scanty dinner, if any, at seven p.m. When Shaw travelled long or short distances, he apparently wrote "catch as catch can" in his usual Pitman shorthand and on pads four by six inches or smaller. "He was lost in thought most of the time, thinking about his plays," said Shaw's gardener Fred Drury. "He always had his notebook with him, and used to fetch it out and write things down in it, as he walked along." [98] Shaw thought he had a gift for "solitariness."

With few exceptions, Shaw usually began a play because some manager, actor, or critic had asked for it or might want it if he did it. Frank Harris, who knew Shaw about fifty years, remarked, "It may be seriously questioned whether Shaw would ever have written a play if there had been no theatres to be kept open and no actors to be obliged." [99] A very few plays originated largely in Shaw's own personal creative need; *Heartbreak House,* for instance, was Shaw's reaction to observing cultured, leisured England before World War I, a privileged class drifting in selfish futility, ideally suited to a Chekhovian treatment, or as Shaw put it, "a Fantasia in the Russian manner on English themes." But the great bulk of Shaw's plays were written to answer someone's need like a cry of "Help!" To illustrate, he finished *Widowers' Houses* and then wrote *The Philanderer* for Jack Grein's Independent Theatre. He wrote *Mrs. Warren's Profession,* a study of a "Madam," when Mrs. Sidney Webb asked him to do a play about "a modern, unromantic, hard-working woman." He wrote *Arms and the Man* to rescue Miss Horniman and Florence Farr and their Old Avenue Theatre from foreclosure. He wrote *Candida* for Janet Achurch; the plays beginning with *John Bull's Other Island* and going through *Androcles and the Lion,* for the desperately dependent Vedrenne-Barker management; *Pygmalion,* for Mrs. Patrick Campbell. Practically all of Shaw's late plays were written for the Malvern Festival specifically honoring him. Shaw implied a basic element in beginning a play when he confided in Ellen Terry, "Everything real in life is based on need." [100]

But the "need," though it began as someone else's, Shaw then made somehow to correspond to his own and the times'. "If a man is a deep writer," Shaw said in self-revelation, "all his works are confessions," and then noting his inseparable attachment to his own times he said, "the best plays are those made of the very stuff of contemporary life in its most deeply felt aspects." [101] To Shaw, every great artist whether

Plato, Aristophanes or Shakespeare, wrote about and for his contemporaries. A play never began with a plot, "that dramatic cancer." "Things occur to me first as scenes with action and dialogue," Shaw told Archibald Henderson, "—as moments developing themselves out of their own vitality." When pressed further, Shaw added:

> My procedure is to imagine characters and to let them rip, but I must warn you that the real process is very obscure: for the result always shows that there has been something *behind* all the time, of which I was not conscious, though it turns out to be the real motive of the whole creation.[102]

Shaw admitted that the arrest of Dick Dudgeon in *The Devil's Disciple* popped into his mind, and this situation called into being the rest of the play. But behind the creation might well have been Shaw's "real motive"—the rebellious Irishman giving England its just due even as the American colonists had—but now the Irishman, Dick Dudgeon, lives by Shaw's view of life as natural history.

The Doctor's Dilemma came to be when an assistant asked the eminent Sir Almroth Wright if Wright could help one more patient with his opsonin treatment for tuberculosis, and Wright had asked, "Is he worth it?"[103] Mrs. Shaw overheard this exchange and told her husband what happened; Shaw had lost his own sister, Elinor Agnes, through tuberculosis contracted from a nursemaid. Doctors in their ignorance at the time did not think tuberculosis contagious. Shaw also had lost a dear friend, James Joynes, and told Archibald Henderson that Joynes "was slaughtered by a medical treatment so grossly and openly stupid and ruinous that I have never forgiven the medical profession for it since"—that is, by crude immobilization, now discredited.[104] Shaw could identify with his sister, Elinor Agnes, with Joynes, and with the artist Dubedat in the play.

As for *Pygmalion's* genesis, Mrs. Patrick Campbell hints in her letters to Shaw that she first suggested Liza Doolittle to him. Shaw had accused her in rehearsal of speaking too carefully onstage, and stung to the quick, she had blurted out at him, "If you will write me a cockney part, I will show you what I can do."[105] Shaw, of course, from his teenage days had studied phonetics with Chichester Bell, hoping to improve his diction in singing. Liza's plight in being socially downgraded because of her cockney speech must have been deep in Shaw's heart; upon arriving in London in 1876, Shaw had a thick brogue that could only have made him something of a laughing stock to English snobs. His mother and sister, Lucy, certainly also had quite a brogue and, like Liza Doolittle, used phonetic drills to correct it; "Your mother will sing one day in London before the Queen," Lee had told the Shaw children according to the biographer Winsten. Lucy had hoped to become a prima donna on the London musical stage; Liza Doolittle, of course, was to be presented to the Queen at court, and the former cockney flower-girl palmed off as a lady. When *The London Observer* of January 11, 1914, pointed out that the plot of *Pygmalion* was to be found in Smollett's novel, *Peregrine Pickle,* Shaw said, "I have never read *Peregrine Pickle . . .*" [106]

The genesis of *Saint Joan* is particularly interesting because Shaw thought this work his best, and his method of genesis was definitely not "to imagine characters and let them rip." A friend of the Shaws, Sir Sidney Cockerell, happened to read T. Douglas Murray's book, *Jeanne D'Arc,* and became so excited by the court records as a possible source for a play by Shaw that he passed his excitement and the book to Mrs. Shaw who, excited in turn, got Shaw to look at the book with a non-committal response. Mrs. Shaw then deliberately took to leaving many different books about Joan of Arc lying about the rooms Shaw frequented. Shaw on impulse picked up these books, for he was "between plays," and well aware, surely, of what his wife was up to. Finally Shaw told his wife that he would do a play about Joan of Arc. Winsten in his book, *Jesting Apostle,* noted Shaw's deep spiritual kinship with Joan—"She stood up in the minority of one against authority, she was above sex . . . and she had belief in her Voices." [107]

Shaw at heart must have felt another powerful identification with Joan. The English in his own case had figuratively burned him at the stake for his anti-imperialist views about World War I and for his defense of Roger Casement, the Irishman the English eventually hanged for allegedly conspiring with the Germans in World War I. Of Shaw's pamphlet, *Common Sense about the War,* Pearson wrote in *Bernard Shaw,* "Yet no work since *The Rights of Man* by Tom Paine, who wrote *Common Sense* about another crisis, has gained for its author such a generous measure of hatred and vituperation." [108] Like Joan, Shaw never recanted.

He based *Saint Joan* on the most contemporary, journalistic source material he could find, the actual court records in Quicherat's *The Rehabilitation of Joan.* "I stuck to the contemporary reports," Shaw told Pearson, "and I did not read a word of the critics and the biographers until I had finished the play." [109]

Characterization

Shaw hunted for his characters in what he called "key situations" in life, picking out contrasted figures to excite conflict. "All his characters are remarkable people," observed Ervine. "The commonplace man or woman did not interest him." [110] The titles of Shaw's best plays show that he centered a play usually upon a single character or two, and required virtuosity in the acting, for instance: *Candida, Caesar and Cleopatra, Man and Superman, Pygmalion, Major Barbara, Saint Joan.*

Asked if he made his characters from composites of his friends and acquaintances, Shaw replied, "I probably never do anything else. But I have never done it consciously." "There is in my plays and indeed in all fiction," Shaw asserted, "an element due altogether to the purely accidental personal experiences of the author which defies exegesis." [111] Shaw noted that even with a conscious model, imaginary people unlike the model, possibly its frustrated selves, crossed brain-cells in the ultimate character. "I exploited you, made money out of you," Shaw wrote Mrs. Patrick Campbell, "got two stage characters out of you (Hesione and Orinthia) and I will perhaps get six more out of your manifold nature." [112]

Shaw acknowledged many conscious models later not easily identified because of his method of cross-breeding, for example: Stopford Brooke, for Morell in *Candida;* Dr. Edward Aveling for Dubedat in *The Doctor's Dilemma;* H. M. Hyndman for Tanner in *Man and Superman;* and Mary Hankinson for Joan of Arc in *Saint Joan.* Shaw also consciously drew models from fiction, for instance: Mrs. Dudgeon in *The Devil's Disciple* from Dickens' Mrs. Clennam; and Mendoza in *Man and Superman* from Sir Arthur Conan Doyle's Brigand who inflicts upon his captives his poetry. Shaw said outright that in *Heartbreak House* he drew his leading characters from stock figures of the Commedia dell' Arte: Mazzini Dunn, to illustrate, from the cowardly Spanish Captain; Alfred Mangan from the stingy old merchant, Pantaloon; Hector Hushabye, from the romantically moonstruck Pierrot; and Hesione Hushabye, from the eternally coquettish Pierrette. Shaw remarked, "my characters are the familiar harlequin and columbine, clown and pantaloon. . ." [113]

Often Shaw used a prototype of himself to cross-breed with his characters. "As a dramatist I have no clue to any historical or other personage," said Shaw, "save that part of him which is also myself." [114] Shaw himself, of course, unmistakably sparkles in the brilliant iconoclasm of the artist, Tanner, of *Man and Superman;* in the fiendishly clever and prophetic Captain Shotover of *Heartbreak House;* and in the witty, imaginative, self-made Larry Doyle of *John Bull's Other Island.* "For stage purposes," said Shaw in his sixties, "there are not many types of character available; and all the playwrights use them over and over again; idiosyncrasies are useful on the stage only to give an air of infinite variety to the standard types." [115]

Having got his models, Shaw developed them through probing: "Indeed, in all the plays my economic studies have played as important a part as a knowledge of anatomy does in the works of Michael Angelo." [116] For Shaw, a dramatic character was in a conclusive way the product of his bank balance in such vital respects as social position, occupation, taste, and life outlook. So for instance, of Mrs. Warren's profession, running houses of prostitution, Shaw says, "I have gone straight to the fact that as Mrs. Warren puts it, 'the only way for a woman to provide for herself decently is for her to be good to some man that can afford to be good to her.'" Shaw found no blackhearted villains in life, nor snow-white angels, either, so he used no such characters in his plays. "In such cheap wares," said Shaw, "I do not deal." [117]

As he let his characters "rip," Shaw claimed they grew by themselves in his imagination and that in his writing he was "as much a medium as Douglas Home." He likened his experience to that of other literary greats:

> Shakespear, like Dickens, like Cervantes, like most geniuses of their type, made the acquaintance of their characters as they went along . . . I see no reason to doubt that the same thing happened during the writing of *Hamlet.* Shakespear began with nothing more definite in his mind than the old zany Hamlet, crazy with grief for the death of his father and horror at the incest of his mother. But when Shakespear got him going, he ran right away with his creator. This does not happen to uninspired writers, who plan everything laboriously beforehand.[118]

Shaw did his best work like other artists when "inspired," but his long apprenticeship and observation of the best practices of others, as a reader and critic, had made him an intensely knowledgeable and disciplined artist who received his "inspiration" well prepared to make the most of it, rather than simply be a passive agent as in "automatic writing." Shaw's muse had been trained to respond almost at call through many years of hard discipline to a very demanding master. Sometimes she only "put in time" as a number of Shaw's less able efforts prove.

As for writing by formula in the manner of the "well-made" play, Shaw conceded that mechanical plays sometimes are more diverting than real plays "just as a clock-work mouse is more amusing than a real mouse, though it will kill the cat who swallows it in good faith." [119] Shaw believed, "No writer of the first order needs the formula any more than a sound man needs a crutch." [120] Even in his simplest mood, the writer does not contrive a plot but tells a story, a narrative with lifelike characters. In a more complex mood, the writer tries to interpret life.

Again and again Shaw declared, "my stories are the old stories." He drew tales, for instance, from folklore and history to write *Man and Superman, Pygmalion, Androcles and the Lion, Back to Methuselah, Man of Destiny, Caesar and Cleopatra,* and *Saint Joan.* An "old" story to Shaw was proof of longevity or even immortality, and by adding his treatment he added to that longevity or immortality, his name.

Shaw's treatment was the freshness of development and viewpoint he gave the old story by interpreting it in terms of his passion to substitute "natural history for conventional ethics and romantic logic." To illustrate, Shaw based his *Man and Superman* on the Mozartian version of the old story of the arch-lover, Don Juan. In terms of natural history, Shaw gave the arch-lover's life a new significance. Woman, the breeder, was basically the huntress in love; man, the bread-winner, was basically the hunted in love; and so, for Shaw, "Don Juan has come to birth as a stage projection of the tragi-comic love chase of the man by the woman . . ." Shaw attributed the play's enormous success to its "complete preoccupation with sex;" [121] intrinsically, the play was what Shaw claimed most managers wanted—"a nice" play about "sex." The play also reflected Shaw's own amorous experiences with women in the game of love, summed up in his words in *Sixteen Self-Sketches,* "I did not pursue women. I was pursued by them." [122]

He never denied the literary ancestors of his characters, but he never made such ancestor-worship his whole future. "I have entered into a great inheritance from the Athenians, from Shakespeare and Molière, from Goethe, Mozart and Wagner, and from the novelists who came to the rescue when the stage had fallen into comtempt," wrote Shaw, "not to mention later legacies from Ibsen and the

Russians; and I have spent this magnificent fortune prodigally in the face of the world." [123]

Each play, Shaw believed, had a structure organic to it. "Real plays," said Shaw, "are no more constructed than a carrot is constructed." [124] The formal organic structure, in which Shaw tended to allow his characters to "rip", moved in one of two alternatives usually. On the one hand, as in *Candida,* Shaw used the unities. "The classic unities have their virtue for those who can handle them," said Shaw, "and are indeed inherent in drama at its highest concentration." [125] On the other hand as in Shakespeare and the movies, Shaw tended to use multiple scenes, showing a story from beginning to end rather than only in its culminating hours; such freedom is found in *Saint Joan.* "No theatre is likely to be generally useful in the future unless its stage is so constructed," said Shaw, "that it can present a play in fifty scenes without a break." [126]

In his preface to *Saint Joan,* Shaw goes into detail about much of his effort to fit Joan's story to the stage. A few examples hint at his conscious artistry. "I have done nothing," said Shaw of Joan, "but arrange her for the stage." [127] But what an arrangement! Shaw made Joan dominate the whole play and gave her death a new significance in terms of natural history: she became the first great Protestant outcry in Catholic Europe's transition from feudalism to nationalism. She heeded her "voices" rather than the Church's voice, and the Church in modern times was to decide her "voices" were not the devil's but a sign of sainthood. So big is Joan's role that Shaw noted, "*Saint Joan* will always be a star play for a big actress." [128]

He compressed fourteen months of historical action into three and a half hours of playing time onstage. He has similarly telescoped places: for instance, historically, before Joan won over the Dauphin to her, the Churchmen put her off for days and then cross-examined her at Poitiers, whereas Shaw presents all this in a single scene.

Faced with fragmentary or conflicting testimony, Shaw made himself the final arbiter. "My Dunois would do equally well for the Duc d'Alençon . . . In view of the things they did in history and have to do again, I can only invent appropriate characters for them in Shakespeare's manner." [129] The Bishop and the Inquisitor in Shaw's play, unlike their monstrously wicked counterparts in Mark Twain and Andrew Lange, are able representatives of the Catholic Church faced with a momentous judgment involving the devil, heresy, damnation, salvation, excommunication, and death at the stake. "If Joan had not been burnt by normally innocent people in the energy of their righteousness," stated Shaw, "her death at their hands would have no more significance than the Tokyo earthquake which burnt a great many maidens." [130]

Shaw admits that he gave his leading characters a far greater understanding of their times than evidence warrants they had, but what Shaw lost in verisimilitude, he believed he gained in essential truth. He wrote of his pivotal characters—the Bishop Cauchon, Inquisitor Lemaître, and Warwick—"the things I represent these three exponents of the drama as saying are the things they actually would have said if they had known what they were really doing." [131] The most meaningful scene of *Saint Joan* to Shaw was the Epilogue which has the spirit of artistic rather than factual truth.

Shaw's Sources of Freshness

Technically speaking, Shaw rated himself "a very old-fashioned playwright." And yet his work is fresh through its distinctively Shavian quality.

The Shavian quality is drawn from Shaw's search for the vital in life. His writing epitomized advanced contemporary thought of his day. "I am a crow," cawed Shaw, "who followed many ploughs. No doubt I seem prodigiously clever to those who have never hopped, hungry and curious, across the fields of philosophy, politics, and art." [132] Shaw did not originate what he had to say so much as assimilate it from others. In this sense, he was always very up-to-the-minute.

The Shavian quality is also drawn from Shaw's wit and insight especially in making discussion a powerful technique in the theatre. "A play with a discussion," asserted Shaw, "is a modern play. A play with only an emotional situation is an old-fashioned one." [133] Shaw used his amazing cleverness and artistry in language to lure and deeply involve the conscience of his audience through parable, irony, epigram, metaphor, paradox, rhetoric, and argument. "It is the technique of playing upon the human conscience," commented Shaw; "and it has been practised by playwrights whenever the playwright has been capable of it." [134] Shaw included among such practitioners Aeschylus, Euripides, Sophocles, and Aristophanes. At best, discussion for Shaw was not to be dragged in like excess baggage but to live as an organic part of the characters' lives:

In . . . *Candida,* you have action producing discussion; in *The Doctor's Dilemma,* you have discussion producing action and that action being finally discussed. In other plays, you have discussion all over the shop. . . . The public now demands a case and an argument, vehemently conducted.[135]

The Shavian quality also is drawn from Shaw's view of life in terms of "natural history" rather than of "conventional ethics and romantic logic." Shaw first formed the credo of his new faith, Creative Evolution, in the preface and action of *Man and Superman* and then elaborated the credo in *Back to Methuselah*. Don Juan in *Man and Superman* is the spokesman of Shaw's prophetic vision:

> I tell you that as long as I can conceive something better than myself I cannot be easy unless I am striving to bring it into existence or clearing the way for it. This is the law of my life. That is the working within me of Life's incessant aspiration to higher organization, wider, deeper, intenser self-consciousness and clearer self-understanding.[136]

In the preface of *Man and Superman* Shaw said, like Don Juan offstage, "This is the true joy of life, the being used for a purpose recognized by yourself as a mighty one; the being thoroughly worn out before you are thrown on the scrap heap . . . ;" and added, "And also the only real tragedy in life is being used by personally minded men for purposes which you recognize to be base."[137]

Declaring himself a "prophet," Shaw as a master of language must have considered himself in the line of biblical succession. Shaw saw in natural history the Life Force trying to perfect itself, with each new life, even cancer and croup bacillus, becoming another experiment.[138] If man through war should be destroyed, in Shaw's opinion the Life Force would regard man's extinction as no more notable than that of the dynosaurs and would simply continue with new experiments in a drive for perfection. Shaw formulated his doctrine by synthesizing Bergson's *élan vitale* or Life Force with Lamarck's view that organic life evolved because it wanted to change. Shaw would have none of Darwin because Shaw believed (though Darwin would deny it) that Darwin excluded God and therefore, of course, the human soul.

Writing and Rewriting

Shaw apparently never worked from a detailed, written scenario, although in the instance of his greatest success, *Saint Joan*, he had an equivalent in history and in the court records. Shaw began the actual writing of the dialogue only when he felt he had a sufficiently strong grasp of his materials. How long it took him to get such a confident grip can only be gauged from his comment: "My method is to take the utmost trouble to find the right thing to say, and then say it with the utmost levity. And all the time the real joke is that I am in earnest." [139] Shaw's prefaces suggest how deeply he plumbed the emotional and intellectual depths of his subject matter.

"I write the dialogue first," recalled Shaw of his manuscript, "leaving the mechanical business of the stage for revision, but I usually find that I have subconsciously seen everything from the start." [140] "A stage direction need not tell an actor *how* to act;" stipulated Shaw in a letter to Louis Wilkinson, "it should tell him *what* he is to act. There is only one effect to be produced; there may be fifty different ways of producing it." [141] Shaw took great care with his stage directions for fear of someday sharing Shakespeare's fate, a victim of interpreters who muddled matters for lack of stage directions.

The master-clue of the effect Shaw worked for in his dialogue is suggested in what he wanted of a play's production. "The beginning and the end of the business from the author's point of view," Shaw said of production in *The Art of Rehearsal*, "is the art of making the audience believe that real things are happening to real people." [142] Shaw thought he knew how to make this come off in the theatre, for he told Frank Harris that "the art of producing plays" was "as much my profession as writing them." [143]

Dialogue for Shaw should obviously help the rest of the production give the effect of real things happening to real people. "I came to seek idiom," said Shaw, "as being the most highly vitalized form of language . . ." He found one of the most effective forms of assertion to be the proverb. "And idiom and proverb he has since used accordingly," observed Shaw's biographer, Colbourne, "until these have become a characteristic of the Shavian style." [144]

"Effectiveness of assertion," to Shaw, "is the Alpha and Omega of style." [145] So great is the power of style that even if time should deny its assertion, the style keeps a work of art alive. Said Shaw, "Darwin has no more destroyed the effectiveness of Job nor of Handel than Martin Luther destroyed the style of Giotto." [146]

Because Shaw found that many people read nothing at all and so understood only modern vernacular English, he confessed that to reach the broadest public with his plays, "I myself . . . discarded my early very classical style for a vernacular one." [147] Shaw conceded that he had mastered his style only after ten years of writing 2,000 words or so a week, with no pains spared to gather the least significant fact about his subject; through this extended apprenticeship of marshaling roughly 1,000,000 words to answer to his call, Shaw claimed the entire vocabulary of the English language finally responded to his bidding "completely and instantaneously." [148]

Shaw found in all truth and certainly in that of his dialogue "indescribable levity." He made use of this often to get a hearing as a clown and to be tolerated as a lunatic. Here is Sergius speaking in *Arms and the Man:*

> Soldiering, my dear madam, is the coward's art of attacking mercilessly when you are strong and keeping out of harm's way when you are weak. That is the whole secret of successful fighting.[149]

And here is Sir Patrick speaking in *The Doctor's Dilemma:*

> When you're as old as I am, you'll know that it matters very little how a man dies. What matters, is how he lives. Every fool that runs his nose against a bullet is a hero nowadays because he dies for his country. Why doesn't he live for some purpose? [150]

And here is Mangan in *Heartbreak House:*

> I knew that the surest way to ruin a man who doesn't know how to handle money, is to give him some.[151]

"The chief mark of Shavian prose," wrote Eric Bentley in *The Playwright as Thinker,* "is its use of ironic anti-thesis and juxtaposition." [152] In his spoken prose, as in the examples of dialogue just cited, Shaw was following a logical extension of his own dictum from 1898: "no conflict, no drama;" ironic anti-thesis and juxtaposition are ideal for promoting conflict in dialogue.

"Opera taught me to shape my plays into recitatives, arias, duets, trios, ensemble finales and bravura pieces," wrote Shaw, "to display the technical accomplishments of the executants." [153] The length of a speech in Shaw's dialogue runs to whatever the occasion warrants within the limits of the audience's endurance. The Inquisitor's famous speech in *Saint Joan* lasts eight minutes. Shaw believed his use of long speeches put him in the dramatic tradition of Sophocles, Shakespeare, and Molière.

As an example of Shaw's skill in giving dialogue the effect of actuality and his use of idiom, proverb, juxtaposition and ironic anti-thesis, here is a passage from *Candida* in which the poet, Marchbanks, romanticizes while the minister's wife, Candida, brings Marchbanks down to earth:

> MARCHBANKS. (*firing up*) Yes, to be idle, selfish, and useless; that is, to be beautiful and free and happy; hasn't every man desired that with all his soul for the woman he loves? That's my ideal; what's yours, and that of all the dreadful people who live in these hideous rows of houses? Sermons and scrubbing brushes! With you to preach the sermon and your wife to scrub.
>
> CANDIDA. (*quaintly*) He cleans the boots, Eugene. You will have to clean them tomorrow for saying that about him.
>
> MARCHBANKS. Oh, don't talk about boots! Your feet should be beautiful on the mountains.
>
> CANDIDA. My feet would not be beautiful on the Hackney Road without boots.
>
> BURGESS. (*scandalized*) Come, Candy! Don't be vulgar. Mr. Marchbanks ain't accustomed to it. You're givin' 'im the 'orrors again. I mean the poetic ones.[154]

Except for *The Admirable Bashville,* which he wrote in blank verse, Shaw wrote all his plays in prose. He claimed he wrote this one, short verse play to show that he could write in one week in verse what would have taken him one month in prose. Gifted with a sense of rhythm, stocked with words and free as Shakespeare was to fool with language, Shaw thought that anyone could pour out blank verse: "this is why whole oceans of dull bombast and drivel have been emptied on the head of England since Shakespear's time," snapped Shaw, ". . . by people who could not have written *Box and Cox* to save their lives."[155] The only blank verse Shaw liked was Shakespeare's; others couldn't compare. Shaw deliberately wrote *Saint Joan* not in verse but in prose—a very daring departure for a high tragedy about characters long dead and somewhat legendary. This choice affirms Shaw's early judgment that prose was harder to write than verse and better suited to give the impression of real things happening to real people. Much of *Saint Joan*'s fresh excitement is in Shaw's handling of the trial before the Inquisition. The cross-examination of Joan becomes a counterpart of discussion, for it relentlessly tries the conscience of the audience and is organic to the play's action and in no way contrived.

Shaw admitted to spending "many grievous, brain-racking days" in specifying the staging of his plays.[156] "I have to plan as carefully as if I were head carpenter as well as author," said Shaw. But Shaw did not always plan on absolute reality. "The wise playwright, when he cannot get absolute reality of presentation," remarked Shaw, "goes to the other extreme and aims at atmosphere and suggestion rather than at direct simulative illusion." [157] No rule, however, was absolutely binding for him. A completely realistic effect, for instance, he thought could blight any poetic illusion of *A Midsummer Night's Dream,* while scenery might help considerably to give *Othello* actuality.

To write a first draft, Shaw usually took two or three months. He worked about four hours a day. *Heartbreak House,* however, was a good three years in coming to life, and other plays, almost as long, even if he was at times "as much a medium as Douglas Home." At first Shaw's wife, Charlotte, and in later years, a professional secretary, would type a fair copy from Shaw's manuscript which was always written in Pitman short-hand. Blanche Patch, Shaw's secretary for about his last thirty years, reported that his manuscripts show he very seldom changed a single word in a first draft.

Revision could be another story. "I have known him to tear a perfectly good manuscript to pieces by the most wholesale revision in response to the spell of a moment's inspiration," said Shaw's authorized biographer, Archibald Henderson, "—though the result may conceivably be worse than the original." [158] Shaw called authors who could not revise "no tradesmen." "I never let a play out of my hands until it is as good as I can make it, and it is sufficiently light to be digested without difficulty," declared Shaw. And he said with pride, "I am like Molière in point of always consulting my cook about my plays. She is an excellent critic." [159] Once a manuscript had been copied, Shaw usually tore up the original in Pitman short-hand; almost none of Shaw's original manuscripts are extant.

As a play came to full life onstage during rehearsal, Shaw revised or didn't revise according to his best judgment. "Rehearsals were a ceremonial performed by Shaw and his casts; upon all others the theatre doors were closed," Patch noticed; [160] "Corrections would invariably be made in the rehearsal copies of the plays, and there might be more when the run had began." [161] During rehearsals, Shaw almost never interrupted or raised his voice. If he thought it warranted, he would simply explain or clearly demonstrate just what he wanted. Rehearsals for Shaw were especially important to test a new play for proper length; usually Shaw over-wrote, and much cutting had to be done. In rehearsing *John Bull's Other Island,* to illustrate, Shaw began with a script 32,000 words long and wound up with one of more conventional length, 18,000 words or so. To cite another instance, in rehearsing *Major Barbara* Shaw found it to be long "beyond human endurance," and after futilely trying to persuade the Vedrenne-Barker management to take two successive evenings to do a single performance, he finally cut *Major Barbara* to a length suitable for one evening.[162]

Shaw might or might not make further revisions after opening night. Once he was satisfied, he would never again make further changes in a script or allow others to make changes. Mrs. Patrick Campbell, for example, in touring the United States with *Pygmalion*, tried to rewrite the play's ending to please the audience by implying a love match between Professor Higgins and Liza Doolittle. Shaw cabled Mrs. Campbell, "Absolutely forbid Campbell interpolation of any suggestion that the middle-aged bully and the girl of eighteen are lovers." [163] In the original Greek myth of *Pygmalion,* of course, the sculptor does fall in love with his statue of the woman of his dreams, and the gods bring the statue to life so his love may be returned. Shaw evidently believed this might be possible with characters living in a pagan and primitive Greece, but not in Edwardian England. When the Theatre Guild decades later tried to get Shaw to cut *Back to Methuselah* so commuters might catch the last train of the evening to return to their homes, Shaw wired back, "Alter the trains." [164]

In his own lifetime, Shaw was finally induced to rewrite his plays somewhat for the talkies. He had through the years refused to sell motion picture rights to producers for fear they would commit mayhem on his brain-children to suit the producer's own "name," some star, the box-office, and a censor. Then in late 1930, Gabriel Pascal, an uninvited, penniless, maverick movie producer, burst in upon Shaw at Ayot. Quite by surprise, Shaw found Pascal to be one of the most entertaining and enterprising people he had ever met in his whole life. As an experiment, Shaw consented to let Pascal make a talking picture of *Pygmalion* with the understanding that Pascal would not change a word of the play. According to Patch, the movie of *Pygmalion* starring Leslie Howard and Wendy Hiller completely renewed Shaw's fame and fortune. Patch believed Shaw owed all this freshening of laurels to the fantastic powers of persuasion of Gabriel Pascal.[165]

Pygmalion won Shaw his first Academy Award for the best screen play of 1938–1939. Shaw had even been persuaded by the incredible Pascal to write a few scenes of continuity to provide an easier transition from the stage to the screen. Heartened by this first success, Shaw allowed Pascal to film *Caesar and Cleopatra* starring Claude Raines

and Vivian Leigh, a project done during three years of World War
II; this time, Shaw not only wrote transitional scenes but also cut his
play to give it more flow.

After Shaw's death in 1950, the greatest single impetus to the renewal of his fame and fortune came when his estate allowed Alan Jay
Lerner and Frederick Loewe to transform *Pygmalion* into *My Fair
Lady,* to date the most successful musical in all theatrical history. *My
Fair Lady* opened in New York City at the Mark Hellinger Theatre
on March 15, 1956 and ran for 2,717 performances, or roughly seven
years on Broadway. World reception of the musical and of the motion
picture has been equally astounding. The irony is that had Shaw been
alive, he very likely would never have allowed Lerner and Loewe or
anyone else to turn any work of his into a musical. In 1926, Theresa
Helburn in the name of the Theatre Guild of New York City had
asked Shaw for permission to turn his play, *The Devil's Disciple,* into
a musical, and Shaw had answered, "My dear Tessie, after my experience with *The Chocolate Soldier,* nothing will ever induce me to
allow any other play of mine to be degraded into an operetta or set to
any music except its own." [166]

"I write prefaces as Dryden did," said Shaw, "and treatises as
Wagner, because I can." [167] Shaw claimed that often his prefaces cost
him more work than his plays, for in the prefaces he exercised his
full powers as both critic and philosopher, two hats which Shaw did
not consider prerequisite to a playwright.[168] Patch reported, "nor did
Shaw ever write his famous prefaces until he had completed the plays
which were their texts." [169] She noted, for example, that while *Saint
Joan* opened in London on March 26, 1924, Shaw did not write the
preface for the play until the following May. Shaw had begun writing
prefaces to his plays in an attempt from 1898 to 1905 to lure a reading
public to them. Thereafter, the public and Shaw so enjoyed the prefaces that Shaw rarely published a play without one.

CHAPTER IV: ACKNOWLEDGEMENTS

My grateful acknowledgement is extended to The Public Trustee and The Society of Authors, Executors of the Estate of Bernard Shaw for permission to use all direct quotations from Shaw's works and from the following sources:

BERNARD SHAW by Frank Harris, Simon and Schuster, 1931

BERNARD SHAW, *His Life and Personality* by Hesketh Pearson. Copyright 1942. Atheneum, 1963. Reprinted by permission of Harper & Row, Inc. and Collins Ltd.

BERNARD SHAW by St. John Ervine, William Morrow and Co., 1956. Reprinted by permission

BERNARD SHAW AND MRS. PATRICK CAMPBELL: THEIR CORRESPONDENCE, edited by Alan Dent. Knopf, Inc. Copyright 1952

BERNARD SHAW'S LETTERS TO GRANVILLE-BARKER, edited by C. B. Purdom, Copyright (c) 1957, The Public Trustee, Executor for the Estate of George Bernard Shaw. Reprinted with the permission of the publishers, Theatre Arts Books, New York

BERNARD SHAW, MAN OF THE CENTURY by Archibald Henderson. Copyright 1956. Reprinted by permission of Appleton-Century

BERNARD SHAW, PLAYBOY AND PROPHET by Archibald Henderson. Copyright 1932. Reprinted by permission of Appleton-Century

GEORGE BERNARD SHAW by G. K. Chesterton, J. Lane Co., and Bodley Head, 1909, 1961

ELLEN TERRY AND BERNARD SHAW, A CORRESPONDENCE edited by Christopher St. John. Copyright (c) 1949, The Public Trustee, Executor for the Estate of George Bernard Shaw. Reprinted with the permission of the publishers, Theatre Arts Books, New York

JESTING APOSTLE by Stephen Winsten, Hutchinson and Co., Ltd., 1956

THE LOVES OF GEORGE BERNARD SHAW by C. G. L. DuCann. Copyright 1963. Reprinted by permission of Funk & Wagnalls Co., Inc. and Arthur Barker, Publishers, Ltd.

THE NEW YORK *TIMES*, June 2, 1912, Letter by Shaw "On the Principles That Govern the Dramatist". (C) 1912 by The New York Times Company. Reprinted by permission.

OSCAR WILDE by Frank Harris with a preface by Bernard Shaw. Copyright 1938. Constable and Co., Ltd.

THE REAL BERNARD SHAW by Maurice Colbourne. Copyright 1939. J. M. Dent Sons, Ltd.

SHAW OF DUBLIN, The Formative Years, by B. C. Rosset, The Pennsylvania State University Press, 1964

SHAW ON THEATRE edited by E. J. West, Hill and Wang, 1958

SHAW THE VILLAGER AND HUMAN BEING, a biographical symposium, narrated and edited by Allan Chappelow. (C) 1961 by Allan Chappelow. All Rights Reserved. Reprinted by permission of The Macmillan Company and Charles Skilton, Ltd.

TABLE-TALK OF GEORGE BERNARD SHAW edited by Archibald Henderson, copyright 1925. Reprinted by permission of Harper & Row, Publishers, Inc.

THIRTY YEARS WITH G. B. S. by Blanche Patch. Copyright 1951. Reprinted by permission of Victor Gollancz, Ltd.

THREE PLAYS OF BRIEUX by Eugene Brieux with a preface by Bernard Shaw. Copyright 1913.

1. Archibald Henderson, *Table-talk of George Bernard Shaw* (New York 1925), 60

2. G. K. Chesterton, *George Bernard Shaw* (London 1961), 251

3. Archibald Henderson, *Bernard Shaw, Playboy and Prophet* (New York 1932), 316

4. Blanche Patch, *Thirty Years with G. B. S.* (London 1951), 221; St. John Ervine, *Bernard Shaw, His Life, Work, and Friends* (New York 1956), 55

5. Stephen Winsten, *Jesting Apostle* (London 1956), 172

6. Winsten, 9, 31

7. B. C. Rosset, *Shaw of Dublin*, the Formative Years (Philadelphia 1964), 245. Earlier biographers had put the inheritance at 4,000–5,000 pounds, a world of difference then.

8. Ervine, 25

9. Bernard Shaw, *Sixteen Self-Sketches* (New York 1949), 27–8

10. Ervine, 17

11. Ibid., 16

12. *Sixteen Self-Sketches,* 29

13. Ibid., 45

14. Ibid., 147

15. Archibald Henderson, *George Bernard Shaw* (London 1911), 39

16. Christopher St. John, *Ellen Terry and Bernard Shaw, a Correspondence* (New York 1949), 196

17. *Sixteen Self-Sketches,* 130

18. Winsten, 18

19. Chesterton, 91

20. *Sixteen Self-Sketches,* 118

21. Patch, 146

22. Chesterton, 206

23. Archibald Henderson, *Bernard Shaw, Man of the Century* (New York 1956), 49, 50, 54

24. Winsten, 33

25. Henderson, *George Bernard Shaw* (London 1911), 40

26. Ibid., 269

27. Winsten, 33

28. Ervine, 58

29. Rosset, p. 274

30. *Sixteen Self-Sketches*, 144

31. Bernard Shaw, "Socialism for Millionaires" (July 1901), A Fabian Society Tract, 15

32. *Sixteen Self-Sketches*, 132

33. Ervine, 124

34. *Sixteen Self-Sketches*, 111

35. *Bernard Shaw, Playboy and Prophet*, 354, 355

36. Bernard Shaw, *Plays Pleasant and Unpleasant* (London 1931), I, v

37. Ervine, 312–3

38. *Sixteen Self-Sketches*, 178

39. Maurice Colbourne, *The Real Bernard Shaw* (London 1939), 71

40. Ervine, 157

41. C. G. L. DuCann, *The Loves of George Bernard Shaw* (New York 1963), 174

42. Ibid., 177–8

43. Ibid., 179

44. *Sixteen Self-Sketches*, 170

45. Allan Chappelow, *Shaw the Villager and Human Being*, a biographical symposium (London 1962), 52

46. Bernard Shaw, *Man and Superman* (New York 1905), vii

47. *Bernard Shaw, Playboy and Prophet*, 784

48. Chappelow, 168

49. DuCann, 196

50. Chappelow, 283; *Bernard Shaw, Playboy and Prophet*, 740

51. Ervine, 592

52. *Sixteen Self-Sketches*, 194

53. Lawrence Langner, *G. B. S. and the Lunatic* (New York 1963), 192, 196

54. William Archer, *The Theatrical 'World' of 1894, preface* by G. B. Shaw (London 1895); E. J. West, *Shaw on Theatre* (New York 1958), 42

55. Bernard Shaw, *Three Plays for Puritans* (New York 1906), xvi, xvii

56. Ibid., xvi

57. Bernard Shaw, *Heartbreak House, Great Catherine, and Playlets of the War* (London 1921), xxxviii

58. Eugene Brieux, *Three Plays of Brieux* with a preface by Bernard Shaw (New York 1909), xxii

59. Ibid.

60. Bernard Shaw, *Dramatic Opinions and Essays* (New York 1906), II, 67

61. *Dramatic Opinions and Essays*, I, 8; *Three Plays for Puritans*, xiv

62. *Heartbreak House, Great Catherine, and Playlets of the War*, xlii

63. Christopher St. John, 159

64. Frank Harris, *Bernard Shaw* (New York 1931), 253

65. *Plays Pleasant and Unpleasant,* II, xvi

66. *Dramatic Opinions and Essays,* I, 33, 413

67. Patch, 57

68. C. B. Purdom, editor, *Bernard Shaw's Letters to Granville-Barker* (New York 1957), 81

69. *Drama* (Winter 1946); West, 259

70. Pearson, 238

71. *Bernard Shaw, Playboy and Prophet,* 756

72. Hesketh Pearson, *Bernard Shaw, His Life* and Personality (New York 1963), 282

73. *Bernard Shaw, Playboy and Prophet,* 370

74. Harris, 175

75. Bernard Shaw, "A Dramatic Realist to His Critics," *New Review* (July 1894); West, 19

76. *Dramatic Opinions and Essays,* I, 242

77. Pearson, 128; *Bernard Shaw, Playboy and Prophet,* 341

78. *Dramatic Opinions and Essays,* I, 239

79. Appendix to *The Quintessence of Ibsenism* (First edition only, 1891); West, 10

80. *Man and Superman,* 22–3; *The Doctor's Dilemma, Getting Married,* and *The Shewing Up of Blanco Posnet* (London 1911), 100

81. Bernard Shaw, *The Simpleton of the Unexpected Isles, The Six against Calais, The Millionairess* (New York 1936), 86

82. Brieux, xxiv; *Plays Pleasant and Unpleasant,* II, vi

83. *The Simpleton of the Unexpected Isles, The Six against Calais, The Millionairess,* 86

84. Christopher St. John, 225

85. *Table-talk of George Bernard Shaw,* 67

86. *Plays Pleasant and Unpleasant,* II, xvi

87. *Three Plays for Puritans,* xxxi

88. Patch, 10

89. Ervine, 310; Pearson, 367; Winsten, 189

90. *Dramatic Opinions and Essays,* II, 67

91. Frank Harris, *Oscar Wilde* with a preface by Bernard Shaw (London 1938), xxxiii

92. *New Republic* (February 22, 1922); West, 152

93. Patch, 219

94. Ibid.

95. Chappelow, 28

96. Patch, 39

97. Chappelow, unnumbered page with photograph before p. 96

98. Ibid., 52

99. Harris, 146

100. Christopher St. John, 89

101. *Sixteen Self-Sketches*, 19; *Malvern Festival Book* (1933); West, 227

102. *Table-talk of George Bernard Shaw*, 63-4

103. *Bernard Shaw, Playboy and Prophet*, 551

104. Ibid., 208

105. Alan Dent, editor, *Bernard Shaw and Mrs. Patrick Campbell: Their Correspondence* (New York 1952), 326

106. *Bernard Shaw, Man of the Century*, 614

107. Winsten, 167

108. Pearson, 319, 320

109. Ibid., 375

110. Ervine, 380

111. *Bernard Shaw, Playboy and Prophet*, 605

112. Dent, 345

113. *Three Plays for Puritans*, xxxv

114. Colbourne, 83

115. Bernard Shaw, "I Am a Classic but Am I a Shakespear Thief?", Hearst's Magazine (September 1920); West, 132

116. *Bernard Shaw, Playboy and Prophet*, 7

117. *Plays Pleasant and Unpleasant*, II, vii

118. *Bernard Shaw, Playboy and Prophet*, 332

119. Brieux, xxiii

120. Ibid., xxiv

121. *Bernard Shaw, Playboy and Prophet*, 518

122. *Sixteen Self-Sketches*, 177

123. West, 134

124. *Table-talk of George Bernard Shaw*, 64

125. Bernard Shaw, "Playhouses and Plays," *New York Herald Tribune* (November 14, 1926); West, 180

126. Ibid.

127. *Bernard Shaw, Playboy and Prophet*, 543

128. Ibid., 542

129. Bernard Shaw, *Saint Joan* (New York 1924), lxxii

130. Ibid., lxxvi, lxxvii

131. Ibid., lxxviii

132. *Three Plays for Puritans*, xxxvi, xxxvii

133. *Bernard Shaw, Playboy and Prophet*, 564

134. Ibid., 597

135. Ibid., 600

136. *Man and Superman*, 129

137. Ibid., xxxi

138. *Bernard Shaw, Man of the Century*, 590

139. Ibid., 294

140. Pearson, 288

141. Harris, 254

142. Bernard Shaw, "The Art of Rehearsal," *Collier's Weekly* (June 24, 1922), 3

143. Harris, 254

144. Bernard Shaw, preface to "Immaturity," *Prefaces* (London 1934), 645; Colbourne, 128

145. *Man and Superman*, xxxv

146. Ibid.

147. *Prefaces*, 739, 740

148. *Bernard Shaw, Playboy and Prophet*, 348

149. Bernard Shaw, *Arms and the Man* (New York 1922), 32

150. *The Doctor's Dilemma, Getting Married*, and *The Shewing Up of Blanco Posnet*, 101

151. *Heartbreak House, Great Catherine* and *Playlets of the War*, 51

152. *The Playwright as Thinker*, 156

153. Bernard Shaw, "The Play of Ideas," *New Statesman and Nation* (May 6, 1950); West, 294; *Drama* (Winter 1946)

154. *Plays Pleasant and Unpleasant*, II, 111

155. Henry L. Mencken, *George Bernard Shaw, His Plays* (Boston 1905), 106, excerpt of Shaw's letter to the *Daily News* following publication of *Three Plays for Puritans*.

156. Pearson, 233, 288

157. Bernard Shaw, *Over-Ruled* (London 1912), 66; *Dramatic Opinions and Essays*, II, 364

158. *Bernard Shaw, Playboy and Prophet*, 777

159. Ibid., 388; Pearson, 225, 226

160. Patch, 51

161. Ibid.

162. Purdom, 74

163. Patch, 125

164. Colbourne, 87

165. Patch, 123

166. Theresa Helburn, *A Wayward Quest* (Boston 1960), 160

167. *Three Plays for Puritans*, xxiii

168. Pearson, 405

169. Patch, 53

Chapter V

John Galsworthy

In 1922, as an established dramatist, John Galsworthy declared, "I am in no sense a student of drama, nor a great playgoer, nor a believer in learning the job of playwriting except by practice." [1] Galsworthy did not attempt and complete his first play until he was thirty-nine years old. He wrote *The Silver Box* in 1906 after writing unsuccessful stories and novels for the preceding ten years. Sheer grit and a sense of predestination carried him through. "For nine years, indeed for eleven years," confessed Galsworthy upon receiving the Nobel Prize for Literature in 1932, "I made not one penny out of what I, but practically no others counted as my profession." [2]

Galsworthy's monumental family chronicle, *The Forsyte Saga,* is usually rated a master-work as likely to survive as any novel in the English language. Galsworthy's plays, however, representing naturalism at its best, as in *Strife* and *Justice,* are now somewhat dated. "What seems to me a great question," said Chesterton, "seems to Mr. Galsworthy a great pain!" [3] And no doubt in some measure because of this, all flippancy aside, the "great question" is no longer the "great pain." There is no certainty that the circumstances that once made *Strife* and *Justice* so timely will not recur, or that the value of the plays as naturalism is less for having possibly helped deter such recurrence. No study of modern playwrights at work can be complete without a good look at this master of naturalism.

I

THE GROWTH OF GALSWORTHY'S
CREATIVE SPIRIT IN LIFE

On Easter Sunday of 1895 at the Gare Du Nord, a railway station in Paris, Ada Cooper Galsworthy said to John Galsworthy, "Why don't you write? You are just the person." [4] This remark was to be quite consequential for the literary world. Ada and John were in love; he was a gentleman lawyer who chose not to practice law, and she was his own cousin's wife. Perhaps in the confidences of their secret affair, Ada had found in her lover a sensitivity, eloquence, and power of observation that his reserve ordinarily hid. Six months earlier, Galsworthy had confided in a friend, "I do wish I had the gift of writing. I really think that it is the nicest way of making money going;" Galsworthy also admitted that he lacked anything to write about. For the ten years following Ada's prophetic remark, their anguished relationship gave him something to write about, the heart to keep writing, and the tormented soul providing thematic material that obsessed his writing the rest of his life. Before John Galsworthy eventually married Ada Cooper Galsworthy, he significantly used the pen-name of "John Sinjohn." [5]

John Galsworthy was born on August 14, 1867, in Parkfield, a porticoed mansion in Surrey, England, the first son of Blanche Bartlett Galsworthy and her husband, "Old John" Galsworthy, a solicitor and director on the boards of several mining and real estate companies. Two years earlier, the couple had had a daughter, Lilian; another daughter, Mabel, and a son, Hubert, followed the birth of "Jack," as young John was called. The Galsworthys were of England's upper middle-class; the elder Galsworthy at the peak of his career was reputed to have a yearly income of 12,000 pounds, a sum worth at least ten times what it is today. The Galsworthy estate where Jack spent his childhood and formative years was a Victorian paradise with gardens, paddocks, a little farmyard, eight indoor and six outdoor servants, and much entertaining.

"My father," said the mature Galsworthy, "really predominated on me from the start and ruled my life." [6] His mother from earliest memories was little more than "a scented, and graciously dressed presence at good-night kiss-times".[7] She was Victorianism incarnate. Galsworthy was to recall of his mother, "the Queen, the Royal family, the Church, the structure of Society, all to her were final." [8] After the first few years of her marriage, Galsworthy's mother was not happy but kept up appearances in the best Victorian tradition, and it was said "her diamonds were always correct". Both of Galsworthy's parents were exceptionally fastidious, masterful, and unyielding. The mother was aloofly loving like a most patrician marquise; the father could be warmly endearing especially with his own children. Commuting daily to London as a solicitor, he made few friends but by today's standards was easily a millionaire. Old John meant his namesake to become a gentleman and a solicitor like him. Neither side of the family had ever produced a creative artist: "so far as I can make out," wrote Galsworthy in a letter to Edward Garnett, "my Dad's forebears were absolutely of the small farmer class for hundreds of years, and all from the same little corner of South Devon, and my Mother's absolutely of the provincial Squire class." [9] Galsworthy thought he got his creative energy from his enterprising father and his sense of form from his often excruciatingly correct mother.

Galsworthy's childhood and schooling were bare of any sign of a creative artist in the making. And of Galsworthy as an adult, R. H. Mottram recalled in *For Some We Loved*, "Never was a man less garrulous, less inclined to anecdote or reminiscence." [10] Galsworthy himself told Barrett Clark, "I can write somewhat better than I can talk." Galsworthy's education followed the course that his father wished for his prospective heir: the elite Bournemouth Preparatory School, Harrow, and New College, Oxford. Perhaps to prove his competitive spirit to his father, Galsworthy at Bournemouth took to football and track with such excess that he strained his heart. After that, he could do nothing more taxing than ride horseback. He loved the racetrack. He made few friends. He took no part in intellectual activities like debating or learned societies. His heart trouble, his gentlemanly dress, and his natural reserve led classmates to rate him as a cynic, a dandy, and a snob.

In 1890, Galsworthy passed his bar examinations with second class honors and was bored. He said, "It does seem to me beastly dull to go on grinding at a profession or business just to make money." [11] Old John, nevertheless, called the tune, and Young John kept on grinding. Galsworthy showed strong independence for a while at Oxford and for a few years afterwards in one respect,—he had a love affair with a young lady named Sybil Carr of whom little more is now known than that she was poor and gave singing lessons. Galsworthy's "predominating" father was to fix that. Once he had passed the bar, his father sent him with his brother Hubert to inspect mining properties in Canada. Following the mining inspection, Galsworthy returned to Sybil. This time his father took good care to send him off on a tour of Australia, New Zealand, and the South Seas. The pretence was that Galsworthy read for the maritime bar and study navigation with the captain. Galsworthy's college chum, Ted Sanderson, went along. "The first mate is a Pole called Conrad and is a capital chap, though queer to look at," Galsworthy wrote home of one who was to become a lifelong friend; "he is a man of travel and experience in many parts of the world, and has a fund of yarns on which I draw freely." [12] As if to make quite sure that Galsworthy had shed Sybil, his father then sent him on a journey to Russia to inspect mines. Sybil was quite shed.

Galsworthy's parents, meanwhile, had their hands full from the romances of their clear-headed and strong-willed daughters, Lilian and Mabel. Lilian's intellectual and artistic bent took her often to the National Gallery in London where she observed a talented, Byronic looking, young painter who on commission of a patron was copying a picture of Bacchus and Ariadne. Somehow Lilian and the painter, Georg Sauter, became acquainted; his parents were Bavarian peasants, and Lilian took him to meet her parents apparently with the idea of getting him some commissions for portraits. Mabel, who was first to be painted, fell in love with Georg, but he and Lilian were already in love. The biographer, Barker, believes that Galsworthy, in observing Georg's intense zeal for his art, discovered how art might give a purpose to his own aimless life. Mabel was eventually to marry an engineer, Thomas Blair Reynolds. And Georg, with the reluctant consent of her parents, married Lilian. The Galsworthy parents set up both daughters and their husbands with homes in Kensington, London. Young composers and instrumentalists flocked to Mabel's house, and painters to Lilian's.

In 1894, upon returning from journeys for his father, Galsworthy joined an Oxford friend, George Harris, to live in a flat on Victoria Street. At his sisters' homes, Galsworthy could see London's artistic Bohemia; at his parents', very rich Victorianism; and from his own flat, London's poverty. Galsworthy got quite an eyeful because his father sent him out collecting rents from family property in London's slums. Dudley Barker noted in his biography, *A Man of Principle,* "Galsworthy repeatedly told his wife, many years later, how distressed he had been to discover the living conditions of some of the people from whom the family's wealth was partly derived." [13] Galsworthy had a special entree to observe quite another side of human nature in that his legal training qualified him to represent his father and to sit on a few Boards of Directors on occasion. His "impersonal eye" took it all in.

For Galsworthy, the greatest single influence of all from 1895 to 1905 was Ada Cooper. An aristocrat in beauty and presence, Ada Cooper was a woman of great sensitivity and femininity. Lilian and

Mabel had told their brother "Jack" the family gossip of Ada's miserable marriage that seemed to have gone wrong for lack of common interest and through sexual incompatibility. Somehow Ada and Galsworthy found themselves in love. The affair began in 1894 when Galsworthy's father was seventy-seven. In those days, the only grounds for Ada's divorce from her husband, a Major, would have to be adultery, and the correspondent had to be named in open court. Possibly Galsworthy and Ada felt the shock of such proceedings might have killed Galsworthy's father, and left them intolerably guilt-ridden for life; his father might also have stopped Galsworthy's yearly income and even cut him out of his will. Ada and Galsworthy kept their love secret until after Galsworthy's father had died of natural causes.

Meanwhile for ten years Old John subsidized his son's apprenticeship to writing. His mother was dead set against Galsworthy's becoming an author, even a famous one. Possibly she felt writing was not a discreet way to hide so many family secrets. Ironically enough, Galsworthy's mother left her husband when he was eighty-six. "Towards the close of their married life," wrote Dudley Barker, "she accused him of taking too great an interest in the young governess of one of his grandsons." [14] In 1904, Galsworthy's father finally died.

The ordeal of ten years of uncertain waiting followed by the public scandal of Ada's divorce on grounds of adultery, and then the couple's ostracism after their marriage, left Galsworthy a much changed man. He had felt the full impact of society's displeasure, and the memory was never to leave his work. His writing showed a deep understanding for suffering humanity in general and for unhappily married women in particular. Throughout his career, Galsworthy was to satirize his social class, but his impersonal eye always saw things in it to admire, too. That class had made him the patrician person he was; and his father had left him financially independent for life—a yearly income of 700 pounds, an immediate legacy of 2,500 pounds, and a large inheritance to come in seven years.

After their honeymoon the Galsworthys practically went into seclusion. In the remote village of Manaton they rented an unmodernized farmhouse named Wingstone, overlooking a beautiful English countryside; their landlord operated the farm. On clear days the Galsworthys could catch a glimpse in the distance of one of England's famous prisons, Dartmoor. With Ada beside him, Galsworthy now set to work at his writing with a dedication and freedom he had never before known.

In 1905 the Vedrenne-Barker management of the experimental Court Theatre in London had already successfully introduced to England such "new" dramatists as Ibsen and Shaw; a contagious stir was in the air. Edward Garnett, the critic and playwright, asked Galsworthy to try a hand at a play for the venturesome spirit of the Court Theatre. In 1906, Galsworthy wrote *The Silver Box,* and the Vedrenne-Barker management immediately accepted this sterling silver cigarette-box of a play, and opened it for the public six weeks later, on September 25, 1906, to extraordinary critical approval over the contents of social justice—one for the rich and another for the poor. *The Silver Box* earned Galsworthy a "name", exciting literary friends, and a sense that he might have many new revelations in him for the theatre.

Galsworthy's total literary output was to be roughly: one-third, novels; one-third, short stories, sketches, poems and essays; and one-third, plays. Only his plays concern this study:

The Silver Box (1906)	*The Little Man**
Strife (1908)	*Hall-Marked**
Joy (1909)	*Defeat**
The Eldest Son	*The Sun**
Justice	*God**
The Little Dream (1911)	*Windows* (1923)
The Patriots (1912)	*Loyalties*
The Pigeon	*A Family Man*
The Fugitive (1913)	*The Forest* (1924)
The Mob (1914)	*Old English* (1925)
A Bit of Love (1915)	*Escape*
The Skin Game (1920)	*The Show*
The Foundations	*Exiled* (1929)
The First and the Last (1921)*	*The Roof*
*Punch and Go**	

The range of these dramatic goods included: comedy, drama, tragedy, allegory, fantasy, tragi-comedy, and extravaganza; those marked with an asterisk were one-acts.

As a dedicated and financially independent writer, Galsworthy tried to live by what he called "the artist theory of life," a notion he elucidated in a letter to Alfred Knopf: "do everything with all your heart, and have no time or inclination left for megrims or nerves." [15] Galsworthy never favored excess, saying, "Be true to your best self." His only children were to be his brain-children. Cleancut, aloof, and patrician, Galsworthy contributed half his income to organized charities and a good half of the rest to private cases. He actively crusaded for progressive reform in such matters as had touched a live nerve in his own life: divorce, minimum wage, woman's suffrage, slum clearance, the docking of horses' tails, and a three year averaging for income tax.

His friends were Joseph Conrad, Edward Garnett, and Gilbert Murray. He was on friendly terms, however, with Barrie, Masefield, Shaw, Belloc, Chesterton, Welles, Cunningham Graham, Nevinson, Walkley, Archer, and Barker. Of his natural reserve Galsworthy said in a speech he prepared but was too ill to deliver upon receiving his Nobel Prize, "I do not believe that I have made a dozen acquaintances in all the Clubs to which I have belonged, and not one single friend." [16] He tended to observe rather than directly involve himself in people's lives; to him, "The one precious thing in life (except love) was "the impersonal eye." [17]

For recreation, Galsworthy was especially fond of horses, dogs, croquet, and classical music—Wagner excluded. His wife loved travel and, although Galsworthy detested it, he catered to Ada's whims, especially to protect her health; she was disposed to asthma, rheumatism, flu, sciatica, neuralgia, and head colds. All their married life she was his secretary, and he in good measure, her nurse. She was to outlive him by twenty-two years.

The Galsworthys usually had a country home and a town house. From 1905 to 1924 their country home was half of Wingstone farm. In 1924 they bought Bury House, a twenty-two room Tudor styled modern mansion with 15 bedrooms and costing 9,000 pounds. In 1906 they had a small town house at Kensington, London; in 1913 they moved to a top floor flat at Adelphi Terrace near Barrie and Shaw; in 1917 they bought a fine town house, Grove Lodge, in Hampstead, London. For all his modesty, Galsworthy came to be as decorated with honors as a Graustarkian General, but his chief distinctions were: the Order of Merit, the Presidency of the P. E. N. (Poets, Essayists, and Novelists) Club and the English Association, seven honorary degrees of Doctor of Literature, a knighthood which he declined as unbefitting a writer, and the Nobel Prize for Literature in 1932.

In 1930, a small persistent growth appeared on the right side of Galsworthy's nose. Distrusting doctors, he first refused any medical care; finally he submitted to radium treatment that seemed to wither away the growth. By December of 1932, as if his nervous system had been crossed up, Galsworthy suddenly found trouble talking and moving. The diagnosis was an inoperable brain tumor. Gaunt, spent, and drugged, Galsworthy on February 1, 1933, breathed his last. As he had willed, he was cremated and his ashes were strewn on the hill-top of his beloved country home, Bury House.

II

COMMERCIAL CONSIDERATIONS AFFECTING GALSWORTHY'S PLAYWRITING

The public taste, to Galsworthy's eye, always hungered for certain ingredients in its literary dishes: novelty, originality, excitement, story, and self-identification—"seeing yourself and your neighbour reproduced . . . satisfied by the creation of character." [18] Two powerful external forces, moreover, like a changing climate were continually affecting the public palate more or less. One force was that of self-conscious literary coteries such as the imagists, trying to make literature respond to their own view of art; a modern equivalent might be the existentialists. The other force was that of world events like prosperity, depression, and war powerfully shifting the public's attention, especially in terms of security and love, by the personal stake involved. A modern equivalent would be the "cold war."

"It is the naked and uncompromising truth that to assess the real, great Public's taste is quite beyond the power of any writer," observed Galsworthy; "he may discover formulas to suit a certain section of the Public, and go on turning out an article to pattern; but that way lies mediocrity or worse." [19] "With every real piece of literary creation," Galsworthy added, "Public Taste gets a fresh jolt; it alters just a little." Hack writing, to Galsworthy, was a prostitution of talent, and it was better for a writer's integrity to earn a living at some other occupation and to write on the side. "I never in my life," said Galsworthy, "have written anything 'to order'." [20] Of course, he had independent means, but Galsworthy believed it was folly for a writer to sell his most precious heritage, his individuality, for a mess of pottage. He said, "the writer who steadily goes his own way, never writes to fulfill the demands of public, publisher, or editor, is the writer who comes off best in the end." [21]

A writer's individuality to Galsworthy was a writer's composite mark of his mood, his imagination, his view of life—his very self. Individuality, nevertheless, did not mean a license to commit literary abuse. "Men make their names," noted Galsworthy, "with *one* book, not with a series of fairly goods." [22] He said, "Take it as a rule that anything you write must be interesting sentence by sentence." Having something worth saying was a must. "Writers generally begin too young," he judged, "and very few who begin very young come to anything." [23] In the drama, furthermore, it is poor craftsmanship to make unwarranted demands; Galsworthy, for instance, advised Edward Garnett against too much scene changing and too great length in *The Trial of Joan of Arc*. He suggested the telescoping of scenes to a few settings and the ruthless cutting of everything superfluous.[24]

Of all Galsworthy's plays, the commercial and incidentally the greatest artistic successes, in America if not always in England, were: *Strife, Justice, The Skin Game, Loyalties,* and *Escape*. The rest, fifteen in all, bit the commercial dust even if in some respects they measured up to artistic stature. By 1910, with the success of *Strife* and *Justice,* Galsworthy became a recognized leader of English dramatists and so his plays tended sooner or later to merit a production even though only one play in four was a commercial success. In 1922, before the financial windfall of his last plays, Galsworthy wrote Kenneth Andres, "As to 'box-office specifications'—if I knew anything about them or paid any attention to them, I suppose I should not have had in London only two commercial successes out of my fifteen plays produced there." [25]

III

AESTHETIC CONSIDERATIONS AFFECTING GALSWORTHY'S PLAYWRITING

Among literary models, Galsworthy most favored Maupassant and Turgenev. Turgenev, best known in the theatre for his *A Month in the Country,* Galsworthy called *"the* man above all others I should like to have known;" he especially scrutinized Turgenev for "an insight into proportion of theme and economy of words." [26] Actually, Galsworthy made no bones about preferring the novel to the drama, for the novel's more leisurely pace with time to work in subtleties of character; he told Barrett Clark, "the effect of a novel . . . is more enduring than that made by a play." [27]

"To quicken the pulses in one way or another," Galsworthy said, "is to me the only purpose, or, to be accurate, by far the chief purpose of dramatic art." [28] The most precious element in art, and so in drama, he thought, was the truth, for "to really stir human nature, a work of art must ring absolutely true, must have lost all the feeling of fake and manufacture." [29] Debased art, like a debased coin, rings false, though some people may accept it. Galsworthy believed that truth involved a relative harmony and proportion in things and was not to be searched out only by argument and syllogism as divining rods.[30] To him, truth could be recognized on the face of things. He implies the best means of testing truth is through its effect: "a dramatist strongly and pitifully impressed by the encircling pressure of modern environment," Galsworthy wrote, "will neither create characters . . . seven feet high nor write plays detached from the problems of his times . . . His only ambition is to present Truth as he sees it, gripping with it his . . . audience to produce in them a sort of mental or moral ferment, whereby vision may be enlarged, imagination livened, and understanding promoted." [31]

In Galsworthy's opinion, authentic art reveals itself in tell-tale signs. He wrote Andre Chevrillon, "The touchstone of things, whether in life or art—especially in art—is actuality. That's what makes Shakespeare so much greater than Milton and all our other poets." [32] Aeschylus, Sophocles, Euripides, Shakespeare—the greatest of dramatists —Galsworthy believed projected the flesh and blood vitality of life in their very own times. Another tell-tale sign of art is individuality: "It must be essentially unlike what has gone before." Galsworthy put this in other words, too—"Flavour! . . . the peculiar and most essential attribute of any work of art!" [33] He noted a further tell-tale sign of art: "the permanence of a novel, a play, a biography depends on the vitality of characters;" Faustus, Hamlet, and Othello, for instance, have taken on lives of their own.[34]

Galsworthy tried to live up to his own ultimate conception of the writer as an artist. "The one precious thing in life (except love)," he wrote Ralph Mottram, "is the impersonal eye." [35] For Galsworthy, the writer lives in loneliness of soul and flourishes in this spiritual isolation. To do his best, he insisted that the writer must respect himself fervently, adjust to the heavy discipline of his art, and never compromise his passion to "make the truest, fairest, best thing" he can; Galsworthy was convinced that the true writer thrives on opposition, arrogance, and originality.[36] Above all, Galsworthy thought that the writer couldn't excite others unless he himself was superior to the ordinary man in observing, feeling, understanding, remembering, and communicating.

As for drama critics, Galsworthy lost no love on them. He said, "I would certainly much rather have the Public's than the Critics' judgment on a play." [37] Galsworthy, in fact, blamed the critics for his many failures as a playwright. He felt they judged his fresh, modern works from a stale, inept, old-fashioned set of standards. "They are a queer crowd anyway," he wrote Denis Mackail as late as December 10, 1929, "and need a chastisement with whips and scorpions. It is the unchastised life that goes to the head. We authors run no risks there." [38]

Galsworthy had no more love for the English censor, the Lord Chamberlain, than he had for the drama critics. When the censor banned the public performance of Shaw's *The Shewing Up of Blanco Posnet,* Galsworthy believed that the power to license was the power to destroy the drama; he joined a move to abolish or greatly restrict the absolute power of the Lord Chamberlain. He knew that the English censor had so limited the creative range of Fielding and Dickens in the imaginative world of playwriting that they simply gave up writing plays. "Artists who wish to do justice to their most original thoughts," said Galsworthy acidly, in testifying to a Parliamentary Committee over *Blanco Posnet,* "have felt that a drama-in-leading-strings was not an occupation for serious men and have turned to other forms of expression." [39]

IV

WORKING METHODS OF GALSWORTHY IN PLAYWRITING

Genesis

"For Heaven's sake, under *no* circumstances, and whatever happens to you," Galsworthy advised a friend, "never write anything unless you must." [40] In settling down to work, Galsworthy was acutely aware of its unpredictable nature, for to him, "all creative work comes in gusts, and fits, and starts, and puffs." [41] He considered that the most trying task of the writer was to keep a brave heart and to carry on. Galsworthy's wife, Ada, was a great help to him in this. "To my wife I dedicate *The Forsyte Saga* in its entirety," wrote Galsworthy giving Ada her special role in his creativeness, "believing it to be of all my work the least unworthy of one without whose encouragement, sympathy, and criticism I could never have become even such a writer as I am." For almost thirty years, Ada also was Galsworthy's secretary, personally typing out copies and revisions of his handwritten manuscript.[42]

Galsworthy favored a fairly fixed schedule to invite his creative "gusts, and fits, and starts, and puffs." He would wake up about 6:30 a.m. and for an hour or so lie in bed just to let his current work run through his mind in flashes. By 8 a.m. he was up, washed and dressed. When staying at his country home, he would usually go for a canter on the downs before breakfast. By 9:15 a.m. he had already scanned his mail and breakfasted on especially his favorite beverage, "the strongest (and only) coffee in all England." [43] From 9:15 a.m. to 11:30 a.m. he settled down to work. In good weather, he would sit on the terrace with a pad on his knee, a pen or pencil in his hand, and a long low table by him with paper and pencil in reserve. He wrote and revised long-hand, smoking cigarettes, or a pipe continually. More likely than not, a pet spaniel or dalmatian lay curled at his feet and he enjoyed as a kind of evocative background his wife softly playing classical music on the piano—especially Mozart. In bad weather, Galsworthy took to his study in a top room of the house. From 11:30 a.m. to 12:30 p.m. he'd go for a walk, because he found walking stimulated his creativeness. From 12:30 p.m. to 2 p.m., Galsworthy lunched. And from 2 p.m. to 4:30 p.m. he was back to work, writing. He rarely wrote for more than four hours a day. After 4:30 p.m., he would relax by playing such games with his wife as croquet, and more often than not, would let her win. At 8:30 p.m. he dined. At Bury House, all meals tended to be long and formal in a patrician sense, even though the food was often simple. Galsworthy ate sparingly and was always rather lean. After dinner, Galsworthy enjoyed listening to music or reading or visiting. By 11:30 p.m. he retired. Tomorrow was another day.

Of his general approach to playwriting, Galsworthy reported, "My own method was the outcome of the trained habit (which I was already employing in my novels) of naturalistic dialogue guided, informed, and selected by a controlling idea, together with an intense visualization of types and scenes." [44] What begins creation for writers? He said, "some match must strike against the surface of their hearts or eyes." [45] The resulting flame, and by implication the lasting scratch, is the reaction of their emotion to experience. They may feel the flash and heat of love, admiration, anger, pity—something that violates their sense of proportion by surprise, peculiarity, sheer drama.

True to his very reserved nature, Galsworthy as a rule was quite reticent about the genesis of his plays. He did, even so, toss out a few clues in some instances. As to the genesis of *Justice,* he recorded that in September 1907 he actually visited Dartmoor Prison, a jail in clear

sight of his country home. What Galsworthy saw at Dartmoor of solitary confinement and "repeaters" so fired him with indignation that
quite a lasting blaze was set in him from that match. He wrote a report, "The House of Silence and Order." He grimly noted, "I mean in
any case to keep on the subject of Solitary Confinement until something is done." [46] His play, *Justice,* was to be his way of doing "something." The "controlling idea" of the play came from personally seeing the "intense visualization of types and scenes" involved in solitary
confinement—a mélange of the human herd in primitive self preserva-
tion goring to death its weaker members even while it mouthed a
faith in "Gentle Jesus." Galsworthy, himself, had experienced something akin to solitary confinement in the ten years he carried on his
secret love affair with Ada and had to live in the guilty solitude and
torment of his soul.

As for the genesis of *Strife,* Barrett Clark recollected that Galsworthy had told him, "One day I saw two men at the club. They
were arguing furiously about no matter what, and neither of them
seemed able to do anything but convince himself that he was right." [47]
Galsworthy went on, "I thought I saw in that fruitless argument, a
play, and I decided that the usual labor-capital dispute would prove
effective in the theatre if I treated it as I intended to treat it." Galsworthy knew of what he wrote to help with the "intense visualization
of types and scenes." He could not have missed seeing the slums during a strike in the neighborhood of his London flat; he undoubtedly
was collecting rents for his father at such a time and listened to many
a story of human suffering relating to why the tenants couldn't pay.
He also knew the executive mind in business, for he had his own
father as a model, and he had sat on the Boards of Directors of various firms as his father's representative.

So critically influential did Galsworthy come to believe was the
"controlling idea" upon the total effect of a play, that he later chose to
follow his initial flash of excitement over such an idea with much
sober thought to find if the fire was really as vital and revealing as it
first seemed. Failure after failure taught Galsworthy that the stage
needed "right" subjects or else the most skillful technique was all to
no avail. The dreary failure of *Joy,* for instance, taught him the futility of writing plays that appealed to only a very limited audience. [48]
Galsworthy was quite aware for all his innate reserve that the commercial theatre expected sex appeal, but he refused to side with D. H.
Lawrence's conviction that the body was "worthwhile;" "the men we

swear by," noted Galsworthy, "—Tolstoy, Turgenev, Tchekhov, Maupassant, Flaubert, France—knew that great truth—they only use the body, and that sparingly, to reveal the soul."[49] Psychoanalysis in Galsworthy's view did not light up the soul so much as show only half-truths in a dim, flickering light.[50] Galsworthy, for instance, firmly believed that a disposition creates a complex rather than the other way around. The problem might be stated: "Does a man act like a mouse because he was born one by disposition or because life has made him a mouse by complexes?"

Very early in creating a play, Galsworthy was concerned with its genre. His best plays like *Justice* and *Strife* are in naturalism. Why did he favor this form? To him naturalism was "the most fastidious and poignant of all dramatic forms." He aimed to give the "illusion of actual life passing on the stage," and this meant there could be absolutely nothing false about it, not a word, for this would break the spell:

> It is easy enough to *reproduce* the exact conversation and movements of persons in a room; it is desperately hard to *produce* the perfectly natural conversation and movements of these persons, when each natural phrase spoken, and each natural movement made, has not only to contribute toward the growth and perfection of a drama's soul, but also to be a revelation, phrase by phrase, movement by movement, of essential traits of character.[51]

Naturalism * to Galsworthy was the quintessence of life and not an indiscriminate heap of its irrelevancies. "To put it another way," he said in *Some Platitudes Concerning Drama,* "naturalism, when alive, indeed to be alive at all, is simply the art of manipulating a long procession of the most delicate symbols . . ."[52]

Incubation

"It is natural to me, when I write plays," commented Galsworthy to Barrett Clark, "to adopt what I can call an 'austere' technique. I must, from some inner necessity, reduce everything I have to say to the barest essentials."[53] In developing his plays, Galsworthy has left evidence of using a variety of devices to advance his 'austere' technique. "I spent last Friday and Saturday in Lewes Prison interviewing convicts undergoing solitary confinement," Galsworthy wrote Edward Garnett of preparing for *Justice,* "—saw 49 in all—and thoroughly confirmed my impression that it is a barbarous thing."[54] When once

* Naturalism is by far the most popular form in movies and vigorously survives onstage in most comedies.

charged with being simply a photographer, Galsworthy replied, "I would humbly say that this is the claim my play has to rise above photography: you are seeing throughout the parts in relation to the whole." [55] Galsworthy believed, like the classicists, that he was seeing life clearly and seeing it whole.

Other devices to encourage incubation have been earlier suggested. Mornings upon waking up, he would lie in bed for an hour or so reviewing some work in mind. At work, he would sit quietly alone in a receptive rather than an expectant mood. "Sat at new story all morning, but only achieved one page," he noted in his diary. [56] Another time, he recorded, "long morning on balcony, thinking out *The Patriots,* four-act play." [57] Galsworthy especially favored walking to help promote his creative work in "gusts, and fits, and starts, and puffs." "Took a walk every day for two to three hours, and some days— about eight—took whole day for long walks," he entered in his notebook of one creative effort. [58] He advised a friend stymied with developing a new work, "This *will* happen whatever one's intentions, and a tramp on the Downs will soon set you right." [59]

Characterization

"Take care of character; action and dialogue will take care of themselves," said Galsworthy in perhaps the most quoted of all his remarks about playwriting. [60] How exactly does he suggest a playwright "take care of character"? "A human being," he says in *Some Platitudes Concerning Drama,* "is the best plot there is . . . He is organic. And so it must be with a good play. Reason alone produces no good plots." [61] But how does a dramatist create a character in the first place? "That profound instinct for the breeding of blood-stock implanted in every English breast," said Galsworthy in his early sixties in the Romanes Lecture at Oxford, "will assist us in understanding how [an author], in the creation of his characters, selects certain salient human traits, and continually reinforces them—just as the blood-stock breeder selects certain strains of blood and gets as many crosses of them as he can without falling into the snare of too close inbreeding." [62]

Galsworthy apparently developed a character as Chekhov did, through reminiscence. Sometimes the analogy to creating a dominant or a recessive strain suited Galsworthy to help explain character creation; but the mystery drove him to another analogy. "If one can imagine the Catacombs at Rome, or the old cellars under the Adelphi, stored to the brim with photographic films," he said in the Romanes Lecture, "one has some notion of what the human sub-conscious mind is like. Every minute, every second, indeed, of our existences, adds to recorded experience." [63] To up-date this analogy, we might today liken the sub-conscious to an enormous and growing bank of computer tapes.

Galsworthy elaborated, "what we know as the creative gifts in literature, or indeed in any art," he said, "is a more than normal power in certain people for dipping into the storehouse and fishing up the odds and ends of experience, together with special aptitude for welding or grouping those odds and ends when they are fished up." [64] Galsworthy believed that minds tended to be either reproductive or creative; the reproductive mind recalled largely conscious experience; the creative mind recalled largely subconscious experience. "When the conscious mind needs something and the subconscious manages to turn it up with reasonable instinctive ease, the result is lively creation of characters." [65] To up-date the analogy, the creative mind not only stores away tapes of memories but through apprenticeship develops a console which becomes accustomed to programming for creation.

In *Candelabra,* Galsworthy has drawn this self-portrait in the act of creating a character:

> I sink into my morning chair, a blotter on my knee, the last words or deed of some character in ink before my eyes, a pen in my hand, a pipe in my mouth, and nothing in my head. I sit. I don't intend; I don't expect; I don't even hope. Gradually my mind seems to leave the chair, and be where my character is acting or speaking, leg raised, waiting to come down, lips opened ready to say something. Suddenly, my pen jots down a movement or remark, another, another, and goes on doing this, haltingly, perhaps, for an hour or two. When the result is read through it surprises me by seeming to come out of what went before, and by ministering to some sort of possible future. Those pages, adding tissue to character, have been supplied from the store cupboard of the subconscious, in response to the appeal of one's conscious directive sense, and in service to the saving grace of one's theme, using the word in its widest sense. The creation of character, however, untrammeled and unconscious, thus has ever the guidance of what perhaps may best be called "the homing instinct." [66]

In *Some Platitudes Concerning Drama,* Galsworthy says more. "And so it is with drama,—no matter what its form—it need only be the 'real thing,' need only have caught some of the precious fluid, revelation, and imprisoned it within a chalice to which we may put our lips and continually drink." [67] *Revelation!* If a human being is the best plot there is, and in a play is created by cross-breeding memories or through the "homing instinct," then plot itself is at its best in the *revelation* of a human being. Revelations may come in a series of minor climaxes advancing to a major climax. Revelation is not to be given away instantly at the raising of each curtain. "No dramatist should let his audience know what is coming," said Galsworthy. The revelation in each scene is obviously best made to promote suspense.

On the other hand, Galsworthy offered a test as it were of the ultimate success of the creation of a character in drama. "The enduring characters in literature," he observed at Oxford in 1931, "are ever such as have kicked free of swaddling clothes and their creators. Theirs is a sublime unconsciousness of the authors of their being." [68] Galsworthy believed, for instance, that the secret of life of such plays as *Oedipus the King, Doctor Faustus* and *Hamlet* was in the extraordinary vitality of their chief characters.

In saying that he worked in the drama, as in the novel, from "a controlling idea, together with an intense visualization of types and scenes," Galsworthy suggested that his characters are blood and flesh and yet representative people associated by probability with the idea and the actual scenes from memories of real life. But contrast is also implied, for how else could Galsworthy escape the static and achieve his notion of the primary aim of the drama: "To quicken the pulses in one way or another . . ."? John Anthony in *Strife,* for example, the aged Chairman, epitomizes reactionary employers bound and determined to fight strikers to their last bite of food; David Roberts, the young and inventive spokesman for his striking union, epitomizes the violently embittered firebrand among union members, determined to fight his skinflint employers to their last cent of profit. The actual scenes of decision, violence, poverty, starvation, death, and family ties crossing strike lines, include the types of people common to such situations.

Galsworthy did not believe in individualizing characters too much for fear of making them simply eccentric or very troublesome to cast. He claimed he never could lift a character right out of life and put him onstage unchanged.

From the start, Galsworthy used contrast in the selection and development of leading characters; in *The Silver Box,* to illustrate, a similar crime of theft but a contrasted punishment involves the wealthy, irresponsible Jack Barthwick and the penniless, unemployed

Jones. In *The Eldest Son,* Sir Cheshire insists that his underkeeper, Dunning, marry the girl Dunning made pregnant, but the baronet forbids his own son to marry his wife's maid whom his son made pregnant. As for *Strife,* the very title announces violent clash of opposites, and this play Galsworthy termed "my most powerful and most impartial stage work." [69]

The unforgivable thing in character-drawing, to Galsworthy, was for an author to suddenly turn his living creations into dummies or marionettes to make the plot work out "right." The effect is a lie, and the whole work rings false. "The dramatist who hangs his characters to his plot, instead of hanging his plot to his characters, ought himself to be depended," said Galsworthy. [70]

Sources of Galsworthy's Freshness

Concerned with life as it truthfully was, Galsworthy wrote of contemporary people faced with daily personal problems and trying to come to terms with them, only to find themselves through accident or choice somehow in conflict with society. "I do not know if it is a discovery of mine," said Galsworthy, "that society stands to the modern individual as the gods and other elemental forces stood to the individual Greek; but one has seen it hinted at so often that one inclines to think it must be." [71]

A distinctive approach in Galsworthy's technique found in such plays as *Strife, Justice* and *Loyalties,* is what he called the *negative method:* "My method is to suggest that the spirit of understanding and sympathy ought to be there by pointing out that it is not. I think by this method one gets less on the nerves of one's reader." [72] He believed that aggressively advocating some specific social reform by a head-on attack against the opposition always aroused only antagonism. A preferable approach, he was convinced, was to invoke the spirit to bring about the reform.

"As a man lives and thinks," said Galsworthy, "so will he write." [73] His most successful plays artistically as well as financially still suggest his deepest convictions and his individuality as a playwright. In *Strife,* the clash between masters and men during a strike portrays the rising strife resulting when extremists refuse to compromise and then, in the tragic waste the conflict finally brings on, the leaders find they are deserted by their own followers and left broken men. In *Justice,* a crime with extenuating circumstances brings on the then customary punishment of solitary confinement and eventually destroys the prisoner's life, because even after he has paid a horrible penalty in suffering, he discovers society refuses to accept him for a new start. In *The Skin Game* the squire class, used to centuries of gentility and domination of the English countryside, clash with the rising industrial class who encroach upon their domination with expanding enterprises, and for all their gentility the squire class is not above a ruthless "skin game" —using unsavory secrets about their enemy to thwart their will, even though innocent human beings are left psychologically skinned alive. In *Loyalties*, a crime by an agreeable war hero with fine friends causes the conflicting loyalties of those affected to refuse to accept the truth, especially since the victim happens to be Jewish; loyalties to class, country, wife, husband, friends, precipitate the action and lead to the war hero's suicide. In *Escape*, an escaped criminal finds a basic and redeeming humanity in individuals rather than in society as a whole.

Writing and Rewriting

"I never make scenarios," said Galsworthy.[74] He believed that reducing a play to a written skeleton from the start would inhibit its spontaneous growth in his mind. But apparently Galsworthy had pretty clearly in mind a rather well developed brain-child before attempting to deliver it in writing. "Admitting that a dramatist should know the trend and ending of his drama before he sits down to write it," Galsworthy noted very late in his career, in May, 1931, "he will be ill advised if he does not give his characters every chance to dictate to him, within that limit."[75]

From his many failures, Galsworthy grew particularly cautious in selecting which plays he would bother to nourish creatively. "It is the ill-mating of forms that has killed a thousand plays," he warned.[76] Ill-mating could only produce a monstrous brain-child. Throughout writing and rewriting, the over-all meaning of the line of action was upper-most in Galsworthy's mind, or as he put it, "A drama must be shaped so as to have a spire of meaning."[77]

"His manner of composition," said H. V. Marrot, Galsworthy's authorized biographer, "was . . . speedy writing followed by a mass of revisions."[78] Galsworthy wrote breathlessly and revised on occasion even twelve times. He said, "never or very rarely can gems be cut perfectly at the first trial."[79] To illustrate, he wrote the whole of his first play, *The Silver Box*, in about six weeks, and *Strife*, *Justice*, and *The Eldest Son* each took about two months. *The Skin Game* he wrote "straight on end" in three weeks. The exact number of revisions of each of these plays is not certain, but records show that in 1911 he wrote eleven revisions of *The Fugitive,* seven of *The Pigeon* and, in between, a whole new play with six revisions.[80] He obviously suited his writing to the inspiration of the moment.

In writing his dialogue, Galsworthy set his imagination "not on the stage but the room or the space where in real life the action would pass." For him, "The soul of good expressions is an unexpectedness which still keeps to the mark of meaning and does not betray the truth." [81] Galsworthy believed that good dramatic dialogue must rely for its fun and pathos strictly upon the character's life. "On the stage," remarked Galsworthy of succinctness, "very little *well placed* does an enormous amount of work. It is largely the art of suggestion, of making the audience themselves do the work for you." [82]

A passage from *Justice* exemplifies Galsworthy's actuality in dialogue. Galsworthy here has his characters express themselves in eloquent pantomime, vocal nuance, exclamation, silence—all to help convey truthfully and powerfully the effect of people overcome by feeling. The occasion is Falder fatally breaking his neck from jumping out a window to escape rearrest; he has become a "repeater" in crime because he could not get a job after his release from prison for a crime inadvertently done out of the goodness of his heart. Ruth, Falder's beloved, for whom he did it all, sees his limp, broken body on the sidewalk:

> (*The three men shrink back out of her way. Ruth drops on her knees by the body.*)
> RUTH: (*in a whisper*) What is it? He's not breathing. (*She crouches over him*) My dear! My pretty!
> (*In the outer office doorway the figures of men are seen standing.*)
> RUTH: (*Leaping to her feet*) No, no! No, no! He's dead! (*The figures of men shrink back.*)
> COKESON: (*Stealing forward, in a hoarse voice*) There, there, poor dear woman! (*At the sound behind her, Ruth faces round at him.*) No one'll touch him now! Never again! He's safe with gentle Jesus! (*Ruth stands as though turned to stone in the doorway, staring at Cokeson who bending humbly before her holds out his hand as one would to a lost dog.*) [83]

"It might be said of Shaw's plays that he creates characters who express feelings which they have not got," Galsworthy once said. "It might be said of mine that I create characters who have feelings which they cannot express." [84] Galsworthy's characters, however, are

almost throttled with emotion only when this seems to him the essence of their actuality. Other times, Galsworthy lets his characters
pour out impassioned, eloquent, and even long speeches as, for instance, when Anthony in *Strife* turns bitterly on his son for taking the
strikers' part:

> There is only one way of treating "men"—with the iron hand. This
> half-and-half business, the half-and-half manners of this generation has
> brought all this upon us. Sentiment and softness, and what this young
> man, no doubt, would call his social policy. You can't eat cake and have
> it! This middle-class sentiment, or socialism or whatever you call it, is
> rotten. Masters are masters, men are men! Yield one demand and they
> will make it six! They are (*he smiles grimly*) like Oliver Twist, asking
> for more. If I were in their place, I should be the same. But I am not in
> their place. Mark my words: one fine morning, when you have given
> way here and given way there—you will find you have parted with the
> ground beneath your feet, and are deep in the bog of bankruptcy; and
> with you, floundering in that bog, will be the very men you have given
> in to.[85]

Needless to say, Roberts, the leader of the strikers, has the occasion to
deliver a speech exactly to the contrary and equally long, bitter, and
eloquently impassioned.

Galsworthy believed that for verse to be good as dialogue it had to
pass the same test as prose: is it true to character and genuinely exciting? Modern blank verse, he found, had "a self-consciousness, a literary emanation" that seemed false to life.[86] He was convinced that
Shakespeare had used blank verse so well that others of less genius
were amateurs at it by comparison.

Usually Galsworthy submitted his work first to the critical judgment of his wife, who naturally would read it in making a fair copy
of the first draft. Then he might read it to a select circle of friends
whose reaction might justify revision. At one time or other he submitted work in an incompleted stage to Joseph Conrad, Edward
Garnett, Gilbert Murray, John Masefield, Granville Barker, and Galsworthy's sisters, Mrs. Sauter and Mrs. Reynolds. For instance, Galsworthy submitted the *Silver Box* in an early draft to Garnett and later
wrote him, "I've adopted your verbal hints practically wholesale. I've
brooded on your larger suggestions—I'm still brooding on them." [87]
And of the same play, he wrote the director, Granville-Barker, "If
you're still of the same opinion as to dropping the curtain on Marlow
and Wheeler—Marlow's 'I set my mind against it,'—I'm now inclined

to agree with you." [88] After receiving Garnett's opinion of an early version of *Strife,* Galsworthy wrote back, "Warm thanks for your letter and criticisms; as usual they are very valuable and mostly tally with my own feelings." [89] And of *The Skin Game,* Galsworthy commented, "I read it out last night to Ada and the Masefields, and the verdict was favorable, though—as usual—it's pretty grim." [90]

Galsworthy usually attended rehearsals of the original productions of his plays to help actors interpret their roles, to answer the director's questions and to rewrite if need be. To illustrate, he had planned to end *Justice* with the death of Falder, the protagonist, so that the audience would feel, "Thank God! He's dead—and *beyond* that awful process going on forever." [91] The producers, Granville-Barker and John Vedrenne, however, favored simply ending the play with Falder's rearrest. Galsworthy to oblige them, rewrote his play to incorporate their suggestions, saw the new ending staged, and felt no discharge of feeling that the first three acts of the play seemed inevitably to intimate and demand. In a quandary, Galsworthy submitted both endings to Gilbert Murray, asking him to pick the better. Murray chose the earlier version ending with Falder's death scene. Galsworthy wrote Murray, "Once more I was refreshed and reinforced by your splendid letter." [92] Vedrenne and Barker then accepted the death scene as the proper end for *Justice.* Throughout rehearsal Galsworthy never hesitated to look upon the stage as his workshop before it became his show-case.

My grateful acknowledgement is extended to the following sources of quotations:

CANDELABRA by John Galsworthy. Copyright 1933. Reprinted by permission of Charles Scribner's Sons

THE CREATION OF CHARACTER IN LITERATURE by John Galsworthy. Copyright 1931. Reprinted by permission of the Clarendon Press, Oxford.

FOR SOME WE LOVED by R. H. Mottram. Copyright 1956. Reprinted by permission of Hutchinson & Co., Ltd.

FORTNIGHTLY REVIEW, December 1909, "Some Platitudes Concerning Drama" by John Galsworthy. Reprinted by permission of CONTEMPORARY REVIEW.

INTIMATE PORTRAITS by Barrett Clark, "John Galsworthy," Dramatists Play Service, 1951, copyright, 1951, by Barrett Clark. Reprinted by permission.

LETTERS FROM JOHN GALSWORTHY 1900–1932, edited with introduction by Edward Garnett. (C) 1934. Charles Scribner's Sons and Jonathan Cape Ltd.

THE LIFE AND LETTERS OF JOHN GALSWORTHY, authorized biography, by H. V. Marrot. Copyright 1935. Reprinted by permission of Charles Scribner's Sons, and William Heinemann Ltd.

THE MAN OF PRINCIPLE, JOHN GALSWORTHY by Dudley Barker. Copyright 1963. Reprinted by permission of William Heinemann Ltd.

MEMORIES OF JOHN GALSWORTHY BY HIS SISTER by M. E. Reynolds. Copyright 1936. Reprinted by permission of Robert Hale Ltd.

THE PLAYS OF JOHN GALSWORTHY: "Justice" by John Galsworthy, copyright 1910 Charles Scribner's Sons; renewal copyright 1938 Ada Galsworthy; "Strife" by John Galsworthy, copyright 1909 by Charles Scribner's Sons, renewal copyright 1937 Ada Galsworthy. Reprinted by permission of Charles Scribner's Sons.

PUBLISHERS WEEKLY, July 4, 1925, "Authors and Their Public" by John Galsworthy

STRAND MAGAZINE, November 1924, "How Our Novelists Write Their Books", a symposium of eminent authors.

CHAPTER V: FOOTNOTES

1. H. V. Marrot, *Life and Letters of John Galsworthy* (London 1935), 791
2. Ibid., 132
3. R. H. Mottram, *For Some We Loved* (London 1956), 39
4. Marrot, 135
5. Mottram, 38, 41
6. Dudley Barker, *The Man of Principle* (London 1963), 19
7. Ibid., 18
8. Ibid.
9. Edward Garnett, editor, *Letters from John Galsworthy 1900–1932* (London 1934), 133–4; Marrot, 24
10. Mottram, 36
11. Barker, 42
12. Ibid., 40
13. Ibid., 43
14. Ibid., 26
15. M. E. Reynolds, *Memories of John Galsworthy* (London 1936), 86
16. Marrot, 132
17. Reynolds, 64
18. John Galsworthy, *Candelabra* (New York 1933), 228.
19. John Galsworthy, "Authors and Their Public," *Publishers' Weekly* (July 4, 1925), 19
20. Marrot, 789
21. Ibid., 137
22. Ibid., 786
23. Ibid., 779
24. Garnett, 183, 186
25. Ibid., 791
26. Barker, 79
27. Barrett Clark, *Intimate Portraits* (New York 1951), 40; Marrot, 189, 720
28. Marrot, 718
29. Reynolds, 71
30. *Candelabra,* 25; Marrot, 708
31. Mottram, p. 280

32. Marrot, 745
33. *Candelabra,* 274, 309
34. Ibid., 307
35. Reynolds, 64
36. John Galsworthy, "Some Platitudes Concerning Drama," *Atlantic Monthly* (December 1909), 769; Marrot, 777
37. Marrot, 624
38. Ibid., 625
39. Marrot, 218
40. Reynolds, 57
41. Ibid., 76
42. Barker, 11, 12
43. Marrot, 533, 587
44. Ibid., 714
45. Ibid., 733
46. Ibid., 250
47. Clark, 37
48. Marrot, 348
49. Ibid., 724
50. Marrot, 803
51. *Atlantic Monthly* (December 1909), 772
52. Ibid.
53. Clark, 40
54. Marrot, 249
55. Marrot, 264
56. Ibid., 320
57. Ibid., 309
58. Ibid., 342
59. Ibid., 482
60. *Candelabra,* 9; *Atlantic Monthly* (December 1909), 770
61. Ibid., 769
62. John Galsworthy, *The Creation of Character in Literature* (Oxford 1931), 19
63. Ibid., 4
64. Ibid., 5
65. *Candelabra,* 292
66. Ibid., 305
67. *Atlantic Monthly* (December 1909), 771
68. *The Creation of Character in Literature,* 27
69. Leon Schalit, *John Galsworthy, a Survey* (London 1929), 7
70. *Atlantic Monthly* (December 1909), 770
71. Marrot, 245–6
72. Reynolds, 79
73. *Atlantic Monthly,* "Some Platitudes Concerning Drama," 769

74. "How Our Novelists Write Their Books," a symposium of eminent authors, *Strand Magazine* (November 1924), 453; William Archer, *Play-Making* (Boston 1923), 36

75. *The Creation of Character in Literature,* 12

76. *Candelabra,* 14

77. Ibid., 3

78. Marrot, 310

79. Reynolds, 55

80. Barker, 190; Marrot, 310

81. *Candelabra,* 171

82. Reynolds, 84

83. John Galsworthy, *The Plays of John Galsworthy* (New York 1925), 173

84. Scribner's Sons, *John Galsworthy, a Sketch of His Life and Works* (New York 1925), 9

85. *The Plays of John Galsworthy,* 101

86. Marrot, 718

87. Ibid., 190

88. Ibid., 192

89. Ibid., 240

90. Ibid., 483

91. Ibid., 252

92. Ibid., 254

Chapter VI

Luigi Pirandello

"THE Great War made me realize the fact that the best form of dramatic action is the stage," recollected Luigi Pirandello in 1926. "Up to then, I simply hated the stage." [1] He had tried his first play, a one-act, *The Epilogue* in 1898 when he was thirty-one years old, and did not score a financial hit until *Right You Are If You Think You Are* in 1918 when he was fifty-one years old. In 1934, Pirandello climaxed his improbable life and career by receiving the Nobel Prize for his "general contribution to letters and arts." "As far as theme is concerned," remarked Eric Bentley, "it seems to me Pirandello says the deepest things the existentialists have more recently been trying to say. And at his best he is a master of stagecraft." [2] Such distinguished writers as Sartre, Giraudoux, Wilder, Miller, Camus, Anouilh, Beckett and Genet suggest in spirit and practice a literary genealogy including Pirandello. Jean-Paul Sartre, for instance, the chief of the whole existentialist movement, when asked who is the most timely dramatist, replied, "It is most certainly Pirandello." [3]

I

THE GROWTH OF PIRANDELLO'S CREATIVE SPIRIT IN LIFE

When Pirandello wrote his first play, *The Epilogue,* in 1898, its only "production" was publication in a Rome newspaper. About ten years later, the Sicilian playwright-producer, Nino Martoglio, and the Sicilian comic, Angelo Musco, opened a repertory theatre in Rome and talked Pirandello into trying a hand at writing Sicilian plays for them. Pirandello's first professional production opened at their theatre in Rome on December 9, 1910, on a bill including *The Epilogue,* retitled *The Vise,* and his now well-known *Sicilian Limes,* both one-acts. These plays were characteristic of his subject matter and themes in plays to come. *The Vise* concerns the mental torment which a good but violently jealous Sicilian businessman, Andrea Fabbri, uses to drive his wife, Giullia, to suicide because he has caught a fleeting glimpse in candlelight of her kissing his business partner, Antonio Serra. The emphasis, suggesting Edgar Allan Poe, is upon passion as hot as the flames of hell and upon psychological analysis as cool as that very light under a spectroscope. In *Sicilian Limes,* a Sicilian peasant, Micuccio Bonavino, who plays piccolo in his home-town band, lavishes his small worldly goods upon training a poor, orphaned girl gifted with a singing voice, Sina Marnis, hoping to make her his own once she is a prima donna; he finds upon visiting Sina in the big city that in her new celebrity, she is so flashily immodest in dress as to be unworthy of his love. The emphasis, suggesting Mark Twain, is upon the poignant illusions of a kind of Sicilian hill-billy clashing with the image that sophisticated, metropolitan success finds necessary for survival. Pirandello's creative spirit was increasingly to turn to playwriting; his life was to temper that spirit into a modern equivalent of the biblical Job's.

Luigi Pirandello drew his first breath on June 28, 1867, on his family's country estate, symbolically not far from a grove of oaks and olives named "the Wood of Chaos" and in view of the magnificent ruins of the ancient Doric temples of Concord and of Hercules at Agrigentum, but also in view of the hovels of the sulphur-miners of Girgenti, then at the mercy of a raging epidemic of cholera. Girgenti, incidentally, is today named "Porto Empedocles." Almost all we know of Pirandello's formative years he himself told his biographer, Frederico V. Nardelli in 1932 for the book, *The Unknown Man (L'uomo segreto)*; much remains unknown.

Pirandello's father, of Greek descent, was a giant with a choleric disposition and the fervor of a veteran under the great Garibaldi. Stefano had reached the rather high local social status of an owner of sulphur mines. Pirandello's mother, born Caterina Ricci Gramitto, was the sister of one of his father's comrades-in-arms. To Sicilians, Garibaldi was "our second Jesus Christ" who liberated Sicily with about 1,000 or so bedraggled volunteers and handed over the kingdom of the oppressive King of Naples to King Victor Emmanuel in the name of Italian unity. Pirandello's father was the youngest of twenty-four sons; but Pirandello, for want of other evidence, seems to have been an only child.

Stefano was anti-clerical and once shot a church-bell whose ringing disturbed his siesta. He beat up an extortionist from the Mafia and was ambushed and shot in the shoulder. He had mistresses, including a cousin whom he would meet in the parlor of a convent on pretence of visiting an aunt, the abbess. Pirandello, then thirteen years old, went to the convent one day to tell off this cousin for making his mother so miserable and, in Sicilian fashion, spat in his cousin's face, when suddenly he saw peeping from under a green curtain, the familiar tips of his father's big, black shoes.[4] The incident, with variations, likely suggested the famous scene at Madame Pace's in Pirandello's *Six Characters in Search of an Author.* Pirandello's father also fought several duels, and duels figure climactically in such notable plays as *The Rules of the Game* and *Each in His Own Way.* Pirandello's mother was a meek, petite, stoical woman. The sweet, affable old lady, Madame Frola, in *Right You Are,* seems in part modelled from her, just as the fierce-looking but kind-hearted son-in-law, Signor Ponza, is modelled in part after his own father and himself.

A few childhood experiences never left Pirandello's soul quite the same. As the only son of a well-to-do father, Pirandello in a new sailor-suit was on his way to church one Sunday when he spotted another child dressed in rags; an impulse of compassion led him to practice the *Bible*'s teaching to clothe the naked. He changed clothes with the child in rags. The child's embarrassed mother at once returned the new sailor-suit; her family was poor but not beggars. Pirandello never forgot the problem of trying to clothe the naked when illusions were somehow peoples' actual clothes.[5]

Another little incident, just the accidental kind that would happen in his plays with profound repercussions, assertedly cost Pirandello his faith in Catholicism. Pirandello's mother, if not his father, regularly attended church, and as a youth, Pirandello bought a church-lottery ticket for two sous to encourage a charity. But afterwards he crossed out his own name on the ticket and wrote in that of an unfortunate boy who had been sick. When the public drawing took place on a Sunday evening in May after the Rosary, the priest read out the winner's name—"Luigi Pirandello." Pirandello insisted in tears that he had given the ticket to the boy who claimed the prize. The curate still insisted that Pirandello with a procession take the prize home—a statuette of the madonna in wax, weeping tears of wax and all under glass. Pirandello's mother returned the prize, and he, according to Nardelli, never went back to church again.[6] What was implied? To Pirandello, the curate's action was not Christ-like but mercenary: the Pirandellos had money. Pirandello could not abide this curate daily helping save his soul. Nakedness of self was to preoccupy him for life: in 1910, a collection of his short stories appeared, *Naked Life;* in 1922, one of his best plays, *To Clothe the Naked;* and late in life, his collection of five of his best plays, *Naked Masks.*

Did he show any early signs of becoming a writer? Apparently an only child, Pirandello until college was schooled entirely by tutors except for a prep school period at Palermo. If the novel, *The Late Mattia Pascal,* in Mattia reflects Pirandello maturing, he had before a successful operation in Rome a left eye he could not control or, in Weaver's translation, given "to gazing into the distance on its own account." [7] Loneliness and shyness might have early driven Pirandello into an intense imaginative life. His family's money allowed him leisure. His homeland invited dreaming. The terrain was mountainous, wildly beautiful, with a rugged coastline. Greeks, Romans, Vandals, Arabs and Spaniards, among others, made Sicily a way-stop on their road of conquest. A feudal system lived on. As in most poor lands, the common folk were elemental. Sicily combined the highest romance with the harshest realities. By late adolescence, Pirandello admitted to writing poetry.

In 1886 after a three months' trial period, Pirandello gave up plans of entering his father's business of mining sulphur. Then as a provincial Sicilian boy, Pirandello for the first time went to the Eternal City, Rome. Here for roughly 3,000 years the human life-stream had moved with every variation of current and content. Rome was real yet swarming with illusions of life of another day. For two years Pirandello attended the University of Rome, majoring in philosophy and philology, a sign of the fusion to come in his literary bent. Then on an impulse preceded by much discontent, as was so often to be true of characters in his plays, Pirandello quarrelled with two professors over their dated teaching methods—Professor Occioni in Latin Literature and Professor Nannerelli in Italian Literature. He was ordered to appear before the faculty council for disciplinary action.

A famous professor of philology, Ernesto Monaci, suggested that he continue his studies at the University of Bonn in Germany. "In October of 1888 I left for Germany," wrote Pirandello, "and remained there two and a half years, that is, until April of 1891." [8] In these few years he published: a collection of poems, *Mal Giocondo* (1889); a possibly definitive Italian translation of Goethe's *Roman Elegies* (1891); another collection of poems, *Springtime of Gaea* (1891)—incidentally dedicated not to his Sicilian intended but to a girl-friend in Bonn named Jenny; and a doctorate dissertation on the dialect of his hometown, *Laute und Sautenwicklung Der Mundart von Girgenti* (1892). Pirandello already had a turn for words and a good ear. Kant, Hegel, and Schopenhauer were especially on his mind.

Pirandello then returned to Rome to make good. With his father's financial support, he tried journalism and free-lance writing. He joined "the Cenacle," a literary camaraderie of young hopefuls and older "arrivals." Luigi Capuana, the celebrated leader of Italian naturalism in literature, "verism," advised Pirandello to give up poetry and to write prose.

When Pirandello was twenty-six, his parents in the Sicilian tradition decided he should marry and picked his bride, Antonietta Portulano, the daughter of the current business partner of Pirandello's father. Signor Portulano, though otherwise balanced, was as a jealous husband rather unbalanced; he likely was the living model in part for many a jealous husband in Pirandello's plays, including the first one in *The Vise,* a play involving two business partners. Pirandello supposedly saw his bride for the first time at the wedding ceremony in January, 1894. The Pirandellos settled down in Rome where Pirandello continued writing. From 1895 to 1899 the couple had three children: Stefano in 1895; Lietta in 1897; and Fausto in 1899.

In 1895, a giant stroke of misfortune started a chain-reaction that was to quite change Pirandello's life. "A man, I have tried to tell something to other men, without any ambition, except perhaps that of avenging myself for having been born," Pirandello wrote in 1935 to Dominico Vittorini. "And yet life, in spite of all that it has made me suffer, is so beautiful! (And here is another positive statement without even a shadow of logic, and yet so true and deeply felt.)" [9] What happened? The family sulphur-mines in Sicily somehow flooded. The combined fortunes of the Pirandellos and the Portulanos were wiped out. Pirandello's wife lost even her dowry, for it, too, had been invested in the mines. Pirandello turned to teaching to support his family. "I have been teaching, alas, for fifteen years at the Instituto Superiore di Magistero Femminile [a girl's high school]," wrote Pirandello in a self-sketch in 1909, as translated by William Murray in the preface to his collection, *One-Act Plays of Pirandello.* "I say alas not only because teaching weighs on me enormously, but also because my greatest desire would be to retire to the country to work." [10]

Pirandello's wife suffered such agonizing pain at the delivery of her third child, Fausto, in 1899, that she was to have no more children and became psychotically jealous of Pirandello, charging him with treachery and infidelity; her own father was so pathologically jealous that her mother had refused to have a doctor at a difficult child-birth and, as a result, died. The mother's death must have haunted the daughter.

Pirandello tried to calm his wildly jealous wife by giving her just about every penny of his meager earnings. "I live in Rome as sheltered a life as possible," said Pirandello. "I go out only a few hours a day toward evening, to get a little exercise, and in the company of a friend or two: Giustino Ferri or Ugo Fleres"—two writers.[11] The Pirandello home became a domestic arena of terrible fits of fury from his increasingly unbalanced and violent wife. Pirandello made too little money to confine his wife to a sanitarium, and besides, the family doctor had compassionately advised it would be better to care for his wife at home. Her torment grew worse when her two sons, Stefano and Fausto, entered the Italian army in World War I. Stefano wound up a prisoner of war in Bohemia, and Fausto became dangerously ill after being drafted while still recovering from an operation. Pirandello's wife persecuted the remaining daughter, Lietta, so viciously, charging her with trying to take over the household, that the girl tried to kill herself with a revolver which by chance jammed. Only in 1918, when Pirandello's plays made a sizeable return, could he afford to send his wife to a sanitarium, and that year she died.

These facts are known. *Their likely implication suggests a traumatic chain-reaction of events.* The loss of the fortune, as today, meant the loss of social status, including property, "friends," and freedom to work at the writing Pirandello loved. The loss of Antonietta's dowry meant to her the loss of her husband's love, for the marriage was arranged. Pirandello teaching in a girl's normal school meant to his very jealous wife that he was surrounded by lovely young ladies with secret assignations; to him it meant he must be most circumspect with the public image of a plaster saint. The wife losing her reason meant the children, too, might lose theirs if driven too far; the frail stuff of every human life has a breaking point. If his demented wife found him at times intolerable, how might she regard their children in whose face she saw his face?

Friends could be few and only in deepest confidence. With a paranoid wife, life for Pirandello was a game of assuming proper roles in changing circumstances altering with the time of day. Reality became shifting appearances. The Don Juan and *bon vivant* of his wealthy bachelor days became an ascetic who for years was condemned to uncertain terrors in his very home.

"I work," Pirandello told one of his admirers as reported in *La*

Grande Revue of March, 1927, "to escape from my own life, whose material aspects bore and disgust me. Once I have released the idea of whatever play or novel I am carrying about, I feel as if God had abandoned me." [12] In the course of his writing career, including twenty-five years concurrent with his teaching, Pirandello did his best to keep from feeling that God had abandoned him. He wrote a grand total of: six novels, more than two hundred and fifty short stories, six books of poetry, two volumes of criticism, and forty-five plays.

Two early works deserve special attention later in this study, for they provide the spiritual reservoir feeding the enormous flow of all of Pirandello's works to come: a novel, *The Late Mattia Pascal* (*Il fu Mattia Pascal*), published in 1904; and the essay, *Humor* (*L'umorismo*), published in 1908.

Pirandello had very limited editorial and public recognition in Italy before 1918. James Joyce and Benjamin Cremieux had "discovered" him in France about 1915, but they themselves were then quite avant-garde. Only recently has an attempt been made to set up some kind of Pirandello canon of his plays. When Vittorini asked Pirandello to fix the dates of some of his writings, Pirandello said, "Dates do not count. An author should stand before the critic as a complete whole." [13] More than two-thirds of these plays were based upon Pirandello's earlier short stories or novels. In the following listing 30 years after his death, titles with one asterisk are one-acts translated into English; titles with two asterisks after them are full-length plays so translated.

Sicilian Limes (1910)*
The Vise (1910) from
   The Epilogue (1898)*
The Doctor's Duty (1912)*
If Not Thus (1913)
The Reason of Others (1915)
At the Exit (1916)*
*Just Think, Giacomino
Liola***
The Jar (1917)*
Cap and Bells
*Right You Are If You Think
   You Are***
The Pleasure of Honesty**
The License*
But It's Not in Earnest
The Rules of the Game**
Grafting (1919)

Man, Beast, and Virtue
Chee Chee (1920)*
*As at First but Better Than
   as at First*
All for the Best
*Mrs. Morli, the First and the
   Second*
*Six Characters in Search of an
   Author* (1921)**
The Imbecile (1922)
To Clothe the Naked**
Henry IV**
The Life I Gave You (1923)
The Other Son*
*The Man with the Flower in
   His Mouth**
*The Festival of Our Lord of
   the Ship* (1924)*

*Each in His Own Way***	*Child of One or of None*
Diana and La Tuda (1926)**	*As You Desire Me* (1930)**
Bellavita (1927)*	*Tonight We Improvise***
The Wives' Friend	*To Find Oneself* (1932)**
Scamandra (1928)	*When One Is Somebody* (1933)**
*The New Colony***	*One Knows not How* (1934)
Lazarus (1929)**	*Giants of the Mountain* (Un-
*I'm Dreaming, but Am I?***	finished) (1936)**

Pirandello's output has been roughly classified into: Sicilian folk-plays, like *Liola;* philosophical tragi-comedy, like *Six Characters;* and modern myths, like *The New Colony*. He had no "periods" but continually mixed the types of plays, although the modern myths first appeared in 1928.

Pirandello's international recognition as a dramatist reached the proportions of a craze from 1922 to 1925. (Shaw thought that crazes at best move in cycles of four years' duration.) "I have lived through the period of the hopes and the bitter disappointments of United Italy," Pirandello told Eleonor Markell for *The New York Times* of November 4, 1923. "My early life was spent under the influence of that first burst of hope and enthusiasm of that liberated, free, united Italy, but I had hardly reached manhood before those hopes faded, that enthusiasm turned to disillusion. This experience turned my mind to deeper subjects." [14]

Then Pirandello noted his distinctive viewpoint of a literary lifetime. "What had appeared reality had proved illusion. I entered that search for truth which is nation-wide today. Each question I submitted to the test—Is it truth, is it illusion?" [15] Mussolini's transformation from a leading communist into the fascist, "Il Duce," Pirandello cited as an example of his own philosophy of changing personality, a by-product of changing circumstances.

When Helen Augur interviewed Pirandello and asked what he read, he answered as reported in *The New York Times* of March 4, 1923, "Very little. Philosophy mostly. Herodotus most of all." When asked about Freud, Pirandello replied, "Why should Italians read about repressions and complexes? We repress nothing." [16] Actually, Pirandello's characters, by being forced through circumstance to behave in a way alien to their nature and to assume a false appearance, are all showing signs of repressions and complexes. Pirandello's doctorate in philosophy and philology from Bonn had probably acquainted him with the best in world dramatic literature as well as in philosophy, especially 19th century German philosophy and Immanuel Kant's doctrine that the appearance of anything for us is *ipso facto* its reality. Later turns in Pirandello's life inclined him by popular identification with such philosophers as Kierkegaard, Pascal, Hegel, Bergson, and Einstein. "Of modern dramatists, I know few," said Pirandello. "Synge is my favorite, and Shaw and Barrie are always a delight." [17] Synge wrote of the Irish peasant with the insight Pirandello brought to the Sicilian peasant. Shaw was a writer of intellectual comedy with philosophical by-play, and Barrie at his best saw poignancy, humor, and fantasy in life. Vittorini reported of Pirandello, "He spoke with great admiration of the American authors Edgar Allan Poe and Mark Twain." [18]

Pirandello never said he admired or read anything of the so-called Italian "Grotesque" literature established by Chiarelli's satirical play, *The Face and the Mask,* written in 1914, and rumored as inspired by *The Late Mattia Pascal.* He hotly resented insinuations that his characters were grotesque; he thought he drew them truthfully from their appearance in life. As for D'Annunzio, the beloved favorite of Italian literature and the stage during all the years that Pirandello was just about left out in a freezing cold, Pirandello said, "He is, I believe, in everything just the opposite of what I am. He is all pose and pathos—and very excellently, almost classically acted repose. For myself I feel that I am of the modern, the throbbing life." [19]

Largely from the royalties of *Six Characters* on the international stage, Pirandello in 1925 founded his own playhouse in Rome by converting a former marionette venture, the Odescalchi Theatre, into The Art Theatre. Mussolini attended the first performance. The venture survived one season, then expired in bankruptcy. Mussolini in 1926, to promote a world-wide image of Italian fascism as a loving patron of the arts, helped underwrite Pirandello's company to tour the capitols of Europe and South America for a season of Italian plays; the venture was successful only artistically. Though late in 1926 Mussolini spoke of making Pirandello "undisputed director" of an ambitious new National Theatre, with playhouses in Italy's largest cities and with a repertory company to challenge even the laurels of the Moscow Art Theatre, the whole plan wound up as just so much cold antipasto without the dinner.

Only after the French government awarded Pirandello the Cross of the Legion of Honor did the Italian government feel obligated by prestige to award Pirandello its own "commenda." France typified civilized Europe in those days; Italy dared not typify less. In April, 1934, an operetta *The Legend of a Changeling Son,* with music by Francesco Malovero and a libretto by Pirandello, opened in Rome and was quickly withdrawn by order of Mussolini, himself. *The Legend* seemed to Mussolini to cast aspersions upon the nature of Italy's current monarchy. An idiot and monster adult king is restored to his throne after being stolen from his crib as a child and replaced by a poor woman's healthy offspring. The return of the idiot-monster King is unnoticed by the people, for they only distinguish actuality from illusion by the trappings anyway. In 1934 Pirandello must have astonished himself and certainly Italy by winning the Nobel Prize for Literature, the only such prize Italy has to this day won.

When Mussolini declared war on Ethiopia in the fall of 1935, Pirandello was visiting the United States with hopes of getting a film production of his *Six Characters;* he was approached in his quarters at the Waldorf Astoria in New York City by Clifford Odets and John Howard Lawson heading a group of writers. They asked him to explain his politics. He handed out a mimeographed statement. "I know nothing of politics," said Pirandello, "and never mix art with politics." Asked what he thought of the Ethiopian War, he answered, "Didn't the Americans take this country from the Indians for the sake of civilization?" [20] He called Ethiopia "the last African region where slavery is still openly and shamefully perpetuated." [21] Both of Pirandello's sons were reservists, and he contributed the gold medal that came with his Nobel Prize, to buy bullets.

What kind of person was Pirandello? "To accomplish as much as I do in the way of turning out books and plays," he said, "I practically live with a pen in my hand. But it is my life—the thing I enjoy." [22] Of medium height and wiry build, with a satyr-like yet benevolently bearded face, Pirandello had the fantastic stamina and nervous energy of a scaled-down Hercules. Calm and modest unless emotionally involved, Pirandello thought, talked, and gestured without inhibition to express full meaning. His restless, small, brown eyes had a bird-like brightness in peering sharply about; his mind's eye peered as sharply within. A born raconteur, he was correct in manner and fastidious in dress. Deeply attached to his children, he took pride in being a Sicilian Italian.

Once he could afford to, he travelled quite a bit. "Let us simply say that I have a horror of being enclosed by custom," he said in an interview for the Parisian weekly, *Candide*. "As soon as I see them lay hold on me I break them. That is why I have traveled so much and traversed two continents." [23] He visited the United States for several months in 1923 and for some weeks in 1935. "The dominating motive in American life for standardizing everything," he said, "can only result in the sacrifice of the rare and the beautiful." [24] "The flaw in the system," he warned, "is that no nation can afford to sacrifice its geniuses for the sake of the mediocre."

Pirandello seemed to have little time for friends except those who directly advanced his work: the leaders of Italian naturalism, Luigi Capuana, and Giovanni Verga, best remembered now for his libretto to Mascagni's opera, *Cavalleria Rusticana;* a drama critic, Giustino Ferri; a humorist, Ugo Fleres; the playwright producer, Nino Martoglio, and his star comic, Angelo Musco; and Marta Abba, Pirandello's protégée and his leading lady at the Art Theatre, for whom he was later to write such starring roles as the beautiful and anguished Strange Lady in *As You Desire Me*. "In the whole course of Italian literature," Pirandello confided to Vittorini in a far from self-demeaning moment, "one constantly finds such contrasts, Dante and Petrarch, Ariosto and Tasso, Goldoni and Matastsio . . . and today myself and D'Annunzio." [25]

At the age of sixty-nine while living at his modest villa in Rome, Pirandello contracted influenza which swiftly developed into pneumonia, and on December 10, 1936, Pirandello died. He regretted leaving unfinished *Memories of My Involuntary Sojourn on Earth*. The fascists sped to his home prepared to put him quickly into a blackshirt, their uniform, and to give him a state funeral for the greater glory of Il Duce, Mussolini. Pirandello botched any such plans by leaving a will stripping his death of any "illusions" civilization might give it. He requested, for instance, "Allow my death to pass in silence;" "Wrap me, naked in a sheet;" "The lowest class of funeral carriage, the one for the poor. . . . And let no one accompany me, neither relatives nor friends;" "Burn me." [26] Until 1951 his ashes were kept in a Greek urn at the Municipal Museum at Agrigento; then they were sealed up in a rock under a favorite pine on a slope before the house where he was born. Was Pirandello a nihilist? In 1935, he told Vittorini:

> I am not sacrilegious. I mean that God is a universal concept existing outside the partial constructions of Him that each sect makes. When this universal concept is enclosed in the Christian God, the Hindu God, and

in as many other gods as there are tribes in Africa and peoples on the earth, the universality of that concept is necessarily offended and dwarfed.[27]

II

COMMERCIAL CONSIDERATIONS AFFECTING PIRANDELLO'S PLAYWRITING

William Murray said of Pirandello's day, "it was not possible then (nor is it now) for anyone to make a living in Italy by purely literary activity."[28] Pirandello must have known this, for he kept his teaching position for about twenty-five years until success in the theatre gave him a bank account that seemed to spell financial independence. Even *The Late Mattia Pascal,* now generally rated his best novel, sold only 2,000 copies in the eighteen years following its publication in 1904; once *Six Characters* succeeded on a world-wide sequence of stages, according to *Publishers' Weekly, The Late Mattia Pascal* sold 100,000 copies in the 2 years following.[29] Pirandello's Art Theatre, which went into bankruptcy after one season in Rome, 1925–26, cost him 600,000 lira; by a conversion table, this was then equal to about $24,000, or in today's inflated dollar, more like $100,000. "I have had no personal gain from my work of the past forty years," Pirandello wrote Marta Abba in April, 1929, "and yet it has brought in a great deal of money. Others took it and made use of it."[30] In 1934, when Pirandello received the Nobel Prize for Literature, then worth $41,138, he said, "Of course, I'm going to keep it. There are poor authors, too."[31]

From 1917–1937, Pirandello's plays were translated into twenty-five foreign languages of such unItalian cultures as Finn, Russian, Lett, Arabic, Hebrew, Japanese and Chinese. *Six Characters,* alone, has to date been translated about 500 times. "As for things in practical life," Pirandello said, "I have always been most inept at taking care of them."

What kept Pirandello writing, though for years it brought in little money? The dictates of talent, escape from a domestic inferno, and also an eye for an actual market suited to his integrity. Pirandello might not have always been as popular as a lottery prize in Italy, but he was still published and performed there. His first professionally produced plays, *The Vise* and *Sicilian Limes,* were suited to and asked for by Martoglio and Musco's Sicilian repertory theatre in

Rome; Pirandello was writing from the heart for his own "paessáni," his countrymen. One-act plays had a ready market to round out an evening's entertainment; after a long melodrama, for instance, would come a short farce to send the public home cheered up.

Pirandello certainly showed some business sense in adapting his proven, original Sicilian short stories into short or long plays, no doubt with a ready customer in Martoglio and Musco and with leading roles tailored with a sharp eye to fit the star comic, Musco. "Italians," said Lander MacClintock in his book, *The Age of Pirandello,* "have long cherished drama in dialect." [32] Comic characters using dialect were old favorites in the Commedia dell'Arte as, for example, the Neapolitan Pulcinelli, the Venetian Pantalone, and the Bolognese Doctore. Martoglio and Musco did just about all of Pirandello's plays until 1921, even adapting the nondialect ones, like *Right You Are,* into Sicilian. Mussolini then frowned on dialect drama as nationally divisive and finally banned it as treason; he wanted uniform mortar to make a monolithic state.

What did Pirandello think the Italian theatre-going public of his day really wanted? He said in his essay, "The New Theatre and the Old," in *Saggi di Luigi Pirandello:*

> Widely patronized not long ago, and almost everywhere in the world, were the illusory glasses of Sardou and Company. Incredible as it may seem, some people continue to use them in our country not without profit and esteem; nothing is more incredible than the truth. . . . But then there arrived from far-off Norway, first on the German market and then on the French, the powerful lenses of Henrik Ibsen, to impose upon everyone their terrible power to investigate ideal and social values. Their vogue lasted a long time, though very few succeeded in adjusting them properly to the nose; then when this difficulty of adjustment was recognized as insuperable the monocles of the Batille-Bernstein factory became the fashion and there is still a fantastic sale for them in all the countries of the world.[33]

Pirandello must have realized that his own "glasses" showing the baffling nature of reality and illusion and of personality, itself, could not but strike the Catholic Italian man in the street like Pontius Pilate's remark, "What is truth?" MacClintock estimates that of Italy's 45,000,000 or so people, a total year's ticket-sale for the legitimate theatre runs to about 5,000,000 seats; actually this is a good average,—1 in 9. Yet Mussolini came to fulminate and gesticulate in his dictatorial certainty that the legitimate theatre was clearly out of touch with the Italian people.

For what particular public did Pirandello believe he was writing? Here is his frank opinion as voiced before the Boston Drama League and reported in the *Boston Transcript,* February 2, 1924, in the words of Pirandello's translator, Arthur Livingston:

> When my plays were first presented, the critics declared them obscure and paradoxical and the crowd in general became convinced that they were fitted only for the small theatres patronized by the intellectuals. I feel that perhaps after all the crowd was right, as my plays all deal with a philosophical concept of life, and few arrive at a correct conception of this idea.[34]

Pirandello was writing for "a small theatre full of intelligent people." "If I had to choose a definite 'ideal' theatre anywhere," he said, "I should choose a small one indeed—the Vieux Colombier." [35] This Parisian playhouse had about 535 seats; Pirandello thought that a house seating 400 or even 300 would be just fine for his plays. "In vast spaces," he said of comedy, "its sparkle is lost." Drama, Pirandello thought, could play to much larger houses.

Pirandello's small audience of intelligent people was not necessarily affluent. "If it is true that the theatre will never die," he wrote Marta Abba, "it is equally true that it must be helped in its competition with other forms of entertainment." [36] He refused to "write down" to the public. "This continual playing down to what the editors and managers assume to be the mentality of the public," Pirandello complained of the United States to Alice Rohe, "has its disastrous effects not only upon the people but upon the writers. Creative genius, in order to maintain its standardized and demanded scale of comforts, has to write down, always down to the superimposed but mistaken level of understanding." [37]

Pirandello must in time have approached his prospective Italian audience like the lion-tamer who keeps putting his head into his favorite animal's mouth as a test of love. T. Y. Ybarra reported Pirandello's own version of perhaps his most important premiere in Italy:

> I remember most especially the first performance at Rome of *Six Characters.* Spectators stood up in their seats and shouted defiance at the actors or at other spectators in the house, and there was a constant undercurrent of growling and hissing as the play progressed. During the intermissions rival factions formed in the corridors, loudly voicing their approval or disapproval of the play, and as it drew toward the close there was such a succession of tempestuous scenes that the thing took on the look of a regular riot.

The climax, however, did not come until the final curtain was rung down. Then a wild hullabaloo broke out in the audience. Scores of spectators, leaning forward from the boxes, shook their fists at me as I came out on the stage, and yelled over and over again: "Buffoon! Buffoon!" So violent did these people become that the police locked the exits from the boxes . . .[38]

Pirandello's Italian theatre audience seemed rather like Americans at a good prize-fight. *Each in His Own Way* and *Tonight We Improvise* work the Italian audience reaction into the actual plays. In the Italian, as in most continental theatres, Pirandello often had to contend with a hostile claque hired by personal enemies and bent on disrupting the performance by such means as whistles and hissing; friendly claques, however, could be hired to counter hostile ones by such means as wild applause and shouts of "Bravo!" These tactics are not unknown at New York City's Metropolitan Opera.

What did Pirandello think the international theatre public wanted? Just what "a small theatre full of intelligent people" wants. He must have felt vastly reassured that his refusal to "write down" to the Italian public had overnight won him a fantastically larger public abroad than he had ever lost at home. "After this late success in the theatrical field, first in Italy, then in Europe and America," wrote Silvio D'Amico of Pirandello, "it was 'discovered' that his narrative works, also, which had been in print for 25 years, were the creation of perhaps the greatest Italian novelist since Boccaccio. His novels and short stories began to be translated as profusely as his dramas."[39] Why the late recognition? "Probably," explained D'Amico, "because he appeared on the literary horizon a quarter of a century ahead of his time."

As earlier suggested, Pirandello in his personal values had gone through the equivalent devastation of a war long before Europe went through World War I. Coincidentally perhaps, he also found himself after World War I quite up to the minute what with Einstein's popularization of a universe of relativity and of Freud's and Jung's discoveries about the universe of the self in terms of sex and identity. Post World War II, Pirandello's view of life won a new public with the existentialists, especially. The atomic stalemate in the world has forced men to examine themselves and their society stripped bare of any illusions if there were to be even a chance of anything surviving.

Pirandello's appeal in the United States was always rather limited to the tributary theatre, with few exceptions. Here is a run-down of his

Broadway record: *Six Characters in Search of an Author,* 1922–23, 136 performances; *The Living Mask (Henry IV* retitled), 1923, 28 performances—and incidentally, the end of Brock Pemberton's plans for producing a Pirandello series; *Right You Are If You Think You Are,* 1927, 28 performances; *As You Desire Me,* 1930–31, 142 performances—and later made into a movie starring Greta Garbo. Paris in 1925 had five Pirandello plays running in one season.

"Writing is a game!" says Pirandello's counterpart, Ludovico, the novelist in the play, *To Clothe the Naked;* "It is something like playing the market where the stocks go up and down." After his death, Pirandello's stocks went down till the mood of post World War II set in. More recently, Pirandello has had several off-Broadway revivals: *Right You Are If You Think You Are,* 1955, 65 performances; *Six Characters in Search of an Author,* 1963–1964, 529 performances; *To Clothe the Naked,* 1967, 30 performances. According to Luciano Codignola in the Spring of 1964 issue of *The Tulane Drama Review,* Italians regard Pirandello as "our greatest playwright," yet the public turns chiefly to opera, movies and television.[40]

Pirandello apparently preferred the Roman theatrical audience with its mobster antics to the drama critics. Critics had ignored him so long that once they "discovered" him, he could only distrust their vision. In an interview reported in *The London Observer* of August 15, 1926, Pirandello said:

> I dislike critics, and I don't believe them. To my mind, "criticism" as an art in itself is utterly unthinkable. If criticism is of intrinsic value itself it automatically becomes an essay. In such cases the critic—I am, of course, thinking of the really talented critic—gives more of his own self than merely the impressions that a book, a piece of music, or a play might exercise on his mind. . . . The only things I do believe in, and the only things that matter are the likes and dislikes of the readers of a book or the onlookers of a play, for these are spontaneous.

Likely Pirandello's bitterest enemy in Italian criticism from 1902 on, when the two first fell out, was the philosopher-aesthetician, Benedetto Croce. "I say that he has exhibited his despair and agitation without going beyond them in his fancy, without transforming them into poetry," Croce wrote Vittorini in a letter in 1935, and when Pirandello had already won the Nobel Prize. "Unhappily, he prided himself on being strong in logic, a philosopher," continued Croce of Pirandello, "and I must confess that rarely have I found a man as unfit as he on this score."[41] "Pirandello and Mah Jong are the two leading New York fads," commented George Jean Nathan in *Screenland* of May, 1924; "Doubtless by the time the ink is dry, both will be in discard and succeeded by the latest Serbian dramatist and strip-poker." Even Burns Mantle, the distinguished drama critic of *The Daily News* of New York, misjudged Pirandello. Mantle's 1922–23 issue of his yearly publication, *Ten Best Plays,* failed to include Pirandello's modern classic, *Six Characters in Search of an Author.* If Pirandello became world famous, it was far more likely in spite of drama critics rather than because of them.

III

AESTHETIC CONSIDERATIONS AFFECTING
PIRANDELLO'S PLAYWRITING

"I do not owe my thoughts to any philosophical book," said Pirandello as reported in an interview in *The Living Age* of August 27, 1925; "They are born in myself. They are born from the labor of my spirit, through observation of the conditions in which men have been put by their birth on earth." [42] If Croce thought Pirandello absurd, Pirandello thought Croce absurd with his attempts to reduce art to systematic logic. Pirandello knew the best philosophical thought; he wound up an empiricist, content to let experience be not simply the best teacher, but as the ultimate test of all learning, the *only* teacher.

"My philosophy? Art is my true philosophy," Pirandello told F. Vinci-Roman at breakfast—a remark that would likely punch most professional philosophers in the mid-riff. "I'm an artist to begin with, and whatever philosophy is in my writings is the irradiation of my art." And then Pirandello suggested how life had taught him: "It is not the philosophical concept that becomes image, but it is the image that becomes philosophy . . ." [43] For a Platonist, Pirandello's reliance upon appearance as the only reality might be the beginning of nothing but error, while today's existentialists would regard Pirandello's view as the only beginning of truth.

"Art is something very special and very concrete. People who erect a system and label it with a word ending in 'ism'," Pirandello said in an interview for the Parisian weekly *Candide,* in 1935, "fall into abstractions. They produce more or less of a caricature." [44] Abstractions like a kind of man-made balloon are at the mercy of whoever inflates them. Pirandello's notions about art are perhaps most conclusively suggested in this passage translated by Murray from posthumous papers:

The idea has no value in art until it acquires feeling, until, in entire possession of the spirit, it becomes a desire strong enough to arouse the images capable of endowing it with a living expression. Art, in short, is life, not a reasoning process. Now, all the founders of a system condemn the artist to reason, instead of to live . . . Art is the living idea, the idea that, in becoming the center of the interior life, creates the body of images in which it clothes itself. The idea *is* nothing without the form, but what is form without the idea, if the idea is what creates it? No formulas, then, for art. Whoever desires to create beauty by a formula deludes himself. Beauty can derive from anything except premeditated reasoning. Since, above all, the artist must be moved, out of his being moved the work of art will be born.[45]

This statement is especially interesting in that in some plays, such as *The Pleasure of Honesty* and *The Rules of the Game,* Pirandello has been accused of being inhumanly logical in some leading characters, for example, Angelo Baldovino and Leone Gala; perhaps Pirandello only drew two philosophers.

As to what form was best for art, Pirandello told Vinci-Roman, "No form of expression is perfect *per se.* The idea is born with its own form . . . It is like the tree that is potential in its seed and cannot be otherwise." When Vinci-Roman told Pirandello that some of his public regarded him as a symbolist, Pirandello in a flash of Sicilian fire replied:

No. I am not a symbolist. Some writers take types for the sake of describing them. That is not sufficient for me. There are others who are not satisfied with man for his own sake. They must see in man a symbol, something imbued with a profound sense of life. Symbolic art is false. A symbolist takes a concept and makes of it an image. A type. He himself does not believe in the reality of his own concept, for he must disguise it. There is no reality in symbolism—no truth.[46]

To these intimations as to the nature of art, Pirandello added one he is certainly most associated with. "All that lives, by the sheer fact of living, has a form and so must die," Pirandello noted of creating *Six Characters,* "all except the work of art which, on the contrary, lives forever insofar as it is form." [47]

And what of the nature of the artist to Pirandello? The artist's eyes almost measured his insight. Pirandello stated in his essay, "The Old and the New Theatre:"

Everybody knows about the simple old peasant who couldn't read but was hopeful when somebody mentioned "reading-glasses." He rushed to

the optician in the nearest city and demanded spectacles. The attitude of
the audience toward plays is the trustful attitude of the old contradino
who thought that the optician who supplied him with glasses would
supply him also with the magic power to read. Imitative dramatists give
the public what it thinks it wants. Great dramatists have never been
concerned with spectacles but with eyes.[48]

Another time, Pirandello equated talent with insight: "by talent I
mean that interior virtue of spirit by which a man discovers for himself what he has not learned from others." Pirandello insisted, "A talent without individuality is not a real talent. And style means individuality, one's own way of thinking, feeling, expressing." [49] From his
own life, Pirandello also demonstrated the artist's need for a rather
demonic drive, a Herculean capacity for work, and the stamina to
survive; for though he entered hell on earth, he did not abandon
hope.

To Pirandello, propaganda was outside the legitimate boundaries of
art and artists. "One must choose between the objectives of art and
those of propaganda," he wrote Marta Abba, as noted in her preface
to *The Mountain Giants and Other Plays.* "The two cannot be practiced together. If they are joined, neither will be successful, for the
realm of art is fancy, invention, imagination, while the effectiveness of
propaganda depends on precise and well documented demonstrable
facts. When art becomes the instrument of definite action and of practical utility, it is condemned and sacrificed." [50] Paradoxically enough,
Pirandello's libretto for *Legend of a Changeling Son* suggests even he
could be accused of propaganda. Talk of illusion and reality!

As an artist, Pirandello always called himself "a humorist." In 1935
he told Vittorini that his essay, *Humor,* written in 1908, contained his
basic views of comedy; "Neither his life concept nor his art had sub-
stantially changed, he insisted," reported Vittorini.[51] Here is Mac-
Clintock's translation of Pirandello's definition of "humor" in *Saggi
di Luigi Pirandello:*

> It consists in the sentiment of the contrary, brought about by the
> special activity of reflexion, which is not concealed, which does not
> become, as it ordinarily does in art, a form of sentiment, but its contrary,
> though it follows the sentiment step by step as the shadow follows the
> body. The ordinary artist pays attention only to the body; the humorist
> pays attention to the body and the shadow, sometimes more to the
> shadow than the body; he watches all the play of this shadow, how it
> lengthens, how it shrinks, almost as if to mock the body, which pays no
> attention to it.[52]

Certainly, if ever a shadow followed anyone about all his life "almost as if to mock the body," it was Pirandello's. Pirandello's conception of humor, derived from his own life, calls for his view of life, itself, a view polarized by his own experience and brought to focus more or less in all of his fiction, especially his plays. Pirandello declared in this passage from an autobiographical sketch written in 1909:

Life is a very sad buffoonery, because, without any possibility of knowing or learning why or from what source, we bear within us the need to deceive ourselves continually with the spontaneous creation of a reality (a different reality for each one of us, and never the same reality for all) which from time to time reveals itself to be vain and illusory. He who once understands the joke does not succeed in fooling himself any longer; but he who cannot fool himself any longer can no longer find zest or pleasure in life. . . . My art is full of compassion for all those who trick themselves, but this compassion cannot help being followed by the ferocious derision of a destiny that condemns man to illusion.[53]

This is Pirandello's opinion of "the human predicament," to use a current existentialist phrase.

Did Pirandello change this attitude much in the balance of his lifetime and so in his writing? In 1924, during a lecture to the Boston Drama League, a member of the audience in the question-and-answer period asked point blank, much to the hearty bursts of laughter from everyone else, "Signor Pirandello, what is your whole philosophy and concept of life?" Pirandello nonplussed, answered:

Life to me is a continuous unbroken flux, to which the human mind gives form by giving it laws, habits and customs. Only in this way can the human mind become aware of itself, and it must give the eternal flux this form. This form, however, is transitory, and soon the flux flows on as if the mind had never been. The tragedy of life is in this breaking away of life from the form which the human spirit has found it necessary to create.[54]

From reading Pirandello's plays, we might paraphrase the above quotation: "Man, a thinking, social animal, makes rules with other men to control his instincts and impulses in society; man's instincts and impulses then break these rules which are soon outdated, and man becomes his own victim."

IV

WORKING METHODS OF PIRANDELLO IN PLAYWRITING

Genesis and Incubation

"For me, to live means to work, to create," Pirandello wrote Marta Abba in October of 1935. "When I shall no longer be able to do this, it will be a thousand times better to die." [55] "I had to escape from . . . ," [56] Pirandello confessed of what drove him to write his most famous play, *Six Characters in Search of an Author.* His escape was from six characters who tormented him, demanding release in a play, after they had already appeared in his short story, *La tragedia d'un personaggi* in *Berecche e la guerra* (1919). The creative urge, however, had exultation in its exercise. "I am in the midst of a burning fever of work," Pirandello informed Marta Abba from Berlin on April 6, 1930, "and I am beginning to feel like a god again." [57] Pirandello developed such potent powers of concentration that he seemed to be able to dim reality and light up his mind's eye with the ease of flicking a switch. "What you really need is *will power, will power, will power,*" he wrote Marta Abba in August, 1926. "And I shall imbue you with it through my own, of which I have so much." Then he spoke of "a gift which I possess in the highest degree of abstracting myself from all contingencies of life." [58]

How did Pirandello approach his working day? His habits were almost ascetic, for, after the loss of his family fortune, he learned to do without. In an autobiographical sketch he wrote at forty-three he said:

> I get up early in the morning and habitually work until noon. After lunch, usually, I go back to my desk at two-thirty and stay there until five-thirty, but, after the morning hours, I do no more writing, unless there is some urgent necessity; I either read or study.

And his recreation?

> I go out only a few hours a day toward evening to get a little exercise and in the company, if possible, of a friend or two . . .
> In the evening, after dinner, I chat a bit with my little family. I read the titles of the articles and the headlines of a few newspapers . . . I very seldom go to the theatre. By ten o'clock every night I am in bed.
> As you can see, there is nothing in my life worth revealing: it is all interior, in my work and my thoughts, which . . . are not happy ones.[59]

Lucio D'Amba, an Italian drama critic who knew Pirandello for over twenty years, gives this reminiscence published in the *Boston Transcript* of March 7, 1925:

> As in a vision, I see him once again, either as he was with his blond beard in his lyrical days, or with the white beard of his philosophical days. I see him sitting at this table, littered with papers, where the sun pours in through two windows towards which he is turned. In the old study which has become old with him, and into which nothing new has been brought. There will Pirandello sit from eight to ten hours a day with hardly half an hour for lunch, a mountain of small cut papers in front of him on his writing table, destined to be written on, his hand on his beard, and to quiet his nerves, the eternal cigarette which is always going out and having to be relighted, his feet in big slippers revealing the inner agitation by the many curves that the points describe on the carpet, with such a distracted and absent manner that at the end of the day one could seriously ask him whether the lunch is there or not.[60]

The "mountain of small cut papers" suggests Pirandello wrote many separate notions as they came to him, and then rearranged them for maximum effectiveness. Evidently, too, Pirandello often did without lunch, quite forgetting to eat it or choosing not to.

> Then at a pause of his work there is a short walk into the town where some business is to be attended to, after which he comes back again, locks himself in his study, where everything is ready from the beard to the cigarette smoke.

Pictures of Pirandello's study taken upon winning the Nobel Prize in 1934 are astonishingly like the study of Ludovico, the novelist, in his play, *To Clothe the Naked* (1922). Pirandello liked staying put in one workshop. He typed all his manuscripts with one finger. He smoked about 120 cigarettes a day. He enjoyed coffee. Italians are said to have three joys in life—"eat well, drink well, and run down the government." Pirandello ate simply but well, and was no teetotaller.

"Can an author ever tell how and why his imagination gives birth to a certain character?" asked Pirandello probing his own creation of *Six Characters* in *The Virginia Quarterly Review* (Leo Ongley's translation). As many artists have done, Pirandello likened the conception of a brain-child to that of a real child. "And in just the same way the artist, who gathers within himself innumerable germs of life, can never say how, or why, or at what precise moment one of these particles of life has lodged in his imagination, there to become a living creature inhabiting a plane of life superior to our voluble and vain daily existence." [61]

When a special correspondent from *The London Observer* (August 15, 1926) asked Pirandello if he worked from a fixed programme, he answered:

> No, I have no fixed programme. *My life consists of impressions, and I always endeavor to reflect these impressions in my writings. I always want to be different and original.* I really could not tell you which of my works is my favorite one. They are all equally dear to me; they are *all the creation of my nerves and energy. To every one of them there is some souvenir attached,* souvenirs which even now have great effect upon me; *they imbue me with feverish energy*—in short, they inspire me.

The italics are added to suggest the key in the genetic code of Pirandello's brain-children. There are other genetic clues dropped in interviews or in the plays themselves. "The theme of all my work," Pirandello told Philip Carr in a story for the *New York Times* of May 24, 1931, "is that imagination is stronger than actuality. What is real for each of us is what he or she believes to be real—," and Pirandello would say no more.[62]

"Any artist who is a true artist never seeks or takes a subject cold bloodedly," remarked Pirandello to the Boston Drama League in 1924. "It must come spontaneously from within himself, and it cannot come by deliberate forethought." "There are authors—and they are not so few—who do write for the pleasure they take in the writing alone, and who look for no other satisfaction. Such writers one might describe as historical" observed Pirandello. "But there are others who, in addition to deriving the pleasure I have described, feel a spiritual need that will not permit them to use characters, events, or scenes which are not impregnated, so to speak, with a special sense of life that gives them a universal significance and value. Such writers are, properly speaking, philosophical. And to this latter group I have the misfortune to belong." [63]

Pirandello by implication was always scrutinizing his prospective brain-children for "a special sense of life that gives them a universal significance and value." He did not give in to every simulated conception without careful examination to find if it would be worth the labor pains of full creation. If he was on guard against life without a universal significance, he also was on guard against universal significance without life. "I hate symbolic art," he said, "for it makes a mechanical structure, an allegory out of all representation, destroying its spontaneity." [64]

Where did Pirandello get the foetal nourishment for his brainchildren? "My life consists of impressions and I always endeavor to reflect these impressions in my writings." His source was his own life: his home in Sicily until the age of nineteen; his two years as a student in Bonn, Germany; his roughly forty-five years in Rome with some interludes of world travel.

"My short stories are full of the conflicts of these realities created by the mind," Pirandello told Helen Augur, "and so most of them are essentially dramatic and could be cast directly into plays." [65] The conflicts in the mind involve the individual's multiple selves. "How can our personality be one," said Pirandello to Vittorini, "when so suddenly we are capable of re-entering primeval life and being reabsorbed by it?" Pirandello was especially intrigued by mental conflicts evolving from sex, a prime mover in nature. "Sexual instinct in its origin is a cosmic force," Pirandello said; "yet when it enters individual life it leads to the most terrifying complications. It makes us betray our friends, break moral laws and conventions." [66] Pirandello elaborated:

> There are four great forces in life whose urge man constantly feels: love, hatred, mystery and the acquisitive instinct.
> We say as fiercely as in the days of the cave man, "This is mine. This woman is mine." As to mystery this is to me the greatest force of all . . . forces emanate from a world that we feel moving beyond time and space . . .[67]

A newspaper story especially might strike harmonic overtones in Pirandello's creative self, exciting it like crystal in sympathetic resonance to a singer's notes, even nearly to shattering. In the play, *Each in His Own Way,* for instance, a spectator says, "This comedy is based on the Moreno affair! Almost word for word! The author has taken it from real life!" And another says, ". . . it's not the first time, you know." [68] Pirandello's *To Clothe the Naked* in its very action suggests a newspaper source. *As You Desire Me* is generally believed based on the notorious Brunelli-Cannella affair with which Pirandello was quite familiar. All these plays, like Pirandello's own life, involve a soul-struggle staked on illusions masking reality.

In the incubation of Pirandello's forty-five plays, only ten or so did not go through a previous stage of growth as a short story, and Eric Bentley believes "twenty-eight might correctly be described as adaptations." [69] "The short story is closer to the theatre than the novel is because it has a synthetic form," Pirandello noted. "Remember all Shakespeare's plays that were drawn from Italian short stories." [70] To Pirandello's delight and possibly surprise, he found his short stories peopled his imaginative world with characters who grew as human beings often over a long period of years. He wrote over 250 short stories; not all grew into plays. But some of his best plays had such an incubation and connote that this stage was usually absolutely necessary for his playwriting:

One Act Plays:

Sicilian Limes (1910) from *Lumie di Sicilia* (1900)
The Doctor's Duty (1912) from a novella in *La vita nuda* (1910)
The Jar (1917) from *La giara* (1909)
The License (1918) from *La patente* (1911)
The Imbecile (1922) from *L'imbecille* (1912)
The Man with the Flower in His Mouth (1923) from *Caffe notturno* (1918) retitled *La morte addosso*
The Other Son (1923) from *L'altro figlio* (1905)
The Festival of Our Lord of the Ship (1924) from *Il signora della nave in noie e il mondo* (1916)

Long Plays:

Just Think, Giacomino (1916) from a novella in *Terzetti* (1912)
Right You Are If You Think You Are (1917) from *La signora Frola e il signor ponza, sua genero* (1916)
Man, Beast and Virtue (1919) from *Richiamo all'obbligo* (1912)
All for the Best (1920) from a novella in *La vita nuda* (1910)
Six Characters in Search of an Author (1921) from *La tragedie d'un personnagi* (1919)

The above list suggests as much as eighteen years or as little as one year might intervene for a short story to emerge as a play. Two of Pirandello's most highly regarded plays do not have any known previous form as a short story or novel: *To Clothe the Naked* (1922) and *Henry IV* (1922). Their characters, stories, themes, and treatment still follow lines that are only variations of his earlier creative work. Pirandello obviously relied upon multiple incubation of plays and of all kinds of writing projects to breed brain-children. In 1934, when asked if he would keep on working after receiving the Nobel Prize, Pirandello said, "Certainly I am going to keep on working. I have dozens of ideas just crying to be put on paper." [71]

Though Pirandello never adapted it into a play, his early and likely best novel, *The Late Mattia Pascal* (1904), showed in its literary blood a genetic code that was vitally present in the form and content of just about all of his plays. Before writing the novel and nearly desperate in his domestic hell, Pirandello actually thought of flight or suicide.[72] The novel can be construed as his sublimated attempt to escape from his marriage by running away, only to find that man is a social animal, and that to lose one's identity by pretending to be somebody else in a new life, is impossible. Even though the anti-hero, Mattia Pascal, wins 82,000 lira at the gaming tables of Monte Carlo after deserting his shrewish, tragi-comic wife and his witch-like mother-in-law, he cannot buy a dog for companionship for fear the need of a dog license will reveal his identity; he cannot report the theft of some of his money to the police lest his true name be discovered; he cannot marry a desirable young lady he falls in love with in Rome, because his birth certificate is needed for the ceremony. He finally goes home to his wife who, as Mattia knows, reported him dead two years earlier when another man's body was found, decayed beyond recognition. Mattia's problem wife, meanwhile, has remarried and had a child. Mattia is left a non-person in society.

The very title of the book has the stamp of Pirandello's virtual lifelong frame of mind. We need only presume Pirandello meant every word of the title to have its full meaning. *The Late* is a reflective jest on the illusory nature of reality, even death. *Mattia* refers to Mathias, a disciple elected in the place of Judas Iscariot, and who later, after being considered a heretic, was imprisoned and blinded by savages, and then rescued by Andrew.[73] *Pascal* refers to the philosopher, Pascal, who said, "There is no man differs more from another than he differs from himself in the course of time;" Pascal believed in experience and reason as opposed to authority, yet wrote in *Pensée,* "nature is as incomprehensible as God Himself who created it."[74]

In this passage of Mattias' reflections, as translated from the Italian by William Weaver, Pirandello suggests further the genetic code of his brain-children: theme, leading characters, situation, story line, minor climaxes and major climaxes, as well as possible variations:

> Alas, today's every reality is necessarily destined to prove an illusion tomorrow, but a necessary illusion, since outside of it, unfortunately, there is no other reality for us. What if the significance consisted precisely in this, that a man or woman, placed by himself or by others, in a painful situation, socially abnormal, absurd if you like, remains in it,

bears it, plays it out in front of others as long as he himself doesn't see it, whether through blindness or through incredible good faith? As soon as he sees it, as if a mirror had been set in front of him, he can no longer bear it, he feels all its horror, and he breaks it, or if he can't break it, he feels that it will kill him.[75]

Pirandello then notes an alternate line of development, actually a basic variation of growth:

> Or if the significance consisted in this: that a socially abnormal situation is accepted, even when seen in a mirror, which in this case holds our own illusion up to us; and then we play it out, suffering all its pain, as long as the performance is possible behind the stifling mask that we have put on ourselves or that others, or cruel necessity, have forced on us; in other words, as long as beneath this mask some keenly felt feeling of ours isn't hurt there? Then the rebellion finally breaks out, and that mask is torn off and trampled underfoot. . . .
>
> They have bared their naked individual faces from beneath that mask which made them the marionettes of themselves or in the hands of others. . . .
>
> What we really are, even we ourselves don't know beyond a certain point.[76]

Some might regard this as a point of view or a bias. Others might charge that this amounts to a formula; life itself is a formula, yet an ultimate mystery.

In considering Pirandello's creative methods, space limits illustrations to plays reputed his best: *Right You Are If You Think You Are, Six Characters in Search of an Author, To Clothe the Naked,* and *Henry IV.*

"Here is a dream: in it I saw a deep courtyard with no exit," recorded Pirandello (Bentley's translation), "and from that frightening image *Right You Are* was born." [77] Pirandello's domestic life at the time had a "no-exit" metaphor in it. The short story basic to the play, preceded the play by at least a year. The setting in the story is the fictional town of Valdana; in the play, it is simply a small Italian town, the capitol of a province. In the Marsica district of Abruzzi, Italy, on January 13, 1915, the town of Avezzano lost over 9,000 of its 11,500 population in an earthquake and made quite a news story; in the play and story, this natural disaster suggested the major reason for the Ponza-Frola despair over loss of loved ones and the destruction of all identification papers.[78]

The newspaper story of the earthquake possibly brought to Pirandello's mind a similar disaster—the flooding of his family's sulphur-mines involving loss of life and bankruptcy. Pirandello's private concern over his demented wife suggests the need for the public not to pry too much into others' misfortunes. As a public employee, Pirandello no doubt found some busybodies trying to pry into his personal life just as they try to pry into the Ponza's personal life. The basic situation of the story and the play follows these "souvenirs," and, "I always want to be different and original," along with the "genetic code" cited from *Mattia Pascal*. The Ponzas and Madame Frola are forced by circumstance into a "painful situation, socially abnormal, absurd if you like," which manipulates them like marionettes and forces them out of consideration for others to mask their true feelings.

And what is the basic situation? Councillor Agazzi, a small town dignitary, has hired as his executive secretary a ferocious looking but truly gentle and capable Signor Ponza, who has his wife living on the fifth floor of a walk-up tenement, and his mother-in-law in a small apartment in the fine building where his employer lives. To the prying women-folk of the Councillor Agazzi, this is an unnatural situation, especially since the aged mother-in-law, Signora Frola, first refuses to receive them, and then is apparently forbidden to visit her own daughter, Signora Ponza, or to have her own daughter visit her. Social pressure manipulates the Ponza's personal lives and Madame Frola's, until rising public curiosity threatens to strip all their illusions and bare their pitiful souls. How much growth the characters took on in transition from short story to play form may be gathered in that the play for the first time shows their action in the high voltage major climax of Act II, and their action in the even higher voltage major climax of Act III.

Six Characters took germ from a novella written two years or so earlier. Pirandello noted:

> Well, a few years ago Fantasia was unfortunately inspired—or it may have been just an unlucky whim on her part—to unload a whole family on me. I don't know where in the world she had fished these people up from, but she insisted that they were material for a perfectly gorgeous novel.
>
> A man of about fifty, in black coat, light trousers, his eyebrows drawn into a painful frown, and in his eyes an expression mortified yet obstinate; a poor woman in widow's weeds, leading a little girl of about four by one hand and a boy of ten or so by the other; a pert, bold young miss, also in black, but an equivocal brazen black it seemed, as she

moved about in a constant flutter of disdainful biting merriment at the expense of the older man, and a young fellow of twenty odd who stood apart from the others seemingly locked within himself, as though holding the rest in utter scorn . . . in short, the Six Characters just as they appear on the stage at the beginning of the play.[79]

This testimony suggests the way characters occurred to Pirandello as a rule: involved in a living relationship, with individual dress, attitudes, and temperament. The characters came specifically, too, for a novel *not* a play:

At once they began telling me their misfortunes, first one, then another, each in turn silencing all the rest, as each in turn shouted out his story; and there they were flourishing their scattered passions in my face, just as in the play they flourished them in the face of the thoroughly misunderstanding Manager . . .

Their story revealed these characters in a "painful situation, absurd, if you like," in the suggested "genetic code."

What was their basic situation? The intellectual Father and the low-born, simple Mother had been married and had a son; the mother then fell in love with the Father's poor and low-born clerk. With her ill-matched husband's approval, the Mother as an experiment went off to live with the clerk by whom she bore three children out of wedlock and then, with her new family, skipped town. The clerk unfortunately died, and the Mother, soon desperately impoverished, returned with her three illegitimate children to her hometown, unknown to her true husband. The Mother's illegitimate daughter, the Step-Daughter, goes to work for a Madam Pace who runs assignations under the guise of a millinery shop. The madam unwittingly arranges for the Father, "an old client," to have a caper with his wife's illegitimate daughter, the Step-Daughter, and just then the Mother walks in.

Pirandello says that at first he listened to the characters tell their story but dismissed them as lacking "a special sense of life that gives them a universal significance and value." The characters, however, especially the Father and the Step-Daughter, at all hours kept house-crashing on Pirandello, demanding their rights. Finally, out of the blue, Pirandello had a great flash of insight—the firing point probably warmed from his viewing life for almost two decades as a game of reality and illusion. He conceived of what amounts to another "painful situation, socially abnormal, absurd if you like," and with a liveliness of "universal significance and value" for his characters:

"Why not," thought I, "represent this unique situation—an author refusing to accept certain characters born of imagination, while the characters themselves obstinately refuse to be shut from the world of art, once they have received the gift of life! . . . why not let them go where the characters of a play usually go to attain full and complete life—on a stage? Let's see what will happen then!"

Well, that's what I did. And of course things turned out just as they had to turn out: there was a mixture of the tragic and comic, of the fantastic and the real, in a situation as humorous as it was novel and complicated . . . It is the vain attempt to improvise on the stage, the carrying out of this demand that constitutes the comedy.[80]

But where was "the universal significance and value?" "All that lives, by the sheer fact of living, has a form and so must die; all except the work of art which, on the contrary, lives forever insofar as it is form." The characters are real; the acting company, illusory. The highly original aspect of the play is that the action certainly takes place inside Pirandello's head, but without the straightforward representation or open statement of Arthur Miller's *Death of a Salesman* or *After the Fall*, which were written decades later. In writing for Martoglio and Musco's stock company, Pirandello must have often imagined his characters meeting particular actors in the company to find if each suited the other to self-realization.

A basic complication of the story of the six characters, "a souvenir," is suggested in that Pirandello's wife once left him, taking along their children, and for three months went back to Sicily. . . . but not with a clerk.[81] The major climax of the second act of *Six Characters* is another "souvenir," in effect a staging of a variation of Pirandello's own childhood traumatic experience when for his "Mother's" sake he came to the convent to tell off the cousin who was carrying on an affair with his "Father." The harrowing complication of the Father unwittingly about to have an assignation with his own "Step-Daughter," has the quality of the last lines of *Oedipus the King* (Gassner's translation):

Therefore with eyes fixed on the end destined for all,
count no one of the race of man happy
until he has crossed life's border free from pain.[82]

Pirandello said of the genesis of *Six Characters:*

The truth of the matter is that the play was conceived in one of those moments of illumination when the imagination acts with untrammelled spontaneity, and when, for a wonder, all the faculties of the mind are working together in superb harmony. No human brain coldly attacking this problem could ever have succeeded, no matter how hard it tried, in grasping and satisfying all the necessities of this form.[83]

Still, the genesis of *Six Characters* came to Pirandello with "souvenirs" and a skill in every slant of its bent from over twenty years of writing fiction and criticism; the genesis did not come, say, to the mind of a migrant apple-picker.

When asked how he happened to write *Henry IV*, Pirandello replied:

> A work of art is usually born as an image rather than as a thought and this was the case with my *Henry IV*. One day many years ago, I happened to see the Roman Hunt Club dressed in medieval costumes riding in a cavalcade to the Villa Doria, and I suddenly wondered what would happen if one of those masqueraders should fall from his horse and lose his reason. From that simple incident grew my *Henry IV*.[84]

"Many years ago" suggests the play took long to incubate. The spiritual harmonics of Pirandello's own life and that of Henry IV are really in sympathetic vibration. The "painful situation, socially abnormal, absurd if you like" which sways and masks trapped lives is again rather complicated, as life itself can be.

The lead is an Italian nobleman dressed as Germany's Henry IV in a medievally costumed hunt. On the hunt the Baron Tito Belcredi, a jealous suitor for Donna Matilda, the Italian nobleman's intended wife, prods the nobleman's horse deliberately with his sword-point so the horse rears and unseats the nobleman who in the fall severely injures his head. When he revives, he believes he is actually Henry IV, the Emperor of Germany who went to Canossa in a hair-shirt and shivered barefoot in winter as penance in the eyes of Pope Gregory VII. The nobleman's family, being rich, humor his insanity. After 12 years of isolation, however, the now aging nobleman comes to his senses but keeps his recovery secret, preferring his new guise of insanity in the face of a faithless, treacherous world that has passed him by and debased everything he valued.

The play opens with the once betrothed of the nobleman, now a widow, the Marchioness Matilda Spina, and with a grown daughter, Frida, strikingly like Matilda in her youth, deciding to try to bring Henry IV to his senses with the aid of an alienist, Dr. Genoni. The former jealous suitor, Belcredi, has now made the widow his mistress.

The "socially abnormal situation, absurd if you like" powerfully influences the characters' lives, forcing them to pretend until their moment of truth. Henry IV is a complex, stoical figure goaded into a mania for revenge. Just as the flooding of the family sulphur-mines unhorsed Pirandello in a sense, so does the rearing accident unhorse Henry IV and begin his chain-reaction of misery of a lifetime. Like Mattia Pascal, Henry IV in a way becomes someone else, but in an escape that is the reverse of the one that Mattia Pascal tries; Henry IV retreats to the past in a fancied nobility, and grows independent of society by living in luxurious isolation, like a perpetual, mad, royal penitent. The "souvenirs" and the "novel" and "original" genetic clues are all there.

To Clothe the Naked, one of Pirandello's most powerful and moving plays, gives further insight into genesis for Pirandello. The old and famous novelist, Ludovico Nota, explains to Ersilia Drei, the young and beautiful but pathetic nobody, why he has offered her a home and help upon her discharge from prison after her attempt at suicide:

> LUDOVICO: Yes, when I read about you in the paper I was, well, fascinated. You know, you stumble by chance into something, or someone drops a casual remark and suddenly, I don't know, you feel something—a wave of sympathy, a moment of understanding—and before you know it you have the germ—the germ of a story, or a novel—

Ludovico then goes on to suggest, as Pirandello's counterpart, his method of spontaneous conception of the whole:

> LUDOVICO: . . . The moment I started to read about you in that newspaper, the novel began to take shape in my head, all of it from beginning to end.
> ERSILIA: But how? So quickly?
> LUDOVICO: In a single instant. And in such a wealth of events, in such detail . . . Oh, it was marvelous: the oriental setting . . . that little villa by the sea . . . you there as governess . . . that little girl falling from the terrace . . . their sending you away . . . the trip back . . . your arrival here . . . the sad discovery . . . all of it, all of it . . . just like that, without ever having seen you or spoken to you.[85]

Ersilia, the genteel nobody, then realizes that even her own story doesn't really depend upon her; given the facts from the newspaper, Ludovico invents action in his imagination that allows him, from having observed and experienced life, to see possible alternatives to her life. He foresees, for instance, Ersilia in her poverty, offering herself for prostitution, even before she tells Ludovico about her humiliating first attempt to make such a "deal."

And what is the powerfully influential "socially abnormal, absurd if you like" basic situation? Ersilia Drei, a young lady of poor family, had been a governess to the child of the Italian Consul in Smyrna, who in time seduced her and made of her, in her weak will, his mistress. One day, even though the thought of the disaster had crossed her mind, Ersilia left the Consul's baby, Mimi, on the flat roof of the Consul's house and went off to an assignation with him. The baby, unwatched, crawled off the roof and was killed in the fall. The Consul's wife, learning the news, then found the Consul and Ersilia "in flagrante delicto." Dismissed, penniless, with no character reference, Ersilia is sent home by boat from Smyrna. She has also incidentally, through an introduction by the Consul, drifted into an earlier affair with a naval cadet. The fact precipitating the whole complex basic situation is that Ersilia in a suicide attempt, to give herself some romantic aura, stated that she was dying for love of the consul from Smyrna. The story, by chance, got into the newspapers; and the play begins with all the men in Ersilia's life forced into motion by society, and Ersilia, herself, must act, too.

Characterization

Pirandello fancied he had a muse:

> As I have written elsewhere, the lively little maid-servant who for years and years now (though it seems as though it were only since yesterday) has been waiting on my writing, is for all that not so new at her work.

This account appeared first in 1925 when "the maid-servant" had already been working for Pirandello over thirty years. She herself has "character," from Pirandello's own creative spirit:

> She is often of a somewhat scornful and jesting humor, this *Fantasia* of mine. If, now and then, she is of a humor to dress in black, there is no denying that her solemn apparel is often extremely odd. . . . Time and again, I've seen her put her hand in her pocket and pull out a fool's cap, red as a cox-comb, and all a-jingle with its tiny bells. This she claps on her head, and off she goes! Here today, and somewhere else tomorrow!—And she persists in bringing back with her the most disgruntled beings imaginable and filling my house with them—men, women, and children, all involved in the most extraordinary and complicated situa-

tions—their plans frustrated, their hopes deluded—in short, people it is often very uncomfortable to deal with.[86]

Where did these "people" come from? A reading of Pirandello's one-acts suggests the whole range of humanity in the life-stream of a Sicilian provincial town like Girgenti. The later long plays suggest a cross-section of the middle-class, as in *Right You Are If You Think You Are,* and of the Roman upper middle-class and titled class, as in *Henry IV* and *Each in His Own Way.* Pirandello drew quite a few highly sympathetic characters in his short plays, like the peasant suitor, Micuccio, in *Sicilian Limes;* the hilarious, gruff old Zi Dima who repairs a huge olive jar in *The Jar* and then is too fat to get out of the mouth; and the old Professor Toti in *Just Think, Giacomino* who, to revenge himself upon a heartless bureaucracy, marries a young lady pregnant by a student and does so in order to guarantee that she will enjoy his pension after his imminent death.

In subsequent long plays there are relatively few leading characters whom we care for intensely: in *Right You Are,* for the affable old lady, Signora Frola, and for Signor Ponza and Signora Ponza. In *The Pleasure of Honesty,* in some special measure we care for Baldovino, contracted to provide an "honest" and gentlemanly husband for the fashionable Countess Maddalena's pregnant daughter, Agata Renni; and in *The Rules of the Game,* somewhat less for the long suffering Leone Gala, who becomes under threat of death less a stoic than a very clever worm who turns on his cheating wife, Silia, and who by sheer wit sends her lover, Guido Venani, to a death Silia had planned for Gala. In *Six Characters,* the Father, the Mother and the Step-Daughter are more pathetic than sympathetic. In *As You Desire Me,* the very beautiful Strange Lady invites profound sympathy and a lurid curiosity, for she is never the same "wife," it appears, after being repeatedly raped by troops in World War I. In *Henry IV,* hardly anyone deeply involves us, even the victimized Henry IV. Pirandello might say that he drew people as he found them, and that in life people tend to be more pathetic than sympathetic; their hearts are better than their heads. Why watch such leading characters? To Pirandello, they are part of the human family.

Usually, as suggested by examples of genesis already cited, the leading characters turned up very early with Fantasia, as in *Six Characters:*

The six characters are not seemingly all in the same stage of formation . . . All six are at the same stage of artistic realization and all six are on the same plane of reality—and this is the strange part of the play. Yet the Father and the Step Daughter and the Son, are realized as *mind,* while the Mother is *nature;* and the Boy who looks on and makes gestures, and the Child, both absolutely inert, are no more than onlookers taking parts by their presence merely. This creates a perspective of another sort . . . those who are most intensely alive, the Father and Step Daughter, naturally come forward and direct and drag along the almost dead weight of the others; of whom one, the Son, is reluctant, while the Mother, like a resigned victim, stands between those two small creatures, the children, who have scarcely any being except that of appearance, and who need to be led by the hand.[87]

Though different characters may each appear in different degrees of development, each character has the rights of a human being. "Every creature born of the imagination, every being art creates, must have his own play," said Pirandello, "that is to say, a play of which he is the hero and for which he is the dominating character. That play is the raison d'être of that particular character." [88]

Pirandello did not think his characters any more abnormal or absurd than everyday people. Normal people, to Pirandello, are an illusion; they exist only by wrapping themselves in so many appearances of conformity that they have really only concealed their differences for highly personal reasons like self-preservation, or the protection of those they love, or the lust for power. "Everybody's a little crazy," Pirandello mused in a conversation with Helen Augur. "Your thoughts, cara signorina, to you are sane and normal. To me they may appear as a little off the high road. My critics see me—a sober, serene man in my own estimation—as a mildly raving madman." [89] For Pirandello, modern man was no more normal than his ancestor, the cave-man. In *The Late Mattia Pascal* we find:

the zoologist, if you introduce him to a man with a wooden leg or a glass eye, will tell you that he doesn't recognize him, because this is not *man.* It is *a* man.

It is also true, however, that we can answer the zoologist by saying that the *man* he knows doesn't exist, and that instead *men* exist, of whom none is exactly like another and some, unfortunately may even have wooden legs and glass eyes.[90]

Pirandello developed a character by a nexus, a concurrence of considerations: the "building oneself up;" the "mirror" effect; the dialectic; and the paradoxical outcome.

Pirandello confided in Vittorini:

My idea of *costruirsi*, to build up oneself, is the fundamental tenet of my art. Marriage, fatherhood, motherhood, and personality have no meaning except that which we give to them. In my plays I have shown how unreal marriage is if held together only by civil and religious ceremonies . . . Such people are not alive or real. They are self-constructed, empty concepts. I have compared one such man to a cigar that has smoked itself out, keeping its shape but being only ashes.[91]

Mattia Pascal says of his attempt at self-escape:

This pursuit, this imaginative construction of a life that had never really been lived but had been pieced together gradually from other lives and from places until it was made mine and felt mine. . . . It was my occupation.[92]

Then Mattia tells of how he went about his "occupation," presumably Pirandello's approach to characterization:

Ah, how many grampas, how many little old men I followed and studied, in Turin, in Milan, in Venice and Florence, putting a little of each into the composition of my own grandfather. I took the bone snuffbox and the checked handkerchief of one of them, the cane of another; a third furnished me with spectacles and a chin-whiskers; a fourth, with his walk and the way he blew his nose; and a fifth supplied his manner of talking and his laugh. The result was a little old man, refined and somewhat crusty, a lover of the arts, a broad-minded Grand-dad . . .[93]

Character, for Pirandello, is always basically "self-built," usually through the sheer need for physical or psychological survival; he found that human motives could be most devious, even labyrinthine. The characters in a Pirandello play grow only as they strip themselves or others strip them of their illusions and reveal their nakedness, a complex and sometimes obscure impulse.

To Pirandello, as in life, *costruirsi* is directly linked to "the mirror effect" in characterization. In commenting upon his drama as "the drama of mirrors," Pirandello told Vittorini:

It is an exaggerated view of a situation that exists in many of my plays. If we present ourselves to others as artificial constructions in terms of what we really are, it is logical that, upon looking at ourselves in a mirror, we see our falseness reflected there, made galling and unbearable in its fixity. That's all that I mean by placing my characters before a mirror and making them say that they would like to spit at themselves.[94]

Hamlet, of course, places his mother, Queen Gertrude, exactly before such a mirror in the famous bed-room scene. Pirandello expanded on the mechanics of "the mirror effect" in an interview for *Living Age:*

> I have had the audacity of placing a mirror in the very centre of the stage. It is the mirror of Intelligence. Man, while alive, lives, but does not see himself. Sentiment by itself is blind; I have therefore so managed that this blind man at a certain moment should open his eyes and should see himself in that mirror and should stand as if frozen by the un-thought of image of his own life.
>
> To live before a looking-glass is not possible. Try to look at yourself in a mirror while you are crying for your deepest sorrow, or while you are laughing for your merriest joy; your tears and your laugh will stop suddenly.
>
> This is the whole secret of that "humorist brain-power" which critics have tried to discover in my theatre. They call me an "over-brained," a "humorist," because I have allowed man to see himself in the actions of his own life.[95]

In "the mirror effect" a character is involved almost invariably with self-discovery; in most plays, a character is involved far more with revelation of character to others. The effect is used most potently by Pirandello in his major climaxes. In *Right You Are,* a kind of play within a play is schemed up by Ponza's employer and the employer's womenfolk to find out, in the major climax of a party in Act II, who is mad, Signor Ponzo or Madame Frola, by forcing their confronta-tion. The inconclusive result leads to scheming up another play within a play to strip Signora Ponza to her true identity in the com-pelling presence of Madame Frola, Signor Ponza, and the Governor.

In *Six Characters,* the characters, led by the Father, again use the play within a play as a mirror; they intrude upon the rehearsals of an acting company and compel the Manager to watch them run through their two scenes of torment. The actors watch as the characters show the Father's unintentional but nearly fulfilled assignation with his wife's illegitimate daughter, and his wife interrupts, crying out, in a phrase that the Father can never outlive: "You brute! You brute! She is my daughter!" Later the actors again watch as the characters show the accidental drowning of the wife's illegitimate child, and the subse-quent suicide by pistol-shot of the ten year old illegitimate Son left to care for the baby sister.

In *Henry IV,* the "mirror effect" again involves a prearranged scene that is the equivalent of a play within a play. Henry IV is to be shocked into reality by the illusion of seeing Frida, almost identical now to her mother in youth, pose in a picture frame and then come walking out of it even at the moment the now aging Marchioness looks on. In *To Clothe the Naked,* the "mirror effect" is done by the device of the newspaper story account of Ersilia Drei's attempted suicide, an account she never expected to see, containing a romantic lie disastrously involving the married Italian Consul in Smyrna and the naval cadet engaged to marry another girl. The "mirror effect" may use not only logic, but all the ways the intelligence has of "knowing." "Reason is an empty vessel," Pirandello told the interviewer for *La Grande Revue* (March, 1927), "if blind instinct does not fill it up." [96] Pirandello detested pure logic as too pat for understanding life fully.

Pirandello's dramatic dialectic, common to almost every one of his leading characters, sometimes incorporates a self-projected raissoneur of sorts, and is actually inseparable from the nexus of "the mirror effect." In his spiritual source-book, *The Late Mattia Pascal,* occurs this most revealing passage as to the validity of the dramatic dialectic:

> isn't it perhaps true that man never reasons so passionately (or so wrongly—not that that changes anything) as when he is suffering? He wants to arrive at the root of his sufferings, he wants to discover who causes them, and whether they are deserved. But when man is happy, doesn't he accept his happiness without reasoning about it, as if it were his right? [97]

This kind of searching self-examination is in *The Book of Job.* Of sometimes projecting himself into a character-raisonneur, Pirandello told Alice Rohe, "But authors always project themselves into their work." [98]

In *Right You Are,* Pirandello projects himself in Laudisi, wryly jesting with his relatives when they think they can distinguish the truth from illusion about Signora Ponza. In *Six Characters,* Pirandello is part of the intellectually philosophic Father, clashing with the Manager over truth and illusion and art and reality as they relate to the sufferings of the six characters. In *Henry IV,* Pirandello again is partly projected in Henry IV, searching his soul as his betrayers try to discern truth from illusion as a motivating force for his chameleon-like life. In *To Clothe the Naked,* Pirandello is in the novelist, Ludovico, stripping Ersilia Drei of those pathetic illusions with which she had clothed herself to keep from dying an unwed, unchaste "nobody." The dialectic probes the soul like a doctor doing an exploratory on the body.

The device of paradox recurs regularly in the major climax of just about all of Pirandello's plays. It almost always is the aftermath of "the mirror effect." The paradox comes in a self-discovery following an excruciating emotional scene leading always to the same crux of the matter, the riddle of life,—"What is truth and what is illusion?" In *Right You Are,* for example, the crescendo of ruthless inquisition as to exactly who Signora Ponza really is, becomes a matter for the police, then the Governor; and finally this is the paradox from "the mirror effect" as Signora Ponza, herself, is summoned, dressed in mourning, and questioned (Bentley's translation):

> SIGNORA PONZA. . . . There has been a misfortune here, as you see, which should remain hidden. Only in this way can the remedy work —the remedy our compassion has provided.
> GOVERNOR. (*moved*) We should like to respect such compassion, Signora. We should wish you to tell us, however—
> SIGNORA PONZA. (*with slow staccato speech*) What? The truth? It is simply this. I am Signora Frola's daughter—
> ALL. (*with gasp of pleasure*) Ah!
> SIGNORA PONZA. (*without pausing, as above*) And I am Signor Ponza's second wife. . . . And to myself I am no one. No one.
> GOVERNOR. No, no, Signora, at least to yourself, you must be either one or the other.
> SIGNORA PONZA. No! To myself—I am the one that each of you thinks I am. (*She looks at them all through her veil just for an instant: and then withdraws. Silence.*)
> LAUDISI. That, my dear friends, was the voice of truth! (*He looks round at them with derisive defiance.*) Are you satisfied? (*He bursts out laughing.*) [99]

In *Six Characters,* at the major climax of the last act showing the child's accidental drowning and the ten year old Son's guilt and suicide, the remaining characters are deeply affected, but the actors see only a bungled attempt at art, and the last line of the Father to the Manager in Storer's translation is: "(*with a terrible cry*) Pretence? Reality, sir, reality!" [100] At the major climax of *Henry IV,* when confronted at once with the young Frida in her mother's likeness, and her aging mother, his old love, Henry embraces the young Frida, realizing again all he has lost; when Belcredi intervenes then Henry, in an impulse exploding from years of accumulated resentment, stabs him to death. Now Henry, though sane, must paradoxically pretend insanity to escape the law, and addressing his retainers who think him mad, says in his last speech,—"here we are . . . together . . . forever!" [101] In *To Clothe the Naked,* Ersilia Drei in successive climaxes first refuses to marry the penitent naval ensign, who mistakenly believed he had deflowered her; then refuses to marry the Italian Consul from Smyrna, who had actually been her first lover, for the guilt of his baby's death is upon her for life. Forced to see herself as she truly is, stripped naked of illusions, Ersilia takes her life by poison, in despair because the public had refused to let her die in peace at her first attempt, clothed in an illusory wedding gown.

The nexus of character development in a Pirandello play also simultaneously develops the story and so the plot. What advice if any did Pirandello give regarding story and plot? In *The Late Mattia Pascal* he wrote:

> Life's absurdities don't have to seem believable because they are real. As opposed to art's absurdities which, to seem real, have to be believable. Then, when they are believable, they are no longer absurd. [102]

If Pirandello had any test for a story, it was to be "believable." "The work of fancy is a work of nature," Pirandello told Vittorini, "an organic and living whole . . ." [103] Once given life, a character becomes an agent as free as a human being. "You remember that woman in *To Clothe the Naked,*" Pirandello told Helen Augur, the newspaper correspondent, in speaking of Ersilia Drei. "Remember how the play ends? That's her fault not mine. I wanted to finish the play in my own way. It seemed my right as a self-respecting dramatist. But no, she wouldn't have it. For days and nights we wrestled and fought over the dénouement, and in the end she won. There's the play, just as she wanted it." [104]

If Pirandello had any specific advice as to plot, the arrangement of the story for maximum dramatic effect, it is implied in his comment to Marta Abba in a letter of September, 1929. "I am still working on the second act of *Come tu mi vuoi (As You Desire Me).* I want it to be better than the first and I want the third to be better than the second." [105]

Sources of Freshness in Pirandello

Pirandello denied he was merely another naturalist. "I have shown the stupidity of placing our sense of reality in this material world of ours," he told Vittorini, "which was the pivotal point of the art mode created by the naturalists." [106] "Pirandello's philosophy of life as illusion and appearance as the only reality, makes his Nobel honors peculiarly appropriate," editorialized *The New York Times* of November 9, 1934. "He fits into an age of relativity and, as it was until only the other day, widespread disillusionment;" and the *Times* later noted Pirandello's "flashing wit of a very high order." [107] Today the relativity continues; the widespread disillusionment has begun to reappear like a blight in the springtime of the world-wide revolution of expectations; the "flashing wit of a very high order" suffers in translation. "He attempted the dramatization of the human mind," noted the *Times*. "This is Luigi Pirandello's unparalleled achievement." [108]

Pirandello is astonishingly fresh today in the wide popular acceptance of concepts he explored as an artist. Consider, for example, today's emphasis of governments, television, radio, movies, advertisers, public relations firms, celebrities, and just people upon phrases like "image," "losing face," "changing image," "building up a new image," "puppet governments." Almost always when the "mirror effect" takes place, the government or personality involved is so shocked upon seeing itself as it actually is or is distorted to be, that it must adapt or die. For Pirandello's common device of the play within a play, or its equivalent, we have today in real life some group dramatizing its plight deliberately for the public communication media to reflect, as in sit-ins, march-ins, and self-immolations.

If Pirandello is charged with being "way out," in that his plays concern people in "a painful situation, socially abnormal, absurd if you like," then what is the situation of governments almost all over the world today, and aren't governments often a reflection of their people? The cold war seems really a gordion knot. At a humbler level, in the course of a lifetime individuals in the United States are far from strangers to Pirandello-like situations: two marriages out of five end in divorce or separation; one person in ten needs treatment at some time in life for a mental illness; the number of chronically ill and handicapped is in the multi-millions; wars hot or cold are accepted as "normal;" and even with American help half of the world is "normally" half-starved. Pirandello will appeal so long as large numbers can honestly say, "I thought I knew people!" or, "It's a crazy world."

When less than his best, Pirandello can be quite exasperating. The earthquake ending of *The New Colony* simulates a mythical, modern nature, called upon as by telephone, and performing a violent disposal of errant humanity. Occasionally, Pirandello seems to be more a prisoner of his method than its master, so that the work seems more formulated than created, as in *Tonight We Improvise*. Some of his char-

acters, like Leone Gala in *The Rules of the Game,* do not seem to
have had a childhood or adolescence that would explain how they
came to be as they are. Pirandello can also be prolix, as in *Henry IV.*
But at his best, Pirandello comes through as a highly original modern
artist. *"Six Characters in Search of an Author,"* said Shaw, "is the
most original and dynamic play ever written in any nation, or at any
time, whether ancient or modern—." [109]

If Pirandello says with Hamlet, "there is nothing either good or
bad, but thinking makes it so," he also says with the mad Ophelia,
"we know what we are but we know not what we may be. God be at
your table." Life cries out for understanding and mercy. A disquiet is
in Pirandello; his concern over, "What is real and what is illusion?"
to many critics is headed only for nihilism. "He did not even allow
himself the comforting assurance the befuddled old lady was able to
get," one critic observed, "when she insisted that if she were she (as
she believed herself to be) then her little dog would know her." Joseph Wood Krutch, in the Cornell University Messenger Lectures of
1952, put Pirandello in the mainstream of modern thought, afloat with
his concern over "the dissolution of the ego" but heading for the falls
of nihilism. Other critics, like Tilgher, Lucas, Starkie, and Mac-
Clintock, find Pirandello tending toward nihilism, if not fully committed. [110]

"All true art contains a philosophy of life that tends toward sound
living," Pirandello told Vittorini. [111] In his posthumous notes Pirandello wrote, "Nietzsche said that the Greeks put up white statues
against the black abyss, in order to hide it. I, instead, topple them in
order to reveal it. . . . It is the tragedy of the modern spirit." [112] The
Greeks' white statues were idealized human beings, illusions taken as
real. Much of his life, Pirandello looked into the "black abyss," but
never jumped. In a sense he suggests we go with him as Dante went
with Virgil on a kind of modern Cook's tour of hell, the human predicament on earth; the pity and terror are meant to be felt as we discard our idealized illusions, and so feel purged, not defeated. To Pirandello, "What we really are, even we ourselves don't know beyond a
certain point." [113] Perhaps someday we shall find for the personality
the equivalent of the radio-telescope for the universe. Meanwhile, we
can only quote a critic of Pirandello who said, "Society is divided into
three parts,—those who understand Pirandello, those who do not, and
those who think they do."

Writing and Rewriting

When Pirandello based a play upon a previously written short story or novel, he was really working from a tentative written scenario. The "pregnancy" with the brain-child might take longer than an elephant's, even running over twenty years sometimes. "Delivery" for Pirandello was merely a matter then of sitting down and typing out the play with little pause or correction. "In my own native Sicily, I have seen washerwomen give birth to a child at the river's edge," said Pirandello, "and five minutes afterwards they were continuing their work! Any creative work that is great should be equally facile." [114] Pirandello told his biographer, Nardelli, that he finished nine plays in one year; for instance, *Just Think, Giacomino,* in three days, *Liola* in one week, and *Right You Are If You Think You Are,* in six days. In a particularly feverish spell of writing Pirandello wrote *Six Characters* in three weeks, and *Henry IV* in the following two weeks. But these works were done only after a literary discipline of a good twenty years or so. Speed, moreover, is no guarantee of quality; many today think Pirandello's chief faults came from writing too much too fast.

What characterized Pirandello's diction in playwriting? His naturalist beginnings, "verism," were modelled from Capuana and Verga. Pirandello saw men's primitive instincts and impulses playing hob with their civilized efforts to control their lives by law; therefore his dialogue had to have the visceral quality of basic, Sicilian reality. Rhetoric, to him, could only be like trying to cross a floor by doing a minuet. Pirandello in 1906 wrote in the preface to the novel of a friend, Alfredo Cantoni, this passage as translated by Vittorini:

> The harm that it [rhetoric] has caused in every age, not only to our literature but also to Latin literature and, hence, in varying degrees, to all Romance literatures, is incalculable. [115]

What do Pirandello's translators into English say of his diction? "Pirandello's language in his plays is generally homely, fragmentary, colloquial to a degree . . . often slangy," said Edward Storer, best known for his successful and likely definitive translation of *Six Characters;* "Italian critics who admire his genius say . . . that his language is not rich and lacks style." [116] "Pirandello's style with its complexities," wrote Starkie, "is highly suggestive, for it is never so much involved with direct meaning as with inferences to be drawn." Starkie also noted Pirandello's stylistic origins as "Sicilian, with that tendency

to jerkiness and incisiveness" and his "complicated psychology . . .
full of reservations and subtle inferences" and his "metaphysics." [117]
"At its best his language is precise and clear, stripped of ornamenta-
tion even at its most torrential," said Murray, "and at times by its very
simplicity, it achieves a beauty that raises it to the level of poetry." [118]
To Bentley, "His strongest weapon is his prose. Its torrential eloquence and pungent force are unique in the whole range of modern
drama;" and Bentley observed, in the preface to *Naked Masks*, "He
gets effects which one would not have thought possible to colloquial
prose . . ." [119] While rhetoric to Pirandello apparently denoted fus-
tian, eloquence meant fluency, power, and aptness.

Pirandello in diction was out to project the "verb," the action, in
character, for drama is "the thing done;" "so that the characters may
leap from the written pages alive, the playwright needs to find the
word which will be the action itself spoken." [120] Here is an illustrative passage of Pirandello's diction from *Six Characters* in the successful stage version done in London and New York, translated by
Storer:

> THE FATHER. But don't you see that the whole trouble lies here. In
> words, words. Each one of us has within him a whole world of
> things, each man of us his own special world. And how can we
> ever come to an understanding if I put in the words I utter the
> sense and value of the things as I see them; while you who listen to
> me must inevitably translate them according to the conception of
> things each one of you has within himself. We think we understand
> each other, but we never really do. Look here! This woman (*indi-
> cating the Mother*) takes all my pity for her as a specially ferocious
> form of cruelty.
> THE MOTHER. But you drove me away.
> THE FATHER. Do you hear her? I drove her away! She believes I
> really sent her away.
> THE MOTHER. You know how to talk, and I don't; but, believe me,
> sir (*to Manager*), after he had married me . . . who knows why?
> . . . I was a poor insignificant woman . . .
> THE FATHER. But, good Heavens! It was just for your humility that
> I married you.[121]

The illustration speaks for itself, and also especially focuses on Pirandello's chief quarrel with diction—the failure of words to communicate between individuals, even when intentions are good. In this respect, Pirandello's diction was a seminal influence on a whole new
generation of avant-garde playwrights, especially Ionesco, Pinter, and
Genet.

Diction for Pirandello is another part of life's confusing game of illusion and reality; words like "people" come with illusory clothing because of different personal associations of the speaker and listener. In *The Man with the Flower in His Mouth,* a much performed one-act play, Pirandello poses the same quandary:

> THE MAN. . . . Ah, yes, the pleasures of the imagination. How do you suppose I happened to think of a doctor's waiting-room?
> COMMUTER. Yes, I really don't—
> THE MAN. You don't see the connection? Neither do I. (*A pause*) It's just that certain seemingly unconnected mental images are peculiar to every one of us. They arise out of experiences and considerations so individual, so private that we simply wouldn't understand each other, if we didn't tacitly agree in everyday conversation to dispense with them. Nothing more illogical than analogies based on such private visions. . . .[122]

And yet Pirandello can use a figure of speech very effectively; so, for example, in this passage referring to cancer of the mouth:

> THE MAN. Death passed my way. It planted this flower in my mouth and said to me, "Keep it, my friend, I'll be back in eight or ten months!" (*A pause*) Now you tell me if, with this flower in my mouth, I can stay calmly and quietly at home, as that poor woman would like me to do.[123]

Pirandello wrote in the vernacular, relying heavily upon idiom and popular turns of phrase, always changing with the liveliness of the times.

He joked to a friend, "Tradutte, traditore!" ("Traitorous translators!") Just to show the problem of translating Pirandello's Italian prose into English, here are a number of current versions of different translations of just the mere title of his play, *Cosi e (se vi pare): Right You Are If You Think You Are; Right You Are If You Think So; And That's the Truth!; As You Like It; And Thinking Makes It So; It is So! (If You Think So).*[124]

Personally, from reading available translations in English, I find his diction varies in several chief effects: simple, basic speech right from a Sicilian peasant's heart; philosophic speculation, cold but illuminating; and emotional scenes, like a powder trail set off in a heated moment and leading to a psychological magazine, where the explosion is an astonishing revelation.

How much did Pirandello rewrite? He left no complete record, but he did rewrite. "I have been able in spite of these stormy days," he informed Marta Abba in a letter of August, 1926, "to reread *Diana e la Tuda* and to rewrite the whole second part of the first act . . ."[125] It is interesting to note that his golden period of playwriting, roughly 1917–1923, came after about seven years of periodic association with the Sicilian repertory company of Martoglio and Musco in Rome; he attended rehearsals and learned his métier with the theatre as his laboratory. When in 1925 he opened his own Art Theatre in Rome, he did some direction, and he could only have learned from observation, especially from the transformation throughout rehearsal.

Pirandello was not an easy man to deal with once his mind was made up. When in 1930 he seemed without honor in his own country, *Living Age* reported, "enemies of Pirandello state that he had only himself to thank because his own company, which he directed for three years, prejudiced all the best actors and producers in Italy against him."[126] In rehearsal, according to Starkie, Pirandello was "inexorable" in subordinating the actor to his will.[127]

My grateful acknowledgement is extended to the following sources of quotations:

THE AGE OF PIRANDELLO by Lander MacClintock. Copyright 1951. Reprinted by permission of the Indiana University Press.

BOSTON TRANSCRIPT, February 2, 1924, "As Pirandello Dissects His Dogmata Before the Members of the Drama League Assembled;" March 7, 1926, "The Man Who Has Wizened into a Mind" by Lucio D'Amba, translated by P. Beaumont Wadsworth

THE CONTEMPORARY THEATRE by Allan Lewis. (C) 1962 by Allan Lewis. Used by permission of Crown Publishers, Inc.

THE DRAMA OF CHEKHOV, SYNGE, YEATS AND PIRANDELLO by F. L. Lucas. (C) 1963. Reprinted by permission of Cassell Ltd.

FORTNIGHTLY, August 1924, "Luigi Pirandello, Dramatist" by Edward Storer

FORUM magazine, June 1924, "Pirandello's Warning" by Alice Rohe

HIGH POINTS IN THE HISTORY OF ITALIAN LITERATURE by Dominico Vittorini. Copyright 1958. Reprinted by permission of David McKay Co., Inc.

THE LATE MATTIA PASCAL by Luigi Pirandello translated by William Weaver. Copyright (c) 1964 by Doubleday & Company, Inc. Reprinted by permission of the publisher and the Sons of Pirandello.

LIVING AGE:

"Pirandello on Writing Plays" (August 29, 1925), reprinted from the London EVENING NEWS by permission

"Pirandello Interviewed" (October 1, 1926), reprinted from the London OBSERVER, Sunday independent newspaper of August 15, 1926, by permission

"Luigi Pirandello" by Daniel-Rops (June 1, 1927), reprinted from La Grande Revue, March 1927 "Pirandello Without Honor" (January 1, 1930)

"Conversation with Pirandello" by A. Rousseaux (February 1935), reprinted from CANDIDE, Paris Topical Weekly

LUIGI PIRANDELLO by Walter Starkie. Copyright 1926, renewed 1954. University of California Press and W. J. M. Dent & Sons

MODERNISM IN THE DRAMA by Joseph Wood Krutch, Cornell University Press, 1953

CHAPTER VI: ACKNOWLEDGEMENTS 277

THE MOUNTAIN GIANTS AND OTHER PLAYS by Luigi Pirandello, translated from the Italian by Marta Abba. (C) 1958. Reprinted by permission of Crown Publishers, Inc.

NAKED MASKS, five plays by Luigi Pirandello, edited by Eric Bentley, a Dutton Paperback, "Six Characters in Search of an Author" translated by Edward Storer. (C) 1922, renewed in the names of Stefano, Fausto and Lietta Pirandello in 1950. Reprinted by permission of E. P. Dutton & Co., Inc. and the Sons of Pirandello.

NEW YORK HERALD TRIBUNE, January 6, 1924, "Luigi Pirandello in Search of Popularity" by Alice Rohe. (C) 1924. Reprinted by permission.

NEW YORK TIMES:
"Who Is Pirandello?" November 5, 1922
"Pirandello's New Play for Duse" by Helen Augur, March 4, 1923
"Playwright of Mussolini's New Italy" by Eleanor Markell, November 4, 1923
"Pirandello, Playboy of Playwrights" by T. R. Ybarra, January 6, 1924
"Great Minds on Little Theatre" by Diana Bourbon, February 10, 1924
"Pirandello and Other Parisian Items" by Philip Carr, May 24, 1931
"Topics of the Times—Pirandello's Nobel Prize," November 9, 1934
"Wit and Wisdom in Pirandello" by Percy Hutchison, November 25, 1934
"Luigi Pirandello Dies at 69," December 10, 1936
(C) 1922, 1923, 1924, 1931, 1934, 1936 by The New York Times Company. Reprinted by permission.

NEW YORK WORLD, March 9, 1924, "Pirandello Breakfasts with Reporter F. Vinci-Roman"

PIRANDELLO'S ONE-ACT PLAYS translated by William Murray. Copyright (C) 1964 by William Murray. Reprinted by permission of Doubleday & Company, Inc. and the Sons of Pirandello.

RIGHT YOU ARE by Luigi Pirandello, translated by Eric Bentley. Copyright 1954. Reprinted by permission of Columbia University Press

THEATRE ARTS MAGAZINE, February 1935, "Luigi Pirandello, Nobel Prize Winner" by Silvio D'Amico; May 1952, "We Need Pirandello Today" by Eric Bentley

TO CLOTHE THE NAKED AND TWO OTHER PLAYS by Luigi Pirandello translated by William Murray. (C) 1962 by William Murray. Reprinted by permission of E. P. Dutton & Co., Inc., and the Sons of Pirandello.

TULANE DRAMA REVIEW, Spring 1964, "Does the Italian Theatre Exist?" by Luciano Codignola. Reprinted by permission.

VIRGINIA QUARTERLY REVIEW, April 1925, "Pirandello Confesses . . ." by Luigi Pirandello, translated by Leo Ongley. (C) 1925 by VIRGINIA QUARTERLY REVIEW, (C) renewed 1953. Reprinted by permission.

1. "Pirandello Interviewed," *Living Age* (October 1, 1926), 81

2. Eric Bentley, "We Need Pirandello Today," *Theatre Arts Monthly* (May 1952), 24

3. Walter Starkie, *Luigi Pirandello* (Berkley 1964), 279

4. F. L. Lucas, *The Drama of Chekhov, Synge, Yeats and Pirandello* (London 1963), 359

5. Ibid., 360

6. Ibid.

7. Luigi Pirandello translated by William Weaver, *The Late Mattia Pascal* (New York 1964), 26, 38

8. Luigi Pirandello translated by William Weaver, *Pirandello's One-Act Plays* (New York 1964), vii

9. Dominico Vittorini, *The Drama of Luigi Pirandello* (New York 1935), vii

10. *Pirandello's One-Act Plays,* vii

11. Ibid.

12. Daniel-Rops, "Luigi Pirandello," *Living Age* (June 1, 1927), 1001–1002

13. Dominico Vittorini, *High Points in the History of Italian Literature* (New York 1958), 264

14. Eleanor Markell, "Playwright of Mussolini's New Italy," *New York Times Magazine* (November 4, 1923), 9

15. Ibid.

16. Helen Augur, "Pirandello's New Play for Duse," *New York Times Magazine* (March 4, 1923), 11

17. Ibid.

18. *High Points in the History of Italian Literature,* 265

19. *Living Age* (October 1, 1926), 81

20. *New York Evening Journal* (July 20, 1935)

21. *New York Times* (July 21, 1935), 21

22. "Who Is Pirandello?" *New York Times* (November 5, 1922), Sect. 8, 1X; Percy Hutchison, "Wit and Wisdom in Pirandello," *New York Times* (November 25, 1934), Sect. 5, 2

23. *Living Age* (February 1935), 514

24. Alice Rohe, "Pirandello's Warning," *Forum* (June 1924), 792

25. *High Points in the History of Italian Literature*, 264

26. *Pirandello's One-Act Plays*, xiii, xiv

27. *High Points in the History of Italian Literature*, 261, 262

28. *Pirandello's One-Act Plays*, viii

29. "Obituary Notes, Luigi Pirandello," *Publishers' Weekly* (December 19, 1936), 2505–2506

30. Luigi Pirandello translated by Marta Abba, *The Mountain Giants and Other Plays* (New York 1958), 15

31. "Pirandello Wins Nobel Literature Prize," *Literary Digest* (November 17, 1934), 8

32. Lander MacClintock, *The Age of Pirandello* (Bloomington 1951), 103

33. MacClintock, 14

34. "As Pirandello Dissects His Dogmata Before the Members of the Drama League Assembled," *Boston Transcript* (February 2, 1924)

35. Diana Bourbon, "Great Minds on Little Theatre," *New York Times Magazine* (February 10, 1924), 6

36. Abba, 28

37. *Forum* (June 1924), 794

38. T. R. Ybarra, "Pirandello, Playboy of Playwrights," *New York Times Magazine* (January 6, 1924), 5

39. Silvio D'Amico, "Luigi Pirandello, Nobel Prize-Winner," *Theatre Arts Monthly* (February 1935), 114–115

40. Luciano Codignola, "Does the Italian Theatre Exist?" *Tulane Drama Review* (Spring 1964), 22

41. *High Points in the History of Italian Literature*, 288–289; *Living Age* (October 1, 1926), 81

42. "Pirandello on Writing Plays," *Living Age* (August 27, 1925), 473

43. F. Vinci-Roman, "Pirandello Breakfasts with Reporter," *New York World* (March 9, 1924)

44. *Living Age* (February 1925), 512

45. *Pirandello's One-Act Plays*, xii, xiii

46. *New York World* (March 9, 1924)

47. Luigi Pirandello translated by Leo Ongley, "Pirandello Confesses . . . ," *Virginia Quarterly Review* (April 1925), 36. Translation authorized by Pirandello.

48. *New York Times Magazine* (March 4, 1923), 11

49. *Pirandello's One-Act Plays*, xi

50. Abba, 27

51. *High Points in the History of Italian Literature*, 259

52. MacClintock, 226

53. *Theatre Arts Magazine* (February 1935), 114–115

54. *Boston Transcript* (February 2, 1924)

55. Abba, 29

56. *Virginia Quarterly Review* (April 1925), 36

57. Abba, 21

58. Ibid., 2

59. *Pirandello's One-Act Plays*, vii, viii

60. Lucio D'Amba, "The Man Who Has Wizened into a Mind," *Boston Transcript* (March 7, 1925); "Died: Luigi Pirandello," *Newsweek* (December 19, 1936), 29

61. *Virginia Quarterly Review* (April 1925), 37

62. Philip Carr, "Pirandello and Other Parisian Items," *New York Times* (May 24, 1931), Sect. 8, 2X

63. *Virginia Quarterly Review* (April 1925), 38

64. Ibid.

65. *New York Times Magazine* (March 4, 1923), 1

66. *High Points in the History of Italian Literature*, 261

67. Ibid., 67, 259

68. Luigi Pirandello, translated by William Murray, *To Clothe the Naked and Two Other Plays* (New York 1962), 322

69. Luigi Pirandello translated by Eric Bentley, *Right You Are* (New York 1954), 133

70. *Living Age* (February 1935), 514

71. *New York Times* (November 9, 1934), 23

72. *New York Times* (November 25, 1934), Sect. 5, 2; Lucas, 361; Starkie, 64; *The Drama of Luigi Pirandello*, 20, 23

73. *International Standard Bible Encyclopaedia* (Grand Rapids 1960), III, 2012

74. Lucien Lévy-Bruhl, *History of Modern Philosophy in France* (Chicago 1924), 86

75. *The Late Mattia Pascal*, 248

76. Ibid., 248, 249

77. *Right You Are*, 133

78. Ibid., 137–147

79. *Virginia Quarterly Review* (April 1925), 37

80. Ibid., 40

81. *The Drama of Luigi Pirandello*, 22

82. Sophocles' *Oedipus the King* translated by John Gassner, *World Drama from Aeschylus to Turgenev* (New York 1963), I, 51

83. *Virginia Quarterly Review* (April 1925), 42, 43

84. *Virginia Quarterly Review* (April 1925) *Boston Transcript* (February 2, 1924)

85. *To Clothe the Naked and Two Other Plays*, 8, 9

86. *Virginia Quarterly Review* (April 1925), 36

87. Ibid., 42

88. Ibid., 43

89. *New York Times Magazine* (March 4, 1923), 1

90. *The Late Mattia Pascal*, 246

91. *High Points in the History of Italian Literature*, 257

92. *The Late Mattia Pascal*, 88

93. Ibid., 89

94. *High Points in the History of Italian Literature*, 258

95. *Living Age* (August 27, 1925), 473

96. Ibid. (June 1, 1927), 1005

97. *The Late Mattia Pascal*, 247

98. Alice Rohe, "Luigi Pirandello in Search of Popularity," *New York Herald Tribune* (January 6, 1924)

99. Luigi Pirandello, *Six Characters in Search of an Author* translated by Edward Storer in *Naked Masks* (New York 1952), 224

100. Ibid., 276

101. Ibid., 208

102. *The Late Mattia Pascal*, 246

103. *High Points in the History of Italian Literature*, 269

104. *New York Times Magazine* (March 4, 1923), 1

105. *High Points in the History of Italian Literature*, 18

106. Ibid., 256

107. *New York Times* (November 9, 1934), 20

108. *New York Times* (November 25, 1934), Sect. 5, 15

109. *Virginia Quarterly Review* (April 1925), 52

110. Hubert Heffner, "Pirandello and the Nature of Man," *Tulane Drama Review* (June 1957), 37; MacClintock, 177, 228

111. *High Points in the History of Italian Literature*, 258

112. *Pirandello's One-Act Plays*, x

113. *The Late Mattia Pascal*, 249; *Living Age* (June 1, 1927), 1002; *New York Times* (December 10, 1936), 27

114. Lucas, 362

115. *High Points in the History of Italian Literature*, 269

116. Edward Storer, "Luigi Pirandello, Dramatist," *Fortnightly* (August 1924), 228

117. Starkie, 246

118. *To Clothe the Naked and Two Other Plays*, xiii

119. *Naked Masks*, xxiii

120. Ibid., 224

121. *Pirandello's One-Act Plays*, 224

122. Ibid., 228

123. *Naked Masks*, xxiv, xx

124. *Right You Are*, 150

125. Abba, 2

126. "Pirandello Without Honor," *Living Age* (January 1, 1930), 544

127. Starkie, 250

Chapter VII

Eugene O'Neill

As a successful playwright, Eugene O'Neill thought that the plays he had written at Harvard in 1914-15 for Professor George Pierce Baker's English 47 Workshop "were rotten." O'Neill still believed that Professor Baker had inspired him to work and to hope, and for this O'Neill owed him "all the finest . . . in memory of gratitude and friendship." [1] "I would say that what has influenced my plays the most," remarked O'Neill in 1932, "is my knowledge of the drama of all time—particularly Greek tragedy . . ." [2] O'Neill was to win three Pulitzer Prizes and, in 1936, the Nobel Prize for Literature. To date, O'Neill is generally acknowledged to be America's greatest playwright. Shaw called him "a fantee Shakespeare," an undisciplined genius. [3]

I

THE GROWTH OF O'NEILL'S CREATIVE SPIRIT IN LIFE

Until O'Neill was twenty-four years old, he had not thought of becoming a dramatist. "If I hadn't had an attack of tuberculosis, if I hadn't been forced to look at myself while I was in the sanitarium, harder than I had ever done before," O'Neill told Hamilton Basso for his profile in the *New Yorker* magazine in 1946, "I might never have become a playwright." Throughout his creative life, O'Neill was to look at himself harder and harder until, to an astonishing degree, he changed his life into his art.

Eugene Gladstone O'Neill was born at Barrett House, a theatrical hotel at the corner of Broadway and 43rd Street, New York City, on October 16, 1888. His father was James O'Neill, a matinee idol of the day, risen to theatrical godhead from a "shanty Irish" childhood. O'Neill's paternal grandfather had come to America a poor farmer with six children and, because of mystical portents of impending death, abandoned his family to return to Ireland to die.

282

"Before he was an actor, he was a machinist," said O'Neill of his father. "He worked in Buffalo, ten hours a day for fifty cents a day." [4] On October 17, 1867, the stage manager of a repertory company on tour through Cincinnati with an Irish comedy, *The Colleen Bawn*, needed supers for a ballroom scene to replace those who had gone on strike; by pure chance he stopped in at a pool-room near the theatre and persuaded the twenty-one year old, itinerant machinist, James O'Neill, to make his first entrance onstage. Edwin Forrest later spotted a real actor in this super.

O'Neill's mother was Ella Quinlan O'Neill, born "lace curtain" Irish. Ella was convent educated, an accomplished pianist, the sweet daughter of a poor Irish immigrant who had succeeded first with a stationery store and later with a liquor and tobacco business in Cleveland, Ohio. James and Ella O'Neill had three children: James, nicknamed Jamie, in 1878; Edmund in 1884; and finally Eugene in 1888. Three months after the O'Neills' wedding in 1875, the marriage almost shattered on the rocks of notoriety. A certain Nettie Walsh who four years earlier, at the age of fifteen, had become James O'Neill's mistress sued him unsuccessfully for bigamy and non-support of her and a son born in 1872.

O'Neill told Croswell Bowen, "One thing that explains more than anything about me is the fact that I'm Irish." [5] With a name like O'Neill he could never forget he was Irish and at a time when the Irish in general were looked down upon as the immigrant servant class. Some of O'Neill's most pronounced traits were just about Irish clichés—his gift of language, his weakness for alcohol, his intense imagination, his love of a good story, his fierce pride in his blood, his clean-cut good looks, his interest in such rougher sports as boxing and football, and his mystical view of life.

But if Eugene O'Neill's creative spirit was Irish, it was still highly individual, molded often by forces over which he had no control. "Gene," as he was called till the age of 7, travelled with his parents while his father toured the United States as a star. Other than his family, Gene's companions during these formative years were restricted largely to the help around railroads and hotels and to an English nurse, Sarah Shandy, who was a walking collection of gruesome tales that delighted Gene. "My father was reciting poetry all the time," O'Neill recollected. "Instead of singing in the bath-tub, he'd break into Shakespeare." [6] Gene believed this somehow helped turn his whole life into a poet's quest. "As a boy," O'Neill reminisced, "I saw so much of the old ranting, artificial romantic stuff that I always had a sort of contempt for the theatre." [7] His contempt for this kind of theatre conditioned him to write for quite another kind. The family summered at their cottage in the seaport town of New London, Connecticut; Gene was early to develop a love of the sea, a friendliness toward seamen and a zest for swimming and sailing.

His father died, as O'Neill put it, believing "that Monte Cristo had ruined his career as an artist." James O'Neill performed the role of Dantes in *The Count of Monte Cristo* 5,678 times because he could not pass up the treasure he found in it each season on tour—$25,000 to $40,000.[8] Edmund O'Neill died when he was only a year and a half old; his brother Jamie had disobeyed his mother and with a bad case of measles gone in to see the baby and infected him fatally. James carried this guilt for the rest of his life and tried to forget it by fast living; he was Gene's boyhood idol and made "sin easy" for his little brother.

After Gene's birth, his mother suffered so much from the physical after-effects that she took to narcotics for relief and wound up a dope-addict. Not until 1914 did Federal law in the United States restrict the free sale of derivatives of morphine. Ella also used dope to escape her loneliness; she refused to mix socially with her husband's acting company, and her former friends cut her off because the theatre was then a kind of automatic fall from grace. When Gene was fourteen years old, he by chance entered a room just as his mother was giving herself a hypodermic of morphine.[9] He talked over her curious behavior with his father and brother, and only then did he see in revelation, like a sudden light through the vista of time, the reason for his mother's crazy and lethargic spells over the years. Gene prayed fervently without avail for his mother's cure; then unable to reconcile her terrible anguish with a merciful God, the boy lost his faith. After he was fifteen, O'Neill stopped attending Catholic church, and personally felt guilty for having through his birth driven his mother from pain into dope addiction. The desolated adolescent O'Neill became as Bowen phrased it, "one who has lost his Faith and who spends his life searching for the meaning of life." [10] O'Neill never stopped searching.

In 1906, his mother had a breast removed because of cancer, a disease dreaded for its commonly fatal recurrence. To all these material and psychological forces molding O'Neill's mind, he confessed that until his mid-twenties he was much given to hard drinking and whoring, the no-account son of a celebrity, mis-shapen from living in his father's giant shadow. O'Neill's shyness, his cruel streak, his self-destructive impulses could well have taken form from the prolonged humiliation of having little identity and much guilt. Eugene O'Neill was Irish but certainly with a difference.

James O'Neill was highly sensitive to his own lack of any formal education. He saw to it that his children received the very best he could afford and that they could profit from. At the age of seven, Gene went to the exclusive St. Aloysius Academy for Boys in the Bronx, on the Hudson, and then to De La Salle Institute in New York City, and finally, when fourteen years old, to the very exclusive Betts Academy in Stamford, Connecticut, where tuition then in 1902 was $500 a school year. His private schooling, though no worse in its isolation from his family than that of any boy's in a private school, is thought to have increased O'Neill's sense of rejection and loneliness. "Always the gloomy one," Captain Francis Dorsey, an intimate friend of the O'Neill family, recalled Gene as a boy. "He never said much, and then spoke softly when he did speak. Brilliant he was, too, always reading a book." [11] At school Gene did mediocre class-work, swam, read on his own, and made very few close friends. He played his share of practical jokes, but spent much time voraciously reading such varied fare as Joseph Conrad, Jack London, Kipling, Wilde, Tolstoi and Dostoievski: adventure, the sea, beauty, mysticism and the dark depths of the human spirit were O'Neill's dish even as a boy. At Betts, O'Neill also developed a discipline he carried into his playwriting—the keeping of voluminous and well-organized notebooks.

"I felt there, instinctively," O'Neill said of entering Princeton University in September, 1906, "that we were not in touch with life or on the trail of real things . . ." [12] O'Neill over-cut his classes and spent wild week-ends with his brother, Jamie, entertaining actresses in New York. One Monday night early in June following a spree in Trenton, O'Neill and some class-mates missed the last trolley to Princeton and could only get a train to Princeton Junction where the station master's dog took to barking. O'Neill heaved bricks at the dog and one flew wild through a window of the station master's house. Princeton's disciplinary committee brought O'Neill up on charges and suspended him for 3 weeks effective his sophomore year; O'Neill promptly left Princeton without bothering to take his freshman finals. O'Neill, incidentally, denied that he threw a beer bottle through a window of the house of Princeton's President at the time, Woodrow Wilson.

O'Neill now set about educating himself. He joined an artist friend in New York City, and at eighteen came across and read Nietzsche's *Thus Spake Zarathustra,* a book he was to make practically his *Bible,* claiming, "*Zarathustra* . . . has influenced me more than any book I've ever read." [13]

Often through family "pull," O'Neill then came to get a series of jobs that were in time to provide him with a file of memories from which to draw many plays. First he was Secretary to the President of a mail order company specializing in "ten cent jewelry." He then fell in love with Kathleen Jenkins who happened to be a Protestant, an artist's model, and a child of divorced parents; O'Neill's parents looked upon Gene's love with holy terror. On October 2, 1909, at Trinity Church in Hoboken, New Jersey, O'Neill secretly married his pregnant Kathleen. About one week later, his unwitting parents, hoping to break up his "affair" with Kathleen, had O'Neill willingly hustled off to Spanish Honduras on a gold prospecting expedition in which they had invested a good sum of money. O'Neill probably embarked for the "gold-fields" with dreams of returning to his Kathleen an instant Croesus. He found nothing in Honduras but jungles alive with reptiles, bugs, beasts, and birds; he literally experienced the world of phantom terrors that was to appear in *Emperor Jones.*

Broke and weak from a violent bout with malaria, O'Neill came back to New York City to learn that Kathleen Jenkins O'Neill on May 5, 1910, had borne him a son, Eugene O'Neill, Jr. O'Neill stopped in to see his wife but found her out; he visited with her mother, held the baby in his arms, cried, and then left. He never again tried to see Kathleen, and he was not to see his son, Eugene Jr., again till 12 years later.

Fed up with the world and especially with himself, O'Neill now headed for the docks around Fulton Street in New York City. He rented a room for $3.00 a month at "Jimmy the Priest's," a water-front dive combining a saloon with a rooming house. "Jimmy the Priest's" catered to seamen, prostitutes, stevedores, truckers, anarchists, junkies, and drifters. O'Neill was twenty-one years old, bitterly at outs with his parents, nearly flat broke, and living on whiskey at five cents a shot and a lunch of free soup. O'Neill prepared for suicide. "It was the lowest moment in my life," he many years later told Eugene O'Neill Jr.[14] In those days it was possible to buy a small dose of veronal without a prescription. O'Neill made the rounds of the neighborhood buying enough small doses to make a lethal one. By afternoon, he returned to his vermin-infested room, locked the door, and took all the

veronal—fortunately wanting in effectiveness because it was an over-
dose. At this point, the story has many versions. In essence, the next
afternoon his forlorn bar-friends went up to his room, knocked,
shouted, and finally broke in the door. They spotted the empty
veronal containers and rushed the still breathing O'Neill off to Belle-
vue Hospital, where his life was saved. Thirty years later, O'Neill recalled these friends at "Jimmy the Priest's" as "the best friends" he
ever had.[15] Their kind appear in *The Iceman Cometh*.

James O'Neill must have felt sorry when informed of his prodigal
son's try at suicide because he sent O'Neill funds enough to join him
in St. Louis as assistant stage manager of his touring company of *The
White Sister*. By the time the company had reached Boston, O'Neill
and his father had had all they could stand of each other. James
O'Neill called his son, Eugene O'Neill, a faithless, ungrateful,
drunken bum, and as a last resort to save him, ordered, "Go before
the mast!" [16] O'Neill went. He signed up to ship from Boston to
Buenos Aires as a common seaman on the Norwegian barque, the
Charles Racine. "I hated a life ruled by the conventions and traditions
of society," O'Neill recalled of his feelings at the time.[17] He turned to
the tiny world of a ship on the vastness of the sea to escape from his
failures in everything he had tried before—education, career, marriage,
and family-life. The trip from Boston to Buenos Aires took the
barque sixty-five days, and Eugene O'Neill daily did the lowest
menial tasks of a common seaman.

At Buenos Aires he tried to get his bearings by drifting from job to
job—draughting, sorting hides, repairing sewing machines—until finally he was again down and out. A desperate fellow bum at the time
attempted to talk O'Neill into joining him in holding up a foreign
exchange currency center, but O'Neill declined because he thought
they were too likely to get caught. The bum tried the hold-up on his
own, and O'Neill told Basso, "He was sent to prison and for all I
know he died there. Nearly everybody's life is determined to a large
extent by just such accidents as these." [18] Finally, O'Neill managed to
sign up as a common seaman with a shipment of mules from Buenos
Aires to Durban, South Africa. From Durban, O'Neill shipped back
to Buenos Aires and then on to New York City; from there, he
shipped for the first time as "able seaman" on a passenger steamer to
Southampton and then back to New York. This ended O'Neill's oc-
cupational career as a sailor.

In New York City, O'Neill found Kathleen Jenkins suing him for divorce, asking no alimony, and charging adultery. O'Neill obliged Kathleen by allowing her lawyer to witness him at a brothel on West 45th Street, in bed with a prostitute. He celebrated his divorce by throwing a big party at "Jimmy the Priest's," and a few days later he woke up with a big head on a train bound for New Orleans where his father was performing Dantes in *The Count of Monte Cristo*. The now much chastened prodigal humbly accepted a bit part and toured for fifteen weeks, then joined his family at their summer home in New London, Connecticut. James O'Neill knew the editor of the New London newspaper, *The Telegraph,* and managed to get his son a job as a reporter; O'Neill later called this writing stint "junk of a low order." [19]

Just before Christmas of 1912, tuberculosis struck O'Neill in the right lung. James O'Neill, though worth between $100,000 and $200,000 in real estate and cash, arranged to have his son, Gene, admitted on December 12, 1912, to Fairfield County State Tuberculosis Sanitarium, a haven for paupers with terminal tuberculosis. After two days, O'Neill found the place impossibly depressing. Upon the advice of Dr. Lynch there and also of a consultant specialist, Dr. James Miller, James O'Neill relented and sent Gene to Gaylord Farm near Wallingford, Connecticut, a progressive sanitarium admitting only patients with good prospects of recovery. On Christmas Eve of 1912, O'Neill entered Gaylord, and what he found there about his creative spirit was to be his Christmas present of a lifetime.

"It was at Gaylord that my mind got the chance to establish itself," O'Neill told J. E. O'Neill for *The Journal of Outdoor Life,* "to digest and valuate the impressions of many past years in which one experience had crowded on another with never a second's reflection." [20] O'Neill read Strindberg's plays, and for the first time felt inspired to write for the theatre himself. O'Neill stayed at Gaylord recovering for six months, and then spent the next sixteen months of convalescence at the Rippins, a home-style boarding house in New London. From his physician in town, Dr. Ganey, O'Neill borrowed and read collections of plays from Aeschylus through Ibsen. O'Neill then was creatively excited enough to write eleven one-act plays and two full length plays. "That's the year I thought I was God," said O'Neill. "I kept writing because I had such a love of it. I was highly introspective, intensely nervous and self-conscious. I was very tense. I drank to overcome my shyness." [21]

James O'Neill was so pleased and no doubt flabbergasted by his son's immersion in playwriting that in 1914 he paid $1,000 out of his own pocket for the publication of *Thirst and Other One-Act Plays*. The drama critic Clayton Hamilton happened to patronize the Rippins, and O'Neill showed him some of his work and asked for his opinion. "Write down what you know about the sea, and the men who sail before the mast," he told O'Neill; "it has not been done in the drama. Keep your eye on life—on life as you have seen it and to hell with the rest." [22] And then Hamilton even persuaded the reluctant James O'Neill to underwrite a whole year at Harvard for Gene in Professor Baker's 47 Workshop, a famous English course in playwriting. James O'Neill was surely thinking with misgivings of what had happened to Gene at Princeton University eight years earlier. A whole year's expenses thrown away!

O'Neill rated the plays he wrote from 1914–15 at Harvard as "rotten." Industrious if not successful, he still most diligently served his apprenticeship but never allowed any of the results to be published: *The Personal Equation, Dear Doctor, The Movie Man, The Sniper, A Knock at the Door,* and *Belshazzar*. After one year, O'Neill left Harvard, claiming he lacked the money to study further. He now went to the Mecca of American Bohemians, New York City's Greenwich Village, where he rented a room for $3.00 a month and settled down to write. He tried to put in about seven hours a day writing. His social life centered on Christopher Street at the Golden Swan Tavern's back-room—nick-named "The Hell-Hole." He would go on one month drunks. He fell in love with a girl named Louise Bryant, but she was already the mistress of the American communist, John Reed, who was to die in his youth of typhus and be enshrined in the Kremlin. To be near Louise, O'Neill followed her to Provincetown, Massachusetts, in the summer of 1916 and quartered with his friend, Terry Carlin, an anarchist. While walking along the beach one day that summer, Carlin happened to meet an acquaintance connected with the Provincetown Players, Susan Glaspell; Susan asked Carlin if he had any plays for the Players to do, and he told her he hadn't but that he had a friend, Eugene O'Neill, with a trunkful of plays. That very evening, Susan Glaspell had the Provincetown Players gathered in her living-room and reading aloud O'Neill's *Bound East for Cardiff* as the moody author sat in the dining-room. After the reading, Susan Glaspell said of the Players, "Then we knew what we were for." [23] Of the plays O'Neill had written from roughly 1913–1916, those so far published but almost never performed are:

Thirst	*Recklessness*	*A Wife for a Life*
The Web	*Abortion*	*Servitude* (only full-length play)
Warning	*The Movie Man*	*Before Breakfast*
Fog	*The Sniper*	

These plays are excellent for an aspiring dramatist to measure his own early efforts against, being, as they are, those of eventually so illustrious a dramatist as O'Neill.

O'Neill became the Provincetown Players' most prolific and promising new playwright. For the next six years they produced his experimental plays, and so surely gave him an incentive to write. Would O'Neill otherwise have given up playwriting for lack of encouragement? "No other American playwright," wrote Edna Kenton, "had such a prolonged preliminary freedom with stage and audience alike." [24] Though admission was charged, the Provincetown Players performed without pay and, like other Provincetown playwrights, O'Neill received no royalties; his father sent him a very modest weekly allowance.

The Provincetown Players were a stage-struck group of talented amateurs rallying to the charmismatic and dedicated leadership of George Cram Cook, assisted by his wife, the gifted playwright, Susan Glaspell. The Players' object was: "to give American playwrights of sincere purpose a chance to work out their ideas in freedom, to give all who worked with the plays their opportunity as artists." [25] The Players thrived on youth, enthusiasm, ingenuity and love of the theatre. Their Playhouse was improvised from an abandoned fish-house at the end of a wharf; the stage was ten feet by twelve, the back-stage opened onto the sea, and the house seated ninety people on backless benches. That memorable summer of 1916 the Players produced their first O'Neill play, the one-act, *Bound East for Cardiff*.

Inspired by the appreciative reception, O'Neill in the winter of 1916–17 wrote for the Players the whole of the sea-oriented *Glencairn Cycle* of one-acts. In 1917, the Players also created their very own playhouse in New York City, this time by converting not an abandoned fish-house but an old stable at 133 Macdougal Street in Greenwich Village. The Provincetown Theatre soon became one of New York City's prime show-cases for new talent. In his six years of association with the Players, O'Neill came to work with and know not only George Cram Cook and Susan Glaspell but also such a galaxy of celebrities to-be as Edna St. Vincent Millay, Edna Ferber, Robert Edmond Jones, Wilbur Steele, Paul Green, James Light, Lawrence Vail, Kenneth

Macgowan, William Zorach and Ann Harding. By 1925 the pioneering example of the Players had helped establish about 1900 little theatres all over the United States.

In autumn of 1917 O'Neill was relaxing at the Swan Tavern's
"hell-hole" when he noticed a new face, a young lady strikingly like
his still unrequited passion, Louise Bryant; mutual friends introduced
O'Neill to this fresh attraction, Agnes Boulton, a divorcee who wrote
stories and had one child. O'Neill struck Agnes Boulton as "sad and
cruel." After walking her home that evening, O'Neill told Agnes at
parting, "I want to spend every night of my life from now on with
you." [26] In those days with "free-love" and "companionate marriage"
in the air, Agnes joined O'Neill and with her "genius," as she called
him, went to spend the winter at Provincetown, Massachusetts, where
the two seemed blissfully contented with love, companionship, and
work.

Because of his latent tuberculosis, O'Neill was not drafted for
World War I. He, himself, viewed the War as a capitalistic scheme
for profits. O'Neill habitually for his writing would take long walks
up and down the beach, and once when a German submarine was
sighted off-shore, he was arrested as a suspected German spy. The
charge, of course, didn't stick, but the experience did, and O'Neill
transformed it creatively into his play *In the Zone*. The Keith Or-
pheum circuit favored this one-act play, and for forty weeks toured it
as a sentimental thriller, paying O'Neill a royalty of $40.00 a week, his
first money earned after five years of playwriting. With this financial
backing O'Neill married Agnes Boulton on April 12, 1918, and only
later did he tell her about his first marriage to Kathleen and about his
son, Eugene O'Neill, Jr. Agnes soon was pregnant, and O'Neill's
Catholic parents, delighted that he had finally settled down, even with
a divorcee, bought the couple Peaked Hill, a luxuriously converted
lighthouse at Provincetown. Here O'Neill lived with Agnes, writing
plays and leaving only for their rehearsal in New York City.

O'Neill's first Broadway production did not come until 1920 when a
group of actors, out of sheer love for the play, performed *Beyond the
Horizon* for a try-out matinee which led Alexander Woollcott to
write, "the play has greatness in it." *Beyond the Horizon* raised such a
harmonious chorus of critical praise that it went on to a full-run and
won O'Neill the Pulitzer Prize for Drama in 1920. O'Neill was thirty-
two years old.

From 1920 to 1923 every single member of O'Neill's immediate family died. James O'Neill died at seventy-four on August 10, 1920, after suffering long from cancer of the intestine; he thought his lot was divine punishment for his worst sins of a lifetime: an illegitimate child fathered in his youth, the wasting of his talent as Dantes in *Monte Cristo,* and the foolish squandering of his wealth in speculating for gold, oil, coal and land. O'Neill's mother died on February 28, 1922, from a brain-tumor. And O'Neill's brother, Jamie, died nearly blind of acute alcoholism at the age of forty-five on November 8, 1923.

Contrary to O'Neill's original wish, Agnes bore him two children: Shane on October 20, 1919; and Oona, on May 13, 1925. O'Neill regarded children as intruders upon his imaginative life as an artist.[27] In 1926 while summering with his family at Belgrade Lakes, Maine, O'Neill met a neighbor's house-guest, Carlotta Monterey. Carlotta was an astonishing beauty, a modestly successful actress, independently wealthy and three times divorced. The following year, in the fall of 1927, O'Neill left his home, Spithead, in Bermuda, to attend rehearsals of his new play, *Strange Interlude,* in New York City, and in his loneliness he looked up Carlotta Monterey. The two fell deeply in love. "I didn't want this to happen," said O'Neill, but he admitted that he always wanted a home properly run and this, Agnes had not given him.[28] "I need you," he told Carlotta, never, "I love you." [29] During this trying time, O'Neill volunteered to be part of a study, *Research on Marriage,* which Dr. Gilbert Van Tassle Hamilton was making of two hundred married couples; O'Neill underwent six weeks of analysis.

From O'Neill's courtship of Agnes Boulton in 1917 until their divorce in 1929, he wrote many plays of very uneven quality and often dedicated his work in the most loving terms to Agnes:

In the Zone * (1917)
*Ile**
*The Long Voyage Home**
*The Moon of the Caribbees**
The Rope * (1918)
*The Dreamy Kid**
*Where the Cross Is Made**
Beyond the Horizon
Chris Christopherson (1919)
The Straw
Diff'rent (1920)
Emperor Jones
Gold

Anne Christie (revised *Chris Christopherson*)
The First Man (1921)
The Hairy Ape
The Fountain (1922)
Welded (1923)
All God's Chillun Got Wings
Desire Under the Elms (1925)
Marco Millions
The Great God Brown
Lazarus Laughed (1926)
Strange Interlude (1927)

The one-act plays are marked with an asterisk. With *Strange Interlude* his greatest commercial success, O'Neill by February of 1928 felt his love for Carlotta Monterey drive him relentlessly to leave his wife and two children. He and Carlotta sailed to England, France, Hong Kong, Manila, and back to France. Reporters hounded them almost wherever they went. By the end of 1929, Agnes finally divorced O'Neill; he then married Carlotta Monterey, and they settled down in the seclusion of a rented six hundred acre estate with forty-five bedrooms and almost no modern conveniences—the Château de Plessis near Tours, France. They rarely entertained, but here O'Neill was able to get away from the world and to write. Carlotta regulated O'Neill's life to promote his maximum creativeness. Some felt that she kept the world so shut out from O'Neill that he and his work suffered for it. Carlotta, however, must have had O'Neill's acquiescence for whatever she did. She commented of O'Neill, "No one could get very far trying to persuade him to do anything." [30] Carlotta was very good for O'Neill's creativeness in playwriting:

Dynamo (1928)	*Long Day's Journey into Night*
Mourning Becomes Electra (1931)	(1941)
Ah, Wilderness! (1932)	*Hughie*
Days Without End (1933)	*A Moon for the Misbegotten*
The Iceman Cometh (1939)	(1943–46)
	A Touch of the Poet
	More Stately Mansions

The last three plays listed were the only ones of a projected cycle of eleven plays to survive; O'Neill deliberately burned up the rest as work he could never finish and wanted no one else to touch. Perhaps O'Neill's dedication to Carlotta of *Long Day's Journey into Night* best shows how much she meant to him: "To Carlotta, again, wife, friend, helper and lover . . ."

O'Neill was a dedicated playwright. What friends and acquaintances he made were somehow related to the promotion of his lifework. "I liked Gene. He was fun to be with," said Shane's wife. "But he wasn't a man you could turn to when you needed help. I think he felt somehow that his children had betrayed him." [31] George Jean Nathan believed that O'Neill's dislike of meeting people amounted almost to terror. Given to moods, O'Neill could invite a friend to dinner and then sit through the whole meal without saying a word. For a real or imagined grievance, he once struck Agnes a blow in the face.

"Gene was such a peculiar mixture," confessed Carlotta. "Sometimes he was so soft-spoken and he had the smile of a child of five; you would forgive him anything. But then he could turn around . . . He was very much of a sadist at times, terribly so." [32] The sadism was followed by agonizing guilt. Carlotta believed O'Neill's moods varied with the moon.

O'Neill's best friends over the years were: the writers Ben De Casseres and Stark Young; the critics, Joseph Wood Krutch, George Jean Nathan, and Brooks Atkinson; the actresses, Lillian Gish and Ilka Chase; the lawyer Winfield Aronberg; the editor at Random House, Saxe Commins; the theatrical manager, Lawrence Langner of the Theatre Guild; the intellectual vagrant, Terry Carlin; and many doctors who treated O'Neill in his years of chronic illness.

Shortly before Christmas of 1936, a series of illnesses began for O'Neill that were to take away the gift of his career that the Christmas of 1912 at Gaylord Farm had by chance given him. First his appendix burst; kidney and prostate trouble followed, then neuritis, then "palsy." In 1937, doctors diagnosed the "palsy" to be Parkinson's disease, and later, an even rarer, degenerative illness of the nervous motor system. After his analysis in 1926 O'Neill quit drinking, but before this, since his college days, he had according to Nathan, Agnes Boulton and the Gelbs gone on many a long drunk of a quart of whiskey or more a day. [33] O'Neill's lack of proper food, sometimes a month at a time, very likely insidiously started the progressive destruction of his motor nerves.

By 1946 O'Neill's handwriting was illegible. He became creatively impotent. For the next seven years, family troubles all but made a Laocoön figure of him, and he steadily wasted away as well. On February 10, 1946, Shane's son, Eugene O'Neill III, aged two months, accidentally strangled to death in his bedclothes; O'Neill refused ever again to see Shane. Treated with dope for a war-connected injury in the Merchant Marine during World War II, Shane became a drug addict, and on August 10, 1948, was arrested for possessing three capsules of heroin; he was given a suspended sentence, then cured; the shade of O'Neill's mother must have seemed near. In 1948, the then seventeen year old Oona married the fifty-four year old multi-millionaire, leftist movie star and genius, Charlie Chaplin, who had been previously married three times and had two sons almost Oona's age. "Oona broke Gene's heart," said Carlotta. [34]

In 1946, O'Neill significantly told Croswell Bowen, "Revenge is the

subconscious motive for the individual's behavior with the rest of society." [35] Eugene O'Neill II, Kathleen's child, had a promising career
as a Greek scholar at Yale, but then turned communist, became an alcoholic rejected in love, and finally in despair took his life in 1950.
O'Neill virtually now withdrew from the world to Carlotta and solitude. Both were increasingly ill, relying more and more on drugs to
kill pain, and alone together so much that O'Neill wound up trying
to have Carlotta committed to an insane asylum. The two reconciled
and Carlotta nursed him through his long, hopeless illness. Except for
his copyrights and the unreleased *Long Day's Journey into Night,*
O'Neill spent everything on doctoring. His weight dropped eventually
to ninety pounds, and he could neither walk nor even hold a cup of
water. Finally at 4:39 a.m. on November 27, 1953, O'Neill at sixty-four
died in Boston. At his request, he was buried in that city at Forest
Hills Cemetery without any religious service, and with only his wife,
his doctor, and his nurse attending the burial. "I planted laurel around
the headstone," said Carlotta, "like the laurel wreaths of the Greek
heroes." [36]

II

COMMERCIAL CONSIDERATIONS AFFECTING
O'NEILL'S PLAYWRITING

In applying to Professor Baker for extraordinary admission to his
course in playwriting at Harvard, O'Neill wrote, "I want to be an
artist or nothing." [37] This was to be O'Neill's commercial credo of a
lifetime in playwriting. By 1926, he could note, "I must confess to having made a darn good thing of my plays financially—a much better
thing for the six years, I am confident, than nine out of ten of the
professional, crafty playwrights of the gamblers' guesses at trade
goods." [38]

In O'Neill's opinion, his best work was the best box-office, but the
best box-office was no sign to him of the best work. Professor Baker,
for instance, in one respect profoundly disappointed O'Neill in his
Harvard days by praising the highly successful playwright, Augustus
Thomas, whom O'Neill considered a contriving hack. "It is too facile
in its conventional technique," O'Neill wrote of his own commercially
successful one-act, *In the Zone,* in a letter to Barrett Clark, "too full of
clever theatrical tricks . . . there is no big feeling for life inspiring
it." [39] At that time O'Neill was content to let the Provincetown Play-

ers perform his *Glencairn Cycle* royalty free; it is also remarkable that he permitted a try-out matinee performance of the play that was to win the Pulitzer Prize for Drama in 1920, *Beyond the Horizon.* By supporting O'Neill through his apprenticeship, O'Neill's father had really underwritten his son's artistic integrity; *Monte Cristo* might have ruined the father as an artist, but its profits helped save the son.

However noble O'Neill's intentions might have been, everything he wrote was not art, and much of it lost a great deal of money for his backers. "One of the most amazing things about Mr. O'Neill," noted Brooks Atkinson in *The New York Times* with some bewilderment, "is his capacity for seasoning his valiant career with bad plays." [40] O'Neill's best works are generally accepted to be his biggest hits: *The Emperor Jones, The Hairy Ape, The Great God Brown, Desire Under the Elms, Strange Interlude, Mourning Becomes Electra, Ah, Wilderness!* and *Long Day's Journey into Night.* In the course of his career, O'Neill earned roughly a million dollars with his plays and at a time when income taxes were low; *Strange Interlude* was his biggest hit, accounting for about $275,000 of his earnings. Beginning with *Marco Millions,* the Theatre Guild in New York City became the exclusive producer on Broadway of everything he wrote in his lifetime. "You can't tell how a play will work out till it's produced," said O'Neill. "If you could, all authors would write hits and turn out as many plays as Lope de Vega"—who supposedly wrote 1,800 or so plays. [41]

III

AESTHETIC CONSIDERATIONS AFFECTING O'NEILL'S PLAYWRITING

From when he first started writing plays, O'Neill believed in himself, and others soon came to believe in him. "That's the year I thought I was God," he said of his initiation into playwriting in 1913. Some of his Harvard classmates saw in him the makings of "America's foremost playwright." The Provincetown Players did his plays out of faith. Agnes Boulton called him "my genius." George Jean Nathan became a one man crusade in his behalf, calling him in print over 220 times "America's best playwright." [42] When Lawrence Langner of the Board of the Theatre Guild visited him in 1935, Langner sensed in O'Neill a consciousness of his own immortality— something Langner had noticed before only in Shaw.

In *The Boston Evening Postscript* of October 21, 1925, O'Neill made this aesthetic declaration of independence which he was to follow to the end of his creative life:

> I rate myself as a beginner with prospects—and in this faith I live: that if I have the "guts" to ignore the megaphone men and what goes with them, to follow the dream and live for that alone, then my real significant bit of truth and the ability to express it will be conquered in time after the struggle has been long and hard enough to merit victory.

O'Neill from experience told Barrett Clark, "a work of art is always happy; all else is unhappy . . ." [43] The exact nature of O'Neill's "significant bit of truth" is suggested in his view of men as told to Oliver Sayler:

> It seems to me that as far as we can judge, man is much the same creature, with the same primal emotions and ambitions, and motives, the same powers and the same weaknesses, as in the time when the Aryan race started toward Europe from the slopes of the Himalayas. [44]

O'Neill saw no hope of improving man except through the imagination and the will of the individual rather than through any political party. "Time was when I was an active socialist, and after that a philosophical anarchist," recollected O'Neill to Sayler. "But today, I can't feel that anything like that really matters." Late in life, O'Neill was convinced that Americans had become so obsessed with material goals that they had forgotten the very secret of happiness—"For what shall it profit a man if he shall gain the whole world and lose his own soul?" [45] What made life worth living in O'Neill's opinion was "a hope worth living and dying for." Man's power to dream, however, was greater than his power to accomplish: "as we progress, we are always seeing further than we can reach." To attain the unattainable was then man's fated and tragic struggle. "What is the theatre for," asked O'Neill, "if not to show man's struggle . . . to conquer life . . . to give it meaning?" [46]

For O'Neill, the proper subject matter of the drama was anything under the sun with one qualification—"Is it the truth as I know it or, better still, feel it?" [47] A playwright, to O'Neill, was little more than a parlor entertainer unless he was concerned with one of the great truths of his day, the sickness of modern times, "—the death of the Old God and the failure of science and materialism to give any satisfying new One for the surviving primitive religious instinct to find a meaning for life in, and to comfort its fears of death with." [48]

In choosing his technique to project his "significant bit of truth," O'Neill used conventional means when these best served his needs. Otherwise, he chose to write "in any manner that fits or can be invented to fit the subject." For him, the one-act form, he said in an interview for *The New York Herald Tribune*, was "a fine vehicle for something poetical, for something spiritual in feeling that cannot be carried through a long play." [49] After finishing the *Glencairn Cycle* of one-act plays in 1918, O'Neill admittedly left the one-act form because it could not go far enough. In 1941, for diversion, he planned a series of one-act plays to be called *By Way of Obit*, but he finished only *Hughie*.

From the one-act form, O'Neill went on to the naturalism of *Anna Christie;* he informed Malcolm Cowley of *The Reporter*, "In telling the story, I deliberately employed all the Broadway tricks I had learned in my stage training." [50] He left naturalism because he felt that it was too limited to appearances. He went on to expressionism as in *The Hairy Ape* and *Emperor Jones* with techniques for dramatizing inner conflicts exemplified in Strindberg's work. O'Neill wrote for the playbill of *The Spook Sonata* produced by the Provincetown Players, opening January 3, 1924:

> Strindberg was the precursor of all modernity in our present theatre
> . . . All that is enduring in what we loosely call "Expressionism"—all
> that is artistically valid and sound theatre—can be clearly traced back
> through Wedekind to Strindberg's *The Dream Play*, *There Are Crimes
> and Crimes*, *The Spook Sonata*.

George Jean Nathan said of O'Neill's technique, "If he stems from anyone, he stems from Strindberg. He carries his emotions to levels that become unnatural." [51] In his address upon receiving the Nobel Prize, as reported in *The New York Times* of December 11, 1936, O'Neill in his words chose:

> to acknowledge with gratitude and pride the debt my work owes to
> that greatest genius of all modern dramatists, your August Strindberg. It
> was reading his plays, when I first started to write back in the winter of
> 1913-14, that above all else gave me the vision of what modern drama
> could be, and first inspired me with the urge to write for the theatre
> myself. If there is anything of lasting worth in my work, it is due to the
> original impulse from him, which has continued as my inspiration down
> all the years since then . . .

O'Neill intensely emotionalized his characters because he thought the best way to project the truth with impact was through the emotions. "They are the result not only of our individual experiences but of the experiences of the whole human race back through the ages," said O'Neill to Mary Mullett for *American* magazine in 1922; "They are deep undercurrents, whereas our thoughts are often only the small individual surface reactions. Truth usually goes deep. So it reaches you through your emotions." [52] O'Neill's search for means to dramatize soul-struggles led him to experiment with such devices as the mask, the aside, and the soliloquy. For greater emotional impact, he also chose to write longer and longer works like *Mourning Becomes Electra* and *Long Day's Journey into Night* and to project a never completed cycle of eleven plays growing from an American family line over many generations. O'Neill's concern with length as a source of power and beauty, he probably saw suggested or corroborated in Aristotle's *Poetics*.

O'Neill found the general level of acting so inadequate in rising to the level of his inspiration that after seeing a play through rehearsal, he hardly ever bothered to see a performance. "I can always do a better production in my mind," he said, "than the one onstage." He told Hamilton Basso that of all the actors who had appeared in his plays, only three fully came up to his conception of the character: "They were Charles Gilpin in *Emperor Jones*, Louis Wolheim in *The Hairy Ape*, and Walter Huston in *Desire Under the Elms*." [53] O'Neill never forgot nor likely forgave the excesses of his father's style; he could only abide a theatre with "sensitive, truthful, trickless" acting. He felt bitter about stars who wanted unacceptable changes in his scripts.

O'Neill had no use for most critics, but a great deal of use for some very few. "Generally speaking the critic of any kind of art is simply a defeated, envious, inferior type who knows nothing whatever about his subject." [54] For O'Neill, the critic's only true function in the theatre was to judge whether or not the play was "inspired." Some critics had helped O'Neill. Clayton Hamilton had advised him to study at Harvard and to write plays about the sea, the very works that were to first make O'Neill a name. The critic George Jean Nathan accepted for publication by the magazine, *Smart Set*, the first O'Neill play to be commercially published, *Moon of the Carribbees*. Even at the height of his powers, as in the writing of *Strange Interlude* and *Mourning Becomes Electra*, before letting a play go into production O'Neill would turn for a respected critical reaction to such figures as George Jean Nathan, Joseph Wood Krutch, and Brooks Atkinson. He carefully deliberated over their suggestions for revision. In the whole world, O'Neill believed that the number of worthwhile critics could be counted on his fingers and toes.

If a critic might have saving virtues, a censor in O'Neill's opinion could have none. Boston, for instance, banned *Strange Interlude*. Here is O'Neill's typical battle-cry against the enemy:

> The history of the theatre censorship proves that it never has much effect on the evils it ostensibly aims to eliminate, while it always ends by becoming a stupid tyranny used by reactionary bigotry and intolerance to suppress all freedom of expression . . . In the light of what has happened in censor-loving Europe and Asia, I think any American should reject with disgust any attempt at censorship in any form whatsoever.[55]

IV

O'NEILL'S WORKING METHODS IN PLAYWRITING

Genesis

As his wife who knew O'Neill most intimately during his period of transition from amateur to professional dramatist, Agnes Boulton in her book, *Part of a Long Story*, gives this record of O'Neill at work in 1917–18 at Provincetown.

> He wanted to write plays, that is understood. He may have even written a few of the earlier ones, which didn't amount to much. But he was undisciplined, he told me, not only in working habits, but in writing, itself—what form to use and how. Then he began consciously to use a method which he kept up for over a year. He read nothing but plays, great plays, melodrama.
>
> Before long he was thinking in dialogue, talking to himself in dialogue, and answering his own thoughts more or less aloud in his low voice, seeing life in scenes and acts—with the curtain going down, perhaps, as he went off to sleep . . . Sometimes I wonder when we did talk, but I know we talked a lot. He talked about his work with me before he wrote it, while he was writing it, and after it was finished.[56]

For over a year then, O'Neill immersed himself in usually the best plays till their techniques became a kind of second nature to his way of thinking. In this period, of course, O'Neill was also writing himself. Reports show other attitudes and habits of O'Neill were creatively helpful to him. To work best, he needed to be happily mated: Agnes Boulton and then Carlotta Monterey were to be to him his "alter ego"—wife, lover, companion, help-mate. O'Neill was so obsessed with "brain-children" that his nursery, as it were, was much too full to be bothered with real children. He worked best in solitude, usually near the sea or at least a view of a river, perhaps because he associated the sea especially with memories of a life-time.

He later adopted a set routine that did not depend on stimulants like alcohol to get him started and keep him going. "You've got to have all your critical and creative faculties about you when you're working," said O'Neill. "I never try to write a line when I'm not strictly on the wagon." [57] After analysis in 1926, O'Neill became a teetotaller. He had drunk spasmodically for at least the previous twenty years. Several times he jumped or fell off the wagon, but only under great emotional stress. "Writing is my vacation from living," O'Neill wrote Dr. Lyman of being deeply occupied in a creative dream world, "—so I don't need vacations." [58] O'Neill nevertheless did vacation with his wife, usually between successive drafts of a play, as with *Mourning Becomes Electra,* but at other times he took his work along.

O'Neill's work day tended to follow rather set ways. By 8 a.m. he'd be out of bed and breakfasting lightly in silence. Then he would settle down to writing in his study until the afternoon. His study tended to be severely simple with his papers and reference books neatly organized and plenty of sharpened pencils handy. He wrote his plays entirely in notebooks, using a precise, minute, pencilled handwriting. By 1 p.m. he was at lunch, and then spent the afternoon relaxing in such activities as walking, fishing, swimming, gardening, or driving his car at high speed—sometimes 90 miles an hour. Probably O'Neill found these doings not only refreshed his spirit but, by their often monotonous and rhythmical nature, helped stimulate the subconscious to solve the day's creative problems. O'Neill was not one to "waste" time. He usually liked to dress informally, except on those rare occasions when the O'Neills entertained. He generally had dinner at 7 p.m. Always quite slender, O'Neill was from all signs a frugal eater.

O'Neill in the course of his life wrote in such a wide variety of locales that his basic needs seem to have been simply solitude, seclusion, peace, and if possible, the sea. His "studies," for instance, ran through this range: Gaylord Sanitarium; a bedroom and a screened porch at the Rippins in New London; an old beach shack at Provincetown

with a sign on the door, "Go to hell;" a $3.00-a-month room on Mac-
dougal Street in Greenwich Village; a simply furnished apartment at
Provincetown; a study in the beautifully converted lighthouse, Peaked
Hill, at Provincetown. With success and changing fortunes, O'Neill's
studies remained simple although his homes were often lavish: in
1922, a thirty-two acre estate at Ridgefield, Connecticut; in 1925, a
thirteen and a half acre estate, Spithead, in Bermuda; in 1929–31, the
rented Château de Plessis on the Loire with 600 acres, 45 bedrooms,
and almost no modern conveniences; in 1932, a custom-built home,
Casa Genotta (a contraction of Gene and Carlotta), in Sea Island,
Georgia; in 1937, another custom built home, Lao Tse (The Right
Way), built to overlook San Francisco Bay. O'Neill's last years were
spent largely in hotels and hospitals in New York and Boston. His
formative years of being on the road with his touring father seem to
have left him a restlessness he never quite lost.

"Oh, the idea usually begins in a small way," O'Neill told Mary
Mullett of the genesis of his plays. "I may have it sort of hanging
around in my mind for a long time before it grows into anything
definite enough to work on. The idea of *Emperor Jones* was in my
mind for two years before I wrote the play." [59]

O'Neill had whole notebooks with just entries for the germination
and growth of his plays. In 1931, for example, to defend himself
against the charge of plagiarism, he submitted a notebook to the court
as evidence; his deposition stipulated: "I respectfully request the court
not to make public the matter in this notebook except that which concerns *Strange Interlude,* as the notebook contains over thirty ideas for
plays not yet written." [60] Georges Lewys lost her suit for $1,250,000,
charging he had plagiarized the story of her book *The Temple of
Pallas-Athenae* to write *Strange Interlude;* she had to pay ruinous
court costs.

By 1943 O'Neill was to have many notebooks filled with entire outlines and ideas for plays he was never to get around to write. After
finishing one play, he had no trouble going on to another. His problem was only to pick the most promising growth from a great deal of
material that had been germinating for years. "I do not think that you
can write anything of value or understanding about the present,"
O'Neill remarked to Karl Schriftgiesser for *The New York Times* regarding *The Iceman Cometh.* "You can only write about if it is
far enough in the past. The present is too mixed up with superficial
values; you can't know which thing is important and which is not.
The past which I have chosen is one I knew . . ." [61]

Reminiscence apparently brought O'Neill a "hunch" he might have a play in the making. In time, a selection and rearrangement of experience took place in his conscious and subconscious mind till a new creative pattern emerged in play form. Consider O'Neill's account of the genesis of *Emperor Jones,* for instance, as reported in *The New York World* of November 9, 1924:

> The idea of *The Emperor Jones* came from an old circus man I knew. This man told me a story current in Hayti concerning the late President Sam. This was to the effect that Sam had said they'd never get him with a lead bullet; that he would get himself first with a silver one. . . . This notion about the silver bullet struck me, and I made a note of the story. About six months later I got the idea of the woods, but I couldn't see how it could be done on the stage, and I passed it up again. A year elapsed. One day I was reading of the religious feasts in the Congo and the uses to which the drum is put here: how it starts at a normal pulse and is slowly intensified until the heartbeat of everyone present corresponds to the frenzied beat of the drum. There was an idea and an experiment. How would this sort of thing work on an audience in a theatre? The effect of the tropical forest on the human imagination was honestly come by. It was the result of my own experience while prospecting for gold in Spanish Honduras.[62]

This is about all O'Neill relates of the genesis of *Emperor Jones.* A mental set seemed induced originally from the story of the old circus man; thereafter, his mind spread a net of a kind for anything O'Neill might experience or recollect related to the possible development of this idea. What he netted, like the use of the drums and the effect of the tropical forest, probably came from much watchful waiting. O'Neill does not tell us when a key revelation in the action of *Emperor Jones* entered his mind: people lost tend to wander in a circle. This revelation must have come very early, for it gives form to the play's whole structure, providing an ironic, natural, and certain end for Brutus Jones, the counterpart of President Sam who fled in panic when pursued by the avenging tribesmen whom he had cheated.

According to the Gelbs, O'Neill's living model for Brutus Jones was Adam Scott, a powerfully built giant of a Negro who was an elder in New London's Shiloh Baptist Church, and who worked in Holt's Grocery, which had a saloon in the rear. "I am a very religious man," said Scott, "but after Sunday, I lay my Jesus on the shelf." [63] Scott exemplified the bravado, religion, and superstition in Brutus Jones. But a powerful strain of Brutus Jones was in O'Neill himself. Mary Heaton Vorse, who knew O'Neill well from his six years with the

Provincetown Players, said, "He could write the epic of fear, *Emperor Jones,* because no one knew more of cosmic fear than Gene, fear of the dark and the universe." [64] O'Neill in a sense also knew what it was to be lost and pursued by his own furies, for he had sailed from Boston to Buenos Aires to Durban and eventually circled back home trying to escape them.

While *Emperor Jones* took about two years to shape up, *The Hairy Ape* emerged complete from conception to first draft in three weeks. Only one other play came to O'Neill at such full speed—*Ah, Wilderness!,* which took only six weeks from complete conception in a dream one night to its finished realization on paper. Both plays were preceded by a great deal of related living. O'Neill told Mary Mullett of the genesis of *The Hairy Ape:*

> It was on two voyages that I got to know the stokers, although it did not really begin aboard ship. There is a class distinction even among the groups that make up the crew of an ocean liner . . . I shouldn't have known the stokers if I hadn't happened to scrape an acquaintance with one of our furnace-room gang at Jimmy the Priest's! His name was Driscoll, and he was a Liverpool Irishman . . . To sailors all over the world, a "Liverpool Irishman" is a synonym for a tough customer. . . . Driscoll came to a strange end. He committed suicide by jumping overboard in mid-ocean. . . . it was the *why* of Driscoll's suicide that gave me the germ of the idea for my play, *The Hairy Ape.*[65]

O'Neill came to believe that Driscoll took his life in utter despair over the failure of all his efforts to "belong." Yank became the lead and Driscoll's counterpart in the play. His efforts to "belong" go into violent motion and emotion when Mildred, a spoiled society girl aboard the ocean steamer, sees him come up from the stoker-hold, grimy with coal dust and very hairy chested: she blurts out before fainting dead away, "Oh, the filthy beast!" Yank's fellow-stokers interpret these words for Yank to mean, "Oh, the hairy ape!" Then in scene after scene of the play, Yank tries to prove to himself he "belongs." But because of his ape-like appearance and basic nature, he is rejected; until, in desperation, he enters the gorilla's cage at the zoo, calls him "brother," and the gorilla embraces Yank, crushing him to death. In death, Yank finally "belongs." "Yank is yourself," said O'Neill, "and myself." [66] The play may very well have derived from that time when his own desperate and futile efforts "to belong" went afoul through his own primitive instincts, and wound up in his own try at suicide.

O'Neill began his plays from a past he knew, often many years in retrospect, which demanded a catharsis or a sublimation. Arthur and Barbara Gelb in their excellent and definitive biography, *O'Neill,* go deeply into this matter, though there are always further depths others may explore. In O'Neill's *Servitude* and *Before Breakfast,* for instance, the leads are men who like O'Neill were trapped into an unhappy marriage. In *Exorcism,* a down and out young man of good family, like O'Neill, tries to commit suicide but his drunken friends save his life, and he finds his death-wish exorcised. Of the *Glencairn Cycle,* O'Neill said frankly, "I have used the members of the same crew through this cycle because, judging from my own experience as a sailor, I thought I had picked out the typical mixed crew of the average British tramp steamer;" [67] the sea which had been O'Neill's escape from life became through his plays his way to fulfillment. No wonder he could say, "a work of art is happy; all else is unhappy . . ."

Gold recalls O'Neill's own disillusionment in the jungles of Honduras. *The Straw* tells of a tubercular young newspaper reporter like O'Neill who meets a tubercular young lady at a sanitarium, and through love the pair find a straw of hope. *The Fountain* deals with the fountain of youth, and *Lazarus Laughed* with resurrection—both plays sublimating O'Neill's grief over the loss of his father, mother and brother, all within three years. *Welded* vivisects the love-hate of O'Neill's jealously possessive marriage to Agnes. *Strange Interlude* concerns O'Neill's study of basic frustrations in love as an aftermath of World War I, and his own analysis, first between 1923 and 1925 with Dr. Smith Ely Jelliffe in New York, then through his neighbor in Bermuda at the time, Dr. Louis Bisch, and then later through Dr. Gilbert Van Tassle Hamilton in New York. *Mourning Becomes Electra* is a psychological study of forces which doom a family to tragedy with only one left to expiate the family's guilt; O'Neill had his own family as an example of such forces at work, and he was the only one left with his own guilt to expiate. *Days Without End* reconciles O'Neill and Carlotta's love-hate by surrendering to Catholicism. *Ah, Wilderness!* O'Neill termed a comedy of "recollection" of his adolescent years in New London, with the Miller family largely drawn from models among his close friends and neighbors, the McGinleys. *The Iceman Cometh* is O'Neill's repayment in part of a debt to the customers at "Jimmy the Priest's" who had saved him from death, were among his "best friends," lived only for illusions and knew the peace that comes from having fallen to their lowest level of being. "It was an obsession with him—this place and his memories of it," wrote

Agnes of 'Jimmy the Priest's'; "and often during the years that we
were together he spoke of wanting to write a play about it and the
men he knew there, but he never did . . . until many years later he
wrote *The Iceman Cometh.*" [68] *Long Day's Journey into Night,*
O'Neill called in his dedication of the play to Carlotta, "a play of old
sorrow, written in tears and blood;" playwriting was his way of making peace with himself and his family even as he had tried to do earlier in *Mourning Becomes Electra.*[69] O'Neill's projected grand cycle
of nine plays was to "form a sort of dramatic autobiography."

Behind the genesis of O'Neill's plays was a great deal of living re-
lived, and then released as art.

Incubation and Characterization

As with so many playwrights, genesis for O'Neill might be a
"hunch" that he had a play while incubation was the certainty. The
two stages, if distinct, are certainly continuous in terms of growth. "I
never try to force an idea. I think about it off and on. If nothing
seems to come of it, I put it away and forget it," observed O'Neill.
"But apparently my subconscious mind keeps working on it, for all of
a sudden, some day, it comes back to my conscious mind as a pretty
well formed scheme." [70] *Strange Interlude,* O'Neill's most successful
play, followed this pattern. A rather detailed account of the "hunch"
and its growth is on record in O'Neill's own words, thanks to the
court records of his "Deposition to the Paris Commission, Answers to
Interrogatories" on August 12, 1930, in Georges Lewys' plagiarism suit
against O'Neill as eventually tried in the U. S. District Court of the
Southern District of New York under Judge John M. Woolsey. Here
is O'Neill's own account:

> it was during the previous summer of 1923 in Provincetown, Massa-
> chusetts, that I heard from an aviator, formerly in the Lafayette Esca-
> drille, the story of a girl whose aviator fiancé had been shot down just
> before the armistice. This girl had gone to pieces from the shock and
> started drinking and having promiscuous sex affairs. She had become
> neurotic and desperate. Finally she had married, not because she loved
> the man, but because she wanted to have a child, hoping through
> motherhood to win back a measure of contentment from life. It was this
> story which forms the basis of the note I made later on and which
> constitutes the plot of the first two acts of the play, *Strange Interlude.*[71]

Even before hearing this true life story, however, O'Neill was alerted
to its usefulness, for it fitted in most aptly to an earlier "hunch:"

I discussed the germ idea which developed into the play—an idea for a series of psychological plays depicting the outer and inner life of a woman from the age of young womanhood until forty-five—I discussed this with George Jean Nathan as far back as the spring of 1923, right after I finished writing *Welded*.[72]

O'Neill made his first preliminary note for *Strange Interlude* in his notebook at Ridgefield, Connecticut, in the fall of 1923, under the heading, "Godfather." The entry is available only in the account of Harry Weinberger, O'Neill's lawyer, speaking in O'Neill's defence at the actual trial:

What do we find in "Godfather"? We find the story of a man marrying a girl and the doctor coming into the story and the woman having a great many children by the doctor, and then confesses to her husband that the doctor is the father of her children, but there is no talk about insanity. The husband goes to the doctor and asks him if it is true, and the doctor denies it and simply blames it on the woman's hysteria or insanity. That is the note of "Godfather" in 1923.[73]

By the summer of 1925, roughly two years later, the material re-emerged in O'Neill's mind "as a pretty well formed scheme:"

The scenario was written in the summer of 1925 at Nantucket, Massachusetts . . . The scenario, photostats of which are attached, consists of the names of the characters, some of which were changed later on when I actually wrote the play. There follows the description of the different scenes of the acts. After which there is description of the main characters as I visualized them at the time. Some of these characters were left out of the play and others added. Finally there is a detailed outline of the plot of each act.[74]

But O'Neill did not hesitate to talk over his play in the course of its incubation, likely to assist that incubation:

While *Strange Interlude* was being written, I discussed its psychological plot with Doctor G. B. Hamilton who was then doing research work on marriage for the Rockefeller Foundation; I discussed the technique of the spoken thoughts used in *Interlude* with Professor George Pierce Baker of Yale University in the spring of 1926 when I was his guest at the time I received my honorary Doctor of Letters Degree. In the summer of 1926 I discussed what I had written up to then with Kenneth Macgowan when he came to see me at Belgrade Lakes, Maine.[75]

During the composition of the scenario O'Neill had crossed out and rewritten as much as half. He let the scenario mature until the spring of 1926 before he began his first draft.

The leading character or characters in an O'Neill play almost invariably turned up in genesis itself and not only gave O'Neill his "hunch" for the play but also the dynamic personality, the natural force unleashed in flesh and blood for the play's whole development through incubation. Yank, for instance, was admittedly inspired by the true story of President Sam and his obsession that he would die only by his own silver bullet; Nina Leeds, by the true story of a girl who desperately searched for happiness first through promiscuity with loves in the image of her fiancé, an aviator shot down before the armistice, and then in marriage. Sometimes, however, O'Neill's leading characters appeared from models in history or legend. Lazarus, for example, is shown in his exultation and its implications after Christ raises him from the dead.

O'Neill viewed life as an endless series of struggles, and to promote an intense clash of wills in his plays he deliberately picked characters in marked contrast to his lead. To illustrate briefly from plays other than those cited, in *Ile,* after two years of futilely hunting for whales, Captain Keeney is obsessed with one thought—not to sail home broken in pride because his ship's hold is unfilled with whale oil; his wife, by contrast, is desperately home-sick because the endless hunt for whales in the monotony of the seas has her edging madness then crossing the border-line. In *Beyond the Horizon,* Robert Mayo gives up his love of the sea for the romance of sex and finds himself tied down to, for him, the dreariness of farm life; his brother, Andrew, by contrast, gives up his love of farming to gamble in the wheat-pit and is financially wiped out. In *Anna Christie,* the old barge captain, Chris Christopherson, hates the sea with a passion and is dead set against his daughter, Anna, marrying a "no good sailor fallar;" Mat Burke, however, a born sailor, is deeply in love with Anna and determined to marry her against her father's bitter will. Not only does O'Neill pick his leads to be opposed by nature, but to suit his declared intent of emotionalizing the truth he gives his leads "the most comprehensive, intense, basic human relationships" such as: husband and wife; lovers; brothers; brother and sister; friends; some bond whose very closeness by blood and affection adds heat and light to the ensuing struggle.

O'Neill chose to develop his characters in terms of their inner lives.

He noted in *American Spectator* of November, 1932, referring to the dramatist: "He must find some method to present this inner drama in his work or confess himself incapable of portraying one of the most characteristic impulses of his time." "There is no conscious use of psychoanalytical material in any of my plays," insisted O'Neill, however, in a letter to the *Saturday Review* of May 28, 1932: "All of them could easily be written by a dramatist who had never heard of the Freudian theory and was simply guided by an intuitive psychological insight into human beings and their life-impulsions that is as old as Greek drama." What O'Neill is saying in essence is that Sophocles did not need Freud at his elbow to write *Oedipus the King.*

Throughout incubation, O'Neill tried to develop his characters to emotionalize yet externalize their inner lives; he tried to turn his characters inside out. In *The Hairy Ape,* he used expressionism to present every scene as seen through the distorted emotional vision of the leading character, Yank; for instance:

> The ceiling crushes down upon the men's heads. They cannot stand upright . . . The men themselves should resemble those pictures in which the appearance of Neanderthal Man is guessed at . . . All are hairy-chested with long arms of tremendous power and low, receding brows above their small, fierce, resentful eyes . . .

Yank sees his fellow stokers as near brutes, but they don't see themselves that way necessarily.

O'Neill also used conventional devices in highly unconventional ways in this and in other plays and always to externalize the inner life. In *Emperor Jones,* for example, O'Neill extended the soliloquy to run sometimes a whole scene; in Brutus Jones' rising panic as he flees his murderous pursuers, O'Neill found reason for Jones' outpouring of delirious hopes, fears, and hallucinations from his racial past. O'Neill adapted the ancient Greek theatre's use of masks so they were not anachronisms in his eyes but "newer and truer characterization . . . For what at bottom is the new psychological insight into human cause and effect but a study in masks, an exercise in unmasking." [76] O'Neil wrote of the masks in his *The Great God Brown:*

> Dion's mask of Pan which he puts on as a boy is not only a defence against the world for the super-sensitive painter-poet underneath it but also an integral part of his character as the artist. The world is not only blind to the man beneath, but also sneers at and condemns the Pan-mask it sees. After that, Dion's inner self retrogresses along the line of Chris-

tian resignation until it partakes of the nature of the Saint, while at the same time the outer Pan is slowly transformed by his struggle with reality into Mephistopheles. It is as Mephistopheles he falls stricken at Brown's feet after having condemned Brown to destruction by willing him his mask, but this mask falling off as he dies, it is the Saint who kisses Brown's feet in abject contrition and pleads as a little boy to a big brother to tell him a prayer.[77]

In *Strange Interlude,* O'Neill extended the aside so that it was continually interwoven with the whole length of a four hour play revealing two selves in each character: "One as he appears and speaks to the world, and the other as he thinks and speaks to himself."

An excellent over-all view of O'Neill's practices in incubating a play in continuity with its genesis, is found in O'Neill's detailed work-diary relating to *Mourning Becomes Electra;* the *New York Herald Tribune* printed almost its full text on November 8, 1931. An interpretation of the work-diary in the context of other circumstances of O'Neill's life at the times of the entries, along with what has already been said of the familiar paths of his approach, suggest the working of his mind in creation.

In 1926 O'Neill read Hugo von Hofmannsthal's play in verse, *Electra,* and was so excited by it that he tried to get Kenneth Macgowan to produce the play; Macgowan declined. Hofmannsthal apparently influenced O'Neill by turning him back to the original Greek sources of literary fecundity. Here is O'Neill's first entry in his work-diary for *Mourning Becomes Electra:*

> Spring, 1926—Modern psychological drama using one of the old legend plots of Greek tragedy for its basic theme—the Electra story?—the Medea? Is it possible to get modern psychological approximation of Greek sense of fate into such a play, which an intelligent audience of today, possessed of no belief in gods or supernatural retribution, could accept and be moved by? [78]

The intensity of Greek tragedy was a controlled but fierce spirit, almost identical with O'Neill's, to emotionalize the truth the better to drive it home by way of the viscera. This first entry also shows O'Neill's typical concern with the inner life—"a modern psychological approximation of Greek sense of fate"—as well as the uncertainty of his "hunch."

Two years later, unforced, the idea began emerging, showing his subconscious had been at work, cell by cell. The knowledge of his own "doomed" family suggested to O'Neill that he could approximate the Greek sense of fate with modern psychology; to spur him to work, he had his own tormenting trial of conscience demanding catharsis. O'Neill at this next entry had, after a one year affair with Carlotta Monterey, sailed away with her, abandoning his second wife and his two children, Shane and Oona:

> October 1928, Arabian Sea, en route for China—the Greek tragedy plot idea, story of Electra and family psychologically most interesting—most comprehensive intense basic human interrelationships—can be easily widened in scope to include still others.

Why had O'Neill rejected the Medea story? Was the association of it with his abandoned wife, Agnes, and his two small children, too hot for his art to handle? Medea kills her two children by her unfaithful husband, Jason. Through the Electra story, O'Neill could parallel his own sense of guilt and retribution as the only one left of his own "doomed" family, the O'Neills.

His next entry came a month later with Carlotta still by him and the newspaper reporters hounding them for news. This entry shows how very early in a play's conception O'Neill settled on his central character and hence his whole viewpoint of the play. He was also very early concerned with the play's ending, most likely to give direction to its development and certainly to its total effect, just as a destination might give to a long journey:

> November 1928, China Sea—Greek plot idea. Give modern Electra figure in play tragic ending worthy of character. In Greek story she peters out into undramatic, married banality. Such a character contained too much tragic fate in her soul to permit this—why should Furies have let Electra escape unpunished?

O'Neill's deep concern with Electra's end from the very beginning is certainly noted here, and especially in the very title of his completed work, like a banner headline, *Mourning Becomes Electra.*

Four months later, O'Neill made his next entry showing the outcome of months of creative deliberation. O'Neill's careful considerations in picking the proper time and place for his story, show his acute concern very early with giving his project of "modern psychological drama" the most probability and verisimilitude. The entry suggests several very big flashes of creative excitement and revelations in which, as usual, a great deal emerged "all of a sudden" and as a "pretty well formed scheme;" it was as if a static charge had to gather in his mind for the giant spark of insight to jump the gap in under-standing. These flashes involved really three basic insights. New Eng-land had actually gone through a period of neo-classic revival and so invoked a kind of spiritual kinship with ancient Greece by its very look. New England Puritanism that made the individual conscience a battle ground for sin and punishment was an unforced modern equivalent for the Furies, the avenging Greek goddesses. And finally by implication, O'Neill had grown up in New England and knew its people in his bones so he could write of them from truthful recollec-tion; most likely this unspoken insight made possible the other two:

> Cap d'Ail, France, April 1929—Greek tragedy plot idea. No matter in what period of American history play is laid, it must remain psycho-logical drama—nothing to do with period except to use as mask—What war? Revolution too far off, too clogged in peoples' minds with romantic grammar school history associations. World War too near and recog-nizable in its obstructing (for my purpose) minor aspects and superfi-cial character identification (audience would not see fated wood because too busy recalling trees)—needs distance and perspective—period not too distant for audience to associate with, yet possessing costume, etc.—possessing sufficient mask of time and space, so that audience will unconsciously grasp at once, it is primarily drama of hidden life forces —fate—behind lives of characters. Civil War is only possibility—fits into picture—Civil War as background for drama of murderous family love and hate.
>
> Greek tragedy plot idea—Lay in New England small seaport ship-building town—family town's best—shipbuilders and owners—wealthy for period—Agamemnon character town's leading citizen. Mayor before war, now Brigadier General in Grant's army—opening act of play day of Lee's surrender—house Greek temple front type that was rage in first half nineteenth-century—(this fits in well and absolutely justifiable not forced Greek similarity)—This home of New England House of Atreus was built in 1830, say, by Atreus character, Agamemnon's father—gro-tesque perversion of everything Greek temple expressed of meaning of life. (New England background best possible dramatically for Greek plot of crime and retribution, chain of fate. Puritan conviction of man born to sin and punishment. Orestes' Furies within him, his conscience, etc.

The extension of this very note shows, too, how O'Neill tried to keep the old Electra legend, yet modernize it without destroying its life-spirit. This is a major problem in using any legendary material; if the story is altered fundamentally beyond popular traditional accep-tance, the playwright might find he has lost the very heart of the mat-ter. The public thinks the new version "not true." O'Neill was especially concerned with preserving the incestuous tradition of the House of Atreus—a tradition not unknown in European royal families—and also in finding a valid, continuous, psychological pattern of behavior in the goings-on; he finds the incest theme and the Oedipus complex inherently extensions of each other and dominating all motivation. The Oedipus complex, of course, is psychiatry's description of the nexus of a son's excessive attachment to his mother, and of a daughter's excessive attachment to her father. Its sentimentalized version is suggested in the popular song, "I Want a Girl Just Like the Girl Who Married Dear Old Dad." In transposing the legend, O'Neill thought in terms of the characters' traditional names in order to keep their identities clearly in mind:

> Departures from Greek story—Electra loves Aegisthus—always fated to be mother's rival in love, always defeated—first for father's love, then for brother's, finally for Aegisthus'—reason for Clytemnestra's hatred for Agamemnon sexual frustration by his puritan sense of guilt turning love to lust (she had romantic love for him before marriage)—omit Iphigenia and Chrysothemis from children—only Orestes and Electra—no Cassandra—keep exact family relationship of Aegisthus (first cousin Agamemnon)—keep general outline of rivalry, hatred, love, lust, revenge in past between Agamemnon's father, Atreus, and Aegisthus' father, Thyestes (in legend Thyestes seduces Aerope, wife of Atreus)—hatred of Atreus for brother—revenge—banishment—(keep general spirit of this but pay no attention to details of legend) Clytemnestra persuades Aegisthus against his will to help her murder Agamemnon (my Aegisthus character weaker, more human, and less evil character, has conscience of sort)—method of murder, poison (woman's weapon)—Aegisthus bears strong facial resemblance to Agamemnon and Orestes—his resemblance to Orestes attracts Clytemnestra—his resemblance to her father attracts Electra—Electra adores father, devoted to brother (who resembles father), hates mother—Orestes adores mother, devoted to sister (whose face resembles mother's) so hates his father—Agamemnon, frustrated in love for Clytemnestra, adores daughter, Electra, who resembles her, hates and is jealous of his son, Orestes—etc.—work out this symbol of family resemblances and identification (as visible sign of the family fate) still further—use of masks (?)

The next month, with his basic parallels to the Greek legend set, O'Neill experienced some added creative insight that for the first time let him glimpse his broad selection and ordering of material as from aerial photo-flashes of his imagination. Now a good three years from the play's germination in Spring of 1926, O'Neill saw the play's total effect clearer than ever and the play as a trilogy. At the same time he noted the modern equivalents for the names of his legendary characters:

> Cap d'Ail, France, May 1929—(Greek plot idea)—Names of characters—use characteristic names with some similarity to Greek ones—for main characters, at least—but don't strain after this and make it a stunt—no real importance, only convenience in picking right names always tough job.
>
> Agamemnon—Asa,(Ezra) Mannon
> Clytemnestra—Christine(?)
> Orestes—Orin
> Electra—Eleonor(?)Ellen(?)Elsa(?)Laodicea—Lavinia(this sounds more like it) Vinnie (Called in family)
> Aegisthus—Augustus(?) Alan Adam(?)
> Pylades—Paul(?) Peter(?)
> Hermione—Hazel—Hesther
>
> Cap d'Ail, France, May 1929—Title—"Mourning Becomes Electra" —that is, in old sense of word—it befits—it becomes Electra to mourn —it is her fate,—also, in usual sense (made ironical here) mourning (black) is becoming to her—it is the only color that becomes her destiny—
>
> Cap d'Ail, France, May 1929—No chance getting full value of material into one play or even two,—must follow Greek practice and make it trilogy—first play Agamemnon's home-coming, and murder—second, Electra's revenge on mother and lover, using Orestes to help her—third play, retribution Orestes and Electra. Give each play a separate title— "Mourning Becomes Electra"—title for trilogy as whole—first play— "Homecoming"—second (?)—third, "The Haunted"

O'Neill made his next note four months before he was even to begin his first draft, demonstrating that his technique in writing a play was determined by his point of view long before the actual writing began, and so actually helped shape the scenario yet to be written:

> Cap d'Ail, France, May 1929—Technique—for first draft use comparatively straight realism—this first draft only for purpose of getting plot material into definite form—then lay aside for period and later decide how to go on to final version—what departures necessary—whether to use masks, soliloquies, asides, etc.

O'Neill knew where he was going and how he proposed to get there. His entire concern for the following four months was in writing a detailed scenario for each play of his trilogy:

> Le Plessis, St. Antoine-du-Rocher, France, June 20, 1929—Finished scenario first play, "Homecoming."

Le Plessis, St. Antoine-du-Rocher, France, July 11, 1929—Finished scenario second play, "The Hunted"—What an advantage it was (from a plotter's standpoint, at least) for authors in other times who wrote about kings—could commit murder without have to dodge detection, arrest, trial scenes for their characters—I have to waste a lot of ingenuity to enable my plotters to get away with it without suspicion!—still, even history of comparatively recent crimes (where they happen among people supposedly respectable), shows that rural authorities easily hood-winked—poisoning of Mannon in "Homecoming" would probably never be suspected (under the same circumstances) even in New England town of today, let alone in 1865.

Le Plessis, August, 1929—Finished scenario third play, "The Haunted" —have given my Yankee Electra tragic end worthy of her—and Orestes, too.

O'Neill investigated the major source material of the Electra story in drama as well as in legend; he had undoubtedly read Aeschylus' trilogy, *The Oresteia,* years before he even thought of writing his own play about Electra. The serious student of drama reads *The Oresteia* the way a serious student of architecture sees the Parthenon. The structure of *Mourning Becomes Electra* shows striking resemblances and likely transpositions from *The Oresteia.* These must have appeared in O'Neill's scenario by and large: the House of Atreus to the House of Mannon; King Agamemnon's palace to General Mannon's New England mansion; the Trojan War to the American Civil War; the Greek Chorus to the hired man and his cronies from town; King Agamemnon to General Mannon; Clytemnestra, the King's wife, to Christine, the General's wife; Electra, the King's daughter, to Lavinia, the General's daughter; Aegisthus, the Queen's paramour, to Captain Adam Brant, the bastard of the General's father out for revenge. The Aeschylean trilogy hints at the subconscious love of daughter for father and son for mother in its leading characters. O'Neill turned this hint into the emotional drive motivating almost the entire action of his trilogy in what psychiatrists term, after the ancient Greek legend, "the Oedipus complex." Aeschylus had the son goaded on by his sister, Electra, to murder the mother who had murdered the father; O'Neill has the son goaded on by his sister, Lavinia, to kill his mother's paramour, and then the mother, in grief over her murdered lover, kills herself. Aeschylus had the Athenian Court and the gods try and then acquit the son of his mother's murder; O'Neill has the son commit suicide over his guilt at having indirectly driven his mother to suicide by his killing of her paramour. Aeschylus had Electra end up an attractive matrimonial prospect for some noble

Greek to continue the illustrious family line; O'Neill has Lavinia end up in perpetual mourning because this is the only way she knows how to really expiate her guilt. In up-dating a story that had proven its essential human truth by surviving about 2,500 years as drama and longer as myth, O'Neill surely realized that he was making his highest bid for literary immortality by identifying the talents of his name with the transcendent life of the story.

Sources of Freshness in O'Neill

Brooks Atkinson, Dean of America's drama critics, in commenting upon O'Neill's receiving the Nobel Prize for Literature in 1936, wrote, "On the general theme of man's angry struggle with nature, he has written the most ruthless and overwhelming plays of our times and added several cubits to the drama." [79] In a television documentary on O'Neill, *The Face of Genius,* broadcast March 14, 1966, Atkinson said of O'Neill, "If you read his plays, many of them are sophomoric, or seem to be sophomoric, but that is not the test. The test is what it is like on the stage. And on the stage it has a kind of reiteration and ponderous face and strength, and that makes very good theatre." [80]

O'Neill drew his chief distinction from sources this study noted earlier. "What is the theatre for," he asked, "if not to show man's struggle . . . to conquer life, . . . to give it meaning?" Yet man by nature has a tragic fate, for his power to dream is greater than his power to accomplish. To O'Neill, "Truth usually goes deep. So it reaches you through your emotions." [81] O'Neill deliberately emotionalized the truth about the inner lives of his characters and then externalized their minds by such dramatic techniques as expressionism, the soliloquy, masks, and the aside. "He regarded it with high seriousness," Arthur Miller remarked of O'Neill's attitude toward the theatre in *The Face of Genius.* "He made it seem as though one could do anything in it, if one had the courage and the talent, whereas most writers never reached that far. He was an example of great courage." Miller noted that O'Neill was "one of the most experimental playwrights we ever had. But, he was not appreciated most of the time."

O'Neill satisfied many if not all drama critics that in such plays as *Mourning Becomes Electra* and *Long Day's Journey into Night* it was possible to write a tragedy in modern times. Through the extraordinary length of these plays O'Neill seemed in agreement with Aristotle's observation in the *Poetics* regarding plot in tragedy (Butcher's translation): "beauty depends on magnitude and order so in a plot, a certain length is necessary, and a length which can be embraced by the memory." Then Aristotle adds, "the greater the length, the more beautiful will the piece be by reason of its size, provided that the whole be perspicuous." [82] Aristotle was quite likely thinking of Aeschylus' *The Oresteia*. The length of O'Neill's best tragedies like some of Shaw's best comedies, such as *Man and Superman,* is rare in modern drama.

During O'Neill's life and after his death quite a few critics have examined the body of his works and pronounced his literary obituary. But like Mark Twain's comment upon reading of his own death, O'Neill's best works say through the popularity of their continued public revival, "The reports of my death are greatly exaggerated." "Robert Benchley, Francis Fergusson, Lionel Trilling, Harold Clurman, Mary McCarthy and Eric Bentley have all had their go at him," said Thomas Curley of O'Neill in *Commonweal* of January 14, 1966. "But with the exception of Trilling's their strictures are either technical . . . or essentially that of Stark Young: 'Those vulgar speeches. God!'" [83] Since O'Neill's death in 1952, what notable commercial productions of his work have there been in New York City alone? *The Iceman Cometh,* Off-Broadway starring Jason Robards, 1955–56, 565 performances. *Long Day's Journey into Night,* starring Fredric March and Florence Eldridge, on Broadway, 1956–57, 390 performances. *Anna Christie* into the musical, *New Girl in Town,* starring Gwen Verdun and Thelma Ritter, on Broadway, 1957–58, 431 performances. *A Touch of the Poet,* starring Helen Hayes, on Broadway, 1958–59, 284 performances. *Ah Wilderness!* into the musical, *Take Me Along,* on Broadway, 1959–60, starring Jackie Gleason, 448 performances. *Desire Under the Elms,* Off-Broadway, 1963–64, 384 performances. *Strange Interlude,* on Broadway, featuring the Actors Studio, 72 performances. *Marco Millions,* Off-Broadway, ANTA, 1964, repertory. *The Iceman Cometh* was done on television in the series, *Show of the Week. Desire Under the Elms* and *Long Day's Journey into Night* were made into movies. A theatre on Broadway was named after O'Neill. Arthur and Barbara Gelb's definitive biography, *O'Neill,* appeared in 1962. *Mourning Becomes Electra* was made into an opera now in The Metropolitan Opera's repertoire. Does this look like literary death or glory?

The chief charge against O'Neill is "melodramadness." Euripides has survived the same charge for about 2,500 years. "Euripedes, faulty though he may be in the general management of his subject," observed Aristotle, "yet is felt to be the most tragic of the poets." [84] The proof to Aristotle? Actual performance and audience reaction. Tolstoy, of course, in *What Is Art?* leveled the charge of "melodramadness" with his literary gun blazing away at Shakespeare.

O'Neill is also charged with ignoring or neglecting man's relation to society. "Most modern plays are concerned with the relation between man and man," Joseph Wood Krutch reported O'Neill saying in a conversation, "but that does not interest me at all. I am interested only in the relation between man and God." [85] This hardly, however, excludes man's relation to man. O'Neill told Croswell Bowen in 1946, "Revenge is the subconscious motive for the individual's behavior with the rest of society. Revulsion drives man to tell others of his sins. . . . It is the furies within us that seek to destroy us. In all my plays, sin is punished and redemption takes place."

Writing and Rewriting

After finishing a scenario, O'Neill would put it aside awhile before attempting a first draft. He finished the scenario of *Strange Interlude,* for instance, in the summer of 1925 but did not attempt a first draft until spring of 1926. "I write the whole play out in long hand. Then I go over it and rewrite it in long hand," said O'Neill. "Then I type it, making a good many changes as I go along. After that, I like to put it away for a few months if possible; then take it out and go over it again." [86] O'Neill here implies that he does at least four drafts of each play, and possibly a fifth at rehearsal. Theresa Helburn, who worked directly with O'Neill during his eighteen years or so of association with the Theatre Guild, noticed that usually he took a year to do three drafts of a full length play and allowed for a three month interval between his first and second draft and then another between his third and fourth draft. In these fallow periods for one play, O'Neill would work on another play or relax.

On his usual work days, O'Neill put in four hours of writing each morning, but with a jet-like drive of inspiration he could work much longer. "I've had a great splurge of writing it," he said of *All God's Chillun Got Wings,* "—and what e'er befall, it's been great sport." [87] Of writing *Strange Interlude,* he said, "I am going great guns on the new one and I want to take full advantage of the favorable spell and get as much done on it as possible." [88] "He was always working on several plays at once," Carlotta said of her husband. "He would work on one until he felt he was stuck, get a thought about another one, and work on that." [89] A single scene in *Strange Interlude* threw him for a loss for a month. In the course of writing and rewriting, he turned to those he trusted for a reaction or a judgment. In drafting *Strange Interlude,* for example, he consulted Professor Baker, Dr. Hamilton, and Kenneth Macgowan.

O'Neill gave his stage directions the most painstaking care. "I've worked out every single detail of the setting and action, and even the lighting," he told Barrett Clark of *Lazarus Laughed.* "Incidentally, I've done the same thing with all my plays, only (with a smile) I didn't get credit for it." [90]

Regardless of which form he wrote in, O'Neill felt he fell short in the gift of words to match the lyric flights and passion of his characters. "Oh, for a language to write drama in!—For a speech that is dramatic," complained O'Neill, "and isn't just conversation!" "I'm so strait-jacketed," he said in outlining *Mourning Becomes Electra,* "by writing in terms of talk!" [91] After the naturalism of *Anna Christie,* O'Neill tried repeatedly to break free of this "strait-jacket." In *Emperor Jones,* for instance, he used theatrical means organic to the play to give the production excitement and eloquence beyond that of the dialogue alone. The relentless, approaching beat of the tom-toms and also Jones' hallucinations of his racial past, for example, magnify the emotional effect of such colloquial speech as this excerpt from a soliloquy of Jones's in mounting terror:

> Oh, Lawd, what I gwine do now? Ain't got no bullet left on'y de silver one. If mo' o' dem h'ants come after me, how I gwine skeer 'em away? Oh, Lawd, on'y de silver one left—an' I gotta save dat for luck. If I shoots dat one, I'm a goner sho! Lawd, it's black heah! Whar's de moon? Oh, Lawd, don't dis night evah come to an end! [92]

In *Lazarus Laughed,* O'Neill used a chorus in free verse to express exultation in the triumph of life over death at the resurrection of Lazarus through faith in Christ:

> CHORUS: (*in a chanting murmur*)
>   Lazarus laughs!
>   Our hearts grow happy!
>   Laughter like music!
>   The wind laughs!
>   The sea laughs!
>   Spring laughs from the earth!
>   Summer laughs in the air!
>   Lazarus laughs! [93]

For more prosaic moments in the same play, O'Neill used realistic dialogue to suggest the vernacular of Greece, Rome, and Palestine in Christ's day.

"My people speak aloud what they think and what others aren't supposed to hear," O'Neill said of *Strange Interlude*. "They speak in prose, realistic or otherwise, . . blank verse, or hexameter or rhymed couplets." [94] A sampling in the predominantly colloquial prose suggests the contrapuntal harmony O'Neill tried to effect:

> PROF. LEEDS: . . . You'll find Nina changed, Charlie, greatly changed! (*He sighs—thinking with a trace of guilty alarm.*) The first thing she said at breakfast . . . I dreamed of Gordon! . . . as if she wanted to taunt me . . . How absurd! . . . Her eyes positively glared. (*Suddenly blurting out resentfully*) She dreams about Gordon.
>
> MARSDEN: (*Looking at him with amused surprise*) Well, I'd hardly call that a change, would you?
>
> PROF. LEEDS: (*Thinking, oblivious to this remark*) But I must constantly bear in mind, that she's not herself . . . that she's a sick girl . . .
>
> MARSDEN: (*Thinking*) The morning news of Gordon's death came . . . Her face like gray putty . . . beauty gone . . . No face can afford intense grief . . . It's only later when sorrow . . . (*With concern*) Just what do you mean by changed, Professor? Before I left she seemed to be coming out of that horrible numbed calm.[95]

O'Neill believed that in his dialogue, and in the very construction of most of his plays, he worked "along the lines of a musical composition." [96] For this reason, he usually hated to cut, claiming it was like excising life from important variations of his theme. But O'Neill, himself, cut mercilessly in a number of notable instances. *Beyond the Horizon* ran for four hours at its first rehearsal, and he cut the running time to two hours. As for *Marco Millions,* "at the last moment before sending it to you," he informed George Jean Nathan, "I reread and decided to rewrite and condense the two nights of the play into one long night." [97] The charge persists that O'Neill deliberately overwrote for fear that he would leave out something important, and then wouldn't cut enough to give his plays a free and easy movement clean of fat; the sluggish pace from his prolixity is supposed to induce "colossal boredom." The same charge persists against Shakespeare and Shaw.

O'Neill's work-diary for *Mourning Becomes Electra* records how in his prime he went about writing and rewriting. "The production of

Electra," noted Arthur and Barbara Gelb, "was in a sense, the climax of O'Neill's career." [98] Thereafter O'Neill finished only six plays, and of the three that reached Broadway in his lifetime only *Ah, Wilderness!* was a hit for both the critics and the public.

While writing *Mourning Becomes Electra,* O'Neill deliberately isolated himself on the 600 acres of the rented estate of the Château de Plessis to observe the United States in "good perspective." "I lived like a trappist monk," he said of his loneliness, except for the imaginary world of his characters.[99] Unlike a trappist monk, however, O'Neill did have a loving wife near. He worked so hard, that in a year and a half he did six drafts of his trilogy, an amount of writing that in sheer physical effort alone was staggering.

Though O'Neill had finished his scenario by August, 1929, he let it lie fallow till the following October. Before starting his first draft, he scanned all the entries of his work-diary to brief himself and noted one entry in particular:

> Cap d'Ail, France, May, 1929—Technique for first draft, use comparatively straight realism—this first draft only for purpose of getting plot material into definite form—then lay aside for period and later decide how to go on to final version—what departures necessary—whether to use masks, soliloquies, asides, etc.[100]

O'Neill's first efforts fumbled things:

> Le Plessis, October, 1929—After several false starts, all rotten, think I have hit right line for first draft now.

Through a demonic inspiration and industry, O'Neill like a man possessed within the next four months or so finished the entire first draft of his trilogy, running in all to twelve acts and three long plays in length. "She has collaborated by keeping the old château running with uncanny efficiency," O'Neill told George Jean Nathan of Carlotta, ". . . A most marvelous wife and friend!" [101] On Februrary 21, 1930, in keeping with his habit of putting a first draft aside for a while, O'Neill went to Italy with Carlotta for a month's vacation.

O'Neill's next entry in his work-diary shows that with each successive draft he was to follow the pattern of being first largely creator and then largely critic, but always partly both. If he could write in the sweep of long spells of inspiration, he was ruthless in his self-appraisal upon reading over what he had written:

Le Plessis, March 27, 1930—Read over first draft of "M. B. E."—scrawny stuff but serves purpose as first draft—parts damned thrilling but lots more lousy—not enough meat—don't like Aegisthus' character—hackneyed and thin—must find new one—not enough sense of fate hovering over characters, fate of family—living in the house built by Atreus' hatred (Abe Mannon)—a psychological fate—reading this first draft I get feeling that more of my idea was left out of play than there is in it!—in my next version I must correct this at all costs—run the risk of going to other cluttered-up extreme—use every means to gain added depth and scope—can always cut what is unnecessary afterwards—will write second draft using half mask and an "Interlude" technique (combination of "Lazarus" and "Interlude") and see what can be gotten out of that—think these will aid me to get just the right effect—must get more distance and perspective—more sense of fate—more sense of the unreal behind what we call reality which is the real reality!—the unrealistic truth wearing the mask of lying reality, that is the right feeling for this trilogy, if I can only catch it! Stick to modern tempo of dialogue without attempt at pretence of Civil Wartime lingo. That part of first draft is right.

O'Neill's compass in the uncertainties of writing and rewriting was his awareness of just what he wanted in the total effect. He found fault and constructively specified possible correctives in this same note. From the somewhat vague and diffuse pattern of the first draft, more and more of the rhythm and balance in the whole structure emerged with deeper implied meanings as from a lifting fog:

Obtain more fixed formal structure for first play which succeeding plays will reiterate—pattern of exterior and interior scenes, beginning and ending with exterior in each play—with the one ship scene at the center of the second play (this, center of whole work) emphasizing sea background of family and symbolic motive of sea as means of escape and release—use townsfolk at the beginning of each play, outside house, as fixed chorus pattern—representing prying, commenting, curious town as an ever-present background for the drama of the Mannon family. Develop South Sea Island motive—its appeal for them all (in various aspects)—release, peace, security, beauty, freedom of conscience, sinlessness, etc.—longing for the primitive—and mother symbol—yearning for prenatal non-competitive freedom from fear—make the Island theme recurrent motive—

If his attention first went to structure, it then went chiefly to characterization. In his leading character especially he wanted only expressions of an inner life and no facile tricks of technique. In the choruslike figures of the townspeople, however, the time limitations of the play compelled O'Neill to settle upon quick characterization by exterior traits. The need for a visual symbol of the incestuous nature of the Mannon family deeply concerned him for its critical influence upon the characters' lives. The same note continues:

> Characterization—Exclude as far as possible and consistent with living people, the easy superficial characterization of individual manner- isms—unless these mannerisms are inevitable fingerprints of inner nature—essential revelations. This applies to main people of trilogy. Townsfolk, on the other hand, should be confined to exterior character- ization—man characters to interior—Peter and Hazel should be almost characterless, judged from either of these angles—they are the un- troubled, contented, "good," a sweet, constant unself-conscious, un- tempted virtue amid which evil passion works, unrecognized by them—(until end)—but emphasized by their contrast. Resemblance of characters by use of masks intensify Mannon family resemblance be- tween Ezra and Orin and Adam (and family portraits), and between Christine and Lavinia—peculiar gold-brown hair exactly alike in Lavinia and her mother—same as hair of the dead woman, Adam's mother, whom Ezra's father and uncle had loved—who started the recurrent motive—strange, hidden psychic identity of Christine with the dead woman and of Lavinia (in spite of her father—Mannon imitative mannerisms) with her mother—and of Adam with the Mannons he hates, as well as of Orin with his father.

O'Neill then noted the place of music in his script, again one with a quintessential meaning though a quite natural form:

> The chanty "Shenandoah"—use this more—as a sort of theme song —its simple sad rhythm of hopeless sea longing peculiarly signifi- cant—even the stupid words have striking meaning when considered in relation to tragic events in play.

O'Neill also reminded himself in this same entry to remove the melodrama of the first draft by sticking to his intended total effect —"a modern psychological play—fate springing from family . . ."

> In my scrawny first draft bare melodrama of plot runs away with my intent—this must be corrected in second draft—the unavoidable entire melodramatic action must be felt as working out of psychic fate from past—thereby attain tragic significance—or else!—a hell of a problem, a modern tragic interpretation of a classic fate without benefit of gods —for it must, before everything, remain modern psychological play— fate springing out of the family—

O'Neill finished his second draft three and a half months later. Ex- hausted, in low spirits, and ready for the dentist, he had worked to

just about the limit of his stamina every day trying to measure up to
the high critical demands he had set for himself in his work-diary
—especially to try "every means to gain added depth and scope"
through asides, soliloquies, and masks:

> Le Plessis, March 31, 1930—Start writing 2nd draft.
> Le Plessis, July 11, 1930—Finished second draft—feel drained out
> —have been working afternoon and night every day without a single
> let-up—never worked so intensively over such a long period as I have on
> this damn trilogy—wish now I'd never attempted the damn thing—bit-
> ten off more than I can chew?—too close to it to see anything but blur of
> words, discouraged reaction natural now—after all do know I was
> deeply moved by each play as I wrote it—this test has always proved
> valid heretofore—to lay it aside now—we are off to Paris tomorrow
> —nice little vacation in dentist's chair scheduled—best anodyne for
> pernicious brooding over one's inadequacies—

A week later with his spirit refreshed, his perspective clear, and his
teeth fixed, O'Neill read over his second draft with some elation but
some severe self-judgment condemning the asides:

> Le Plessis, July 18, 1930—Read the trilogy—much better than I
> feared—but needs a lot more work before it will be anything like
> right—chief thing, thought asides now seem entirely unnecessary—don't
> reveal anything about the characters I can't bring out quite naturally in
> their talk or their soliloquies when alone . . .

The very next day O'Neill again read over the second draft. In self-
criticism, he now not only disliked the asides but also the pattern of
his soliloquies and his use of half-masks. It seems as if he reluctantly
confirmed the fears he must have felt the day before:

> Le Plessis, July 19, 1930—Read trilogy again—don't like the soliloquies
> in their present disjointed, thought-prose formula—and my use of half-
> masks in the main protagonists seems to obscure meaning of resem-
> blance between characters instead of dramatically intensifying this mean-
> ing. . . . Rewrite all soliloquies in plays along this line—introduce new
> ones so that soliloquies will recur in a fixed pattern throughout, fitting
> into structural pattern repeated in each play—try for prose with simple,
> forceful, repeating accent and rhythm which will express driving, in-
> sistent, compulsion of passions engendered in family past, which consti-
> tutes family fate.

Affirming his comment, "Writing is my vacation from living so I
don't need a vacation," O'Neill went right on from his disappointing

second draft into his third draft. In his work-diary he noted exactly what he wanted to do and how. He plainly did not dash wildly into writing in some kind of creative panic and without design:

> Le Plessis, July 20, 1930—Start rewriting, cutting out all asides, stylizing soliloquies as per new conception—think I have hit on right rhythm of prose—monotonous, simple words, driving insistence—tom-tom from "Jones" in thought-repetition.

Driven by a creative zeal, O'Neill finished his third draft in less than two months and again passed critical judgment on his own work:

> Le Plessis, Sept. 16, 1930—Finished rewriting—lay aside for awhile —one thing I am certain of now, omitting asides has helped enormously.

Following his usual habit, O'Neill set his third draft aside, reread it with a fresh eye, and wrote a candid self-criticism. He felt he had failed in his main object in the third draft—to save the soliloquies by modifying them in prose:

> Paris, Sept. 20, 1930—Read and carefully re-read this last stylized soliloquies version—absolutely convinced they won't do—feel as I felt about asides in version before this—that they held up plays, break rhythm, clog flow of dramatic development, reveal nothing of characters' motives, secret desires or dreams that can't be shown directly or clearly suggested in their pantomime or talk—some of these soliloquies are gratifying as pieces of writing in themselves (most of them are not), but even they don't belong—have no inherent place in structure—they must come out.

Although O'Neill's creative drive must have felt deterred, delayed, and even depressed in the bog of the failure of the asides, the masks, and the soliloquies, he apparently found his way out. He hit upon a refined modification of each of these devices, and he would likely never have hit upon the refinement without the crude failure to suggest it:

> Paris, September 21, 1930—Scheme for revision and final version—in spite of labor on this stylized conception am glad I did it—time not wasted—learned a lot—stylized solil. uncovered new insights into characters and recurrent themes—job now is to get all this in naturally straight dialogue—as simple and direct and dynamic as possible—with as few words—stop doing things to these characters—let them reveal themselves.

> Keep mask conception but as Mannon *background* not foreground
> —what I want from this mask conception is a dramatic, arresting,
> visual symbol of the separateness, the fated isolation of this family, the
> mark of their fate which makes them dramatically distinct from the rest
> of the world—I see now how to retain this effect without the use of built
> masks—by make-up—in *repose* (that is, *background*) the Mannon faces
> are like life-like death-masks (death-in-life motive, return to death-birth
> peace yearning that runs through plays)—this can be gotten *very* effec-
> tively by make-up as can also the family resemblance. (Make-up isn't a
> lost art in the European theatre, why should it be in ours?—only our
> shiftless inefficiency)—I can visualize the death-mask-like expression of
> characters' faces in repose suddenly being torn open by passion as ex-
> traordinarily effective.

Within another two months O'Neill had written his fourth draft,
appraised it, felt well on his way, but still was ready to experiment. A
good measure of success had spurred him on to his goal:

> Le Plessis, St. Antoine du Rochers, Nov. 19, 1930—Read last ver-
> sion—fairly well satisfied—got right line to it at least—and quality I
> want—but needs considerable work yet—several new ideas I want to try
> out—may bring added value—not sure—only way try and see—start on
> this at once.

O'Neill completed his fifth draft three months later and found he had
gone all the way around Robin Hood's barn, so to speak, for he was
obviously trying to say too much:

> Le Plessis, Feb. 7, 1931—Read over—don't like most of new stuff—all
> right but introduces too many added complications—trying to get added
> values has blurred those I had—too much of muchness—would need
> another play added to do it right—and would be wrong even then!
> —can't crowd intuitions, all hidden aspects of life forms into one
> work!

O'Neill's revision of his fifth draft could not have been very extensive
because he finished it in about two weeks:

> Le Plessis, Feb. 20, 1931—Revision finished—off to Canary Islands now
> for sun and sea vacation.

O'Neill had been working from the beginning of his revision of his
first draft on March 27, 1930, to the completion of the 6th draft of his
trilogy on February 30, 1931, with apparently no let up except for a
few days between successive drafts. Even on his vacation in the Ca-

nary Islands with his wife, he took his trilogy along, evidently in typed script. He wrote a self-appraising note as usual, this time highly encouraging though suggesting improvements chiefly through cutting, condensing, and strengthening passages.

> Las Palmas, Canary Islands, March 8, 1931—Read typed script—looks damned good to me—funny how typed pages bring out clearly values that too-long familiarity with long-hand had rendered vague and un-dynamic. But plenty of work to do, no vacation here—script much too long, of course, needs condensing and cutting throughout—must rewrite end of "The Hunted"—weak now—Christine's talk to Lavinia toward end bad stuff—first scene of Act I "The Haunted" also needs rewriting and pointing up—flabby and faltering as now written—end of scenes one and two "The Hunted" need work.

O'Neill's last revision before submitting the play to the Theatre Guild took him about one month, and he must have thought highly of it, to submit it finally for production:

> Paris, Apr. 9, 1931—All work finished—script off to Guild.

It appears that O'Neill deliberately chose not to read his trilogy again until four months or so later when the proofs came through and he was fresh enough to judge reasonably whether or not he had achieved his intent to the best of his ability:

> Northampton, Long Island, August 1931—Read over galley proofs after nearly four months of not looking at this trilogy, get fairly fresh impact—moved by it—has power and drive, and the strange quality of the unreal quality I wanted—main purpose seems to me soundly achieved—there is a feeling of fate in it or I am a fool—a psychological modern approximation of the fate in the Greek tragedies on this theme—attained without the benefit of the supernatural.
>
> Northport, September 1931—work on second galleys—several points strike me—work I did at Canary Islands was of great value in most of results—but feel now a few things eliminated there should be restored—Lavinia's last appeal to Peter near very end—some things in Act II which helped to clear it up—this Act II of "The Haunted" is weak spot still—needs rearranging—but will postpone final decision on this until I hear cast read plays—then it will hit my ear.

At this stage, O'Neill submitted his script to Brooks Atkinson for a reaction; Atkinson thought the audience would be "overwhelmed by the first play, disappointed by the second, and the third would be better than the second." [102] O'Neill must have kept Atkinson's comment in mind during rehearsal and revised accordingly, for Atkinson hailed *Mourning Becomes Electra* at its premiere as "a masterpiece."

Mourning Becomes Electra went into rehearsal on the second week of September, 1931, and required seven weeks to mount. In the course of rehearsal, O'Neill drastically changed his mind about how the play could be most effectively produced. He had suggested that the Guild take three successive nights to do the trilogy. From seeing the play in rehearsal, however, the Guild decided that "the unity and suspensive action of *Mourning Becomes Electra* would be aided if the plays were presented in a single day." [103] O'Neill must have cut his trilogy to less than half its original length. He attended rehearsals almost every day. He sat in the front row of the theatre with Carlotta, made notes, and answered questions. "He listens to the director's ideas," Theresa Helburn of the Guild's Board reported in reference to cutting, "but he takes the script home and brings it back the next day cut or not cut —as the case may be." [104] "You see, Mr. O'Neill kept changing and changing the lines at every rehearsal," said Alice Brady of her fears about playing Lavinia opening-night. "He even made some minor changes on the day of the opening performance. So that every time I'd think of a line, I'd wonder with horror whether that was the line which had been cut or changed in the script." [105]

The trilogy opened at the Guild Theatre on October 27, 1931. Performances began at 5 P.M., allowed for a quarter hour intermission between *The Homecoming* and *The Hunted* and another quarter-hour between *The Hunted* and *The Haunted*. The trilogy ended at mid-night. Almost unanimous critical reaction called the play "a masterpiece." [106] The Pulitzer Prize for 1931, however, went to the Kaufman-Ryskind-Gershwin musical comedy, *Of Thee I Sing. Mourning Becomes Electra* had a Broadway run of 150 performances, and the book version became a best seller. Counting O'Neill's many changes in the script during rehearsal as amounting to a single major revision, O'Neill had in all written a minimum of eight drafts to realize fully his intent in *Mourning Becomes Electra*.

Under the spell of creative excitement, O'Neill could work at writing and rewriting for long periods like a man possessed by demons who would give him no peace until he finally released them through his best efforts in writing.

My grateful acknowledgement is extended to the following sources of quotations:
AMERICAN magazine, November 1922, "The Extraordinary Story of Eugene O'Neill" by Mary B. Mullett
AMERICAN SPECTATOR, November 1932, "Memoranda on Masks" by Eugene O'Neill
BOSTON EVENING POSTSCRIPT, October 31, 1925, "A Letter to George Jean Nathan" from Eugene O'Neill, written June 20, 1920, reprinted in THE THEATRE OF GEORGE JEAN NATHAN by Isaac Golberg, Simon and Schuster, 1926
CENTURY magazine, January 1922, "The Real Eugene O'Neill" by Oliver Sayler
COMMONWEAL magazine, January 14, 1966, "The Vulgarity of O'Neill" by Thomas F. Curley. Reprinted by permission.
EUGENE O'NEILL AND HIS PLAYS, a Survey of His Life and Works, edited by O. Cargill, N. B. Fagin, W. J. Fisher, New York University Press and Peter Owens Ltd., 1961
EUGENE O'NEILL, THE CURSE OF THE MISBEGOTTEN by Croswell Bowen. (C) 1959. Reprinted by permission of McGraw-Hill Book Co., Inc.
EUGENE O'NEILL: THE MAN AND HIS PLAYS by Barrett H. Clark. (C) 1926, 1929, 1947. Dover Publications, Inc.
GEORGE PIERCE BAKER AND THE AMERICAN THEATRE by Wisner Payne Inne, Harvard University Press, 1954
NEW YORK HERALD TRIBUNE:
"Bound East for Cardiff" by Heywood Broun, January 30, 1917
"Damn the Optimists" by Eugene O'Neill, February 13, 1921
"O'Neill Talks about His Plays," March 16, 1924
"O'Neill's Own Story of 'Electra' in the Making," November 8, 1931
Reprinted by permission of the New York Herald Tribune Company, Inc.
NEW YORK TIMES:
"A Letter from O'Neill on BEYOND THE HORIZON," April 11, 1920
"O'Neill Defends His Play of Negro Life," by Louis Kantor, May 11, 1924
"The Playwright Explains" by Eugene O'Neill, February 14, 1926
"Nathan in Court Tilt Aids O'Neill Defense," March 17, 1931

"Mourning Becomes Electra" by Brooks Atkinson, October 27, 1931
"Prof. George P. Baker" by Eugene O'Neill, January 13, 1935
"En—Nobeling O'Neill" by Brooks Atkinson, November 22, 1936
"A Talk with Mrs. O'Neill" by Seymour Peck, November 4, 1956
(C) 1920, 1924, 1926, 1931, 1935, 1936, 1956 by The New York Times Company. Reprinted by permission.
NEW YORK WORLD: November 9, 1924, article on the origin of EMPEROR JONES by Eugene O'Neill; February 21, 1926, "I Knew Him When" by John V. A. Weaver
NEW YORKER magazine, March 13, 1948, "Profile: The Tragic Sense, III" by Hamilton Basso. Reprinted by permission.
NINE PLAYS OF EUGENE O'NEILL. Copyright 1932. Reprinted by permission of Random House, Inc., and Jonathan Cape Ltd.
O'NEILL by Arthur and Barbara Gelb. (C) 1962. Reprinted by permission of Harper & Row Publishers, Inc., and Jonathan Cape Ltd.
O'NEILL, A Critical Study by Sophus Keith Winther. Copyright 1934. Reprinted by permission of Random House, Inc.
PART OF A LONG STORY by Agnes Boulton. Copyright (c) 1958 by Agnes Boulton Kaufman. Reprinted by permission of Doubleday & Company, Inc., and Peter Davies Ltd.
THE ROAD TO THE TEMPLE by Susan Glaspell. Copyright 1927. Reprinted by permission of Curtis Brown Ltd.
SATURDAY REVIEW OF LITERATURE, May 28, 1932, "A Letter from Eugene O'Neill;" November 21, 1936, "O'Neill an Impression" by Theresa Helburn. Reprinted by permission of SATURDAY REVIEW.
THE THEATRE OF GEORGE JEAN NATHAN by Isaac Goldberg. Copyright 1926. Reprinted by permission of Simon and Schuster.
U. S. District Court, Southern District of New York City, Georges Lewys complainant against Eugene O'Neill, Boni and Liveright Inc., Horace Liveright Inc., and The Theatre Guild Inc. Defendant's Deposition to Paris Commission, Answers to Interrogatories, August 12, 1930. And Closing Speeches and Court's Opinion. Opinion of Judge John M. Woolsey.
VARIETY, March 16, 1966, "Atkinson, Miller, Quintero TVcast on Eugene O'Neill" by Guy Livingston. Reprinted by permission.

1. Eugene O'Neill, "Professor George P. Baker," *New York Times* (January 13, 1935), Sect. 9, X
2. Theresa Helburn, "O'Neill, an Impression," *Saturday Review of Literature* (May 28, 1932), 758
3. Arthur and Barbara Gelb, *O'Neill* (New York 1962), 474–5
4. Hamilton Basso, "Profile: The Tragic Sense, III," *New Yorker* (March 13, 1948), 37–8
5. Croswell Bowen, "The Black Irishman," *PM* (November 3, 1946) reprinted in Cargill, Fagin, Fisher, editors, *Eugene O'Neill and His Plays* (New York 1961), 65
6. *New Yorker* (March 13, 1948), 47
7. Gelb, 64
8. Ibid., 177–8, 50
9. Ibid., 72–3
10. Cargill, 64–5; Gelb, 55, 72
11. Cargill, 64
12. Gelb, 112
13. Ibid., 121
14. Croswell Bowen, *Eugene O'Neill, Curse of the Misbegotten* (New York 1959), 42; Agnes Boulton, *Part of a Long Story* (New York 1958), 202
15. Gelb, 187–8; Cargill, 61
16. *Curse of the Misbegotten,* 45
17. Mary B. Mullet, "The Extraordinary Story of Eugene O'Neill," *American Magazine* (November 1922), 116
18. *New Yorker* (March 13, 1948), 37–8
19. J. F. O'Neill, "What a Sanitorium Did for Eugene O'Neill," *Journal of Outdoor Life* (June 1923), 192; Gelb, 231
20. Ibid.
21. Cargill, 71; Gelb, 250
22. *Curse of the Misbegotten,* 74–5
23. Susan Glaspell, *The Road to the Temple* (New York 1927), 254
24. George Cram Cook, *Greek Coins* (Doubleday & Co., New York 1925), reprinted in Cargill, 34

25. Glaspell, 251

26. Boulton, 21

27. Gelb, 582

28. Ibid., 655

29. Ibid., 623

30. Ibid., 938

31. Ibid., 849; Boulton, 224

32. Ibid., 868

33. Ibid., 78, 114, 123, 202, 293; Boulton, 20, 61, 99, 157–8; Bowen, *Curse of the Misbegotten,* 89

34. Gelb, 852

35. Cargill, 82

36. Gelb, 943

37. Wisner Payne Inne, *George Pierce Baker and the American Theatre* (Cambridge 1954), 193

38. Isaac Goldberg, *The Theatre of George Jean Nathan* (New York 1926), 161

39. Barrett Clark, *Eugene O'Neill, the Man and His Plays* (New York 1947), 56, 57

40. Gelb, 780

41. Ibid., 591

42. "Nathan in Court Tilt Aids O'Neill Defense," *New York Times* (March 17, 1931); *New York World* (February 21, 1926), reprinted in Cargill, 29

43. Clark (New York 1929), 146

44. Oliver Sayler, "Interview with O'Neill," *Century Magazine* (January 1922), 358

45. *New Yorker* (March 13, 1948), 40

46. "Eugene O'Neill Defends His Play of Negro Life," *New York Times* (May 11, 1924), Sect. 9, X5; Eugene O'Neill, "Damn the Optimists," *New York Herald Tribune* (February 13, 1921), reprinted in Cargill, 104

47. Clark (New York 1929), 99

48. George Jean Nathan, *The Intimate Notebooks of George Jean Nathan* (New York 1931, 1932), reprinted in Cargill, 115

49. "O'Neill Talks about His Plays," *New York Herald Tribune* (November 16, 1924), reprinted in Cargill, 110

50. Malcolm Cowley, "A Week-end with Eugene O'Neill," *The Reporter* (September 5, 1957), reprinted in Cargill, 46

51. Helen Deutsche and Stella Hanau, *The Provincetown* (New York 1959), reprinted in Cargill, 113; *New York Times* (March 17, 1931), 26

52. *American Magazine* (November 1922), 34

53. *New Yorker* (March 13, 1948), 44; Cargill, 111–112; Gelb, 559

54. Gelb, 556

55. Ibid., 734

56. Boulton, 315–316; Gelb, 333, 795

57. Clark (New York 1927), 29; Cargill, 58

58. Gelb, 235; Boulton, 101, 112

59. *American Magazine* (November 1922), 118

60. *Defendant's Deposition to Paris Commission, Answers to Interrogatories,* 4–5

61. Gelb, 873

62. Clark (New York 1947), 71–72

63. Gelb, 203

64. Mary Heaton Vorse, *Time and the Town* (Dial, New York 1942), 122

65. *American Magazine* (November 1922), 114

66. Ibid., 118

67. *New Yorker* (March 13, 1948), 36

68. Boulton, 200

69. Gelb, 841; Seymour Peck, "A Talk with Mrs. O'Neill," *New York Times* (November 3, 1956), reprinted in Cargill, 92–93

70. *American Magazine* (November 1922), 118

71. *Deposition to Paris Commission,* 4

72. Ibid.

73. Lewys vs O'Neill, *Closing Speeches and Court's Opinion,* 54

74. *Deposition to Paris Commission,* 4

75. Ibid., 6

76. "Eugene O'Neill, The Mask and the Face," *New York Times* (January 7, 1934), Sect. 10, 2X

77. Eugene O'Neill, "The Playwright Explains," *New York Times* (February 14, 1926), Sect. 8, 2X; *Theatre Guild Magazine,* vol. 6, 23

78. Eugene O'Neill, "O'Neill's Own Story of 'Electra' in the Making," *New York Herald Tribune* (November 8, 1931), VII, 2; for further notes in a few instances from the work-diary, see Sophus Keith Winther's *O'Neill, a Critical Study* (New York 1931) and also editor Horst Frenz's *American Playwrights on Drama* (New York 1965)

79. Brooks Atkinson, "En-Nobeling O'Neill," *New York Times* (November 22, 1936), Sect. 11, X

80. Guy Livingston, "Atkinson, Miller, O'Neill Quintero TVcast on Eugene O'Neill," *Variety* (March 16, 1966), 71

81. *American Magazine* (November 1922), 118

82. J. H. Smith and E. W. Parks, editors, *The Great Critics,* an anthology (Norton, New York 1932), 11

83. Thomas F. Curley, "The Vulgarity of O'Neill," *Commonweal* (January 14, 1966), 443

84. Smith and Parks, 16

85. *Commonweal* (January 14, 1966), 443

86. *American Magazine* (November 1922), 118

87. Goldberg, 157

88. Ibid.

89. Gelb, 792

90. Clark (New York 1947), 117
91. Gelb, 698
92. Eugene O'Neill, *Nine Plays by Eugene O'Neill* (New York 1932), 29
93. Ibid., 388
94. Clark (New York 1947), 111
95. *Nine Plays by Eugene O'Neill,* 480
96. Gelb, 677–678
97. Goldberg, 158
98. Gelb, 756
99. Gelb, 723
100. *New York Herald Tribune* (November 8, 1931), Sect. VII, 2
101. Gelb, 723
102. Ibid., 743
103. Ibid., 747
104. *Saturday Review of Literature* (November 21, 1936), 10
105. Gelb, 751
106. Ibid., 751–752, 756

Chapter VIII

Tennessee Williams

In the September 3, 1955, issue of *Saturday Review,* Tennessee Williams replied to a questionnaire sent out by Henry Hewes surveying playwrights' working methods:

> I feel that the loneliness and privacy of any kind of creative writing, even writing for such a public thing as the stage, must be defended with Quixotic ardor. You may interpret this as my own tiny squeal of protest against all efforts to interrogate, to pigeonhole, to classify and document a thing that depends on seclusion till its completion for its safety.[1]

Williams' ardor for secrecy toward creativeness has proven somewhat Quixotic as he, himself, intimated it would, for in one way or another, Williams and others have since revealed a great deal about his working methods—piece-meal.

"Tom had fanatical and inexhaustible energy in his writing," a friend, Clark McBurney, recalled of Williams' years of apprenticeship. "He may have written 100 unsuccessful plays." [2] After the disastrous failure in 1940 of his *Battle of Angels,* he kept writing while fearing "the culminating disaster" his notebooks hinted at—heart failure or madness.[3] And then on March 31, 1945, following in his words "the very, very rough years I barely got through," Williams at the age of thirty-four scored his first Broadway hit, *The Glass Menagerie.* He learned to write plays the hard way—though perhaps there is no other way.

To date, Williams' plays have won four Drama Critics' Circle Awards, a record for any living playwright. Drama critics still differ violently as to the present and lasting merits of this most prolific and financially successful of all current American playwrights. *Time* magazine on December 1, 1961, typical of one body of opinion declared, "In his most famous plays, he has hallucinated a vast but specious pageant of depravity in which fantasies of incest, cannibalism, murder, rape, sodomy and drug addiction constitute the canon of reality." [4] In the March 9, 1962, issue, *Time* ironically recanted in this statement typical of the opposite body of critical opinion: "The fact is that Tennessee Williams . . . is a consummate master of theatre. His plays beat with the heart's blood of the drama: passion. He is the greatest U. S. playwright since Eugene O'Neill . . ." [5]

The Library of Congress had asked Williams that it be made the permanent repository of all his literary records. According to Audrey Wood, Williams' literary agent, "the University of Texas in Austin now has all of Tennessee Williams' manuscripts and the papers and letters pertaining to them." Athens can be where you make it as Athenians themselves found out.

I

THE GROWTH OF WILLIAMS' CREATIVE SPIRIT IN LIFE

"My conversion to the theatre," confessed Williams in his preface to *Battle of Angels,* "arrived as mysteriously as those impulses that enter the flesh at puberty." [6] In 1935 while recovering from an illness at his grandparents' home in Memphis, Tennessee, Williams collaborated with a young lady, Dorothy Shapiro, to write a play about two sailors on shore leave who pick up a couple of girls. The Garden Players of The Rose Arbor Theatre in Memphis presented the comedy, *Cairo! Shanghai! Bombay!,* and Williams recollected, "That was when I first realized that this was a medium that was most attractive. I discovered the thrill of people reacting to my work right in front of my eyes." [7] The next April in St. Louis at his mother's urging, Williams wrote a short play to enter the local Webster Groves' Theatre Guild Playwriting Contest, and he won first prize—an engraved, silver cake-dish. The Guild Players also successfully produced Williams' prize-winning play, *The Magic Tower,* portraying an artist and his wife who are happy in their "magic tower," a garret flat, until the artist loses faith in his star. Williams said, "I wrote plays, which I started to do because, being a lonely person, I could in this way provide myself with company." [8] Williams was then twenty-five years old.

He showed early signs of a literary hankering. He loved stories and was good at making them up to amuse his playmates. Of the movies, he said, "When I was little, I used to want to climb into the screen and join the action. My mother had to hold me down." [9] One day his mother asked him why he was digging a deep hole in the backyard, and the little child answered, "I'm diggin' to de debbil,"[10]—a preoccupation some think Williams has never given up. When he was 11, his mother bought him a second-hand typewriter for ten dollars. He learned to type hunt-and-peck fashion. "I began writing poems and short stories when I was 12. It came quite naturally to me,' said Williams, "because I led such an intense inner life."[11]

Tennessee Williams, christened Thomas Lanier Williams, was born in a doctor's private hospital in the little town of Columbus, Mississippi, on Palm Sunday morning, March 26, 1911. His date of birth is often given as March 26, 1914, because Williams himself gave this date, fibbing to qualify to enter The Group Theatre Playwriting Contest which was open only to those 25 or under. His mother was Edwina Dakin Williams, and his father, Cornelius Coffin Williams. A sister, Rose, had been born two years before "Tom."

On the mother's side, the Dakins numbered doctors, lawyers, and a preacher, all tracing their blood-line to German Quakers who had spent the American Revolution in Canada as Tories. On the father's side, the blood-line flowed from American frontiersmen and Indian fighters of East Tennessee, a great grandfather who was right hand man to Andrew Jackson, and a grandfather who repeatedly ran for Governor of Tennessee and never won. Williams has described his father's family as "violent and aggressive," but it had a poet, Sidney Lanier, who was hailed as the true voice of the post-bellum Southern aristocracy for his sad, chivalric lyrics—the postlude, no doubt, of violence and aggression.[12] At the time of Tom's birth, his father was a traveling salesman with a clothing line. His mother was a housewife, reared to be articulate, lovely, decorative and useless in the Southern tradition of a lady; menial work was for colored domestics. Williams said, "I think my father was crazy about my mother, but she did not reciprocate to the same degree, I think. My mother is a Puritan. I'm a Puritan, too, but I'm a rebellious Puritan."[13]

Until Williams was eight years old, his family lived with his mother's parents, the Episcopal Reverend Walter Dakin and his wife, in an atmosphere of Southern Puritanism which Williams recalled as even "more fractious" and "old-fashioned" than the severe New England brand. The Reverend Dakin heeded his "calls" and took the Williams family with him to Columbus, Mississippi, then to Nashville, Tennessee, then to Canton, Ohio, and then to Clarksdale, Mississippi, all before Williams was eight. This relative homelessness as a child might help explain Williams' fondness for keeping on the move in spells as an adult. Williams' father wanted a manly son in the military tradition of his fighting family; Williams was growing up in a parish milieu his mother called "perfect peace" and "an atmosphere of sweetness and light," playing with his older sister, Rose.[14]

Shocks were in store for Tom. At five, in a peevish moment he called Ozzie, the colored nurse whom he dearly loved, "Nigger!" and she left the Williams home never again to return.[15] To this day, Williams is dead set against discrimination, and the guilt for his childhood misdeed persists. At five, diphtheria hit Tom very hard and left him with complications of Bright's disease, a palpitating heart, and paralysis of the legs for about two years. For comfort and company, Tom turned more and more to the world of books where even with paralyzed legs he could move freely through imagination. "He developed a curious faculty," reported Lincoln Barnett for *Life* magazine of February 16, 1948, "of visualizing scenes with his eyes closed in bed at night." [16]

When Tom was eight, his father got a desk job with the International Shoe Company in St. Louis, and for the first time the Williams family had their very own home. Robert Rice, who, incidentally, is Elmer Rice's son, interviewed Williams for a fine series of articles in the *New York Post* in 1958 and wrote, "He is convinced that life in St. Louis made him the nervous, baffled, lonely man he is—Williams was by then 'delicate and sissified'—his own words." [17] Although he earned a good salary, Williams' father was downright stingy toward his family. Williams said of his father's pay-check, "I guess he drank it and gambled it and had himself a ball." [18] If Dionysian traits can be inherited, Williams certainly got them from his father. In her very candid book, *Remember Me to Tom,* Williams' mother noted of her husband, "My sons have inherited some of his best qualities—honesty, perseverance, integrity." [19]

Cornelius worked very hard and rose to sales manager in the shoe business, no mean accomplishment in time of depression. He also played very hard and made his home the scene of week-end-long poker games with his heavy drinking cronies in the booming, salty, fun-loving spirit of traveling salesmen. "Cornelius was not shocked by *Streetcar,*" declared Mrs. Williams, ". . . for he was a veteran of many a *Poker Night* as the play was originally called." [20] When Mrs. Williams called her husband to account for all these goings on in front of the children, Cornelius took his pleasure to clubs and hotelrooms. Mrs. Williams said of life with her husband, "it was like walk-

ing on eggs every minute of the day and night. The most trivial act
might spin him into a tantrum . . ." [21] Once a month, usually when
the bills fell due, the parents really had things out. "In my ears often
echo the words of fury I heard so many times," Mrs. Williams recalled her husband saying, " 'Take the children and go! Go home.
Just get out!' " Once in a drunken rage her husband even threatened
to kill her, smashing into the bedroom door she had locked to get
away from him.[22]

Tom found more and more in his reading an imaginative world
and a refuge. By the age of nine he had read Dickens, all the Waverly
novels of Scott, and Shakespeare. "I loved Shakespeare . . . I loved
the violence. I was mad about *Titus Andronicus,*" said Williams of
the bard's grisliest play, littered with murders and mutilations.[23] In
1919, Edwina bore Cornelius another son, Dakin. She felt her husband
loved only Dakin and taunted Tom as a weakling, "no good" and
"Miss Nancy." "The love of reading," observed Williams, "gave me a
great love of writing." In 1958 after some "analysis," Williams said,
"My father was a totally honest man. He had a strong character and a
sense of honor. . . . Maybe I hated him once but I certainly don't any
more." [24] Williams believes his fighting blood came from his father.

At school, Williams did well in English but almost failed math. Of
the effect upon his schoolmates of his delicate health and his writing
poems and stories, Williams commented, "I remember gangs of kids
following me home yelling 'Sissy!'—and home was not a very pleasant refuge." [25] Williams' sanctuary from school and home was the
public library. His confidant was his sister, Rose, who had grown into
a shy, delicate, imaginative and beautiful girl. Rose quit Sunday school
because the more prosperous children, once they found she lived in a
shabby neighborhood, "snobbed" her.[26] In St. Louis, what counted
most was not family background but money.

When Tom was twelve, Rose matured into womanhood and tended
to confide in him less. By his senior year in high school, Tom had become attached to a class-mate, Hazel Kramer, whom he later told his
mother was "much the deepest love of my life." At fifteen, Tom won
third prize of $5.00 from *Smart Set* magazine for his essay published
in the May 1927 issue and titled "Can a Good Wife Be a Good
Sport?" The adolescent Williams pretended to be a traveling salesman
who, unexpected by his wife, came home from the road and found
she was a party girl. At sixteen, Tom for $35.00 sold *Weird Tales*
magazine his story *The Vengeance of Nitocris* drawn from a comic

book version of an incident in Herodotus. In Williams' version, Queen Nitocris of Egypt invited her enemies to dinner in a subterranean chamber, excused herself, and then had the subterranean chamber flooded. "I don't have to tell you," suggested Williams, "that it set the key-note for most of the work that has followed." [27]

Williams graduated from high school in January of 1929, and his father immediately broke up his attachment to Hazel Kramer. Williams then entered the University of Missouri as a journalism major, pledged Alpha Tau Omega fraternity largely to please his father, and in his third year both failed R.O.T.C. and so neglected his other studies for writing and fraternity life that in disgust his father withdrew him from the University. Cornelius got his son a job with the International Shoe Company paying $65.00 a month for routine, clerical work. To Williams, "It was a living death." Every morning he dusted thousands of pairs of shoes in the sample room, and every afternoon he entered factory orders by a numeral code. Evenings, after dinner, Williams came to life in the seclusion of his room with cigarettes and a pot of black coffee, writing far into the morning.[28] Two years later a doctor spotted a heart condition in him, and soon after that, upon returning from a movie with Rose, Williams had a possibly psychosomatic seizure that paralyzed his limbs. He recovered at a hospital, quit the job he hated, convalesced at his grandparents' in Memphis, and there in 1935 collaborated with a neighbor, Dorothy Shapiro, to write his first play, *Cairo! Shanghai! Bombay!*

In the fall of 1935 Mrs. Williams, defying her husband, paid for her son's tuition so he might take his degree at Washington University in St. Louis. Willard Holland, the Director of the Mummers, a community theatre group in St. Louis, had heard of Williams' writing and got him to do a curtain-raiser, *Headlines,* for the Mummers' production of Irwin Shaw's *Bury the Dead.* In 1937 and 1938 the Mummers did two of Williams' long plays, *Candles to the Sun* and *The Fugitive Kind.* "He had no sense in those days of plot construction or story line whatsoever," Holland said of Williams, "but his people were really fantastic," and writing "just poured out of him." [29] Williams entered the playwriting contest at Washington University and upon failing to win even an honorable mention, he reminisced in maturity, "I stormed into Carson's office. (He was a good professor.) I screamed at him. I forget what my parting shot was, but I remember it was quite a shot—I surprised myself." [30] Williams then transferred to the University of Iowa to complete his degree and especially to study playwriting with Professor E. C. Mabie. This time, Williams' grandmother underwrote his tuition.

Meanwhile in 1937, Williams' sister Rose was stricken with schizophrenia. In desperation for a possible cure, her parents allowed doctors to perform a lobotomy upon her. Lovely and remote, Rose was left beyond cure; she entered a mental hospital, her lot for life.

At the University of Iowa, Williams earned his meals waiting on table at the cafeteria of the State Hospital. He wrote radio scripts for the University's radio station and a full length play, *Spring Storm,* for Professor Mabie's playwriting seminar. Williams read aloud this outspoken play about adolescent love to his playwriting class for a reaction. A long embarrassed silence followed. Finally Professor Mabie said, "Well, we all have to paint our nudes!"[31] In 1938, Williams took his B.A. at the University of Iowa. He was twenty-seven years old.

Williams now headed for Chicago with the hope of getting on the W.P.A. Writer's Project there; the country was in the doldrums of the great depression of the '30's. "My work lacked 'social content' or 'protest'," reminisced Williams of his failure to get on the Project. "And I couldn't prove my family was destitute."[32] Williams returned to St. Louis long enough to write *Not about Nightingales,* a full length play based on a true story of convicts who, after wildly rioting, were confined for discipline in a hot-room called "The Klondike," and possibly by accident were roasted to death. Williams then headed for New Orleans where he tried again without success to get on the local W.P.A. Writer's Project.

The winter of 1938-39 spent in New Orleans in the French Quarter was for Williams his revelation of a lifetime. He found himself in his phrase "a rebellious Puritan." Williams earned his keep by working in a restaurant selling meals for $.25. Frequenting the French Quarter, he ran across lonely and drifting human flotsam and jetsam—whores, gamblers, merchant seamen, artists, jazz musicians, alcoholic old ladies, homosexuals, hoboes, pimps, junkies—a catalogue of desperate people struggling for survival against the odds of the great depression. "I found the kind of freedom I had always needed," Williams told Robert Rice of the experience of that winter in New Orleans. "And the shock of it against the Puritanism of my nature has given me a subject, a theme, which I have never ceased exploiting."[33]

The year 1939 also convinced Williams that he was really on his way as a professional writer. He submitted all four of his full length plays and *American Blues,* a group of short plays about New Orleans, to The Group Theatre Playwriting Contest. Then in very early spring of 1939, Williams left New Orleans with a friend, a clarinetist, who offered him a free-ride to a squab ranch the clarinetist's aunt owned about six miles from Los Angeles. Once arrived, Williams supported himself by clerking at Clark's Bootery near the new MGM studios and by plucking squab at two cents a bird. On March 29, 1939, he received word from The Group Theatre that he had won a Special Award of $100 for the "first three sketches in *American Blues.*" With a new sense of being, Williams quit shoe-clerking and headed for Laguna Beach to write *Battle of Angels.* He then followed the advice of one of the contest judges, Molly Day Thacher, and picked Audrey Wood to be his literary agent, but only after he first gave Audrey Wood a chance to examine critically a full display of his current wares.

In 1939 as Williams' agent, Audrey Wood sold his story, *The Field of Blue Children,* a recollection of adolescent love, to *Story* magazine. For the first time the author's name appeared not as "Thomas Williams" but "Tennessee Williams." "I changed it to Tennessee Williams, the justification being mainly that the Williamses had fought the Indians for Tennessee," noted Williams in the First Supplement of *Twentieth Century Authors,* "and I had already discovered that the life of a young writer was going to be something similar to the defense of a stockade against a band of savages." [34]

On December 20, 1939, Williams received a Rockefeller Playwriting grant of $1,000. In the spring of 1940, he enrolled in the Advanced Playwriting Seminar at The New School for Social Research with John Gassner and Theresa Helburn of The Theatre Guild conducting the course. Williams' *Battle of Angels* excited Gassner to say, "one of the most promising scripts I have read in years." The Theatre Guild opened the play in Boston on December 20, 1940, and closed it there as a debacle; the battle was over before Broadway. *Battle of Angels* almost left the twenty-nine year old Williams a fatality.

Williams continued writing. Often what thoughts took over his mind? Death, madness, an operation for a cataract on his left eye, the heart condition that made him 4-F to his draft board in World War II, the Guild's rejection of the revised *Battle of Angels,* the desperate struggle to write and yet earn a subsistence by running an elevator or bell-hopping, or waiting table, or ushering at the movies. To buoy his sinking spirits, his one-act plays meanwhile won some recognition.

Moony's Kid Don't Cry appeared in Margaret Mayorga's *Best One-Act Plays of* 1940; *The Lady of Larkspur Lotion* in Mayorga's *Best One-Act Plays of* 1941; *At Liberty* and *This Property Is Condemned,* in Kozlenko's *American Scenes,* 1941.

In May, 1943, while Williams was ushering at New York's Strand Theatre for $18.00 a week, Audrey Wood contracted with MGM to hire Williams as a script writer at $250 a week for six months. He was assigned to a Lana Turner vehicle, *Marriage Is a Private Affair* which he retitled for his own pleasure *The Celluloid Brassiere.* His script was turned down. He then submitted his original script, *The Gentleman Caller,* with a note saying that a movie on this script would run twice as long as *Gone with the Wind.* He received his script rejected with a note saying that *Gone with the Wind* had already been done once. He was then assigned to write for the child star, Margaret O'Brien, but he said child stars made him vomit. MGM by now had had enough of Williams' scripts and his nausea; in a grandiose gesture of contempt, they dismissed him with four months' pay coming. Williams hurried off to Malibu Beach and expanded *The Gentleman Caller* into the play, *The Glass Menagerie.* What MGM had declined to take as its right by contract, it later bid very high for in the market place and lost to Warner Brothers.

Eddie Dowling read and produced *The Glass Menagerie,* which opened to rave notices first in Chicago on December 26, 1944, and then in New York City on March 31, 1945. *The Glass Menagerie* won Williams the Pulitzer Prize, the Drama Critics' Circle Award, and the Award of the American Institute of Arts and Letters, among other awards. Williams had arrived, and the literary world of the theatre gave him its most distinguished fanfares and symbols of distinction.

Success reassured Williams about his talent but never freed him of the heavy burden of family troubles that inadvertently had helped to create or would help to create his plays. He assigned half his rights to *The Glass Menagerie* to his mother, but according to his mother, his father deeply resented this for making her independent of him. Williams took on all financial responsibility for Rose, who was to remain in a mental hospital beyond cure after her lobotomy.

In 1947 *A Streetcar Named Desire* established Williams' fame and fortune on the stages of the world, but that very year his father separated from his mother, refusing to live in the same house with "the old buzzard," her aged and retired father, the Reverend Walter Dakin. Cornelius was to die alone at Memphis after a spree in his hotel room in 1957, and Williams' brother Dakin said of the funeral, "Neither Tom nor I shed a tear."[35] Williams, however, confided in his friend, Maxwell, "That is not true. I cried."[36] Cornelius was largely the model for the Delta "drummer," Mr. Charlie Colton, in *The Last of My Solid Gold Watches,* in some aspects the model for Stanley Kowalski in *Streetcar,* and especially the model for Big Daddy in *Cat on a Hot Tin Roof.* The Reverend Walter Dakin died in 1955 at 98, to the end often visiting and traveling with Williams for about six months each year. He was apparently the model for the spent old man in *Night of the Iguana.*

In 1956 while visiting Italy, Williams was almost killed when, after downing a thermos of martinis, he demolished his white Jaguar, crashing into a tree at seventy miles an hour. He miraculously came out with little more than two black eyes. In 1957, after the failure of *Orpheus Descending,* Williams went into "analysis" for a year.

Come success or failure, Williams has always been a prolific writer of short plays, long plays, poems, and short stories. His one-act plays by date of publication are:

Moony's Kid Don't Cry (1939)	*Lord Byron's Love Letter*
The Dark Room	*The Strangest Kind of*
The Case of the Crushed Petunias	*Romance* (1945)
The Long Stay Cut Short or	*The Long Good-Bye*
The Unsatisfactory Supper	*Hello from Bertha*
This Property Is Condemned	*Talk to Me Like the Rain*
(1941)	*Something Unspoken*
The Lady of Larkspur Lotion	*Ten Blocks on the Camino*
The Last of My Solid Gold	*Real* (1948)
Watches (1943)	*I Rise in Flame, Cried the*
Twenty-Seven Wagons Full	*Phoenix* (1951)
of Cotton (1945)	*Suddenly Last Summer* (1959)
The Purification	*The Mutilated* (1966)
Portrait of a Madonna	*Gnadiges Fraulein*
Auto Da Fé	

Williams' professionally produced long plays, by year of their opening on the road, or on Broadway when no road tour preceded are:

Battle of Angels (1940)	*Orpheus Descending* (1957)
The Glass Menagerie (1944)	*Sweet Bird of Youth* (1959)
You Touched Me! (1945)	*Period of Adjustment* (1960)
A Streetcar Named Desire (1947)	*Night of the Iguana* (1962)
Summer and Smoke (1948)	*The Milk Train Doesn't Stop Here*
The Rose Tattoo (1951)	*Any More* (1963) (revised, 1964)
Camino Real (1953)	*The Seven Descents of Myrtle*
Cat on a Hot Tin Roof (1955)	(1968)

Selected poems of Williams appear in: *Five Young American Poets,* 1944; and *In the Winter of Cities,* 1956. His short stories are: *One Arm and Other Stories,* 1948; *Rock Candy and Other Stories,* 1954; and a novelette, *The Roman Spring of Mrs. Stone,* 1950.

Williams is a dedicated writer. "I'm rather selfish in picking my friends anyway," he said, "that is, I prefer people who can help me in some way or another, and most of my friendships are accidental . . . I don't want to be like most people. And I do think there is the problem of personal integrity involved." [37] Over the years, his closest friends have been: Audrey Wood, his agent; Margo Jones, the director and producer; James Laughlin, his publisher; Elia Kazan, the director; Carson McCullers, the novelist-playwright, and William Inge, the playwright; Cheryl Crawford and Irene Selznick, the producers; Diana Barrymore, Tallulah Bankhead, and Laurette Taylor, actresses. Less celebrated but close friends have included: Paul Bigelow, Paul Moor, Donald Windham, Gilbert Maxwell, and Frank Merlo—Williams' secretary and companion for about fourteen years. Quite a few of these friends are now dead. Williams considers himself by nature a very lonely person. He has a number of pets: a parrot; and two bulldogs named "Mr. Moon" and "Baby Doll"—possible echoes of his father's favorite bull-dog, "Jiggs," a symbol of fighting tenacity with humorous overtones.

Only five foot seven inches tall and weighing a plump 150 pounds, Williams has the deceptively bland look of a balding bank clerk or an insurance agent. His face actually bears a striking resemblance to one of the very few authentic likenesses of Shakespeare, the Droeshout engraving which appeared as a frontispiece of *The First Folio* in 1623. As a celebrity, Williams likely for self-protection has grown decidedly ambiguous—very trusting yet suspicious, truly kind yet self-centered, somewhat helpless yet self-reliant, fear-ridden yet courageous, absent-minded yet sharp-eyed, remote yet gregarious, gentle yet wrathful, Bohemian yet Puritanical. In fact, he has the ambiguity of some of his best characters. In his book, *Tennessee Williams and Friends,* Maxwell Gilbert, who has known Williams for about twenty-five years in "our long, roller-coaster relationship," has concluded that "always he is the champion, in any area of human endeavor, of the misfit, abused, downtrodden underdog," and that however ambiguous Williams may be, "it is the good, generous, compassionate, kindly self that is most often in residence. . . ." [38] Of Williams' generosity, Audrey Wood confided in Maxwell, "No, it's not just one or two people, by any means. It's a whole group he's helping, and it goes on all the time." [39]

Still, Maxwell observed, "it is never easy for him to establish a deep, warm contact with anyone . . ."[40] Williams' only permanent home is a cottage in a remote part of Key West, Florida, and a two-room apartment in New York City's West 70's. Very high strung, he relieves his tensions by traveling, swimming, drinking about half a fifth of martinis or bourbon daily and by taking tranquilizers. Using a cigarette holder, he smokes about two packs of cigarettes a day and his left eye is nearly blind, in spite of five operations to save it from cataracts.

Williams regards his reputation in the theatre with healthy doubt. "All reputations in the theatre are inflicted reputations," he said in Ben Gross' column of *The Daily News* of March 3, 1958, ". . . nobody is as good as publicity makes them appear . . ."[41] He himself is most aware of his true nature and his public image which he believes is all done with mirrors—a limited view multiplied on a grand scale by the press and all the other media of communication. The reflection can be the difference between that of the Versailles Hall of Mirrors and that of the Coney Island Fun-House.

II

COMMERCIAL CONSIDERATIONS AFFECTING WILLIAMS' PLAYWRITING

Financially the most successful of current American playwrights, Tennessee Williams has so far had only four solid hits, that is, plays enjoying a Broadway run of from one to two full years: *The Glass Menagerie, A Streetcar Named Desire, Cat on a Hot Tin Roof,* and *Night of the Iguana. The Rose Tattoo* ran for 306 performances but Williams considers it a failure. Williams' other plays, which had less than 100 performances and failed to repay their full investment are: *Battle of Angels, You Touched Me!, Summer and Smoke, Camino Real, Orpheus Descending, Sweet Bird of Youth, The Milk Train Doesn't Stop Here Any More,* and *Slapstick Tragedy*—a bill of *The Mutilated* and *Gnadiges Fraulein.* According to Williams' mother, "he always believed he is headed straight for the poorhouse."[42] Community theatre, summer theatre, foreign theatre, Off-Broadway revivals, Broadway revivals, amateur theatre, and movie production, however, have made many of Williams' Broadway flops profitable enough so that in his best years he has grossed an average of $200,-

ooo. Williams in 1959 said, "I've been paying between 87 and 90 per cent in income taxes."

Williams' reaction to the movie treatment of his plays as told to Joe Hymans in Hollywood on December 23, 1959, suggests how helpless he or any big name is today once the movies have bought the film production rights: *The Glass Menagerie*, "butchered;" *A Streetcar Named Desire*, "a great picture;" *Baby Doll*, his least successful movie based on two short plays, vulgarized by pantomimic sequences he never wrote in; *Cat on a Hot Tin Roof*, "weak dramatization" but, "I've been living off it for a long time;" *The Rose Tattoo*, "bawdy rather than poetic;" *Suddenly Last Summer*, "filled out on the screen," "a fabulous job" of play structure by Gore Vidal and Sam Spiegel; *The Fugitive Kind (Orpheus Descending)*, a big "art picture." [43] "I'm not going to write films any more," Williams insisted after doing the screen version of *The Fugitive Kind*. "One's energy and one's creative life are too short to create anything in one medium and then go back and create it in another." [44]

"I've never written for money," said Williams. "I always write to express myself," he said in discussing his art and morals in *The New York Herald Tribune* of March 3, 1957. "But I want to succeed also as an entertainer." [45] Accused by critics like George Jean Nathan of deliberately writing for a "succèss de scandale," Williams has replied, "I like strong effect and boldness, and perhaps sometimes I go overboard, but I never do it for commercial reasons. I do it only to make a point more strongly." [46] Strindberg and O'Neill did the same. Williams' plays have involved so far incest, insanity, adultery, rape, homosexuality, suicide, Lesbianism, cannibalism, castration, cancer, and lobotomy, among other subjects. *The Old Testament*, Homer, Greek tragedy, and Shakespeare have similar and often identical subject matter. George Jean Nathan still rated Williams as "a kind of D. H. Lawrence in diapers" and "rather a dramatic opportunist plainly out for the big money." [47] One has only to read Williams' earliest short plays in *American Blues* and *Twenty-Seven Wagons Full of Cotton And Other One-Act Plays* to realize that in the years when Williams was nearly starving as a playwright, he was fascinated almost exclusively by the very same subject matter and thematic material that eventually won him fame and fortune.

Once he signed with her in 1939, Audrey Wood became his commercial and artistic foster-mother, helping him gain grants, work, awards, and recognition. "He was wonderful, he'd do anything," she said of Williams.[48] "This man understood we must get through a certain period. I never in my life had such a hunch on anybody." [49] That period took six years of nurturing before Williams came of age with *The Glass Menagerie*. Probably at Audrey Woods' suggestion, Williams took care to use only one set with very few characters —only four in fact—to help sell his play by minimizing the financial risks of production. Incidentally, whether he has succeeded or failed with his plays since his association with Audrey Wood, he has written only of life he has known. In *American Blues*, he knew the people he wrote of. He has admitted that he did not know nor had he ever even met the characters of his earlier efforts like: the sailors of *Cairo! Shanghai! Bombay!*; the munitions makers of *Me, Vashtya*; the coal-miners of *Candles to the Sun*; or the convicts of *Not about Nightingales*.

Williams had abiding faith in Audrey Wood. From the start he gave her power of attorney over his financial affairs and, after nearly twenty-five years with her, he said in *Esquire* magazine of December 1962, "Audrey can call the shots better than any producer on or off Broadway." [50] In his eyes, she always works for "the best possible realization of a work." [51] So, for instance, she kept *The Glass Menagerie* in her office for three weeks before she finally decided that the producer to give the play its best chance for success was Eddie Dowling, who had earlier succeeded with Saroyans' *The Time of Your Life*. Today, according to Williams, Audrey Wood is the most successful and powerful agent in playwriting in New York. Upon submitting a new play to her, he thinks if it is good, as with *Cat on a Hot Tin Roof*, he hears from her very shortly and enthusiastically. Otherwise he has to wait two or three weeks.

Even Audrey Wood, however, did not fully foresee the reaction of Boston to *Battle of Angels*. Williams said, "The thing is, you can't mix up sex and religion as I did in *Battle of Angels*, but you can always write safely about mothers . . ." [52] Hollywood, of course, almost always mixes up sex and religion but never as Williams had done —having a small-town sheriff's wife paint a portrait of Christ with the facial features of her secret passion and that of the local ladies—an itinerant shoe-clerk. Williams' troubles in production, it so happened, were compounded in Boston at the play's opening on December 20, 1940, when the blasphemed audience was driven choking into the wintry streets by an over-stoked smoke-effects machine gone beserk at the *Battle's* immolating moment. Said Williams, "I never heard of an audience getting so infuriated." [53]

For maximum insurance against a Broadway failure, Williams has repeatedly used try-out productions at the community theatre level, and then revised accordingly. "I try to maintain two covenants with an audience: not to deceive and not to bore," Williams told John Cruesemann of *The London Express* in 1959. "I think now I do not bore so much as annoy and that at least has the merit of a positive reaction."[54] Some of Williams' try-out productions have been: *You Touched Me!* at the Cleveland Playhouse, 1943; *Stairs to the Roof,* the Pasadena Playhouse, 1945 and again in 1947—a long play that was never to reach Broadway; *Summer and Smoke,* the Dallas Theatre, 1946; *Sweet Bird of Youth,* the Studio M Playhouse, Coral Gables, Florida, 1956; *Night of the Iguana,* Festival of Two Worlds in Spoleto, Italy, 1959; *Night of the Iguana* and *Period of Adjustment,* the Coconut Grove Playhouse, Florida, 1960; and *The Milk Train Doesn't Stop Here Any More,* the Festival of Two Worlds at Spoleto, Italy, 1962.

Williams said in the program note of the Studio M Playhouse's try-out production of *Sweet Bird of Youth:*

> All the while this work has been in rehearsal it has been also undergoing continual changes in dialogue and structure, even in basic theme and interpretation of character. . . . By grace of unusual circumstance at least a year's work has been condensed into the space of a few weeks. . . . It has been of enormous value to me. I hope it is a precedent, not just one adventure. At the same time, you may feel a sense of collaboration with us in the first making of something which is still being made.

Williams obviously rewrote not only on the basis of rehearsal but emphatically on the basis of the audience's reaction to the try-out performance.

After a series of rather staggering financial failures on Broadway, Williams in 1958 allowed at a much reduced financial risk the Off-Broadway production at the 299-seat York Theatre of two short plays billed as *Garden District: Something Unspoken* and *Suddenly Last Summer.* The venture was small but very successful. "On Broadway someone's always shouting at you, 'For God's sake, cut here, cut there, make it shorter. Don't you know that if the play goes beyond a certain minute we'll have to pay the stage-hands double?'"[55] Williams has since chosen to return to the risks of Broadway, explaining, "it's much easier to get the best director and the finest stars . . . in a Broadway production."[56] But on or Off-Broadway, the commercial effect of the critical notices led Williams to sound off: "This hatred of notices has got worse . . ." "This business of having to aim at bringing in a Broadway blockbuster every time you do a play," he fumed, "is exhausting, demoralizing, vitiating, and corrupting." [57] In 1959 he noted of his reaction to drama critics, "That awful having to wait for the verdict which in New York can be absolutely decisive, humiliates me to a degree that enrages me." [58]

In musing over the motives of the prehistoric artist who did the superb drawings of bison on the walls of caves in Southern France, Williams concluded not writing, "nor any form of creative work was ever meant by nature to be a man's way of making a living . . . when it becomes one, it almost certainly loses a measure of purity." [59]

III

AESTHETIC CONSIDERATIONS AFFECTING WILLIAMS' PLAYWRITING

"In my opinion," said Williams, "art is a kind of anarchy, and the theatre is a province of art . . ." [60] He specified that art is benevolent anarchy in providing life with "something which is missing," for instance, a criticism of life. From his experience with the Mummers in St. Louis, Williams recalled, "It was like a definition of what I think theater is. Something wild, something exciting, something that you are not used to. Offbeat is the word." Vacuous pretentiousness has paid off handsomely in painting, for example, "But the theatre, which is called the charlatan of the arts," Williams noted in the preface to *Summer and Smoke*, "is paradoxically the one in which the charlatan is most easily detected. He must say intelligibly what he has to say," remarked Williams of the playwright, "and unless it is well worth saying, he does not have a Chinaman's chance of surviving. Even cheap entertainment is honest." [61] "Great theatre," Williams further observed, "is the highest and purest form of religion and should be fostered and respected because it is concerned with truth." [62]

"It is only in his work that an artist can find reality and satisfaction," Williams told R. C. Lewis for *The New York Times* (November 30, 1947), "for the actual world is less intense than the world of his invention . . ." To the present, in more than thirty-five years of writing, Williams has with very few exceptions not passed a single day without working at least three hours or more. "All artists are eccentric," asserted Williams. "The very fact of needing to be an artist is eccentric. That's why it's so hard for me to conform to the taste of

Pollyannas." [63] Writing, to Williams, is "a very lonesome profession." He, moreover, has since early in his career felt it was in his stars to write. "I have never for one moment doubted," he stated in the preface to *Battle of Angels,* "that there are people—millions!—to say things to. We come to each other gradually with love. . . . With love and with honesty, the embrace is inevitable." [64]

As for his subject matter, Williams said, "If the writing is honest, it cannot be separated from the man who wrote it." A writer's work is his very identity. "It isn't so much his mirror as it is the distillation, the essence of what is strongest and purest in his nature whether that be gentleness or anger, serenity or torment, light or dark." [65] A writer's integrity and his work are one flesh and spirit: "you could flay the skin off a writer whose work is organic," said Williams, "and you still would not get out of him a sincere or workable recantation of his faith in what he is doing, however abominable that work may be, or strike you as being." [66]

Williams is against censorship. "The biologist," he noted, "will tell you that progress is the result of mutations . . . another word for freaks." "Maybe 90 per cent of the freaks will be just freaks," he added, but, "Eliminate them . . . and we'll be left standing in the dead center of nowhere." [67]

The greatest threats to the writer as an artist Williams found, from his own experience, paradoxically to be both financial success and financial failure. Following the financial success of *The Glass Menagerie,* for three months Williams was increasingly morose and cynical; then he realized that his body was still pitched from years of poverty to mere physical survival and that his new opulent surroundings and money were actually terrifying him—"Security is a kind of death, I think, and it can come to you in a storm of royalty checks beside a kidney shaped pool in Beverly Hills or anywhere at all that is removed from the conditions that made you an artist . . ." [68] Thereafter Williams avoided posh living for a relatively simple, almost Spartan life, although he usually travels first-class. Financial failure also threatened Williams as an artist as if the public by staying away from his work was saying, "We don't need you any more."

Following the precipitous disaster of *Orpheus Descending* on Broadway in 1957, Williams felt his best work long done and nothing but more decline ahead. When Maxwell told Williams of deep frustration, disappointment, and worse in writing, Williams said, "I still don't think you should feel too bad, though. Think about me—up there in that hotel room, *killing* myself, and for what? Just to stay where I am." *"Orpheus* brought all my problems to a head," said Williams. "I knew I must find help or crack up, so I went to an analyst and poured out all my troubles and felt the most enormous relief." Analysis meant survival as an artist.

As Williams views life, "We are all civilized people, which means that we are all savages at heart but observing a few amenities of civilized behavior." [69] Whitney Bolton in *The Morning Telegraph* (January 26, 1959), reported Williams as saying, "People are violent. I remember you were appalled at the cannibalism in *Suddenly Last Summer*. But life is cannibalistic. Truly. Egos eat egos, personalities eat personalities . . ."

For Williams, the passing of time is a haunting challenge that no one can escape. "I think life is a process of burning oneself out, and time is the fire that burns you," he told Robert Rice; "But I think the spirit of man is a good adversary." [70] Man is by lot unhappy. "All of us are sentenced to solitary confinement inside our skins for life," he said; "those are the great moments in life when we escape from the prison of our skin." [71] However people try to hide it, Williams sees them as not dignified but humble, frightened and guilty at heart. He thinks his plays come to the public on a wave length their spirit is tuned to—"I understand you. You and I are brothers, the deal is rugged, but let's face and fight it together." [72] What, for instance, makes the deal "rugged?" "Do they work together, God and the devil? I sometimes suspect there's a sort of understanding between them which we won't understand until Doomsday," confessed Williams.[73]

He, himself, had said of his job as a routine clerk in the stock-room of the International Shoe Company in St. Louis, "It was a living death." Could he have written *The Glass Menagerie* without that job? Of the pity and terror in his plays, he remarked in discussing *Sweet Bird of Youth,* "If there is any truth in the Aristotelian idea that violence is purged by its poetic representation on the stage, then it may be that my cycle of violent plays has had a moral justification after all." [74] He has vowed his writing always purges him psychologically. All this comprises Williams' view of life and so in a sense his justification for portraying what he believes to be the truth onstage.

"The writing and theatre world," Williams wrote his mother, "is a flock of sheep. They never get interested until someone else is. You have to distribute things around several places to work up any enthusiasm." When Mike Wallace of *The New York Post* (December 30, 1957), asked Williams, "You haven't enjoyed your fame?" Williams answered, "It never seems real to me." Williams has few if any illusions about the aesthetics let alone the commerce involved in his profession.

In 1958 Williams told Robert Rice that the writers who had helped him most as an artist were Hart Crane, D. H. Lawrence, Rainer Maria Rilke, and Anton Chekhov. Elsewhere Williams has intimated or elaborated his debt to each. Hart Crane was a modern approximation of Shakespeare and Whitman. D. H. Lawrence was "probably the greatest modern monument to the dark roots of creation." Rilke was a modern poet concerned mostly with decay through time and valor to the end. And Williams wrote Paul Bigelow of Chekhov that *The Sea Gull* was "probably the first really modern poetic play as well as the greatest." [75] By intimation in his introduction to Carson McCullers' *Reflections in a Golden Eye,* Williams considers himself in the American Gothic tradition of Poe, Melville, and Hawthorne. In *The New York Times* of November 6, 1960, he suggested a powerful new influence on his writing, Proust, "who made out of his life . . . possibly the greatest novel of our time, *The Remembrance of Things Past.*" In fact, Williams found Proust's genius even greater than Chekhov's or Joyce's in "transposing the contents of life into a creative synthesis." Williams recommended that "within the limits of each, the writers of our times can use the method of Proust."

As an artist, Williams is open to new techniques. He has decided, however, that, "Expressionism and all the other unconventional techniques in drama have only one valid aim, and that is a closer approach to truth." [76] Unconventional techniques for their own sake only distract. Drama that limits itself to reproducing life is on a par with photography; "Everyone should know nowadays the unimportance of the photographic in art: the truth, life, or reality is an organic thing which the poetic imagination can represent or suggest in essence . . ." Plays of essence, in Williams' opinion, have the quality of sculpture at its very best; "A play may be violent, full of motion, yet it has that special kind of repose which allows contemplation." [77] So, for example, Williams thinks that Willy Loman in real life might be a bore, but reduced to his essence in *Death of a Salesman* Willy is organic in a detached way that commands attention.

Drama critics have come to trouble Williams profoundly. They unmercifully panned *Battle of Angels* in Boston in 1940 with the *Globe's* man typically commenting "One of the most incredible dramas ever presented in Boston," and another critic terming it "a half-wit living a defensive life against predatory women." [78] But critics helped save *The Glass Menagerie* from being possibly junked. The play opened in Chicago to rave notices, yet by the second week business had so dropped off that the producers, Dowling and Singer, seriously considered closing the play and not even bothering to take it into New York. Then Claudia Cassidy of *The Chicago Tribune* and Ashton Stevens of *The Chicago Herald* so loudly and persistently in their drama columns rang out the play's praises that by the third week the public filled the houses. After the Broadway failure of *Summer and Smoke,* Williams denounced the critics for denying him as a playwright the tolerance and patience he needed to develop. "Painters have it better. They are allowed to evolve new methods, new styles, by a reasonable gradual process," complained Williams bitterly in a letter in Irving Hoffman's column, "Tales of Hoffman," featured in *The Hollywood Reporter.* "They are not abused for turning out creative variations of themes already stated. If a certain theme has importance, it may take a number of individual works to explore it fully . . ."

IV

WORKING METHODS OF WILLIAMS IN PLAYWRITING

Genesis

"It has always been compulsive with me," Williams said of his writing. "Otherwise I would have gone off my trolley." [79] In his story on *Sweet Bird of Youth* in *The New York Times* of March 8, 1959, Williams recalled, "At the age of fourteen, I discovered writing as an escape from a world of reality in which I felt acutely uncomfortable. It immediately became my place of retreat, my cave, my refuge. From what?" He continued, "From being called a sissy by the neighborhood kids, and Miss Nancy by my father, because I would rather read books from my grandfather's large classical library than play marbles and baseball and other normal kid games, a result of a severe childhood illness and of excessive attachment to the female members of my family who had coaxed me back into life." Williams had grown up handicapped as the aftermath of diphtheria. Severe psychic wounds then drove Williams to write, it seems, to sublimate the pain of his trauma. To this, Williams recollected in 1962, "I've always been obsessed with dying of cancer, dying of heart trouble. I think it's good for a writer to think he's dying. He works harder." [80] Chekhov, of course, did to the very end.

From experience, Williams has noted that for the writer in middle-age the only safety to preserve the conditions that made him an artist was by "living in a remote place, particularly on an island in the tropics, or in a fugitive way of life, running like a fox from place to place. I have tried both and am still trying both." [81] He has written on the move in rooming houses, hotel-rooms, steamship cabins, beaches—almost anywhere over a good share of the world that is quiet, agreeable and offers sunshine and swimming. Of New York, he said, "there are too many diverting things going on." Of Rome, "I want to have peace in the middle of people, and here I find it." Of New Orleans, "My happiest years were there . . . I was desperately poor . . . hocked everything but my typewriter to get by . . ." [82] His small white cottage in Key West and his two-room apartment in New York's West 70's are so far his only rather fixed homes. Both are simple. Here is a description of his studio, "the madhouse," at Key West:

> I have a six foot work table, and across the room there is a divan for relaxation or contemplation. All the walls in the workroom are covered with theatrical posters, and at either end of the room are bookshelves —lots of them—to hold manuscripts, side by side with conch shell and other treasures I find along the sea shore. I love to entertain here.[83]

At work, Williams follows a daily routine with the discipline yet freedom that comes with proven habits. In the January, 1962, issue of *Theatre Arts* magazine, Williams told Lewis Funke and John E. Booth, "I will wake up at around seven—around daybreak—and I'll make my coffee, and I'll go into what I call the 'madhouse'—in Key West, it's a studio . . ." Asked how many hours he worked, he replied, "Three and a half as a rule . . . But then if the afternoon is very boring, I'll come home and start again. But I've discovered that in the afternoons I'm only good for about half an hour. I can't, you know, by that time I've had it." [84] Williams' exhaustion he explained another time: "A playwright is especially tense. He has to work up the same tenseness as the characters in his play." [85] After his morning stint, to relax Williams has a martini or some bourbon, drives to the beach, swims or just takes it easy for two or three hours. By early evening, Williams has a fine dinner, usually prepared by his cook at home. This dinner is literally the only meal Williams eats.[86] His mother observed this and so did his grandfather, the Reverend Walter Dakin. Perhaps

from his days when he nearly starved, Williams found he works best
on an absolutely empty stomach except possibly for coffee drunk more
or less continually. In this respect he recalls Ibsen's breakfast of coffee
and one slice of bread, and Chekhov's own diet during working hours,
"Coffee in the morning and chicken broth at midday. If I don't my
work suffers." Strindberg, Shaw, and O'Neill also ate very sparingly
when working and were always quite lean.

Working on an empty stomach is a critical factor for Williams to
get his creative spirit limber enough to go. It is true that Williams has
also admitted to taking the tranquillizer, "Miltown," and drinking a
martini or bourbon to relax when he is especially tense.[87] His work,
he finds, naturally tends to make him tense. A relaxed body, playwrights have commonly found, as in sitting or lying in bed, seems to
free the mind for its own activities. Though Williams told Funke and
Booth in 1962 that he worked only three and a half hours a day as a
rule, he told a reporter for *Newsweek* (April 1, 1957), "I write because I love writing. It's what I know how to do, and I work eight
hours a day. What else is there?." Perhaps the implication is that if
Williams' current creation excites him enough, he is quite capable of
putting in a long working day. Or perhaps he only tires more easily
with the years.

How does Williams start his plays? He said in 1960, speaking of
any artist, "the source, the fountain-head of his work, can only be his
life." [88] In an early notebook from the 1940's he wrote, "A period
that is rich in neuroses is also rich in invention." [89] In 1948 he confided in *Life* magazine's Lincoln Barnett, "Every artist has a basic
premise pervading his whole life, and that premise can provide the
impulse to everything he creates. For me," Williams went on, "the
dominating premise has been the need for understanding and tenderness and fortitude among individuals trapped by circumstance." [90]

Williams has put a further floodlight on genesis of his plays in discussing *Cat on a Hot Tin Roof* in *The New York Herald Tribune* of
April 17, 1955:

> My characters make my play. I always start with them. They take
> spirit and body in my mind. Nothing that they say or do is arbitrary or
> invented. They build the play about them like spiders weaving their
> webs. . . . I live with them for a year and a half or two years, and I
> know them far better than I know myself, since I created them and not
> myself.

Emphasizing his need to know his characters from long intimacy, Williams has said, "I have to understand the characters in my play in order to write about them because if I just hate them, I can't write about them," and then he said in self-condemnation, "That's why Boss Finely wasn't right in *Sweet Bird of Youth* . . ."[91] Detailing what most excites him about a character, Williams reminisced, "The ambiguity, the mysterious contractions in the heart and life of a human being, is a thing that could almost be called my most obsessive concern as a playwright." [92] With the passing of time, Williams has grown more critical of promising material for plays or else his material is running low, for he said, "It takes me, say, two years to do what I would do in one year before." [93] The genesis of a play for Williams, therefore, begins specifically with not only deep personal identification but with "organic" characters Williams lives with for possibly a year or two or even longer—a method markedly like Ibsen's, Strindberg's, Chekhov's, Pirandello's, and O'Neill's.

"My longer plays," Williams told an interviewer for *Newsweek* (March 23, 1959), "emerge out of earlier one acters or short stories . . . I work over them again and again." Here are notable instances of this practice that Williams uses to nurture new growth from old roots. His story, *Portrait of a Girl in Glass,* is the essence of *The Glass Menagerie.* His two short plays, *The Lady of Larkspur Lotion* and *Portrait of a Madonna,* suggest basic traits of Blanche in *A Streetcar Named Desire.* The story, *The Yellow Bird,* underwent a creative metamorphosis to become *Summer and Smoke.* The short play, *Ten Blocks on the Camino Real,* was the spirit and substance of the real estate and people of *Camino Real.* The story, *Three Players of A Summer Game,* provided the first crude sketches of Brick and Maggie in *Cat on a Hot Tin Roof.* The short story, *Night of the Iguana,* has more than a little of the dominant characters, action, and mood that grew first into a short play and then into the long play, *Night of the Iguana. The Milk Train Doesn't Stop Here Any More* is based upon an original short story of similar trackage, *Man, Bring This Up Road.*

"The thing I hate about starting a new play," Williams told Barnett, "is that there's always so much waste. So many things don't strike fire." [94] And Williams added, "It's hard to get new subjects to write about." "It takes five or six years to use something out of life," Williams noted in *Time* of March 9, 1962. "It's lurking in the unconscious—it finds its meaning there." Apparently the tried and proven way for Williams to "strike fire" is to turn to characters and situations complying with his current deep tensions. These characters more likely than not emerge almost full grown since he has left them in his world of fiction years earlier, and called upon them at intervals to see how they were coming along. And then suddenly, he senses they have gathered a deep meaning for him. Williams has a test for creative fire in his material, that is, in his characters. *"Dynamic* is a word in disrepute at the moment," he said in the preface of *Camino Real,* "and so, I suppose is the word *organic,* but those terms still define the dramatic values that I value most." [95]

Because of the limitations of space in this study, examples of Williams' working methods will be drawn with few exceptions from three works that he and his critics usually consider his best to date and so likely show his methods at top form: *The Glass Menagerie, A Streetcar Named Desire* and *Cat on A Hot Tin Roof.*

Of the genesis of *The Glass Menagerie,* Williams has said, "It was derived from years of living." [96] In *Tennessee Williams and Friends,* Maxwell suggests feelings of great power in Williams which it appears to me especially demanded catharsis. After his sister's lobotomy, Williams felt the operation to have been, in Maxwell's words, "a mistaken gesture of mercy which he can never condone, forgive or forget." He had grown up very close to his sister, Rose. Once after visiting her where she is confined, Williams with Gilbert Maxwell and Diana Barrymore rode home in silence except that Diana Barrymore cried convulsively; then upon arrival, Williams let out his still latent anguish, as Maxwell recalled the words:

> She was the best of us all, do you understand? More beautiful, more intelligent, sweeter and warmer than anyone. Not one of us was fit to stoop and tie her shoes. . . . The torments this girl has endured are not to be mentioned; yet she stands there before you, triumphant, with her head up and her shoulders back and looks you in the face and silently tells you, this brave little creature, "Look at me. Somehow, I came through, I am here. . . ." [97]

"I do not take characters from life," Williams has asserted of his playwriting, "only possibly some of my family, the female members, that is." He has called Amanda Wingfield "an exact portrait of my mother." [98] *Portrait of a Girl in Glass* and *The Glass Menagerie* are drawn directly from Williams' memories of his family life in St. Louis during the ordeal of the great depression of the 1930's. The play's Tom Wingfield working in the warehouse has a counterpart in Tom Williams working as a stock-room clerk for The International Shoe Company and trying desperately to keep up his writing while he yearns for excitement, adventure, and escape from his "living death." Unlike Amanda in *The Glass Menagerie,* Mrs. Williams was not deserted by her husband, but about once a month when the bills fell due, by her own word, he would order her and the children out of the house; and eventually the parents were to separate. Suggesting Mrs. Williams' predicament, Amanda is an aging Southern belle, living in a world of recollections of lost social gentility and coping desperately with penny-pinching reality; she also plays martyr, nag, and loving mother to Tom while pressing him to bring home a "gentleman caller" for her daughter.

Laura, modelled from Rose, is crippled and painfully shy in her fragile loveliness. While Rose was committed permanently to a mental hospital, Williams gave her counterpart, Laura, a different disability: she has become withdrawn over self-consciousness from a foot crippled by a childhood disease; and in fact, Williams' own withdrawal came on from the crippling aftermath of diphtheria in childhood. Rose, like Laura, actually did go to a secretarial school for awhile, but left because of her "heart;" and Rose, like Laura, did have a glass menagerie. Rose's room, like Laura's in the story and in the play, looked out on a sunless, dreary alley, symbolic of her reality, where night after night stray dogs chased stray cats up a dead-end and tore them to pieces to the sound of hair-raising screeches and yelping. To brighten things, Williams had helped Rose paint her furniture white, hang white curtains, and set up white shelves to display the colored glass animals that lent an air of delicate magic to the room. The very origin of these little glass animals could only suggest to Williams a "gentle-man caller" who did not fall in love with Laura. "She wore a crown of stars on her head and a gown of green tarleton flounces covered with little tinkling glass ornaments, mostly animals," Mrs. Williams recalled of Rose's dress at a masquerade party given by wealthy relatives of her husband in Knoxville.[99] Rose in search of a suitor was dressed as a Christmas tree. The symbolism of the glass animals and their likeness to his sister's fragile nature was certainly far from lost on so perceptive a writer as Williams. Williams' friend, McBurney, recalled that Mrs. Williams used to "command" Tom to bring home gentlemen callers for Rose—like Jim Delaney in the story and Jim O'Connor in the play.[100] To Williams' embarrassment, his mother then would often entertain the callers with highflown gentility while Rose was shyly silent. Williams must have felt a powerful catharsis in writing *The Glass Menagerie;* his play gave Laura a new hope in life for the lost hope of Rose. Williams still preserved in his play the full poignancy of his relation to his sister.

He also provided a justification for his own "desertion" of his family in the guise of Tom Wingfield, the merchant seaman who writes; actually, the "desertion" was strictly in the imaginative world, for Williams' father always provided for his family, if often meanly. And Tom Wingfield in the play knew in his heart that his mother, Amanda, and his sister, Rose, would somehow go on living without his support. Indeed, the fact that Williams gave his mother half of the rights to *The Glass Menagerie* shows that he never abandoned her in spirit nor had she failed him in his imaginative life. As narrator, Tom Wingfield gives the whole play its highly lyrical and touching viewpoint of a confessional in memory. The basic method of genesis of *The Glass Menagerie* was that of Chekhov—reminiscence with artistic license to produce a fresh creative synthesis from "years of living."

When Williams was asked how he had come to write *A Streetcar Named Desire,* he answered, "Perhaps my unconscious could tell. I can't." [101] He conceded, however, "It is New Orleans where I've lived off and on since 1938 which has provided me with more material than any other part of the country." He recalled, "I lived near the main street of the Quarter which is named Royal. Down this street, running on the same tracks are two street cars, one named *Desire* and the other named *Cemeteries.* Their indiscourageable progress up and down Royal struck me as having some symbolic bearing of a broad nature on life in the Vieux Carré—and everywhere else for that matter . . ." [102] The streetcar, *Cemeteries,* actually wound up in a neighborhood named *Elysian Fields,* a further unforced symbolism Williams incorporated into what his play had to say. The title was originally *Poker Night,* suggesting the poker-game as basic to the play's germ life. Williams had seen his father and his cronies in many such a poker-game; and the lusty, earthy-humored, hard-drinking, fearfully tempered father certainly had some of the traits of the far less well born Stanley Kowalski; for to Williams, all men are basically primitive. The fights Williams' parents had over the week-end long poker parties and the hard drinking suggest Kowalski's apish drunkenness and ugliness, and Blanche and Stella's revulsion.

Blanche Dubois had several models. One is Mrs. Hardwicke-Moore, the lead in *The Lady of Larkspur Lotion,* a fading ex-belle of the old South, nourished by delusions as she waits for dividends from her mythical rubber plantation in Brazil. Another model for Blanche is Lucretia Collins, the lead in *Portrait of a Madonna*. Lucretia is a southern spinster with visions of being repeatedly raped by men breaking into her room; although an ardent Episcopalian and a church-worker, she winds up denouncing her church and defending one rapacious lover even as a doctor and an attendant lead her off to a mental asylum. Blanche is also modelled from Rose in her loveliness, gentility, and eventual madness. In composite, these ladies suggest Blanche in her cornered pretensions of gentility, her sexual decline, her hopeless fight for a new start, and her harsh end. The importance of Blanche as a prime-mover in the genesis of *Streetcar* is implied in Williams' letter to the Editor of *Theatre Arts* magazine (October, 1955) in which he calls Blanche "the greatest lady of my life." Echoing Williams' obsession with the ambiguity of character, he said, "In some respects, Blanche who went to the madhouse was the most rational of all the characters I've created, and in almost all ways she was the strongest. She certainly fought on a much more desperate field than Maggie the Cat fights on. She fought with all odds against her and with unfailing valor, with gallantry that persisted and even reached its peak at the final curtain."

Like *The Glass Menagerie,* for Williams *A Streetcar Named Desire* had something "well worth saying." Suggesting Chekhov's great theme of the aristocracy in transition in *The Cherry Orchard, A Streetcar Named Desire* dramatized the passing of the last vestiges of Southern aristocracy in the spirit which Williams likened to "the fall of Rome to the blue-eyed marauders of the North."[103] Just as *The Cherry Orchard* in a sense was the story of Chekhov's own life, detailing the decline of the Russian nobility and the rise of the serf class from which Chekhov came, so in a sense *A Streetcar Named Desire* was Williams' story detailing the decline of a bygone Southern elite of planters, and the rise of the common man.

The genesis of *Cat on a Hot Tin Roof* is bound up with the mysterious motive Brick Pollitt has for being disgusted with his wife, Maggie, as portrayed in Williams' story, *Three Players of a Summer Game*. In the story, Brick for a never stated reason becomes an alcoholic, and his wife, Maggie, takes over more and more of his obligations in running the plantation. The doctor treating Brick for alcoholism then falls victim of a tumor on the brain, doubtless, cancer; with the tacit consent of the doctor's wife, Brick gives the doctor a merciful, lethal hypodermic. While Maggie is out of town over the matter of a relative's funeral, Brick takes the doctor's wife as mistress, manages her estate, and plays croquet with her orphaned daughter. At Maggie's return, Brick goes back to her and his alcoholism and ends up in jail, deprived of his driver's license and mumbling for Maggie. Maggie has taken his masculinity from him and left him a handsome weakling, a kind of embattled D. H. Lawrence relationship to his mistress (later his wife), Frieda; Williams had drawn this somewhat parallel circumstance in *I Rise in Flame, Cried the Phoenix,* a play which preceded *Cat on a Hot Tin Roof* by two years, and possibly had a bearing upon it.

In writing *Cat on a Hot Tin Roof,* Williams dropped the doctor, his wife, and their child from the action, and concentrated on a more manly Brick and a more feminine Maggie. The motive for Brick becoming alcoholic is made plain as the root of the play's whole action: the fiercely possessive Maggie, jealous of Brick's devotion to his best friend, Skipper, deliberately gets Skipper drunk to seduce him, and when he proves impotent, charges him with being a homosexual. Skipper then in effect commits suicide. Brick in revulsion at what Maggie has done, and stricken with the loss of his best friend, takes to alcohol and refuses to sleep with Maggie. His ambivalence or ambiguity suggests Williams' note, "a period that is rich in neuroses is also rich in invention."

The rest of the Pollitt family, Big Daddy, Big Mama, Gooper, Mae, and their five "no-neck" monster children, are introduced in *Cat on a Hot Tin Roof* for the first time. Big Daddy has a startling resemblance to Williams' father, Cornelius—big, stout, domineering and exulting in his lustiness, bawdiness, booming voice, love of gain, and basic integrity. Big Daddy hates the sham and hypocrisy of Gooper and Mae in their scheming to inherit his estate; and to get the truth out of Brick about his ambiguous relationship to Skipper, he flays him alive psychologically in the climactic scene of Act II. This big scene again suggests the inventiveness of Williams' neurosis at work. Cornelius for years had repeatedly turned on his son, taunting him as "Miss Nancy" and "no good;" Big Daddy became a sublimation of Cornelius, far more understanding toward his favorite son, Brick, than Cornelius ever was toward Williams. Emerging as a kind of purgation of Williams' one time hatred for his father, Big Daddy seems Williams' wish-fulfillment of what he would have liked his own father to have been. Big Daddy intimates that homosexuality is latent in Brick; Brick, like a loving but revengeful Williams, then turns on Big Daddy and tells him a terrible truth in turn—Big Daddy is dying of cancer, and the family has kept the news from him. So in a way, Williams was also expressing his death-wish for Cornelius. In a startling similarity of Cornelius' attitude toward Mrs. Williams, Big Daddy claims he never cared for his wife, Big Mama, but slept with her for animal warmth.

The greed, lies, taunting and sham of Gooper and Mae reflect what helped make Williams the "nervous, baffled, lonely" person he says he is from his years in St. Louis. The Williams family was cruelly snubbed and humiliated for being "poor;" Rose stopped going to Sunday school because, "The girls snobbed me." The major climax and the very end of the play is an echo of D. H. Lawrence's faith in unashamed sex as man's mystical way to freedom and the affirmation of the primal life urge in the face of death. What Williams felt he had to say was certainly "well worth saying" and very big, indeed. When confronted with the certain death of the father he loves, Brick in his ambiguity toward his father, his wife, and his best friend, chooses not death but survival. He will procreate. This partial rationalization of some of the genesis of *Cat on a Hot Tin Roof* is founded on some of Williams' most powerful experiences "creatively synthesized," chiefly regarding: his father, St. Louis' philistinism, cruelty, lies, and cowardice that will not face life and fight gallantly to the end. *Cat on a Hot Tin Roof* helps through art to answer the question Williams said his analyst put to him after a few sessions in 1958—"Why are you so full of hate, anger and envy?" [105]

Is Williams guided by a theme in genesis? "I have never been able to say what was the theme of my play," he said of *Summer and Smoke*, "and I don't think I have ever been conscious of writing with a theme in mind. . . . Usually when asked about a theme, I look vague and say, 'It's a play about life.'" [106] Williams, however, told a reporter for *The Washington Evening Star*, "I think, without planning to do so, I have followed the developing tension and anger and violence of the world and time that I live in through my own steadily increasing tensions as a writer." Early in the creation of a play, Williams must at least have some notion of the total effect he might want. He called *The Glass Menagerie*, "a play whose interest does not depend on incident or situation but holds its audience through the revelation of quiet and ordinary truths." [107] In working on *A Streetcar*

Named Desire, he thought of it as "a tragedy of incomprehension" and of wanting to say, "If you don't watch out, the apes will take over." Of *Cat on a Hot Tin Roof,* he wrote, "What I want most of all is to catch the quality of existence and experience. I want people to think 'This is life.' I want to offer them my own individual attitude toward it." [108]

Incubation and Characterization

"The stages in the making of a play are long and devious as a rule," wrote Williams in a program note in 1956 for the April try-out of the Studio M Playhouse's production of *Sweet Bird of Youth.* When does genesis end and incubation begin? Apparently only when Williams is reasonably sure that he really has a play—that his characters, "trapped by circumstance" and needing understanding, tenderness, and fortitude, have something "well worth saying," or else the play "does not have a Chinaman's chance of surviving." This realization can only come when Williams finds the right major climax, for the major climax is by its nature the most dramatic statement of what the play's whole struggle is trying to say through its outcome. In his best plays, this method of growth seems implied, for Williams always brings down the curtain almost immediately after the major climax. "When I get an idea, I work on it at white heat," Williams told an interviewer for *The Miami Herald.* "It doesn't take me long to do a first draft, but I work over my plays a lot." [109]

In the year and a half to two years that Williams has said it takes him to write a full length play, the growth of his characters is his chief preoccupation. He told John Cruesemann:

> For the one real quality which I believe I have is possessing an almost fragmental mind, a multiple split personality, if you like. I can pick up all sorts of signs from people and spot what they are like.
>
> I believe I can get myself into the situation of almost anyone. This way I bulid up characters in my own mind from those probings. [110]

Williams' own self is intensely involved in the process. "In fact, I can't expose a human weakness on the stage," he said, "unless I know it through having it myself. I have exposed a good many human weaknesses and brutalities and consequently I have them." [111] Williams creates his characters from reminiscence, but his models are drawn not only from life but from history and from fiction—themselves drawn from life—like Lord Byron and Don Quixote in *Camino Real.*

In general, he likes to create characters who are, as he put it, "deeply troubled;" the merely sordid and petty do not interest him in a protagonist. "I think most of us have deep troubles," Williams said in 1957. "I've yet to find people I didn't think were deeply troubled. This is the age of anxiety." "A writer's view of the world," he elaborated, "is always affected by his own state of being. I am an anxious, troubled person. I can't write about anything I don't feel." [112] In discussing *Orpheus Descending* in *Newsweek* Williams said, "Frankly, there must be some limitations in me as a dramatist. I can't handle people in routine situations. I must find characters who correspond to my own tensions." [113]

As it is, Williams has chosen with few exceptions to write of people seldom sunny but usually drawn from the deep South. Asked why he wrote so much of these people, he answered, "Because I know and understand their moods and personalities better and because I am both familiar and in complete sympathy with the flavor and mode of their speech." [114] To him, his characters are not unrepresentative because they happen to be southerners, as for instance in *Cat on a Hot Tin Roof*. "Their problems and feelings and the inner tragedy of their whole tortured lives," said Williams, "would be very much the same if the story were laid elsewhere." [115]

In his best plays, Williams concentrates upon a single character or sometimes two, but seldom more than three, and these leading characters are in varying degrees of subtle contrast with one another or lesser characters. The contrast promotes the tensions to make "dynamic" and "organic" action. In *The Glass Menagerie,* for instance, the leading character, Tom Wingfield, is an unhappy, frustrated dreamer, deeply attached to his withdrawn sister, Laura, and hating his dehumanizing warehouse job even as he despises his mother's tricks to manipulate him and to have him take up the burden of supporting the family his father had deserted; by contrast, the lesser character, Jim O'Connor, the "Gentleman Caller," is a down-to-earth go-getter, somewhat ordinary and yet a good young man who faces his short-comings and who is doing his best to better himself by practical education. Laura, the lovely, crippled, shy, self-effacing young lady is contrasted with her mother, Amanda, the loquacious, domineering, faded belle, who martyrizes herself with pity in order to try to move her children to her will. In *A Streetcar Named Desire,* the leading female character, Blanche DuBois, is contrasted markedly with the lesser character, her sister Stella. Blanche, full of pretensions of her family's vanished gentility, tries to find a solution by marrying a poetic homosexual who kills himself when she taunts him with her discovery; then Blanche in guilt and loneliness, turns to nymphomania, prostitution, dipsomania, and finally seduction of one of her high school students. Stella, unlike Blanche, has given up any illusions of retaining her lost aristocratic social status and has married, not a weakling poet, but a lusty Polish truck-driver, Stanley Kowalski, who makes sex her narcotic and a family a certainty. Stanley Kowalski, the male lead, is contrasted not only with Blanche but with the much lesser role of Mitch, a mama's boy and Stanley's close friend, who thinks of marrying Blanche but then declines once the vindictive Stanley exposes her lurid past. In *Cat on a Hot Tin Roof,* the leading male character, Brick Pollitt, is sharply contrasted with the almost equally strong role of Big Daddy, his father. Brick, born to every material advantage, rejects his wife sexually because her jealous possessiveness has driven his best friend, Skipper, to suicide by intimating homosexuality, and thereby driven Brick to alcoholism, childlessness, and world weariness. Big Daddy, however, is coarse, piratical, self-made, domineering, lusty, blustering, realistic; he never liked his wife but slept with her for animal comfort, accepts life's lies and treachery, fights them his own way, and is determined to get at the truth and face it. Maggie, the female lead and Brick's wife, is contrasted not only with him, but with the much lesser role of Mae, the wife of Gooper, Brick's brother. Maggie is pretty, vivacious, charming, possessively loving, resilient, a woman who has fought her way into society from the wrong side of the railroad tracks and is determined to fight to save her marriage and to have children, too; Mae, however, is unattractive, strident, sneaky, greedy, and a deliberate breeder of five "no-neck" children to impress Big Daddy with her fertility in providing him with heirs.

Certainly one of Williams' chief models in dramatic technique is Chekhov. "Williams' plays have been compared with those of Anton Chekhov," wrote Lincoln Barnett who interviewed Williams, "and he readily acknowledges the great Russian as his dramaturgic mentor." [116] In the bulk of Williams' plays, not withstanding, far more unusual things happen than in Chekhov. The characterization may be Chekhovian, but emerging action strongly suggests Ibsen's technique of characters in climactic confrontation, crossed with Strindberg's emphasis upon normal characters becoming abnormal under the terrible stress of circumstance, as in *The Father.*

In constructing his plays to be "dynamic" and "organic," Williams must be aware of the most common charge brought against him by such drama critics as John Mason Brown and Walter Kerr—weakness of structure. Even in *Suddenly Last Summer,* for instance, which moves to its major climax with great artfulness of character drawing, Kerr found the starving children turning upon Sebastian, who had used them for his pleasure, as incredible cannibalism. "But life is cannibalistic," was Williams' defense. "In *Suddenly Last Summer,* it was more symbolic than actual, but many persons felt I meant it actually." [117] Kerr believed Williams made an unwarranted switch from the believable to the suddenly symbolic in the major climax.

Structurally in his most successful plays, Williams has usually worked for a straight narrative line based upon a series of revelations of character. He wrote of *Camino Real,* "I am not at all sure that it isn't the one I love most of my plays, though I know it commits the huge structural error of deviating from a straight narrative line." [118] Williams also implies the overall structure he works for through incubation; he remarked of Daniel Mann's direction of *The Rose Tattoo* as contrasted with how Elia (Gadge) Kazan would have done it, "Gadge would have demanded a stronger, tighter script from me. Danny was willing to take a chance on the script submitted." Williams told Funke and Booth of construction in general, "I have always tried to find the dénouement that seemed predicated . . . by the play as a whole." In all of Williams' most acclaimed plays, the major climax comes very near the play's end.

To Williams, "using a symbol is just a way of saying a thing more vividly and dramatically than I could otherwise;" he told Henry Hewes, "I don't believe in using symbols unless they clarify." [119] In developing his best plays, he has used symbolism through all the elements of production in concert: setting, lighting, illustrative action, diction, silence, sound effects, music, dance, and so on. His symbols are most effective when apparently most natural and least obtrusive. In *Camino Real,* many critics complained that his symbolism was either painfully obvious or downright confusing. Williams, however, has said of the dreamlike free flow of symbols in that play, "it is the result of painstaking design, and in this work I have given more conscious attention to form and construction than I have in any work before. Freedom is not achieved simply by working freely." [120]

His symbolism has come off best in *The Glass Menagerie, A Streetcar Named Desire,* and *Cat on a Hot Tin Roof.* To illustrate, the

symbolism of setting in *The Glass Menagerie* not only uses the gauze
screen, the conventional stage device to lend a slight blur to a "memory scene," but also the display of Laura's little glass animals on the
what-not setting their fragile note: "They stood for all the small and
tender things that relieve the austere pattern of life," said Williams,
"and make it endurable for the sensitive." [121] The slum alley with the
ash-cans suggests the Wingfield's immediate outlook as seen from
their tenement apartment. The fire escape landing is the porch and
entrance to the apartment, suggesting Tom's escape from the hell of
his circumstance that has trapped him. The light on Laura has a "peculiar pristine clarity such as light used in early religious portraits of
female saints or madonnas." [122] Across the alley is the Paradise Dance
Hall from which flows intermittent waltz and tango music and where
couples living a drab life go for escape, change, and adventure, winding up with sex in the alley. As for symbolic illustrative action, Jim
O'Connor dances with Laura, bumps into a table, knocks off a glass
unicorn, picks it up and observes that now that its horn is knocked
off it is no longer a "freak" but like all other horses. The lost horn of
the unicorn does not disturb Laura, and the implication is plain that
with self-confidence she too can get rid of her morbid shyness and no
longer be a "freak."

In *A Streetcar Named Desire,* Stanley Kowalski's first entrance and
speech, near the very beginning of the play, symbolically sets the
play's whole key-note and gives a glimpse of his character as a breed
of cave-man. Stanley tosses a blood-stained package of meat to his
wife, Stella, and yells, "Catch!" [123] Blanche's opening lines, soon after
her arrival in the poor but raffish section of New Orleans where her
sister Stella lives, symbolize a variation on the play's key-note as well
as the whole course of Blanche's life. "They told me to take a streetcar
named Desire, and then transfer to one called Cemeteries," she says,
". . . and get off at—Elysian Fields." [124] Blanche's favorite song symbolizes her dependence upon illusion for survival—"It's Only a
Paper Moon." Guilt-ridden by her 'dirty' past, Blanche during meaningful pauses and silences is given to too much bathing, and washing of
her hands. When Mitch takes off the pink paper Chinese lantern that
Blanche bought to cover the plain white light bulb, he symbolically at
last sees Blanche as she really is—fading, wrinkled, dissipated. "I don't
want realism. I want magic," she tells Mitch. ". . . *Don't turn the
light on!"* [125] To get rid of Mitch when he tells her he knows all
about her and then tries to take her, she yells, "Fire!" again and

again, and he runs off.[126] But Blanche is literally left in the flames of her personal hell. Stanley's drunken violence in raping Blanche, once he is sure of her past promiscuity, symbolizes his brutality in shattering the fragile illusions of Blanche's last ditch fight to adjust to the harsh, real world. The blue-eyed vandal has raped the decadent Roman lady.

In *Cat on a Hot Tin Roof,* the setting of Brick and Maggie's bedroom is heavily shuttered as if hiding the truth of the Pollitt's marriage from the light of day. Brick has a broken ankle from trying hurdles on the local athletic field at three in the morning, the crippling outcome of trying to relive memories of his old glory in his present disillusionment with life. Brick is left hobbling on crutches for three acts, crippled in his human relations. At the end of the play, Maggie takes away Brick's alcohol, his symbol of escape, and finally gets him to bed with her, the symbol of procreating. Big Daddy's incurably malignant cancer is kept from him by lies, like so many figurative cancers of a rapaciously successful figure in society. The "no-neck" five children of Gooper and Mae symbolize, in their song and dance routine at Big Daddy's birthday party, the hypocritical merriment of their greedy parents. The very names of the characters, as always in a Williams' play, have symbolic overtones. "Brick" for instance, suggests the wall he presents to communication as well as the popular connotation of a good fellow. "Big Daddy" suggests the benevolent despot who acts a bit like God on his 28,000 acres of "the richest land this side of the Nile." "Maggie," for Margaret, suggests the fighting Irish up from the shanty side of the railroad tracks and determined to keep fighting for her rights in the highest local society. And so it goes—symbols in Williams in profusion and at their best when "dynamic" and "organic" to the action.

Williams said of his characters, "They build the play about them like spiders weaving their webs. . . . I live with them for a year and a half to two years . . ."[127] If most plays take Williams that long, some take much longer. *Orpheus Descending,* for example, based on his failure, *Battle of Angels,* was more than he could leave lost. "Well, nothing is more precious to anybody than the emotional record of his youth," he said. And Williams admitted of *Battle,* "it never went into the trunk, it always stayed on the work bench"—for seventeen years![128]

In developing a play, Williams might have three or four projects which he works at intermittently but are concurrently in the back of

his mind. In the course of a visit to the Orient, to illustrate, he told a
reporter for *Variety* (September 30, 1959) that he was working on
and off at such plays as *Period of Adjustment, Night of the Iguana,*
and *The Milk Train Doesn't Stop Here Any More*:

> I skip about among them. I usually get bored with one, I get stuck. I
> arrive at a point where I can't continue. I put it aside and come back to
> it again with a fresh point of view.
>   I usually run a month on one before I switch to another. That way I
> finish two plays simultaneously. It's also a psychological advantage. If
> one of them flops, I still have another chance.

When asked in 1962 what he would work on after the opening of
Night of the Iguana, Williams said, "Oh, there are always unfinished
scripts lying around. I just reach in, you know."

Sources of Freshness in Williams

The citation of America's National Institute of Arts and Letters in
awarding Williams a prize of $1,000 on May 19, 1944, states:

> To Tennessee Williams, born in Mississippi, in recognition of his dra-
> matic works, which reveal a poetic imagination and a gift for charac-
> terization that are rare in the contemporary theatre.

The Sidney Howard Memorial Award of $1,500 given Williams in
Washington, D. C., in January of 1946, noted: "He has the sense of
poetry and of character of which great drama is made." [129] Williams'
two Pulitzer Prize Awards are for *A Streetcar Named Desire* and *Cat
on a Hot Tin Roof.* His four New York City Drama Critics' Circle
Awards—more than any other living American playwright has received—tally up: *The Glass Menagerie, A Streetcar Named Desire,
Cat on a Hot Tin Roof* and *Night of the Iguana.* At least the first
two are modern classics, and possibly the third. Williams' detractors
are many and this study has already suggested their chief charges. An
artist is not a miracle man. Even Shakespeare wasn't. Parents have no
way of quite anticipating the nature of their children. An artist, too,
must take what brain-children come, though preventing some.
    Williams' "poetic imagination" and "gift for characterization" from
which "great drama is made," both depend upon Williams' point of
view as an artist. "I dare to suggest from my P O V (point of
view)," he said in *The New York Times Magazine* (June 12, 1960),
"that the theatre has made in our time its greatest artistic advance
through the unlocking and lighting up and ventilation of the closets,

attics, and basements of human behavior and experience." In his plays which speak for themselves, Williams has opened up some places of the mind which the commercial theatre largely regarded as nailed shut, taboo. For Williams, truth has no taboos, and the view of the dramatist is rightfully the whole of life, "provided it is presented with honest intention and taste." Censorship, to Williams, is "perilously close to a degree of cultural fascism." [130]

Williams' "poetic imagination" and "gift for characterization" possibly are most noticeable in the power of his lyric diction and the total effect of his plays. That diction at best can be sheer dramatic poetry in prose within the play's context, as for instance, Blanche's comment to Mitch in *A Streetcar Named Desire* when she thinks she has found in him, and he in her, the love to redeem their incomplete lives: "Sometimes—there's God—so quickly." [131]

The power of Williams' total effect depends upon all the elements of production in concert, often projecting the essence of living in unforced symbols. His characters are his chief obsession, and in his best plays the action is "dynamic" and "organic," depending upon a series of revelations of truth of character to lead to the major climax very near the end of the play. This kind of structure, as in *The Glass Menagerie* and also *A Streetcar Named Desire,* uses only scenes rather than act divisions—seven scenes in *The Glass Menagerie* and eleven in *A Streetcar Named Desire.* The method requires profound insight into the heart and soul of a character. It moves in an almost hypnotic drift of suggested or implied meaning. It is the fulfillment in terms of drama of Williams' statement, "The ambiguity, the mysterious contractions in the heart and life of a human being, is a thing that could almost be called my most obsessive concern as a playwright." "I like strong effects and boldness," he confessed, "and perhaps sometimes I go overboard, but I never do it for commercial reasons. I do it only to make a point strongly." [132] Brooks Atkinson has in *The New York Times* paid Williams such tribute as one possessing "a terrifying knowledge of the secrets of the mind," "a poetic writer who could look through the polite surfaces of life into the pain that froze the hearts of lonely people," and, "Mr. Williams has made art of malignance and maleficence."

Writing and Rewriting

With his own short stories and short plays as a spring-board for a long play, Williams must dive into the writing with a scenario of sorts on paper and certainly in mind. "It doesn't take me long to do a first draft," he said, "but I work over my plays a lot. I do a lot of talking to myself when I write, trying out the sound of dialogue. Neighbors must think I always have a roomful of company."[133] If Williams follows the line of a scenario, it is only a tentative course open to change in the swim of things. "I prefer a play not to be a noose but a net with fairly wide meshes," he said of writing *The Rose Tattoo*. "So many of its instants of revelation are wayward flashes, not part of the plan of the author but struck accidentally off, and perhaps these are closest to being a true celebration of the inebriate god"—Dionysius, of course.[134] For Williams, incubation obviously continues through writing and rewriting.

Instants of revelation occurring as wayward flashes or not, Williams still expects some angles of character to remain in shadow or even in darkness. "Some mystery should be left in the revelation of character in a play," he said, "just as a great deal of mystery is always left in the revelation of character in life, even in one's own character to himself."[135] Yet Williams warned, "This does not absolve the playwright of his duty to probe and observe as clearly and as deeply as he legitimately can, but it should steer him away from 'pat' conclusions, facile definitions, which make just a play, not a snare for the truth of human experience."[136] The classic example, of course, of a character profoundly realized but still never free of shadows is Hamlet. The value of a day's output is unpredictable for Williams. In *Time* (March 9, 1962), he told an interviewer that "out of a year's writing days, there are only five good ones." These are likely the days with the wonderful "wayward flashes" made possible perhaps by the gathering static charge of the probing of other days.

To understand Williams' use of dialogue, we must keep in mind his comment, "I think of writing as something more organic than words, something closer to being and action."[137] At best, Williams' dialogue is the mark of that rarity of writers, the combination of dramatist and poet. His poetry is not in his verse but in his prose. He tried verse in only one early short play, *The Purification,* a tragedy about a brother and sister's incest. Some samples might suggest why Williams gave up verse for diction:

"THE JUDGE: Rain's the treatment for a forest fire.
　　　　　　　For violent deeds likewise the rain is needed.
　　　　　　　The rain I speak of is the rain of truth.
　　　　　　　For truth between men is the only purification."
"SON:　　　　　The truth?

> Why ask me for that?
> Ask it of him, the player—
> For truth is sometimes alluded to in music.
> But words are too loosely woven to catch it in."
>
> "RANCHER: 'Woman,' I said to her, 'Woman, what keeps you alive?
> What keeps you sparkling so, you make-believe fountain?' " [138]

The characters plainly tend to talk alike with a literary self-consciousness that rings false to life. Thereafter Williams used verse only in his poems. "But poetry doesn't have to be words, you see," he told Funke and Booth in 1962. "In the theatre, it can be situations, it can be silences. Colloquial, completely unheightened language can be more poetic, I think." [139] Perhaps the most moving line in the whole of *A Streetcar Named Desire* is Blanche's last speech when thought of in the context of the play—she is led off by the doctor and the matron to the state mental hospital: "Whoever you are—I have always depended on the kindness of strangers." [140]

In his dialogue as in all other elements of his plays, Williams tries to be "dynamic" and "organic." His dialogue may move in such short spurts as monosyllabic give-and-take of characters or go on to varying lengths of speeches up to the record stretch of the twenty-minute speech of Catherine Holly in *Suddenly Last Summer* when, under the release of truth serum, she spews out her full story of long repressed horrors. This speech held the audience enthralled. "Sometimes what Kazan refers to as the arias," said Williams, "sometimes they come off very well, and other times, they stop the play." [141] Williams also frankly admitted, "My great bête noir as a writer has been a tendency to what people call . . . to poeticize. You know that's why I've written so many Southern heroines. They have a tendency to gild the lily, and they speak in a rather florid style which seems to suit me because I write out of emotion and I get carried away by the emotion." [142] If Williams' dialogue moves in any direction of change, he suggested it would be toward the elusive, allusive, symbolic, spare style of such "new wave" playwrights as Pinter. "It's something that drives me crazy with jealousy," said Williams, "I love it . . . I say, 'Oh God, if I could write like that!' " [143]

Deprived of his lyric and usually Southern diction, Williams would likely be in deep trouble trying to invoke his special magic. He, himself, suggests that it is no accident that the overwhelming number of characters in his plays are at home and quite themselves talking a strain of lyric speech; Southerners, earthy foreigners, romantics, and off-beat types, all find figurative language natural to their lips, and such characters people Williams' plays. Consider, for instance, Southerners like the Wingfields in *The Glass Menagerie,* the DuBois sisters in *A Streetcar Named Desire,* the Pollitts in *Cat on a Hot Tin Roof;* such earthy Americans as Stanley Kowalski and his friends in *A Streetcar Named Desire,* or Serafina delle Rose and her Sicilian suitor Alvaro Mangiacavallo in *The Rose Tattoo;* such romantic archetypes as Kilroy, Don Quixote, Lord Byron, and the Gypsy Esmeralda in *Camino Real;* such renegade southerners and off-beat romantics as Maxine Falk, T. Lawrence Shannon, Nonno, and Hannah Coffin in *Night of the Iguana.* In *Period of Adjustment,* Williams approximated routine characters in routine situations, and the diction was noticeably flat.

Williams has not said exactly how long a first draft tends to take him but simply, "It doesn't take me long . . . ;" nor has he said exactly how many revisions he tends to make but only, "I work over my plays a lot." The story behind *Night of the Iguana* suggests how much he relies upon time to help him fully realize a character, and therefore how much he even welcomes revision to reveal growth by "wayward flashes." A trip to Acapulco in 1940 gave Williams the first raw material for *Iguana.* By 1946, he had written the short story. By 1959, he had turned it into a one-act play which was tried out at Spoleto Theatre Festival in Italy. *Time* magazine reported four separate versions of the long play followed, and said, "to compare them is to watch sand turning into Baccarat crystal." [144] In considering that *Orpheus Descending* never left Williams' desk for seventeen years, it is clear that he knows no fool-proof system of transmuting his material into crystal, diamonds, or what you will. Like all writers, he is at the mercy of his inspiration, and tries above all, to make each work the best he can.

As a veteran of Broadway, Williams in 1957 recollected three phases that the playwright tends to go through in revising his script during rehearsal. In his first phase, the playwright tends to be a "nobody" working with many "somebodies"; largely out of fear, "He will permit lines, speeches, sometimes even whole scenes to be cut from his script because a director has found them difficult to direct or an actor has found them difficult to act," noted Williams. [145] "He will put in or build up a scene or a star at the sacrifice of the play's just proportions." But even the new playwright reaches his limit. "Intimidation having bottled him up until now," Williams observed, "he now pops off with unnecessary violence . . ."[146] After the Guild optioned *Battle of Angels,* Williams wrote his mother, "I have to do a lot of revision to meet their requirements, many of which seem foolish to me at the present moment, but I am not telling them so."[147] Williams revised *Battle of Angels* extensively before the Guild's failure with it, and afterward, too, without getting the Guild to do another production. He made relatively few if any important revisions of *The Glass Menagerie* in rehearsal. When Louis Singer, Eddie Dowling's coproducer of the play, asked Williams to change the play's ending for 'box-office' reasons to a happier prospect for Laura, Williams refused. "There is only one important difference between the original and the acting version of the play," Williams said pointedly in the preface to the acting version, "—the deleted screen."[148] Williams' original script had suggested the use of a movie screen on which titles would be projected as chapter headings for each scene viewed in memory.

The playwright's second phase follows his first notable success. Now, right or wrong, he fights for his script as if it were "Holy Writ," all in the name of artistic integrity.

What brings on the third phase? "It may take only one failure, it may take two or three, to persuade him that his single assessment of his work is fallible . . ."[149] After the success of *The Glass Menagerie,* Williams had a failure in his collaboration with Donald Windham, *You Touched Me!* based on a D. H. Lawrence story. The playwright's third phase comes in acknowledging that there are "vitally creative minds in other departments of the theatre than the writing department, and that they have much to offer him." Williams had admitted, for example, that what Laurette Taylor was to *The Glass Menagerie,* Elia Kazan was to *A Streetcar Named Desire.* In one instance, a star, in the other, a director, lifted the script beyond Williams' own awareness of its potential in conception; "he has now recognized that there are elements of the incomplete in his nature," said Williams of the playwright's third phase, "and in the work it produces."[150]

Cat on a Hot Tin Roof is a good instance of Williams' revising in the third phase. The play is now available in two versions: the first approximately as Williams submitted it to Kazan; and the second, the Broadway acting version. Kazan had found three shortcomings in the first version: the powerful and vital character, Big Daddy, failed to appear in the third act; Brick, the romantic lead, had no change of

character, even after Big Daddy had practically vivisected him to find
the true reason for his not sleeping with Maggie; and Maggie was not
clearly enough a sympathetic figure to the audience. "It was only the
third of these suggestions," wrote Williams, "that I embraced whole-
heartedly from the outset because it so happened that Maggie the Cat
had become steadily more charming to me as I worked on her characterization." [151] Williams, nevertheless, still rewrote Act III to meet
Kazan's other objections lest Kazan, Broadway's foremost director at
the time, turn down the script. "The reception of the playing script,"
Williams noted of the play's public reaction, "has more than justified,
in my opinion, the adjustments made to that influence"—Kazan's. Big
Daddy in Burl Ives' overwhelming performance on Broadway all but
made the play his, and his exclusion from Act III is hard to imagine
without very seriously damaging the total effect. It would have been
as if one were watching a family drama with the father, as it were,
the center of the solar system, and in the third act, the sun were quite
removed. Maggie's more sympathetic quality through revision allowed
the audience someone to "root for." And Brick's capitulation to Maggie's trick to get her to become pregnant is made more plausible as a
kind of truce in Brick's war with Maggie—a truce so that Big Daddy
might die with some measure of happiness. The revisions were relatively small in size but of major effect.

Act III of the Broadway acting version begins with a repeat of Big
Daddy's words that closed Act II; this shows a direct continuity with
Act II and re-emphasizes Big Daddy's view of all the people around
him: "(*shouts as he goes on dr on gallery*) All—lyin'—dyin'—liars!
Liars! Liars!" [152] Then follows a series of scenes substantiating Big
Daddy's outburst, the same largely in both versions. Gooper, Mae, and
Margaret try to tell Big Mama the truth painlessly—that Big Daddy is
dying of cancer. And soon the family is in a terrible hassle over
Gooper's plans to take over Big Daddy's plantation—all 28,000 acres of
it. In the Broadway version, Big Daddy then reenters. Throughout
the third act (and only in the Broadway version) a violent thun-
derstorm had been gathering, awakening Big Daddy—a kind of
symbol of the equivalent psychological storm raging in his family. Big
Daddy implies that when he was supposedly in bed, he was near
enough to overhear Gooper's machinations in the living-room. Big
Daddy reaffirms his power. Then before the whole family, Maggie announces her birthday present to Big Daddy, the fulfillment of his
dream—Maggie is going to have a baby by Brick. Rejoicing, Big
Daddy exits, saying he's going to see his lawyer in the morning, im-

plying the revision of his will to favor his prospective new heir. In the original version, Big Daddy was not present when Maggie announced she was going to have a baby. In both versions, Gooper and Mae imply Maggie is lying because they have heard no sounds of love-making through the wall of Brick and Maggie's bed-room, adjoining theirs. In the Broadway version, Brick is now more determined than ever to make his father's dream come true; Brick says of Maggie to Gooper and Mae, "How d'ya know we're not silent lovers." [153] Mae and Gooper then cynically exit.

In both versions, Maggie then makes her deal with Brick. In the early version, she tells him that she has locked up his liquor and that he'll get none until she first has conceived from him—it's her time. Brick then gives in as the play closes with the lines:

> MARGARET: Oh, you weak people, you weak, beautiful people!— Who give up!—What you want is someone to— (*She turns out the rose silk lamp*) take hold of you—Gently, gently, with love! (*The curtain begins to fall slowly*) I *do* love you, Brick, I *do*.
> BRICK: (*smiling with charming sadness*) Wouldn't it be funny if that was true? [154]

In the Broadway version, Maggie dramatically grabs the liquor bottles from the bar, and the crippled Brick watches her send the bottles flying out the opened doorway to smash on the walk. Maggie then tells Brick there's no more liquor in the house, that he's lost his driver's license, and that if he tries to go to Ruby Lightfoot's gin mill, she'll have him stopped by the troopers on the highway. She promises, however, that if he makes her lie to Big Daddy come true, then she'll get him all the liquor he wants. The closing lines of the Broadway version are:

> MARGARET: Oh, you weak, beautiful people who give up with such grace. What you need is someone to take hold of you—gently, with love, and hand your life back to you, like something gold you let go of—and I can! I'm determined to do it—and nothing's more determined than a cat on a tin roof—is there? Is there, baby? (*She touches his cheek gently*) [155]

The Broadway version not only makes Maggie more likeable but re-states at the very end,—which is the play's major climax,—just what Williams wanted the play to say about life: a loving and possessive wife will see to it that humanity survives by procreating in spite of all the lying, envy, greed, and hypocrisy in the world about them.

My grateful acknowledgement is extended to Audrey Wood, Literary Agent for Tennessee Williams at Ashley Famous Agency, Incorporated; she read, corrected, and amended the manuscript and granted permission to use all source material in her final jurisdiction. My gratitude is also extended to the following sources of quotations:

NEW YORK DAILY NEWS, March 3, 1958, Ben Gross' Column, "What's on—A Famous Playwright Prays before Premieres"

THE DARK AT THE TOP OF THE STAIRS by William Inge with an introduction by Tennessee Williams. (C) 1958. Reprinted by permission of Random House, Inc.

ESQUIRE magazine, April 1956, "From the Journal of George Jean Nathan"; December 1962, "The Agent as Catalyst" by Tennessee Williams; April 1963, "No Time Like the Present"

THE HOLLYWOOD REPORTER, Irving Hoffman's column, "Tales of Hoffman," a letter from Tennessee Williams written after the failure of SUMMER AND SMOKE. Reprinted by permission.

LIFE magazine, February 16, 1948, "Tennessee Williams" by Lincoln Barnett. (C) 1948 Time Inc. Reprinted by permission.

THE MORNING TELEGRAPH, January 26, 1959, "Of Suddenly Last Summer" by Whitney Bolton. Reprinted by permission.

NEW YORK HERALD TRIBUNE:

"Critics Say, 'Evasion,' Writer Says, 'Mystery,' " by Tennessee Williams, April 17, 1955

"Williams in Art and Morals" by Don Ross, March 3, 1957

"Joe Hyams in Hollywood—Tennessee Williams Turns Critic," December 23, 1959

"SWEET BIRD OF YOUTH Violent in Tennessee Williams Style" by Don Ross, March 8, 1959

Reprinted by permission.

NEW YORK POST, December 30, 1957, "Mike Wallace Asks Tennessee Williams 'What Makes You Angry?' "; Excerpts from "A Man Named Tennessee" series by Robert Rice in *The New York Post,* Copyright 1958, New York Post Corporation

NEW YORK TIMES:

"A Playwright Named Tennessee" by R. C. Lewis, December 7, 1947

"Questions Without Answers" by Tennessee Williams, October 3, 1948

"A Writer's Quest for Parnassus" by Tennessee Williams, August 13, 1950

"Williams' Wells of Violence" by Tennessee Williams, March 8, 1959

"News and Gossip Gathered on the Rialto" by Lewis Funke, December 6, 1959

"Tennessee Williams Presents His POV," June 12, 1960

"Prelude to a Comedy" by Tennessee Williams, November 6, 1960

(C) 1947, 1948, 1950, 1959, 1960 by the New York Times Company. Reprinted by permission.

NEW YORK WORLD TELEGRAM AND SUN, May 25, 1959, "Tennessee Williams' Aim: Not to Deceive or to Bore" by Tennessee Williams as told to John Cruesemann of the LONDON EXPRESS

NEW YORKER, April 14, 1945, "The Celluloid Brassiere"

NEWSWEEK magazine, April 1, 1957, "The Play, Only the Flashes;" March 23, 1959, "Talk with the Playwright." Reprinted by permission.

THE PLAYBILL FOR "WEST-SIDE STORY," September 30, 1957, "Author and Director, a Delicate Situation" by Tennessee Williams. Reprinted by permission

REMEMBER ME TO TOM by Edwina Dakin Williams as told to Lucy Freeman. Copyright 1963. Reprinted by permission of G. P. Putnam's Sons.

SATURDAY REVIEW:

"Tennessee Williams—The Last of Our Solid Gold Bohemians" by Henry Hewes, March 28, 1953

"American Playwrights Self-Appraised" compiled by Henry Hewes, September 3, 1955

Reprinted by permission.

STUDIO M PLAYHOUSE PLAYBILL, April 1956, "Author's Note" by Tennessee Williams for try-out of SWEET BIRD OF YOUTH at Coral Gables, Florida

TENNESSEE WILLIAMS by Signi Falk. Copyright 1961. Twayne Publishing Co.

TENNESSEE WILLIAMS AND FRIENDS by Gilbert Maxwell. Copyright (C) 1965 by Gilbert Maxwell. All rights reserved. The World Publishing Co. Reprinted by permission.

TENNESSEE WILLIAMS, The Man and His Work by Benjamin Nelson. Copyright 1961. Ivan Obolensky, Publishers, Inc.

TENNESSEE WILLIAMS, REBELLIOUS PURITAN by Nancy Tischler. Copyright 1961. Citadel Press, Inc.

THEATRE ARTS MONTHLY:

"Tennessee Williams: Ten Years Later," July 1955

"Letters to the Editor," a letter from Tennessee Williams, October 1955

"Offstage Commentary" by Tennessee Williams, May 1958

"Williams on Williams" by Lewis Funke and John E. Booth, January 1962 TIME magazine, December 1, 1961, "A Small Thing But His Own;" March 9, 1962, "Angel of the Odd." Reprinted by permission.

VARIETY:

"Tennessee Williams Touring Orient, Working in Mornings on 4 Scripts" by Dave Jampel, September 30, 1959

"Tennessee Williams Sez He's Finished Scripting Pix; Hates to Re-create," November 4, 1959

"All Artists Are Eccentric" by Tennessee Williams, July 27, 1960

Reprinted by permission.

VOGUE magazine, March 15, 1951, "Tennessee Williams Explains His Elusive, Brilliant, Allusive Comedy, THE ROSE TATTOO"

Works of Tennessee Williams:

BATTLE OF ANGELS by Tennessee Williams, *Pharos* magazine, Spring 1945. Copyright 1945 by Tennessee Williams.

CAMINO REAL by Tennessee Williams. Copyright 1953 by Tennessee Williams. All rights reserved. Reprinted by permission of the publisher, New Directions Publishing Corporation.

CAT ON A HOT TIN ROOF by Tennessee Williams. Copyright 1955 by Tennessee Williams. All rights reserved. Reprinted by permission of the publisher, New Directions Publishing Corporation.

THE GLASS MENAGERIE by Tennessee Williams. Copyright 1945 by Tennessee Williams and Edwina D. Williams. All rights reserved. Reprinted by permission of the publisher, New Directions Publishing Corporation.

ORPHEUS DESCENDING by Tennessee Williams. Copyright (c) 1955, 1958 by Tennessee Williams. All rights reserved. Reprinted by permission of the publisher, New Directions Publishing Corporation.

THE ROSE TATTOO by Tennessee Williams. Copyright 1950 by Tennessee Williams. Copyright 1951 by Tennessee Williams. All rights reserved. Reprinted by permission of the publisher, New Directions Publishing Corporation.

A STREETCAR NAMED DESIRE. Copyright 1947 by Tennessee Williams. All rights reserved. Reprinted by permission of the publisher, New Directions Publishing Corporation.

27 WAGONS FULL OF COTTON & OTHER PLAYS by Tennessee Williams. Copyright 1945 by Tennessee Williams. Copyright 1953 by Tennessee Williams. All rights reserved. Reprinted by permission of the publisher, New Directions Publishing Corporation

CHAPTER VIII: FOOTNOTES

1. "American Playwrights Self-Appraised," *Saturday Review* (September 3, 1955), 18
2. Robert Rice, "A Man Named Tennessee," *New York Post* (April 29, 1958), M-2
3. Ibid. (April 30, 1958), M-2; Edwina Dakin Williams as told to Lucy Freeman, *Remember Me to Tom* (New York 1963), 138
4. "A Small Thing But His Own," *Time* (December 1, 1961), 76
5. "Angel of the Odd," *Time* (March 9, 1962), 53
6. Tennessee Williams, *Battle of Angels, Pharos* magazine (Spring 1945), 110
7. *New York Post* (April 29, 1958), M-2
8. "Tennessee Williams' Aim: Not to Deceive or to Bore," as told to John Cruesemann of the *London Express,* reprinted in *New York World Telegram and Sun* (May 25, 1959)
9. *New York Post* (April 25, 1958), M-2
10. Edwina Williams, 13
11. *New York World Telegram and Sun* (May 25, 1959)
12. *New York Post* (April 24, 1958), M-1, M-2
13. Ibid., M-2
14. Edwina Williams, 17, 21, 26
15. Lincoln Barnett, "Tennessee Williams," *Life* magazine (February 16, 1948), 116
16. Ibid.
17. *New York Post* (April 25, 1958), M-2
18. Ibid.
19. Edwina Williams, 34
20. Ibid., 189
21. Ibid., 35
22. Ibid., 57, 205
23. *New York Post* (May 4, 1958), M-2; Edwina Williams, 39, 202
24. *New York Post* (April 25, 1958), M-2
25. *Life* (February 16, 1948), 118
26. Edwina Williams, 30
27. Tennessee Williams, "Williams' Wells of Violence," *New York Times* (March 8, 1959), Sect. 2, X3

28. Paul Moor, "A Mississippian Named Tennessee," *Harper's* magazine (July 1948), 65; *Life* (February 16, 1948), 121; Edwina Williams, 64

29. *New York Post* (April 29, 1958), M-2

30. *New York Post* (April 28, 1958), M-2

31. Edwina Williams, 96; Tennessee Williams, *Orpheus Descending* with *Battle of Angels* (New York 1955), vii

32. *New York Post* (April 30, 1958), M-2

33. Ibid.

34. *Twentieth Century Authors, First Supplement* (New York 1955), 1087

35. *Edwina Williams,* 202

36. Gilbert Maxwell, *Tennessee Williams and Friends* (New York 1965), 222

37. Nancy Tischler, *Tennessee Williams, Rebellious Puritan* (New York 1961), 115

38. Maxwell, 329, 333

39. Ibid., 304

40. Ibid., 102

41. Ben Gross's Column, *New York Daily News* (March 3, 1958); "Offstage," *Theatre Arts* magazine (May 1958), 11

42. Edwina Williams, 254; *New York Herald Tribune* (March 8, 1959), Sect. 4, 9

43. "Joe Hyams in Hollywood—Tennessee Williams Turns Critic," *New York Herald Tribune* (December 23, 1959), 13

44. "Tennessee Williams Sez He's Finished Scripting Pix; Hates to Re-create," *Variety* (November 4, 1959)

45. "Tennessee Williams in Art and Morals," *New York Herald Tribune* (March 3, 1957), IV, 2

46. Ibid.

47. "From the Journal of George Jean Nathan," *Esquire* (April 1956), 48

48. *New York Post* (April 30, 1958), M-2

49. Ibid.

50. Tennessee Williams, "The Agent as Catalyst," *Esquire* (December 1962), 260

51. Ibid.

52. "The Celluloid Brassiere," *New Yorker* (April 14, 1945), 18

53. Ibid.

54. *New York World Telegram and Sun* (May 25, 1959)

55. Don Ross, *"Sweet Bird of Youth* Violent in Tennessee Williams' Style," *New York Herald Tribune* (March 8, 1959), Sect. 4, 1

56. Lewis Funke and John E. Booth, "Williams on Williams," *Theatre Arts Monthly* (January 1962), 19

57. *New York Herald Tribune* (March 8, 1959), Sect. 4, 1

58. *New York World Telegram and Sun* (May 25, 1959)

59. Tennessee Williams, "Prelude to Comedy," *New York Times* (November 6, 1960), Sect. 2, X

60. Tennessee Williams, *27 Wagons Full of Cotton and Other One-Act Plays* (New York 1945), vii

61. Tennessee Williams, "Questions Without Answers," *New York Times* (October 3, 1948), Sect. 2, X

62. *Current Biography* (1946), 646

63. *Variety* (July 27, 1960); Ibid. (September 30, 1959)

64. Tennessee Williams, *Cat on a Hot Tin Roof* (New York 1955), viii

65. William Inge, *The Dark at the Top of the Stairs* with a preface by Tennessee Williams (New York 1958), vii

66. "Tennessee Williams Presents His POV," *New York Times Magazine* (June 12, 1960), 78

67. *27 Wagons Full of Cotton and Other One-Act Plays,* xii

68. Tennessee Williams, *The Glass Menagerie* (New York 1949), xviii, xiv

69. *New York Times* (March 8, 1959), Sect. 2, X

70. *New York Post* (April 30, 1958), M-2

71. *New York Daily News* (March 3, 1958)

72. *New York Times Magazine* (June 12, 1960), 78

73. Tischler, 301

74. *New York Times* (March 8, 1959), Sect. 2, X3

75. Nelson, 76; *New York Times Magazine* (December 7, 1947), 19

76. *The Glass Menagerie,* ix

77. Tennessee Williams, *The Rose Tattoo* (New York 1950), vii

78. *Harper's* magazine (July 1948), 64; *New York Times Magazine* (December 7, 1947), 19

79. *Theatre Arts Monthly* (January 1962), 73; *New York Post* (April 21, 1959), M-2; Edwina Williams, 252

80. *Time* (March 9, 1962), 54

81. *New York Times* (November 6, 1960), Sect. 2, X3

82. Tennessee Williams, "A Writer's Quest for Parnassus," *New York Times Magazine* (August 13, 1950), 35; Edwina Williams, 103, 110, 193

83. Edwina Williams, 218–219

84. *Theatre Arts Monthly* (January 1962), 73

85. Edwina Williams, 222–223

86. Ibid.

87. *Theatre Arts Monthly* (January 1962), 73

88. *New York Times* (November 6, 1960), Sect. 2, X3

89. Edwina Williams, 132

90. *Life* (February 16, 1948), 116

91. *Theatre Arts Monthly* (January 1962), 19

92. *Esquire* (December 1962), 216

93. *Theatre Arts Monthly* (January 1962), 73; *New York Times Magazine* (December 7, 1947), 67

94. *Life* (February 16, 1948), 113

95. Tennessee Williams, *Three Plays of Tennessee Williams* (New York 1955), 162

96. Edwina Williams, 149

97. Maxwell, 28, 256–257

98. *Time* (March 9, 1962), 55

99. Edwina Williams, 54, 55; *New York World Telegram and Sun* (May 25, 1959)

100. *Time* (March 9, 1962), 56; *Life* (February 16, 1948), 116

101. R. C. Lewis, "A Playwright Named Tennessee," *New York Times Magazine* (December 7, 1947), 19

102. Ibid.

103. Tischler, 140

104. Edwina Williams, 207

105. *New York Times* (March 8, 1959), Sect. 2, X3

106. *New York Times* (October 3, 1948), Sect. 2, X3

107. *Life* (February 16, 1948), 118; Edwina Williams, 193; *New York Times Magazine* (December 7, 1947), 67

108. *New York Herald Tribune* (March 3, 1957), Sect. 4, 2

109. Edwina Williams, 223

110. *New York World Telegram and Sun* (May 25, 1959)

111. *New York Times* (March 8, 1959), Sect. 2, X3

112. *New York Herald Tribune* (March 3, 1957), Sect. 4, 1

113. "The Play, Not the Flashes," *Newsweek* (April 1, 1957), 81

114. "Tennessee Williams, Ten Years Later," *Theatre Arts* (July 1955), 96

115. Ibid.

116. *Life* (February 16, 1948), 116; Ben Nelson, *Tennessee Williams* (New York 1961), 76

117. Whitney Bolton, "Suddenly Last Summer," *Morning Telegraph* (January 26, 1959); Tischler, 176

118. "Letters to the Editor," letter from Tennessee Williams, *Theatre Arts Monthly* (October 1955), 3

119. Henry Hewes, "Tennessee Williams—the Last of Our Solid Gold Bohemians," *Saturday Review* (March 28, 1953), 26

120. *Three Plays of Tennessee Williams,* 161

121. *Life* (February 16, 1948), 118

122. *Glass Menagerie,* xix

123. Tennessee Williams, *A Streetcar Named Desire* (New York 1948), 10

124. Ibid., 11

125. Ibid., 60, 135

126. Ibid., 140

127. Tennessee Williams, "Critics Say, 'Evasion,' Writer Says, 'Mystery,'" *New York Herald Tribune* (April 17, 1955), Sect. 4, 2

128. *Life* (February 16, 1948), 113; *Orpheus Descending* with *Battle of Angels,* vi, x

129. *Harper's* magazine (July 1948), 67

130. Edwina Williams, 154

131. *A Streetcar Named Desire,* 110

132. *New York Herald Tribune* (March 3, 1957), Sect. 4, 2

133. Edwina Williams, 223

134. "Tennessee Williams Explains His Elusive, Brilliant, Allusive Comedy, *The Rose Tattoo,*" *Vogue* (March 15, 1951), 96

135. *Theatre Arts* (July 1955), 96

136. Ibid.

137. *Cat on a Hot Tin Roof,* viii; *Pharos* magazine, 121

138. *27 Wagons Full of Cotton and Other One-Act Plays,* 32, 40, 51

139. *Theatre Arts* (January 1962), 18

140. *A Streetcar Named Desire,* 165

141. *Theatre Arts* (January 1962), 18

142. Ibid.

143. Ibid.

144. *Time* (March 9, 1962), 53

145. Tennessee Williams, "Author and Director, a Delicate Situation," Playbill for *West-Side Story* (September 30, 1957), 9

146. Ibid.

147. Edwina Williams, 115

148. *New York Times Magazine* (December 7, 1947), 19

149. Playbill for *West-Side Story* (September 30, 1957), 10

150. Ibid.

151. *Cat on a Hot Tin Roof,* 152

152. Ibid., 112

153. Ibid., 194

154. Ibid., 149–150

155. Ibid., 197

Chapter IX

A Cursory Study of Modern Playwrights

I

GROWTH OF THE PLAYWRIGHTS' CREATIVE SPIRIT

Born or Made?

To DAVID BELASCO, "playwriting is the most complex of all the arts." [1] To Eugene Ionesco who is poles apart from Belasco in his dramaturgy, "nothing is more difficult than to write for the theatre." [2] In *The Writer* (April, 1962), Jean Kerr said in Howard Teichmann's article, "Myths of Present Day Playwriting," "No question of it," referring to playwriting as a form of fiction; "The play is by far the most difficult." Arthur Kober added, "And how!" Ibsen, Strindberg, Chekhov, Shaw, Galsworthy, Pirandello, O'Neill, and Williams were all undoubtedly born gifted and yet had to serve usually a long and sometimes a very discouraging apprenticeship. Even diamonds in the rough have to be meticulously cut and polished to bring out their finest hidden fire. Whether the most difficult or not, playwriting is a formidable art.

Pinero thought that, like the poet, the dramatist had to be born but still needed long study and discipline. Belasco thought the same. "It would be difficult to say whether it can be learned or taught," surmised Jacinto Benavente, "just as it would be embarrassing to be asked whether it is easy or difficult to be a playwright." Benavente insisted, "Natural predisposition, no matter how fundamental, must be supplemented by study." [3] Rachel Crothers noted "only the gifted can be helped." [4] In Clayton Hamilton's opinion, the playwright needed talent and also "a dozen years of unremitted, unremunerated labor." "I believe that you can teach the technique of playwriting by exploring successful plays and discovering how they work and why they work," said Robert Anderson, who taught playwriting for four years at the American Theatre Wing. "But the artistry, that certain quality

which lifts a play—making it particular—this you cannot teach." [5]
Lawrence Langner believed there were not nor could there be child
prodigies among dramatists because playwriting required not only a
gift but long discipline and, above all, an understanding of human nature through experiencing maturity. Belasco and Maugham both
thought, incidentally, that good plays earn fortunes because of the
rarity of genuine playwrights.

"I will not be able to calculate the debt I owe television for the
amount of sheer craft I have learned," said Paddy Chayefsky. "I have
achieved a discipline and preciseness of thinking . . ." [6] Through five
years of adapting and writing television plays, Chayefsky picked up
playwriting. "In America they have college courses in writing of
plays. Do you approve of this?" a Warsaw University student asked
Arthur Miller when he lectured there in 1965. "I came from one myself," Miller replied, "so I approve. You have an audience and you can
see whether something is reaching people. It's a way to try your
wings." And then Miller cautioned, "But I wouldn't take early success
too seriously. And it's very difficult to make playwriting academic.
Audiences are very critical, and they get bored with boring plays." [7]

Nature of the Playwright

"I have a pet theory of my own, probably invalid," said the late
Moss Hart in his autobiography, *Act One,* "that the theatre is an inevitable refuge of the unhappy child." [8] "All authors are neurotic,"
wrote George Abbott on the same note in his autobiography, *Mister
Abbott.* "I'll even go further: everybody in the creative side of the
theatre is neurotic." [9] Ibsen, Strindberg, Chekhov, Shaw, O'Neill, Williams, all had unhappy childhoods for exceptionally long periods.
When driven to an inner life, they made the most of their loneliness
by fantasies, reading, story-telling and related forms of play. Whether
a playwright needs to have an unhappy childhood to drive his imagination to create a make-believe world, remains a moot point.

Suggesting other traits characteristic of the playwright, Maugham
noted a newspaperman's nose for a good story and a sense of how to
point it up with vivid detail. "The Press," Maugham warned, "in fact,
kills the individuality of those who write for it," and he thought reviewing did, too.[10] Maugham believed a great playwright needed an
eye that caught the universal and the individual. Hart thought the
playwright had to have a gift for story-telling; even in childhood,
Hart found he could hold his playmates spellbound with his stories.

The playwright, in Benavente's view, had an endless, sympathetic curiosity about human nature and a memory for richly stocking details. As for the playwright being an idler, Benavente remarked, "But in this apparent idleness the great works of the spirit have been born, for all life is labor to the man who is a true artist; his mind is unceasingly active . . ." [11] John Van Druten regarded the playwright as "more interested in people than in things or places," and as given to using these observations creatively.[12] Saroyan thought the playwright needed "eagerness, faith, industry, goodness, severity, real objectivity, courage," and Saroyan added emphatically, "To look sharply means to know what you and things are about, and that is the beginning of criticism." [13] To Thornton Wilder, the mark of the true story teller in the *Bible,* in Plato, and in the playwright was "an instinctive coupling of idea and illustration." [14] Lillian Hellman thought the playwright had to be a dedicated artist of "high seriousness" with an able partner in the unconscious. "The playwright has to have character. His wife has to have character, too," said Robert Anderson in his article, "The Playwright and His Craft," in the May, 1955, issue of *The Writer.* "It is the kind of character that will not be shattered by disappointments, cruelty, lack of attention . . ." "I believe that to become a playwright," summed up Anderson, "it takes talent, time, character, humility, and work." "Playwriting in the United States," Edward Albee declared after the success of *Who's Afraid of Virginia Woolf?* "demands (talent aside) extraordinary ego, guts, and gall." [15]

Early Signs and Inclinations

"A teacher of elocution who advertised in my uncle's paper failed to pay her bill," recalled Howard Lindsay of his childhood in Atlantic City at the age of three. "I was sent to work it out. This condition continued for about four years, and I have always believed it was these early experiences as an elocutionist that made me determined to become an actor."[16] Acting led Lindsay to playwriting. Benavente in childhood wrote skits for his own puppet theatre. Rachel Crothers admitted writing plays for her paper dolls and wrote and produced a five-act melodrama at the age of twelve. Edmond Rostand as a boy was devoted to his marionette theatre and to poetry. Arthur Schnitzler as a child was scribbling skits and plays, and at nine finished a five-act tragedy. Owen Davis wrote *Diamond Cut Diamond or The Rival Detectives* at the age of nine; one character survived the mayhem of the first act only to commit suicide later. As a child, Oscar Wilde already showed such a gift for language and story-telling that his mother called him "my genius." Richard Rodgers at four could play piano by ear and at fourteen wrote his first song, *My Auto Show Girl*. Robert Emmet Sherwood began writing at seven and for one year edited his own magazine, *Children's Life,* and at ten, wrote his first play, *Tom Ruggles' Surprise*. Terence Rattigan was a stage-struck child often seeing and reading plays; at ten, he wrote his first play, a drama about Caesare Borgia. James Thurber took to writing at the age of ten with *The Intrepid Boy-Scout,* and started drawing at fourteen. John Van Druten confessed to writing his first long play, *Anne Boleyn,* at the age of seven. "I have been writing since I was a child," said Lillian Hellman.[17] At the age of ten, Jean Anouilh was already writing verse plays largely imitating Rostand, and Anouilh completed his first long play at sixteen. Christopher Fry wrote a farce at eleven, a poem at twelve, and his first verse drama at fourteen. William Inge became stage-struck at seven when he learned a monologue his sister was tirelessly practising. "At eleven or twelve," said Arthur Laurents, "I wrote my first short story, completely in dialogue: apparently I always wanted to be a playwright."[18] Edward Albee wrote his first play at the age of twelve, a full length sex-farce, *Aliqueen;* he was not to try another play until *Zoo Story* about eighteen years later.

"I cannot remember the time I did not want to write," remarked Susan Glaspell, "and creative effort began while still in grammar school."[19] "I have been writing since I was sixteen years old," said Carson McCullers; "My first effort at writing was a play."[20] Alan Jay Lerner was writing lyrics and songs and decided upon a theatrical career at the age of eleven. Friedrich Duerrenmatt wrote his first play, *Es Stet Geschriben,* at sixteen, and won a prize with it. Noel Coward was only eighteen when he had his first commercial production, a failure called *The Rat Trap;* he had earlier received $2,000 for working on his melodrama, *The Last Trick,* which remained unproduced. Bayard Veiller, best remembered for *Within the Law,* wrote his first play at eighteen, submitted it to the producer, Augustin Daily, and Daily told Bayard that he didn't think a play could be that bad. William Saroyan started writing at thirteen. Clifford Odets quit high school at fifteen to enter radio as announcer, writer, and actor. Sidney Kingsley wrote one-act plays of social problems as a high school student at Townsend Harris Hall in New York City.

Sometimes a playwright shows an early sign or inclination not by writing a play but perhaps by a yen for a contributing art or craft, which like a tributary stream comes to feed the main talent by finding it through time. Ivor Novello published his first song at fifteen and came into fame and fortune with *Keep the Homes Fires Burning* at twenty-one. Russel Crouse at seventeen became a news and sports reporter for the Kansas City, Missouri, *Star*. Gabriele D'Annunzio published *Prima Verse*, his first volume of poems, at the age of sixteen. T. S. Eliot published a comic narrative in ottava rima, "A Fable for Feasters," in his prep school newspaper, *The Smith Academy Record*, when he was seventeen. Max Shulman was active on the newspaper staff at Central High School in St. Paul. "Mine was the same old story of hanging around little acting groups," Lorraine Hansberry said of her high school days," and developing the feeling that the theatre embraces everything I like all at one time." [21] Paddy Chayefsky worked on the De Witt Clinton High School periodical. Garson Kanin helped support himself by playing sax and clarinet, performed for vaudeville and burlesque shows, and then was a master of ceremonies in summer camps and night clubs. At sixteen, Paul Vincent Carroll began a five year association with the Abbey Players of Dublin. "I learned at the Abbey Theatre the rudiments of playmaking," he said, "and that unquenchable love of the drama that is the chief impetus of my life." [22] Jan de Hartog at eighteen became a sub-inspector for the Amsterdam Harbor Police and, to wile away his night watches, wrote sea stories which Amsterdam newspapers came to accept. The Municipal Theatre called de Hartog in to give technical advice on a sea play, and he soon took to playwriting. John Osborne tutored juveniles touring the English provinces with the play, *No Room at the Inn,* and then Osborne became an actor himself, and so eventually a playwright. Harold Pinter took to acting after his drama teacher at Hackney Downs Grammar School in London encouraged him. Pinter had been writing poetry since he was thirteen. John Howard Lawson at nineteen received a small payment from George M. Cohan and Sam H. Harris for an option on an ill-fated play.

An impressive number of playwrights confirmed earlier signs of a gift for playwriting in their college years or showed their inclination only then. Ferenc Molnar wrote short stories and plays while studying at the Royal College of Science in Budapest, and later as a law student at the University of Budapest and that of Geneva. Hugo von Hofmannsthal, who was to write the librettos for many of Richard Strauss's operas, wrote three poetic dramas during his student days at the University of Vienna, all under pseudonyms. George Abbott became interested in playwriting after writing the Varsity show at the University of Rochester. Martin Flavin in his short stay at the University of Chicago centered his activities around the dramatic club. Philip Barry at Yale wrote and had produced his only one-act play. Bertolt Brecht wrote skits and one-act plays and saw them produced in his student days at the Universities of Munich and Berlin. As a Yale undergraduate, Thornton Wilder wrote some plays later published in his collected one-acts. Robert Emmet Sherwood edited the *Vanity Fair* issue of *The Harvard Lampoon.* "I wrote my first play in the ten days of spring vacation," recalled Arthur Miller of his University of Michigan days. "I had seen but one play in my life and had read the tragedies of Shakespeare." Miller also noted by way of self-revelation, "A book that changed my life was *The Brothers Karamazov,* which I picked up I don't know how or why, and all at once I believed I was born to be a writer. This was after I had graduated from high school and was working in a warehouse on Tenth Avenue in Manhattan." [23] Miller was an editor on the University of Michigan's newspaper and won the $500 Avery Hopwood Award in playwriting. Robert Anderson wrote musical shows for the Harvard Hasty Pudding Club and was also chosen class poet. Alan Jay Lerner collaborated on the Harvard Hasty Pudding Club shows *Proudly We Hail* and *Fair Enough.* T. S. Eliot edited *The Harvard Advocate,* contributed poetry, and was class odist. William Inge believed that the most valuable experience of his college years came in the musical comedies in which he had a chance to test his creative talents at the University of Kansas. Max Shulman edited *Ski U Mah,* the humor magazine of the University of Minnesota, and wrote a daily column for the college newspaper.

Sometimes a marked gift for the drama fails to reveal itself until well after college years. Lawrence Langner as a full fledged patent agent, helped organize the Washington Square Players, the forerunners of the Theatre Guild, and for them, wrote one-acts like *Matinata.* William Butler Yeats influenced Synge, then in his late twenties, to try a hand at folk plays about the Aran Islands. A. A. Milne with three volumes of essays to his credit from *Punch,* in 1915 found time at an army training camp to write a play for himself and other soldiers to put on. Albert Camus, following his graduation from the University of Algiers, took active part from age twenty-two to twenty-five as an actor and manager in Algiers' theatre life. As a full fledged lawyer, Maurice Maeterlinck at the age of twenty-seven wrote his first play, *La Princesse Maleine,* and two years later wrote his now famous one-acts, *L'Intruse* (*The Intruder*), and *Les Aveugles* (*The Blind*). Some of the best of playwrights showed no specific bent for the drama until their mid-twenties or even their late thirties, for instance: Shaw, Wilde, O'Neill, Galsworthy, Pirandello, Williams, Drinkwater, Giraudoux, Maxwell Anderson, Lindsay and Crouse. In every instance, however, they had a previous discipline in the writing of poetry, stories, or even novels.

The Playwright's Age at First Success *

How long, rocky, and studded with pitfalls is the road to a playwright's first success? Enough playwrights have succeeded before the age of thirty to really hearten the optimists. To date, Shelagh Delaney has scored the earliest smash-hit of any modern playwright; her first play, *A Taste of Honey*, based on her rough draft of a novel, scored a sensational English success when she was nineteen and won the New York Drama Critics' Circle Award for the best foreign play of 1961-62. Elmer Rice was to make about $100,000 from his play, *On Trial*, a smash-hit when he was twenty-two. Rice, however, while studying law and serving a law clerkship, had in collaboration with a friend, Frank Harris, earlier written two full-length plays that failed to win a production: *A Defection from Grace* and *The Seventh Commandment*. Richard Rodgers made good at twenty-three with his music and Larry Hart's lyrics contributing to *The Garrick Gaieties,* an experimental production of The Theatre Guild conceived to help pay for the Gobelin tapestries in the Guild's new theatre by running for Sunday performances only; the first *Gaieties* went into a full run of 214 performances. Rodgers had earlier written the music for some twenty amateur shows sponsored by churches, synagogues, girls' schools, and Columbia University.

John Van Druten arrived with *Young Woodley* at twenty-four; and so did Noel Coward with *The Vortex*. Van Druten, however, had earlier failed with *The Return Half,* a collaboration with John Gielgud. Coward had had a failure, *The Rat Trap,* and also an unproduced play, *The Last Trick.* Albert Camus, Terence Rattigan and Jean Kerr came through at twenty-five. Camus scored an artistic victory with *Caligula;* he had earlier published essays, *L'Envers et*

* Runs and profits are not always available; producers often conceal them unless compelled by law as now in the United States to divulge them to protect investors. Sometimes artistic success alone, as with John Millington Synge, merits mention.

L'Endroit and *Les Noces.* Terence Rattigan smiled with *French Without Tears;* he had an earlier failure, *First Episode,* written in collaboration with Philip Heimann, and Rattigan had previously written five full-length unproduced plays. *French Without Tears* ran in London for 1,090 performances. Jean Kerr and her husband, Walter Kerr, co-authored a revue at Washington's Catholic University, *Thank You, Just Looking.* George Abbott saw the revue and produced it on Broadway as *Touch and Go.* She had earlier co-authored two Broadway failures: *Song of Bernadette* and *Jenny Kissed Me.* Edmond Rostand and Moss Hart succeeded at twenty-six: Rostand with *The Romancers,* later to be the basis of the long-run Off-Broadway musical, *The Fantasticks;* and Moss Hart with George S. Kaufman as collaborator in *Once in a Lifetime.* Rostand had earlier failed with *Le Gant Rouge* in collaboration with Henri Lee; Hart had failed with *The Beloved Bandit* and had written at least five full-length unproduced plays. Sidney Kingsley, Alan Jay Lerner and John Osborne won their first laurels at twenty-seven. Kingsley did it with *Crisis,* retitled *Men in White,* which waited three years for a production; Lerner collaborated with Frederick Loewe in the musical, *The Day before Spring,* and had had an earlier failure, *What's Up?;* John Osborne scored with *Look Back in Anger* after an earlier modest success, *The Devil Inside.*

Jacinto Benavente, Rachel Crothers, Oscar Hammerstein II, Max Shulman and Herb Gardner made their mark at twenty-eight. Benavente rated with *El Nido Ajeno* although, incidentally, none of his plays, not even *The Bonds of Interest,* has been commercially successful in the United States. Crothers succeeded with *The Three of Us* after four earlier misses: *Nora, The Point of View, Criss Cross* and *The Rector.* Hammerstein II made good with the musical, *Wildflower,* after earlier disappointment with a four-act drama and fair luck as a collaborator on the books and lyrics of five musicals: *Always You, Jimmie, Tickle Me, Queen of Hearts* and *Daffy Dill.* Max Shulman collaborating with George Abbott scored with the musical, *Barefoot Boy with Cheek;* Shulman had earlier written several successful satirical novels including *Barefoot Boy with Cheek.* Herb Gardner came home with *A Thousand Clowns* after having done cartooning and having had a novel published, *A Piece of Action.* Frederick Lonsdale, Samson Raphaelson, Lillian Hellman and Lorraine Hansberry arrived at twenty-nine: Lonsdale in collaboration with Frank Curzon with *The Balkan Princess;* Raphaelson with *The Jazz Singer;* Hellman with *The Children's Hour;* and Hansberry with *A Raisin in the Sun.* Lonsdale previously had only middling luck with *The Early Worm, The Best People* and *The King of Caldonia.* Hellman had an unproduced collaboration with Louis Kronenberger, *The Dear Queen.* Hansberry had a drawer of unproduced short and long plays.

If the past is any sign of the future, it is not in their twenties but in their thirties that playwrights have their best chance of first succeeding. Clifford Odets, Harold Rome, Peter Ustinov, Harold Pinter, and Anthony Newley made their first real success at thirty. Odets did it with *Awake and Sing,* which waited two years for a production; Ustinov with *The Love of Four Colonels;* Rome with *Pins and Needles;* Pinter with *The Caretaker;* and Newley with *Stop the World—I Want to Get Off,* a collaboration with Leslie Bricusse. Odets had had a sensational success the previous year with his short play, *Waiting for Lefty.* Rome had helped write and produce at least nine amateur musicals at a Catskill Mountain summer resort, Green Mansions. Ustinov had been writing and acting in his own sketches for over ten years. Pinter had written such radio and TV plays as *The Room, The Dumbwaiter, A Slight Ache,* and had had a failure in the first production of *The Birthday Party.* Newley had been acting chiefly in films since he was seventeen.

Ivor Novello, Ferenc Molnar, Lynn Riggs, Robert Emmet Sherwood, Philip Barry, Edward Chodorov and Friedrich Duerrenmatt registered their first hit at thirty-one. Novello entered with *The Rat,* a collaboration with Constance Collier. Molnar succeeded with his finest play, *Liliom.* Riggs had a more artistic than financial success, *Green Grow the Lilacs,* later to be the basis for the book of the musical, *Oklahoma!* Sherwood scored with *The Road to Rome,* Barry with *Paris Bound,* Chodorov with *Kind Lady,* based on Hugh Walpole's short story, "The Silver Mask,' and Duerrenmatt with *Die Ehe Des Heren Mississippi (The Wedding of Mr. Mississippi).* Novello had been singing, composing music, acting, and writing intermittently for well over a decade. Molnar had earlier written *The Devil,* which helped establish his reputation in drama. Riggs had previously had three try-out productions of plays that never reached Broadway: *Rancor, Domino Parlor* and *Roadside.* Sherwood was editor of the now defunct humor magazine, *Life.* Barry had earlier seen small success or outright failure with: *You and I, The Youngest, In a Garden, White Wings,* and *John.* Chodorov had had a disappointment, *Wonder Boy,* in collaboration with Arthur Barton, and had done screen writing. Duerrenmatt had been writing plays, radio scripts, suspense stories and novels for about fifteen years.

August Strindberg, Eugene O'Neill, George S. Kaufman, William Saroyan, Jean Anouilh, Arthur Miller, Gore Vidal and Peter Shaffer first won wide public approval at thirty-two: Strindberg with *Master Olof* in its original prose version, written at twenty-three rather than in the ensuing, much revised, verse version; O'Neill with *Beyond the Horizon;* Kaufman with *Dulcy* in collaboration with Marc Connelly; Saroyan with *The Time of Your Life;* Anouilh with *Antigone;* Miller with *All My Sons;* Vidal with *Visit to a Small Planet,* based on his TV play of that name; Shaffer with *Five Finger Exercise.* Strindberg had earlier had a best-selling novel, *The Red Room,* and a near failure, *The Secret of the Guild.* O'Neill had earlier written at least six long plays and many one-acts, largely destroyed as unworthy, and he had had the Off-Broadway success of his one-acts, *The Glencairn Cycle.* Kaufman had earlier written an unproduced farce, *Going Up;* an unproduced collaboration with Irving Pichel, *The Failure;* a collaboration with Larry Evans, *Someone in the House,* a failure; and a solo effort, *The Butter and Egg Man.* Saroyan had won recognition as an artist for his short play, *My Heart's in the Highlands,* and for his short stories, *Daring Young Man on the Flying Trapeze.* Anouilh had previously had failures or small success with ten full length plays including: *Jezebel, Le Bal des Voleurs, Le Sauvage, Le Voyageur, Sans Baggages, Léocadia,* and *Oreste.* Miller had survived a Broadway flop, *The Man Who Had All the Luck,* and had written radio plays for *Columbia Workshop* and *Cavalcade of America,* as well as had two novels published. Vidal had written several novels and many TV plays for *Omnibus, Studio One* and *Philco Playhouse.* Shaffer had written *The Salt Land* and *The Prodigal Father.*

The age of thirty-three marked the first notable success for John Millington Synge, Arthur Schnitzler, W. Somerset Maugham, Sidney Howard, Clare Boothe, Carson McCullers, Paddy Chayefsky, and Brendan Behan. Synge scored with his one-act folk tragedy, *Riders to the Sea,* now rated a modern classic. Schnitzler did *Libelei;* he had barely missed success with *Anatol* and for fifteen years had sporadically written short stories and playlets. Maugham succeeded with *Lady Frederick,* a play he had written ten years earlier and which won attention only after recognition of many short stories and novels, including *The Bishop's Apron,* based on his own *Loaves and Fishes.* Howard reached his goal with *They Knew What They Wanted,* later to be the basis of the musical, *The Most Happy Fella.* Boothe arrived with *The Women* after an earlier outright failure, *Abide with Me.* McCullers met good fortune with *Member of the Wedding;* Chayefsky, with *In the Middle of the Night,* based on his own TV play of that name; Behan, with *The Quare Fellow,* drawn from his prison experiences incurred for the Irish Army of Independence. Synge had earlier written the one-act, *In the Shadow of the Glen.* Maugham had written at least five full length plays before *Lady Frederick* reached production. McCullers at twenty-three had written her novel, *The Heart Is a Lonely Hunter.* Chayefsky had been working at some form of script in every entertainment media for the previous twelve years or so, writing most notably the TV play, *Marty.* Behan had published his reform school experiences, *Borstal Boy.*

Maxim Gorki, Paul Green, S. N. Behrman, Tennessee Williams, Robert Bolt, and Edward Albee were thirty-four before their first sizeable success. Gorki rose with *The Lower Depths.* Green had largely an artistic success with *In Abraham's Bosom.* Behrman arrived with *The Second Man,* which took him eleven years to sell. Williams came home with *The Glass Menagerie;* Bolt, with *Flowering Cherry;* and Albee, with *Who's Afraid of Virginia Woolf?* Gorki was already established as one of Russia's foremost writers of stories and novels. Green had earlier published a book of one-act plays. Behrman had two unproduced collaborations, one with J. Kenyon Nicholson, and another with Owen Davis. Williams had failed with *Battle of Angels* and had written at least seven full length plays and many one-acts. Bolt had written plays for radio. Albee roughly two years earlier had scored a nationally acclaimed Off-Broadway hit with bills of his short plays, *The Zoo Story, The American Dream* and *The Death of Bessie Smith.*

Ben Hecht, Ruth and Augustus Goetz, and Neil Simon achieved their first big success at thirty-five: Hecht, in collaboration with Charles MacArthur, put out *Front Page;* Ruth and Augustus Goetz as man and wife collaborated in adapting Henry James' novel, *Washington Square,* into *The Heiress;* Neil Simon soloed in *Come Blow Your Horn.* Hecht had previously published a collection of his one-act plays, *The Wonder Hat,* and had a Broadway flop, *The Egotist.* The Goetzes had marked time with *Franklin Street* and *The One-Man Show.* Neil Simon had written for Leonard Sillman's *New Faces* and for such topflight TV shows as *Caesar's Hour, Sergeant Bilko* and *The Gary Moore Show.*

John Drinkwater, Maxwell Anderson, Bella and Samuel Spewack, Robert Ardrey, Mary Coyle Chase, and Rober Woodruff Anderson celebrated their first playwriting success at thirty-six: Drinkwater, *Abraham Lincoln;* Maxwell Anderson, *What Price Glory?,* in collaboration with Laurence Stallings; the Spewacks, *Boy Meets Girl;* Ardrey, *Thunder Rock;* Chase, *Harvey;* Robert Anderson, *Tea and Sympathy.* Drinkwater had experienced an earlier failure, *Sar Taldo's Bride,* and written at least ten other plays. Maxwell Anderson had failed in *White Desert.* The Spewacks had some success with: *War Song, Poppa, Clear All Wires, and Spring Song*—none running over 100 performances. Ardrey had failure or middling success earlier in *Star Spangled, How to Get Tough about It* and *Casey Jones.* Chase had earlier flopped with *Now I've Done It,* and had unproduced tragedies, fantasies, and comedies. Robert Anderson had written at least twenty one-act plays and composed many amateur musicals as well as adapted a good forty plays for radio and television.

For A. A. Milne, Rose Franken and William Inge, impressive success came first at thirty-seven. Milne's was *Mr. Pim Passes By;* Franken's, *Another Language;* Inge's, *Come Back, Little Sheba.* Milne had earlier written at least six plays including the short *Wurzel Flummery.* Franken had on her hands an unproduced play, *Fortnight.* "I made two separate tries," said Inge, "both failures, before writing *Come Back, Little Sheba."*

Henrik Ibsen, Anton Chekhov, Oscar Wilde, Bernard Shaw, Jean-Paul Sartre, John Patrick, and Samuel Taylor won their real success as playwrights only when they were thirty-eight years old. Ibsen came through with *Brand* after failure or little success with nine earlier long plays. Chekhov soared with *The Sea-Gull;* Wilde registered with *Lady Windermere's Fan;* Shaw, with *Arms and the Man;* Taylor with *The Happy Time,* based on a book by Robert Fontanne; Patrick with *The Hasty Heart.* Chekhov had earlier had fair success with *Ivanov,* disaster with *The Wood Demon,* and much success with his one-act farces, especially *The Boor.* Wilde, curiously enough, had previously written only "tragedies," including two incredibly bad works in blank verse, *Vera or The Nihilists* and *The Duchess of Padua.* His far superior *Salome,* while in production with Sarah Bernhardt, was banned by the Lord Chamberlain. Shaw's earlier plays, *Widowers' Houses, The Philanderer* and *Mrs. Warren's Profession,* had only a small avant-garde public. Sartre succeeded with *Huis Clos (No Exit);* he had previously written his now famous novel, *La Nausée*

(*Nausea*), a collection of short stories, *Le Mur* (*The Wall*), and a long play, *Les Mouches* (*The Flies*) based on the Orestes legend. Patrick had survived two Broadway failures, *Hell Freezes Over* and *The Willow and I.*

George Abbott was thirty-nine when in collaboration with Philip Dunning, he wrote the smash-hit, *Broadway,* that ran for 603 performances; earlier he had had mild success with three other collaborations. Murray Schisgal also was thirty-nine when he succeeded with *Luv;* he had earlier had an Off-Broadway hit, a bill of two short plays, *The Typists* and *The Tiger,* and had written numerous one-acts.

An impressive number of playwrights did not arrive until their forties. Jerome Lawrence was forty and his collaborator, Robert E. Lee, was thirty-seven when their *Inherit the Wind* finally reached Broadway and success after a wait of five years. The pair had had an earlier fair success with *Look, Ma, I'm Dancin';* both were also top-flight radio and TV writers and producers for roughly five years. Abe Burrows was also forty when in collaboration with Jo Swerling he wrote the book for the musical, *Guys and Dolls,* based on some Damon Runyon stories; for the previous ten years or so he was a popular comedy writer for radio and TV. Galsworthy was forty-one when *Strife* won him wide distinction; two years earlier, he had earned some name with *The Silver Box* and had written the first of the Forsyte novels, *The Man of Property.* Thornton Wilder, Russel Crouse, and Christopher Fry scored their first hit at forty-one: Wilder, with *Our Town;* Crouse in collaboration with Howard Lindsay with the revision of the book of the musical, *Anything Goes;* and Fry, with *The Lady's not for Burning.* Wilder was long established as a Pulitzer Prize-winning novelist, a short story writer, and a writer of one-act plays. Crouse had earlier co-authored a fair success with Corey Ford, *Hold Your Horses,* and a failure, *The Gang's All Here;* Lindsay was forty-five at the time of the successful *Anything Goes* and had earlier had three plays produced on Broadway with fair success and all collaborations with Bertrand Robinson: *Tommy, Your Uncle Dudley* and *Oh Promise Me.* Fry had earlier written a number of full length plays for special church occasions.

David Belasco and James Barrie were famous at forty-three: Belasco through *Madame Butterfly,* a collaboration with John Luther Long and later to be the basis of the book for Puccini's opera. Barrie arrived with *Quality Street,* quickly followed by *Peter Pan.* Before this, Belasco had gone awry with *La Belle Russe;* Barrie had had small success with *Walker, London* and *The Professor's Love Story*, but extraordinary success with such one-acts in vaudeville as *The Twelve Pound Look*. Samuel Beckett reached distinction as a dramatist at forty-four with *Waiting for Godot*, often considered a modern classic. He had earlier published poems, short stories, novels and short plays. Joseph Fields arrived at forty-five in collaboration with Jerome Chodorov with *My Sister Eileen*, based on Ruth McKenney's autobiographical stories; both men were veterans of Hollywood as scenario-writers. James Thurber's first big hit came at the age of 46 in collaboration with Elliot Nugent—*The Male Animal*. Thurber was already a celebrity for his humorous writings and drawings in *The New Yorker* magazine.

Jean Giraudoux also succeeded at forty-six with *Siegfried,* an adaptation of his novel, *My Friend from Limousin;* he was then a long established short story writer and novelist. Eugene Ionesco did not stir up wide public favor until *Rhinoceros* when he was forty-seven; about ten years before this, he had made an avant-garde reputation with *The Bald Soprano,* followed by other short plays such as *The Chairs* and *The Lesson.* Graham Greene made good in the theatre at forty-eight with *The Living-Room;* he was already a proven novelist of such accomplishment as *The Power and the Glory.* E. Y. (Yip) Harburg arrived on Broadway at forty-nine as co-author of the book and lyrics for *Finian's Rainbow,* having for almost fifteen years written sketches and lyrics especially for the *Ziegfeld Follies* and for *Earl Carroll's Vanities.*

Relatively few playwrights have scored a first popular success after reaching the age of fifty, and yet the number is notable. Pirandello had his first financial hit at fifty-one with *Right You Are If You Think You Are;* over the previous twenty years or so, he had been quite productive but only very modestly successful in writing short stories, novels, criticism, poetry and plays. Dore Schary wrote his first Broadway hit at fifty-three, *Sunrise at Campobello;* by then, however, he had already reached such heights as executive producer of about 350 films for MGM and RKO. Agatha Christie succeeded as a playwright at fifty-three with her mystery, *Ten Little Indians,* adapted from one of her own novels; she had long been famous for mysteries which others adapted into successful plays, such as *Love from a Stranger.* Meredith Willson made good with his musical, *The Music Man,* at fifty-five, culminating a career of roughly thirty years as a musician and radio and TV personality.

Robinson Jeffers proved himself a dramatist at the age of sixty with his free adaption of Euripides' *Medea;* he had earlier written *The Tower Beyond Tragedy,* an adaptation of the Electra legend, and had been an internationally known poet with many awards and at least fourteen volumes to his credit. T. S. Eliot came through with *The Cocktail Party* when he was sixty-two years old; at forty-seven, he had scored a great artistic success with *Murder in the Cathedral* and later had a failure, *Family Reunion;* Eliot had also received the Nobel Prize for Literature in 1948 in recognition of his trail-blazing in modern poetry. Frances Goodrich and Albert Hackett, a wife and husband team of collaborators, arrived very big with the wife in her sixties and the husband, fifty-five, and their achievement, the adaptation of *The Diary of Anne Frank.* Twenty-five years earlier, the Hacketts had a mild success with *Up Pops the Devil* and then had other works on unsuccessfully such as *Great Big Doorstep;* they also earned many credits as screen-writers. William Archer wrote his smash-hit melodrama, *The Green Goddess,* at sixty-five; Archer had for a good thirty years been a highly successful English drama critic and once abandoned a collaboration with Shaw, which later became *Widowers' Houses.* Enid Bagnold made her mark of celebrity in the theatre with *The Chalk Garden* at sixty-six; she had for decades been a very successful novelist with such credits as *Serena Blandish* and *National Velvet,* and had adapted a number of her novels into somewhat successful plays notably *Lottie Dundass.* Archibald MacLeish scored his first big hit, *J. B.,* at the age of sixty-seven, although the play was published two years earlier; he had previously had a Broadway failure, *Panic,* and had written distinguished verse drama for radio, such as *The Fall of the City,* and had twice received the Pulitzer Prize for Poetry. Laurence Housman, brother of A. E. Housman, first succeeded with *Victoria Regina* at sixty-nine. Laurence Housman had long been known for his stories and poems, and it is estimated that thirty of his plays were censored by the Lord Chamberlain for dealing with biblical subjects or with living members of the English royal family.

Birthplace

Where does the record show that playwrights are most likely to be born and so, incidentally, even be reared in the formative years—in a small community or in a metropolis?

Many continental playwrights were native sons of small towns or relatively small cities. Galsworthy hailed from Kingston, Surrey, England. Noel Coward spent his early childhood in Teddington on the Thames. Clemence Dane, best recalled for *A Bill of Divorcement,* is from southern, rural England; Agatha Christie, from Torquay, Devon; Patrick Hamilton of *Angel Street* fame is from Sussex near Hove; Anthony Newley, from Heckney; Ivor Novello, from Cardiff, Wales; Emlyn Williams, from Mostyn, Flintshire, Wales; Lawrence Langner, from Swansea, South Wales; Frederick Lonsdale, from Jersey in the Channel Islands; Sir James Barrie, from Kiriemuir in Forfarshire, Scotland; William Archer, from Perth, Scotland. Lennox Robinson, perhaps best remembered for *The White Headed Boy,* is from Douglas, County Cork; Vincent Carroll of *Shadow and Substance* renown is from a small seaside resort, Blackrock, near Dunalk in County of Louth, Ireland; St. John Ervine is from Belfast; Lady Gregory, from Roxborough; Shelagh Delaney, from Salford near Manchester. Chekhov was a product of Taganrog on the Sea of Azov, Russia; Maxim Gorki, of Nizhni Novgorod, Russia; Henrik Ibsen, of Skien, Norway; Jan de Hartog, of Haarlem, Holland; Bertolt Brecht, of Augsburg, Bavarian Swabia; Ferenc Molnar, of Budapest, Hungary; Ernst Toller, now best remembered for *Masse Mensche* (*Man and the Masses*), of Samotschin, Poland; Luigi Pirandello, of Girgenti, Sicily; Gabriele D'Annunzio, a favorite playwright of Eleonora Duse especially for *La Gioconda,* of Pescara (Abruzzi), Italy; and Friedrich Duerrenmatt, of Konolfingen, Switzerland. Many of France's most distinguished playwrights were from small towns: Albert Camus, from Mondovi, Algeria; Jean Giraudoux, from Bellac in Limousin, France; Paul Claudel from Villeuve-sur-Fere-en-Tardenois in Aisne, a town of about 300 people.

On the contrary, however, many other continental playwrights were born in large cities, usually in their nation's capitol, where steady theatrical fare was not unusual or often easily available. Christopher Fry is from Bristol; Peter Shaffer, from Liverpool; Robert Bolt, from Manchester; John Drinkwater, Alfred Sutro, Lord Dunsany, Granville-Barker, A. A. Milne, Terence Rattigan, Peter Ustinov, John Osborne and Harold Pinter were all open to the exciting stimulation of London. Bernard Shaw, Oscar Wilde, John Millington Synge, Sean O'Casey, Brendan Behan, and Samuel Beckett were Dubliners. Henri Bernstein, W. Somerset Maugham, Eugene Brieux, Jacques Deval, Jean-Paul Sartre are all Parisians. Edmond Rostland hailed from the port city of Marseilles; Jean Anouilh from Bordeaux. Maurice Maeterlinck came from Ghent, Belgium's Catholic and tradition-steeped city; Arthur Schnitzler and Hugo von Hofmannsthal, from sophisticated, gay Vienna; Jacinto Benavente, from Madrid; Sascha Guitry, from St. Petersburg; Bella Cohen, later Bella Spewack, from Bucharest, Roumania; Samuel Spewack, from Bachmut, Russia; Eugene Ionesco, from Bucharest.

As for American playwrights, an impressive roster came from small towns or relatively small cities with a strong local flavor: Owen Davis, from Bangor, Maine; S. N. Behrman, from Worcester, Massachusetts; Harold Rome, from Hartford, Connecticut; Howard Lindsay, from Waterford, New York, although when he was three his family moved to Atlantic City, New Jersey; Frances Goodrich, from Belleville, New Jersey; Gore Vidal, from the United States Military Academy at West Point from which his family soon moved to Washington, D. C., where he grew up; Charles MacArthur, from Nyack, New York; George Abbott, from Forestville, New York; Maxwell Anderson, from Atlantic, Pennsylvania, with much rearing in the Middle West where his father's "calls" took him; Jean Kerr, from Scranton, Pennsylvania; Hatcher Hughes, from Polkville, North Carolina and Paul Green, from Lillington, North Carolina; Laurence Stallings, from Macon, and Carson McCullers, from Columbus, Georgia; Russel Crouse, from Findlay, Ohio, although he attended primary and secondary schools in Toledo; Robert E. Lee from Elyria, Ohio; Edna Ferber, from Kalamazoo, Michigan; Rachel Crothers, from Bloomington, Illinois; Archibald MacLeish, from Glencoe, Illinois; Thornton Wilder, from Madison and Ben Hecht from Racine, Wisconsin; Susan Glaspell, from Davenport, Iowa; Meredith Willson, from Mason City, Iowa; William Inge, from Independence, Kansas; Lynn Riggs, from Indian Territory near Claremore, Oklahoma; Tennessee (Thomas) Williams, from Columbus, Mississippi; William Saroyan, from Fresno, California; Sidney Howard, from Oakland, California; Rose Franken, from Gainesville, Texas.

At least an equally impressive roster of American playwrights were from or near a metropolis. The New Yorkers are an especially numerous lot: Percy Mackaye, Eugene O'Neill, Bayard Veiller, Joseph Fields, Lorenz Hart, Richard Rodgers, Oscar Hammerstein II, Elmer Rice, Robert Emmet Sherwood, Albert Hackett, Edward and Jerome Chodorov, Moss Hart, Sidney Kingsley, Samson Raphaelson, Joseph Kesselring, John Howard Lawson, Arthur Laurents, Arthur Miller, Alan Jay Lerner, Robert W. Anderson, Paddy Chayefsky, Abe Burrows, Murray Schisgal, Herb Gardner and Neil Simon. Edward Albee, though born in Washington, D. C., was reared near New York City in Larchmont with much wintering in Florida and Arizona. Philip Barry and Garson Kanin were both Rochesterians. George S. Kaufman, Mary Roberts Rinehart, and Robinson Jeffers were all children of Pittsburgh. Clifford Odets, Ruth and Augustus Goetz, and George Kelly, hail from Philadelphia; John Patrick, from Louisville, Kentucky; Lillian Hellman, from New Orleans; James Thurber from Columbus and Jerome Lawrence from Cleveland, Ohio; Augustus Thomas and T. S. Eliot, from St. Louis, Missouri; Max Shulman, from St. Paul, Minnesota; Robert Ardrey, Samuel Taylor, and Lorraine Hansberry, from Chicago, Illinois. Clare Boothe, though a New Yorker by birth, was largely a Chicagoan by rearing. Mary Chase, creator of *Harvey,* is a Denverite. David Belasco was born in San Francisco and attended a monastery school in Victoria, British Columbia, which led to his wearing his collar reversed as an adult.

It seems a playwright is just about as likely to be born and therefore often reared in a small community as in or near a metropolis. The media of communication in the last generation or so make it more and more possible for a potential playwright from even a remote crossroads community to see or hear or read exceptional examples of drama in some form. Movies, radio, television, long playing records of the original cast, community and college theatres, pocket books, and public libraries have made the best drama often available where little if any used to be.

Education

How much formal education have playwrights had? Maxim Gorki (Maxim the Bitter) had only two years of formal schooling—from age eight through nine. Because of his family's poverty and a chronic eye infection from the age of five through twelve, Sean O'Casey had only three years of formal schooling; "really began to try to teach myself all I wanted to know," he remarked, "when I was thirteen years of age." [24] He learned both from his brothers' and sisters' discarded schoolbooks and from reading first-rate authors he found in secondhand bookshops, for instance, Shakespeare, Milton, Byron, Scott, Burns, Shelley and Keats.

"It is in the theatre," said Maugham, "that the dramatist really learns his business." [25] And a good many playwrights seem to confirm him, for they lacked even a formal high school education, though today their plays are often studied in colleges and universities. Sascha Guitry made his first of almost a lifetime of stage appearances at the age of five in the role of Pierrot Jr., in a pantomime; formal schooling was spasmodic. Augustus Thomas' father came to manage the New Orleans St. Charles Theatre, and so Augustus came to see the greats of his day perform, and he went onstage as a juvenile in resident stock. At eleven, David Belasco joined the professional theatre and stayed with it through life, whether barnstorming or making stars or fortunes. At thirteen, Granville-Barker entered the combination dramatic school and stock company at Margate, and at fourteen appeared on the London stage and continued not only acting, but also translating, producing and writing criticism of plays. Noel Coward attended Surrey and then Chapel Royal School in Clapham, and embarked on a career of acting, singing, composing lyrics and music, and playwriting. At fifteen, Moss Hart quit school to take active part in amateur theatricals in New York City and in summer camps, and to write whole shows he helped stage. Odets at fifteen also quit school to join an amateur theatre group, do radio work, and eventually wind up among the organizers of The Group Theatre as one of its actors. Though Saroyan never finished high school, he admitted reading almost every book in his hometown library and as a poor boy sneaked into about every theatrical production that came to town.

Peter Ustinov attended The London Theatre School and acted in repertory and often in his own sketches. Brendan Behan was expelled from the Christian Brothers' School in Dublin and for a while attended a Dublin technical school; at sixteen he was found guilty of possessing explosives with intent to blow up the battleship, *King George V,* in Liverpool harbor. Behan often attended his uncle's theatre in Dublin. At sixteen, Hecht ran away from Racine, Wisconsin, to Chicago and got into newspaper reporting, beginning with *The Chicago Journal.*

An impressive number of playwrights completed only the formal equivalent of high school and then made life, itself, their classroom. Patrick Hamilton went onstage at seventeen; Lennox Robinson took to working with Dublin's Abbey Theatre; Bayard Veiller at sixteen became advance agent for touring theatrical attractions; Eugene Brieux, who was to write *Damaged Goods,* went into clerking; John Drinkwater started work with the Northern Assurance Company in Nottingham. Edna Ferber went right from high school in Appleton, Wisconsin, to reporting for *The Appleton Daily Crescent* at $3.00 a week, and Russel Crouse at seventeen became a reporter for *The Cincinnati Commercial Tribune*. Agatha Christie was privately educated. Laurence Housman at eighteen went to London for art training. Bella Spewack graduated from Washington Irving High School in New York. Carson McCullers went to New York to study possibly at Columbia University or Julliard Institute, "But on the second day," she said, "I lost all my tuition money on a subway." [26] She never went to college. Gore Vidal finished Philips Exeter Academy's course of study and after a stint in the army, took to writing on his own. Anthony Newley went directly into acting in films at seventeen and branched into stage, radio, and TV work. At eighteen Christopher Fry became a schoolteacher for one year and then for the next eight years or so toured in repertory theatre as an actor. John Osborne did not attend a university but took to acting in repertory and later managed a small theatrical company at a seaside resort. Ibsen and Shaw, of course, never went beyond the equivalent of high school in formal education.

Quite a few playwrights entered a training school or college or university and soon left or never took a degree. Ernst Toller studied for a short period at the Universities of Munich, Berlin, and Grenoble. Bertolt Brecht applied himself to natural sciences and medicine at the Universities of Munich and Berlin with literature a major interest. George S. Kaufman tried law for a few months. Howard Lindsay completed a year at Harvard and then six months at the American Academy of Dramatic Arts in New York, and quickly landed a job acting. Richard Rodgers put in a year at Columbia University where his work on the Varsity show led him to be hailed by faculty and press as a musical prodigy; he left Columbia for a year of private study under Frank Damrosch at the Institute of Musical Art. Samuel Spewack completed two years at Columbia University, then went directly into newspaper reporting for *The New York World*. Edward Chodorov had a very short stay at Brown University. Jan de Hartog went to the Amsterdam Naval College for three months and was then dismissed with the note, "This school is not for pirates." Terence Rattigan studied for three years at Trinity College, Oxford University, where he had a scholarship, but left to do only playwriting. Lillian Hellman had three years at New York University; Mary Chase, two years at the University of Denver, one year at the University of Colorado, and then marriage; Harold Pinter, a very short stay at the Royal Academy of Dramatic Art in London, at that time to him—"a terrible atmosphere of affectation and unreality, ankle bands and golden hair." [27] Friedrich Duerrenmatt studied at the Universities of Bern and Zurich, and then as he told Joseph Morgenstern of *The New York Times,* "all of a sudden I began to write, and I just had not time to finish my university degree." Lorraine Hansberry studied painting for a year or so at the Art Institute of Chicago, tried Roosevelt College briefly, studied painting on her own in Mexico, then finally took to writing at the New School for Social Research in New York City. Edward Albee put in a year and a half at Trinity College, Hartford, Connecticut, where he explained that he lacked the interest to qualify for a degree, and the College agreed with him. Eugene O'Neill, of course, had one year at Princeton University and then, six years later, one year at Harvard in Professor Baker's English 47 Workshop, a graduate course in playwriting.

The record shows, however, that the great majority of playwrights have completed some specialty school or taken a college degree of some kind. Mary Roberts graduated from the Pittsburgh Training School for Nurses at nineteen and four days later married Dr. Stanley Marshal Rinehart. Clemence Dane studied chiefly portraiture for three years at the Slade School in London and one year in Dresden. Meredith Willson graduated from the Institute of Musical Art now known as Julliard School of Music. Garson Kanin completed two years at the American Academy of Dramatic Arts in New York City. Those who took a B. A. degree or its approximation are: Percy Mackaye, Harvard University; Rachel Crothers, Illinois State Normal School, and then added study at Wheatcroft School of Acting in New York City; Gabriele D'Annunzio, the College of Prato in Tuscany and the University of Rome; George Abbott, the University of Rochester, and then a year at Harvard in the 47 Workshop; A.A. (Alan Alexander) Milne, Trinity College, Cambridge; John Millington Synge, Trinity College, Dublin; John Howard Lawson, Williams College; Susan Glaspell, Drake University; James Thurber, Ohio State University, interrupted by World War I; Samson Raphaelson, the University of Illinios; Robert Emmet Sherwood, Harvard University; Frances Goodrich, Vassar College; Robert Ardrey, University of Chicago; Jean Giraudoux, L'École Normale Supérieure in Paris; Lynn Riggs, the University of Oklahoma; Paul Vincent Carroll, St. Patrick's Training College, Dublin; Sidney Kingsley, Cornell University; John Patrick, Holy Cross in New Orleans, then Harvard and Columbia; Albert Camus, the University of Algiers; Arthur Miller, the University of Michigan; Arthur Laurents, Cornell University; Tennessee Williams, the University of Missouri, the University of Washington in St. Louis, and the University of Iowa; Abe Burrows, College of the City of New York, New York University's School of Finance; Graham Greene, Balliol College, Oxford; Max Shulman, the University of Minnesota; Alan Jay Lerner, Harvard University and two summers of study at the Julliard School of Music; Paddy Chayefsky, City College of New York and Fordham University; Peter Shaffer, Cambridge University; Robert Bolt, Manchester University; Herb Gardner, Carnegie Institute of Technology and Antioch College.

A number of playwrights took not only a B. A. or its approximation but also an M. A. or its approximation: William Archer, B. A., George Watson's College, Edinburgh, M. A., the University of Edinburgh; James Barrie, B. A. and M. A., the University of Edinburgh; Oscar Wilde, one year at Trinity, Dublin, four years at Oxford; Laurence Stallings, B. A., Wake Forest College, M. of S., Georgetown University; Maxwell Anderson, B. A., University of North Dakota, M.A., Stanford University; S. N. (Samuel Nathaniel) Behrman, B. A., Clark College, 47 Workshop at Harvard, M. A., Columbia University; Philip Barry, B. A., Yale, three years at Harvard, chiefly in the 47 Workshop; Sidney Howard, B. A., University of California at Berkeley, 47 Workshop at Harvard; Paul Green, B. A., University of North Carolina, further study at Cornell University; Jerome Lawrence, B. A., Ohio State University, M. A., University of California at Los Angeles; Robert E. Lee, Northwestern, Ohio Wesleyan, and Drake Universities, B. A., and graduate study; Emlyn Williams, B. A. and M. A., Christ College, Oxford; Samuel Beckett, B. A. and M. A., Trinity College, Dublin; T. S. Eliot, B. A. and M. A., Harvard University with added study at the University of Paris; Thornton Wilder, two years at Oberlin College, B. A., Yale, M. A., Princeton; Harold Rome, two years at Trinity College, Hartford, Connecticut, B. A., Yale, one year law at Yale, M. F. A. Architecture, Yale, with drama and music courses worked in; William Inge, B. A., University of Kansas, M. A., Peabody College for Teachers, Nashville, Tennessee; Robert W. Anderson, B. A. and and M. A., Harvard University; Jean Kerr, B. A., Marywood College, Scranton, Pennsylvania, M. F. A., Catholic University, Washington, D. C.; Samuel Taylor, five years at the University of California at Berkeley.

Three playwrights took a doctorate: Luigi Pirandello, University of Rome with the degree completed at the University of Bonn, Germany; Hugo von Hofmannsthal, University of Vienna; Jean-Paul Sartre (degree "aggregé") École Normale Supérièure, Paris.

A few playwrights took an M. D. degree: Anton Chekhov, the University of Moscow; W. Somerset Maugham, the University of Heidelberg as an unmatriculated student, and six years at St. Thomas' Hospital, London; Arthur Schnitzler, the University of Vienna. Robinson Jeffers practically earned an M. D. then changed his mind: B. A., University of Pittsburgh and Occidental College, Los Angeles; three years studying medicine at the University of Southern California; one year of forestry, University of Washington.

An unusually large number of playwrights took a law degree and practiced law little or not at all: Jacinto Benavente, the University of Madrid; Ferenc Molnar, the Law Faculty of Budapest University, and then of Geneva University; John Galsworthy, New College, Oxford; Edmond Rostand, College Stanislaus, Paris; Maurice Maeterlinck, the University of Ghent; Paul Claudel, L'École de Sciènce Politîque, Paris; John Van Druten, London University; Archibald MacLeish, B. A., Yale, M. A., Tufts College, law degree, Harvard; Elmer Rice, New York Law School; Joseph Fields, New York University; Oscar Hammerstein II, B. A., Columbia University, law degree, Columbia University; Murray Schisgal, Brooklyn Law School. Jean Anouilh studied law for a year and a half at the Sorbonne of the University of Paris, then left for lack of funds.

Certainly a sizeable number of playwrights had only the equivalent of a formal high school education or even less. With the decline of the road and resident stock companies, however, it appears that playwrights tend more and more to formal college or university training to give them a means of livelihood to fall back on if playwriting doesn't prove to be their métier.

Work Other Than Playwriting

Through their somewhat long and often trying apprenticeship, playwrights have usually had to earn a living by some other means than playwriting.

Sean O'Casey had perhaps the humblest of jobs to support him and his mother, a common laborer's, until he was forty-four years old. As a self-taught human being who fought an almost lifelong battle against the threat of blindness, O'Casey represents an extraordinary triumph of the human spirit to realize itself. Brendan Behan was a house-painter and a professional revolutionary for Irish independence.

Joseph Fields, Eugene O'Neill, Maxim Gorki, Frederick Lonsdale, Lynn Riggs, Tennessee Williams, Lorraine Hansberry, Abe Burrows, Shelagh Delaney and Edward Albee drifted from job to job, usually well into their twenties before definitely finding themselves. Edward Albee, to illustrate, wrote continuity for radio station WNYC's music programs for over a year, was an office boy at Warwick and Legerly Advertising Agency, sold records at Bloomingdale's Department Store, clerked at a Schirmers music store, was counterman in the luncheonette at the Manhattan Towers Hotel, and delivered messages for Western Union—the job he liked best.

A number of playwrights entered professions only to abandon them or to practice them sparingly. Chekhov, Schnitzler, and Maugham were doctors. Galsworthy, Maeterlinck, Rostand, MacLeish, Rice and Van Druten were lawyers. Hecht and Synge were violinists. Housman and Dane were painters. Willson was a flutist with the New York Philharmonic Orchestra. Burrows was an accountant. Schnitzler, Pirandello, Dunsany, Maxwell Anderson, MacLeish, Riggs, Green, Wilder, Kesselring, Robert Anderson, Sartre, Inge, Ionesco and Beckett were at one time or other teachers at the preparatory school or college level. Wilder, for instance, taught French for seven years at Lawrenceville School in Lawrenceville, New Jersey, and also taught comparative literature at the University of Chicago, and lists his profession as "teacher." Samuel Beckett taught French at Trinity College, Dublin, and later became James Joyce's secretary. Robert Anderson taught English and drama at Harvard for three years and then taught playwriting for The American Theatre Wing for four years. A few playwrights have been in diplomacy: Giraudoux spent about ten years in the French Ministry of Foreign Affairs; Philip Barry put in a dull six months at the American embassy in London; MacLeish in World War II was with the United States Office of War Information; Robert Emmet Sherwood assisted in writing Roosevelt's speeches.

An especially large number of playwrights first earned a living through the use of words in some job or succession of jobs in journalism: proof-reading, reporting, feature writing, press agentry, writing a humor column, advertising, reviewing, and editing. Playwrights who came into their own assisted by such disciplines include: Strindberg, Chekhov, Shaw, Archer, Pirandello, Wilde, D'Annunzio, Barrie, Milne,

Synge, Drinkwater, Kaufman, Howard, Maxwell Anderson, Riggs, Boothe, Hellman, Chodorov, Crouse, Behrman, Camus, Chase, Inge, Anouilh and Simon. Compelled to leave college for lack of money, for example, Anouilh went to work for a Parisian advertising firm, *Publicité D'Amour:* "For three years I wrote copy for products ranging from noodles to automobiles," said Anouilh. "I consider advertising a great school for playwriting. The precision, conciseness and agility of expression necessary in writing advertisements, helped me enormously." [28] Sherwood rose to editorship of the now defunct humor magazine, *Life.* MacLeish for about ten years wrote articles for *Fortune* magazine. S. N. Behrman was once press agent for The Theatre Guild. Mary Coyle Chase for four years was a free lance correspondent for the International News Service and the United Press. T. S. Eliot for over thirty years worked for the publishers, Faber and Faber Ltd., and became an editor.

Often while engaged in journalism, though not necessarily, many playwrights first earned public recognition and some of their livelihood as poets, essayists, short story writers and novelists. This was true of: Strindberg, Chekhov, Gorki, Galsworthy, Pirandello, D'Annunzio, Benavente, Synge, Rostand, Maugham, Milne, Schnitzler, Molnar, Dane, Maxwell Anderson, Giraudoux, MacLeish, Wilder, Rice, Crouse, Fields, Franken, T. S. Eliot, Arthur Miller, Patrick Hamilton, Max Shulman, Jan de Hartog, and Gore Vidal. Arthur Miller's first literary success, for instance, was *Focus,* a novel which sold 90,000 copies. MacLeish won two Pulitzer Prizes in poetry. Shulman made good with a novel lampooning college life, *Barefoot Boy with Cheek,* which he and George Abbott rewrote into a successful musical.

Relatively few playwrights have earned a good deal of their living from the theatre before succeeding in playwriting. Benavente toured with a circus and became its impresario. Lindsay joined a touring company of *Polly of the Circus* for three years and then for five years was with Margaret Anglin's stock company as stage manager, then actor, then director. Fry for about eight years was with repertory troupes touring England. Kanin was George Abbott's assistant. Pinter for about ten years acted in English repertory. Osborne for about eight years was actor and later manager in English repertory. Hellman and Kingsley had been play-readers and scenario readers for producers.

A growing number of playwrights in recent years have in some form practised their craft and helped earn a living by writing for radio, television or the movies. The roster includes: Robert W. Anderson, John Patrick, Meredith Willson, Friedrich Duerrenmatt, Arthur Miller, Christopher Fry, Paddy Chayefsky, Arthur Laurents, Alan Jay Lerner, Abe Burrows, Harold Pinter, Neil Simon, Arthur Kober, Gore Vidal and Peter Shaffer. "As for the radio and TV scripts," confessed Robert Anderson of adapting a good forty plays to these media, "it was doing them that made a professional writer of me." [29] Arthur Laurents recalled, "a show a week for a half year of *Army Service Forces Presents,* and for over a year for *Assignment Home.* It is an enormous strain to write what amounts to a new one-act play every week for almost two years, particularly when you are both trying to say something and to write well. But it is also wonderful training and discipline." [30] Duerrenmatt wrote detective stories, radio scripts, motion picture scenarios and even novels and criticism while playwriting remained his primary interest.

Until they succeed, aspiring playwrights have supported themselves by a very wide range of work. The great majority, however, have somehow been directly or indirectly involved with some kind of use of words. If their work could possibly be related to the theatre, to observing human nature under test, or to mastering their style, it was all to the good; "if I hadn't had to bother about earning a living and could have given all my time to poetry," said T. S. Eliot, who worked first in a bank and then for decades in publishing, "it would have had a deadening influence on me . . ." [31] Work other than playwriting undoubtedly helps feed the writer's imagination.

Residence at Late Apprenticeship

Should the aspiring playwright live in or near the theatrical center of his country during what he hopes is his late apprenticeship?

Playwrights who spent their late apprenticeship largely in London were: Shaw, Wilde, Archer, Barrie, Coward, Dunsany, Granville-Barker, Milne, T. S. Eliot, Pinter, and Osborne. D'Annunzio and Pirandello chose to live in Rome. Ibsen lived in Rome and Munich. Strindberg lived in Stockholm. Chekhov made Moscow his home and Gorki, St. Petersburg. Maugham, Riggs, Anouilh, and Sartre favored Paris. Benavente lived in Madrid and Schnitzler in Vienna.

Playwrights who made New York City their home previous to their success were: O'Neill, Belasco, Crothers, Maxwell Anderson, Franken, Howard, Crouse, Lindsay, Kingsley, Kaufman, Hecht, MacArthur,

Connelly, Kelly, Behrman, Rice, Hellman, Boothe, Moss Hart, Raphaelson, Lorenz Hart, Joseph Fields, Saroyan, Burrows, Lerner, Robert Anderson, Tennessee Williams, Inge, Chayefsky, Hansberry and Albee.

Certainly an impressive number of playwrights found it wise to make their national centers of drama the locale for their late apprenticeship. Once these playwrights succeeded, nevertheless, in many instances they worked at homes in the country or by the sea, and sometimes, like Williams at Key West, Florida, a good distance away from the theatrical center of their country.

II

COMMERCIAL CONSIDERATIONS AFFECTING PLAYWRITING THESE DAYS

Vital Statistics of Broadway and Off-Broadway

It is no secret that a successful playwright can earn millions. Jean Kerr, for instance, has already earned over $1,000,000 gross from her comedy, *Mary, Mary*. Neil Simon, however, a relative newcomer, seems to be breaking all records for a playwright. "Neil Simon is the new Midas author of Broadway," noted *Variety* (March 16, 1966) in Hobe Morrison's article, "with royalties of around $20,000 a week, or at a rate of over $1,000,000 a year." Simon's income was then drawn from three productions current on Broadway: two comedies, *Barefoot in the Park* and *The Odd Couple;* and the book for a musical comedy, *Sweet Charity*, based on a Fellini movie. Simon added another scoring entry that season, *Star-Spangled Girl*. Simon also received royalties from tributary theatre productions of his comedy, *Come Blow Your Horn*, and the musical, *Little Me*. Only Cole Porter and Irving Berlin, doubling as composer and lyricist in their time, did as well as Simon. Simon's next work, *Plaza Suite*, 3 one-act comedies, was also a hit.

A hit play which becomes the basis of a television series, like *I Remember Mama*, Lawrence Langner estimated to be worth a million to the author in this subsequent medium alone. A single hit play, as a matter of fact, involves a potential compounding of rights that amount to the biggest of all jackpots from writing: royalties from Broadway production, from stock and touring company production, from foreign, semi-professional and amateur production, from moving picture, radio and television production, from adaptation into a musical comedy, from LP recording, and from publication in hardcover and paper-backs. Success in playwriting, it must be said, is a formidable victory to win. And yet the odds against winning the Irish Sweepstakes are much greater, and this has not ended the sweepstakes or reduced the betting. Laurel wreaths are always waiting for the hit playwright. He or she has only to come forward.

Richard Maney in a moment of hyperbole has estimated that if all the plays written in the United States alone in any one year were piled on top of each other, they would rise higher than the Empire State Building. Writing plays is a kind of recurrent fever with uncounted tens of thousands who are stage-struck and believe they have at least one good play in them. With increasing leisure and the rise of community and college theatres, playwriting contests have become almost as common as forsythia in April. There are 5,000 or so organized theatrical groups in the United States; the tributary theatre may feed the professional theatre the way the bush leagues feed the major leagues in sports, although community theatres want above all to be cultural community centers.

All the figures soon to be cited are open to the variations of the market place, but they approximate the truth these days even if the details may vary from day to day. The figures may be translated into European equivalents if costs are converted to from one-half to one-third of their American original; the lower wages in foreign countries and the conversion rate of the dollar account for the discrepancy.

In the United States, theatrical trade publications usually release a prospectus before each season intimating roughly 200 productions as optioned and Broadway-bound. From figures gathered by Sam Zolotow of *The New York Times* (June 21, 1965), the number of productions that actually opened on Broadway each season as averaged over the previous 21 seasons, was 50—excluding revivals, return engagements, foreign and miscellaneous productions, and failures on the road to New York. In the 1963-4 season, 63 productions opened. In the 1964-65 season, only 52 opened. In the 1965-6 season, according to *Variety* (June 22, 1966), 68 productions opened.

Productions fail to open chiefly, as Richard Maney sees it, because the producer can't raise the money or sign the proper star. The entire Broadway season each year involves a round investment of $10,000,000, more or less a million. As averaged over a ten year period, 1 play in 4 scores a smash-hit. In some seasons, like 1963-64, however, as *Fortune* magazine noted, "While no accurate industry statistics are available, it is claimed . . . as high as 80% resulted in loss to investors."[32]

As a rule, only smash-hits survive in the financially rarified air of Broadway; the others die quickly without the most extraordinary oxygenating. David Merrick has earned the title "Barnum of Broadway" for his nostrums. When his musical production, *Fanny,* got bad notices in some critical New York newspapers, Merrick employed the huckstering techniques of Madison Avenue to earn back fully in 17 weeks the $250,000 production cost, and in time *Fanny* became so healthy as to shower her investors with over a million dollars in earnings.

Theatre owners generally contract for 30% of a play's box-office gross with a stop clause stipulating that, at a gross less than half the theatre's potential, a play is subject to eviction. With intimate comedies playing to a $7.50 top and the most lavish musicals to a top of $9.90—not counting a premium added by ticket brokers—the public is not in a mood to patronize much of anything but smash-hits. Broadway now has only 36 theatres available to house legitimate plays and musicals, according to *The Rockefeller Panel Report of 1965.* A theatre owner has little if any trouble at the height of the season finding a new tenant. "It's largely dependent upon the cast, the director, the producer, but above all the script," said John Shubert on the subject of securing a theatre to house a new production. The Shuberts control 18 of the available theatres, and John Shubert insists, "Reputations don't count for much. When it comes to getting a theatre, 'The play's the thing'." [33] Out of town theatre notices are usually critical in making up a theatre owner's mind as to whether or not to book a new production; he doesn't want his tenants to die on him immediately so that his theatre gets the reputation of a morgue.

The Broadway theatre is big business, and its economics are deceptively involved. The average cost of mounting a one-set show is from $100,000 to $125,000. Some of the biggest hits have cost less: *Man for All Seasons,* $60,000; and *Who's Afraid of Virginia Woolf?,* $55,000. Rumored hits do not always make money. "Except for that period of four weeks," noted Jed Harris, the producer of *Our Town,* referring to the play's run after winning the Pulitzer Prize, "the show actually had more losing weeks than profitable weeks during its entire New York engagement." [34] *Our Town* ran for a year in New York only because, as Jed Harris let out in his book, *Watchman, What of the Night?,* the cast took a cut in salary.

A play with a break-even point over weekly expenses of $23,000 has a slim chance if any of making money for its backers. Chayefsky's

Gideon ran for over 8 months in the 1958–59 season, yet returned only 85% of its investment. *Night of the Iguana* lost money on Broadway but more than repaid its investors through sale of the movie rights for $250,000, of which the investors received 40%. Whatever the investors get back, the playwright's standard contract of The Dramatists Guild nets him a varying percentage of each week's box-office gross: 5% of the first $5,000; 7.5% of the next $2,000; 10% of all over $7,000; this broadly averages out to 9% of the gross. Some playwrights, whose names alone have drawing power, might contract for more. In *Performing Arts: The Economic Dilemma*, William Baumol and William Bowen conclude from financial statements as submitted by the League of New York Theatres for 30 straight plays between 1961–65, "the author of a drama earns more than the producer or the investors. Frequently author's royalties were more than 10 times the producer's reported income."

The average cost of mounting a musical on Broadway these days is from $250,000 to $550,000. Costs keep rising. In 1949, *South Pacific* opened for $225,000; in 1956, *My Fair Lady* required $360,000; and in 1963, the flop, *Jennie*, $550,000; in 1965, another flop, *Kelly*, $650,000.[35] A musical today with a break-even point over $50,000 a week can be a grim business unless it is a very big hit. *Hello, Dolly!*, playing to packed houses from almost the start, has such high running expenses that its profits could not be more than $14,500 for a sold-out house each week; after more than a year, its investors had still not started earning a profit. *Golden Boy* and *Baker Street* each cost over $500,000 to mount, and tickets had to be priced at a top of $9.90 because a potential gross in excess of $90,000 a week was necessary if the backers were ever to recoup their investment; the backers, incidentally, didn't recoup. The best theatre seats are generally sold to people with expense accounts cushioned to absorb the financial shock. Usually benefits will buy out a whole house to raise money for a cause.

Even as it struggles for survival with over 30 craft unions, Broadway is repeatedly charged with pricing itself out of the market. In round figures, of the 54 playhouses available in the 1930's, only 36 were available in the 1963–4 season. And of the 142 productions a season in the 1930's, the average so far in the 1960's is now down to some 50 or so "new" productions a season. Of the 590 commercial theatres for plays on tour in 1927, barely 200 remain available. And of attendance at the legitimate theatre in the 1930's of roughly 12,000,000 customers, including those from road tours, all that is now left of this total with a much larger population is roundly 8,000,000. Community, university, college, and summer theatres sooner or later offer the same plays and musicals at prices far less than those of second-string Broadway or touring companies. In fact, in 1964, according to the *Rockefeller Panel Report of 1965,* there were some 5,000 organized amateur theatrical groups; loosely formed amateur groups producing only sporadically, numbered roughly 35,000. There were only in 1964 some 50 professional year-around organizations and almost all of the major ones were nonprofit and relied in part on subsidy of some foundation; to illustrate, New York's Lincoln Center Repertory, New York's APA-Phoenix Theatre, Washington's Arena Stage, San Francisco's Actor's Workshop, and Houston's Alley Theatre. There were in 1965, 266 summer theatres of which 156 were bonded with Actors' Equity. The theatre-going public is willing to pay the high cost of attending the legitimate theatre only when it offers smash-hits as a rule with stars in the leads; otherwise that public will find a reasonable substitute in less professional local efforts, or in an old movie of the work on television.

To avoid the great risks of Broadway, a new breed of producers in New York has turned to Off-Broadway with its avant-garde audience willing to stand the hard seats and other discomforts of improvised playhouses in Greenwich Village or scattered throughout the City. In 1962–63, Off-Broadway offered 102 productions; in 1964–65, 54 productions. In 1965–66, 92 productions. Many of these productions were revivals of Euripides, Ibsen, Chekhov, O'Neill, Wilder, and Williams, or show-cases for Beckett, Genet, and Pinter. If anything, the chances of scoring a hit Off-Broadway are less than on, for Off-Broadway can only afford the less proven talent. Walter Kerr estimates that, Off-Broadway, 1 out of 9 productions is a hit. Off-Broadway's productions like Broadway's continue to spiral up in cost. In the early 1950's, a producer Off-Broadway could stage a one-set play with a few characters for about $10,000; the same production, it is now estimated, would cost nearer $15,000 to $20,000. Theatrical unions still allow Off-Broadway to pay help much less than Broadway minimums to give employment and a show-case to new talent; an Off-Broadway lead, for instance, may earn as little as $75.00 a week. No Off-Broadway house may seat more than 299 people, or wage scales automatically rise to Broadway levels.

Perhaps the best known producing team to go from Off-Broadway to Broadway is Clinton Wilder and Richard Barr who successfully produced Edward Albee's one-act plays, *The Zoo Story, The Death of Bessie Smith* and *The American Dream* as Off-Broadway fare. *The Death of Bessie Smith* and *The American Dream* on one play-bill cost them only $11,500. "Our basic rule," said Barr, "is never to spend a nickel where we can use our imagination or ingenuity instead." [36] Only the "most incredible hit" Off-Broadway can count on more than twelve weeks of sold-out business; the limit of 299 seats confines the maximum weekly gross to between $5,000 and $6,000. If weekly operating expenses rise to near the weekly gross, even the biggest hit has trouble paying off a production cost as high as $20,000.[37] Off-Broadway offers the playwright a minimum of $150 a week regardless of gross, or 6% of the gross if that is higher than the minimum. "Most important of all, you are reminded that the play is really the thing," Barr told John Keating of *Theatre Arts* (September 1961). "On Broadway, it is such a hassle getting a theatre and a star and a play all ready at the same time that you are frequently forced into rehearsal . . . before the play is ready." Many Off-Broadway playwrights deliberately limit their plays to very few characters and simple settings. This economy made through extreme ingenuity in their dramaturgy, is just about their only hope for expediting a professional production. Even Off-Broadway producers expect to make money, or at least to stay in business and not go flat broke.

In the season of 1966, a new variation in production has come upon the New York theatrical scene. "In my earlier days of producing," Merrick told Lewis Funke of *The New York Times* (February 13, 1966), "I risked my backers' dollars producing serious ventures. I don't do that any more." Merrick, who prefers producing to buying yachts or country homes, said, "With a *Cactus Flower* or a *Hello, Dolly!* I can support my foundation. Instead of turning over 70 per cent of my income in taxes I have been able to contribute to and build up the foundation." [38] In the 1966 season, The David Merrick Arts Foundation and Merrick's liking for the "unconventional, offbeat play" brought Broadway such distinguished work as: The Royal Shakespeare Company's production of *The Persecution and Assassination of Marat as Performed by Inmates of the Asylum of Charenton under the Direction of the Marquis de Sade;* The English Stage Company's production of *Inadmissible Evidence;* and an Irish import, *Philadelphia, Here I Come!* Funke noted of Merrick's success with these ventures, "Bland and at ease, Mr. Merrick was not in the mood to chide his colleagues. But there is no doubt that others could follow suit and stop bemoaning the fate of the serious theater on Broad-way."[39] Those whom Broadway has greatly helped could, if they would, modestly help Broadway, and without the interference of government that comes usually with any subsidy.

Merrick's Foundation notwithstanding, there is still a contingent of students of the theatre who, like Eric Bentley in his book, *The Playwright as Thinker,* would say, "What I shall urge is that the temples be left to the money-changers to wallow in; the true faith must survive—if at all—elsewhere." Bentley continues, "The hope of the theater—I shall maintain—lies outside the commercial theater altogether."[40] Brecht's circuitous approach to the Broadway scene with *The Caucasian Chalk Circle* illustrates Bentley's hope in action. In 1945, Samuel French Publishers commissioned Brecht to write the play. Although *Chalk Circle* has since been widely performed throughout the world, in the United States for long it has received only repertory and college theatre production; Bentley had said, "we are led to the Little Theater as to a home."[41] Then on March 24, 1966, the The Repertory Company of Lincoln Center, produced *The Caucasian Chalk Circle* in Bentley's translation to score its one hit of the whole 1965–66 repertory season and in a huge theatre for a run of over three months. Bentley implies that plays like *The Caucasian Chalk Circle* would never have even been written let alone produced had they depended strictly upon encouragement from the Broadway commercial theatre.

The Producer

What every producer or "theatrical manager," as he used to be called, really wants is a smash-hit. Even those interested chiefly in artistic success, like the producers of The Repertory Company of Lincoln Center, have to be interested as well in the box-office to survive. The Lincoln Center's Repertory Company dismissed its first producers for box-office reasons. A man may become a producer if he has at least one talent or ability—that of raising enough money to mount the play that excites him. To pick a winner and stage it, a producer at best should have the experience, know-how and drive of a George Abbott who has acted in, written, directed, and produced plays with phenomenal success for about forty years, especially farce, melodrama, and musical comedy. Abbott, himself, it should be mentioned, once had an unbroken string of 16 financial failures. A producer earns usually about half of the gross profits of a first-class production, and about 20% of subsidiary profits. "A theatrical producer without a good play," said Sam Harris, "is like a good jockey on a bad horse." [42] A wise producer knows when to sit out a race.

A gathering of current producers might include such a motley lot as stage-struck business men risking a possibly painless tax-loss, speculators in burlesque, doting relatives of a playwright, sugar daddies of stars or lesser luminaries, art connoisseurs, gamblers, scholars, hangers-on, and men who usually not only own theatres but have produced plays professionally for many years. According to Richard Maney, about twenty producers are established enough on Broadway so that over the years their names recur in theatrical news; some well known producers like Merrick, for instance, do more than one production a season. This means that of some 50 productions of "new" plays or musicals in an average Broadway season, about one-half of the producers are also "new" to Broadway. A survey by *Fortune* magazine (February 1938), showed approximately the same proportion of old and new producers each season even then; from the season 1934–35, *Fortune* said, "It's a twenty-seven to one shot the novice will fail." The occurrence of few new names among successful producers these days suggests the odds are still forbidding. Small wonder that bad plays still get produced and good plays fail for lack of judgment like a major error in the casting.

In their search for a smash-hit, most producers automatically reject certain genres of plays. "Again, every experienced dramatist," noted Elmer Rice in his book, *The Living Theatre,* "is well aware that plays of excessive length, plays written in verse, plays dealing with abstract ideas or with 'depressing' subjects are not very good box-office prospects." [43] After more than forty years on the shifting Broadway scene, Richard Maney, the dean of New York's theatrical press agents, wrote in his book *Fanfare,* "Tragedies, classic or contemporary, rarely pay off. They're box-office poison." [44] He also observed that producers usually regard melodrama and farce as a king of second-rate goods. "Satire," George S. Kaufman once wryly remarked, "is something that closes on Saturday night in Wilmington." As for plays whose primary rather than secondary concern is a social message, even The Theatre Guild never made them pay. "If you want to send a message," the Broadway gag goes, "call Western Union." Revues also rarely pay off. In the last twenty years or so, there have been only a handful of successful revues among them *Call Me Mister, Lend an Ear, Second City, La Plume de Ma Tante, Beyond the Fringe, Wait a*

Minim, and these operated on low budgets without big names. In the 1964–5 season, 14 productions were musicals. A dozen dramas were produced, and all but one, *The Subject Was Roses,* failed. Of seven revues, only Victor Borg's *Comedy in Music* was a big success, but it was more a one man show than actually a revue. Maney says of producers, "They're suspicious of all categorical labels save 'comedy' and 'musical comedy'." [45]

Is there no tell-tale mark of a smash-hit? Broadway's most successful producer, George Abbott, is said to have earned throughout his career over twenty million dollars. From 1935 to 1965, with the exception of a week or two, he has always had at least one play running on Broadway—either as an actor, director, co-author, producer or some combination of these capacities. According to Hal Prince, the very successful producer who learned production with Abbott, "He has ditched a half-dozen of his own shows during out of town tryouts because he hates to waste time whipping a dead horse." [46] It's too easy for Abbott to find a new, live horse that looks like a winner. Still leading the field in hits, Abbott said, "my whole training and experience makes me place construction, or story line, first, and words second." [47] And he added, "The difference between the passable success and the smash-hit is that the latter never lets down—that in it each scene leads to the next with interest, so that when it is over there is a feeling of wanting more, a feeling that no matter how long the show is it has been a short evening." [48] Abbott has also said that one other sign of a smash-hit is the excellence of those who collaborated to mount it; the one-hit playwright and the one-hit producer, to Abbott, are those who bluffed and bragged that the success was "my hit" and who then failed disastrously without the contributing talents of those with a more consistent record of success. Abbott cited as a fine, practical view for a producer the salty comment of George M. Cohan to Sam Harris about an actor who in rehearsal peeved Cohan: "We'll never use that son-of-a-bitch again—unless we need him." [49] Emphasizing how difficult it is to accurately assay the commercial or artistic gold in any theatrical work, Abbott with all his acumen saw The Theatre Guild's opening of *Oklahoma!* in New Haven and liked it, but then admitted that he did not realize he was seeing, in his phrase, "an epochal production."

Next to George Abbott, perhaps the most seasoned veteran of Broadway's battles of production is Theresa Helburn who recently died. For over forty years, she was on the Executive Board of The Theatre Guild and directly involved with selecting plays for production. By 1942, after being in business for over twenty years, The Theatre Guild had suffered a series of fourteen virtual failures that left the once bursting treasury dwindled to a mere $30,000. Theresa Helburn then pushed through or around every obstacle to turn Lynn Riggs' *Green Grow the Lilacs* into the musical, *Oklahoma!,* and so literally saved the life of The Theatre Guild.

During its most profitable years, the first fifteen or so of its life, the Guild picked scripts for production by having all six Board members read them and then vote at a meeting for or against production with an open statement as to the why's and wherefore's. The Board, it was hoped, represented a microcosm of the Broadway audience: Lawrence Langer, law; Maurice Wertheim, banking; Lee Simonson, scene design; Helen Westley, acting; Philip Moeller, directing; Theresa Helburn, business. The Board finally gave up this system after "irreconcilable differences," and then Helburn and Langer took over play selection. "There was only one standard we set ourselves," said Helburn of the Board before it dissolved in the mid-thirties, "one criterion we applied to our choice of a play: Does it say enough to us and say it well enough to deserve the work and expense of production?" [50] And she remarked ruefully, "I can't remember a case when it did not prove to be a mistake to produce a play which had failed to arouse majority approval on its own merits." [51] Even so, the Board made blunders; for instance, they turned down Elmer Rice's *Street Scene.* The most successful plays, Helburn recalled, were those which the Board had voted unanimously to produce, though each member may have given a different reason for the choice. The blind spots of some Board members were usually made up for by the vision of others; all Board members were mercilessly honest.

Helburn also attributed the Guild's high average of success—two out of five as contrasted with the usual producer's one out of four—to the Board's system of "manager rehearsals." The Board would attend periodic run-throughs of the current play in rehearsal to review critically the casting, the direction, and any matters that might ruin a production unless corrected in time. As for the outcome of a production, Helburn, near the conclusion of her long career admitted in her book, *A Wayward Quest,* that neither she nor any theatrical manager she ever knew could be sure of a play's reception until after the curtain had come down upon opening night. "Only the public can tell," she said of a play's fate. "And what the public decides is an unending surprise." [52]

For one more authority as to the nature of a hit play to a producer, listen to Lawrence Langner who was with The Theatre Guild's Board from its beginning in 1920 to his death about forty years later: "The most effective stories for the theatre are usually those which affect one or two characters who are in the central position of the story," he wrote in *The Play's the Thing:* "The story line of a single character who moves along the play and is its central figure usually results in a fine acting role for an actor or actress as well as a unified play . . ." [53] In a well constructed play, to Langner, the action kept building from scene to scene and reached its major climax near the very end. "The resolution which arrives toward the end of the play constitutes an ending which satisfies the audience by reason of our greater understanding of the nobility of the human spirit in the case of high tragedy," noted Langner, "or the solution, or the suggestion of a solution, of the human problem involved in the case of comedy." [54]

Incidentally, The Theatre Guild's apparently beautiful system of production, had it seems in its very nature the critical flaws of its own demise. Five of the Guild's finest playwrights, Elmer Rice, Robert Emmet Sherwood, Maxwell Anderson, S. N. Behrman, and Sidney Howard found, in Sherwood's term to Ward Morehouse, relating to the Guild's system, "never ending wrangling and jangling;" [55] Elmer Rice details the story in *Minority Report.*

To get a play to a producer, the playwright must first submit it to a reputable play agent who screens incoming scripts and has access to play producers. Producers refuse to read unsolicited manuscripts because of the danger of plagiarism suits or the wasting of precious time from reading indiscriminately. A good agent is a kind of assay office of a script's commercial possibilities. If a producer reads and likes a script, he may option it for a limited time, usually six months, for a pre-emptive fee. The play agent's standard commission is 10% for being the playwright's business agent in any commercial exploitation of the play. If the play finally goes into production, the playwright signs the regulation Dramatists Guild contract guaranteeing the playwright terms already mentioned. A hit comedy grossing $30,000 a week, for instance, will in round figures earn the playwright 9% of the gross or $2,700 a week.

If a producer fails to raise the money required to stage the script, he may drop his option and never produce the play. Play investors or "angels," as they are euphemistically called, are people with usually $250.00 and up to invest. Established producers have a preferred list of this theatrical heavenly host, just as established playwrights have a preferred list of producers. Loyalties founded on previous good fortune often last at least for one more try with the same producer, and recognized quality seldom goes begging. In bygone days, a producer occasionally was so very enthusiastic over a script that he would finance the whole production out of his own pocket. Brock Pemberton, for instance, did this until a series of flops almost undid him. His judgment then became chastened enough to look for reassuring "angels." The producer who dared completely underwrite his own production is today on Broadway, like the dinosaur in natural history, an extinct species.

Arnold Maremont, who called himself "a most consistent angel," made a survey of 18 typical angels to find what caused the mutation into this breed of investor. Maremont decided that angels wanted chiefly the thrill of creative identification with the theatre. What money angels invested in a show, they could afford to lose as a tax write-off usually, but they were also flushed with the same hectic fever of winning that goes with betting on a horse-race or a poker-hand. "Howard Gotbetter, a New York theatrical lawyer," reported an interviewer for *Fortune* magazine of November, 1964, "says that many 'invest for a variety of nonbusiness reasons,' the glamour of being associated with a Broadway show, the prestige associated with reading scripts, attending backers' auditions, buying opening night seats, for other ego purposes, and in large part because they are stage-struck." [56]

"There have been two overlapping stages in theater backing," reported *Business Week* magazine of February 2, 1963; "Traditionally backing came from individuals—either several affluent 'angels' or up to 50 to 100 small contributors who joined to put up total production costs (today an average $100,000 for a play; $300,000 to $500,000 for a full-size musical)." [57] Furthermore, "This method still accounts for about 80 per cent of new shows." The other 20 per cent, especially musicals, rely upon financing by motion picture companies or recording companies eager to pre-empt rights to a prospective smash-hit. The Columbia Broadcasting System, for instance, invested the full $360,000 for *My Fair Lady* to secure album rights and 40% of the profits. Capitol Records put up the whole $400,000 for *The Unsinkable Molly Brown*.[58] To draw angels to invest, producers often use the device of a cocktail party or buffet supper at a good sized apartment where the guests may be refreshed and see an audition of the work. New ideas for hatching angels keep cropping up, like The Theatrical Investing Service, organizing about 1,200 petty investors with an ante of from $100 to $1,000; it is unknown how long this incubator will last.

Producers have sometimes failed to raise money to produce plays that other producers in time turned into bonanzas. Oscar Serlin, to illustrate, had to drop his option on *Arsenic and Old Lace* because he could not raise the money to produce it; it was to run for about five years on Broadway. "There were endless exhausting auditions," Margaret Cullman recalled of raising money for the eventual smash-hit musical, *Kiss Me Kate.* "But by and large, the audience continued to keep their money in stocks and bonds."[59] Oscar Serlin almost failed to raise the $35,000 to produce *Life with Father* in 1939, a play that was to run for over seven years on Broadway, breaking all long-run records to the present; such knowledgeable investors turned Serlin down as: Alfred Knopf, Cary Grant, Alice Duer Miller, Benny Goodman, Goodman Ace, B. P. Schulberg, Mrs. Otto Kahn, and Leland Hayward.[60] In 1943, the Theatre Guild in rising desperation gave three huge cocktail parties to try to round up enough backers to stage *Oklahoma!,* but failed to corral representatives of MGM, Paramount, and Twentieth Century Fox, not to mention almost a Who's Who in the Theatre. Lee Shubert, for example, declined on the grounds that no successful musical ever had a murder in it, and a Broadway ticket-broker said, "No legs, no jokes, no chance." Frantic, the Guild induced their scene designer, Lemuel Ayers, to take a percentage of the gross rather than a flat fee, and thereby made him in time the highest paid scene designer in all theatrical history. *Oklahoma* had 2,248 performances on Broadway alone.

If producers at times have gone begging to support an eventual smash-hit, eventual smash-hits have also gone begging for a producer. Consider as illustrations: *Abie's Irish Rose, Street Scene, Journey's End, Personal Appearance, The Barretts of Wimpole Street, Tea and Sympathy, Inherit the Wind, Look Back in Anger* and *Come Blow Your Horn.* Over twenty American producers turned down *The Barretts of Wimpole Street.* Twelve rejected *Inherit the Wind,* and it lay unproduced for five years until Margo Jones of the Dallas Arena Theatre did it as a try-out. The biggest Broadway producers of comedy turned down *Come Blow Your Horn* until Michael Ellis tried it out at the Bucks County Playhouse, where it made such delightfully funny music for the audience, that Ellis took it to Broadway.

The Play-Going Public

Whoever works in the commercial theatre directly depends upon the play-going public for a living. In opening or shutting its wallets and purses, this public literally dictates a production's life and death. To design a play without considering the play-going public that must support it is to build a ship without any intention of submitting it to the hazards of water. The playwright's indignation at the water will never keep the leaky ship afloat. After over twenty-five years of experience in the theatre, Moss Hart in his *Act One* said: "the actual fate of a play is almost always sealed by its first audience." [61] The words, "almost always," suggest that a resourceful playwright in a crisis might mend the assorted sized holes in his play before it lists or founders like a rock in the expert eyes of the drama critics. To transfer a poorly received play unchanged from city to city, hoping that a more favorable public reception depends only on latitude and longitude, is plain folly, as Hart found from his own first commercial failure, *The Beloved Bandit*. "Audiences do not vary that widely," commented Hart, "nor, for that matter, do critics." [62] Hart became fully convinced that theatre audiences could intuitively sense a play's weakness or an actor's shortcomings with the speed and precision of lightning. What "stinks" in Philadelphia will smell no better in Detroit or Chicago or eventually in New York. "Somehow at the end of that first fifteen minutes," wrote Hart, "an invisible bell seems to ring in the theatre, and if the play has not captured them by then en masse," he said of the audience, "they become a disparate group of people who are never welded together again." [63]

A pool of opinion helps give a composite view of what the playwrights and producers have from observation thought the public really wanted in the theatre. Because romantic young ladies and their escorts made up by far most of the play-going audience in Belasco's day, he thought that a play that pleased youth in love was a guaranteed success, and yet the play had to deal with "the dramatic material of the present" and relate somehow to "the theme of universal interest." [64] Even lovers want to be the latest. In a like vein, Frederick Lonsdale thought that all the public really wanted was another love story. To Dunsany, the public was yearning for a chance to let its spirit soar on sheer inspiration for an hour or so. Rachel Crothers thought the public came to the theatre to forget its troubles and come out refreshed enough to face life again. In Thornton Wilder's opinion, "The theatre partakes of the nature of festival." [65] The public came for fun and excitement amounting to something; the highly mixed audience limited the playwright to common concerns in living.

Maxwell Anderson believed "the playwright must pluck from the air about him a fable which will be of immediate interest to his time and hour, and relate it in a fashion acceptable to his neighbors." [66] Anderson furthermore was convinced, "And there is only one condition that makes possible a Bach, an Aeschylus, or a Michelangelo—it is a national interest in and enthusiasm for the art he practices." [67] From studying the masterpieces of the drama, Anderson at first decided that the secret of their lasting popular appeal was in their heroes who acted for race survival, that is, for the public good. The popularity of such plays as *Antigone* and *Saint Joan,* however, led Anderson to further decide that the public wanted "to claim a kinship with a higher morality than that which hems them in." [68] Survival of the race was fine, but a faith in man's soul as God-given was the only thing that could give survival, itself, meaning.

"We discovered in the long run," remarked Theresa Helburn from her years with The Theatre Guild, "that much of the public was weary of tired formulas and standardized productions, that the thinking few had become many, that there were enough of them to constitute an important theatrical audience." [69] Oscar Hammerstein II noticed the same phenomenon: "The great hits are not those that have been written to formula, but those that have been trail-blazers." [70] *Rose Marie,* for instance, had a killing in it. "Experience has taught me," Hammerstein also noted after a good forty years in the theatre, "that audiences follow the story. . . . If it isn't firm, then all the jokes and all the songs and the chorus and the beautiful production all fall in a heap." [71] In Harold Clurman's judgment, the public is so eager to find something new in life, that the old plays in the sense of repertory or revivals are rarely profitable.

Some playwrights, however, have a less pleasant view of the wants of the play-going public. "The dramatist must share the prepossessions of his audience, the example of Lope de Vega and Shakespeare is there to prove it," said Maugham, as he chose to work largely in the freer medium of the novel.[72] For Maugham, theatre audiences were intellectually at least thirty years behind the times and interested only in the preoccupations of the human race for survival,—birth, love, death, and destiny. "The most important trend in American playwriting at the present moment," said Arthur Miller in 1955, "is that seats cost up to eight dollars each, and the house is full of the bored." [73] Seats have since gone up to $9.00. Miller thought that a $.75 ticket would bring back to the theatre the universal audiences that made possible the great drama of Classical Greece and Elizabethan England.

"I would submit that 'The Theatre of the Absurd,' in the sense that it is truly the contemporary theatre facing as it does man's condition as it is, is the Realistic theatre of our time," declared Edward Albee in *The New York Times Magazine* of February 25, 1962; "and the supposed Realistic theatre—the term used here to mean most of what is done on Broadway—in the sense that it panders to the public need for self-congratulation and reassurance and presents a false picture of ourselves to ourselves, is with an occasional very lovely exception, really and truly 'The Theatre of the Absurd'." "It is evident then," said Jean-Paul Sartre, condemning the play-going public of the commercial theatre, "that the dictatorship of the bourgeoisie has created a bourgeois theatre." [74] And to Bertolt Brecht, the Western world's commercial theatre was declining into "a branch of the bourgeois narcotics traffic." [75]

Broadway's Opening-Night Audience

An opening-night audience on Broadway is in the mood of a Roman emperor at the gladiatorial games, ready above all for "thumbs up" or "thumbs down." The most influential members of that gathering are the "Caesars," the drama critics representing the leading newspapers in New York City. Cafe society and celebrities from stage, screen, radio, and television contribute a good sprinkling of exhibitionists and eccentrics. Producers who rejected the script, actors who were not cast, directors who were passed up, and the disillusioned and envious, according to Maney, come ready for willing ill toward the offering. The bulk of the audience is somehow professionally involved in the theatre. Many first-nighters, however, are friends and relatives of those with a stake in the production's success, and this group in its overeagerness to applaud too hard and to laugh too loud and long at the slightest occasion, is markedly partisan. The reaction of the audience at the closing curtain tells the play's fate. Synthetic ovations are as spurious as the dubbed in laughter that falsifies audience reaction to TV comedy. "If the audience competes with the reviewers in the dash to the exits," Maney calculates, "it's an evil omen. But if it remains fixed in its seats through ten or twelve curtain calls, I count the day won." [76] So infectious is a hit play that Moss Hart believed even those who came to the premiere with ill will were won over in the end. To Brooks Atkinson, "Most first-night audiences are . . . easy victims to all the blandishments of good theatrical craftsmanship and remarkably alert to every impulse of humor." [77] "A good play seems in its first performance better than it would seem in any other performance," observed the distinguished English drama critic, Max Beerbohm, "and a bad play seems worse."

Within two hours after the closing curtain has come down, the decisive drama reviews begin to appear in the morning newspapers— *The New York Times* and *The Daily News*. Another review appears in New York's only current afternoon newspaper, *The Post*. Trade journals also come through with notices: *The Wall Street Journal* for the financially slanted; *The Journal of Commerce* for the business world; *Women's Wear Daily* for the garment industry; *The Saturday Review* for the literary minded; and *The Morning Telegraph* for the horse-racing fans. Other drama reviews also appear and can become quite consequential in providing the play's press agent with quotable excerpts to lure the public to the box-office: the TV networks whose drama reviewers sound off within an hour of the play's final curtain; gossip columnists like Walter Winchell, Leonard Lyons, and Ed Sullivan; and magazines of current events like *Life, Look, Newsweek, Time* and *The New Yorker*. A typical Broadway opening night provides about 65 pairs of tickets, a single pair for each representative of some aspect of the communications industry.

Elmer Rice remarked, "lasting success is the product of what is quaintly known as 'word of mouth'." The praise for hits reverberates throughout the land, and so does the condemnation for flops. The theatre becomes a very hard place to keep one's head in success or failure. The acute dangers are almost instant, utter deflation or inflation of the playwright's ego.

The storms of argument over the validity of drama critics abate periodically but never for long. Somehow there lingers in the air the spirit of Boswell quoting Doctor Johnson, "Criticism is a device by which one may grow important and formidable at the expense of others." Maxwell Anderson, once a journalist himself, fired point blank at drama critics after a series of failures—"the Jukes family of journalism." The late Percy Hammond, long a drama critic, once said, "Dramatic criticism is the venom from contented rattlesnakes." [78] A more moderate view is that of John Gassner, who has been a producer and drama critic, if not an author. Says Gassner, "the critic whose praise is indiscriminate will not hold his followers." [79] People will resent being misled to spend good money for cheap goods. To Gassner, the critic is essentially the guardian of the theatre's excellence. "Whether or not the critic reaches a large public," argues Gassner, "he certainly reaches the playwright, the producer, the director, and the actors. He penetrates to the very heart of the theatre by speaking to its creators." [80] No drama critic in his right mind would try to kill off the theatre with bad notices, thinks Richard Maney, because to do so would kill off the drama critic's own privileged job.

For those interested, the merits and foibles of individual drama critics may be gathered by reading back issues of their reviews in bound volumes, *New York Theatre Critics Reviews*. Men of integrity, it is plain, sometimes see the same production with a quite opposite reaction. Brooks Atkinson, for example, wrote of the Bernstein-Hellman musicalization of Voltaire's *Candide,* "a brilliant musical satire," but Walter Kerr called it "a spectacular disaster." [81] How two such eminent critics can differ so markedly, some try to explain as simply personal prejudice, myopia, childhood, indigestion, wife trouble, or just the phases of the moon. Whether they admit it or not, drama critics will occasionally get on the kind of very high horse Anatole France gave them in defining criticism as, "The adventures of a soul among masterpieces." If drama critics—or reviewers, as they are sometimes termed—were to allow only masterpieces to survive on the Broadway stage each season, few if any plays could or would survive. Ironically, when a modern masterpiece does come along like the now generally acknowledged *Our Town,* critics may not even recognize it. It did not get the New York Drama Critics' Circle Award of 1937–38. In fact, for one week before *Our Town* reached Broadway, the play in its Boston run lost over $10,000. "And for absolutely no better reason," said its producer, Jed Harris, "than that the critics in Boston were too stupid to appreciate what was being offered them." [82] With bad Boston notices, *Our Town* almost failed to get a first-class house in New York City. Only through friendship did Gilbert Miller offer Jed Harris his theatre for one performance and extend the offer to a full week when Ina Claire, scheduled to open at the Gilbert Miller Theatre, chose to keep her own play on the road longer for polishing.

"Politics, they say, is the art of the possible," remarked Jed Harris. "The theatre is, of course, the art of the impossible." [83] According to Richard Maney, incidentally, Jed Harris himself declined to invest in the now classic *Oklahoma!* after seeing its opening night in New Haven.

John Mason Brown wrote in his book, *The Worlds of Robert E. Sherwood:*

> The fatal flattery of criticism is that it raises its sights when faced with authors who have raised theirs. . . . It means that to try for the indifferent is to gain tolerance and to aim at the best is to invite dismissal.[84]

Brown in *The New York Post* reviewed Sherwood's only likely classic, *Abe Lincoln in Illinois,* as "rotten," but has since reversed himself even to writing Sherwood's biography. Critics may take comfort in their lack of omniscience in that even the United States Supreme Court has a majority and a minority opinion and on occasion has reversed itself years later. "It is inhuman to judge everything alongside of perfection," said Peter Ustinov epitomizing the chief charge against the critics. "Sometimes one must be thankful that there is anything at all." [85]

One thing perhaps should forever make the tribe of drama critics feel less omniscient, and writers, too. "The absence of any reasoned criticism of the plays during the first half of the seventeenth century," wrote C. F. Johnson in *Shakespeare and His Critics,* "is less remarkable than the fact that so many writers ignore Shakespeare's existence entirely. . . . Francis Bacon, Sir Walter Raleigh, Daniel, Warner, Drayton, John Donne. . . ." [86] There may be a Shakespeare industry today among pundits of literature and the stage, but in Shakespeare's day there was barely the merest handicrafting by such otherwise quite unknown men as Francis Meres in his *Palladis Tamia.* The greatest dramatic and literary genius of the English language went unrecognized by the watchers of the literary sky for such an astral phenomenon. It took a fellow dramatist, Ben Jonson, to write in the commendatory verse prefacing *The First Folio* in 1623:

> Soul of the age,
> Th' applause, delight, the wonder of our stage,
> My Shakespeare, rise . . .
> He was not of an age, but for all time.

Could what happened once happen once again? "The critics of the nineteenth century had two first-rate chances—Ibsen and Wagner," wrote Shaw in 1905 to his biographer, Henderson. "For the most part they missed both. Second best, they could recognize; but best was beyond them."

No matter how stoutly the critics may defend themselves against their detractors, the two most coveted critical awards in the American theatre are monuments to a fierce and alienating quarrel among the critics themselves: the Pulitzer Prize and the Drama Critics' Circle Award. Upon his death in 1911, Joseph Pulitzer, the distinguished publisher of *The St. Louis Post-Dispatch* and *The New York World,* left money for many yearly prizes in writing and, among them, a Pulitzer Prize Award for "the original American play performed in New York City which shall best represent the standards of good morals, good taste, and good manners." The first Pulitzer Prize in Drama was awarded in 1917. The jurors' identification was and is kept secret to prevent undue outside interference. To be official, the jurors' choice had to be approved by the fourteen member Advisory Board which, by Pulitzer's will, was drawn from the Board of Trustees of Columbia University. Through freedom granted them in Pulitzer's will, the Advisory Board in 1929 modified their criteria for the drama award to read: "To an original American play performed in New York which shall represent in marked fashion the educational value and power of the stage, preferably dealing with American life." [87]

In 1935 the Pulitzer Prize in Drama went to Zoe Akins' play, *The Old Maid,* adapted from the novel by Edith Wharton. This choice outraged the conscience of the drama critics of New York City, for it by-passed such original American plays of that season as Lillian Hellman's *The Children's Hour,* Clifford Odets' *Awake and Sing,* and Robert Emmet Sherwood's *The Petrified Forest.* As Helen Deutsch suggested, the New York City drama critics and reviewers organized a circle of twelve leading practitioners to pick, in their opinion, "the best American play of the year." To win this award, a play had to poll at least nine of the twelve critics' votes. By 1965, however, the rules of the game had changed so much that the panel had increased to nineteen, and a play could win the award with only a plurality; the critics were so divided and adamant in their choice that *The Subject Was Roses* won the Drama Critics' Circle Award by polling only five of the total nineteen votes then cast. Since 1935, the Pulitzer Prize

Award in Drama and the Drama Critics' Circle Award have agreed roughly one time in three.

With the critics so at odds in their own circle, and their own Award so often at odds with the Pulitzer Award, no wonder theatre-folk themselves are often in an excruciating quandary before and sometimes after the criticisms or reviews come out. George Abbott said, "in general, critics are honest men doing their very best, sitting through a dozen tedious plays to see one exciting one . . ." [88] Other theatre-folk are deeply disturbed over the power of critics. "It's not wise for a playwright to say too much about drama critics," observed Edward Albee after the mixed notices of *Tiny Alice,* "because unfortunately they have totalitarian power and authority." [89] "Intelligent reviewers are disturbed over this state of affairs," remarked Elmer Rice in *The Living Theatre,* "for, recognizing their own fallibility, they feel that the responsibility imposed upon them is too heavy, particularly since there seems to be no general agreement as to the function of the critic." [90] Maxwell Anderson, who carried on a verbal vendetta for a few years with the critics, said of their power, "They operate a censorship. . . . It's unhealthy because it's undemocratic. The people of a democracy should decide for themselves what plays they will see." [91]

Early in February, 1965, when a student at Warsaw University asked the visiting lecturer, Arthur Miller, what an ideal critic should look like, Miller answered, "He should be small and invisible, deaf and dumb. . . . I never learned anything from critics. They are for the public and not for artists." [92] Is Miller alone? In its issue of June 15, 1966, *Variety* reported that after the London critics in general had panned the new play, *A Bond Honored,* adapted from the Spanish of Lope de Vega by one of England's most distinguished current playwrights, John Osborne, Osborne sent this telegram to each of the newspapers concerned:

> The gentleman's agreement to ignore puny theatre critics as bourgeois conventions that keep you pinned in your soft seats is a thing that I fall in with no longer. After 10 years it is now war. Not a campaign of considerate complaints in private letters, but open and frontal war that will be as public as I and other men of earned reputation have the considerable power to make it.[93]

Of course, this war hidden or open never really ended, and probably began with the first playwright. Playwrights, ironically, fathered drama critics, for without playwrights there could be no drama critics. Drama criticism at best is a troublesome profession involving commerce dependent upon an aesthetic judgment, and one has only to read aesthetics to find how caked with blood that battlefield is and how the fallen can rise to vanquish the victor.

III

AESTHETIC CONSIDERATIONS AFFECTING PLAYWRITING THESE DAYS

The Function of the Drama

What is the function of the drama in a free society? Opinions vary with the playwright's spirit. "The first thing I try to do is to make a play live:" said Sean O'Casey, "live as a part of life, and live in its own right as a work of drama." [94] "Playwrights and poets have had, are having a share in squeezing the mind of man into visions of woe and great lamentations," complained O'Casey in sharp disagreement with some avant-garde trends. "They labor hard to get us all down." [95] For Synge, drama should be "a dinner where the food we need is taken with pleasure and excitement;" the best of Molière and Ben Jonson, Synge noted in his preface to *The Tinker's Wedding,* had the freshness of "blackberries on hedges," and taught no lessons and solved no problems any more than a symphony does.[96] "A farce and a tragedy are alike in this," observed Yeats, "that they are a moment of intense life;" there is Walter Pater in this. "He takes it for granted," said William Inge of the playwright, "that the audience comes to the theatre not to be told something but to find out something for themselves." [97]

Benavente thought the theatre was meant to project the life of the soul. For Dunsany, the theatre's chief concern was to surprise the audience with truth. Belasco thought that the theatre was not a soapbox or a lecture platform but a place to tell the audience a good story that was truthful and up to the minute. To Sidney Howard, "The drama does not spring from a literary impulse, but to satisfy the brave, ephemeral, beautiful art of acting . . ." "When such a love becomes the obsession of genius," Howard declared in the preface of his *Lucky Sam McCarver,* "then great plays are written and great dramatists appear, as Ibsen, Shakespeare and Chekhov appeared." [98] To Howard the dramatist was in essence a vicarious actor. John Howard Lawson conceived of drama as a mirror of current social conflict.

Maxwell Anderson construed the drama's valid function to be just what it was in the days of Aeschylus and Aristophanes: tragedy exulted in the god in man, a declaration of faith; and comedy exulted in the animal in man, a Dionysian revel. "The fact is, I entered the theatre thinking of it as a church," wrote William Gibson who first scored with *Two for the Seesaw,* "and emerged thinking of it as a brothel." [99] Gibson, of course, shortly afterward returned to the theatre with hardly a prostitution of playwriting, *The Miracle Worker.*

In his existentialist view of the world, Sartre at first thought it was enough for him to be "sequestered," to write in an attic as one abandoned by an indifferent universe; by 1961, however, he had decided that if the spectacle of life were to be justified, he must come "out of the attic." Sartre then turned to writing as "an act of personal engagement," committing himself to improve the lot of men. "Engaged literature," declared Sartre in *The Tulane Drama Review* of March 1961, "requires a personal commitment and anonymous heroism." [100] In writing *Rhinoceros,* Ionesco implied his conception of the drama's function: "I tried to achieve the expression of the strangeness in which all human existence seems to be bathed." Ionesco elaborated, "I have no wish to save humanity—to wish to save it is to kill it—and there are no solutions." [101]

John Osborne, on the contrary, feels that he may not be an expert on housing, schools, or pensions, but as a human being he is qualified to be concerned with such questions, for example, as "—how do people live inside those houses?" [102] "Imaginative literature has nothing to say to those who do not recognize—who cannot be *reminded.* . . . Of all the arts the theatre is best endowed to awaken this recollection within us—," said Thornton Wilder.[103] "By whatever means it is accomplished," said Arthur Miller, "the prime business of a play is to arouse the passions of its audience so that by the route of passion may be opened up new relationships between a man and men, and between men and Man." [104] Miller also said, "My aim is what it has been from the beginning—to bring to the stage the thickness, awareness, and complexity of the novel." [105]

What do these individual judgments amount to? For the most part, they say essentially that the drama should delight us and make some implied sense out of living. "For we are only an industry of entertainment, really," said William Inge epitomizing the matter, "with the potential of discovering truth and beauty at once making life a little richer as a consequence." [106]

The Subject Matter of the Drama

The individuality as to the drama's proper function, makes for individuality as to the drama's proper subject matter. Our times are called "The Age of Anxiety." And the spirit of the age tends to polarize all subject matter to this viewpoint from within. We are involved in a continuous game of search, discovery, and uncertainty in widening cycles of our expanding consciousness through knowledge. For over a thousand years religious faith had God in His Heaven, even if through machinations of the Devil all was not right with the world. Man was the direct creation of God, and the earth, the center of the universe. After Copernicus, the earth was no longer the center of the universe. After Darwin, man appeared more the product of evolution than of God's direct creation; a vast variety of all manner of life was also evolving distinct from man. After Adam Smith, the world seemed safe for man's private enterprise. After Karl Marx, much of the world has come to view economics as an endless conflict heading for communism or anarchy. After the success of American democracy, freedom seemed man's natural right and happiest state. After fascist and communist dictatorships, man's service to the state was preached as his only right and only lot. After Freud, the mysteries of the human mind clearly showed powers molding individual conduct sometimes beyond the individual's will. After Einstein, we are an instant in time, and our solar system, one of an incalculable number. With electricity, machines, radio, television, computers, atomic power, automation we have half the world starving, population explosions, mass education, racial conflicts, and the threat of nuclear war. What do playwrights favor as the subject matter of this Age of Anxiety?

Jean Anouilh has created *Becket,* Archibald MacLeish *J. B.,* and Robert Bolt *A Man for All Seasons.* "They have sensed," said John Mason Brown in *Dramatis Personae,* of these playwrights who have found a noble spiritual strain in man, "that people are what they prove to be in the moments of being most cruelly tested." [107] Like modern man, the leading characters in these plays all live in a time that tries men's souls and especially their own. The unscrupulous playboy, Becket, once installed as Archbishop of Canterbury, finds in his conscience that he must defy the expedient wishes of the very man who made him Primate, his best friend, King Henry II; and rather than break faith with his vows to God, Becket accepts martyrdom. J. B., like the biblical Job, is run through a gauntlet of trials of our time by

Mr. Zuss and Nickles, suggesting God and the Devil, but J. B.'s spirit, though all but broken, emerges triumphantly strengthened, if less deist than humanist. When compromise means that life itself is meaningless, for then faith is a mockery, Sir Thomas More, who is master of compromise in all things but his faith, refuses to approve of the marriage of Henry VIII to Anne Boleyn, though he knows the choice will cost him his head.

Poles apart from this subject matter of current drama which finds that man as a reasoning animal has a soul exalting him under supreme test, is the subject matter of the existentialists. To date, Broadway's only popular successes in this genre have been Ionesco's *Rhinoceros* and Albee's *Who's Afraid of Virginia Woolf?* In *Rhinoceros* life is viewed as a witty, frightening, farcical tragedy in which peoples' desire to get ahead in the world leads them to imitate and then in essence become rhinoceroses, charging and stomping out all opposition. Of all humanity portrayed in the play, only the leading male character temporarily resists transformation at the play's very end. *Who's Afraid of Virginia Woolf?* shows how two unhappily married couples psychologically flay each other alive, in a marathon drinking bout freeing them of all inhibitions, at the same time purging them of their modern conflicts. Though some salutary purpose may be read into Albee's and Ionesco's plays, they belong to "The Theatre of the Absurd," and according to Ionesco, "Absurd is that which is devoid of purpose." "Cut off from his religious, metaphysical, and transcendental roots, man is lost," wrote Ionesco, influenced by Sartre and Camus especially; "all his actions become senseless, absurd, useless." [108]

In a conversation with Gielgud reported in *The Atlantic Monthly* of April, 1965, Albee seems to have aligned himself with Sartre's "engaged" position. "I've always thought that it was one of the responsibilities of the playwright," said Albee, "to show people how they are and what their time is like in the hope that perhaps they'll change it." [109] In his book, *The Theatre of the Absurd,* Martin Esslin wrote of this kind of theatre's view of man, "It attempts to make him face up to the human condition as it really is . . . for the dignity of man lies in his ability to face reality in all its senselessness; to accept it freely, without fear, without illusions—and to laugh at it." [110]

Some plays of the Theatre of the Absurd that have won high artistic if only modest commercial success on Broadway are: Samuel Beckett's *Waiting for Godot;* Edward Albee's *Tiny Alice;* and Harold Pinter's *The Caretaker* and *The Homecoming.* The activity of the

Theatre of the Absurd has been overwhelmingly in avant-garde productions Off-Broadway. The line between the existentialists and the apparently more conservative playwrights is still a blurred one at times; Schisgal, the author of *Luv,* a big Broadway hit, asserted that his comedy was existential.

The subject matter of the great bulk of modern drama these days lies between these two poles, the one viewing man with a God-given soul, the other viewing man as devoid of purpose however courageous he is in laughing about it or in helping his fellow man by being "engaged."

Maugham thought the playwright got little thanks for writing on current social and political ideas; ideas already accepted, bore the audience like Nora's right to self-respect and fulfillment in *A Doll's House,* and ideas unaccepted, repel the general public as perfect nonsense. Maugham excelled in high comedy such as *The Circle.* "The ability to laugh at its own pretensions and shortcomings," said S. N. Behrman, one of America's few writers of high comedy, "is the true mark of a civilized nation, as it is of the civilized man." [111] Behrman specified the nature of his subject matter:

> There is an idea that the characters of high comedy must be rich, well dressed, and socially elevated. This is not necessarily true. . . . The immediate concerns of the characters in a high comedy may sometimes be trivial; their point of view must never be. Indeed, one of the endless sources of high comedy is seriousness of temperament, and intensity of purpose in contrast with the triviality of the occasion.[112]

"I believe there is a certain amount of morality, of propaganda in all good writing," said Lillian Hellman. "I assure you . . . that both *The Children's Hour* and *The Little Foxes* were designed as dramas of morality first and last." [113] Charged with using melodrama, Hellman countered, "But when violence is actually the needed stuff of the work and comes toward a large end, it has been and always will be in the good writer's field." [114] "I believe that the best plays are about people and not about things," was Terence Rattigan's position which launched a free-for-all symposium in the March 4, 1950 issue of *New Statesman and Nation* magazine. "From Aeschylus to Tennessee Williams," said Rattigan, "the only theatre that has ever mattered is the theatre of character and narrative." [115] As for ideas in a play, to Rattigan, "They definitely take third place to character and narrative . . ." He cites late Ibsen and early Shaw as not the best of models.

"The plays written around the new life," replied O'Casey to Rattigan, "must be currents in the mainstream of drama, must be an offspring of the great tradition." Ibsen and Shaw, to O'Casey, "brought a dead drama back to a serious and singing life again." [116] "One cannot write about people without writing about things," insisted O'Casey; ". . . Even the atom bomb, so far away from us, is very close to us all." The very aged Shaw joined in the full battle with his powder dry—"Without a stock of ideas, mind cannot operate and plays cannot exist. The quality of a play is the quality of its ideas." [117] "The battle of the 'schools' is a sham battle," judged Ben Levy. "There are only good plays and bad plays." And then Levy shed this light, "Looking along the line of masterpieces, I should say the first essential of a great play is a heated intellectual or poetic imagination, and preferably both." [118] Christopher Fry in this fray declared himself at loss to understand the passion for trying to pigeon-hole drama and said, "what we should want is more of all of them, not all of one of them." [119]

It is in totalitarian countries like Russia and Red China that the play of ideas in the sense of didactic drama as a weapon of the state is most popular by edict; drama like other arts in such countries has one chief function—to promote the state ideology or be considered subversive. Totalitarian countries seem to share Émile Zola's view of the theatre stated in his essay, *Naturalism in the Theatre:* "No better instrument for propaganda exists." [120] The nearest a totalitarian oriented playwright has come to American acceptance is Bertolt Brecht whose "epic realism" and Berliner Ensemble in East Berlin have made him especially popular in Central European countries. Although it failed on Broadway in 1933, Brecht's *Three Penny Opera* based on John Gay's *The Beggar's Opera* had a run of 2,611 performances Off-Broadway at the Theatre De Lys in the 1950's. Plays of Brecht that have failed on Broadway but scored an artistic success for many are: *Mother, Galileo,* and *Mother Courage*. Brecht's most successful long play in America has been *The Caucasian Chalk Circle* done in the Spring of 1966 for a three month run by the Lincoln Theater Center Repertory Company; the tributary theatre has easily excised the play's ideological frame-work. *Galileo* had a second, limited run under the Lincoln Center aegis in the spring of 1967.

Kenneth Tynan, the drama critic, noted that Brecht is not only extremely difficult to translate from German into English but possibly even more difficult to give adequate production. In developing his epic realism, Brecht tried to fuse all kinds of devices to imply socialist doctrine of the moment, for instance, a great many scenes, multiple settings, oriental elisions, movie clips, slides, live and recorded music, choral effects, lights, dance, all in an often complex sequence aimed to shake up the audience to think rather than to lull it into an imaginary world of vicarious experience. Brecht told the skeptical Mordecai Gorelik, "I am the Einstein of the new stage form." [121] Like his mentor, Erwin Piscator, Brecht tried to turn the theatre into a kind of peoples' tribunal.

"The greater my concern with social problems, the more resolutely I became a socialist, the more clearly I recognized the limit to any possibility of happiness that can be fought for and attained by individual and social strength of will," confessed Ernst Töller as translated by Marketa Goetz in *The Tulane Drama Review* of March, 1959. "As long as we are not able to overcome lightning and earthquakes, fires and hail storms, hunch backs and ugly faces, blind eyes and crooked souls, sterility and death, we ought to become humbler." [122] Perhaps no more poignant example of the limitations of ideological doctrine, as the full answer to the complex needs of human life, is found than in the suicide of Karl Marx's own daughter, Eleonor Marx-Aveling over a very unhappy marriage with a socialist, Dr. Edward Aveling.

The modern theatre, especially since the thirties, has had some highly successful plays dealing with social comment directly or by implication. Sidney Kingsley's *Dead End* dramatized in hard-hitting terror and pathos the vicious dead-end plight of too many slum "kids" in New York City's totally depressed neighborhoods often directly in sight of luxury apartments. Giraudoux's *Mad Woman of Chaillot* condemned exploiters of the earth's treasure, using a grotesque modern fable that sends them to hell looking for riches. Hellman's *The Little Foxes* showed the human destruction left by predatory greed in a Southern family of fine surface gentility. Miller's *All My Sons* posed the individual's trial of conscience in choosing during war-time between honorable ruin or dishonorable profits. Miller's *Death of a Salesman* delineated the deterioration of a soul that lives and dies by a popular code of success. His *The Crucible* captured the moment of intense life when, in a time of mass hysteria, a good and decent man must choose between saving his life by lying or losing his life by telling the truth. Lorraine Hansberry's *Raisin in the Sun* depicted the struggle of a matriarchal Negro family in Chicago trying to fulfill itself in a dominant white society. James Baldwin's virulently anti-white *Blues for Mr. Charlie* and his kindlier *Amen Corner* were commercial failures if in some respects artistic successes. "We are probably in the most problem-conscious period of world history," summed up John Gassner, ". . . Yet the theatre of this mid-century period has had less to say about the world and has been a poorer reflector of its tensions than ever before in our century."[123]

Only very recently have there been marked signs of a new trend originating in Germany and using facts like squadrons of Furies aimed at the viscera and conscience of the audience. The movement took on formidable life with Rolf Hochhuth's *The Deputy,* dramatizing Pope Pius XII's alleged failure to speak out against Hitler's systematized murder of Europe's Jews. The late Erwin Piscator, who first produced *The Deputy* at the Freie Volksbühne Theater in Berlin—a theater his enemies called 'the Piscatoire'—insisted, "this form was adopted because the facts of our great catastrophe overwhelmed the writers. They had to start with careful documentation."[124] Peter Weiss joined the movement with his play of tape-worm length title, nicknamed *Marat/Sade,* which was to win *The New York Drama Critics' Circle Award of* 1966. *Marat/Sade,* while not strictly documentary, dramatized the social and metaphysical problems of the modern world by an imaginative historical parallel; a play within a play, staged by the extreme individualist, the Marquis de Sade, as cathartic therapy is performed by the inmates of a madhouse and amuses well-to-do Parisians looking for entertainment after the French Revolution; in a mad world, the action reveals how the disgruntled revolutionist, Charlotte Corday, repeatedly tries and finally assassinates the extreme rationalist of social revolution, Jean-Paul Marat, in his bath. The play's dominant theme suggests how, with the best intentions, men are led to commit horrible atrocities only to find they have made a worse world; the people for whose good the revolution took place are never ready to receive or recognize it, and so make a mess of matters. Peter Weiss's *The Investigation,* based on the actual Auschwitz atrocity trials, is purely of the genre of historical documentary—a genre incidentally, that is very close to Shaw's *Saint Joan,* Miller's *The Crucible,* and Lawrence and Lee's *Inherit the Wind.*

Certainly there is a wide divergence of opinion among playwrights as to the proper subject matter for the drama these days. "The theatre usually reflects the temper of the times," said Elmer Rice. "The present trend of plays dealing with sadism and violence, with children and the problems of childhood and with sheer escapism," diagnosed Rice, "are indicative of the world climate of destructiveness and de-

spair and unwillingness or inability to come to grips with adult problems." [125] But Moss Hart probably tells the other half of the story:
"Every play is basically an expression of the playwright's personality
at that particular moment." [126]

*ACKNOWLEDGMENTS AND FOOTNOTES FOR CHAPTER
IX ARE AT THE CLOSE OF THE ENTIRE CURSORY STUDY,
THE END OF CHAPTER XI.*

Chapter X

A Cursory Study of Working Methods

Genesis

THE cursory study uncovered only a few instances in which playwrights have directly or indirectly told how they encouraged their creativeness. Lord Alfred Douglas, for instance, who was Oscar Wilde's close friend from the writing of *Salome* through *The Importance of Being Earnest,* reported that Wilde was never sober from four in the afternoon until three each morning, yet neither was Wilde drunk. "The more he drank, the more he talked," said Lord Douglas, "and without whiskey he could neither talk nor write."[1] Wilde also smoked cigarettes by the thousands, saying "abstinence from tobacco is mere torture to me."[2] Of writing *The Time of Your Life* in only six days and six nights, William Saroyan noted in the preface to the play, "The cigarettes smoked were Chesterfields . . . the cigars were panatelas . . . ten cents straight. The food was Automat food . . . The liquor was Scotch."[3] Saroyan suggests Wilde's creation in great bursts of energy driving him to exhaustion under the spur of proven stimulants.

Neil Simon, who has had four comedy hits in a row,—*Come Blow Your Horn, Barefoot in the Park, The Odd Couple,* and *Star Spangled Girl*—with the last three running simultaneously, is of the relatively Spartan school in creative habits. He doesn't smoke, and his working diet consists only of coffee, cookies, and dry roasted peanuts—suggesting a deliberate attempt to stimulate yet sustain himself on a relatively empty stomach. This diet is rather like George S. Kaufman's in collaborating with Moss Hart: nothing during working hours but an occasional piece of "home-made" fudge, as Kaufman put it, "for energy." Said Moss Hart, "Mr. Kaufman cared very little about food . . . indeed, his lack of concern with food was quite unlike anyone else's I have ever known."[4] This echoes Ibsen, Che-

442

khov, Shaw, and Williams' relatively complete abstention from food when working.

Physical inactivity also stimulates some playwrights to creative activity. Reminiscent of O'Neill, Maugham reported of the years he was an invalid from tuberculosis, "My imagination was never more nimble;" Maugham hinted that a playwright's deepest sensibilities may operate best from "want of exercise or a sluggish liver." [5] Noel Coward wrote the whole of *Private Lives* while recovering from an attack of flu in Shanghai. Among the more or less dedicated pacers to stimulate creativeness are not only Ibsen, Strindberg, Chekhov, Galsworthy, and O'Neill, but also Fields, Lindsay, Crouse, and Kaufman. As a young man, St. John Ervine used to walk as much as twenty miles a day to stimulate his circulation to a warm glow which he believed helped him identify with the deepest feelings of his characters. Ervine told Lawrence Langner that after losing a leg in World War I he could no longer write deeply emotional plays because of having to give up long walks; Ervine now could succeed only with high comedy.

Some few playwrights of Wilde's spasmodic creativeness worked without any set daily routine, but the great number like Ibsen, Strindberg, Chekhov, Shaw, Galsworthy, Pirandello, O'Neill and Williams, followed a routine working day. T. S. Eliot, for instance, worked regularly from 10 a. m. to 1 p. m.: "I found that three hours a day is about all I can do of actual composing. I could do polishing perhaps later." [6] Speaking of Neil Simon, the director Stanley Prager said, "Simon works at his writing the way other people work in a grocery store." [7] Simon appears at his rented office at 10 a. m. and stays until nightfall.

O'Neill's mentor at Harvard, Prof. George Pierce Baker, said of playwriting, "Undoubtedly, he who begins with a story is nearer his goal than he who begins with an idea or a character." [8] Shakespeare, of course, knew this and used this insight for almost every play he wrote. The story that fires the creative excitement may come to the playwright in chance ways. The love story of Elizabeth Barrett and Robert Browning so fascinated Hugh Walpole, for instance, that he persuaded Rudolph Besier to collaborate with him on a play about it. Walpole somehow became disenchanted with the notion and simply gave it all to Besier to do with as he pleased. And Besier alone wrote *The Barretts of Wimpole Street*. From reading Ludwig Fulda's fifty-year old play, *Die Seerauber,* Alfred Lunt saw an excellent role for him to star in and persuaded S. N. Behrman to modernize the play with this in mind; and so began S. N. Behrman's *The Pirate*—"a world famous pirate with an itch for respectability retires to a small community, marries, and becomes the village censor."[9] Maugham's ailing friend, John Colton, happened to be staying at the same hotel in Hollywood as Maugham and asked Maugham for something to read before going to bed. Maugham handed Colton his story, *Sadie Thompson.* Instead of putting him to sleep, the story kept Colton awake almost all night with its potential as a play. The next morning, Maugham agreed with Colton that there was a play in *Sadie Thompson*—good for a six night run. With Maugham's permission, Colton on his own adapted *Sadie Thompson* into the play, *Rain,* which ran on Broadway for over 700 performances, and has been revived periodically ever since.

To cite a few more instances of stories striking the magic of a creative fire in a playwright, *The Children's Hour* came about from Lillian Hellman reading "The Great Drumsheugh Case" in William Roughead's anthology of criminal law trials; Hellman's play shows the baneful influence of a child upon the lives of many adults. Clarence Day's autobiographical tales about his family provided Russell Crouse and Howard Lindsay with the enthusiasm and raw material to write *Life with Father,* which incidentally was to have an all-time record run on Braodway, 3,224 performances. Ruth McKenney's autobiographical stories gave Joseph Fields and Jerome Chodorov the content and spirit of *My Sister Eileen.* And Kathryn Forbes recollections of her childhood provided John Van Druten with the characters, the action, the theme, the settings, and even some of the dialogue for his best loved play, *I Remember Mama.* The Tevye stories of Sholom Aleichem provided Joseph Stein with the stuff of life to create the book for the musical, *Fiddler on the Roof.* Sir Arthur Conan Doyle's stories of the adventures of Sherlock Holmes stirred Jerome Coopersmith to the creative excitement to shape up the book for the musical *Baker Street.*

Plays sometimes begin from deep personal anxieties trying to find a sublimation or resolution. Arthur Laurents told Gilbert Millstein of *The New York Times* that Laurents' plays were all "a reflection of the state I was in at the time."[10] To illustrate, *Home of the Brave* grew from Laurents' World War II combat experiences, which were intensified by the suffering he endured from his hypersensitivity toward discrimination he met as a Jew. Lorraine Hansberry wrote her

Drama Critics' Circle Award play, *Raisin in the Sun,* from searing
memories of her own trials as a Negro trying to realize herself in a
dominantly white world; her family had moved into a white neighborhood when she was eight years old. She had written three other
plays before *Raisin* but *Raisin* had a new slant, examining the effect
of money upon individual members of a Negro family, with moving
into a white neighborhood only a secondary effect.

From visiting the English town of West Hamm shortly after a
Nazi bombing raid in World War II, Archibald MacLeish was
haunted for years by the implication of what he had witnessed. "The
bombs fell here and there," MacLeish recalled of some families that
had been previously bombed out four times. "They followed some of
these people for no rhyme or reason, and this condition of meaningless suffering and persecution that one couldn't explain bothered me
more and more."[11] Here was a universal theme of war. "What attracted me to the story of Job in the first place," said MacLeish, "was
the end of the *Book of Job*—Job's action."[12] God restores the absolutely stricken Job with not only double the goods He took away
from him but gives Job a new wife and children more beautiful than
those he had lost. In picking up his will to live after life had done its
worst to him, Job became in MacLeish's eyes like the people of West
Hamm, a triumph of the human spirit in extreme adversity. "Only
God's giving implies Job's acceptance. And it was the acceptance that
haunted my mind," noted MacLeish. *"The Book of Job* is a human
triumph. Its answer is not dogma but an act."[13] MacLeish did not
get his story "right" until a good ten years after witnessing the results
of the bombing of West Hamm. The ultimate meaning, too, took
years to evolve. On May 8th, 1955, MacLeish delivered one of a series
of six talks by distinguished laymen at the service of the Congrega-
tionalist First Church of Christ in Farmington, Connecticut, and Mac-
Leish's conclusion on his subject, *The Book of Job,* is really the
revelation of his play:

> Man, the scientists say, is the animal that thinks. They are wrong.
> Man is the animal that loves. It is in man's love that God exists and
> triumphs: in man's love that life is beautiful: in man's love that the
> world's injustice is resolved. . . . Our labor always, like Job's labor, is to
> learn through suffering to love . . . to love even that which lets us
> suffer.[14]

Next to stories, doubtless associated with the playwright's dominant
state of mind at the time, perhaps the most common way in which

plays begin is from a dynamic central character or characters in a basic comic or serious situation. Joseph Kesselring, the author of *Arsenic and Old Lace,* which had a Broadway run of 1,444 performances, said:

> I got the idea for *Arsenic* by deliberately selecting my grandmother as a focal point and trying to imagine the most improbable thing she could possibly do. She was a saintly old lady of the Whistler's Mother type, who raised fourteen children and lived to be eighty-four. First I thought of having her as a bootlegger on the side, but that seemed pretty commonplace, and after that I considered having her a secret writer for the horror pulp magazines, but that seemed to lack novelty, and I'm sure it has been done before. Then murder occurred to me—a poisoner on the wholesale basis—and that was *Arsenic.*[15]

The sweet old lady in the play only out of kindness poisons stray, lonesome, homeless, old men so they won't have to worry any more. The play came near the end of the great depression of the '30's, and the general public thought the notion very funny.

George Axelrod said of the genesis of *The Seven Year Itch,* "As everybody who writes down words on paper for a living, knows, once in awhile you get an idea that's a natural. One that can't miss." "As I say, the idea came in one piece. The summer bachelor. The girl upstairs. The wife we only see in the hero's imagination. The whole business," reminisced Axelrod, who had finished sexing up a paper back mystery novel for a book publisher in January of 1953 when the brainstorm over *The Seven Year Itch* hit him.[16] "In about twenty minutes I had typed out a scene-by-scene synopsis which—with two minor changes—is exactly the way the show is running today." [17] Interestingly enough the play, conceived in mid-winter, concerned sex and summer vacation. The leading characters and the basic comic situation of *The Seven Year Itch* are common in any metropolitan city in summer: a husband seven years married must stay in the city to work while his wife is off to the country on vacation with the children and, of course, the husband entirely through accident—in this instance a falling tomato plant that almost kills him—happens to meet a very attractive young lady in the apartment above and gets the seven year itch—a yen for extramarital activity.

To cite another instance, here in a half minute are the leading characters, the basic comic situation, and the true-to-life, ever-timely theme of Neil Simon's comedy, *The Odd Couple,* just as he dictated it into his tape recorder before writing the play, as reported by Alan Levy:

Two men—one divorced and one estranged and neither quite sure why their marriages fell apart—move in together to cut down on their alimony and suddenly discover that they're having the same conflicts and fights that they had in their marriage.[18]

But this half minute of dictation had a great many years of living behind it. Simon's own parents were separated and, after the children grew up, divorced. And in the vicinity of his summer home at Amagansett, Long Island, Simon saw so many marriages fall apart that he put up a "For Sale" sign on his house. Simon's genius, according to director, Mike Nichols, is "comedy and reality; extremely distorted but recognizable, not zany behavior."[19] When asked where he got his plays, Simon answered, "From life. From my head." He had not pulled his plays like rabbits out of a hat, however much it might have appeared to others that way.

A central character or characters in a basic serious situation has the life-giving start of many distinguished plays. "I am moved to write a new play only when I find, sometimes with a little shock to myself," said William Inge, "that I have seen inside a person's heart. Then, with a little feeling of identification, I can begin."[20] Inge asserted, "If I wrote plays of theme and idea, I don't think I would be able to write of people themselves as fully as I hope to." "I have been most concerned with dramatizing something of the dynamism I myself find in human motivations and behavior," said Inge. He likened a play so drawn, to "a journey in which every moment should be as interesting as the destination."[21]

The basic situation which Inge gets his characters into may take years to develop until it is "right." *Picnic,* for instance, began as *Front Porch,* which he called "an incongruous mixture of reality and contrivance," portraying middle-class women in a protectively feminine world, sitting on a front porch, pretending men never existed. Two years later, a fresh look at *Front Porch* turned it into *Picnic* when Hal, a virile vagabond, entering as a new character, creates a new basic situation by acting as a catalyst on the old one: his protectively masculine world collides with the women's protectively feminine world.

Edward Albee's typical experience in genesis is stated so in a report of *Newsweek* of February 4, 1963: "He thinks first of a situation and of characters."[22] The situation might not be the basic situation but the major climax which implies the basic situation. *Who's Afraid of Virginia Woolf?,* to illustrate, first occurred to Albee in "the exorcism of the child." "I knew I wanted an exorcism at the end of the play," said Albee. "I wouldn't start without a fairly general idea of where I was going, but I let the reality of the people take over the situation." [23]

Edward Albee has said that a play might take him anywhere from six months to two years and a half before it is quite conceived. "I try to let the unconscious do as much work as possible," confessed Albee, "since I find that's the more efficient part of my mind." [24] When Albee returns to a play after allowing it a fallow period in which to grow, "I try to turn off anything except the reality of the characters in the situation. I like to exclude the symbolism. I don't plan ahead,— saying this is going to represent that." He elaborated, "I have the characters improvise the dialogue in my mind. I put them in a situation outside the play. I like to pretend I'm giving them free rein." [25]

A variant in genesis, to be confirmed by the experience of Arthur Miller, is Sherwood's complex of his own true character and a play that, though a failure, became a seminal source of Sherwood's best writing. In *The Worlds of Robert E. Sherwood,* John Mason Brown wrote of *Acropolis* depicting the Athenian-Spartan conflict of freedom against tyranny:

> Out of it, he acknowledged, came *The Petrified Forest, Idiot's Delight;* and *Abe Lincoln in Illinois,* and from it he took lines for them and his paraphrase of the noble words spoken by Pericles over the Athenian war dead, which he included in Dr. Valkonen's letter of farewell in *There Shall Be No Night.*[26]

A failure may live in the playwright's mind to indirectly beget success. Though Sherwood conceived and wrote the whole of *The Petrified Forest* in four weeks, his best play, *Abe Lincoln in Illinois,* evolved from a childhood of idolizing Lincoln and from later reading intensively about him, especially Carl Sandburg's *The Prairie Years* which he read no less than five times. Sherwood, himself six feet seven inches tall, wrote in his diary during rehearsal of *Idiot's Delight,* "I believe in two things, true Democracy & true Christianity. I hope to God neither of them dies before I do." [27] A central character with whom Sherwood's very soul identified, and the crucial pertinence to democracy in an impending life and death struggle with the tyranny of Nazi fascism, organically shaped *Abe Lincoln in Illinois* to finally come of age. John Mason Brown reports:

> To his Aunt Lydia he confided that he was "not concerned with Abraham Lincoln's position in history—because no one needs to elabo-

rate on that. It was his remarkable character. It seems to me that all the contrasted qualities of the human race—the hopes and fears, the doubts and convictions, the mortal frailty and superhuman endurance, the prescience and the neuroses, the desire for escape from reality, and the fundamental unshakable nobility—were concentrated and magnified in him as they were in Oedipus Rex and in Hamlet. Except that he was no reaction of the poetic imagination. He was a living American, and in his living words are the answers—or the conceivable answers—to all the questions that distract the world today." [28]

Brown in his book on Sherwood goes into the full creation of Sherwood's best work. The play had a Broadway run of 472 performances.

"The very impulse to write, I think, springs from an inner chaos crying for order, for meaning," observed Arthur Miller of the genesis of his own plays, "and that meaning must be discovered in the process of writing or the work lies dead as it is finished." [29] For each play he has finished, Miller admits at least one play or more remains unfinished. He has found no way of forcing the bloom. How much of a creative synthesis Miller has made in turning his own life into his art, he implies in what he said of *After the Fall,* in which the public tended to identify Maggie as the counterpart in many ways of Marilyn Monroe. "I would only say now that despite appearances," noted Miller, "this play is no more and no less autobiographical than *All My Sons, Death of a Salesman, The Crucible* or *A View from the Bridge.*" [30] Among living American playwrights, Miller is usually rated as second only to Tennessee Williams, with the chief runners-up in Albee, Inge, and Chayefsky. Miller's approach to the genesis of his plays merits special attention.

All My Sons and *Death of a Salesman* Miller traces to roots growing from his first play to reach Broadway, a failure in 1944, *The Man Who Had All the Luck. The Man Who Had All the Luck,* like almost all of Miller's plays, took its first sign of life from a true story. Miller knew of a young mid-Westerner who supposedly had all the luck and who, after prospering greatly, grew more and more convinced that others were out to rob him, and finally, in despair, committed suicide. Among this play's characters were two friends whom Miller, as he lay musing on the beach one day, thought of making brothers; the relation of these sons to their father struck Miller "with a fullness of feeling I had never known before." "The crux of *All My Sons,* which would not be written until nearly three years later, was formed," recollected Miller, "and the roots of *Death of a Salesman* were sprouted." [31] Miller had always been fascinated by the wonder of how things got to be as they are, and in the failure of *The Man Who Had All the Luck* he turned to his model for wonder, Fyodor Dostoievsky's *The Brothers Karamazov*. Miller discovered that "if one reads its most colorful, breathtaking, wonderful pages, one finds the thickest concentration of hard facts." [32] Miller has ever since tried to carry this insight into heavily documenting the growth of his characters.

A story true to life set *All My Sons* into a life of its own. A pious mid-Western lady visiting the Millers chatted away in the living-room about a manufacturer in her neighborhood who, though World War II was in full crisis, sold the United States Army defective machinery; when the manufacturers' own daughter found out what her father had done, she informed on him, and in so doing, destroyed the manufacturer's whole family. Almost the moment Miller heard this story, he felt an intense creative stir in his own mind and had turned the daughter into a son and had the climax of his second act of *All My Sons*. Miller deeply identified with the story because he knew the middle-class people and the very neighborhood in which they had spent their lives. "Something was crystal clear to me for the first time since I had begun writing plays," said Miller, "and it was the crisis of the second act, the revelation of the full loathesomeness of an antisocial action." [33] This crisis guided Miller from that moment through the two years it took him to document his characters in their living relation to society, so that what preceded and what followed the crisis would be believable. "You can't understand anything unless you understand its relations to its context," said Miller, ". . . That much for good or ill the great depression taught me." [34] "It was the unveiling of what I believed everybody knew," said Miller of the vital theme of *All My Sons*, "and nobody publicly said." [35]

The genesis of Miller's most performed play, *The Crucible,* is intriguing for showing how a creative excitement grew from quite a combination of somewhat related matter: a deeply troubled state of mind, an earlier play that failed to go much beyond a rough draft, a heavily documented true story, and a "hunch" which allowed Miller to identify intensely with his leading character, John Proctor. In 1950, Miller found himself profoundly distraught. Senator Joseph McCarthy's "witch-hunt" for communists and fellow-travellers had brought the whole United States to such hysteria through all the media of communication that unproven allegations and innuendos were destroying the innocent as well as the guilty. For his one-time association with left wing causes during the great depression and World War II, when Russia was America's ally, Miller now found himself victimized. "Astounded, I watched men pass me by without a nod whom I had known rather well for years," related Miller, aware that these peoples' terror had been planned and engineered deliberately.[36] Miller said of this intense realization on his part, "it underlies every word in *The Crucible*."[37]

As a student at the University of Michigan in late 1930, Miller had unsuccessfully tried to write a play about the Salem witch-hunt. This old play now crossed Miller's mind and hit him as especially apt to give "order" and "meaning" to his "inner chaos," for it was modern, relevant, and yet detached through perspective. For "wonder" as to how the Salem witch-hunt came about, Miller turned to the best source of facts available, the actual court records of the Salem trials for witch-craft. "I doubt I should ever have tempted agony by actually writing a play on the subject," said Miller, "had I not come upon a single fact."[38] This fact was that Abigail Williams, a former servant of the Proctors and a prime-mover of the hysteria among the children, denounced Elizabeth Proctor as a witch but, even when urged to do so by the prosecution, refused to denounce Elizabeth's husband, John Proctor. Miller read into Abigail's action the reason to focus his entire play upon the story of John and Elizabeth Proctor and Abigail Williams. Miller powerfully identified with John Proctor. "It was like my own situation then," said Miller, "trying to tell people that the great 'issues' which the hysteria was allegedly about were covers for petty ambitions, hardheaded political drives, and the fantasies of very small and vengeful minds."[39]

"I believe *After the Fall*," said Miller, "to be a dramatic statement of a hidden process which underlies the destructiveness hanging over this age."[40] Miller has so far not told of the genesis of this play, but that of his other plays intimates much of the pattern. McCarthyism had made Miller a victim in a time ready for this national hysteria, so that Miller said of his horror at America surrendering its soul, "It underlies every word of *The Crucible*." When the American movie's sex symbol, Marilyn Monroe, took her life, in a sense Arthur Miller was somewhat her victim; she was his wife and they were separated at the time. News stories over every media of communication, gossip, self-recrimination and self-examination could only be natural, and perhaps provided the impulse to write—"an inner chaos crying for order, for meaning."

Marilyn Monroe as a prime-mover in the genesis of *After the Fall* is implicit in Miller's comment about her counterpart, Maggie, "she most perfectly exemplifies the self-destructiveness which finally comes when one views oneself as pure victim." [41] Maggie, like Marilyn, had been victimized by her parents, the Puritanical code of sex, and others exploiting her as an entertainer. *After the Fall* suggests, too, Miller's attempt through art to provide a written memorial to Marilyn Monroe as the very title of his article for *Life* of February 7, 1964, suggests: "With Respect for Her Agony—but with Love." Miller, furthermore, has again and again admitted drawing his plays in part from stories true to life.

The basic situation at the start of the play is identified with Miller's own life. Miller has said, "A great drama is a great jurisprudence;" the leading character, a successful New York lawyer and plainly Miller's counterpart, stands alone on the stage of his mind and opens the play; in torment, guilt, and doubt, this lawyer named Quentin turns to the audience as to a father confessor or an analyst he has long known, and unburdens his soul. After two disastrous marriages, dare Quentin try again? Miller, after two disastrous marriages, was to try again; the play is an affirmation of life, for Miller early in his career said, "pessimism, [is] a philosophy in which I do not believe." [42] Quentin doesn't.

"The play grew from simple images," Miller wrote of *Death of a Salesman*. "The play's eye was to revolve from within Willy's head, sweeping endlessly in all directions like a light on the sea." [43] This is just what happens to Quentin in *After the Fall*. He is onstage for the whole three hours of the play's action, and everything is seen through his eyes. "The image was in direct opposition to the method of *All My Sons*—a method one might call linear or eventual, in that one fact or incident creates the necessity for the next," wrote Miller of creating *Death of a Salesman,* calling this new form "a confession," and literally "the process of Willy Loman's way of mind." [44] *Death of a Salesman,* in fact, was first titled *Inside of His Head,* a mass of half laughable contradictions. The whole pattern of genesis and development of *After the Fall* strikingly parallels that for *Death of a Salesman*—the form of confession, the images, the way of thinking, even the technique of the fluidity of memories. "There was too much to say to waste precious stage time with feints and preparations . . . ." wrote Miller of avoiding the clumsy machinery of trivia so necessary to the realistic technique.[45] In *After the Fall,* Quentin's mind through recall brings back, free of time and space, critical incidents in his life related to his present crisis by association, inference, or drift of meaning. Quentin, for instances, quarrels with his first wife, meets Maggie on a park bench, visits the site of a German concentration camp. The staging of *After the Fall* requires that this be picked out with only a shifting beam of light in settings of lavalike formations of the mind, lacking even the scenery of *Death of a Salesman.*

"Yet for all this honesty," Tom Prideaux of *Life* magazine says, like so many critics of *After the Fall,* "the cards in the play are stacked in favor of Quentin." [46] As a highly sensitive and perceptive writer, Miller must have very well known that the critics and much of the public would take exactly this stand. Miller has written, "Indeed, it is one of the play's major points that there is not and cannot truly be a divestment of guilt." [47] A complex of forces seems to have operated in giving life and form to *After the Fall.* A living memorial to Marilyn Monroe as well as implications of Miller's own public atonement seem potently involved.

Incubation

The broad review suggests that in the incubation of a play as in genesis—and the two are always continuous and sometimes virtually identical—there are two distinct creative tendencies. One, like Oscar Wilde's, creates almost spontaneously and as a whole in relatively a short time. "I can only think in stories," said Wilde to Gide. "The sculptor does not search to translate his thoughts into marble; he thinks in marble directly." [48] The other tendency, like Henrik Ibsen's, usually is far slower, laborious, but likely surer of genuine organic growth. It is possible to show both dispositions. Elmer Rice, for instance, conceived and wrote *The Adding Machine* in seventeen days; he took about three years to get *Street Scene* really under way.

"The process with me is purely automatic and spontaneous as dreaming," said the once famous but now almost forgotten Henry Arthur Jones of fusing theme, character, and action. "I haven't any dramatic technique," Paul Green asserted early in his career; "I merely tell a story, episode by episode." [49] Green is best remembered in the theatre for his Pulitzer prize-winning play, *In Abraham's Bosom,* and for his "symphonic dramas"—literally a "sounding together" of all the elements of theatre in epic pattern—like *The Lost Colony,* which opened in an amphi-theatre off Roanoke Island in North Carolina and had a run during summer seasons of over 600 performances. "For, after all, drama is storytelling," said Green in his book *Dramatic Heritage;* "Of whatever sort, it is storytelling in action." [50] A prolific dramatist of about 300 plays but now recalled chiefly for his co-adaptation of Edith Wharton's novel *Ethan Frome,* Owen Davis said, "The story comes to me as Topsy came to an unappreciative world—'Born growed.'" [51] Thorton Wilder had said, "The dramatist must be by instinct a story-teller." [52]

Among the most distinguished modern playwrights to develop plays in relatively spontaneous and full generation is Noel Coward. In 1929, for instance, before leaving New York City to sail for the Orient, Coward promised Gertrude Lawrence that he would write a play to star her with him. In the weeks en route to Yokohama, Coward mulled over the possibilities and wound up only with uncertainties. Then one evening shortly after arriving in Shanghai, Coward wearily went to bed; "the moment I switched out the lights," related Coward in his autobiography, *Present Indicative,* "Gertie appeared in a white Molyneux dress on a terrace in the South of France and refused to go again until four a. m., by which time *Private Lives,* title and all, had constructed itself." [53] Coward from disappointing previous experience was very wary of giving in uncritically to such fantastically fast growth of a whole play. "In 1923, the play would have been written and typed within a few days of my thinking of it, but in 1929, I had learned the wisdom of not welcoming a new idea too ardently," confessed Coward, "so I forced it into the back of my mind, trusting to its own integrity to emerge again later on when it had become sufficiently set and matured." [54] Coward was not to write another *Private Lives* ever again in his lifetime, though *Design for Living* perhaps came close. The hint is that though a play may form almost spontaneously as a whole, once the rich experience in life, that was waiting only for a catalyst to appropriate it, is used up, new plays of comparable quality do not necessarily follow, although variations of it may.

Coward's play with music, *Cavalcade,* suggests that, if need be, he could compromise the spontaneous method of generation with that of the carefully documented method to create a play. While searching for the stuff for an epic drama, Coward happened to look at an old photograph of English troops embarking for the Boer War. He then talked over the period with Peter Stern, a friend with rich memories of that time. Coward recalled

> My original story was different from what finally emerged but the shape was the same, New Year's Eve 1899 to New Year's Eve 1930. Events took precedence first in my mind, and against them I moved a group of people—the bright young people of the nineties, the play was to finish with their children—the same eager emptiness, but a different jargon. After awhile, I realized that the play should be bigger than that . . . Presently my real characters appeared in two classes. The Marryots and Ellen and Bridges.[55]

From the very start of creating *Cavalcade,* Coward not only had a sequence of historical events to guide the main line of action but also an awareness of the power of popular music to help him. "The emotional basis of *Cavalcade* was undoubtedly music," he admitted. "The whole story was threaded onto a string of popular melodies. This ultimately was a big contributing factor to its success. Popular tunes probe the memory more swiftly than anything else." [56] The story of the people affected by the events and the music underwent quite a few changes. Coward chronicled that originally Jan Marryot had not only the children, Joe and Edward of the final draft, but others—"these fell away, stillborn, . . . discouraged by my firm determination to keep the whole thing as simple and uncomplicated as possible, and gradually the whole story completed itself in my mind." [57] Though Coward said he dreamed up the basic story line rather quickly, he plodded through thousands of pages of historical material to carefully document his characters' lives so that they would live in, rather than seem fictitious aliens to, the events of their time. He said:

> I started at an earlier date than 1899, feeling that to work slowly through the seventies, eighties, and nineties would give my people a more solid background than if I just let them appear, untouched by any past experience whatever, in leg of mutton sleeves.[58]

"It takes me a year to make a play," said Sir Arthur Wing Pinero, now almost forgotten except perhaps for *The Second Mrs. Tanqueray;* "six months to get acquainted with the characters, and six months to build the plot and write the dialogue. All that time, I have to seclude myself from the companionship of friends and live only with the imaginary people of my story." [59] Pinero here suggests a creative tendency to develop a play through relatively slow growth. "I try to turn off anything except the reality of the characters in the situation," said Edward Albee in words strikingly similar to Pinero's, though the two are as far apart as a Victorian valentine from an Existential "weltschmerz." [60] Albee admits to carrying his characters and their situation around in his head for from six months to the two and a half years or so in which he allows his characters to grow into a play. Albee relies upon fallow periods as if he feels it is not good for a play to be forever pulling it up by the roots to see how it is growing. "I try to let the unconscious do as much work as possible," Albee told John Gielgud, "since I find that's the more efficient part of my mind." So intense is Albee's imaginative world that he says, "When I'm writing a play, the people I'm writing about are real people. Real people seem imaginary." [61] Once his characters take shape, Albee improvises with them in new situations to test them for full credibility; in this way, he apparently tries to create an extension of their lives in the play just as real people have an extension of their lives from whatever story we may know of them. "And when they start behaving on their own and take over from me, and seem quite natural and believable in an improvised situation," said Albee, "then I suppose I know it's time to start writing the play." [62]

Lillian Hellman and Arthur Miller are perhaps the most established and distinguished playwrights to use the relatively slow method of organic growth so dear to Ibsen, and to Chekhov, too, in his long, late plays, though this approach does not shut out great flashes of insight. "It took a year and a half of stumbling stubbornness," Hellman recalled of *The Children's Hour*, ". . . and I thought again of the world of the half-remembered, the half-observed, the half-understood which you need so much as you begin to write." [63] Hellman reminisced, "the play went through twelve revisions "—a reference to *The Children's Hour*—"and in the course of incubation lost a third set and three or four characters. *Days to Come* once had a scene in the town's main street; in *The Little Foxes,* Addie had a daughter and Horace had another disease; *Watch on the Rhine* started in Ohio." [64] To illustrate her thorough preparation, Hellman noted that in writing *Watch on the Rhine* she gathered from four to five hundred single-spaced typewritten pages of memoranda. "I always do much more research than I really have to, but it makes me feel more sure in writing," she told C. Hughes for *The New York Times*. "If you know your people well, they say what they have to say for you almost of their own accord when it comes to writing them down." [65]

Before the failure on Broadway in 1944 of his play, *The Man Who Had All the Luck,* Miller calculated he had previously written seven long, unproduced plays, and in no instance spent more than three months on any one play. The Broadway failure changed Miller's whole approach to playwriting. Meaning in the story rather than the story for its own sake now obsessed him. "Do you feel that the best way to present a universal is in terms of a really specific story?" Philip Gelb asked Miller about fourteen years later, in a symposium published in the *Tulane Drama Review* of May 1958. "It is the best way! It is the hardest way, too," answered Miller. "The ability to create the universal from the particular is not given to many authors, nor to any single author many times. You have to know the particular in your bones to do this." [66] Even though Miller began *All My Sons* with full awareness of the climax of his second act, it took him about two more years to fashion the play. "My approach to playwriting, and the drama itself, is organic," said Miller, in effect summing up the whole change. "The underlying poem of a play I take to be the organic necessity of its parts," continued Miller. "Which is to say that I prize the poetic above all else in the theater, and because I do, I insist that the poem truly be there." [67] This view, of course, approximates that found in Aristotle's *Poetics.*

Throughout incubation, to reveal the "wonder" of how things got to be as they are, Miller works for "the thickest concentration of hard facts." Miller admittedly, like Ibsen as well as Dostoievsky, chose to very heavily document the past so the present could be understood as its living outcome. *All My Sons* took two years; but sometimes incubation went much faster for Miller, especially when he knew the particular "in his bones," as he did for his finest play to date, *Death of a Salesman*. Here is the account of Allan Seager who interviewed Miller for *Esquire* of October, 1959:

> Miller was at work one night on another play. It was a warm evening in May and suddenly the character of the man who was to become Willy Loman drifted into his head, a memory of a man he had known. The accretion of ideas and emotions around this figure seemed to be instantaneous, and Miller wrote two-thirds of the first draft that night. The last third took him three months.[68]

Off-hand this suggests that *Death of a Salesman* represents a relatively spontaneous creation; Miller, himself, thought so, until months later he happened to be going through his files and found a forgotten manuscript from his University of Michigan days—about the same man. Whoever this man was—Miller never identified him—to know him in his bones he must have known him as a very close friend or blood relative. This man incubated in Miller's unconscious a good ten years from one play to emerge almost full grown in the "spontaneous" creation of *Death of a Salesman*.

Miller usually spends his work day in his study, which is either a simple office in his New York City apartment or a cabin behind his country home in Roxbury, Connecticut. He uses dime-store, spiral notebooks to enter whatever might cross his mind relevant to his hunch from genesis. The thoughts come in spasms or even in a hodge podge of experience that only Miller can relate to, such as: homely truths, snatches of dialogue, portions of action, incidents or dreams of childhood, scraps of poetry, pictures of settings, creative flashes of the whole or its parts. Here is a smattering from his notebooks:

> M: You ought to pay more attention to your wife.
> D: That's all I do. I never knew you had to cultivate a wife until recently.
> M: Well, you don't just plant them and let them grow by themselves.
> D: Tells of his unhappiness.
> Then . . .
> 1. God! Who would ever have believed I would need sixty thousand dollars a year to live! And I'm not even living.[69]

Between entries in his notebook, Miller may break off to do whole scenes on his typewriter whenever he feels ready, but what comes out may prove abortive.

The social implications of his plays never leave Miller, for he sees man and society as inseparable, and the international acceptance of his plays suggest much human truth in what he sees. "The fish is in the water," says Miller, "the water is in the fish." [70] "There are two questions I ask myself over and over when I'm working," noted Miller to Seager: "'What do I mean? What am I trying to say?'" [71] The meaning for Miller at best should be found not explicitly in the play but implicitly, and so in the minds of the audience even as they view the play as a whole.

A favorite device of Miller to develop his characters during incubation is "giving them their heads," as Seager put it, "to say anything that might be remotely relevant to his purposes, not that these purposes were yet entirely clear." [72] For one untitled play, Miller had about a thousand pages of typewritten scenes in which he let his characters improvise within his imagined purpose.[73] But still the meaning of what he was driving at might elude him. For each three plays he has finished, Miller has admitted to being stymied by three others. Stymied, he might turn to other work, as he did to the movie, *The Misfits*. His mind, meanwhile, at a subliminal level seems trained enough to continue to work on its own till someday the needed breakthrough of insight flashes. "I look things up all the time," said Miller of his encyclopedia, "to remind myself of details, to face the fact that there's so little I can really know . . ."[74] That pertinent detail might touch off the flash of insight from "the thickest concentration of hard facts."

To try to guarantee a more or less continual output, many playwrights like Miller use the device of keeping notebooks and working intermittently at different works to allow their unconscious minds to help solve creative problems as a capable silent partner. Among the keepers of often voluminous notebooks or their equivalent are: Strindberg, Chekhov, O'Neill, Williams, Synge, Jones, Molnar, Davis, Belasco, Moss Hart, Hellman, and Maugham. Maugham, for instance, deliberately travelled a great deal to stock his memory with promising raw material for his imagination to feed upon, lest the day come when it might otherwise starve. "I kept my eyes open for character, oddness, and personality," Maugham said of his entries in his ever handy little notebook. ". . . I accepted every experience that came my way. . . . I do not think I ever hestitated to do anything because it was uncomfortable or dangerous."[75]

Perhaps an exemplary use of Maugham's notebook is shown in the creation of his story, *Sadie Thompson,* adapted by John Colton into the minor classic, *Rain.* On a voyage from Honolulu to Pago Pago in the South Seas at an indeterminate date, Maugham made entries about several of the ship's passengers:

> This is what I said of Miss Thompson: "Plump, pretty in a coarse fashion, perhaps not more than twenty-seven. She wore a white dress and a large white hat, long white boots from which the calves bulged in cotton stockings." There has been a raid on the Red Light district in Honolulu just before we sailed, and the gossip of the ship spread the report that she was making the journey to escape arrest.[76]

On that same boat, Maugham saw a missionary of whom he made this entry:

W. The Missionary. He was a tall thin man, with long limbs loosely jointed, he had hollow cheeks and high cheek bones, his fine large dark eyes were deep in their sockets, he had full sensual lips, he wore his hair rather long. He had a cadaverous air and a look of suppressed fire. His hands were large, with long fingers, rather finely shaped. His naturally pale skin was deeply burned by the tropical sun.[77]

Maugham also made a note about the missionary's wife, "Mrs. W.:"

She was a little woman with her hair very elaborately done, New England; not prominent blue eyes behind gold-rimmed pince-nez, her face was long like a sheep's, but she gave no impression of foolishness, rather of extreme alertness. She had the quick movements of a bird. . . . He was a medical missionary. She spoke of the depravity of the natives in a voice which nothing could hush, but with a vehement unctuous horror, telling me of their marriage customs which were obscene beyond description. She said, when first they went it was impossible to find a single good girl in any of the villages. She inveighed against dancing. I talked with the missionary and his wife but once, and with Miss Thompson not at all.[78]

Even before the ship reached Pago Pago, Maugham had dreamed up this synopsis for his note-book as printed recently in his volume, *Selected Prefaces and Introductions:*

A prostitute, flying from Honolulu after a raid, lands in Pago Pago. There lands also a missionary and his wife. Also the narrator. All are obliged to stay there owing to an outbreak of measles. The missionary, finding out the girl's profession, persecutes her. He reduces her to misery, shame, and repentance, he has no mercy on her. He induces the Governor to order her return to Honolulu. One morning he is found with his throat cut by his own hand and she is once more radiant and self-possessed. She looks at men and scornfully exclaims, "dirty pigs."[79]

Ironically, John Colton, not Maugham, saw a long-run play in the story, *Sadie Thompson,* that basically follows the notes cited. This example from Maugham's notebook, however, nicely illustrates Maugham's genesis through incubation as recorded in his book, *The Summing Up:* "The physical traits of a man influence his character and contrariwise his character is expressed, at least in the rough, in his appearance;" and also Maugham's confession, "I have taken living people and put them into situations, tragic or comic, that their characters suggested (I might well say that they invented their own stories.)"[80] Maugham customarily let his notes lie fallow: "It was not till four years after I had made my notes for it that I wrote the first of the stories I had conceived in the South Seas."

Keeping notebooks helps continual incubation. Playwrights also try to stimulate new growth by allowing work to lie fallow as they apply themselves intermittently to plays at different stages of growth. Such creative agriculturalists of a kind include: Strindberg, Chekhov, Shaw, Synge, Galsworthy, O'Neill, Williams, Howard, Hart, Kaufman, Rice, Sherwood, Simon, and Albee. *"The Tinker's Wedding,"* recollected Synge, for instance, "was written a few years ago about the time I was working at *Riders to the Sea* and *In the Shadow of the Glen*." [81] "I am eager to go ahead with four plays," said Sidney Howard, "and eager to get on to a novel." [82] While writing *First Lady* with Katharine Dayton, George S. Kaufman took one break of five months to do other playwriting with Moss Hart, and took other shorter breaks to do scenarios for Hollywood. In the three years he was working on *Come Blow Your Horn,* Neil Simon was also on the writer's payroll of a number of TV shows—*Caesar's Hour, Sergeant Bilko,* and *The Gary Moore Show.* In the course of working on *Who's Afraid of Virginia Woolf?,* Edward Albee busied himself at intervals with adapting Carson McCuller's novella, *The Ballad of the Sad Cafe,* writing *The Substitute Speaker* and keeping *Tiny Alice* somehow in the back of his mind, for *Alice* emerged in production while *The Substitute Speaker* has yet to utter a word in public.

Characterization

As the study of genesis suggested, a playwright almost invariably finds his central character or characters in whatever set off his creative heat and light—a true life story, a traumatic experience, a character or characters in a basic comic or serious situation, a major climax, or a leading character's point of view. The titles of many masterpieces of dramatic literature, moreover, plainly advertise the wisdom of centering a play upon usually a single dynamic character, for instance: *Oedipus The King, Medea, Lysistrata, Everyman, Dr. Faustus, Hamlet, Tartuffe, Hedda Gabler, Uncle Vanya, Saint Joan, Mourning Becomes Electra, Cat on a Hot Tin Roof.* The modern theatre, however, is so obsessed with love as the only guaranteed common concern of the highly mixed theatre audiences that the playwright usually does well to focus upon two characters or sometimes even three; but one character must still dominate the action, or else the audience, for want of emphasis by the playwright, tends to lack a point of view, a vision of life that is found to distinguish the best of plays.

Chekhov and Shaw, out of high regard for central roles and respect for the wonder of talent, deliberately wrote for stars, and so did

Wilde, Maugham, Belasco, Coward, Anderson, Kaufman, Hart, Sherwood, Behrman and Jeffers, among others. Proven and promoted as the most gifted actors in particular roles, stars through their aura help draw the public to the box-office and so to the play. Shakespeare, of course, knew this and wrote many of his greatest leading roles like Romeo, Hamlet, Macbeth, and Lear for the brightest star of Shakespeare's current company, Richard Burbage. In his *Poetics,* Aristotle delineated the nature of the central figure, the tragic hero, from observing the drama of his day. Maxwell Anderson in *The Essence of Tragedy* is concerned with this same central figure and his fortunes in modern times. The titles of many of the best comedies of such fine craftsmen as Kelly, Kaufman and Hart, Van Druten, and Lindsay and Crouse show a deep concern with a central character or characters, for instance: *The Show-Off, The Man Who Came to Dinner, I Remember Mama, Life with Father.*

"The play had achieved that kind of universal identification," said Van Druten of his three character comedy, *The Voice of the Turtle,* "that is every playwright's best desire which can almost never be achieved by aiming at it." [83] Van Druten implies such character drawing can only be done through total honesty. Amanda in *The Glass Menagerie* and Willy Loman in *Death of a Salesman,* Van Druten believed to be among the most memorable and moving of characters in modern drama because the author had seen in each instance a character part, and drawn it with such total honesty that the audience everywhere identified with it simply as a human being true to life. Van Druten warned against the distortion that must come from a playwright hating or falling in love with a character. "Consider your heroine going to the bath-room," Van Druten suggested.[84] Perhaps he might have added, "Consider your villain in his bassinet."

Maugham's approach to drawing a lifelike representative lead came to him from his experience as a medical student in the dissecting room. When Maugham couldn't find a nerve where it should have been, the demonstrator soon found it elsewhere and explained to the complaining Maugham, "The normal is what you find but rarely." [85] Maugham, like Turgenev, always began with a living model and cross-bred through reverie the honest oddity that makes the whole world kin. "The writer does not copy his originals," said Maugham; "he takes what he wants from them, a few traits that have caught his attention, a turn of mind that has fired his imagination, and therefrom constructs his character . . ." [86] When tested by an imagined circumstance they suggest, the characters act and react. Said Maugham, "Reverie is the groundwork of creative imagination." [87] But the upshot of the reverie is always in the back of Maugham's mind, for he said, "to display the development of character . . . is the chief concern of fiction of the present day." [88] And the best kind of development was also plain to Maugham in time. "There is nothing more beautiful than goodness," he noted, "and it has pleased me very often to show how much of it there is in persons who by common standards would be relentlessly condemned." [89] Of all values, Maugham found only goodness was lasting and deeply moving; goodness was its own reward and beyond a price. Beauty, Maugham observed, dated with the needs of the age, as the basement storage rooms of art museums bear witness. Truth varies with the culture.

Wilder, in selecting his leading characters for *Our Town,* suggests he was quite aware of the importance of saying what was on his mind. "It is an attempt," he said of *Our Town,* "to find a value above all price for the smallest events in our daily life." [90] But Wilder was also aware of the need for the individual and the representative in his characters, for he noted in the original appearance of the article in *Harper's* (October 1957):

> As an artist (or listener or beholder) which "truth" do you pre-fer—that of the isolated occasion or that which includes and resumes the innumerables? Which truth is more worth telling? Every age differs in this. . . . The theatre is admirably fitted to tell both truths.[91]

And in discussing the character of Emily, Wilder wrote:

> Emily's joys and griefs, her algebra lessons and her birthday pres-ents—what are they when we consider all the billions of girls who have lived, who are living, and who will live? Each individual's assertion to an absolute reality can only be inner, very inner. . . . Our claim, our hope, our despair are in the mind— [92]

Innumerable girls may feel *like* Emily. In her own *mind,* there is still *one* Emily. Wilder also suggests his approach to character drawing in his comment, "I began writing one-act plays that tried to capture not verisimilitude but reality." [93]

"Where there is no one in a play with whom the audience can iden-tify," cautioned Langner of the lead, "it generally fails." [94] Langner believed that merely commonplace people doing commonplace things in a commonplace way make soap opera, not masterpieces of drama.

The stage demands vivid, thrilling leads, preferably two starring roles, a man and a woman playing opposite each other and whose character the playwright so skillfully dramatizes that the audience knows what makes them "tick."

Marc Connelly, who collaborated with George S. Kaufman in *Dulcy* and other plays, said of their method of selecting a comic lead and, incidentally, other characters too:

> George and I are chiefly interested in character, the spiritual growth which can be shown through dramatic action. After we have our major character, usually someone who will personify certain grand assininities that occur in life, we sit down and say, "What would the people be who would associate with a man like that?" [95]

Incidentally, from a study of comedies Kaufman did with such collaborators as Connelly, Lardner, and Hart, Carl Carmer spotted a tendency to rely sometimes on a rather proven formula which still requires a fine gift of humor to bring off:

> The formula involves the selection of a main character, an easily recognizable type, loveable as a rule, but utterly lacking in common sense, a protagonist at whom the audience may laugh with the jolly feeling of superiority and tolerance. The unpleasant complications which confront the character as a result of his stupidity are completely overcome at the end of the play with a magnificent stroke of luck, frequently occasioned by this very thick-headedness. From *Dulcy* onward, no matter who the collaborator, this recipe has served to fill the theatres of Broadway. Sometimes it works more successfully than others.[96]

Carmer also took care to note, "Fortunately for modern American drama, Kaufman has not always seen fit to rub his Aladdin's Lamp." [97] Certainly, as in *You Can't Take It With You,* Kaufman could write without the "formula."

After some phenomenal success and then much appalling failure, Maxwell Anderson, while confessing that he had a poor head for theory, turned again to dramatic theory and dramatic literature to find, if any, the general laws in great drama which determine the tragic hero and the main action. Anderson had come to distrust his "dramatic instinct." "A play should lead up to and away from a central crisis," concluded Anderson, paralleling Aristotle's *Poetics,* "and this crisis should consist in a discovery by the leading character which has an indelible effect on his thought and emotion and completely alters his course of action." [98] Aristotle's definition of tragedy, in S. H. Butcher's famous translation, suggests Anderson's continuity of dramatic tradition:

> Tragedy then, is an imitation of an action that is serious, complete, and of a certain magnitude, in language embellished with each kind of artistic ornament, the several kinds being found in separate parts of the play; in the form of action, not of narrative; through pity and fear effecting the proper purgation of these emotions.[99]

And then admittedly paralleling Aristotle's concern with the hero's tragic fault, Anderson remarked of the modern tragic hero, "when he makes his discovery . . . he must change for the better." [100] If the awakening is for the worse, like Troilus' conclusion from Cressida's faithlessness that all women are faithless, then the play fails. With goodness and badness denoting moral differences, Aristotle also observed, "Comedy aims at presenting men as worse, tragedy as better than in actual life." Aristotle had described the tragic hero:

> a man who is not eminently good and just yet whose misfortune is brought about not by vice or depravity, but by some error or frailty. He must be one who is highly renowned and prosperous—a personage like Oedipus, Thyestes, or other illustrious men of such families.[101]

For Anderson, "From the point of view of the playwright then, the essence of a tragedy, or even of a serious play is the spiritual awakening, or regeneration, of his hero." [102] Anderson admitted his conclusion could only be an attempt to answer the sphinxlike questions of the drama. Yet he, like Maugham, in emphasizing or implying the need for the leading character's regeneration in terms of goodness, is actually echoing the age-old emphasis of religion upon the need for the soul's rebirth, although in modern times no specific religious dogma might necessarily be involved; it is as if the public wanted to believe that a man and therefore mankind can be better than what it is through the power of human goodness. "Conscience is the most powerful of all instincts," Shaw, himself, asserted, "and the love of God the most powerful of all passions." [103] Anderson and Maugham's emphasis upon the leading character's spiritual renaissance imply that the public comes to the theatre looking for the stuff of race survival and faith, rather than of suicide and despair. It is most strange, it seems, that so many aspiring playwrights who exult in negativism in their plays should ask the public to pay money to be told that life is not worth living, while the playwrights, themselves, are quite willing to use that money presumably to enjoy life.

"More than any other art, Theater asks for relevance," noted Miller of the imperative need for a leading character to be as immediate in peoples' lives as tomorrow's newspaper. "Before a play is art it is a kind of psychic journalism, a mirror of its hour," Miller observed, "and this reflection of contemporary feeling is exactly what makes so many plays irrelevant to later times." [104] "What finally survives, when anything does," Miller concluded from personal experience with his own plays, "are archetypal characters and relationships which can be transferred to the new period." [105] How quintessentially he had created Willy Loman in *Death of a Salesman,* for instance, only time could prove. *"Death of a Salesman* was hardly noticed when it opened in Paris some 15 years ago," Miller recollected in *The New York Times* of August 15, 1965, in mulling over what makes plays endure. "A new production now is a great success. In 1950 Willy was a man from Mars. Today, the French are up to their necks in time payments, broken washing machines, dreams of fantastic success, new apartment houses shading out the vegetables in the backyard, and the chromed anxiety of a society where nothing deserves existence that doesn't pay." [106]

Granted relevance and a quintessential vitality, what other prime requisites does Miller look for in a central character? "I take it that if one could know enough about a human being," wrote Miller covering just about every leading character in his plays, "he could discover some conflict, some value, some challenge, however minor or major, which he cannot find it in himself to walk away from or turn his back on." [107] The less a central character can walk away from the play's central conflict, the more, in Miller's view, he tends to the tragic in his utter zeal. "From this flows the necessity for scenes of high and open emotion," said Miller in echo of his faith in the theatre's need for passion, "and plays constructed toward climax rather than the evocation of a mood alone or of bizarre spectacle . . ." [108] The construction of a play toward a major climax of commitment in a hero's life need not at all be contrived if done properly; it is just what a corps of investigators does when reconstructing a crime like the real one in Capote's novel, *In Cold Blood,* or in discovering a miracle drug like Fleming's happening on penicillin, or in authenticating a religious revelation like that of Bernadette.

The central character's action must be organically conceived from such prismatic views of life as memory, association, imagination, logic, chance, and feeling, all operating on facts and people. The organic story involved is literally created largely backward. Aristotle had observed, "Character is that which reveals moral purpose, showing what kind of things a man chooses or avoids." [109] "The structure of these plays," Miller said candidly in the preface of his *Collected Plays,* relating to the need of his central character to make a critical commitment, ". . . in this respect, is to the end that such a conflict be discovered and clarified. . . . Time, characterization, and other elements are treated differently from play to play, but all to the end that that moment of commitment be brought forth, that moment when, in my eyes, a man differentiates himself from every other man . . ." [110]

The universality that Miller works for in his heroes must be inherent in their actions. Willy Loman, for example, was to Miller an average American, not in that Willy committed suicide, but in that his terrible conflicts were those of the common man in the street, and his suicide results from his inability to realize his ideals in any other way. In Miller's opinion, even the corner grocer could be a tragic hero, "providing of course, that the grocer's career engages the issues of, for instance, the survival of the race, the relationships of man to God —the questions, in short, whose answers define humanity and the right way to live so that the world is a home . . ." [111] Ambiguity in a central character who must make a commitment, strikes Miller as adolescent refusal or inability on the playwright's part to analyze adulthood. In Miller's view, indeed, tragedy appeals to the public because in facing death men actually gain strength to live.

"Contrast is the dramatist's method while he is working," said Lord Dunsany, expressing a general opinion and practice suggesting how the dramatist selects a character to play opposite the central character.[112] Supporting characters would obviously be chosen by their likelihood of associating with the central characters and on the basis of contrast, too, so as to promote the conflict that is indispensable to drama. "The essential character of drama," wrote John Howard Lawson after exhaustive study of the theory and technique of dramatic literature, "is social conflict—persons against other persons or individuals against groups, or groups against groups, or individuals or groups against social or national forces—in which the conscious will, exerted for the accomplishment of specific and understandable aims, is sufficiently strong to bring the conflict to the point of crisis."[113] Granville-Barker, a foremost authority on Shakespeare, concluded, "He works by means of contrast between character and character, by tension and relaxation, climax and anti-climax, by changes of tone and pace, by every sort of variation between scene and scene." [114] And in his book, *On Dramatic Method,* Granville-Barker also noted, "The discovery which turned Shakespeare from a good dramatist to a great one was that the outward clashing of character with character is poor material beside the ferment in the spirit of man, confined by law or custom or inherited belief, or netted round by alien circumstance or wills but quickening in their despite." [115]

Benavente thought the most effective contrast in characters came from relating them closely by circumstance, for instance, as blood relatives and dear friends. Aristotle had anticipated much of this as usual in saying:

> But when the tragic incident occurs between those who are near or dear to one another—if, for example, a brother kills or intends to kill, a brother, a son his father, a mother her son, a son his mother, or any other deed of the kind is done—these are the situations to be looked for by the poet.[116]

"Every scene I write has to have conflict," said Neil Simon. *"The Odd Couple* starts with a poker game—which is a conflict. I'm impatient with plays that take 10 or 15 minutes for the slow development of situation before moving into high gear. I prefer to start with a funny conflict," continued Simon, "and let the audience say to itself, 'We're in good hands.' Then it sits back and relaxes and lets the characters and the comedy develop." [117] Simon's leading characters in *The Odd Couple* are two men who share a somewhat common experience—one is divorced and the other, separated; but contrasting in this close circumstance, one man is basically very sloppy around the house, and the other is fastidious to a fault. Here in the contrast of leading characters is a basic conflict.

How many characters should a playwright have in his cast? Enough. Van Druten said, "The actual number to be used in a piece can only be determined by the type of piece and the exigencies of the plot, but the fewer an author has, the more time he will have to create them fully and in the round." [118] New playwrights, on Broadway and Off-Broadway, too, have repeatedly used all their ingenuity to shape their play's story into a plot requiring very few characters in a single set, not only to show excellence in fully dramatized portraiture but also to lure wary producers to take a chance on their unproven talent.

To illustrate, William Gibson's *Two for the See-Saw* had two characters and one multiple set; Edward Albee's *Who's Afraid of Virginia Woolf?* four characters and one set; Murray Schisgal's *Luv,* three characters and one set; Frank Gilroy's *The Subject Was Roses,* three characters and one set. A play with few characters onstage may through the playwright's resourcefulness fill the stage with the psychologically felt presence of many other characters who shape the lives of the onstage characters in ways critical to the play's action. Van Druten's *Voice of the Turtle* had only three characters in the cast, but a good thirty-six offstage characters helped people the stage psychologically. Langner, however, has warned of the difficulty of finding actors good enough to sustain an audience's attention for two hours in a play with only two or three in the cast.

To write a character, know a character. Ironically, this knowledge can only come for many playwrights largely in the actual writing and rewriting itself. All the leading playwrights came to know their characters admittedly by consciously or unconsciously using models for cross-breeding. "You can never know enough about your characters," said Maugham in a probing note.[119] "I have never yet been able to write a play," said Van Druten, "without knowing the full offstage lives of every character . . ."[120] "The more thoroughly the environment is realized," thought Lawson, "the more deeply we understand the character."[121] Sidney Kingsley, of course, made his setting for *Dead End* a living force that could be seen to visually shape somewhat the very lives of his "dead-end kids." To Thornton Wilder, "the idea, for a born story-teller, can only be expressed imbedded in its circumstantial illustration;" this implies that the basic way to develop a character is through illustrative action.[122] Saroyan damned playwrights who falsify their characters with trumped up action. He said, "the author is a liar," and added, "The play he writes is always technically excellent . . . It's just no good though."[123]

In the broad survey, playwrights have come up with quite a few added hints that have served them well in characterization and may serve others. "Drama that truthfully reflects life," believed Belasco, "requires the use of child actors."[124] "Would you pay $3.50 to spend an evening with five people you didn't like?" asked George M. Cohan in his hey-day, and the price would have to be doubled or almost tripled today.[125] "There is a well known producer," said Arthur Hopkins, "who always sums up failures by saying, 'There was no one to root for.'" If the audience doesn't really care about any leading character, why should it sit through a play to find out what happens? Rachel Crothers, in a bid for honesty, urged shunning cliché and stock characters like "hicks who talk through their noses and all that." [126]

Maugham believed that for stage characters to be lifelike they had to be like human beings, neither all good nor all bad, and acting with strong motivation rather than by unaccountable impulse. People in life, however, Maugham found to be too complicated and inconsistent for the stage to portray fully with either credibility or acceptance, and this, in fact, is one big reason that Maugham turned from plays to writing novels. "I knew the man and reported him overfaithfully," confessed Sidney Howard of Joe in *They Knew What They Wanted,* ". . . I stuck so close to him . . . that he ceased to be theatric and became improbable . . ." "It is always dangerous to stick too close to an original," Howard wrote Barrett Clark.[127] It is even more dangerous to make characters out of clichés. "The Negro, as primarily presented in that past, has never existed on land or sea," wrote Lorraine Hansberry in 1960, in a plea for honest character drawing of Negroes as human beings in plays. "Thus for three centuries in Europe and America alike, buffoonery or villainy was his only permissible role in the hall of entertainment or drama," she pointed out of the stage stereotype of the Negro.[128] Other minorities have also suffered from stage stereotypes at one time or another, and naturally deeply resented it as a travesty on their dignity as human beings.

"Every human being has his own gallery which he himself is," said Clifford Odets to Michael Mendelsohn in an interview for *Theatre Arts* magazine of June, 1963. "The more gifted the human being, the larger his gallery of characters. What is that gallery of characters?" queried Odets. "It is a group of characteristics or relationships to certain key psychological types outside of yourself," answered Odets. "You're lucky if you have six or seven of them. If you're an ardent young man, it's easy to write an ardent young man." [129] The writer's problem is how to make additions to his gallery without having the public reject him as "not himself."

Action

The word "drama" originally meant "the thing done." Action is still the soul of drama. "Action speaks louder than words," applies to characters as well as to people, for a play more or less imitates life.

Life's one certainty, of course, is uncertainty. In a play, this uncertainty is called "suspense." From over 40 years of playwriting and play production, Langner concluded: "given characters which live on the stage, *suspense interest* is the one essential of the play which cannot be dispensed with."[130] The more comprehensive the conflict of the central character, the more the total personality is involved, the more is at stake, the greater is the suspense. A classic example of suspense is *Hamlet,* for Hamlet is involved in total conflict: against himself, against his circumstance, against his associates, against the girl he loves, against his family, against his God, against his destiny. Common sense tells us that if an audience is to sit in a theatre for two hours or more, its concern over the outcome of the main conflict had better increase because if "nothing happens" for long, the audience loses interest. Suspense should mount with the main conflict so that the major climax is worked into very near the end of the play, for after this major excitement is spent, the audience is about ready to go home. An anti-climax makes sense only to let the audience in on the "fall-out" of the major climax, and it had usually better not take long.

However he goes about it, the development of an organic main action in a play is the playwright's most formidable task. In his *Poetics,* Aristotle used the term "organic" in the sense of an action having a beginning, a middle and an end, like an organism, no part removable without impairing or crippling the whole. He said:

> the plot, being an imitation of an action, must imitate one action and that a whole, the structural union of the parts being such that, if any one of them is displaced or removed, the whole will be disjointed and disturbed. For a thing whose presence or absence makes no visible difference, is not an organic part of the whole.[131]

To Aristotle, the action of the plot should be "necessary or probable."[132] Arthur Miller uses the term *organic action* almost identically, calling it the *poem* of a play, and like Aristotle, the play's prime element: no *poem,* no play. A corollary is, no truthfulness to the human nature of the characters, no *poem. Poet,* of course, literally means *maker* or *creator;* a *poem* is a *creation,* not a *contrivance.* Miller elaborated on the nature of the *poem* of a play in his speech, "The Shadow of the Gods," which was first printed in *Harper's* (August 1958); he tells what a memorable thing of a lifetime he learned from reading *The Brothers Karamazov:*

The book said to me, "There is a hidden order in the world. There is only one reason to live. It is to discover its nature. The good are those who do this. The evil say that there is nothing beyond the face of the world, the surface of reality. Man will only find peace when he learns to live humanly, in conformity to those laws which decree his human nature." [133]

"In the case of any play of mine that was any good," Sherwood wrote his niece, Lydia, "I knew the principal characters intimately—had lived with them and slept with them—long before I had any remote notion of the plot." [134] "Inevitability," said Rachel Crothers, referring to the unity of action drawn from human nature, "I believe is the greatest quality in playwriting, not surprise and invention." [135] And Maugham succinctly concluded, "I think the secret of playwriting can be given in two maxims: stick to the point, and whenever you can, cut." [136] Maugham, of course, had said, "You can never know enough about your characters . . . People are hard to know." [137]

Through the painful failure of *Days to Come,* after her gratifying success with *The Children's Hour,* Lillian Hellman had to learn again to respect the limitations of organic action. "I wanted to say too much," she admitted, ". . . I returned to the amateur's mistake: everything you think and feel must be written at this time, because you may never have another chance to write it." [138] Owen Davis believed that no good story should take more than 200 words to tell, because more than that was hard for an audience to recall. "Keep in mind," Davis cautioned, "that no part of a play—and this is especially true of farce—is effective when it is not convincing. The more belief you create in your characters and situations, the greater your success." [139] "The first law of the stage, whether in writing a play or playing a part," said Belasco in tune with Davis, "is to convince the audience of the truth and logic of the work." [140] Without credibility to human nature, all is lost. Only "organic action" can give such credibility.

A favorite maxim of 19th century dramatists was, "A man's character is his fate." Depending upon the character's view of his life's source of conflict, however, the maxim might be rephrased with many variations; for example, "A man's character and God are his fate;" "A man's character and society and God are his fate;" "A man's character and heredity and chance are his fate." The viewpoint might even change with personal experience of the character.

One of the most helpful techniques to develop action from character with suspense is "squeezing" a situation, as an old term goes, or "thinking over" characters in a situation, to "think it out," as common sense might put it. The practice is so common among playwrights that no one can really lay claim to originating it. It is basically the way people choose creatively in mulling over a variety of courses of action to anticipate the outcome of a conflict with different persons concerned. It involves scrutiny, perception, memory, deduction, induction, intuition, in fact, every means of "knowing." It seems to operate largely subconsciously—"in back of the head." Aristotle suggests it is based on signs and probabilities. Poker players, businessmen, generals, and lovers, for instance, more or less "think over" to "think out" character in a situation so that, by permutation and combination of possibilities, they might anticipate action leading toward or away from a major climax, and so best "know" their prospects. In a play as in life, changing forces might well change the outcome.

To Aristotle, plot was "the arrangement of the incidents" and "the soul of tragedy." [141] Plot at best is an arrangement or reordering of a well thought out organic story, to be dramatically most effective. Aristotle observed from actual plays "the most powerful elements of emotional interest in tragedy—Peripeteia or Reversal of Intentions, and Recognition scenes—are part of the plot." [142] The combination of reversal and recognition, it is implied, is more powerful than either alone. To illustrate, in the major climax of *Oedipus the King,* the brilliant but impulsive King Oedipus finally discovers with certainty and horror that he, himself, is the utterly "unclean" man he has hunted down throughout the play, for Oedipus learns he has unknowingly killed his own father and married his own mother, and by so offending the gods brought the plague on his own city of Thebes; in the reversal this self-recognition brings, Oedipus in expiation for his guilt chooses to deliver his people from the plague by blinding himself and by then going into exile as maximum atonement. To the imaginative playwright, the recognition of character through choice of action, and the reversal of an intended action are especially the stuff to look for in "thinking over" character in a situation. The intent of the discipline is that one insight will consciously or unconsciously provide somehow a chain-reaction to another insight leading to or away from a meaningful major climax. This "thinking over" to "think out" is exactly what Edward Albee, for example, does when he lets his characters improvise in a new situation to test their credibility and choice of action, and so reveal their most likely growth. It is also what Arthur Miller does in writing possibly a thousand pages of typewritten scenes in which he lets his characters improvise within his imagined purpose, the better to know his characters and to find out what they are driving at. In fact, it is this element of "thinking over" and "thinking out" that is suggested in Aristotle's comparing history to poetry, that is, life to art:

> The true difference is that one relates what has happened, the other what may happen. Poetry, therefore, is a more philosophical and a higher thing than history; for poetry tends to express the universal, history the particular.[143]

A scene vital to the main action the critic Sarcey called "a scène a faire," a scene to be done or an obligatory scene, "a scene that the public has been permitted to foresee and to desire from the progress of the action"—and whose omission, of course, the public will resent.

The most important obligatory scene is the major climax resolving the whole conflict. When should an obligatory scene about a secret best be revealed? William Archer believed that an audience should be let in on a secret as soon as possible unless the secret is far more dramatic if let out later, as in *Oedipus the King*. It is plain that in *Hamlet*, for instance, the audience is best let in on Hamlet's secret very early in the action through the scene between Hamlet and his father's ghost. Otherwise, *Hamlet* would not be nearly so good a play. Once in on Hamlet's secret, the audience finds that its suspense grows steadily. The audience knows what Hamlet's own Mother and step-father, King Claudius, do not know for some time—Hamlet's sworn intent to find by feigning madness if Claudius really killed Hamlet's father and, if Claudius is guilty, to avenge the murder by his own hand.

When a playwright begins with a major climax in mind, as Maxwell Anderson and Arthur Miller admittedly have done on occasion, then "thinking over" character in a situation has a head start in guaranteeing the play's successful growth. When Anderson is sure of the big scene combining discovery and reversal resulting in his hero's spiritual regeneration, or when Miller is sure of the big scene of commitment of his hero showing his relation as a man to men or as a man to God in terms that make the world his home, then these playwrights are taking a valuable precaution, indeed. Aristotle long ago observed of plots that the untying of the knot, that is, the resolution of the action, is much more difficult to do satisfactorily than the tying of the knot, that is, the complication of the action. Sometimes, even beginning with a good major climax, playwrights for all their scrutiny and deliberation of character in a situation, still fail to evolve the needed growth for a good organic action making the major climax credible and therefore effective. After all, even in life investigators sometimes fail to reconstruct the true story of, say, the Brink's bank robbery, or to discover the miracle drug to kill cancer, or to find until too late the drift into a war. Some things elude the human mind possibly for lack of a powerful enough searchlight.

A situation in itself is only a basic circumstance, a kind of piece of geography in the landscape of a play. What makes all the difference is who comes upon the setting and what they do within its limits. Put Hamlet in Macbeth's place and King Duncan would never have been murdered. Put Macbeth in Hamlet's place, and King Claudius might have died in the first act—with Lady Macbeth, of course, sharpening the fatal dagger. Carlo Gozzi, the popular writer of farce and comedy in the 18th century, could count up only 36 possible situations in playwriting. Goethe and Schiller managed to find only 20. What matters, obviously, is not so much the situation as the characters put to test through it. Here is the full scope of the drama's potential—as varied as life itself.

A good first act is considered easiest to construct. An old Broadway saying goes, "Hell is paved with good first acts." "It is desirable in my opinion," said Langer, "at the very beginning of the play, or somewhere close to the beginning, to introduce the theme in a direct or indirect manner, as may best serve the purposes of the play." [144] "As a rule, the writing of a second act seems to drag on forever," said Moss Hart. "It is the danger spot of every play—the soft underbelly of playwriting, as Mr. Churchill might put it—and it is well to be aware of it. . . . It is the second acts that separate the men from the boys." [145] Formulas for plots are suspect in the theatre because they seem to mechanically force characters into action which their own free will should rightfully choose. And yet some formulas for plot persist, as if they had something vital to the all important element of suspense in them. George M. Cohan's formula was: "In Act 1, get your characters up a tree; in Act 2, throw stones at them; and in Act 3, get them down again." [146] Langner thought this formula best suited to comedy and suggested a few refinements. In Act 1, believed Langner, get the characters up a tree right away, show their true nature, and clearly focus on the tree, that is, the problem that "trees" your characters. In Act 2, begin by throwing small stones, steadily increase their size till, by the end of the act, the characters are to all appearances about to be knocked clean out of the tree. In Act 3, the characters manage somehow on their own to climb gradually down to the ground, but never with safe footing assured until the very end. "I also emphasize," noted Langner, "that the curtain situations or so called curtains for plays, whether they consist of two, three, or four acts, are of extreme importance to the success of any play."[147] Weak curtains lose an audience for the next act; strong curtains bring them back stimulated from talking over the play and eager for the next act, or satisfied with the final curtain.

"Good construction builds the story act by act," said Crothers, "always climbing, always advancing . . ."[148] To best hold the audience's attention, the major climax obviously should come as late as possible in the third act of a three act play, or in an equivalent position in a play otherwise divided.

Writers and often readers are so often taken in by the early stages of a play's action, that the emergence of a play's organic action might be likened to the actual delivery of a brain-child. The first act, the head, might look very good indeed; the second act, the torso, might appear quite vigorous; the third act, the legs, however, complete the effective life of the whole organism on earth. Only the third act and, by implication, the whole play can reveal the true state of the brain-child—whether handicapped, a monster, or wonderfully healthy in its way. Judging a play's whole action before the third act, *indeed, the whole play, is read aloud* or *seen,* is as premature as deciding a child's faculties as excellent before it is quite born. And freakish plays are far more common than freakish children, for nature has been at the business of making healthy babies infinitely longer than any playwright has been at the business of making healthy brain-children.

The aspiring playwright is bound to rely upon models of action and structure if only to give him a second nature awareness of the best practises. "After Ibsen, Chekhov is the most widely imitated playwright in the contemporary theatre . . . ," wrote Walter Kerr in his book of 1955, *How Not to Write a Play.*[149] Then with the effect for many of tossing a bomb at a public statue, Kerr noted, "Ibsen, himself, has at no time had a mass following in this country, neither in his matinee beginnings nor in the heyday of his convinced imitators."[150] The chief reasons Kerr gives for this are that Ibsen deliberately chose in his plays not to please but rather to upset and to infuriate. Then Kerr, again for many, does another bit of bomb-tossing: "Chekhov has never been popular. A difficult 'prestige' dramatist in his own country, an 'Arts theater' admiration in London, he is almost without peer in his power to chill American audiences." [151] Kerr's chief objection to Chekhov is that the broad American public does not take to his rather static drama. Kerr concedes that Williams and Miller among others have profited from aspects of Ibsen and Chekhov, but insists that in terms of cycles and of styles, the time is long overdue for new models for aspiring playwrights. Kerr frankly means to toss a few bombs to clear the playwrights' landscape of statues he feels are obstructing any new prospect. Kerr also includes early Shaw among his targets, for having so intellectualized the theatre to make it a place where William Morris might enjoy going of an evening, that the rest of the public except for the "intellectuals" have been driven away. Granted that the drama must experiment or die for lack of growth, what new models does Kerr offer? "The next accent is likely to be less mechanistic, more humanistic, less concerned with evolving a sociological slide-rule and more concerned with seeking some understanding of the complex cantankerous personal soul," wrote Kerr.[152] But is this not the general drift of much modern drama from Ibsen on through the "intellectuals?"

"What is precious in the Ibsen method," Arthur Miller specified of his own indebtedness to Ibsen and by implication providing an answer to Kerr, "is its insistence upon valid causation . . . This can be scoffed away only at a price, and the price is a living drama." [153] Ibsen, himself, wanted no one's slavish imitation, and said of any attempt to monopolize the "eternal verities," "Aesthetics are as great a curse to poetry as theology to religion." [154] "The paths paved by me will remain safe and sound," said Chekhov to Kuprin, "therein is my only merit;" and despising lies as he did, Chekhov told Kuprin, "The drama must either degenerate completely or assume a completely new form." [155] Chekhov's technique of characterization has left every modern playwright of distinction more or less in his debt. Though he called himself "a very old fashioned playwright," Shaw also noted that his plays were "sui generis," of their own kind, suggesting his emphasis upon experiment chiefly through his fresh interpretation of life.[156]

Kerr has deliberately overstated his case to blast slavish imitators of far less talent from blindly trying to mimick their masters. "To this day, a repertory company organizing itself around the usual Shakespeare, Shaw, and Ibsen," calculated Kerr, "tends to make a little money with Shaw, break even with Shakespeare, and break its neck with *The Wild Duck*." [157] Kerr would never urge dropping Shakespeare because repertory only broke even on him. Kerr must know that few if any repertory companies make money on any revivals. " 'Old' plays are rarely profitable," commented producer-director Harold Clurman; "their publicity value has gone out of them." [158] Kerr says, "My guess is by working with the universal audience, we may get universal plays." He cites Sophocles, Shakespeare, Molière, for instance, as having taken this route to the summit. Television certainly offers universal audiences; Abe Burrows, Neil Simon, Inge, Chayefsky, and Robert Anderson, among others, have come along by this route although much of television was and still is a "wasteland," designed primarily to sell a product rather than to scale new heights of the drama.

To Kerr, only musical comedy in the legitimate theatre today shows signs of genuine growth as a popular dramatic form. Musical comedy delights the general public by frankly exploring the make-believe nature of the theatre through such conventions as unreal backgrounds with plenty of color, staging flowing freely in time and space, the action soaring to the poetry of the lyrics, the melody of the music, and the excitement and rhythmic movement of the dance. Thornton Wilder suggests the drama's possibilities of change in his comment found in *The Intent of the Artist:*

> The history of the theatre shows that in its greatest ages the stage employed the greatest number of conventions. The stage is fundamental pretense and it thrives on the acceptance of that fact and in the multiplication of additional pretense.[159]

Wilder follows his own approximation of this in about all of his one-act plays, as well as in *Our Town* and *The Skin of Our Teeth.* "I began writing one-act plays that tried to capture not verisimilitude but reality," he said.[160] "In *The Happy Journey to Trenton and Camden* four kitchen chairs represent an automobile and a family travels seventy miles in twenty minutes." [161] "I am not an innovator, but a rediscoverer of forgotten goods," acknowledged Wilder, "and I hope a remover of obtrusive bric-a-brac." [162] "But when a form of art has reached what perfection it is capable of and then decays, there is nothing to do but return to its origins," said Maugham, viewing the modern drama of Ibsen. "The early drama amuses the eye with spectacle and dancing, and the ear with verse and music," said Maugham. "I think the modern playwright would do well to call in these allied arts to his help." [163] "A playwright's responsibility," said Albee, "is to

write plays which have some relationship to the historical continuum
of the theatre . . ."[164]

Since Ibsen and Strindberg, the drama's most exciting changes of
form came in the movies and promise to come in television, and these
new media depend upon great, new technological advances offering
fantastic flexibility. As to startling freshness, if the success of past experiments is any sign of the future, the models of action in new
drama are far more likely to be minor variations rather than major
mutations, paralleling the evolution of man in the family of primates.
Examples of new and imaginative drama also suggest that change in
form is intrinsic in the organic nature of a particular play, for instance, as in *Our Town, The Glass Menagerie, Murder in the Cathedral, The Caucasian Chalk Circle, Rhinoceros, Waiting for
Godot,* and *The Royal Hunt of the Sun.* The pioneering success in
each instance is no guarantee of its proof as a stencil for future playwriting; the very mood of experiment of these works suggests a free
creative spirit exultant. The pressure for modern dramatists to work
in new forms is perhaps an attempt to somehow find in the theatre an
equivalent for the advances in science through the electron and the
fission and fusion of the atom. The basic material of the drama is still
human beings and, though techniques change, human nature must always remain at least human if it is to be recognizable onstage. This
some avant-garde drama seems to have lost sight of. And yet the theatre is the place for the unexpected. "Man hopes," said Emerson;
"Genius creates."[165]

Writing and Rewriting

Before beginning the actual writing of a first draft, playwrights
have usually gathered the results of genesis and incubation into some
kind of scenario. "No, I do not work from a synopsis," said
Maugham. "I turn an idea over in my mind until I get tired of it.
Then I write straight ahead, and the first draft usually takes me a
month or six weeks to get down on paper. In this way, I keep the
spontaneity of the story."[166] Wilde, who thought only in terms of
stories, would work and rework a story out aloud by testing it on his
friends as he did, for example, with *Salome,* until he felt it was in
good enough shape to be written. Wilde, however, did on occasion
write scenarios, for he sold the one for *Mr. and Mrs. Daventry* to no
less than twelve different, unsuspecting purchasers because he was
desperate for money. George M. Cohan would often write down only

a bare sketch of a play's action and then, suggesting the approach of the commedia dell'arte and some movie directors today, call actors as for a rehearsal, brief them on the characters, have the actors improvise following the sketch of the action, and in this way, eventually develop the play in detail. "Before beginning to write a play," said Pinero, "I always make sure, by means of a definite scheme, that there is a way of doing it; but whether I ultimately follow that way is a totally different matter." [167] Lillian Hellman and Arthur Miller from their heavily documented preparation, imply they usually work from a written scenario yet are committed to numerous revisions as the only way to important revelations that often give a play its finest qualities. But Miller could write very fast sometimes. A mere acquaintance, Martin Ritt, acting in the Broadway version of Odets' blighted *The Flowering Peach,* asked Miller to write some one-acts for the cast to put on for invited Sunday matinees only. "I had never written one-acters," recollected Miller, "but I said I would think about it." He certainly did. "Within the next three or four weeks I wrote *A Memory of Two Mondays* and *A View from the Bridge.*" [168]

Some playwrights write their first draft with astonishing speed, and these tend to be the very ones who rely largely upon relatively spontaneous generation of the whole play in a short time. Wilde wrote the whole first draft of *Salome* in French in a single day, and the whole of *The Importance of Being Earnest* in three weeks, and then hardly changed a line. Coward, while convalescing from the flu in Shanghai, wrote the first draft of *Private Lives* in four days. Saroyan wrote the entire first draft of *The Time of Your Life* in six days, writing day and night to exhaustion. Those who nurture their play's growth with detailed reality, like Hellman and Miller, usually work more slowly. Hellman, for instance, termed her writing *The Children's Hour* "stumbling stubbornness,"—"about fourteen complete rewrites;" and Miller spoke of writing *The Crucible* as having "tempted agony."

"A very great play," thought Miller, "can be mimed and still issue forth its essential actions and their rudiments of symbolic meaning." [169] Dialogue to Miller is only an extension of the organic action of a play—intense, for example, or anything else—only if the organic action is. When other elements of the theatre, like lights, music, business can express organic action better than words, Miller implies dialogue is better not used. Miller says he has written his plays to be performed rather than for the library. So important is the "poem," the organic action of a play in his eyes, that he thinks a playwright (presumably O'Neill) may fall short in his diction and yet the effect is not ruinous. "Speech is a kind of action," said Lawson, "a compression and extension of action." [170] If to Aristotle plot was "the soul of tragedy," diction by implication was evidence of the body and the soul, for Aristotle says that reading alone can convey the power of tragedy: "For the power of tragedy, we may be sure, is felt even apart from representation and actors." [171]

As a springboard in the continuum of dramatic tradition in dialogue, what did Aristotle observe to be the best style for diction? He says in his *Poetics:*

> The perfection of style is to be clear without being mean. The clearest style is that which uses only current or proper words: at the same time it is mean. . . . That diction, on the other hand, is lofty and raised above the commonplace which employs unusual words. By unusual, I mean strange (or rare) words, metaphorical, lengthened—anything, in short, that differs from the normal idiom.[172]

Aristotle noted in particular what to us likely accounts for much of the genius in the language of the Bible and of Shakespeare:

> But the greatest thing by far is to have a command of metaphor. This alone cannot be imparted by another; it is the mark of genius—for to make good metaphors implies an eye for resemblances.[173]

Almost all modern plays use prose for their dialogue. People talk in prose, and the popular faith in science to solve life's problems has led to a search for truth in the facts of prose. New revelations of God are looked for often in such factual realities as color television, the H-Bomb, or a chemical cure for mental illness, rather than in impassioned modern prophets in a continuation of the biblical succession. The dramatist still needs a touch of the poet in his dialogue to catch life's passion and mystery. "If he is a real dramatist, he must be at once poet and lyric poet," remarked Benavente in *The Yale Review.* "The art of dialogue is a question wholly of rhythm. Dialogue without rhythm is dialogue without a soul." [174] Music, of course, uses basically rhythm and sound to conjure any mood. Observe, for example, the rhythm of Chopin's *Funeral March* and that of Rodgers and Hammerstein's *The Surrey with the Fringe on Top,* and the disastrous change in mood if the rhythms were exchanged.

"The dramatist who is not a poet," said Lawson, "is only half a dramatist."[175] To Lawson, dramatic poetry "must evolve out of the richness and imagery of contemporary speech."[176] "Dramatic dialogue has two obvious ends," wrote Granville-Barker, "the telling of the story and the disclosure of character," and then he suggested what only poetry can do: "But there is another not so obvious: it must be made to stimulate our imagination and emotion—and here mainly, comes in the need for some artifice of form."[177] "In a good play," noted Synge in his preface to *The Playboy of the Western World,* "every speech should be as fully flavored as a nut or apple, and such speeches cannot be written by anyone who works among people who have shut their lips on poetry."[178] "The fewer words the character speaks," judged Rachel Crothers implying the evocative quality of only poetry, "and the more he shows of himself by them, the better the writing." "Very great dialogue," Crothers noted, "is the rarest gift, and is the flower, the crowning touch of drama."[179] "The talk must be succinct. It must give an impression of reality, not a copy," said Maugham, who advised the playwright, "whenever you can, cut."[180] In Lawson's opinion, "Compression is not only achieved by hot violent words, but by sudden contrasts, by breaks, pauses, moments of unexpected calm."[181] James Barrie, when urged by Clayton Hamilton to print his plays, replied, "There isn't anything to print. The best moments always happen when nobody is saying anything."[182] Barrie had seen to that.

The example of conversation, itself, and the testimony of playwrights provide other hints to writing good prose dialogue. Speeches, as a rule, should be very short, one thought to a speech, so that the give and take of speakers has the liveliness of a tennis match. Exclamations can be superably expressive, like Medea's animal cry of torment near the opening of Robinson Jeffers' *Medea,* projecting a complete expression of the character's state of being as Judith Anderson did the leading role. Long speeches suggest an emotional range from sluggishness to exalted eloquence. Good dialogue, like good talk, wastes no words, is specific, in the active voice, uses language true to the speaker's nature and gets things done. "When I was writing *In the Shadow of the Glen,*" said Synge, "I got more aid than any learning could have given me from a chink in the floor of the old Wicklow house where I was staying that let me hear what was being said by the servant girls in the kitchen."[183] "Reality on stage is highly selective reality, chosen to give form," said Albee in effect qualifying

Synge's experience; "Real dialogue onstage is impossible. Make a tape recording of people and try to put that onstage." [184]

"Like a bee," said Preston Sturges recalling an old comedian's advice, "a good line should carry the sting in its tail." [185] "I have seen far, far better heads on umbrellas," for instance, is a better comic line than, "I have seen umbrellas that have better heads on than you have." For good continuity or drift, Preston Sturges inserted a word or thought in each speech for the following speaker to relate or "hook" on to. Lawson viewed dialogue as an extension of the main organic action, moving in cycles of expectation, preparation, and accomplishment of change, and always toward and then eventually away from the major climax. The common terms for such a cycle are the "build-up" and the "come-off."

When many characters in a play use witticisms, the suggestion comes through that the playwright himself is showing-off and intruding upon his characters. "Unless I can get rid of those damned witticisms," said Maugham, "the public will never really laugh at the characters or even the situations." In *The Importance of Being Earnest,* Oscar Wilde, who was one of the world's truly great conversationalists of all time, and who said, "I have put my genius into my life, and only my talent into my work," still relied upon character and situation to provide a choice moment for his witticisms to sparkle most brilliantly in their setting. The similar sparkle from so many of Wilde's characters, however, is suspiciously more the author's than the characters'. Consider, for instance, these excerpts:

> ALGERNON: The very essence of romance is uncertainty. If ever I get married, I'll certainly try to forget it.
> GWENDOLYN: Whenever people talk to me about the weather, I always feel quite certain that they mean something else.
> MISS PRISM: The good ended happily, and the bad unhappily. That is what fiction means.
> LADY BRACKNELL: I do not approve of anything that tampers with natural ignorance. Ignorance is like a delicate, exotic fruit; touch it and the bloom is gone.

Only Wilde could somehow get away with this, for of its kind, *The Importance of Being Earest* is certainly a classic. Shaw observed that Wilde was a "thorough" playwright in that he played with everything in terms of epigrams. Shaw commented, "As far as I can ascertain, I am the only person in London who cannot sit down and write an Oscar Wilde play at will." [186] Clayton Hamilton and John Van

Druten both concluded from experience that the biggest laughs in a play always came not from simply a gag line but from character or from the reaction of character to a situation.

Maugham, Barker, and Maxwell Anderson have, each in his own way, regretfully noted that serious plays written in prose dialogue tend to a short if a full life. Pinero and Jones epitomized this to Maugham in their identical comment of the public, "They don't want me any more." Langner noted that comedy with the moment its chief concern, seemed to date much faster than tragedy with its chief concern in basic, intense, human relationships. Among serious plays, moreover, only those with dialogue in verse have survived for centuries. Maugham, Barker, and Maxwell Anderson—each came to believe that verse alone had the power to rise quickly, to rocket as it were through its pulse of memorable language to the highest flights of emotion and imagination. And yet only a handful of dramatic poets have kept that firing power and thrust through the centuries: Aeschylus, Sophocles, Euripides, Aristophanes, Marlowe, and Shakespeare. Others today fizz more than they rocket—like Kydd and Webster— and are museum pieces more dead than alive. A first-rate dramatic poet, in fact, is perhaps the greatest of rarities combining two rarities, the dramatist and the poet, in one man. A first-rate translator of dramatic poetry is almost as great a rarity, requiring a mastery of word-magic equal to that of the original poet if the spell is to work. In modern drama, time has yet to test the longevity of such successful dramatists in verse as Maxwell Anderson, T. S. Eliot, Archibald Mac-Leish, Robinson Jeffers, and Christopher Fry.

Because so much stock has been put in the potential of verse for modern drama, the matter deserves special focussing for clarification. "Until a play has risen to a certain level of emotion," said Maxwell Anderson, "it seems most natural to write the dialogue in prose; but, after this emotion has been superseded, I find it impossible to restrain myself from writing verse." [187] Anderson thinks prose is the language of information and verse the language of emotion. When the emotion calls for it, Anderson has chosen to write almost exclusively in blank verse in the modern idiom, as illustrated in this passage in which Mio in *Winterset* pours out his heart and soul:

> . . . For my heritage,
> they've left me one thing only, and that's to be
> my father's voice crying up out of the earth
> and quicklime where they stuck him. Electrocution
> doesn't kill you know. They eviscerate them

with a turn of the knife in the dissecting room.
The blood spurts out. The man was alive. Then into
the lime-pit, leave no trace. Make it short shrift
and chemical dissolution. That's what they thought
of the man that was my father.

As Marlowe and Shakespeare knew well, and no doubt Anderson, too, the iambic pentameter of blank verse is the rhythm most common to conversation. In fact, Aristotle had observed: "For the iambic is, of all measures, the most colloquial; we see it in the fact that conversational speech runs into iambic form more frequently than into any other kind of verse."[188] Since Anderson's death, his plays have not often been revived, although old movies of these plays are periodically seen on television. Anderson's most ambitious and successful efforts in verse were: *Winterset, High Tor, Elizabeth the Queen, Mary of Scotland,* and *Anne of the Thousand Days.* Perhaps someday when Anderson may be played as royalty-free as Shakespeare, Anderson will be played more than now.

T. S. Eliot's *Murder in the Cathedral* promises to be perhaps the most durable of the modern verse plays. Like Anderson's efforts for the most part, Eliot in this instance uses the traditional stuff of high tragedy: characters long dead or legendary in a story that has fascinated the public for centuries and arouses pity and terror. The remoteness of medieval times and the costumes of the period made his use of verse apt. Eliot was persuaded that the 19th century poets such as Tennyson who had attempted poetic drama failed not for want of theatrical technique but because, in imitating Shakespeare, they used blank verse. To Eliot, "The rhythm of regular blank verse had become too remote from the movement of modern speech."[189] *Murder in the Cathedral* is Eliot's modern vision of the martyrdom of Thomas à Becket in his cathedral at Canterbury, England, at the climax of a power struggle with his King, and uses modern free verse with conversational directness, idiom, familiar terms, and electrifying imagery in keeping with the characters and mood. The style is distinctly Eliot's, who is generally considered the greatest poet of modern times. In foretelling the assassination of the Archbishop of Canterbury, this passage from the chorus of hysterical women—a highly theatrical device when divided among separate speakers—epitomises Eliot's diction:

I have smelt them, the death-bringers, senses are quickened
By subtile forebodings; I have heard

> Flutings in the night-time, fluting and owls, have seen at noon
> Scaly wings slanting over, huge and ridiculous. I have tasted
> The savour of putrid flesh in the spoon. I have felt
> The heaving of earth at nightfall, restless, absurd.[190]

For special effects, Eliot has not hesitated to vary his prosody, as when the Archbishop speaks in a contemplative mood using assonance and rhyme:

> While I ate out of the King's dish
> To become servant of God was never my wish.
> Servant of God has chance of greater sin
> And sorrow, than the man who serves a king.[191]

The language is never used for display but to express the intense, inherent drama of the action and to reveal character. The rhythms are varied all through the work in keeping with the drama's nuances of thought and feeling. "The two prose passages in *Murder in the Cathedral*," said Eliot in the First Theodore Spencer Memorial Lecture at Harvard on November 12, 1950, "could not have been written in verse. Certainly, with the kind of dialogue verse which I used in that play, the audience would have been uncomfortably aware that it was verse they were hearing." [192] The sermon of the Archbishop on the meaning of the mass on Christmas morning is in prose because to Eliot, "A sermon cast in verse is too unusual an experience for even the most regular church goer . . ." [193] The speeches of justification by the knights who murdered the Archbishop are also in prose and, according to Eliot, aimed to "shock the audience out of their complacency." [194] In performance, the auditorium lights are turned full up, suggesting audience participation and a kind of fascistic double-talk in the knights' prose which uses language not to reveal thought but to conceal it.

Why did Eliot use verse at all in *Murder in the Cathedral?* He believed that verse is unique in its power at moments of greatest intensity to border on feelings that only music can actually give full voice. "We can never emulate music," cautioned Eliot, "because to arrive at the condition of music would be the annihilation of poetry, and especially dramatic poetry." [195] A perfect verse drama, in Eliot's opinion, would combine action and words as the equivalent of drama and music. "To go as far in this direction as it is possible to go, without losing that contact with the ordinary everyday world with which drama must come to terms," noted Eliot, "seems to me the proper aim of dramatic poetry." [196] The tangential nature of drama to music, of course, has been noted by many dramatists, for instance, Strindberg, Wilde, Shaw, and O'Neill. Suggesting his own experimental spirit of suiting the verse to the organic nature of each distinct project, Eliot in his one commercial success in verse, *The Cocktail Party,* did revert to blank verse but strictly in the modern idiom.

In *J. B.,* Archibald MacLeish used the traditional material of high tragedy. MacLeish updated the story of Job in terms of the modern equivalent of the characters and the afflictions; J. B., for instance, to begin with was a highly prosperous and fortunate American business-man with a fine family. Providing a kind of morality play frame-work, two unemployed actors in a circus tent portray Mr. Zuss and Mr. Nickles, the counterpart of God and the Devil, and decide to test J. B.'s faith in God by inflicting him with a series of devastating mis-fortunes fresh from the news-wires. For his dialogue, MacLeish chose verse in the contemporary American spirit—"nervous . . . excited . . . vivid"—even as he had described it in the preface of his play, *Panic,* written over twenty years earlier.[197] In *The Atlantic Monthly* of February, 1955, MacLeish remarked in the original printing of *The Poet as Playwright,* "An audience does not accept poetry of the end of *Antony and Cleopatra* because, 'I could talk in poetry too!' but because there are no other words than these to say what is being said." And MacLeish set up a traffic light as to when to use or not use poetry onstage—"Until it can people the stage again with actions which are at once poetry *and* drama, poetic drama will not exist." [198] In his successful poetic drama, *J. B.,* MacLeish uses diction with much idiom and usually four accents to a line of an unfixed number of syl-lables. Here is a sample of the diction as the modern businessman, J. B.—his wealth wiped out, his children dead, his body diseased, and his wife fled,—speaks at his life's nadir in utter desolation:

> The hand of God has touched me. Look at me!
> Every hope I ever had,
> Every task I put my mind to,
> Every work I've ever done,
> Annulled as though I had not done it.
> My trace extinguished in the land,
> My children dead, my father's name
> Obliterated in the sunlight everywhere . . .
> Love, too, has left me.[199]

The market for verse in the commercial theatre has proven relatively small. Christopher Fry showed much promise in *The Lady's Not for Burning,* but a series of commercial failures turned him to the more dependable income and the far greater public of movie scripts in prose, like those of *Ben Hur* and *The Bible.* Robinson Jeffers in *Medea,* written specifically for Judith Anderson and based upon Euripides' version, has scored a superb tour de force with Judith Anderson performing in bravura incandescence rare to the stage in the fierce fire of the title role.

Modern verse in dialogue strikes the general public as often unnatural, strained, artificial. Plays like *Our Town, The Glass Menagerie* and *Death of a Salesman* show that modern dramatic prose at its best in concert with the other elements of the theatre, like action, song, dance, music, lights, symbols, may even better than verse project the essence of dramatic poetry—a succinct evocation of thought and feeling. The entry of a modern Shakespeare on the scene might change the whole picture. "The most pervasive and usually the most effective poetry," John Gassner judged of the theatre, "is not one of words, but of the theatrical organization of the play and the production elements . . ."[200]

When a playwright has finished his first draft, whether in prose or verse, how much rewriting is required? Theresa Helburn in almost forty seasons of production with the Theatre Guild never knew one American playwright except Eugene O'Neill whose work needed only cutting to be ready for production. When does or should all the required rewriting take place? Some takes place after the first draft and before the playwright even submits the play to his agent, for he has a standard of professional competence to maintain. Coward, for example, put aside the first draft of *Private Lives* for a few weeks to gain a fresh perspective and then revised the play in one week. More rewriting may take place after the playwright has submitted the play to a prospective agent who then may suggest revisions; Williams revised some of his early plays at the suggestion of Audrey Wood, for he realized he had "a certain period" to go through. More rewriting may take place to please a prospective producer; Neil Simon revised *Come Blow Your Horn* four times in unsuccessful attempts to try to satisfy such producers as Herman Shumlin, Saint Subber, and George Abbott. More rewriting may take place after the cast first reads the script aloud; actors, for instance, may find some speeches hard to read, not clear, don't play, and so on.

"A good play is hardly ever finished," even Oscar Wilde conceded;

"It must be fitted to the stage." [201] "From the time I finish writing until the first performance," said Miller, "everything is a compromise." [202] To illustrate, he had written Willy Loman with a small man in mind, but a large man, Lee J. Cobb, proved brilliant in the try-out and got the role. Miller had visualized the set for *Death of a Salesman* one way but, he admitted, "When I saw Jo Mielziner's sketches for the set and his ideas about the lighting, I knew they were better than anything I had imagined." [203] Rewriting almost always takes place after the first complete run-through in rehearsal; when acted out as a whole, the play may be gauged fairly accurately as to effective life. The director, the producer, the star and the author then usually confer to decide such questions as total effect, interpretation, motivation, cutting, building up a role, and polishing exit and entrance lines. "I could mention quite a few important authors," said Langer in his book, *The Play's the Thing,* "who are deeply indebted to their actors, directors, and producers for extremely valuable suggestions." [204]

The most rewriting of all usually takes place after the opening night of the try-out when the audience has finally had a chance to show what it thinks of every moment in the play by its running reaction to the performance. "It is an axiom of the profession of the theatre," remarked David Belasco, "that only by performing it publicly can all the imperfections of a play be detected." [205] During a try-out, perhaps the most commonplace remark in the theatre is, "It needs a lot of work." "The rustling of programs, coughing, the shuffling of feet," warned Belasco, "all these tell their story more plainly than words can express. Each means revision, blue-penciling, or transposition." [206] Moss Hart said of the audience's reactions, "they are the surest barometer of a play's weakness or of an actor's inadequacy that I know." [207]

So unpredictable is the outcome of a try-out that it is said to conform to "Murphy's Law," which according to Abe Burrows means, "If something can go wrong, it will." Jed Harris, for instance, said of Thornton Wilder's reaction to Harris' still acclaimed production of *Our Town* in its try-out, "And his detestation reached such shrill heights on the opening night in Princeton that all further communication between us lapsed." [208] George Abbott found that try-outs and crises generally go together and that, even if a play runs reasonably well for the audience, actors will somehow develop personality clashes. Try-outs like ship-launchings reveal leaks, listing, imbalance, and outright foundering. The problem is to correct the trouble within the deadline of the try-out before the fault in the eyes of the exacting Broadway critics endangers the launching of the whole enterprise.

There are basically three different kinds of try-outs and sometimes all three are more or less used: the summer theatre try-out is usually the least expensive and allows the playwright the most time for revision before a Broadway production is scheduled; the Broadway preview is a less expensive try-out than a road tour and allows the playwright relatively little time for revision; the out of town, pre-Broadway tour is the most expensive kind of try-out but allows possibly even a half year or so for a musical, like *Oliver,* to be revised, or over a month for a play, like *The Odd Couple.* Neil Simon's *Come Blow Your Horn,* for example, had a summer theatre try-out at Michael Ellis' Bucks County Playhouse, and on the basis of the audience "loving the play," Ellis—after Simon had made some revision—took the play to Broadway. *Who's Afraid of Virginia Woolf?* had only a preview try-out at the Longacre Theatre; the attentiveness of the audience proved that, though the play ran for three hours, it did not need to be cut more for the opening.

The pre-Broadway road tour, followed by a week or so of Broadway previews is the commonest method of trying out a play these days. Simon rewrote the third act of *The Odd Couple* five times in the pre-Broadway road tour. The resultant play illustrates the inadvertent, almost intuitively guided way in which critical rewriting may come about. After the Boston opening, the dean of Boston's drama critics, Eliot Norton, interviewed *The Odd Couple*'s author, Neil Simon, its director, Mike Nichols, and the stars, Walter Matthau and Art Carney, on Norton's half hour television show. Eliot, among other remarks, asked, "Did the third act run down?" [209] While Nichols and Matthau defended the third act, Simon asked what Norton missed in the resolution. "I'm just looking for one more big scene before it happens. I was thinking about those two English sisters who have a wonderful scene with Mr. Matthau and Mr. Carney in the second act," said Norton. "When the third act curtain went up, I felt badly about those two girls not being around any more." [210] Within two days, Simon came up with a ten page scene, later cut to six, to fill Norton's request; in two days the scene was worked into the performance, and two weeks later in Washington the same scene still was undergoing tinkering. Simon brought the English sisters back onstage in the third act in a scene in which they defend Carney against Matthau but feud on their own and so point up the play's whole theme with a new variation—"living together can be hell—whether togetherness involves husband and wife, an odd couple like Matthau and Carney, or even two congenial sisters." [211]

The standard contract of the Dramatists Guild prevents any tampering with a play's script without an author's consent. In the midst of the possible cross-currents of interest of the playwright, the producer, the director, the stars, not to mention others with a high stake in the successful launching of the venture, no wonder playwrights are sometimes at loss in a try-out as to what to rewrite and what to leave alone. Neil Simon wrote in all fifteen versions of *Come Blow Your Horn* but far fewer for *The Odd Couple.*

"I can leave the stage when I am directing," reported Clifford Odets of the insight directing gave him in rewriting his own plays, "and go to my hotel room out of town, as I did in *The Country Girl,* and three or four nights before the New York opening, in Boston, rewrite the last 15 pages which made the play successful." [212] Moss Hart, however, cautioned against the added wear and tear upon the author who is also his own director. An author might have to stay up all night revising, and then a good share of the next day be directing the cast in the revisions, and then be up watching the audience's reaction that night, and then possibly have to do more revision with a fearful series of such cycles ahead. The strain conceivably could be very hard on the heart. Odets and Moss Hart were both to die in middle-age of heart attacks. Noel Coward has had better luck.

ACKNOWLEDGMENTS AND FOOTNOTES FOR CHAPTER X ARE AT THE CLOSE OF THE ENTIRE CURSORY STUDY, THE END OF CHAPTER XI.

Chapter XI

A Cursory Study of Collaboration

COLLABORATION in playwriting is based on the sensible idea that sometimes two heads are better than one. Collaborators should need and want to work together. George S. Kaufman and Moss Hart, for instance, first collaborated when Hart as an undisciplined talent, at the age of twenty-five, followed the writing of six unproduced plays with the first draft of a potential hit beyond his own skill to fully realize, *Once in a Lifetime*. Kaufman had much earlier had two unsuccessful collaborations and tried collaboration again with Marc Connelly when managers turned down Kaufman's solo effort, *Going Up*. John Toohey, an associate of the manager George C. Tyler, found Kaufman's dialogue so snappy and his sense of comic situation so good that Toohey sold Tyler on the idea of joining Kaufman and Connelly to collaborate on *Dulcy*. George Abbott, to cite another instance, chose collaboration only after producers again and again rejected his plays with the comment that his dialogue and construction were good, but his ideas were not. "I was not a successful playwright," admitted Abbott, "until I took parasitical advantage of other people's ideas." [1] The theatre, of course, is the most collaborative of all the arts. Though Shakespeare was an adaptor rather than a collaborator in almost all his best work, he obviously "took parasitical advantage of other people's ideas." The collaborator and the adaptor are close kin, and either title has won great literary distinction and success in the theatre.

How do collaborators work? The evidence suggests they "play it by ear." When William Archer heard Shaw read aloud the first two acts of Shaw's dialogue set to Archer's plot for *Widowers' Houses*, Archer fell asleep, and the collaboration was through. Shaw and Archer had "played it by ear:" Archer heard Shaw's dialogue, Shaw heard Archer's snoring. Moss Hart, who said, "writing is the loneliest of the professions," found collaboration far more agreeable than working

492

alone. Hart, moreover, suggests he took every care to encourage harmony in working with Kaufman, for though their relationship bordered on the personal, Kaufman of aloof disposition never encouraged the intimacy of close friendship.

Bella and Samuel Spewack, who wrote the book for the musical *Kiss Me Kate,* were married; their working relationship had to be played by ear to keep in tune with the wedding march. Lawrence Langner believed that if one collaborator, for example, is gifted in structure while the other excells in characterization, each should respect the other's forte if the collaboration is to survive. "Our working rule is simple," wrote Jerome Lawrence and Robert E. Lee of their collaboration in such plays as *Inherit the Wind* and their adaptation of the novel, *Auntie Mame,* into the play, and the movie, *Auntie Mame,* and then into the musical *Mame:* "Both must approve everything. Corollary: The one who doesn't approve, has the burden of improving, to the approval of the other." [2] Even the viewpoint of Lawrence and Lee is eye to eye. "As we see it," they stated, "the playwright in mid-century is more and more the interpretive journalist, the prober into our times." [3] If collaborators don't see eye to eye, the result can literally be cross-eyed.

Very likely the best way to promote collaboration is for it to succeed. "When the basic idea of a play was a good one," noted Hart of collaborating with Kaufman, "our collaboration worked well, and when it was not, it did not work at all." [4] Even success doesn't always preserve a collaboration. Kaufman and Hart did not collaborate on another play after their success with *George Washington Slept Here.* A recently much publicized example suggests the very sensitive adjustment of collaborators. After the death of Oscar Hammerstein II, Richard Rodgers in 1964 tried to collaborate with Alan J. Lerner on a musical. Lerner's usual collaborator, Frederick Loewe, had chosen retirement after a severe coronary attack. Rodgers and Lerner, however, soon parted without creating a single work together. On the other hand, in 1942, Larry Hart, for over fifteen years Rodgers' collaborator, chose for personal reasons not to collaborate with Rodgers in writing the musical, *Oklahoma!,* and so Rodgers teamed up with Oscar Hammerstein II. "What happened between Oscar and me was almost chemical," Richard Rodgers told his biographer, David Ewen. "Put the right components together and an explosion takes place. Oscar and I hit it off from the day we began discussing the show." [5] And yet under agreeable circumstances, Rodgers had been just as content with Hart. "We have never had any sort of contract," Rodgers said of working with Hart. "Obviously then, what has kept us together and will probably continue to do so is a mutual respect, a mutual responsibility, and a mutual aim." [6] Even the most successful and distinguished of collaborators can only "play it by ear."

Genesis

Genesis in collaboration has one indispensable condition: collaborators must communicate somehow to set up a contagious excitement. To illustrate, the most famous play about World War I, *What Price Glory?*, began as a casual conversation to fill in a lull in the to-do of the editorial rooms of *The New York World* where Lawrence Stallings and Maxwell Anderson made a living trying to write up the larger significance of current affairs. Stallings, incidentally, had been a literary editor for the *World* the previous year and had written a novel as well as news stories on the drama; Anderson had had a Broadway failure, a poetic drama, *White Desert*. For the fun of it, Stallings told Anderson of a pet notion he had to write a musical comedy about his experiences as a marine in the American occupation of Haiti. Anderson was intrigued enough to lead Stallings on to tell more and more anecdotes, especially about his experiences with the Fourth Brigade of the Second Division of Marines and their lives and loves in France during World War I. The more Stallings talked, the more Anderson grew convinced that a really big story was not in a musical about the Marines' occupation of Haiti, but in Stallings' World War I experiences in France, and Anderson told Stallings so. The two in a contagious fever of enthusiasm made copious notes between editorializing, and Anderson took these notes and wrote the whole first draft of the play in six nights at the reading room of the New York Public Library, 42nd Street and Fifth Avenue. Anderson's own apartment was small and crowded, what with a wife and two little children at a rather noisy age. *What Price Glory?* spontaneously took on body and soul from an unexpected joint enthusiasm.

Collaborators must not only communicate but must allow for chance and time to mature potentially exciting material. Referring to *You Can't Take It with You, I'd Rather Be Right,* and *The Man Who Came to Dinner,* Moss Hart told an interviewer for *The New York Times* of October 29, 1939, "For it is a matter of actual fact that all of the afore-mentioned plays (to say nothing of several others) were not the plays we meant to write at all. Some heaven-sent chance happened to swerve us."[7] Hart, for instance, told of how four years earlier he and Kaufman had met in Pasadena, each teeming with ideas for a new collaboration; "on the basis of a chance remark that had been dropped by one of us two years before that, and as idly recalled," said Moss Hart, "we were deep in the first act of what turned out to be *You Can't Take It with You*."[8] A mere interruption, thought Hart, like a telephone ringing, and *You Can't Take It with You* might never have been written.

Kaufman and Hart at the critical moment had just cooled to what at first had seemed like a "hot" idea for a play to be called *Washington Jitters*. "What about your other idea?" asked Kaufman. "You mean the one about the mad family?" replied Hart. The two had talked over the idea the previous winter in New York. "It was then only the merest germ," the interview with Hart reported, "simply the notion of building a comedy around a group of utterly mad but lovable people, each of whom did the thing nearest to his or her heart's desire and the hell with what the other folks thought." The rest of *You Can't Take It With You* came to life with the spontaneity of a "natural." "In this particular play," reportedly, "the characters came first."[9] In roughly three days of running discussion, Kaufman and Hart nurtured every member of the Sycamore household into reasonably full growth, complete with eccentricities and hobbies. The characters then created the play so spontaneously for their creators that within that very week Kaufman and Hart sent this unprecedented wire to their producer, Sam Harris: "DEAR SAM WE START WORK ON NEW PLAY TOMORROW MORNING STOP CAN YOU TIE UP AT ONCE JOSEPHINE HULL GEORGE TOBIAS FRANK CONLAN OSCAR POLK STOP WE ARE ENGAGING HENRY TRAVERS HERE STOP MOSS AND GEORGE."[10] The keen visualisation of the roles in terms of the very actors who would play them must have helped write the play and especially given it nuances. "When an idea is sound," noted Hart in his late years, "it writes easily . . ."

The collaboration of Jerome Lawrence and Robert E. Lee suggests a somewhat opposite approach to genesis because of the nature of the material involved: a heavy reliance upon detailed documentation to substantiate an exciting hunch, as with *Inherit the Wind*. This play, of course, is based upon the world famous "Monkey Trial" in Dayton, Tennessee, on July 10-21, 1925. A school teacher named John Thomas Scopes allowed himself to become a test case against Tennessee's Butler Law forbidding any teacher in a publicly supported school or college "to teach any theory that denies the story of the divine creation of man as taught in the *Bible,* and to teach instead that man has descended from a lower order of animals." [11] The lawyer and revivalist preacher, William Jennings Bryan, prosecuted Scopes with the fervor of a fundamentalist Christian, and Clarence Darrow, America's best known criminal lawyer at the time, defended Scopes with the reasoned view of not only Darwin but of science as it pertained to the *Bible.* The story was old news about twenty-five years later, but what brought it to the collaborators' minds as living history was a study that one of them was making for his master's thesis, examining the difference in the way Maxwell Anderson treated the Sacco-Vanzetti case in two plays: *Gods of Lightning,* documentary in spirit; and *Winterset,* in the spirit of poetic license. What Anderson had done for Sacco and Vanzetti in *Winterset,* Lawrence and Lee suddenly realized they might do for Scopes, Darrow, and Bryan in *Inherit the Wind,* for these people in a sense were human beings representing great forces in conflict in modern thought. Lawrence and Lee reported in *Theatre Arts* magazine of August, 1957:

> For more than a year we haunted libraries and secondhand bookstores. We read the complete files of the *New York Times* and the *Chattanooga Times,* the day-to-day and hour-to-hour accounts of Dayton's sweltering carnival. We searched out every book on the Darrow-Bryan clash and even uncovered a stinging essay from the more remote viewpoint of George Bernard Shaw. We tried to learn about Bryan, Darrow and Mencken as if they were father, brother, and son. Our notes would have made six plays. Having allowed the juices to flow through us, we put aside the facts and allowed the fiction to take over.[12]

The collaborators took the poetic license of finding a larger, lasting meaning in the trial. They used none of the actual names and very few actual quotes of the trial.

With musicals costing $250,000–$500,000 these days, to minimize the risk the genesis of a musical has been reduced largely to a search for proven material that excites creative talent to collaborate on the book, the music, and the lyrics. "Success," observed Langner of a musical, "almost invariably depends upon a good book, which is even rarer to find than a good score." [13] Musicals with good books but undistinguished scores, like *Baker Street,* somehow reasonably survive but almost never does a musical with a good score but a poor book survive. A quick glance at the best musicals over the years suggests a very heavy reliance of collaborators upon proven material to excite genesis: *Porgy and Bess* from *Porgy; Carousel,* from *Liliom; My Fair Lady* from *Pygmalion; Kismet* from *Kismet; West-Side Story* from a modern equivalent of the Romeo and Juliet story; *Oliver* from *Oliver Twist; Fiddler on the Roof* from the Tevye stories of Sholom Aleichem; *Baker Street* from the Sherlock Holmes stories of Sir Arthur Conan Doyle; *Cabaret* from *I Am a Camera* adapted by John Van Druten from the Berlin stories by Christopher Isherwood. To excite genesis for a musical, prospective material should have a considerable lyric line and plenty of excitement that naturally calls for song and dance to do what words alone cannot do. A composer, or lyricist, or writer of the book—sometimes these functions are combined in one or two or three people—may try to spot these places in a potential script and then set up a contagious creative excitement among collaborators.

Oklahoma! provides an example of the genesis of a musical suggesting the circuitous and chance route often involved even for what was to become a classic American musical. *Oklahoma!* really began with the fervent faith of Theresa Helburn in the potential of Lynn Riggs' *Green Grow the Lilacs* to make a good musical and thereby save The Theatre Guild from imminent bankruptcy in 1942. The Guild had produced *Green Grow the Lilacs* on January 25, 1931, and so Helburn had a good idea of the visual appeal of the story and the setting for a musical. The play, however, had a Broadway run of only 64 performances. What the Guild had done to make *Porgy* into *Porgy and Bess,* Helburn believed the Guild could do to make *Green Grow the Lilacs* into an equally fine musical. The fact that *Porgy and Bess* had been a financial failure in 1935 did not deter Helburn; perhaps she figured that if the Guild were to go down in a sea of debt, it was best to go down with its finest colors proudly flying. Helburn had Rodgers and Hart in mind to do the songs; they had written songs for two early Guild experimental successes, *The Garrick Gaieties*. The Guild in effect had opened Broadway to Rodgers and Hart, and now ironically, Rodgers and Hart were the Guild's hope to keep from being itself closed to Broadway.

"I decided the moment had come for the fulfillment of my dream," said Helburn with escape from the nightmare of the Guild's possible bankruptcy no doubt also on her mind, "the production of a totally new kind of play with music, not a musical comedy in the familiar sense, but a play in which music and dancing would be aids to and adjuncts of the plot itself in telling the story." [14] As the unswerving master spirit in the venture, Helburn then talked to Rodgers and Hart of doing what she had in mind with Riggs' play about cowboys and farmers in Indian Territory. Though Rodgers was enthusiastic, Hart felt unsuited to the folk material and gave Rodgers full freedom to pick another collaborator. Rodgers picked Oscar Hammerstein II.

Hammerstein came with excellent yet forbidding credentials. In 1927, he had with Jerome Kern written the classic musical, *Showboat,* based on Edna Ferber's novel and in essence an American folk play with music. By 1942, although he had a great many famous songs to his credit as a lyricist, Hammerstein had nothing but a record of failure in musicals on Broadway for the previous ten years. In first conferring with Rodgers, Hammerstein confided that he had once tried to get Jerome Kern interested in doing a musical on the Riggs play but that Kern found too many problems in the script. Helburn's creative excitement had spread in full blaze to Rodgers and revived an earlier excitement in Hammerstein. Now all three believed—producer, book and lyric writer, and composer. Rodgers and Hammerstein II had so much faith in their collaboration that though they had a standard Guild contract if the new musical were to succeed, they were content to accept only a few hundred dollars for all their labors if the musical failed.

Developing the Play

George S. Kaufman had many collaborators in his life-time, for instance, Marc Connelly, Moss Hart, Morrie Ryskind, Edna Ferber, Katharine Dayton, and Leueen McGrath. His method of incubating a play was generally about the same; perhaps "doctoring" a play is a more apt term, for often a very promising first draft of some playwright might be submitted to Kaufman for collaboration to bring to full realization. The torment of Kaufman almost "losing a patient" varied from play to play, but the method of treatment didn't. As Moss Hart recalled, "Our working hours were from eleven in the morning until five thirty or six in the evening . . ." during the creation of *Once in a Lifetime.*[15] Working in his study, Kaufman would begin each session like a surgeon meticulously washing his hands, according to Hart, "as though the anatomy of a play were a living thing whose internal organs were to be explored surgically." Kaufman's basic approach to play doctoring was "cut down to the bare bones," noted Hart, ". . . to get a clean look at it, until we could glimpse what was wrong and had an idea of how to solve it." [16] Dialogue could be valid only to fill out the right organic structure. While working, Kaufman would pace while Hart would man the typewriter. Occasionally Kaufman ate his own home-made fudge for energy and found creative stimulation somewhat Yogi fashion from the relaxation and the flow of blood to his head in lying prone on his back on the floor of the study. Kaufman and Hart's deliberations led to excisions and new growth in the action and yet, "an outline or scenario," Hart admitted, "is an imprecise instrument at best." [17] A character taking over in the writing, for instance, might give the play a new emphasis that called for marked changes elsewhere.

Kaufman so much liked Katharine Dayton's first draft of a play about Washington's social whirl that he consented to collaborate with her. Here is Dayton's recollection of her first work session with Kaufman:

> For five hours we walked and we walked and we walked around my apartment . . . At the end of that time, we really had an outline of a play of which, incidentally, only our two chief women characters and our Secretary of State survived to reach *First Lady*.[18]

So demanding was Kaufman that he would begin each work session with the comment, "Do you want to see if we have a play?" [19] Kaufman helped develop *First Lady* by periodically setting it aside to be nurtured by his unconscious mind while he went off to work with Morrie Ryskind on *Merrily We Roll Along*.

"We did our arguing and battling before anything was set on paper," said Edna Ferber of developing the action to create *The Land Is Bright* with Kaufman.[20] To gather authentic detail for another collaboration, *Stage-Door*, Ferber even posed as a lady from Boston and visited The Rehearsal Club, a theatrical residence for aspiring actresses in New York City, and asked many questions on the pretense of looking for proper accommodations for a niece planning to study acting in town.

"The method of collaboration that the men used for *Oklahoma!*," wrote Stanley Green in his biography, *The Rodgers and Hammerstein Story*, "set the model for all of their shows. After spending months talking over the story line and the places that they thought required songs, the men would then part." [21] Each would work on his own. After Hammerstein finished a lyric, he would phone or mail it to Rodgers who would then set music to it. But each brought to his part of the collaboration an attitude they kept through the years.

Rodgers had in his phrase "an almost psychopathic fear of something called Formula." From authoring the books and lyrics of roughly twenty-five musicals previous to *Oklahoma!,* Hammerstein could not but acquire Rodgers' hatred of "Formula." "In less than fifteen years," Rodgers recalled while still collaborating with Hart in 1940, "we have watched teams of writers and teams of producers enter the field, grow enormously successful, and quietly fade from the picture because of Formula. . . . 'This is the way we did it the last time. It worked, so let's try it again.' " [22] Rodgers then thought that a better fate than formula musicals would be to go into a business where a formula counts, like a hat shop. In developing the story line of *Oklahoma!,* Rodgers and Hammerstein kept faith with Theresa Helburn and with themselves. They decided that the folk story of the play must determine the musical techniques, and not the clichés of musical comedy determine the folk story. "We realized that such a course was experimental, amounting almost to a breach of an implied contract with a musical comedy audience," said Hammerstein. "Once we made the decision everything seemed to work right, and we had the inner confidence people feel when they have adopted the direct and honest approach to a problem." [23]

Traditionally, musicals called for a very early display of chorus girls. Riggs' folk story offered no such chance in the first act and so Rodgers and Hammerstein introduced no such display then. The collaborators avoided other clichés like gags, scanty dress for the girls, big production numbers not organic to the action, and non-violent conflict. They kept every element of production as organic as in a good play. For instance, in faithfulness to the story they kept Jud's murder, unconventional though it might be for a musical. "Experience has taught me," Hammerstein observed in his late years with the incredible success of *Oklahoma!* a good fifteen years behind, "that audiences follow the story. . . . If it isn't firm, then all the jokes and all the songs and the chorus and the beautiful production all fall in a heap." [24] The epochal success of *Oklahoma!* as a musical making everything germane to the text, set the basic pattern for America's best musicals following World War II. *Oklahoma!* ran for over five years on Broadway and for over ten years on the road, not to mention a world-wide popularity in almost every civilized capitol city. No producer could ignore the organic book and lyrics that brought in such a fantastic flow of gold to the box-office.

Jerome Lawrence and Robert E. Lee have said of developing their plays in collaboration:

> We belong to the peripatetic school of playwriting. Good plays are basically good conversation. We converse a play. We talk about it for months, even years, before beginning the actual writing. During this time, we play Boswell to each other, taking copious and usually disorganized notes.[25]

Through talking out each idea at great length, the pair has found that what might first have seemed an attractive notion for a play actually lacks the substance to fill a whole evening's entertainment. "Most of the failures of responsible dramatists," Lawrence and Lee believe, "are plays that should not have been written." [26] "How many authors in middle age," they assert, "find themselves writing the same old characters through slightly different situations?" [27] Talking out a play tends to prevent such circular thinking. The pair are committed to absolute honesty as they alternate as creator and critic, allowing the special gift of each to prevail in moments of doubt which call for a special gift to resolve. So complete is the merging of talents in developing a promising idea that these collaborators contend it is impossible to tell from the completed work what each alone has contributed. Likely the most important thing of all they give each other is renewed faith. They were almost the only ones who thought successful plays could be made from the "Monkey Trial" in Dayton, Tennessee, and from the novel, *Auntie Mame*. *Auntie Mame* was to run for 639 performances on Broadway, score another hit as a movie, and then in 1966, with Lawrence and Lee doing the book, score still another hit as the musical, *Mame*.

Writing and Rewriting

With the scenario more or less plotted on paper or in mind, collaborators are then ready for the actual writing of the script. Again they "play it by ear," keeping attuned to every means to promote harmony and to avoid discord.

Roi Cooper Megrue said, "For the most part collaborators meet to discuss and part to write." [28] Working solo on a script is especially favored by those who through long habit are accustomed to working best and fastest alone. The collaborators meet to discuss after each in turn has done his stint on a new draft. The meeting may take place through one or a variety of means: person to person, mail, telegram, telephone, or whatever the ingenuity of collaborators can devise and is convenient to both.

Maxwell Anderson wrote the whole first draft of *What Price Glory?* on his own, with Stallings' and Anderson's copious notes to guide him. Anderson took only six nights to do it at the reading room of the Public Library. Then he simply handed Stallings the script to read and rewrite. Stallings had been in the Marine Corps and knew the ways and the idiom of Marines; Anderson had been draft exempt as a married man with two children. Stallings' rewriting gave Anderson's first draft the authentic detail it needed. "The dug-out in his hands," reported an interviewer for *The New York Times* of Stallings' revision, "began to resemble a real dug-out and the people in it emerged as startling, true counterfeits of the frightened and brave and lofty and shallow and stalwart and maimed boys and men who really lived in it." [29] How many separate revisions and then joint discussions the script went through, the collaborators never said specifically. "*What Price Glory?* was finished according to legend in three weeks," said Roi Cooper Megrue, "but it had two authors." [30]

In the actual writing of *The Pursuit of Happiness,* Langner did the first draft, and his wife, Armina Marshall, the second draft—a revision of the first, of course. The couple then took turns rewriting until the seventh draft which they rewrote together. Philip Barry and Elmer Rice followed a similar routine in writing their mystery play, *Cock Robin,* but their entire contact between drafts consisted of letters, telephone calls, and telegrams.

After months of discussion in which they settled on their scenario, Rodgers and Hammerstein parted to write. Hammerstein worked best alone in his study on his farm in Pennsylvania, applying himself to the book and the lyrics. Rodgers worked best alone at his home in New York City or at his country place in Connecticut, applying himself to the music and waiting for Hammerstein to write him a lyric before Rodgers attempted the melody. Hammerstein realized that to allow time for song and dance, the book of a musical had to use dialogue far more succinct than that of a play. "A professional toils, and sweats and polishes," said Hammerstein of his labors. "He doesn't submit his work to anyone until he has done everything he can think of to make his song good." [31] Once satisfied with a lyric, Hammerstein would phone Rodgers and read it to him, or possibly mail it to Rodgers.

Much has been made of the fantastic speed with which Rodgers wrote some of his finest melodies. Hammerstein admitted to taking three weeks to write the lyric for *Oh, What a Beautiful Morning!* while Rodgers with the lyric in hand completed the waltz music for the lyric in less than ten minutes. What is often quite overlooked, is that through months of discussion of the story with Hammerstein and also of settling on the position of possible songs as well as their likely nature, Rodgers would be most sensitively pre-conditioned and attuned to Hammerstein's lyrics long before they arrived. Rodgers would write a melody in a burst of spontaneity because his subconscious mind had been relating to it for months or more.

If many distinguished collaborators have met to discuss and then parted to write, at least as many or more have met to discuss and continued to meet to write. Some, like Kaufman, in playing their collaboration by ear, have shown even from fragmentary reports their sensitive adjustment to different collaborators. Marc Connelly gave this account to *The Saturday Evening Post:*

> We discuss everything together. After we have decided on the plot and trimmings, someone says, "I'll start on this act and you do the second." If the play happens to be around a crisis, we work that out first. Before we part to do any work, however, we get an anchor—a good architect's blueprint of what the whole round plan of the play will be.[32]

Connelly continued, "Things which seemed to be all right to us individually turn out to be overwritten or underwritten or cloudy." Kaufman and Connelly would plainly alternate as critic and creator in a congenial fashion. Suggesting their exacting professionalism, Connelly recalled, "—we pay a call on a particular character—go through the whole piece, paying attention to him or her alone, to see if everything he says is consistent with his personality as we've conceived it." [33] This is how *Dulcy,* for example, was written.

Kaufman's practice in writing *First Lady* in collaboration with Katharine Dayton, shows a variation. "The truth is that George Kaufman does his best writing walking around," reported Dayton, "and his best cutting sitting down. Don't ask me why—he just does, that's all." [34] One task, of course, is largely creative, while the other is largely critical. "Warmth, depth, height, length, breadth, life, and love and Laska were put into and taken out of *First Lady,*" recalled Dayton of the struggle of her and Kaufman obviously working in the same room together to make *First Lady* live. "The great brass Kaufman scrap baskets were filled and emptied," said Dayton, "as Ol' Massa cut and cut and cut." [35]

Edna Ferber remarked of collaborating with Kaufman on *Stage-Door,* "Every single speech was discussed and sometimes acted out before it was written." The collaborators worked from 11 a.m. to 3 p.m. each day for about two months. In writing *You Can't Take It with You,* Kaufman and Hart made and kept a verbal agreement to spend ten days doing each act together, writing and testing their dialogue out loud as they went along. The task took a month.

Just as in solo authorship, collaborators rewrite as much as seems needed. And if the rewriting of collaborators proves to be of no avail during the pre-Broadway road tour, a producer sometimes calls in a play doctor whom he hopes can diagnose the trouble and correct it with some kind of miracle drug. Sometimes in spite of the most frantic doctoring on the road, an ailing production simply dies; the ill-fated musical *Kelly,* for example, cost $650,000 to mount and opened on Broadway, February 6, 1965, and after one performance, closed. Sometimes, a play doctor seems to perform wonders; the musical, *Golden Boy,* was seriously ailing on its pre-Broadway road tour, but William Gibson was called in to perform play surgery and administer medications, and somehow *Golden Boy,* with Sammy Davis as star, acquired a reasonably healthy 14 karat gold quality.

Perhaps the classic instance of collaborators "playing it by ear" to rewrite a failure into a success during a road tour try-out, is Kaufman and Hart's *Once in a Lifetime.* A two week try-out in Atlantic City and Brooklyn's Brighton Beach in the spring of 1930 showed from audience reaction that only the first half of *Once in a Lifetime* was good comedy and the second half was not. Frantic rewriting and rehearsal failed to notably improve the second half. Kaufman finally felt his energy and resourcefulness exhausted and frankly told Hart that *Once in a Lifetime* was all his for the taking. Hart knew that what George S. Kaufman had abandoned, no manager would care to touch. In desperation the next day, Hart went to Brighton Beach and took along a writing pad, a pencil, a bagful of sandwiches, and some soda pop. Whatever did it—possibly the adrenalin from his desperation along with a return to the approximate spot where Hart had written the play's first draft—Hart finished his day with enough related creative flashes of insight to quite excite the exhausted Kaufman to further revision. The play's scenery was hopefully stored in a warehouse.

For the next two months of that summer of 1930, Hart lived and worked in Kaufman's home in New York City.

When *Once in a Lifetime* opened its pre-Broadway tour in Philadelphia that fall, the first two acts played like a smash-hit, but the third act was way wide of the mark. With success so near and his professional pride at stake, Kaufman like a man demoniacally possessed, set to work with Hart to revise the third act. After each evening's performance, the collaborators would spend the rest of the night revising the third act; by the following 11 a.m. the revisions would be typed and Kaufman would be rehearsing them with the cast onstage. The audience's reaction to the revision would then carefully be watched in the play's next performance. The audience continued to leave the theater glum. Kaufman and Hart continued their frantic attempts to save the play, but nothing seemed to work. Time had all but run out before the scheduled Broadway opening. "Comedies usually have to be ninety-five per cent air tight," Kaufman told Hart, "at least that's my experience." [36] Kaufman rated their play as seventy per cent "air-tight." On the fifth day before the play's Broadway opening, as Moss Hart related in *Act One,* the house receipts in Philadelphia dwindled to $104.85, which means practically an empty theatre. After the performance that evening, Kaufman had to go to New York City on urgent business. Sam Harris, the producer of *Once in a Lifetime,* had a talk with Hart over a glass of beer; he told Hart that *Once in a Lifetime* was one of the noisiest plays he had ever been around. "I think they're longing to see that stage just once," said Harris of the audience, "with maybe two or three people on it quietly talking the whole thing over." [37]

Hart left Harris and in a desperate hunt for a creative brainstorm to save his play, Hart went for a walk. By 4 a.m., he was still walking; he happened to find he was passing a children's playground, and to rest his feet, he sat on a swing. Soon he was swinging himself higher and higher in the moonlight when abruptly, as he put, "I thought I saw clearly where we had gone wrong, and then in a sudden flash of improvisation, exactly the right way to resolve it." [38] The revision would mean junking $20,000 worth of scenery from the gaudy Pigeon's Egg cafe setting of the third act, and in its place, using the scenery of the first act's Hollywood studio and the pullman train. Hart's new third act would show the aftermath of the mania Hollywood was suffering from the technological revolution brought on by the "talkies." The third act would show this aftermath through its effect upon the lives of the author, Vane, played by Kaufman, and the actress May Daniels, played by Jean Dixon, as they flee Hollywood and return East after having "had it." When Kaufman returned to Philadelphia the next day and heard what revisions Hart had in mind, he first balked but then gave in; without a new third act, Kaufman and Hart knew that *Once in a Lifetime* was a certain flop. "When an idea is sound," said Hart of rewriting the whole third act of the play in one day, "it writes easily, and I struck pay dirt early." [39] Polished with Kaufman on the following night, rehearsed the next morning and afternoon, and tried out the last night of the play's run in Philadelphia, the third act now worked like a charm on the quite tiny paying audience. *Once in a Lifetime* scored a smash-hit in New York City on its opening night at the Music Box Theatre, September 23, 1930. A photo-finish revision of the whole third act had literally saved the play. Such an experience shows what revision at best can do.

CHAPTERS IX, X, XI: ACKNOWLEDGEMENTS

My grateful acknowledgement is extended to the following sources of quotations:

Books

ACT ONE by Moss Hart. Copyright 1959. Reprinted by permission of Random House, Inc. and Secker & Warburg Ltd.

AMERICAN PLAYWRIGHTS ON DRAMA edited by Horst Frenz, a Dramabook, Hill and Wang, 1965

AROUND THEATRES by Max Beerbohm, Knopf, 1930

THE ART OF PLAYWRITING, a compilation of a series of lectures by modern playwrights. Copyright 1928. Reprinted by permission of Pennsylvania University Press.

THE BIOGRAPHICAL ENCYCLOPAEDIA AND WHO'S WHO OF THE AMERICAN THEATRE edited by Walter Rigdon, James H. Heineman, Inc., 1966

COLLECTED PLAYS by Arthur Miller with a New Essay on His Dramatic Technique. Copyright 1961. Reprinted by permission of Viking Press and Ashley Famous Agency, Inc.

THE COMPLETE SHORT STORIES OF W. SOMERSET MAUGHAM, EAST AND WEST, VOL. I. Copyright 1934 by W. Somerset Maugham. Copyright 1938 by W. Somerset Maugham. Reprinted by permission of Doubleday & Company, Inc., William Heinemann Ltd., and A. P. Watt and Son, The Literary Executor for the Estate of W. Somerset Maugham.

CURRENT BIOGRAPHY YEARBOOK, the H. W. Wilson Co., issues 1940–1965.

THE DARK AT THE TOP OF THE STAIRS by William Inge. Copyright 1958. Reprinted by permission of Random House, Inc. and William Inge.

DECLARATION edited by Tom Maschler, "They Call It Cricket" by John Osborne, E. P. Dutton and Co., Inc., and MacGibbon and Kee Ltd., 1957

DRAMATIC HERITAGE by Paul Green, Samuel French, 1953

DRAMATIS PERSONAE by John Mason Brown, Viking Press, 1963

DRAMATIC TECHNIQUE by George Pierce Baker, Houghton Mifflin Co., 1919.

THE ESSENCE OF TRAGEDY AND OTHER FOOTNOTES AND PAPERS,

THE PERFORMING ARTS: PROBLEMS AND PROSPECTS, Rockefeller Panel Report on the future of theatre, dance, music in America, McGraw-Hill Book Co., 1965

THE PLAYBOY OF THE WESTERN WORLD by John Millington Synge, Maunsel & Co., Ltd., 1907

PLAY-MAKING, A MANUAL OF CRAFTSMANSHIP by William Archer, Dover Publications, 1960. Reprinted by permission.

THE PLAY'S THE THING by Lawrence Langner. Copyright 1960. Reprinted by permission of G. P. Putnam's Sons and Longmans, Green & Co.

THE PLAYWRIGHT AS THINKER by Eric Bentley. Copyright 1946. Reprinted by permission of Harcourt, Brace & World, Inc.

PLAYWRIGHT AT WORK by John Van Druten. Copyright 1953. Reprinted by permission of Harper & Row, Publishers, Inc.

PLAYWRIGHTS ON PLAYMAKING by Brander Mathews, Charles Scribner's Sons, 1923.

PLAYWRIGHTS ON PLAYWRITING, edited by Toby Cole. Copyright 1961, A Dramabook, Hill and Wang.

Reprinted by permission of the publishers from T. S. Eliot's POETRY AND DRAMA, Cambridge, Mass.: Harvard University Press, Copyright 1951, by the President and Fellows of Harvard College.

PRESENT INDICATIVE by Noel Coward. Copyright 1937 by Noel Coward. Reprinted by permission of Doubleday & Company, Inc. and Curtis Brown Ltd.

PROBLEMS OF THE PLAYWRIGHT by Clayton Hamilton, copyright 1917, 1945. Reprinted by permission of Holt, Rinehart and Winston, Inc.

PRODUCING THE PLAY by John Gassner, Dryden Press, 1941. Reprinted by permission of Holt, Rinehart and Winston, Inc.

RICHARD RODGERS by David Ewen, Henry Holt and Co., 1957

THE ROAD TO THE TEMPLE by Susan Glaspell. Copyright 1927. Reprinted by permission of Curtis Brown Ltd.

THE RODGERS AND HAMMERSTEIN STORY by Stanley Green, John Day Company, Inc., 1963

SELECTED PREFACES AND INTRODUCTIONS by W. Somerset Maugham, copyright 1963. Reprinted by permission of Doubleday & Company, Inc., William Heinemann Ltd., and A. P. Watt and Son, The Literary Executor of the Estate of W. Somerset Maugham.

SHAKESPEARE AND HIS CRITICS by C. F. Johnson, Houghton Mifflin Co., Inc., 1909

SO YOU'RE WRITING A PLAY by Clayton Hamilton, Little, Brown and Co., 1935.

THE SUMMING UP by W. Somerset Maugham. Copyright 1938 by W. Somerset Maugham. Reprinted by permission of Doubleday & Company, Inc., William Heinemann Ltd., and A. P. Watt and Son, The Literary Executor of the Estate of W. Somerset Maugham.

Periodicals

Allan Seager. Copyright 1959. Reprinted by permission of Ashley Famous Agency, Inc.

FORTUNE magazine, February 1938, "Theatre Business;" November 1964, "The Hard Life of an Angel." Reprinted by permission.

HARPER'S magazine:

"A Platform and a Passion or Two" by Thornton Wilder, October 1957, Copyright (c) 1957 by Thornton Wilder; used as a preface to THREE PLAYS by Thorton Wilder. Reprinted by permission of Harper & Row, Publishers, Inc., and Brandt & Brandt

"The Shadows of the Gods" by Arthur Miller, August 1958. Reprinted by permission of Harper & Row, Publishers, Inc., and Ashley Famous Agency, Inc.

"What Happens Out of Town" by Jean Kerr, June 1960

HARPER'S WEEKLY, March 29, 1913, "Dramatizing the Present" by David Belasco

LIFE magazine:

"Perennial Hatcher of Hits and Talents" by Tom Prideaux, January 18, 1960

"A Desperate Search for a Troubled Hero" by Tom Prideaux, February 7, 1964

"With Respect for Her Agony but with Love" by Arthur Miller, February 7, 1964. Reprinted by permission of Ashley Famous Agency, Inc.

(C) 1960, 1964 by TIME, Inc. Reprinted by permission of LIFE.

LITERARY DIGEST, August 4, 1934, "The Playwright Is the Thing" by Sam H. Harris

LIVING AGE, May 1931, "Maugham Discusses Drama"

MADEMOISELLE, March 1963, "Five Playwrights Talk about How They Got There"

NEW STATESMAN AND NATION:

"Concerning the Play of Ideas" by Terence Rattigan, March 4, 1950

"The Play of Ideas" by Ben Levy, March 25, 1950

"The Play of Ideas" by Sean O'Casey, April 8, 1950

"The Play of Ideas" by Christopher Fry, April 22, 1950

(C) 1950 by NEW STATESMAN. Reprinted by permission.

NEW YORK HERALD TRIBUNE:

"Stage Asides: Miss Hellman Tells of Her Latest Play, THE LITTLE FOXES" by Lucius Beebe, March 12, 1939

"Stage Asides: Arsenic and Mr. Kesselring" by Lucius Beebe, June 15, 1941

"It Appears Two Persons Wrote Latest Kaufman-Ferber Play," November 23, 1941

"The Playbill: Lillian Hellman" by Otis L. Guernsey, October 24, 1943

"CRY OF THE PEACOCK Was a Paris Hit" by Michael Horton, April 2, 1950

Reprinted by permission of New York Herald Tribune Co., Inc.

512   CHAPTERS IX, X XI: ACKNOWLEDGEMENTS

NEW YORK TIMES:

"*What Price Glory* and Its Authors," September 14, 1924

"First Night Amenities" by J. Brooks Atkinson, February 1, 1931

"It Must Be Such Fun to Work with George S. Kaufman" by K. Dayton, December 8, 1935

"En-Nobeling O'Neill" by Brooks Atkinson, "Tuesday Evening at 8:30" by Noel Coward, November 22, 1936

"Why YOU CAN'T TAKE IT WITH YOU," December 20, 1936

"How A. W. Came to Dinner and Other Stories" by Moss Hart, October 1939

"Life with Fathers" by Alison Smith, December 10, 1939

"A Score of Years and One" by Richard Rodgers, May 5, 1940. Reprinted by permission of Richard Rodgers.

"Women Playmakers" by C. Hughes, May 4, 1941

"Research for a Comedy" by John Van Druten, December 6, 1942

"A Tribute to Fulda" by S. N. Behrman, February 7, 1943

"Characters Offstage" by John Van Druten, December 5, 1943

"What Makes Comedy High?" by S. N. Behrman, March 30, 1952. Reprinted by permission of Brandt and Brandt.

"The World of Eugene Ionesco" by Eugene Ionesco, June 1, 1958

"O'Casey's Credo" by Sean O'Casey, November 9, 1958

"Ten Playwrights Tell How It All Starts" by Gilbert Millstein, December 6, 1959

"Which Theatre Is the Absurd One?" by Edward Albee, February 25, 1962. Literary Agent, William Morris Agency.

"Polish Students Question Arthur Miller" by David Halberstam, February 17, 1965

"What Makes Plays Endure?" by Arthur Miller, August 15, 1965. Reprinted by permission of Ashley Famous Agency, Inc.

"The Theater Today: No Place for Drama" by Sam Zolotow, June 21, 1965

"Doc Simon's RX for Comedy" by Alan Levy, March 7, 1965. Reprinted by permission of Alan Levy.

"Merrick Gets His 'Subsidy'" by Lewis Funke, February 13, 1966

(C) 1924, 1931, 1935, 1936, 1939, 1943, 1958, 1959, 1962, 1965, 1966 by The New York Times Company. Reprinted by permission.

NEWSWEEK magazine:

"Talk with the Author," October 29, 1962

"Albee: Odd Man in on Broadway," February 4, 1963

"History Onstage," January 31, 1966

(c) 1962, 1963, 1966. Reprinted by permission.

SATURDAY EVENING POST:

"The First Three Acts the Hardest" by K. Sprohle and Roi Megrue, January 16, 1926

"Playwriting" by Owen Davis, September 27, 1930

"How to Become a Playwright" by Alva Johnson, March 15, 1941

SATURDAY REVIEW:
"Seventeen Playwrights Self-Appraised" compiled by Henry Hewes, May 7, 1955
"American Playwrights Self-Appraised" compiled by Henry Hewes, September 3, 1955
"Why Men Become Angels" by Arnold Maremont, February 23, 1957
"What's Right with the Theatre?" by John Mason Brown, May 11, 1963, with excerpt from H. M. Brown's book, DRAMATIS PERSONAE, Vanguard Press Reprinted by permission.
THEATRE ARTS magazine:
"Paul Green" by Barrett H. Clark, October 1928
"Playmaker to Broadway" (George S. Kaufman) by Carl Carmer, October 1932
"How to See" by William Saroyan, March 1941
"Letters from Sidney Howard" by Barrett H. Clark, April 1941
"4 Parts in 8 Weeks" by George Axelrod, January 1954. Reprinted by permission of George Axelrod.
"PICNIC—from FRONT PORCH to Broadway" by William Inge, April 1954. Reprinted by permission of William Inge.
"INHERIT THE WIND: The Genesis and Exodus of the Play" by Jerome Lawrence and Robert E. Lee. Reprinted by permission of Jerome Lawrence and Robert E. Lee
"Forgotten Anger" by William Inge, February 1958. Reprinted by permission of William Inge.
"Which One Can't Spell?" by Jerome Lawrence and Robert E. Lee, June 1958. Reprinted by permission of Jerome Lawrence and Robert E. Lee.
"More on the Playwright's Mission" by William Inge, August 1958. Reprinted by permission of William Inge.
"The Men Behind J. B." by Archibald MacLeish, April 1959. Reprinted by permission of Archibald MacLeish.
"Second Wind" by William Gibson, October 1959
"Me Tink Me Hear Sounds in de Night" by Lorraine Hansberry, October 1960
"The Book Had Better Be Good" by Oscar Hammerstein II, November 1960
"A Producer Should Produce" by John Keating, September 1961
"Odets at Center Stage", talk with Michael J. Mendelsohn, May 1963
"Odets at Center Stage", talk with Michael J. Mendelsohn continued, June 1963
THE TULANE DRAMA REVIEW:
"Death of a Salesman—A Symposium with Arthur Miller, Gore Vidal, Richard Watts, John Beaufort, Martin Dworkin, David W. Thompson, and Richard Gelb," May 1958, 67
"My Works" by Ernst Toller, translated by Marketa Goetz, March 1959, p. 221
"Discovering the Theatre" by Eugene Ionesco, translated by Leonard Pronko, September 1959, 7, 9, 11
"Beyond Bourgeois Theatre" by Jean-Paul Sarte, March 1961, 3

"An Interview with Jean-Paul Sartre" by Oreste F. Pucciani, pp. 14, 16

"Does the Italian Theatre Exist?" by Luciano Codignola, Spring, 1964, p. 21

VARIETY, March 16, 1966, "No. 1 Broadway Playwright, Neil Simon's 3 Current Clicks" by Hobe Morrison; June 15, 1966, "John Osborne Raps Back in Anger as London Critics Belt His 'Bond'; Kretzmer Sez 'That's Show Business' "

THE WRITER magazine:

"The Playwright and His Craft" by Robert Anderson, May 1955

"Myths of Present Day Playwriting" by Howard Teichmann, April 1962

Reprinted by permission of THE WRITER.

THE YALE REVIEW, October 1923, "The Playwright's Mind" by Jacinto Benavente. Reprinted by permission of THE YALE REVIEW.

CHAPTER IX: FOOTNOTES

1. David Belasco, *The Theatre Through Its Stage Door* (New York 1919), 50
2. Eugene Ionesco, "Discovering the Theatre," *Tulane Drama Review* (September 1959), 7
3. Jacinto Benavente, "The Playwright's Mind," *Yale Review* (October 1923), 60
4. *The Art of Playwriting,* 121
5. "Robert Anderson," *Current Biography* (1954), 22
6. "Paddy Chayefsky," ibid. (1957), 110
7. David Halberstam, "Polish Students Question Miller," *New York Times* (February 17, 1965), 36
8. Moss Hart, *Act One* (New York 1959), 6
9. George Abbott, *Mister Abbott* (New York 1963), 233
10. W. Somerset Maugham, *The Summing Up* (New York 1938), 178
11. *The Yale Review* (October 1923), 60
12. John Van Druten, "A Note about Myself," *New York Times* (December 6, 1925), Sect. 8, X
13. William Saroyan, "How to See," *Theatre Arts* (March 1941), 203
14. Thornton Wilder, "Some Thoughts on Playwriting," *The Intent of the Artist* (Princeton 1941), 86
15. "Five Playwrights Talk about How They Got There," *Mademoiselle* (March 1963), 215
16. "Howard Lindsay," *Twentieth Century Authors, First Supplement,* 584
17. "Lillian Hellman," *Twentieth Century Authors,* 634
18. "Arthur Laurents," *Twentieth Century Authors, First Supplement,* 556
19. "Susan Glaspell," *Twentieth Century Authors,* 541
20. Ibid., 868
21. "Lorraine Hansberry," *Current Biography* (1959), 166
22. "Paul Vincent Carroll," *Twentieth Century Authors,* 253
23. "Arthur Miller," *Twentieth Century Authors, First Supplement,* 669
24. "Sean O'Casey," *Twentieth Century Authors,* 1039
25. "Maugham Discusses Drama," *Living Age* (May 1931), 305
26. "Carson McCullers," *Twentieth Century Authors,* 868

27. "Harold Pinter," *Current Biography* (1963), 326
28. Michael Horton, *"Cry of the Peacock* Was a Paris Hit," *New York Herald Tribune* (April 2, 1950), Sect. 5, 1
29. "Robert Anderson," *Current Biography* (1954), 22
30. "Arthur Laurents," *Twentieth Century Authors, First Supplement,* 556
31. *Writers at Work* (New York 1963), 106
32. "The Hard Life of an Angel," *Fortune* (November 1964), 96
33. Howard Teichmann, "Myths of Present Day Playwriting," *The Writer* (April 1962), 36
34. Jed Harris, *Watchman, What of the Night?* (New York 1963), 83
35. *Fortune* (November 1964), 100
36. John Keating, "A Producer Should Produce," *Theatre Arts* (September 1961), 12
37. Ibid., 13
38. Lewis Funke, "Merrick Gets His 'Subsidy,' " *New York Times* (February 13, 1966), Sect. 2, 16X
39. Ibid.
40. Eric Bentley, *The Playwright as Thinker* (Cleveland 1955), xx
41. Ibid., 246
42. Sam Harris, "The Playwright's the Thing," *Literary Digest* (August 4, 1934), 23
43. Elmer Rice, *The Living Theatre* (New York 1959), 165
44. Richard Maney, *Fanfare* (New York 1957), 280
45. Ibid.
46. Tom Prideaux, "Perennial Hatcher of Hits and Talents," *Life* (January 18, 1960), 61
47. *Mister Abbott,* 248
48. Ibid.
49. Ibid., 176
50. Theresa Helburn, *A Wayward Quest* (Boston 1960), 100
51. Ibid., 103
52. Ibid., 101
53. Lawrence Langner, *The Play's the Thing* (New York 1960), 46
54. Ibid.
55. John Mason Brown, *The Worlds of Robert E. Sherwood* (New York 1965), 273
56. *Fortune* (November 1964), 98
57. "Broadway's Hottest Producers," *Business Week* (February 2, 1963), 90-9
58. Ibid.
59. "How the Angels Wing along the Rialto," *New York Times Magazine* (Dec. 8, 1963), 28
60. *Fanfare,* 90, 91
61. *Act One,* 326

62. Ibid.

63. Ibid., 74

64. David Belasco, "Dramatizing the Present," *Harper's Weekly* (March 29, 1913), 18

65. *The Intent of the Artist,* 108

66. *The Essence of Tragedy,* 31; *Offbroadway,* 47

67. *The Essence of Tragedy,* 26

68. Ibid., 31

69. *A Wayward Quest,* 103–4

70. Oscar Hammerstein, "The Book Had Better Be Good," *Theatre Arts* (November 1960), 19

71. Ibid.

72. *The Summing Up,* 153, 154

73. "American Playwrights Self-Appraised," *Saturday Review* (September 3, 1955), 19

74. Jean-Paul Sartre, "Beyond Bourgeois Theatre," *Tulane Drama Review* (March 1961), 3

75. *Playwrights on Playwriting,* 72; from Bertolt Brecht's "Kleines Organum fur das Theater," Versuche, translated by John Willett

76. *Fanfare,* 250–1

77. J. Brooks Atkinson, "First Night Amenities," *New York Times* (February 1, 1931), Sect. 8, X

78. *Time* (March 9, 1962), m-7

79. John Gassner, *Theatre at the Crossroads* (New York 1960), 110

80. Ibid., 113

81. *New York Theatre Critics' Reviews* (1956), 179, 180

82. Jed Harris, *Watchman, What of the Night?,* 79

83. Ibid., 19

84. *The Worlds of Robert E. Sherwood,* 305

85. "Seventeen Playwrights Self-Appraised," *Saturday Review* (May 7, 1955), 48

86. C. F. Johnson, *Shakespeare and His Critics* (Cambridge 1909), 42

87. *Fanfare,* 183

88. *Mister Abbott,* 196

89. "John Gielgud and Edward Albee Talk about Theatre," *Atlantic* (April 1965), 67

90. *The Living Theatre,* 229

91. *Current Biography* (1953), 18

92. *New York Times* (February 17, 1965), 36

93. "John Osborne Raps Back in Anger," *Variety* (June 15, 1966), 67

94. "Sean O'Casey's Credo," *New York Times* (November 9, 1958), Sect. 2, X

95. Ibid., X3

518 CHAPTER IX: FOOTNOTES

96. *The Works of Synge* (Dublin 1910), I, 135
97. William Inge, "More on the Playwright's Mission," *Theatre Arts* (August 1958), 19
98. Sydney Howard, *Lucky Sam McCarver* (New York 1926), xvi, xvii
99. William Gibson, "Second Wind," *Theatre Arts* (October 1959), 20
100. Oreste F. Pucciani, "An Interview with Jean-Paul Sartre," *Tulane Drama Review* (March 1961), 16
101. Eugene Ionesco, "The World of Eugene Ionesco," *New York Times* (June 1, 1958), Sect. 2, X3
102. John Osborne, "They Call It Cricket," *Declaration* (New York 1958)
103. *Harper's* (October 1957), 48
104. *Collected Plays,* 53
105. *Twentieth Century Authors, First Supplement,* 670
106. William Inge, "Forgotten Anger," *Theatre Arts* (February 1958), 94
107. John Mason Brown, "What's Right with the Theatre," *Saturday Review* (May 11, 1963), 21
108. Martin Esslin, *The Theatre of the Absurd* (New York 1961), xix
109. *Atlantic Monthly* (April 1965), 62
110. *Saturday Review* (May 11, 1963), 20
111. S. N. Behrman, "Query: What Makes Comedy High?" *New York Times* (March 30, 1952), Sect. 2, x
112. Ibid.
113. Lucius Beebe, "Stage Asides," *New York Herald Tribune* (March 12, 1939), vi, 1
114. Lillian Hellman, *Four Plays* (New York 1942), xii
115. Terence Rattigan, "Concerning the Play of Ideas," *New Statesman and Nation* (March 4, 1950), 241, 242
116. Sean O'Casey, "The Play of Ideas," ibid. (April 8, 1950), 397–8
117. Bernard Shaw, "The Play of Ideas," ibid. (May 6, 1950), 510
118. Ben Levy, "The Play of Ideas," ibid. (March 25, 1950), 338
119. Christopher Fry, "The Play of Ideas," ibid. (April 22, 1950), 458
120. Toby Cole, editor, *Playwrights on Playwriting* from Émile Zola's "Le Naturalisme au Théâtre," translated by Samuel Draper, 9
121. Mordecai Gorelik, "Brecht," *Theatre Arts* (March 1957), 73.
122. Ernst Toller translated by Marketa Goetz, "My Works," *Tulane Drama Review* (March 1959), 101
123. *Theatre at the Crossroads,* 36
124. "History Onstage," *Newsweek* (January 31, 1966), 81–2
125. *Saturday Review,* "American Playwrights Self-Appraised," 19
126. Ibid.

CHAPTER X: FOOTNOTES

1. Lord Alfred Douglas, *Oscar Wilde and Myself* (London 1914), 71

2. Frank Harris, *Oscar Wilde, His Life and Confessions* (New York 1916), II, 490; Robert Sherard, *Oscar Wilde* (London 1905), 53

3. William Saroyan, *The Time of Your Life* (New York 1939), 9

4. *Act One,* 284

5. W. Somerset Maugham, *The Summing Up* (New York 1938), 201, 260

6. *Writers at Work,* 101

7. Alan Levy, "Doc Simon's Rx for Comedy," *New York Times Magazine* (March 7, 1965), 55

8. George P. Baker, *Dramatic Technique* (Cambridge 1919), 54

9. S. N. Behrman, "A Tribute to Fulda," *New York Times* (February 7, 1943), Sect. 2, X2

10. *New York Times Magazine* (December 6, 1959), 63

11. Ibid.

12. "The Men Behind J. B.," *Theatre Arts* (April 1959), 61

13. Ibid., 62

14. Archibald MacLeish, "The Book of Job," a sermon delivered at First Church of Christ, Farmington, Connecticut, May 8th, 1955, 9

15. Lucius Beebe, "Stage Asides: Arsenic and Mr. Kesselring," *New York Herald Tribune* (June 15, 1941), VI, 2

16. George Axelrod, "4 Parts in 8 Weeks, a Hit in a Hurry," *Theatre Arts* (January 1954), 33

17. Ibid.

18. *New York Times Magazine* (March 7, 1965), 42

19. Ibid.

20. William Inge, *"Picnic*—from *Front Porch* to Broadway," *Theatre Arts* (April 1954), 33

21. *4 Plays,* vii, viii

22. "Albee: Odd Man in on Broadway," *Newsweek* (February 3, 1963), 52

23. "Talk with the Author," *Newsweek* (October 29, 1962), 53

24. *Atlantic Monthly* (April 1965), 64

25. *Newsweek* (February 4, 1963), 52

26. *The Worlds of Robert E. Sherwood,* 295

519

27. Ibid., 329

28. Ibid., 370

29. Arthur Miller, *Collected Plays* (New York 1961), 38

30. Arthur Miller, "With Respect for Her Agony but with Love," *Life* (February 7, 1964), 66

31. *Collected Plays*, 15

32. Ibid.

33. Ibid., 17

34. Arthur Miller, "The Shadows of the Gods," *Harper's* (August 1958), 36

35. *Collected Plays*, 17

36. Ibid., 39, 40

37. Ibid., 40

38. Ibid., 31

39. Ibid., 24

40. *Life* (February 7, 1964), 66

41. Ibid.

42. *Collected Plays*, 38

43. Ibid., 29

44. Ibid., 23

45. Ibid., 31

46. Tom Prideaux, "A Desperate Search by a Troubled Hero," *Life* (February 7, 1964), 64c

47. *Life* (February 7, 1964), 66

48. Andre Gide, *Oscar Wilde* (Paris 1947), 25

49. Barrett Clark, "Paul Green," *Theatre Arts* (October 1928), 732

50. Paul Green, *Dramatic Heritage* (New York 1953), 17

51. Owen Davis, "Playwriting," *Saturday Evening Post* (September 27, 1930), 97

52. *The Intent of the Artist*, 86

53. Noel Coward, *Present Indicative* (New York 1937), 320

54. Ibid.

55. Ibid., 341

56. Ibid.

57. Ibid., 341–342

58. Ibid., 342

59. Clayton Hamilton, *Problems of the Playwright* (New York 1917), 84

60. *Newsweek* (February 4, 1963), 52

61. Ibid.

62. Ibid.

63. *Four Plays*, viii

64. Ibid., vii

65. C. Hughes, "Women Play-Makers," *New York Times Magazine* (May 4, 1941), 27, 102

66. "Death of a Salesman," a symposium, *Tulane Drama Review* (May 1958), 67
67. *Collected Plays,* 8
68. Allan Seager, "The Creative Agony of Arthur Miller," *Esquire* (October 1959), 23
69. Ibid., 25
70. Ibid.
71. Ibid.
72. Ibid., 23
73. Ibid.
74. Ibid., 25
75. *The Summing Up,* 202
76. W. Somerset Maugham, *Selected Prefaces and Introductions* (New York 1963), 46
77. Ibid.
78. Ibid., 47
79. Ibid.
80. *The Summing Up,* 83, 215
81. *Works of Synge,* I, 136
82. Barrett H. Clark, "Letters from Sidney Howard," *Theatre Arts* (April 1941), 278
83. John Van Druten, *Playwright at Work* (New York 1953), 100
84. Ibid., 104
85. *The Summing Up,* 68
86. Ibid., 213
87. Ibid., 82
88. Ibid., 221
89. Ibid., 58
90. *Harper's* (October 1957), 50
91. Ibid., 49
92. Ibid., 50
93. Ibid.
94. *The Play's the Thing,* 70
95. *Saturday Evening Post* (January 16, 1926), 58
96. Carl Carmer, "George Kaufman: Playmaker to Broadway," *Theatre Arts* (October 1932), 808
97. Ibid., 811
98. *The Essence of Tragedy,* 7
99. J. H. Smith and E. W. Parks, editors, *The Great Critics* (New York 1932), 9
100. *The Essence of Tragedy,* 9
101. *The Great Critics,* 16
102. *The Essence of Tragedy,* 10

103. Archibald Henderson, *Bernard Shaw: Man of the Century*, 770
104. Arthur Miller, "What Makes Plays Endure," *New York Times* (August 15, 1965), Sect. 2, X
105. Ibid.
106. Ibid., X3
107. *Collected Plays*, 7
108. Ibid.
109. *The Great Critics*, 10
110. *Collected Plays*, 7
111. Ibid., 31
112. *The Art of Playwriting*, 60
113. *The Theory and Technique of Playwriting*, 168
114. Granville-Barker, *On Dramatic Method* (New York 1956), 161
115. Ibid., 92–93
116. *The Great Critics*, 16
117. *New York Times Magazine* (March 7, 1965), 63
118. John Van Druten, "Characters Offstage," *New York Times* (December 5, 1943), Sect. 2, X5
119. *The Summing Up*, 93
120. John Van Druten, "Research for Comedy," *New York Times* (December 6, 1942), Sect. 8, X2
121. *The Theory and Technique of Playwriting*, 280
122. *The Intent of the Artist*, 86
123. *The Time of Your Life*, 209, 210
124. *The Theatre Through Its Stage Door*, 132
125. Bayard Veiller, *The Fun I've Had* (New York 1941), 42
126. Rachel Crothers, "That Times Square Veteran," *New York Times* (March 15, 1931), Sect. 9, X
127. *Theatre Arts* (April 1941), 276, 277
128. Lorraine Hansberry, "Me Tink Me Hear Sounds in de Night," *Theatre Arts* (October 1960), 69, 10
129. "Odets at Center Stage," talk with Michael J. Mendelsohn, *Theatre Arts* (June 1963), 78
130. *The Play's the Thing*, 118
131. *The Great Critics*, 12
132. Ibid., 14
133. *Harper's* (August 1958), 37
134. *The Worlds of Robert E. Sherwood*, 262
135. *The Art of Playwriting*, 123
136. *The Summing Up*, 123
137. Ibid., 93
138. Hellman, *Four Plays*, ix
139. *Saturday Evening Post* (September 27, 1930), 25, 98
140. *Theatre Through Its Stage Door*, 50

141. *The Great Critics,* 10
142. Ibid.
143. Ibid., 12
144. *The Play's the Thing,* 53
145. *Act One,* 371
146. *The Play's the Thing,* 133
147. Ibid., 143
148. *The Art of Playwriting,* 123
149. *How Not to Write a Play,* 32
150. Ibid., 31
151. Ibid., 33
152. Ibid., 26
153. *Collected Plays,* 21
154. *The Collected Works of Henrik Ibsen,* III, 8
155. Kotelianksy, *Literary and Theatrical Reminiscences* (New York 1927), 4; Gorky, *Reminiscences of Tolstoy, Chekhov, and Andreyev* (New York 1921), 78
156. *Table-talk of George Bernard Shaw,* 67
157. *How Not to Write a Play,* 31
158. Harold Clurman, *Lies Like Truth* (New York 1958), 273
159. *The Intent of the Artist,* 94
160. *Harper's* (October 1957), 50
161. Ibid.
162. Ibid., 51
163. *Selected Prefaces and Introductions,* 40
164. *Mademoiselle* (March 1963), 215
165. Ralph Waldo Emerson, *Complete Works* (Cambridge), I, 83
166. "Maugham Discusses Drama," *Living Age* (May 1931), 305
167. Archer, *Play-Making,* 36
168. *New York Times* (August 15, 1965), Sect. 2, X
169. *Collected Plays,* 8
170. *The Theory and Technique of Playwriting,* 297
171. *The Great Critics,* 10, 11
172. Ibid., 27
173. Ibid., 29
174. *The Yale Review* (October 1923), 57
175. *The Theory and Technique of Playwriting,* 298
176. Ibid., 289
177. *On Dramatic Method,* 37
178. *The Playboy of the Western World,* vii
179. *The Art of Playwriting,* 129
180. *Living Age* (May 1931), 305
181. *The Theory and Technique of Playwriting,* 297
182. Clayton Hamilton, *So You're Writing a Play* (New York 1917), 239–240

183. *The Playboy of the Western World,* vi

184. *Newsweek* (October 29, 1962), 53

185. Alva Johnston, "How to Become a Playwright," *Saturday Evening Post* (March 15, 1941), 83; *So You're Writing a Play,* 255

186. *Dramatic Opinions and Essays,* I, 12

187. *So You're Writing a Play,* 227

188. *The Great Critics,* 7

189. T. S. Eliot, *Poetry and Drama* (Cambridge 1951), 27

190. T. S. Eliot, *Murder in the Cathedral* (London 1935), 64–5

191. Ibid., 45

192. Ibid., 29, 30

193. Ibid., 30

194. Ibid., 30

195. Ibid., 43

196. Ibid.

197. Archibald MacLeish, *Panic* (New York 1935), vii

198. Archibald MacLeish, "The Poet as Playwright," *Atlantic Monthly* (February 1955), 52

199. Archibald MacLeish, *J. B.* (Boston 1956), 119–120

200. *Theatre at the Cross-roads,* 9

201. *Chicago Sun* (July 3, 1910)

202. *Esquire* (October 1959), 26

203. Ibid.

204. *The Play's the Thing,* 96

205. *The Theatre Through Its Stage Door,* 87

206. Ibid.

207. *Act One,* 74

208. *Watchman, What of the Night?,* 82

209. *New York Times Magazine* (March 7, 1965), 63

210. Ibid.

211. Ibid.

212. "Odets at Center Stage," *Theatre Arts* (June 1963), 19

1. *Mister Abbott,* 89
2. Jerome Lawrence and Robert E. Lee, "Which One Can't Spell?" *Theatre Arts* (June 1958), 64
3. Ibid.
4. *Act One,* 305
5. David Ewen, *Richard Rodgers* (New York 1957), 209
6. Richard Rodgers, "A Score of Years and One," *New York Times* (May 5, 1940), Sect. 10, 3X
7. Moss Hart, "How A. W. Came to Dinner and Other Stories," *New York Times* (October 29, 1939), Sect. 9, X
8. Ibid.
9. "Why *You Can't Take It With You,*" *New York Times* (December 20, 1936), Sect. 11, 4X
10. Ibid.
11. Sherwin D. Smith, "The Great Monkey Trial," *New York Times Magazine* (July 4, 1965), 9
12. Jerome Lawrence and Robert E. Lee, "Inherit the Wind: the Genesis and Exodus of the Play," *Theatre Arts* (August 1957), 34, 94
13. *The Play's the Thing,* 174
14. *A Wayward Quest,* 282
15. *Act One,* 288
16. Ibid., 280, 386
17. Ibid., 367
18. Katherine Dayton, "It Must Be Such Fun to Work with George S. Kaufman," *New York Times* (December 8, 1935), Sect. 10, X3
19. Ibid.
20. "It Appears Two Persons Wrote the Latest Kaufman-Ferber Play," *New York Herald Tribune* (November 23, 1941), VI, 2
21. Stanley Green, *The Rodgers and Hammerstein Story* (New York 1963), 103
22. *New York Times* (May 5, 1940), Sect. 10, X3
23. *Richard Rodgers,* 210
24. Oscar Hammerstein, "The Book Had Better Be Good," *Theatre Arts* (November 1960), 19

25. *Theatre Arts* (June 1958), 63
26. Ibid.
27. Ibid., 64
28. *Saturday Evening Post* (January 16, 1926), 58
29. *"What Price Glory* and Its Authors," *New York Times* (September 14, 1924), Sect. 8, X
30. *Saturday Evening Post* (January 16, 1926), 58
31. *The Rodgers and Hammerstein Story,* 103
32. *Saturday Evening Post* (January 16, 1926), 58
33. Ibid.
34. *New York Times* (December 8, 1935), Sect. 10, X3
35. Ibid.
36. *Act One,* 390
37. Ibid., 392
38. Ibid., 392–393
39. Ibid., 396

Appendix

"Enter the theatre with the same seriousness as you would medicine or law. Be patient, work hard, grow as a human being because talent is worthless unless there is a heart and mind and soul behind it."
—Robert Woodruff Anderson to aspiring playwrights

"Read plays, see plays, think plays, talk plays; read all good dramatic criticism."
—John Van Druten to aspiring playwrights

Key Questions and Answers in Playwriting

If the word and example of the foremost playwrights can't help you in playwriting, whose word and example can?

(The following series of key questions were designed to act as a self-help guide in playwriting; the answers are to be found on the pages indicated directly after each question. This approach allows for quickly finding answers to individual questions uppermost in the aspiring playwright's mind as personal needs vary. The piece-meal method of answering found in this approach should exercise the playwright's mind in selecting and reordering material imaginatively to suit his or her creative purpose in playwriting itself.)

1. What personal need or creative drive starts a play? ix; Ibsen, 4, 21–23; Strindberg, 82, 83; Chekhov, 122, 123, 125–126, 129, 130; Shaw, 180–182; Galsworthy, 211, 214–216; Pirandello, 236, 250; O'Neill, 282–283, 300, 301, 303; Williams, 336, 354–355; Cursory Study, 387

2. What should I write about? Ibsen, 19, 21, 24, 38; Strindberg, 82–83, 87–88; Chekhov, 128, 130; Shaw, 179, 182; Galsworthy, 216–218; Pirandello, 252, 253; O'Neill, 297, 302; Williams, 341, 353, 357; Cursory Study, 435–441

3. How vital is timeliness to a play? Ibsen, 12, 16, 19, 26–27, 30, 39; Strindberg, 74, 79–80; Chekhov, 128–129; Shaw, 179–180, 189; Pirandello, 244; O'Neill, 299, 363; Williams, 425–426; Cursory Study, 466, 477–479

4. How important is truth in a play? Ibsen, 20, 39, 44; Strindberg, 72, 74, 78, 81, 100–101; Chekhov, 127; Shaw, 179, 189; Galsworthy,

213, 221; Pirandello, 253, 255, 267, 271; O'Neill, 297; Williams, 350, 353, 370-372; Cursory Study, 434-441

5. What part does "sex" have in successful plays? Ibsen, 7, 11, 19, 20, 38; Strindberg, 59, 63, 83, 91; Chekhov, 124, 127, 131; Shaw, 162, 173-175, 178, 187; Galsworthy, 205, 216-217; Pirandello, 234-235, 253; O'Neill, 297, 299, 305, 309, 318; Williams, 347, 351, 353, 356; Cursory Study, 434-435

6. How much can diet and stimulants influence a playwright? Ibsen, 12, 23; Strindberg, 64, 84, 85; Chekhov, 129; Shaw, 180, 181; Galsworthy, 215; Pirandello, 251; O'Neill, 301; Williams, 355-356; Cursory Study, 442-443

7. Do I need the discipline of a routine working day? Ibsen, 22-24; Strindberg, 83-85; Chekhov, 129; Shaw, 181-182; Galsworthy, 214-215; Pirandello, 250-251; O'Neill, 301-302; Williams, 355-356; Cursory Study, 442-443

8. Is poor health necessarily bad for playwriting? Ibsen, 12; Strindberg, 62-63, 69-70; Chekhov, 118-119; Shaw, 161, 170-171; Galsworthy, 210-211; Pirandello, 234-236; O'Neill, 288, 292, 294; Williams, 338, 340, 354-355; Cursory Study, 443

9. Should I talk to others about some play I am writing or thinking of writing? Ibsen, 26-27; Strindberg, 89-90; Chekhov, 132-133, 135-137; Shaw, 194; Galsworthy, 224-225; Pirandello, 275; O'Neill, 300, 307, 319, 327-328; Williams, 335, 347-349, 375-376; Cursory Study, 489, 491

10. How has the genesis of plays come about? Ibsen, 21-33; Strindberg, 82-96; Chekhov, 129-145; Shaw, 180-184; Galsworthy, 214-217; Pirandello, 250-262; O'Neill, 300-306; Williams, 354-364; Cursory Study, 442-453

11. Why keep a notebook? Ibsen, 27-32; Strindberg, 89; Chekhov, 130; Shaw, 182; O'Neill, 302-303; Williams, 335, 356; Cursory Study, 458-461

12. How may symbolism be used in a play? Ibsen, 9, 18-19, 41-42; Strindberg, 89-91, 94-97; Chekhov, 131, 137, 142-143; Shaw, 186-190; Galsworthy, 217, 220; Pirandello, 246-247; O'Neill, 309-311, 313; Williams, 351, 358-360, 365, 367-369; Cursory Study, 448, 457, 464-465, 470, 478, 486

22. Are good plays ever written with specific stars in mind for the leading roles? Ibsen, 16–17; Strindberg, 77; Chekhov, 124, 126; Shaw, 176, 182–183; Pirandello, 240, 242; O'Neill, 299; Williams, 349; Cursory Study, 461–462, 488, 495

23. Should a scenario be written before attempting to write the dialogue? Ibsen, 42; Strindberg, 84–85, 101–102; Chekhov, 137–138, 148; Shaw, 187, 190–191; Galsworthy, 222; Pirandello, 272; O'Neill, 307, 314–315, 318, 321; Williams, 371–372; Cursory Study, 479–480

24. Are good plays sometimes written very quickly? Ibsen, 34; Strindberg, 68, 70–71, 101–102; Chekhov, 132, 145, 151; Shaw, 194; Galsworthy, 222; Pirandello, 272; O'Neill, 304, 318–319, 326–327; Williams, 371–372; Cursory Study, 446–447, 453–454, 457, 480, 502, 505, 506

25. What makes for good dialogue? Ibsen, 43; Strindberg, 102–106; Chekhov, 145–148; Shaw, 191–193; Galsworthy, 217, 223–224; Pirandello, 272–274; O'Neill, 319–320; Williams, 372–374; Cursory Study, 480–484

26. What are the advantages and disadvantages of using verse in dialogue? Ibsen, 43–44; Strindberg, 80, 101, 105; Chekhov, 127–128, 137, 144, 146; Shaw, 193; Galsworthy, 224; Pirandello, 272–274; O'Neill, 316, 319–320; Williams, 370–374; Cursory Study, 419, 481–488

27. What good can come of rewriting? Ibsen, 44–51; Strindberg, 101–102, 106; Chekhov, 145–146, 148–152; Shaw, 194–196; Galsworthy, 222–225; Pirandello, 275; O'Neill, 318, 328; Williams, 371–372, 374–377; Cursory Study, 488–491, 501–506

28. Why collaborate?   492–493

29. How collaborate in the genesis of a play?   494–498

30. How collaborate in developing character and action?   498–501

31. How collaborate in writing and rewriting?   501–506

32. If a play does not succeed, may it indirectly lead to another play that does succeed? Ibsen, 9–10; Strindberg, 99–100; Chekhov, 123–125, 148–150; Shaw, 174–175; Galsworthy, 212; Pirandello, 255–256; O'Neill, 296, 304–306; Williams, 346, 354, 370; Cursory Study, 448–450

33. How necessary is a try-out to a play's success? Williams, 348–349; Cursory Study, 488–491, 504–506

34. Can "pot-boiling" still make for good playwriting? Ibsen, 15; Strindberg, 73; Chekhov, 122–124; Shaw, 176; Galsworthy, 211–212; Pirandello, 241–242; O'Neill, 295–296; Williams, 343, 347, 350; Cursory Study, 387, 409–411, 461

35. How do I get my first production? Ibsen, 5–6; Strindberg, 66, 77; Chekhov, 123–124; Shaw, 167; Galsworthy, 209; Pirandello, 230–231, 240–241; O'Neill, 289–290; Williams, 336; Cursory Study, 392–400

36. What are the vital economics of Broadway and of Off-Broadway? 412–418

37. What does a producer want in a play? Ibsen, 15–16; Strindberg, 73–74; Chekhov, 123–126; Shaw, 173–175; Galsworthy, 211; Pirandello, 242–243; O'Neill, 295–296; Williams, 346–347; Cursory Study, 418–425

38. Have ultimate hits gone begging for producers? 424–425

39. What does the play-going public want in a play? Ibsen, 15–16; Strindberg, 73–74; Chekhov, 124, 126; Shaw, 174–175; Galsworthy, 211; Pirandello, 243; O'Neill, 295–297; Williams, 346–347, 350; Cursory Study, 425–428, 489, 491

40. Should a playwright "write down" to the public or expect the public to "grow up" to the playwright? Ibsen, 15–16; Strindberg, 74–75; Chekhov, 123–125; Shaw, 174–175; Galsworthy, 211–212; Pirandello, 242–243; O'Neill, 295–296; Williams, 347, 351; Cursory Study, 477–479

41. What characterizes the playwright as an artist? Ibsen, 18–20; Strindberg, 77–82; Chekhov, 127–129; Shaw, 178–180; Galsworthy, 212–214; Pirandello, 246–249; O'Neill, 296–300; Williams, 350–354; Cursory Study, 387–388

42. How have playwrights regarded critics? Ibsen, 9–12, 15, 17–18; Strindberg, 81–82; Chekhov, 126–127; Shaw, 177; Galsworthy, 213–214; Pirandello, 245–246; O'Neill, 299–300; Williams, 349–350, 353–354; Cursory Study, 427–432

43. Are playwrights born or made? 386–387

A Suggested Pattern of Play Analysis*

I. Check-points in a play
   A. Is the theme or key-note of the play struck very soon? (Langner: "It is desirable, in my opinion, at the very beginning of the play, or somewhere close to the beginning, to introduce the theme in a direct or indirect manner, as may best serve the purpose of the play.")
   B. Is the theme or basic implication about life sounded and resounded yet with an ultimate sense of revelation? (Maugham: "I think the secret of playwriting can be given in two maxims: stick to the point and whenever you can cut." Miller: "The very impulse to write, I think, springs from an inner chaos crying for order, for meaning, and that meaning must be discovered in the process of writing or the work lies dead as it is finished." Williams: "Usually when asked about a theme, I look vague and say, 'It's a play about life,'" and, "I prefer a play not to be a noose but a net with fairly wide meshes. So many of its instants of revelation are wayward flashes . . .")
   C. Is the exposition exciting and apparently artless? (Shaw: "no conflict, no drama." Exposition should set tone and suspense as to outcome of the conflict implied or stated. Chekhov: "An artist observes, selects, guesses, and combines—and this in itself presupposes a problem.")
   D. How soon is the basic situation revealed? (Usually, the sooner the better. All plays involve a basic situation or circumstance. Wilder: "The dramatist must be by instinct a story-teller.")
   E. At what point in the story does the plot begin for the most effectiveness? (Shaw: "The classic unities have their virtue for

---

* This pattern of analysis is easily adaptable to a one-act play by allowing for its basic difference from a full-length play—a less extended main action from less intensively developed main characters. Tennessee Williams, suggesting the one-act as a stage of growth for a full-length play, has repeatedly worked one acts into full-length plays.

535

those who can handle them and are indeed inherent in drama at its highest concentration." Consider Albee's *Who's Afraid of Virginia Woolf?* By contrast, all of Shakespeare, such plays as Shaw's *Saint Joan,* and most movies, to emphasize action as most vital to drama, show the story happening before our eyes rather than only in the most intense culmination of its last hours.)

F. Does one central character or perhaps two give the play a distinctive viewpoint? (The titles of masterpieces of dramatic literature advertise the value of a strong central character or two to focus the audience's attention.)

  1. Is the leading character's entrance built up? (Such a build-up can offer a field of reference for the play's viewpoint.)

  2. Does the leading character bear widely recognized identification for the audience? (Chekhov: "The stage reflects in itself the quintessence of life . . ." Langner: "Where there is no one in a play with whom the audience can identify, it generally fails." Wilder: "Imaginative literature has nothing to say to those who do not recognize—who cannot be reminded . . . Of all the arts the theatre is best endowed to awaken this recollection within us . . .")

  3. Does the leading character have extraordinary vitality? (Galsworthy: "That's what makes Shakespeare so much greater than Milton and all our other poets." Miller: "What finally survives, when anything does, are archetypal characters and relationships which can be transferred to the new period.")

  4. Is the conflict of the leading character or characters more or less a total involvement of personality? (The more varied the conflict, the chances are the greater the suspense as to outcome. Langner: "given characters which live on the stage, *suspense interest* is the one essential of the play which cannot be dispensed with." Granville-Barker: "The discovery which turned Shakespeare from a good dramatist to a great one was that the outward clashing of character with character is poor material beside the ferment in the spirit of man, confined by law or custom or inherited belief, or netted round by alien circumstance or wills but quickening in their despite.")

5. Does the lead offer an excellent chance for acting? (Shaw: "As I write my plays, it is continually in my mind and very much to my taste . . . to provide an exhibition of the art of acting.")

G. How are characters contrasted to promote conflict? (Shaw: "no conflict, no drama." Lord Dunsany: "Contrast is the dramatist's method while he is working." Granville-Barker of Shakespeare: "He works by means of contrast between character and character, by tension and relaxation, climax and anti-climax, by changes of tone and pace, by every sort of variation between scene and scene.")

H. Are there enough characters? (Van Druten: "the fewer an author has, the more time he will have to create them fully and in the round." Marc Connelly of collaborating with George S. Kaufman: "After we have our major character, usually someone who will personify certain grand assininities that occur in life, we sit down and say, 'What would the people be who would associate with a man like that?'")

I. Is the story up-to-the minute and a good one? (Williams of the playwright: "He must say intelligibly what he has to say, and unless it is well worth saying, he does not have a Chinaman's chance of surviving." Miller: "Before a play is art, it is a kind of psychic journalism, a mirror of its hour, and this reflection of contemporary feeling is exactly what makes so many plays irrelevant to later times.")

J. Is the action of the story rearranged into a good plot for maximum dramatic effect? (Chekhov: "The large number of revisions need not trouble you, for the more of a mosaic a work is, the better. The characters stand to gain by this." Shaw: "Real plays are no more constructed than a carrot is constructed." Galsworthy: "A human being is the best plot there is . . ." Williams: "*Dynamic* is a word in disrepute at the moment, and so, I suppose is the word *organic,* but those terms still define the dramatic values that I value most.")

1. Is the action unified? (As Aristotle first noted, an action is organic when like an organism, no part may be removed without impairing the whole.)

2. Are the minor climaxes revelations of character or circumstance leading to reversal of intended action? (To Aristotle and since, discovery and reversal are the chief means

of moving the line of conflict forming the main action; combined as in the major climax of *Oedipus the King*, discovery and reversal are likely the most powerful of all means.)

3. Is the major climax valid? (Strindberg: "a dramatist generally begins his work at the end." Williams of *Camino Real*: "it commits the huge structural error of deviating from a straight, narrative line," and of *The Rose Tattoo*, "Gadge [Elia Kazan] would have demanded a stronger, tighter script from me." A major climax of spiritual renaissance in the leading character is stated or implied as desirable in Shaw, Maugham, Maxwell Anderson and Miller.)

4. Does the action escalate to the major climax with proper tension?

   a. How much fat may be cut away? (Shaw in rehearsal found *Major Barbara* to be long "beyond human endurance" and cut it to a length suitable for one evening.)

   b. Are there good entrances and exits for characters? (These are emphatic moments like beginnings and endings and imply special importance.)

   c. Are there strong act endings? (Weak act endings literally lose an audience; they may go home. Shaw: "The theatre is a place which people can only endure when they forget themselves, that is when their attention is entirely captured . . .")

   d. How soon after the major climax does the play end? (As a rule, the sooner the better. Worthington Minor: "Anti-climax is allowable only when the implications of the climax are too far-reaching to be fully absorbed at that moment." Anti-climax implies "fall-out" as, for instance, in *The Cherry Orchard*.)

K. Is the dialogue a true extension of the action of the play's characters? (George Abbott: "my whole training and experience makes me place construction, or story line, first, and words second." Lawson: "the dramatist who is not a poet is only half a dramatist." To Shaw, idiom is "the most highly vitalized form of language" and the proverb is one of "the most effective forms of assertion." Maugham: "The talk must be succinct. It must give the impression of reality, not a copy." Preston Sturges: "Like a bee, a good line should carry the sting in its tail.")

L. Are the basic elements of the theatre's make-believe such as dance, music, setting, lights, costumes, actors, used to their fullest dramatic potential in the play? (Gassner: "The most pervasive and usually the most effective poetry is not one of words but of the theatrical organization of the play and the production elements." Williams: "using a symbol is just a way of saying a thing more vividly and dramatically than I could otherwise." "As for symbolism," Archer noted in recollecting Ibsen, "he says that life is full of it . . ." Wilder: "The history of the theatre shows that in its greatest ages the stage employed the greatest number of conventions.")

II. The total effect.

A. Does the play "come off"? (Tolstoy in his book, *What Is Art?*, the outcome of a 25 year quest in the wilderness of aesthetics, concluded: "Art is a human activity consisting in this, that one man consciously, by means of certain external signs, hands on to others feelings he has lived through, and that other people are infected by these feelings, and also experience them." Galsworthy: "To quicken the pulses in one way or another is to me . . . by far the chief purpose of dramatic art." Williams of the theatre: "Something wild, something exciting, something that you are. not used to. Offbeat is the word.")

  1. Is the play reasonably clear? (Galsworthy: "It is the ill-mating of forms that has killed a thousand plays." Williams of the playwright: "He must say intelligibly what he has to say . . . ")

  2. Is the play sincere? (Ibsen: "The great thing is to become honest and truthful in dealing with one's self . . . All the rest simply leads to falsehood." Galsworthy: "a work of art must ring absolutely true, must have lost all the feeling of fake and manufacture." Williams: "the theatre which is called the charlatan of the arts is paradoxically the one in which the charlatan is most easily detected. Even cheap entertainment is honest.")

  3. Is the play individual? (Galsworthy: "Flavour . . . the peculiar and most essential attribute of any work of art!")

    a. In style? (Shaw: "Effectiveness of assertion is the alpha and omega of style.")

b. In view of life? (Strindberg of art: "a piece of nature seen through a temperament.")

c. In impact? (Read the last paragraph of any capable review.)

Introduction To Suggested Reading Lists

"Read."—Lillian Hellman to aspiring playwrights

Ibsen, Chekhov, O'Neill, Williams, Fry, Ionesco, Odets, Pinter and Albee, not to mention a good many other modern playwrights, began their playwriting with one-acts and made their first mark that way. O'Neill called the one-act "a fine vehicle for something poetical, for something spiritual in feeling that cannot be carried on through a long play." Noel Coward in his series of nine one-act plays, *To-Night at 8:30,* felt it no come-down, even at the height of his powers, to write one-act plays. James Thurber in his late years adapted some of his best stories into one-act plays or revue sketches to create *The Thurber Carnival.* "My longer plays," said Williams, "emerge out of earlier one acters or short stories . . . I work over them again and again." Robert W. Anderson's latest Broadway hit is a collection of four one-act comedies—*You Know I Can't Hear You When the Water's Running.* And Neil Simon's newest smash-hit is *Plaza Suite,* a trio of one-act farce-comedies.

To help acquire a sense of form, the aspiring playwright should read the best of one-act plays, and this appendix provides such a selected list. The aspiring playwright on his or her own might freely expand or contract the list. Expansion is a better course. An open mind is more likely to be well stocked than a closed one; comparative anatomy courses have assorted organs and even freaks pickled in glass jars however unattractive they may appear as objects of art.

A selected list of suggested readings in criticism then follows. This list should be turned to as one turns to food out of actual hunger. There is no point in gorging oneself to nausea or to be overwhelmed by the sheer size of the range of nourishment offered in criticism or in plays, either. It is well to remember, too, that plays as witnessed by the classical Greeks, preceded rather than followed criticism. Too much criticism offered or taken when the aspiring playwright feels no need or power to cope with it, is of very dubious value in helping him along; it is better for the playwright to seek the advice after groping and stumbling on his or her own. Some criticism is a historically dated, theatrical smorgasbord, stale, dried out, and inept for our time. But other criticism, however old, is as refreshing and wholesome as the best of food and drinking water.

Following the selected reading list in criticism, this appendix then offers three recourses in the range of a balanced diet in the reading of long plays: anthologies of the drama; long-run productions with their genre and run noted; and prize-winning award plays with their genre and run noted—Pulitzer Prize Plays and Drama Critics' Circle Prize Plays. The plays in these lists should be read as avidly by a student of playwriting to acquire a sense of form as a law student would read law cases to acquire a sense of law. The anthologies, with their emphasis upon masterpieces, provide the stuff of survival; the greatest commercial successes suggest the keenest public taste and appetite; the prize-winning plays note the critics' view of the drama's yearly achievement as art. The three reading lists sometimes have identical entries.

Special insights may be picked up from scrutinizing the lists of long-run and prize-winning plays. The list of long-run plays on Broadway, for example, shows how musicals and comedies are by far the most popular genres in terms of the total number of hits running 500 or more performances in the last 65 years as covered by Burns Mantle's series, *Best Plays,* and continued by John Chapman, Henry Hewes, and Otis Guernsey Jr. A trend and a precedent are suggested in this break-down of genres of productions running 500 or more performances in their initial Broadway run:

Musicals	66	Comedies	53
Variety Shows	6	Dramas	32
Revues (Burlesque, Mu-		Farces	4
sical, Topical)	9	Murder Mysteries	4

Some modern classics like Ibsen's *Hedda Gabler,* Chekhov's *The Cherry Orchard* and Shaw's *Man and Superman* are not on the list of long-runs on Broadway, but they are repeatedly revived in repertory, Off-Broadway, and in college theatres, and suggest the stamina to survive for centuries. A good look at the Pulitzer Prize Play Awards shows this break-down in terms of genres:

Dramas	25	Melodramas	1
Comedies	9	Musicals	4
Folk-Fables	1		

The listing of plays which won the New York Drama Critics' Circle
Award since the Award's beginning in 1935–1936, shows this break-
down:

Dramas   20   Comedies   5

The Drama Critics' Circle has given distinct recognition to musicals
by granting them a separate category of award and so far has given
this award 18 times. This comparative totaling of genres of productions shows that the critics have especially favored drama in granting
their coveted yearly awards to plays, while the public has tended to
favor musicals and comedies in extending their patronage to long
lines at the box-office. Another insight is implied in the grand total
to date of some 170 hits with runs of 500 performances or more in
the Broadway season over the last 65 years or so. A solid year's run
of 8 performances a week,—6 evenings and 2 matinees—totals 416;
a play, therefore, to hit the 500 performance mark must run at least
15 months. This implies, of course, that in the last 65 years or so,
only some 170 hits to date have had an initial Broadway run of over
15 months.

The suggested pattern of play analysis based upon the text is meant
to be used preferably *after* having read a play through once; the first
time should be to give the play a fair chance to work its magic without the reader stopping the show to x-ray its innards. After the first
reading comes the x-ray eye toward the form. Admittedly the more
sophisticated the reader becomes, the more prone the reader is to
analysis of plays read. The study suggests many refinements to possibly improve on this pattern of analysis.

A SELECTED LIST OF ONE–ACT PLAYS *

"A short play, having a great advantage over a long one in that it can
sustain a mood without technical creaking or over-padding deserves a
better fate, and if, by careful writing, acting, and producing, I can do a
little toward reinstating it in its rightful pride, I shall have achieved one
of my sentimental ambitions."
—Noel Coward of his series of one-act plays, *To-Night at 8:30*

Albee, Edward: *The American Dream, The Death of Bessie Smith,
The Sandbox, Zoo Story, Box Mao Box*
Anouilh, Jean: *The Apollo of Bellac, Cecile*

* Available in anthologies or as indicated in catalogs of: Samuel French, Inc.,
25 W. 45th St., N.Y., N.Y.; or Dramatists Play Service, Inc., 440 Park Ave
South, N.Y., N.Y.

Anderson, Robert W., *You Know I Can't Hear You When the Water's Running*

Barrie, Sir James M.: *The Old Lady Shows Her Medals, The Twelve Pound Look*

Beckett, Samuel: *Krapp's Last Tape, Endgame*

Binet, Stephen V.: *The Devil and Daniel Webster*

Brecht, Bertolt: *The Exception and the Rule*

Chekhov, Anton: *The Boor, The Marriage Proposal, On the Harmfulness of Tobacco, Swansong, The Tragedian In Spite of Himself, The Wedding*

Conkle, E. P.: *Sparkin'*

Coward, Noel: *Fumed Oak, Hands Across the Sea, Red Peppers, Ways and Means*

Dunsany, Lord: *A Night at an Inn, The Queen's Enemies*

France, Anatole: *The Man Who Married a Dumb Wife*

Fry, Christopher: *A Phoenix too Frequent, Thor without Angels*

Galsworthy, John: *The Little Man*

Glaspell, Susan: *Suppressed Desires* (in collaboration with her husband, George Cram Cook), *Trifles*

Inge, William: *A Boy in the Basement, Glory in the Flower, Incident at the Standish Arms, The Mall, Memory of Summer, A Social Event*

Ionesco, Eugene: *The Bald Soprano, The Chairs, Jack, The Lesson*

Kaufman, George S.: *If Men Played Cards as Women Do, The Still Alarm*

Koppit, Arthur: *Oh, Dad, Poor Dad, Mamma's Hung You in the Closet and I'm Feelin' so Sad*

MacLeish, Archibald: *Air Raid, The Fall of the City, The Secret of Freedom*

Maeterlinck, Maurice: *The Blind, The Intruder*

Millay, Edna St. Vincent: *Aria Da Capo*

Miller, Arthur: *A Memory of Two Mondays*

Milne, A. A.: *The Ugly Duckling*

Morton, John J.: *Box and Cox*

Odets, Clifford: *Waiting for Lefty*

O'Neill, Eugene: *Bound East for Cardiff, Hughie, Ile, In the Zone, The Long Voyage Home, Moon of the Caribbees*

Perl, Arnold: *A Tale of Chelm, Bontsche Schweig, The High School* (Three one-acts adapted from the Tevye stories and titled *The World of Sholom Aleichem*, part basis of the musical, *Fiddler on the Roof*), *Tevye and His Daughters*

Pinter, Harold: *The Collection, The Dumbwaiter, The Lover, The Night Out, The Room, A Slight Ache*
Pirandello, Luigi: *The Man with the Flower in His Mouth*
Rostand, Edmond: *The Romancers* (basis of *The Fantasticks*)
Saroyan, William, *The Man with the Heart in the Highlands*
Sartre, Jean Paul: *No Exit*
Schisgal, Murray: *The Tiger, The Typists*
Schnitzler, Arthur: *Anatol* (cycle of one-act comedies)
Shaw, Bernard: *Androcles and the Lion, Village Wooing*
Shaw, Irwin, *Bury the Dead*
Simon, Neil, *Plaza Suite*
Strindberg, August: *Miss Julie, The Stronger, The Bond*
Synge, John M.: *In the Shadow of the Glen, Riders to the Sea*
Thurber, James: *A Thurber Carnival* (A revue—*The Unicorn in the Garden, Mr. Preble Gets Rid of His Wife, If Grant Had Been Drinking at Appomattox, File and Forget, The Secret Life of Walter Mitty*)
Wilde, Oscar: *Salome*
Wilder, Thornton: *The Happy Journey*
Williams, Tennessee: *Hello from Bertha, The Lady of Larkspur Lotion, The Last of My Solid Gold Watches, Lord Byron's Love Letter, Portrait of a Madonna, Something Unspoken, Suddenly Last Summer, 27 Wagons Full of Cotton, Slapstick Tragedy*
Yeats, William B.: *Cathleen Ni Houlihan*

A SELECTED LIST OF COLLECTIONS OF ONE-ACT PLAYS

American Blues by Tennessee Williams, N. Y., Dramatists Play Service, 1948
Best One-Act Plays, selected with an introduction by Margaret Mayorga, 1937–1952, N. Y., Dodd, Mead & Co.
Eight Plays from Off-Off-Broadway, edited by Nick Orzel and Michael Smith, Indianapolis, Bobbs-Merrill, 1966
English One-Act Plays of Today, selected and introduced by Donald Fitzjohn, Cambridge, Oxford University Press, 1962
Four Plays by Eugene Ionesco, translated by Donald Allen, N. Y., Grove Press, 1958
One-Act: Short Plays of the Modern Theatre, edited by Samuel Moon, N. Y., Grove Press, 1961

Representative One-Act Plays by British and Irish Authors, edited by Barrett H. Clark, Boston, Little, Brown and Co., 1935

Seven Plays by Bertolt Brecht, edited with an introduction by Eric Bentley, N.Y., Grove Press, 1961

24 Favorite One-Act Plays, edited by Bennett Cerf and Van H. Cartmell, Garden City, N.Y., Doubleday, 1958

Thirty Famous One-Act Plays, edited by Bennett Cerf and Van H. Cartmell, Garden City, N.Y., Doubleday, 1958

27 Wagons Full of Cotton and Other One-Act Plays by Tennessee Williams, Norfolk, Conn., New Directions, 1953

The Zoo Story, The Death of Bessie Smith, The Sand-Box: Three Plays by Edward Albee, N.Y., Coward McCann, 1960

The Zoo Story and Other Plays by Edward Albee, London, Jonathan Cape, 1962

A SELECTED LIST OF DRAMATIC CRITICISM

"I have learned that what matters most is doing whatever you do with all your heart . . . Do it as if your life depended on it, and first thing you know, you'll have made a life out of it. A good life, too."
—Theresa Helburn in *A Wayward Quest*

Anderson, Maxwell, *Off-Broadway,* William Sloan Assoc., Inc., N.Y., 1947

Barker, H. Granville, *On Dramatic Method,* Hill and Wang, N.Y., 1956

Beerbohm, Max, *Around Theatres,* Knopf, N.Y., 1930

Clark, Barrett H., editor, *European Theories of the Drama,* an anthology of dramatic theory and criticism from Aristotle to the present, N.Y., Crown Publishers, 1947

Craig, E. Gordon, *The Art of the Theatre,* London, Heinemann and Co., Ltd., 1957

Gassner, John, *Producing the Play,* N.Y., the Dryden Press, 1960

Kerr, Walter, *Pieces at Eight,* N.Y., Simon and Schuster, 1957

Kerr, Walter, *The Theater in Spite of Itself,* N.Y., Simon and Schuster, 1963

Nathan, George J., *The Magic Mirror: Selected Writings on the Theatre,* N.Y., Knopf, 1960

New York Theatre Critics' Reviews, a yearly compilation from 1940

Nicoll, Allardyce, *The Theatre and Dramatic Theory,* N.Y., Barnes and Noble, 1962

Shaw, Bernard, *Dramatic Opinions and Essays,* London, Constable and Co., 1898

Tolstoy, Lev. N., *What Is Art?* translated by Aylmer Maude, vol. 18 of *The Works of Leo Tolstoy,* Oxford University Press, Tolstoy Society, 1928–1937

Ward, A. C., editor, *Plays and Players,* essays on the theatre, London, Oxford University Press, 1952

Warrington, John W., *Aristotle's Poetics,* London, Dent; N. Y., Dutton's Everyman's Library

A SELECTED LIST OF ANTHOLOGIES OF THE DRAMA

"He wanted to write plays, that is understood. He may even have written a few of the earlier ones, which didn't amount to much. But he was undisciplined, he told me, not only in working habits, but in writing itself,—what form to use, and how. Then he began consciously to use a method which he kept up for over a year. He read nothing but plays, great plays, melodrama . . . Before long he was thinking in dialogue and answering his own thoughts more or less aloud in his low voice, seeing life in scenes and acts—with the curtain going down perhaps, as he went off to sleep."

—Agnes Boulton Kaufman, the second wife of Eugene O'Neill, in her book, *Part of a Long Story*

Chief European Dramatists, selected and edited by Brander Mathews, Boston, Riverside Press, Cambridge, 1944

Chief Patterns of World Drama, Aeschylus to Anderson, introduction by William Smith Clark II, Houghton, Mifflin Co., Riverside, Cambridge, 1946

A Modern Repertory, edited by Harlan Hatcher, N. Y., Harcourt, Brace and Co., 1940

A Treasury of the Theatre, vol. I, *World Drama from Aeschylus to Turgenev;* vol. II, *Modern European Drama from Henrik Ibsen to Jean-Paul Sartre;* vol. III, *Modern British and American Drama from Oscar Wilde to Arthur Miller,* edited by John Gassner, N. Y., revised, Simon and Schuster, 1963

Long Runs On Broadway

> "I am willing to trust to the decision of the multitude and I hold it
> as difficult to combat a work which the public approves as to defend
> one which it condemns."
> —Molière

In the following table, the genre of each production is indicated by
a key letter or letters directly after the title: M for musical; V for
variety show; R for revue whether burlesque, musical or topical; C for
comedy; F for farce; D for drama; and MM for murder mystery. The
genres *melodrama* and *tragedy* are so forbidding at the box-office that
very few modern plays bear them, choosing rather to be called *drama*.
Producers also like their plays to be called if possible *comedy* rather
than *drama* unless they have a solid hit; when *The Two Mrs. Carrolls*
opened, it was billed as *comedy* but once it became a big hit, it was
admittedly *drama*. Almost all dramas are seasoned with touches of
comedy; and comedies, representing a laughable view of life as they
do, are touched with drama. This breakdown into genres suggests
why producers today tend to favor musicals and comedies to make
big money, for these genres have proven to have the best chance with
the widest public. Actually the table shows there is room for almost
any big work in any genre. Incidentally, the run cited is drawn from
the records of Burns Mantle and succeeding editors of the yearly publication, *Best Plays;* these figures do not always agree with those in
*The Biographical Encyclopaedia and Who's Who of the American
Theatre* (1966).

Title	Run	Title	Run
Life with Father (C)	3,224	*Abie's Irish Rose* (FC)	2,327
Tobacco Road (CD)	3,182	*Oklahoma!* (M)	2,212
My Fair Lady (M)	2,717	*Harvey* (C)	1,775

Title	Run	Title	Run
Hello, Dolly! (M)	1,756*	Anna Lucasta (CD)	957
South Pacific (M)	1,694	Kiss and Tell (C)	957
Born Yesterday (C)	1,642	The Moon Is Blue (C)	924
Mary, Mary (C)	1,572	Bells Are Ringing (M)	924
The Voice of the Turtle (C)	1,557	Luv (C)	902
		Can-Can (M)	892
Barefoot in the Park (C)	1,532	Carousel (M)	890
Fiddler on the Roof (M)	1,472*	Hats Off to Ice (V)	889
Arsenic and Old Lace (FC)	1,444	Fanny (M)	888
The Sound of Music (M)	1,443	Follow the Girls (M)	882
How to Succeed in Business without Really Trying (M)	1,417	Camelot (M)	873
		The Bat (MM)	867
		My Sister Eileen (C)	865
Hellzapoppin' (V)	1,404	White Cargo (D)	864
The Music Man (M)	1,373	Song of Norway (M)	860
Funny Girl (M)	1,346	A Streetcar Named Desire (D)	855
Angel Street (MM)	1,295		
Lightnin' (CD)	1,291	Comedy in Music (R)	849
The King and I (M)	1,246	You Can't Take It with You (C)	837
Guys and Dolls (M)	1,200	La Plume de Ma Tante (R)	835
Mister Roberts (C)	1,157		
Annie Get Your Gun (M)	1,147	Three Men on a Horse (F)	835
The Seven Year Itch (C)	1,141		
Pins and Needles (R)	1,108	The Subject Was Roses (CD)	832
Kiss Me Kate (M)	1,070		
Pajama Game (M)	1,063	Inherit the Wind (D)	806
The Teahouse of the August Moon (C)	1,027	No Time for Sergeants (C)	796
Damn Yankees (M)	1,019	Fiorello! (M)	795
Never Too Late (C)	1,007	Where's Charley? (M)	792
Man of La Mancha (M)	984*	The Ladder (D)	789
Any Wednesday (C)	983	Mame (M)	777*
Cactus Flower (FC)	966*	Oliver (M)	774
A Funny Thing Happened on the Way to the Forum (M)	964	State of the Union (C)	765
		The First Year (C)	760
		Two for the See-Saw (C)	750
The Odd Couple (C)	963	Death of a Salesman (D)	742

* Continuing run as of May 7, 1968.

Title	Run	Title	Run
No Strings (M)	580	*Within the Law* (D)	541
Brother Rat (C)	577	*The Music Master* (D)	540
Show Boat (M)	572	*Pal Joey* (M)	540
The Show-Off (C)	571	*What a Life!* (C)	538
Sally (M)	570	*The Red Mill* (M)	531
Golden Boy (D)	568	*The Solid Gold*	
One Touch of Venus (M)	567	*Cadillac* (C)	526
Happy Birthday (C)	564	*The Boomerang* (C)	522
Look Homeward		*Rosalinda* (M)	521
Angel (D)	564	*Chauve Souris* (V)	520
The Glass Menagerie (D)	561	*Blackbirds* (R)	518
Wonderful Town (M)	559	*Sunny* (M)	517
Rose Marie (M)	557	*Victoria Regina* (D)	517
Strictly Dishonorable (C)	557	*Half a Sixpence* (M)	512
A Majority of One (C)	556	*The Vagabond King* (M)	511
Sunrise at		*The New Moon* (M)	509
Campobello (D)	556	*Shuffle Along* (M)	504
Toys in the Attic (D)	556	*Carmen Jones* (M)	503
Jamaica (M)	555	*The Member of the*	
Stop the World I Want		*Wedding* (D)	501
to Get Off (R)	555	*Personal Appearance* (C)	501
Ziegfeld Follies (R)	553	*Panama Hattie* (M)	501
Dial M for Murder (MM)	552	*Bird in Hand* (C)	500
Good News (M)	551	*Sailor Beware* (M)	500
Let's Face It (M)	547	*Tomorrow the World* (D)	500
Milk and Honey (M)	543	*Room Service* (F)	500

LONG RUNS OFF–BROADWAY

Title	Run	Title	Run
The Fantasticks (M)	2,990*	*Leave It to Jane* (M)	928
The Threepenny		*A View from the*	
Opera (M)	2,611	*Bridge* (D)	780
The Blacks (D)	1,408	*The Boy Friend* (M)	763
Little Mary Sun-		*The Mad Show* (RV)	760
shine (M)	1,143	*The Knack* (C)	685

* Continuing run as of May 7, 1968.

Title	Run	Title	Run
The Balcony (CD)	672	*Krapp's Last Tape* and	
The Pocket Watch (CD)	624	*Zoo Story* (D)	532
Hogan's Goat (CD)	607	*Six Characters in Search*	
The Trojan Women (D)	600	*of an Author* (D)	529
The Crucible (D)	571	*Happy Ending* and	
The Iceman Cometh (D)	565	*Day of Ascence* (C)	504
The Hostage (CD)	545	*The Boys from*	
		Syracuse (M)	500

PULITZER PRIZE–WINNING PLAYS, THEIR GENRE AND RUN

"To an original American play performed in New York which shall represent in marked fashion the educational value and power of the stage, preferably dealing with American life."
—Criteria of the Advisory Board of Awards

1917–1918...*Why Marry?* (C) by J. Lynch Williams (120)

1918–1919...No award

1919–1920...*Beyond the Horizon* (D) by Eugene O'Neill (160)

1920–1921...*Miss Lulu Bett* (C) by Zona Gale (198)

1921–1922...*Anna Christie* (D) by Eugene O'Neill (177)

1922–1923...*Icebound* (D) by Owen Davis (171)

1923–1924...*Hell-Bent for Heaven* (D) by Hatcher Hughes (122)

1924–1925...*They Knew What They Wanted* (CD) by Sidney Howard (414)

1925–1926...*Craig's Wife* (D) by George Kelly (360)

1926–1927...*In Abraham's Bosom* (D) by Paul Green (116)

1927–1928...*Strange Interlude* (D) by Eugene O'Neill (426)

1928–1929...*Street Scene* (D) by Elmer Rice (601)

1929–1930...*The Green Pastures* (Fable) by Marc Connelly based on Roark Bradford's stories (640)

1930–1931...*Alison's House* (D) by Susan Glaspell (41)

1931–1932...*Of Thee I Sing* (M) by George S. Kaufman, Morrie Ryskind, Ira and George Gershwin (441)

1932–1933...*Both Your Houses* (D) by Maxwell Anderson (104)

1933–1934...*Men in White* (D) by Sidney Kingsley (351)

1934–1935...*The Old Maid* (D) by Zoë Akins (305)

1935–1936...*Idiot's Delight* (CD) by Robert E. Sherwood (300)

1936–1937...*You Can't Take It with You* (C) by Moss Hart and George S. Kaufman (837)

1937–1938...*Our Town* (D) by Thornton Wilder (336)

1938–1939...*Abe Lincoln in Illinois* (D) by Robert E. Sherwood (472)

1939–1940...*The Time of Your Life* (CD) by William Saroyan (185)

1940–1941...*There Shall Be No Night* (D) by Robert E. Sherwood (181)

1941–1942...No award

1942–1943...*The Skin of Our Teeth* (D) by Thornton Wilder (359)

1943–1944...No award

1944–1945...*Harvey* (C) by Mary C. Chase (1,775)

1945–1946...*State of the Union* (C) by Howard Lindsay and Russel Crouse (765)

1946–1947...No award

1947–1948...*A Streetcar Named Desire* (D) by Tennessee Williams (855)

1948–1949...*Death of a Salesman* (D) by Arthur Miller (742)

1949–1950...*South Pacific* (M) by Richard Rodgers, Oscar Hammerstein II, and Joshua Logan, based on James Michener's *Tales of the South Pacific* (1,694)

1950–1951...No award

1951–1952...*The Shrike* (D) by Joseph Kramm (161)

1952–1953...*Picnic* (C) by William Inge (477)

1953–1954...*The Teahouse of the August Moon* (C) by John Patrick (1,027)

1954–1955...*Cat on a Hot Tin Roof* (D) by Tennessee Williams (694)

1955–1956...*The Diary of Anne Frank* (D) by Frances Goodrich and Albert Hackett, based on Anne Frank's *Diary of a Young Girl*

1956–1957...*Long Day's Journey into Night* (D) by Eugene O'Neill (390)

1957–1958...*Look Homeward, Angel* (D) by Ketti Frings, based on Thomas Wolfe's novel (564)

1958–1959...*J. B.* (D) by Archibald MacLeish (364)

1959–1960...*Fiorello!* (M) by Jerome Weidman, George Abbott, Sheldon Harnick, Jerry Bock (795)

1960–1961...*All the Way Home* (D) by Tad Mosel (333)

1961–1962...*How to Succeed in Business without Really Trying* (M) by Abe Burrows, Willie Gilbert, Jack Weinstock and

Frank Loesser, based on Shepherd Mead's novel (1,095)
1962–1963...No award
1963–1964...No award
1964–1965...*The Subject Was Roses* (CD) by Frank Gilroy (834)
1965–1966...No award
1966–1967...*A Delicate Balance* (D) by Edward Albee (133)
1967–1968...No award

NEW YORK DRAMA CRITICS' CIRCLE AWARD PLAYS, THEIR GENRE, AND RUN

"to the best American play of the year"—Criteria of the Drama Critics' Circle (The Award was later extended to include two more categories: "to the best foreign play of the year," and, "to the best musical of the year.")

Year	American Play	Foreign Play	Musical
1935–1936	*Winterset* (D) (195)		
1936–1937	*High Tor* (CD) (171)		
1937–1938	*Of Mice and Men* (D) (207)	*Shadow and Substance* (D) (274)	
1938–1939	No award	*The White Steed* (D) (136)	
1939–1940	*The Time of Your Life* (C) (185)	No award	
1940–1941	*Watch on the Rhine* (D) (378)	*The Corn Is Green* (D) (477)	
1941–1942	No award	*Blithe Spirit* (F) (657)	
1942–1943	*The Patriots* (D) (173)	No award	
1943–1944	No award	*Jacobowsky and the Colonel* (C) (417)	
1944–1945	*The Glass Menagerie* (D) (561)	No award	
1945–1946	No award	No award	*Carousel* (890)
1946–1947	*All My Sons* (D) (328)	*No Exit* (D) (31)	*Brigadoon* (581)
1947–1948	*A Streetcar Named Desire* (D) (855)	*The Winslow Boy* (D) (215)	No award

Year	American Play	Foreign Play	Musical
1948–1949	Death of a Salesman (D) (742)	The Madwoman of Chaillot (CD) (368)	South Pacific (1,694)
1949–1950	The Member of the Wedding (D) (501)	The Cocktail Party (C) (409)	The Consul (93)
1950–1951	Darkness at Noon (D) (186)	The Lady's not for Burning (CD) (151)	Guys and Dolls (1,200)
1951–1952	I Am a Camera (D) (214)	Venus Observed (C) (86)	Pal Joey (540)
1952–1953	Picnic (C) (477)	The Love of Four Colonels (C) (141)	Wonderful Town (559)
1953–1954	The Teahouse of the August Moon (C) (1,027)	Ondine (Fantasy) (117)	The Golden Apple (125)
1954–1955	Cat on a Hot Tin Roof (D) (694)	Witness for the Prosecution (MM) (645)	The Saint of Bleecker Street (92)
1955–1956	The Diary of Ann Frank (D) (717)	Tiger at the Gates (D) (217)	My Fair Lady (2,717)
1956–1957	Long Day's Journey into Night (D) (390)	Waltz of the Toreadors (C) (132)	The Most Happy Fella (676)
1957–1958	Look Homeward, Angel (D) (564)	Look Back in Anger (C) (407)	The Music Man (1,375)
1958–1959	A Raisin in the Sun (C) (530)	The Visit (D) (189)	La Plume de Ma Tante (R) (835)
1959–1960	Toys in the Attic (D) (556)	Five Finger Exercise (C) (337)	Fiorello! (795)
1960–1961	All the Way Home (D) (334)	A Taste of Honey (C) (334)	Carnival (719)
1961–1962	The Night of the Iguana (D) (316)	A Man for All Seasons (D) (638)	How to Succeed in Business without Really Trying (1,095)
1962–1963	Who's Afraid of Virginia Woolf? (D) (664)	No award	No award
1963–1964	No award	Luther (D) (211)	Hello, Dolly! *
1964–1965	The Subject Was Roses (CD) (832)	No award	Fiddler on the Roof *
1965–1966	No award	Marat/Sade (D) (145)	Man of La Mancha *
1966–1967	No award	The Homecoming (CD) (328)	Cabaret *
1967–1968	No award	Rosencrantz and Guildenstern Are Dead (D) *	Your Own Thing *

* Run continuing. Your Own Thing is the first Off-Broadway musical to win the New York Drama Critics' Circle Award.

PLAYWRITING ENDOWMENTS

Did endowments help the most talented of playwrights? They unquestionably helped Ibsen and Williams. Shaw, Galsworthy, and O'Neill suggest the advantages of having money in the family; without such money, it is a moot point as to whether these men could or would have continued playwriting until they arrived.

Have endowments helped make playwrights these days? Unquestionably it seems there is room for a modern, democratic equivalent of the patron in the western European tradition of the Renaissance. Playwrights take an indeterminate time to yield results. John Golden, for instance, after World War II, put up funds for five playwriting fellowships to allow promising young playwrights to finish scripts with a notion of then having the right to option any script first. None of the scripts, in Golden's opinion, turned out good enough to produce. On the other hand, the New Dramatists Committee, which has been actively functioning from 1950 to the present, has had a longer chance to prove itself, and among its illustrious "graduates" are such more or less well known names as: Robert Anderson, Horton Foote, William Inge, Joseph Hayes, Ronald Alexander, Michael Stewart, Paddy Chayefsky, Arnold Schulman, William Gibson, Robert Thom, Jack Gelber, Don Appell, Joe Masteroff, Burt Shevelove, William Snyder, David Rayfiel, John Lewis Carlino, and James Baldwin. The annual operating budget to allow roughly forty members a year to work with the committee is $50,000; membership is allowed to run for three years for a playwright and then is open to renewal depending upon progress proven. The founders of the New Dramatists Committee are: Howard Lindsay, Richard Rodgers, Russel Crouse, Moss Hart, John Golden, John Wharton, Michaela O'Harra and Oscar Hammerstein II. Current supporters of the New Dramatists Committee are: the New York State Council on the Arts, Sam S. Shubert Foundation, John Golden Fund, Richard Rodgers Foundation, Rodgers and Hammerstein Foundation, Play of the Month Guild, Dramatists Guild Fund, McKnight Foundation, William and Mary Frank Foundation, New York Foundation, William C. Whitney Foundation, Gilbert Miller Foundation, Scherman Foundation, Leonard and

Sophie Davis Foundation, Abe Wouk Foundation, Actors Equity Fund, Irving Berlin Foundation. Individual donors have also helped and continue to. The program of the New Dramatists Committee includes: craft discussions with professionals; play-readings of new dramatists' plays by professional actors with a round-table critique of the effort; a follow through observation from start to finish of a professional Broadway production; guest admission by courtesy of the management for new dramatists to see almost all Broadway and Off-Broadway productions each season. Two other organizations in New York City which are currently functioning in a somewhat similar way to the New Dramatists Committee are the Playwrights Unit of the Actors Studio and the Playwriting Workshop sponsored by Edward Albee and his producers, Wilder and Barr. The addresses of these organizations are:

New Dramatists Committee Inc. The Playwriting Workshop
130 W. 56th St.   Circle in the Square
N. Y., N. Y.   159 Bleecker Street
                               N. Y. 12, N. Y.

The Playwrights Unit
Actors Studio
432 West 44th St.
N. Y. 36, N. Y.

CONTESTS

The winning of prizes in playwriting contests has encouraged some of the most distinguished modern playwrights. Arthur Miller, for instance, won the Avery Hopwood Memorial Award of $500 for two years at the University of Michigan, in 1936 and in 1937, and in 1938 he won second honor and the $1,250 Theatre Guild National Award. Tennessee Williams, on the other hand, won no prizes in playwriting at Missouri University, Washington University, or the University of Iowa. What opened many doors to him in the professional theatre and gave him new hope was the special award of $100 he won in 1939 from entering the Group Theatre Playwriting Contest. To keep informed of current playwriting contests, aspiring playwrights may consult:

American National Theatre and Academy
245 W. 52nd St.
New York, N. Y. 10019

Playwrights Program
American Educational Theatre Association
726 Jackson Place, N. W.
Washington, D. C. 20566

The Writer
8 Arlington St.
Boston, Mass. 02116

Dramatists Guild Quarterly
234 W. 44th St.
New York, N. Y. 10036
(members only)

Index